African Americans
A Concise History

COMBINED VOLUME

Darlene Clark Hine
Northwestern University

William C. Hine
South Carolina State University

Stanley Harrold
South Carolina State University

PEARSON

Boston   Columbus   Indianapolis   New York   San Francisco   Upper Saddle River
Amsterdam   Cape Town   Dubai   London   Madrid   Milan   Munich   Paris   Montréal   Toronto
Delhi   Mexico City   São Paulo   Sydney   Hong Kong   Seoul   Singapore   Taipei   Tokyo

Editor-in-Chief: Dickson Musslewhite
Publisher: Charlyce Jones Owen
Editorial Assistant: Maureen Diana
Program Manager: Beverly Fong
Managing Editor: Ann Marie McCarthy
Project Manager: Emsal Hasan
Director of Marketing: Brandy Dawson
Executive Marketing Manager: Wendy Albert
Operations Specialist: Mary Ann Gloriande
Director of Media: Brian Hyland
Digital Media Editor: Thomas Scalzo
Senior Art Director: Maria Lange
Interior Design: S4Carlisle Publishing Services
Cover Design: Redkite Productions
Cartographer: International Mapping
Full-Service Production and Composition: S4Carlisle Publishing Services
Full Service Project Manager: Mary Tindle
Manager, Rights and Permissions: Barbara Ryan
Printer/Binder: Courier/Kendallville
Cover Printer: Lehigh Phoenix

Credits and acknowledgments for materials borrowed from other sources and reproduced, with permission, in this textbook appear on pages **C-1** to **C-4.**

Many of the designations by manufacturers and seller to distinguish their products are claimed as trademarks. Where those designations appear in this book, and the publisher was aware of a trademark claim, the designations have been printed in initial caps or all caps.

Library of Congress Cataloging-in-Publication Data
Hine, Darlene Clark, author.
  African Americans, combined volume : a concise history / Darlene Clark Hine, William C. Hine, and
Stanley Harrold. — Fifth edition.
       pages cm
  Includes index.
  ISBN 978-0-205-96906-7
  1. African Americans—History—Textbooks.   I. Hine, William C.   II. Harrold, Stanley.   III. Title.
  E185.H534 2013
  973.0496073—dc23

                                                          2013025099

Student Edition:
ISBN 10:   0-205-96906-2
ISBN 13: 978-0-205-96906-7

Instructor Review Copy
ISBN 10:   0-205-96907-0
ISBN 13: 978-0-205-96907-4

Volume 1
ISBN 10:   0-205-96977-1
ISBN 13: 978-0-205-96977-7

Volume 2
ISBN 10:   0-205-96948-8
ISBN 13: 978-0-205-96948-7

Volume 1 a la carte
ISBN 10:   0-205-97288-8
ISBN 13: 978-0-205-97288-3

Volume 2 a la carte
ISBN 10:   0-205-97287-x
ISBN 13: 978-0-205-97287-6

Dedicated To

Alma J. Clark McIntosh
(1951–2012)

Roy Harrold
(1950–2011)

Peter J. Hine
(1953–2012)

Brief Contents

Contents

CHAPTER 16

Conciliation, Agitation, and Migration: African Americans in the Early Twentieth Century, 1895–1928 341

CHAPTER 17

African Americans and the 1920s, 1918–1929 372

Maps, Figures, and Tables

Maps

Figures

Tables

Preface

"One ever feels his two-ness,—an American, a Negro; two souls, two thoughts, two unreconciled strivings; two warring ideals in one dark body." So wrote W. E. B. Du Bois in 1897. African-American history, Du Bois maintained, was the history of this double-consciousness. Black people have always been part of the American nation that they helped to build. But they have also been a nation unto themselves, with their own experiences, culture, and aspirations. African-American history cannot be understood except in the broader context of American history. Likewise, American history cannot be understood without African-American history.

Since Du Bois's time, our understanding of both African-American and American history has been complicated and enriched by a growing appreciation of the role of class and gender in shaping human societies. We are also increasingly aware of the complexity of racial experiences in American history. Even in times of great racial polarity, some white people have empathized with black people and some black people have identified with white interests.

It is in light of these insights that *African Americans: A Concise History* tells the story of African Americans. That story begins in Africa, where the people who were to become African Americans began their long, turbulent, and difficult journey, a journey marked by sustained suffering as well as perseverance, bravery, and achievement. It includes the rich culture—at once splendidly distinctive and tightly intertwined with a broader American culture—that African Americans have nurtured throughout their history. And it includes the many-faceted quest for freedom in which African Americans have sought to counter white oppression and racism with the egalitarian spirit of the Declaration of Independence that American society professes to embody.

Nurtured by black historian Carter G. Woodson during the early decades of the twentieth century, African-American history has blossomed as a field of study since the 1950s. Books and articles have appeared on almost every facet of black life. Yet this survey is the first comprehensive college textbook of the African-American experience. It draws on recent research to present black history in a clear and direct manner, within a broad social, cultural, and political framework. It also provides thorough coverage of African-American women as active builders of black culture.

African Americans: A Concise History balances accounts of the actions of African-American leaders with investigations of the lives of the ordinary men and women in black communities. This community focus helps make this a history of a people rather than an account of a few extraordinary individuals. Yet the book does not neglect important political and religious leaders, entrepreneurs, and entertainers. It also gives extensive coverage to African-American art, literature, and music.

African-American history started in Africa, and this narrative begins with an account of life on that continent to the sixteenth century and the beginning of the forced migration of millions of Africans to the Americas. Succeeding chapters present the struggle of black people to maintain their humanity during the slave trade and as slaves in North America during the long colonial period.

The coming of the American Revolution during the 1770s initiated a pattern of black struggle for racial justice in which periods of optimism alternated with times of repression. Several chapters analyze the building of black community institutions, the antislavery movement, the efforts of black people to make the Civil War a war for emancipation, their struggle for equal rights as citizens during Reconstruction, and the strong opposition these efforts faced. There is also substantial coverage of African-American military service, from the War for Independence through American wars of the nineteenth and twentieth centuries.

During the late nineteenth century and much of the twentieth century, racial segregation and racially motivated violence that relegated African Americans to second-class citizenship provoked despair, but also inspired resistance and commitment to change. Chapters on the late nineteenth and early twentieth centuries cover the Great Migration from the cotton fields of the South to the North and West, black nationalism, and the Harlem Renaissance. Chapters on the 1930s and 1940s—the beginning of a period of revolutionary change for African Americans—tell of the economic devastation and political turmoil caused by the Great Depression, the growing influence of black culture in America, the emergence of black internationalism, and the racial tensions caused by black participation in World War II.

The final chapters tell the story of African Americans in the closing decades of the twentieth century and the dawn of the twenty-first century. They portray the freedom struggles and legislative successes of the civil rights movement at its peak during the 1950s and 1960s and the electoral political victories of the black power movement during the more conservative 1970s and 1980s. Finally, there are discussions of black life in the twenty-first century and the election and reelection of Barack Obama, the first African-American president of the United States.

In all, *African Americans: A Concise History* tells a compelling story of survival, struggle, and triumph over adversity. It will leave students with an appreciation of the central place of black people and black culture in this country and a better understanding of both African-American and American history.

WHAT'S NEW IN THE FIFTH EDITION

Every chapter in the fifth edition of *African Americans: A Concise History* has been revised and improved with updated scholarship. A new feature at the end of each part, **Connecting the Past**, examines important milestones of the African-American experience over time. These six featured essays examine the evolution of the black church, the development of black autobiography, black migration, desegregation of the military, and black culture. There are new in-depth MyHistoryLab activities that explore events and issues using interactive maps on a key event within the chapters.

Chapter Revision Highlights

Chapter 1 The section on the "Birth of Humanity" has been revised as has the section entitled "The Ancient Manuscripts of Timbuktu."

Chapter 2 There is more information on "African Women on Slave Ships." The discussion of "seasoning" has been clarified.

Chapter 3 The section on "The Spanish Empire" has been eliminated and replaced with "The Spanish, French, and Dutch," which emphasizes the role of Africans and people of African descent in those areas of the New World. There have also been revisions made to the section on "The British and Jamestown."

Chapter 5 The section on "The War of 1812" has been revised. A new featured essay, **Connecting the Past**, "The Great Awakening and the Black Church," follows the chapter.

Chapter 7 "The Jacksonian Era" has been reworked.

Chapter 8 To clarify the text, two headings have been changed: "A Country in Turmoil" to "The Path Toward a More Radical Antislavery Movement;" and "Political Paranoia" to "Slavery and Politics."

Chapter 10 There is a new featured essay, **Connecting the Past**, exploring "The Narrative of Frederick Douglass and Black Autobiography," which follows the chapter.

Chapter 11 The number of casualties sustained in the Civil War has been revised upward to 750,000 in keeping with recent research as has the number of black men who served in the U.S. Navy during the Civil War.

Chapter 12 The discussion of the devastating impact that the Civil War had on the South has been expanded, and there is more information on widespread disease among African Americans following the War.

Chapter 13 There is a new section on the Ellenton riot in South Carolina in 1876. There is a new featured essay, **Connecting the Past**, on voting rights and politics, which follows the chapter.

Chapter 14 The discussion of memories of the Civil War among black and white people has been revised. There is more information on the desire among black people to acquire land.

Chapter 15 There is additional information on the origins of the term "buffalo soldiers" and on black women in the west including black "cowgirls."

Chapter 16 There is a revised discussion of Booker T. Washington's dinner with President Theodore Roosevelt in 1901. Information has been added on the Great Migration, and there is a new table on migration, as well as a new quote from Ida B. Wells anticipating the Chicago race riot in 1919.

Chapter 17 There is a new featured essay, **Connecting the Past**, on migration and its impact, which follows the chapter.

Chapter 18 A new discussion of medical experimentation on people besides those involved in the Tuskegee Syphilis Experiment has been added with information about the syphilis experiments in Guatemala and in the Indiana prison population.

Chapter 19 The Bibliography has been updated with new studies and information about Don Cornelius, creator of "Soul Train."

Chapter 20 There is new information on black radar specialists at Camp Evans during World War II. There is also a new photo of President Eisenhower and Dr. Walter S. McAfee of Camp Evans. A new featured essay, **Connecting the Past,** on the significance of the desegregation of the military, which follows the chapter.

Chapter 21 The discussion on Rosa Parks has been expanded as has that of black women's activism against rape and sexual violence before the 1955-1956 bus boycott.

Chapter 22 The Introduction to the chapter has been rewritten. There have been revisions to the discussion of the black power movement "From Bullets to Ballots." A new chart of black elected officials has been added.

Chapter 23 The discussion of the impact of the Recession of 2008–2011 on black women and black communities has been revised and expanded.

Chapter 24 There is a new discussion of the four stages in the evolution of black politics. Information on the reelection of Barack Obama to a second term is new as is a map of voters and a demographic chart of the 2012 electorate. There is also a new chart depicting select accomplishments of President Obama's first term. There is an added a new featured essay, **Connecting the Past**, on the significance of black culture, which follows the chapter.

ABOUT *AFRICAN AMERICANS: A CONCISE HISTORY*

The many special features and pedagogical tools integrated within *African Americans: A Concise History* are designed to make the text accessible to students. They include a variety of tools to reinforce the narrative and help students grasp key issues.

Chronologies are included throughout the chapters to provide students with a snapshot of the temporal relationship among significant events.

1861–1863
THE STEPS TO EMANCIPATION

April 1861
Fort Sumter is attacked; Civil War begins

May 1861
General Butler refuses to return escaped "contrabands" to slavery

August 1861
General Fremont orders emancipation of slaves in Missouri; Lincoln countermands him

August 1861
First Confiscation Act frees captured slaves used by Confederate Army

April 1862
Congress provides funds for compensated emancipation; border states spurn the proposal

May 1862
Lincoln revokes General Hunter's order abolishing slavery in South Carolina, Georgia, and Florida

Summer 1862
Lincoln concludes that Union military victory requires emancipation

September 22, 1862
Lincoln issues Preliminary Emancipation Proclamation after Battle of Antietam

January 1, 1863
Emancipation Proclamation takes effect

Voices boxes provide students with first-person perspectives on key events in African-American history. Brief introductions and study questions help students analyze these primary source documents and relate them to the text.

VOICES   A Black Nurse on the Horrors of War and the Sacrifice of Black Soldiers

Susie King Taylor was born a slave in Georgia and learned to read and write in Savannah. She escaped to Union forces in 1862 and served as a nurse and laundress with the First South Carolina Volunteers. In these passages, written years later, she recalls her service with the black men who went into combat and pays tribute to them.

It seems strange how our aversion to seeing suffering is overcome in war,—how we are able to see the most sickening sights, such as men with their limbs blown off and mangled by the deadly shells, without a shudder; and instead of turning away, how we hurry to assist in alleviating their pain, bind up their wounds, and press the cool water to their parched lips, with feelings only of sympathy and pity. . . .

I look around now and see the comforts that our younger generation enjoy, and think of the blood that was shed to make these comforts possible for them, and see how little some of

them appreciate the old soldiers. My heart burns within me at this want of appreciation. There are only a few of them left now, so let us all, as the ranks close, take a deeper interest in them. Let the younger generation take an interest also, and remember that it was through the efforts of these veterans that we older ones enjoy our liberty today.

1. How does Taylor describe what men in combat endure?
2. Who is the object of Taylor's criticism, and why does she offer it?

SOURCE: Susie King Taylor, *Reminiscences of My Life in Camp* (Boston: Taylor, 1902), 31–32, 51–52.

 Read on MyHistoryLab Document: An African-American Army Laundress Describes Her Service, 1902

Marginal glossary terms throughout the chapter guide the student to key terms for review.

The First South Carolina Volunteers

View on MyHistoryLab Closer Look: Black Union Soldiers

First South Carolina Volunteers This black military unit consisted of former slaves recruited in the South Carolina and Georgia low country in 1862 and 1863 for service with Union military forces in the Civil War.

Second Confiscation Act The 1862 Act freeing all slaves of rebel owners.

Some Union officers recruited black men long before emancipation was proclaimed and before most white northerners were prepared to accept, much less welcome, black troops. In May 1862 General David Hunter began recruiting former slaves along the South Carolina coast and the sea islands, an area Union forces had captured in late 1861. But some black men did not want to enlist, and Hunter used white troops to force black men to "volunteer" for military service. He managed to organize a 500-man regiment—the **First South Carolina Volunteers**.

Through the summer of 1862, Hunter trained and drilled the regiment while awaiting official authorization and funds to pay them. When Congress balked, Hunter disbanded all but one company of the regiment that August. The troops were dispersed, unpaid and disappointed. The surviving company was sent to St. Simon's Island off the Georgia coast to protect former slaves.

Although Congress failed to support Hunter, it did pass the **Second Confiscation Act** and the **Militia Act of 1862**, which authorized President Lincoln to enlist black men. In Louisiana that fall, two regiments of free black men, the Native Guards, were accepted for federal service, and General Benjamin Butler organized them into the Corps d'Afrique. General Rufus Saxton gained the approval of Secretary of War Edwin Stanton to revive Hunter's dispersed regiment and to recall the company that had been sent to St. Simon's Island.

Connecting the Past essays examine important milestones of the African-American experience over time: evolution of the black church, the emergence of black autobiography, black migration, desegregation of the military, and black culture.

SUPPLEMENTARY INSTRUCTIONAL MATERIALS

The supplementary package that accompanies *African Americans: A Concise History* provides instructors and students with an array of resources that combine sound scholarship, engaging content, and a variety of pedagogical tools and media to enrich the classroom experience and students' understanding of African-American history.

Instructor's Manual

The Instructor's Manual provides instructor resources—lecture and discussion topics, MyHistoryLab resources, and audio/visual resources for each chapter—organized around the learning objectives from the text. The Instructor's Manual is available to adopters for download at Pearson's Instructor Resource Center, www.pearsonhighered.com/irc.

Test Item File

Test materials include multiple-choice, essay, and short-answer questions correlated to the learning objectives from the text. The test item file is available to adopters for download at Pearson's Instructor Resource Center, www.pearsonhighered.com/irc.

My Test

This online test management program allows instructors to select from testing material in the Test Item File to design their own exams. They are available to adopters for download at Pearson's Instructor Resource Center, www.pearsonhighered.com/irc.

PowerPoint Presentations

PowerPoint presentations correlated to the chapters of *African Americans: A Concise History* include a full lecture script, a wealth of images and maps, and links to the full array of MyHistoryLab media. They are available to adopters for download at Pearson's Instructor Resource Center, www.pearsonhighered.com/irc.

MyHistoryLab™

MyHistoryLab is a state-of-the-art interactive and instructive solution, designed to be used as a supplement to a traditional lecture course in African-American history, or to completely administer an online course. MyHistoryLab provides access to a wealth of resources, all geared to meet the individual teaching and learning needs of instructors and students. Highlights of MyHistoryLab include:

- The tools you need to engage every student before, during, and after class. An assignment calendar and gradebook allow you to assign specific activities with due dates and to measure your students' progress throughout the semester.

- The **Pearson e-Text** lets students access their textbook anytime, anywhere, and anyway they want, including *listening online*. The e-Text for *African Americans: A Concise History* features integrated videos, Explorer activities, documents, images, maps, and interactive self-quizzes.

- A **Personalized Study Plan** for each student, based on Bloom's Taxonomy, arranges activities from those that require less complex thinking—like remembering and understanding—to more complex critical thinking—like applying and analyzing. This layered approach promotes better critical thinking skills, helping students succeed in the course and beyond.

New Features of MyHistoryLab

Two exciting new features of MyHistoryLab are Explorer and MyHistoryLibrary.

- **Explorer** activities connect with topics from the text, engaging students with data visualizations, comparisons of change over time, and data localized to their own communities.

- **MyHistoryLibrary** features 200 documents that enable students to explore the discipline more deeply. Multiple-choice questions for each reading help students review what they've learned—and allow instructors to monitor their performance. The documents are available as e-Texts and audio files.

Acknowledgments

In preparing *African Americans: A Concise History,* we have benefited from the work of many scholars and the help of colleagues, librarians, friends, and family.

Special thanks are due to the following scholars for their substantial contributions to the development of *The African-American Odyssey,* from which this concise edition has been crafted: Hilary Mac Austin, *Chicago, Illinois;* Brian W. Dippie, *University of Victoria;* Thomas Doughton, *Holy Cross College;* W. Marvin Dulaney, *College of Charleston;* Sherry DuPree, *Rosewood Heritage Foundation;* Peter Banner-Haley, *Colgate University;* Robert L. Harris, Jr., *Cornell University;* Wanda Hendricks, *University of South Carolina;* Rickey Hill, *Mississippi Valley State University;* William B. Hixson, *Michigan State University;* Barbara Williams Jenkins, formerly of *South Carolina State University;* Earnestine Jenkins, *University of Memphis;* Hannibal Johnson, *Tulsa, Oklahoma;* Wilma King, *University of Missouri, Columbia;* Karen Kossie-Chernyshev, *Texas Southern University;* Frank C. Martin, *South Carolina State University;* Jacqueline McLeod, Metropolitan State University of Denver; Freddie Parker, *North Carolina Central University;* Christopher R. Reed, *Roosevelt University;* Linda Reed, *University of Houston;* Mark Stegmaier, *Cameron University;* Robert Stewart, *Trinity School, New York;* Matthew Whitaker, *Arizona State University;* Barbara Woods, *South Carolina State University;* Andrew Workman, *Mills College;* Deborah Wright, *Avery Research Center, College of Charleston.*

We are grateful to the reviewers through six editions who devoted valuable time to reading and commenting on *The African-American Odyssey* and *African Americans: A Concise History.* Their insightful suggestions greatly improved the quality of the text: Leslie Alexander, *The Ohio State University;* Carol Anderson, *University of Missouri, Columbia;* Abel A. Bartley, *University of Akron;* Jennifer L. Baszile, *Yale University;* James M. Beeby, *West Virginia Wesleyan College;* Richard A. Buckelew, *Bethune-Cookman College;* Claude A. Clegg, *Indiana University;* Gregory Conerly, *Cleveland State University;* Delia Cook, *University of Missouri at Kansas City;* Caroline Cox, *University of the Pacific;* Mary Ellen Curtin, *Southwest Texas State University;* Henry Vance Davis, *Ramapo College of NJ;* Roy F. Finkenbine, *Wayne State University;* Dr. Jessie Gaston, *California State University, Sacramento;* Abiodun Goke-Pariola, *Georgia Southern University;* Robert Gregg, *Richard Stockton College of NJ;* Keith Griffler, *University of Cincinnati;* John H. Haley, *University of North Carolina at Wilmington;* Robert V. Hanes, *Western Kentucky University;* Julia Robinson Harmon, *Western Michigan University;* Ebeneazer Hunter, *De Anza College;* Eric R. Jackson, *Northern Kentucky University;* Wali Rashash Kharif, *Tennessee Technological University;* John W. King, *Temple University;* Joseph Kinner, *Gallaudet University;* Lester C. Lamon, *Indiana University, South Bend;* Eric Love, *University of Colorado-Boulder;* John F. Marszalek, *Mississippi State University;* Kenneth Mason, *Santa Monica College;* Andrew T. Miller, *Union College;* Diane Batts Morrow, *University of Georgia;* Ruddy Pearson, *American College;* Walter Rucker, *University of Nebraska, Lincoln;* Josh Sides, *California State University, Northridge;* Manisha Sinha, *University of Massachusetts, Amherst;* John David Smith, *North Carolina State University at Raleigh;* Marshall Stevenson, *Ohio State University;* Betty Joe Wallace, *Austin Peay State University;* Matthew C. Whitaker, *Arizona State University;* Harry Williams, *Carleton College;* Vernon J. Williams, Jr., *Purdue University;* Leslie Wilson, *Montclair State University;* Andrew Workman, *Mills College;* Marilyn L. Yancy, *Virginia Union University.*

We wish to thank the following reviewers for their insightful comments in preparation for the revision of *The African-American Odyssey,* which is the basis for the concise edition: Leslie Alexander, *The Ohio State University;* Lila Ammons, *Howard University;* Beverly Bunch-Lyons, *Virginia Technical College;* Latangela Crossfield, *Clark Atlanta University;* Linda Denkins, *Houston Community College;* Lillie Edwards, *Drew University;* Jim Harper, *North Carolina Central University;* Dr. Maurice Hobson, *University of Mississippi;* Alyce

Miller, *John Tyler Community College*; Zacharia Nchinda, *University of Wisconsin, Milwaukee*; Melinda Pash, *Fayetteville Technical Community College*; Charmayne Patterson, *Clark Atlanta University*; Matthew Schaffer, *Florence Darlington Technical College*; Denise Scifres, *City Colleges of Chicago, Center for Distance Learning*; Linda Tomlinson, *Fayetteville State University*; Angela Winand, *University of Illinois, Springfield*; Erica Woods-Warrior, *Hampton University*.

Many librarians provided valuable help tracking down important material. They include Avery Daniels, Ruth Hodges, Doris Johnson, the late Barbara Keitt, Cathi Cooper Mack, Mary L. Smalls, Ashley Till, and Adrienne Webber, all of Miller F. Whittaker Library, South Carolina State University; James Brooks and Jo Cottingham of the interlibrary loan department, Cooper Library, University of South Carolina; and Allan Stokes of the South Caroliniana Library at the University of South Carolina. Dr. Marshanda Smith and Kathleen Thompson provided important documents and other source material.

Seleta Simpson Byrd of South Carolina State University and Marshanda Smith of Northwestern University provided valuable administrative assistance.

Each of us also enjoyed the support of family members, particularly Barbara A. Clark, Robbie D. Clark, Emily Harrold, Judy Harrold, Carol A. Hine, and Thomas D. Hine.

Finally, we gratefully acknowledge the essential help of the superb editorial and production team at Prentice Hall: Charlyce Jones Owen, Publisher, whose vision got this project started and whose unwavering support saw it through to completion; Maureen Diana, Editorial Assistant; Rochelle Diogenes, Editor-in-Chief of Development; Maria Lange, Creative Design Director; Ann Marie McCarthy, Senior Managing Editor; and Emsal Hasan, Project Manager, who saw it efficiently through production; Marianne Gloriande, Manufacturing Buyer; Wendy Albert, Senior Marketing Manager; Beverly Fong, Program Manager; and Monica Ohlinger Group, who pulled together the book's supplementary material.

We owe a special and heartfelt debt of gratitude to our development editor, the late Gerald Lombardi. Gerald worked closely and conscientiously with us for five editions. This is a better book because of his efforts.

D.C.H.
W.C.H.
S.H.

About the Authors

Darlene Clark Hine

Darlene Clark Hine is Board of Trustees Professor of African-American Studies and Professor of History at Northwestern University. She is a fellow of the American Academy of Arts and Sciences, as well as past president of the Organization of American Historians and of the Southern Historical Association. Hine received her BA at Roosevelt University in Chicago, and her MA and Ph.D. from Kent State University, Kent, Ohio. Hine has taught at South Carolina State University and at Purdue University. She was a fellow at the Center for Advanced Study in the Behavioral Sciences at Stanford University and at the Radcliffe Institute for Advanced Studies at Harvard University. She is the author and/or co-editor of 20 books, most recently *The Black Chicago Renaissance* (Urbana: University of Illinois Press, 2012), *Black Europe and the African Diaspora* (Urbana: University of Illinois Press, 2010), co-edited with Trica Danielle Keaton and Stephen Small; *Beyond Bondage: Free Women of Color in the Americas* (Urbana: University of Illinois Press, 2005), co-edited with Barry Gaspar; and *The Harvard Guide to African-American History* (Cambridge: Harvard University Press, 2000), co-edited with Evelyn Brooks Higginbotham and Leon Litwack. She co-edited a two-volume set with Earnestine Jenkins, *A Question of Manhood: A Reader in U.S. Black Men's History and Masculinity* (Bloomington: Indiana University Press, 1999, 2001); and with Jacqueline McLeod, *Crossing Boundaries: Comparative History of Black People in Diaspora* (Bloomington: Indiana University Press, 2000). With Kathleen Thompson she wrote *A Shining Thread of Hope: The History of Black Women in America* (New York: Broadway Books, 1998), and edited with Barry Gaspar *More Than Chattel: Black Women and Slavery in the Americas* (Bloomington: Indiana University Press, 1996). She won the Dartmouth Medal of the American Library Association for the reference volumes co-edited with Elsa Barkley Brown and Rosalyn Terborg-Penn, *Black Women in America: An Historical Encyclopedia* (New York: Carlson Publishing, 1993). She is the author of *Black Women in White: Racial Conflict and Cooperation in the Nursing Profession, 1890–1950* (Bloomington: Indiana University Press, 1989). She continues to work on the forthcoming book project *The Black Professional Class: Physicians, Nurses, Lawyers, and the Origins of the Civil Rights Movement, 1890–1955.*

William C. Hine

William C. Hine received his undergraduate education at Bowling Green State University, his master's degree at the University of Wyoming, and his Ph.D. at Kent State University. He is a Professor of History at South Carolina State University. He has had articles published in several journals, including *Agricultural History, Labor History*, and the *Journal of Southern History*. He is currently writing a history of South Carolina State University.

Stanley Harrold

Stanley Harrold, Professor of History at South Carolina State University, received his bachelor's degree from Allegheny College and his master's and Ph.D. degrees from Kent State University. He is co-editor of *Southern Dissent*, a book series published by the University Press of Florida. In 1991–1992 and 1996–1997 he had National Endowment for the Humanities Fellowships. In 2005 and 2013 he received NEH Faculty Research Awards. His books include *Gamaliel Bailey and Antislavery Union* (Kent, Ohio: Kent State University Press, 1986), *The Abolitionists and the South* (Lexington: University Press of Kentucky, 1995), *Antislavery Violence: Sectional, Racial, and Cultural Conflict in Antebellum America* (co-edited with John R. McKivigan, Knoxville: University of Tennessee Press, 1999), *American Abolitionists* (Harlow, U.K.: Longman, 2001), *Subversives: Antislavery Community in Washington, D.C., 1828–1865* (Baton Rouge: Louisiana State University Press, 2003), *The Rise of Aggressive Abolitionism: Addresses to the Slaves* (Lexington: University Press of Kentucky, 2004), *Civil War and Reconstruction: A Documentary Reader* (Oxford, U.K.: Blackwell, 2007), and *Border War: Fighting Over Slavery before the Civil War* (Chapel Hill: University of North Carolina Press, 2010). He has published articles in *Civil War History, Journal of Southern History, Radical History Review*, and *Journal of the Early Republic*.

Africa ca. 6000 BCE–ca. 1600 CE

((•)) **Listen to Chapter 1 on MyHistoryLab**

The ancestral homeland of most black Americans is West Africa. Other parts of Africa—Angola and East Africa—were caught up in the great Atlantic slave trade that carried Africans to the New World from the sixteenth to the nineteenth centuries. But West Africa was the center of the trade in human beings. Knowing the history of West Africa therefore is important for understanding the people who became the first African Americans.

That history, however, is best understood within the larger context of the history and geography of the African continent. This chapter begins, therefore, with a survey of the larger context. It emphasizes aspects of a broader African experience that shaped life in West Africa before the arrival of Europeans in that region. It then explores West Africa's unique heritage and the facets of its culture that have influenced the lives of African Americans from the Diaspora—the original forced dispersal of Africans from their homeland—to the present.

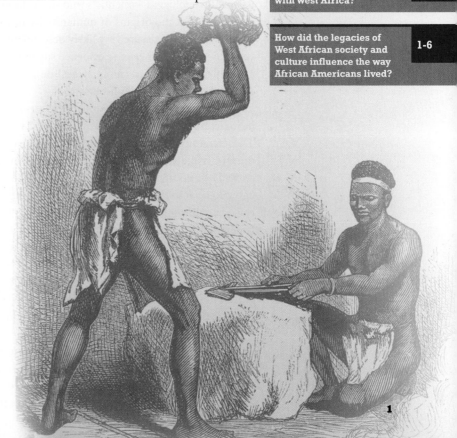

West Africans were making iron tools long before Europeans arrived in Africa.

A Huge and Diverse Land

1-1   What are the geographical characteristics of Africa?

From north to south, Africa is divided into a succession of climatic zones (see Map 1–1). Except for a fertile strip along the Mediterranean coast and the agriculturally rich Nile River valley, most of the northern third of the continent consists of the Sahara Desert. For thousands of years, the Sahara limited contact between the rest of Africa—known as sub-Saharan Africa—and the Mediterranean coast, Europe, and Asia. South of the Sahara is a semidesert region known as the Sahel, and south of the Sahel is a huge grassland, or **savanna**, stretching from Ethiopia west to the Atlantic Ocean. Much of the habitable part of West Africa falls within the savanna. The rest lies within the northern part of a **rain forest** that extends east from the Atlantic coast over most of the central part of the continent. Another region of savanna borders the rain forest to the south, followed by another desert—the Kalahari—and another coastal strip at the continent's southern extremity.

The Birthplace of Humanity

1-2   Where and how did humans originate?

Paleoanthropologists—scientists who study the evolution and prehistory of humans—have concluded that the origins of humanity lie in the savanna regions of Africa. All people today, in other words, are very likely descendants of beings who lived in Africa millions of years ago. Fossil and genetic evidence suggests that both humans and the forest-dwelling great apes (gorillas and chimpanzees) descended from a common ancestor who lived in Africa about 5 to 10 million years ago.

The earliest known *hominids* (the term designates the biological family to which humans belong) were the *Ardipithecines*, who emerged about 4.5 million years ago. These creatures walked upright but otherwise retained primitive characteristics and did not make stone tools. But by 3.4 million years ago, their descendants, known as *Australopithecus*, used primitive stone tools to butcher meat. By 2.4 million years ago, *Homo habilis*, the earliest creature designated as within the *homo* (human) lineage, had developed a larger brain than *Ardipithecus or Australopithecus*. *Homo habilis* (*habilis* means "tool using") used fire and built shelters with stone foundations. Like people in **hunting and gathering societies** today, they probably lived in small bands in which women foraged for plant food and men hunted and scavenged for meat. Recent discoveries suggest *Homo habilis* may have spread from Africa to the Caucasus region of southeastern Europe. A more advanced human, *Homo erectus*, who emerged in Africa about 1.6 million years ago, spread even farther from Africa, reaching eastern Asia and Indonesia.

Paleoanthropologists agree that modern humans, *Homo sapiens*, evolved from *Homo erectus*, but they disagree on how. According to a multiregional model, modern humans evolved throughout Africa, Asia, and Europe from ancestral regional populations of *Homo erectus* and archaic *Homo sapiens*. According to the out-of-Africa model, modern humans

savanna A flat, nearly treeless grassland typical of large portions of West Africa.

rain forest A dense growth of tall trees characteristic of hot, wet regions.

hunting and gathering societies Small societies dependent on hunting animals and collecting wild plants rather than on agriculture.

1-1
1-2
1-3
1-4
1-5
1-6

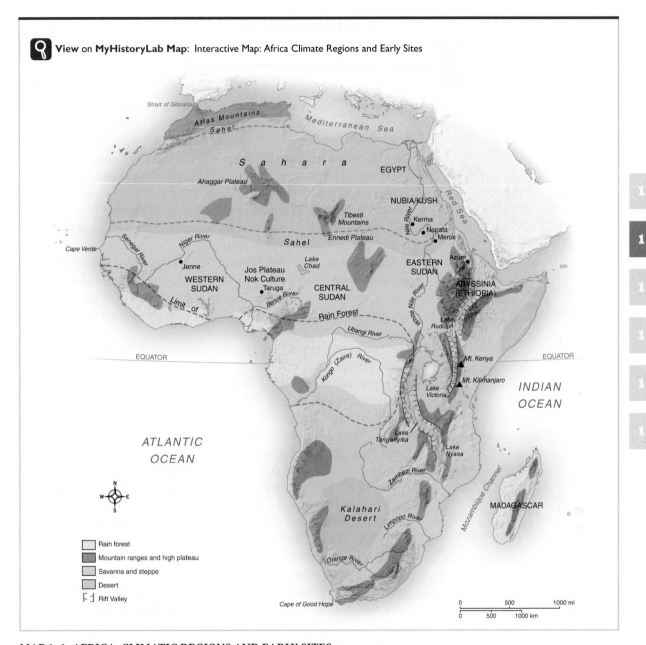

View on **MyHistoryLab Map**: Interactive Map: Africa Climate Regions and Early Sites

1-1
1-2
1-3
1-4
1-5
1-6

MAP 1–1 AFRICA: CLIMATIC REGIONS AND EARLY SITES
Africa is a large continent with several climatic zones. It is also the home of several early civilizations.

What impact did the variety of climatic zones have on the development of civilization in Africa?

emerged in Africa some 200,000 years ago and began migrating to the rest of the world about 100,000 years ago, eventually replacing all other existing hominid populations. Both of these models are consistent with recent genetic evidence, and both indicate that all living peoples are closely related.

Ancient Civilizations and Old Arguments

1-3   **Why are ancient African civilizations important?**

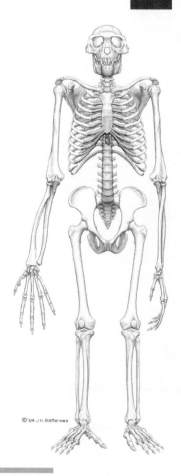

This drawing is based on a partial, fossilized skeleton discovered at Afar, Ethiopia, in 1994. The anthropologists who found the remains concluded in 2009 that the bones are those of a female *Ardipithecus ramidus* (nicknamed "Ardi") who lived 4.5 million years ago. Ardi shows that hominids diverged from apes much earlier than previously believed and fortifies existing evidence that human origins lay in Africa.

hierarchical Refers to a social system based on class rank.

hieroglyphics A writing system based on pictures or symbols.

patrilineal Descent through the male line.

patriarchal A society ruled by a senior man.

The earliest civilization in Africa and one of the two earliest civilizations in world history is that of ancient Egypt (see Map 1–1), which emerged in the Nile River valley in the fourth millennium BCE. Mesopotamian civilization, the other of the two, emerged in the valleys of the Tigris and Euphrates rivers in southwest Asia. In both regions, civilization appeared at the end of a long process in which hunting and gathering gave way to agriculture. The settled village life that resulted from this transformation permitted society to become increasingly **hierarchical** and specialized. Similar processes gave rise to civilization in other parts of the world.

The race of the ancient Egyptians and the nature and extent of their influence on later Western civilizations have long been a source of controversy. That controversy reflects more about the racial politics of recent history than it reveals about the Egyptians themselves, who did not regard themselves in ways related to modern racial terminology.

The argument over the Egyptians' race began in the nineteenth century when African Americans and white reformers sought to refute claims by racist pseudoscientists that people of African descent were inherently inferior to people of European descent. Unaware of the achievements of West African civilization, those who believed in human equality used evidence that the Egyptians were black to counter assertions that African Americans were incapable of civilization.

During the last two decades of the twentieth century, a more scholarly debate occurred between Afrocentrists and traditionalists. Afrocentrists regarded ancient Egypt as an essentially black civilization closely linked to other indigenous African civilizations to its south. They maintained not only that the Egyptians influenced later African civilizations but also that they had a decisive impact on the Mediterranean Sea region, including ancient Greece and Rome. Therefore, in regard to philosophy and science, black Egyptians originated Western civilization. In response, traditionalists claimed that modern racial categories have no relevance to the world of the ancient Egyptians. The ancient Greeks, they argued, developed the empirical method of inquiry and notions of individual freedom that characterize Western civilization. Not under debate, however, was Egypt's contribution to the spread of civilization throughout the Mediterranean region. No one doubts that in religion, commerce, and art, Egypt strongly influenced Greece and subsequent Western civilizations.

Egyptian Civilization

Egypt was, as the Greek historian Herodotus observed 2,500 years ago, the "gift of the Nile." This great river's gentle annual flooding regularly irrigated its banks, leaving behind deposits of fertile soil. The Nile also provided the Egyptians with a transportation and communications artery, while their desert surroundings protected them from foreign invasion.

Egypt became a unified kingdom around 3150 BCE. Between 1550–1100 BCE, it expanded beyond the Nile valley, creating an empire over the coastal regions of southwest Asia as well as over Libya and Nubia in Africa. During this period Egypt's kings began using the title *pharaoh*. After 1100 BCE, Egypt fell prey to a series of outside invaders. With the invasion of Alexander the Great's Macedonian army in 331 BCE, Egypt's ancient culture began a long decline under the pressure of Greek ideas and institutions (see Map 1–2). Finally the Roman Empire conquered Egypt in 30 BCE.

Before decline began, Egypt had resisted change for thousands of years. Pharoahs presided over a hierarchical society. Beneath them were classes of warriors, priests, merchants, artisans, and peasants. Scribes, who mastered Egypt's complex **hieroglyphic** writing system, staffed a large bureaucracy. Egyptian society was also **patrilineal** and **patriarchal**. Egyptian women nonetheless held a high status compared with women in much of the rest of the ancient world. They owned property independently of their husband, oversaw household slaves, controlled the education of their children, held public office, served as priests, and operated businesses. Several women became pharoah, one of whom, Hatshepsut, reigned for 20 years (1478–1458 BCE).

A complex polytheistic religion shaped Egyptian life. Although there were many gods, two of the more important were the sun god Re (or Ra), who represented the immortality of the Egyptian state, and Osiris, the god of the Nile, who embodied each person's immortality. Personal immortality and the immortality of the state merged in the person of the pharoah, as expressed in Egypt's elaborate royal tombs, the most famous of which are the Great Pyramids at Giza.

Nubia, Kush, Meroë, and Axum

To the south of Egypt in the upper Nile valley, in what is today the nation of Sudan, lay the ancient region known as Nubia. As early as the fourth millennium BCE, the black people who lived there interacted with the Egyptians. Archaeological evidence suggests that grain production and the concept of monarchy may have arisen in Nubia and then spread north to Egypt. But Egypt's population always greatly exceeded Nubia's, and during the second millennium BCE, Egypt used its military power to make Nubia an Egyptian colony and control Nubian copper and gold mines.

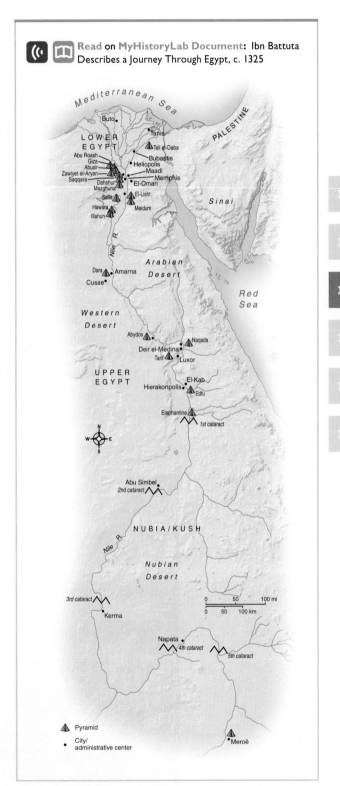

Read on MyHistoryLab Document: Ibn Battuta Describes a Journey Through Egypt, c. 1325

MAP 1–2 ANCIENT EGYPT AND NUBIA

What does this map indicate about the relationship between ancient Egypt and Nubia/Kush?

1-1

1-2

1-3

1-4

1-5

1-6

Egyptian religion, art, hieroglyphics, and political structure influenced Nubia. Then, with Egypt's decline during the first millennium BCE, the Nubians established an independent kingdom known as Kush. During the eighth century BCE, the Kushites took control of upper (meaning southern because the Nile flows from south to north) Egypt, and in about 750 BCE, the Kushite king Piankhy added lower Egypt to his realm. Piankhy became pharaoh and founded Egypt's twenty-fifth dynasty, which ruled until the Assyrians, who invaded Egypt from southwest Asia in 663 BCE, drove the Kushites out.

Kush itself remained independent for another thousand years until 540 BCE when a resurgent Egyptian army destroyed Kerma, and the Kushites moved their capital southward to Meroë. The new capital became wealthy from trade with East Africa, with regions to the west across Sudan, and with the Mediterranean world by way of the Nile River. The development of a smelting technology capable of exploiting local deposits of iron transformed the city into Africa's first industrial center.

Kush's wealth attracted powerful enemies, and in 23 BCE a Roman army invaded. But it was the decline of Rome and its Mediterranean economy that hurt Kush the most. As the Roman Empire grew weaker and poorer, its trade with Kush declined, and Kush, too, weakened. During the early fourth century CE, it fell to the neighboring Noba people, who in turn fell to the kingdom of Axum, whose warriors destroyed Meroë.

Located in what is today Ethiopia, Axum emerged as a nation during the first century BCE as **Semitic** people from the Arabian Peninsula settled among a local black

Semitic Refers to languages, such as Arabic and Hebrew, native to southwest Asia.

1-1

1-2

1-3

1-4

1-5

1-6

📖 **Read** on **MyHistoryLab Document:** Herodotus on Carthaginian Trade and on the City of Meroë

The ruined pyramids of Meroë on the banks of the upper Nile River are not as old as those at Giza in Egypt, and they differ from them stylistically. But they nonetheless attest to the cultural connections between Meroë and Egypt.

population. By the time it absorbed Kush during the fourth century CE, Axum had become the first Christian state in sub-Saharan Africa. By the eighth century, shifting trade patterns, environmental depletion, and Islamic invaders combined to reduce Axum's power.

West Africa

1-4 Why is West Africa significant for African-American history?

The immediate birthright of most African Americans, then, is to be found not in the ancient civilizations of the Nile valley—although those civilizations are part of the heritage of all Africans—but thousands of miles away among the civilizations that emerged in West Africa during the first millennium BCE.

Like Africa as a whole, West Africa is physically, ethnically, and culturally diverse. Much of West Africa south of the Sahara Desert falls within the savanna that spans the continent from east to west. West and south of the savanna are extensive forests. These two environments—savanna and forest—were home to a variety of cultures and languages. Patterns of settlement in the region ranged from isolated homesteads and hamlets to villages, towns, and cities.

West Africans began cultivating crops and tending domesticated animals between 1000 BCE and 200 CE. Those who lived on the savanna usually adopted settled village life well before those who lived in the forests. The early farmers produced grains while tending cattle and goats. By 500 BCE, some West Africans produced iron tools and weapons.

From early times, the peoples of West Africa traded among themselves and with the peoples who lived across the Sahara Desert in North Africa. This extensive trade became an essential part of the region's economy and had two other important results. First, it was the basis for the three great western Sudanese empires that successively dominated the region, from before 800 CE until the beginnings of the modern era. Second, it drew Arab merchants, and the Islamic religion, into the region.

Ancient Ghana

The first known kingdom in western Sudan was Ghana (see Map 1–3). Founded by the Soninke people in the area north of the modern republic of Ghana, the kingdom's origins are unclear. Because they possessed superior iron weapons, the Soninke dominated their neighbors and forged an empire through constant warfare. Ghana's boundaries reached into the Sahara Desert to its north and into modern Senegal to its south. But the empire's real power lay in commerce.

Ghana's kings were known in Europe and southwest Asia as the richest of monarchs, and trade produced their wealth. The key to this trade was the camel, introduced into Africa from Asia during the first century CE. The camel's ability to endure long journeys on small amounts of food and water dramatically increased trade across the Sahara between western Sudan and the coastal regions of North Africa.

Ghana traded in several commodities. From North Africa came silk, cotton, glass beads, horses, mirrors, dates, and especially salt. In return, Ghana exported pepper, slaves, and especially gold. The slaves were usually war captives.

1-1

1-2

1-3

1-4

1-5

1-6

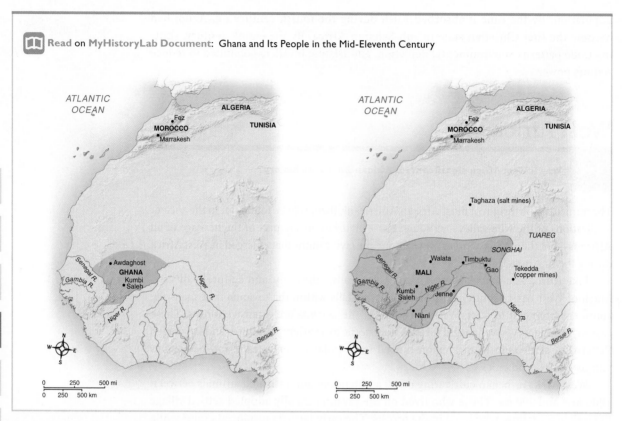

Read on MyHistoryLab Document: Ghana and Its People in the Mid-Eleventh Century

MAP 1–3 THE EMPIRES OF GHANA AND MALI
The western Sudanese empires of Ghana and Mali helped shape West African culture.
Ghana existed from as early as the fourth century CE to 1076. Mali dominated western
Sudan from 1230 to 1468.

**What does this map suggest concerning the historical relationship
between ancient Ghana and Mali?**

Before the fifth century CE, Roman merchants and Berbers were West Africa's chief partners in the trans-Sahara trade. As Roman power declined and Islam spread across North
Africa during the seventh and eighth centuries, Arabs replaced the Romans. Arab merchants
settled in Kumbi Saleh, Ghana's capital, which by the twelfth century had become an impressive city. There were stone houses and tombs and as many as 20,000 people. Kumbi Saleh had
several mosques, and some Soninke converted to Islam, although it is unclear whether the
royal family joined them. Muslims dominated the royal bureaucracy and introduced Arabic
writing to the region.

Commercial and religious rivalries led to Ghana's decline during the twelfth century.
The Almoravids, who were Islamic Berbers from what is today Morocco, had been Ghana's
principal competitors for control of the trans-Sahara trade. In 992 Ghana's army captured
Awdaghost, the Almoravid trade center northwest of Kumbi Saleh. Driven as much by religious fervor as by economic interest, the Almoravids retaliated in 1076 by conquering
Ghana. The Soninke regained their independence in 1087, but a little over a century later
the Sosso, a previously tributary people, destroyed Kumbi Saleh.

VOICES Al Bakri Describes Kumbi Saleh and Ghana's Royal Court

Nothing remains of the documents compiled by Ghana's Islamic bureaucracy. As a result, accounts of the civilization are all based on the testimony of Arab or Berber visitors. In this passage, written in the eleventh century, Arab geographer Al Bakri describes the great wealth and power of the king of Ghana and suggests there were tensions between Islam and the indigenous religion of the Soninke.

The city of Ghana [Kumbi Saleh] consists of two towns lying in a plain. One of these towns is inhabited by Muslims. It is large and possesses twelve mosques. . . . There are imams and muezzins, and assistants as well as jurists and learned men. Around the town are wells of sweet water from which they drink and near which they grow vegetables. The town in which the king lives is six miles from the Muslim one, and bears the name Al Ghaba [the forest]. The land between the two towns is covered with houses. The houses of the inhabitants are of stone and acacia wood. The king has a palace and a number of dome-shaped dwellings, the whole surrounded by an enclosure like the defensive wall of a city. In the town where the king lives, and not far from the hall where he holds his court of justice, is a mosque where pray the Muslims who come on diplomatic missions. Around the king's town are domed buildings, woods, and copses where live the sorcerers of these people, the men in charge of the religious cult. . . .

Of the people who follow the king's religion, only he and his heir presumptive, who is the son of his sister, may wear sewn clothes. All the other people wear clothes of cotton, silk, or brocade, according to their means. All men shave their beards and women shave their heads. The king adorns himself like a woman, wearing necklaces and bracelets, and when he sits before the people he puts on a high cap decorated with gold and wrapped in a turban of fine cotton. The court of appeal [for grievances against officials] is held in a domed pavilion around which stand ten horses with gold embroidered trappings. Behind the king stand ten pages holding shields and swords decorated with gold, and on his right are the sons of the subordinate kings of his country, all wearing splendid garments and their hair mixed with gold. . . . When the people professing the same religion as the king approach him, they fall on their knees and sprinkle their heads with dust, for this is their way of showing him their respect. As for the Muslims, they greet him only by clapping their hands.

1. **What does this passage indicate about life in ancient Ghana?**
2. **According to Al Bakri, in what ways do customs in Kumbi Saleh differ from customs in Arab lands?**

SOURCE: *Roland Oliver and Caroline Oliver,* Africa in the Days of Exploration *(Upper Saddle River, NJ: Prentice Hall, 1965), 9–10. Reprinted with permission.*

1-1
1-2
1-3
1-4
1-5
1-6

The Empire of Mali, 1230–1468

Following the defeat of Ghana by the Almoravids, western Sudanese peoples competed for political and economic power. This contest ended in 1235 when the Mandinka, under their legendary leader Sundiata (c. 1210–1260), defeated the Sosso at the Battle of Kirina. Sundiata then forged the Empire of Mali.

Mali was socially, politically, and economically similar to Ghana. It was larger than Ghana, however, and centered farther south, in a region of greater rainfall and more abundant crops. Sundiata also gained control of Wangara's gold mines, making Mali wealthier than Ghana had been. As a result, Mali's population grew to eight million.

To administer their vast empire at a time when communication was slow, Mali's rulers relied on personal and family ties with local chiefs. Commerce, bureaucracy, and scholarship also helped hold the empire together. Mali's most important city was Timbuktu, which had been established during the eleventh century beside the Niger River near the southern edge of the Sahara.

By the thirteenth century, Timbuktu had become a major hub for trade in gold, slaves, and salt. It attracted merchants from throughout the Mediterranean world and became a center of Islamic learning. The city had several mosques, 150 Islamic schools, a law school, and many book dealers. It supported a cosmopolitan community and impressed visitors with its religious and ethnic tolerance.

Mali reached its peak during the reign of Mansa Musa (r. 1312–1337). One of the wealthiest rulers the world has known, Musa made himself and Mali famous when in 1324 he undertook a pilgrimage across Africa to the Islamic holy city of Mecca in Arabia. With an entourage of 60,000, a train of one hundred elephants, and a propensity for distributing huge amounts of gold to those who greeted him along the way, Musa amazed the Islamic world. After his death, however, Mali declined. In 1468, one of its formerly subject peoples, the Songhai, captured Timbuktu, and their leader, Sunni Ali, founded a new West African empire.

Read on **MyHistoryLab**
Document: Leo Africanus
Describes Timbuktu, c. 1500

1-1

1-2

1-3

1-4

1-5

1-6

Read on **MyHistoryLab Document:** Al-Umari Describes Mansa Musa of Mali, c. 1330

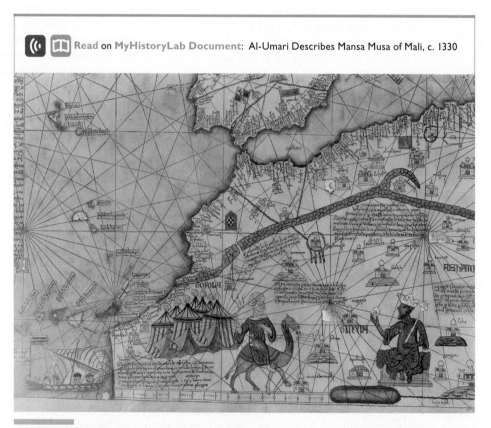

Mansa Musa, who ruled the West African Empire of Mali from 1312 to 1337, is portrayed at the bottom center of this portion of the fourteenth-century Catalan Atlas. Musa's crown, scepter, throne, and the huge gold nugget he displays symbolize his power and wealth.

The Empire of Songhai, 1464–1591

Like the Mandinka and Soninke before them, the Songhai were great traders and warriors. They built the last and largest of the western Sudanese empires (see Map 1–4). Sunni Ali required conquered peoples to pay tribute but otherwise let them run their own affairs. Nominally a Muslim, he—like Sundiata—was reputedly a great magician who derived power from the traditional spirits.

When Sunni Ali died by drowning, Askia Muhammad Toure led a successful revolt against Ali's son and made himself king of Songhai. The new king (r. 1492–1528) extended the empire north into the Sahara, west into Mali, and east to include the trading cities of Hausaland. He centralized the administration of the empire, replacing local chiefs with members of his family, substituting taxation for tribute, and establishing a bureaucracy to regulate trade.

A devout Muslim, Muhammad Toure used his power to spread the influence of Islam within the empire. During a pilgrimage to Mecca in 1497, he established diplomatic relations with Morocco and Egypt and recruited Muslim scholars to serve at the Sankore Mosque at Timbuktu. The mosque became a center for the study of theology, law, mathematics, and medicine. Despite these efforts, by the end of Muhammad Toure's reign Islamic culture remained weak in West Africa outside urban areas. Peasants, who made up 95 percent of the population, spoke a variety of languages, continued to practice indigenous religions, and remained loyal to their local chiefs.

Songhai reached its peak of influence under Askia Daud (r. 1549–1582). However, as the political balance of power in West Africa changed rapidly, Songhai failed to adapt. Since the 1430s, adventurers from the European country of Portugal had been establishing trading centers along the Guinea Coast, seeking gold and diverting it from the trans-Sahara trade. Their success threatened the Arab rulers of North Africa, Songhai's traditional partners in the trans-Sahara trade. In 1591 the king of Morocco, hoping to regain access to West African gold, sent an army of 4,000—mostly Spanish mercenaries armed with muskets and cannons—across the Sahara to attack Gao, Songhai's capital. Only 1,000 of the soldiers survived the march to confront Songhai's elite cavalry. But the Songhai warriors' bows and lances were no match for firearms, and the mercenaries routed them. Its army destroyed, the Songhai empire fell apart. When the Moroccans soon departed, West Africa lost a government powerful enough to intervene when the Portuguese, other Europeans, and the African kingdoms of the Guinea Coast became

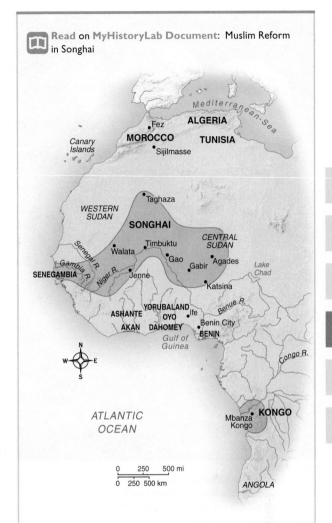

Read on **MyHistoryLab Document**: Muslim Reform in Songhai

MAP 1–4 WEST AND CENTRAL AFRICA, C. 1500
This map shows the Empire of Songhai (1464–1591), the Kongo kingdom (c. 1400–1700), and the major kingdoms of the West African forest region.

How did the western Sudanese empires' geographical location make them susceptible to slave trading?

The Nok people of what is today Nigeria produced terra-cotta sculptures like this one during the first millennium BCE. They also pioneered, between 500 and 450 BCE, iron smelting in West Africa.

more interested in trading for human beings than for gold.

The West African Forest Region

The area known as the forest region of West Africa extends 2,000 miles along the Atlantic coast from Senegambia in the northwest to the former kingdom of Benin (modern Cameroon) in the east. Among the early settlers of this region were the Nok, who, in what is today southern Nigeria, created around 500 BCE a culture noted for its ironworking technology and its terra-cotta sculptures. But significant migration into the forests began only after 1000 CE, as the western Sudanese climate became increasingly dry.

Because people migrated south from Sudan in small groups over an extended period, the process brought about considerable cultural diversification. A variety of languages, economies, political systems, and traditions came into existence. Some ancient customs survived, such as dividing types of agricultural labor by gender and living in villages composed of extended families. Nevertheless, the forest region became a patchwork of diverse ethnic groups with related but various ways of life.

Colonizing a region covered with thick vegetation was hard work. In some portions of the forest, agriculture did not supplant hunting and gathering until the fifteenth and sixteenth centuries. In more open parts of the region, however, small kingdoms emerged centuries earlier. Although none of these kingdoms ever grew as large as the empires of western Sudan, some became powerful. Their kings claimed semidivine status and sought to extend their power by conquering and assimilating neighboring peoples.

The peoples of the forest region are of particular importance for African-American history because of the role they played in the Atlantic slave trade as both slave traders and victims. Space limitations permit only a survey of the most important of these peoples, beginning with those of Senegambia in the northwest.

The inhabitants of Senegambia shared a common history and spoke closely related languages, but they were not politically united. Parts of the region had been incorporated within the empires of Ghana and Mali and had been exposed to Islamic influences. Senegambian society was strictly hierarchical, with royalty at the top and slaves at the bottom. Most people were farmers.

Southeast of Senegambia, the Akan states emerged during the sixteenth century. The rulers used gold from mines they controlled to purchase slaves who did the difficult work of cutting trees and burning refuse. The rulers then distributed the cleared fields to settlers. In return the settlers gave the rulers a portion of their produce and provided services. When Europeans arrived, the rulers used gold to purchase guns. The guns in turn allowed the Akan states to expand. During the late seventeenth century, one of them, the Ashantee, created a well-organized and densely populated kingdom, comparable in size to the modern country of Ghana. By the eighteenth century, this kingdom dominated the central portion of the forest region and used its army to capture slaves for sale to European traders.

To the east of the Akan states (in modern Benin and western Nigeria) lived the people of the Yoruba culture. They gained ascendancy in the area as early as 1000 CE by trading kola nuts and cloth to the peoples of the western Sudan. The artisans of the Yoruba city of Ife gained renown for their fine sculptures. Ife was also notable for the prominent role women played in commerce. During the seventeenth century, the Oyo people, employing a well-trained cavalry, imposed political unity on part of the Yoruba region. They, like the Ashantee, became extensively involved in the Atlantic slave trade.

West of the Oyo were the Fon people, who formed the Kingdom of Dahomey, which rivaled Oyo as a center for the slave trade. The king of Dahomey was an absolute monarch who, to ensure the loyalty of potential rivals, took thousands of wives for himself from leading families.

At the eastern end of the forest region lay the Kingdom of Benin, which controlled much of what is today southern Nigeria. The people of this kingdom shared a common heritage with the Yoruba, who played a role in the kingdom's formation during the thirteenth century. Throughout Benin's history, the Obas (kings), who claimed divine status, struggled for power with the kingdom's hereditary nobility.

After reforming its army during the fifteenth century, Benin expanded to the Niger River in the east, to the Gulf of Guinea to the south, and into Yoruba country to the west. The kingdom peaked during the late sixteenth century. European visitors noted the size and sophistication of its capital, Benin City. The city's wealthy class dined on beef, mutton, chicken, and yams. Its streets, unlike those of European cities of the time, had no beggars.

Benin remained little influenced by Islam or Christianity, but like other coastal kingdoms, it joined in the Atlantic slave trade. Beginning in the late fifteenth century, the Oba allowed Europeans to trade for gold, pepper, ivory, and slaves. Initially, the Oba forbade the sale of his subjects, but his large army—the first in the forest region to have European firearms—captured others for the trade as it conquered neighboring regions. By the seventeenth century, Benin's prosperity depended on the slave trade. As the kingdom declined during the eighteenth century, it began to sell its own people to European slave traders.

To Benin's east was Igboland, a densely populated but politically weak region along the Niger River. The Igbo people lived in one of the stateless societies common in West Africa. In these societies, families rather than central authorities ruled. Village elders provided local government, and life centered on family homesteads. Igboland had long exported fieldworkers and skilled artisans to Benin and other kingdoms. When Europeans arrived, they expanded this trade, which brought many Igbos to the Americas (see Map 1–5).

1-1
1-2
1-3
1-4
1-5
1-6

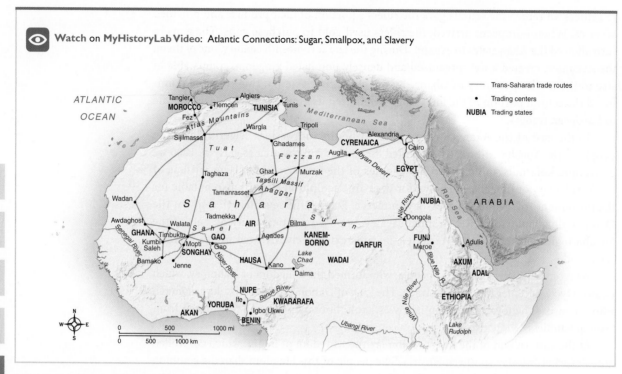

MAP 1–5 TRANS-SAHARAN TRADE ROUTES
Ancient trade routes connected sub-Saharan West Africa to the Mediterranean coast.
Among the commodities carried southward were silk, cotton, horses, and salt. Among
those carried northward were gold, ivory, pepper, and slaves.

**What was the significance of the trans-Saharan trade in West African
history?**

Kongo and Angola

1-5 **What did Kongo and Angola have in common with West Africa?**

Although the forebears of most African Americans originated in West Africa, a large minority came from Central Africa. In particular, they came from the area around the Congo
River and its tributaries and from the region to the south that the Portuguese called Angola.
The people of these regions had much in common with those of the Guinea Coast. They
divided labor by gender, lived in villages of extended families, and gave semidivine status
to their kings.

During the fourteenth and fifteenth centuries, a number of states formed in the area
to the north and south of what is today the border between the Democratic Republic of
the Congo and Angola. By far the most important was Kongo Kingdom, which controlled
much of the Congo River system. In addition to farming and fishing, this kingdom's wealth
derived from access to salt, iron, and trade with the interior. Nzinga Knuwu was king when
Portuguese expeditions arrived in the late fifteenth century, seeking chiefly to trade for
slaves. His son Nzinga Mbemba tried to convert the kingdom to Christianity and remodel it
along European lines. The resulting unrest, combined with Portuguese greed and the effects

VOICES A Dutch Visitor Describes Benin City

Benin City was one of the few towns of the Guinea Coast that were open to European travelers before the nineteenth century. As this account by a Dutch visitor in 1602 suggests, many of them compared it favorably to the cities of Europe.

The town seemeth to be very great; when you enter into it, you go into a great broad street, not paved, which seems to be seven or eight times broader than the Warmoes street in Amsterdam; which goeth right out and never crooks. . . . It is thought that street is a mile long [this is a Dutch mile, equal to about four English miles] besides the suburbs. At the gate where I entered on horseback, I saw a very high bulwark, very thick of earth, with a very deep broad ditch. . . . Without this gate there is a great suburb. When you are in the great street aforesaid, you see many great streets on the sides thereof, which also go right forth. . . . The houses in this street stand in good order, one close and even with the other, as the houses in Holland stand. . . . Their rooms within are four-square, over them having a roof that is not close[d] in the middle, at which place the rain, wind, and light come in, and therein they lie and eat their meat; they have other places besides, as kitchens and other rooms. . . .

The King's Court is very great, within it having many great four-square plains, which round about them have galleries, wherein there is always watch kept. I was so far within the Court that I passed over four such great plains, and wherever I looked, still I saw gates upon gates to go into other places. . . . I went as far as any Netherlander was, which was to the stable where his best horses stood, always passing a great long way. It seems that the King has many soldiers; he has also many gentlemen, who when they come to the court ride upon horses. . . . There are also many men slaves seen in the town, that carry water, yams, and palm-wine, which they say is for the King; and many carry grass, which is for their horses; and all of this is carried into the court.

1. **According to the Dutch visitor, how does Benin City compare to Amsterdam?**
2. **What seems to impress the Dutch visitor most about Benin City?**

SOURCE: *Roland Oliver and J. D. Fage,* A Short History of Africa *(Penguin Books 1962, Sixth Edition 1988). Copyright Roland Oliver and J. D. Fage, 1962, 1966, 1970, 1972, 1975, 1988. Reprinted with permission.*

1-1
1-2
1-3
1-4
1-5
1-6

---

of the slave trade, undermined royal authority. The ultimate result was the breakup of the kingdom and the disruption of the other Kongo-Angola states.

West African Society and Culture

1-6 **How did the legacies of West African society and culture influence the way African Americans lived?**

West Africa's great ethnic and cultural diversity makes it hazardous to generalize about the social and cultural background of the first African Americans. The dearth of written records from the region south of Sudan compounds the difficulties. But by working with a variety of sources, including oral histories, traditions, and archaeological studies, historians have pieced together a broad understanding of the way the people of West Africa lived at the beginning of the Atlantic slave trade.

Watch on MyHistoryLab
Video: West African States

Families and Villages

By the early sixteenth century, most West Africans were farmers. They usually lived in hamlets or villages of extended families and clans called **lineages**. Depending on the ethnic group involved, extended families and lineages were either patrilineal or **matrilineal**. In patrilineal societies, social rank and property passed in the male line from fathers to sons. In matrilineal societies, rank and property, although controlled by men, passed from generation to generation in the female line. A village chief in a matrilineal society was succeeded by his sister's son, not his own.

Within extended families, **nuclear families** (husband, wife, and children) or in some cases **polygynous families** (husband, wives, and children) acted as economic units. In other words, nuclear and polygynous families existed in the context of broader family communities composed of grandparents, aunts, uncles, and cousins. Elders in these extended families had great power over the economic and social lives of their members. Villagers' few possessions included cots, rugs, stools, and wooden storage chests. Their tools and weapons included bows, spears, iron axes, hoes, and scythes. Households used grinding stones, baskets, and ceramic vessels to prepare and store food.

Farming in West Africa was not easy. Drought came often on the savanna. In the forest, diseases carried by the tsetse fly sickened draft animals, and agricultural plots (because they had to be cleared by hand) averaged just two or three acres per family. Although private landownership prevailed, West Africans generally worked land communally, dividing tasks by gender. Among the Akan of the Guinea Coast, for example, men cleared the land of trees and underbrush, and women tended the fields, planting, weeding, and harvesting. Women also cared for children, prepared meals, and manufactured household pottery.

Women

In general, men dominated women in West Africa. As previously noted, men often had two or more wives, and, to a degree, custom held women to be the property of men. But West African women also enjoyed an amount of freedom that impressed Arabs and Europeans. In ancient Ghana, women sometimes served as government officials. Later, in the forest region, they sometimes inherited property and owned land—or at least controlled its income. Women—including enslaved women—in the royal court of Dahomey held high government posts. Ashantee noblewomen could own property, although they themselves could be considered inheritable property. The Ashantee queen held her own court to administer women's affairs.

Women retained far more sexual freedom in West Africa than was the case in Europe or southwest Asia. Ibn Battuta, a Muslim Berber who visited Mali during the fourteenth century, was shocked to discover that West African women could have male friends and companions other than their husbands or relatives.

Sexual freedom in West Africa was, however, more apparent than real. Throughout the region **secret societies** instilled in men and women ethical standards of behavior. The most important secret societies were the women's *Sande* and the men's *Poro*. They initiated boys and girls into adulthood and provided sex education. They established standards for personal conduct by emphasizing female virtue and male honor.

Class and Slavery

Although many West Africans lived in stateless societies, most of them lived in hierarchically organized states headed by monarchs who claimed divine or semidivine status. Most of these

---

lineage A type of clan, typical of West Africa, in which members claim descent from a single ancestor.

matrilineal Descent traced through the female line.

nuclear family A family unit consisting solely of one set of parents and their children.

polygynous family A family unit consisting of a man, his wives, and their children.

secret societies Social organizations that have secret ceremonies that only their members know about and can participate in.

1-1
1-2
1-3
1-4
1-5
1-6

monarchs' power was far from absolute, but they commanded armies, taxed commerce, and accumulated wealth. Beneath the royalty were classes of landed nobles, warriors, bureaucrats, and peasants. Lower classes included blacksmiths, butchers, weavers, woodcarvers, and tanners.

Slavery had been part of this hierarchical social structure since ancient times. Although common throughout West Africa, slavery was less so in the forest region than on the savanna. It took many forms and was not necessarily a permanent condition. Like people in other parts of the world, West Africans held war captives to be without rights and suitable for enslavement. In Islamic regions, masters had obligations to their slaves similar to those of a guardian for a ward. They were, for example, responsible for their slaves' religious well-being. In non-Islamic regions, the children of slaves acquired legal protections, such as the right not to be sold away from the land they occupied.

Slaves who served either in the royal courts of a West African kingdom or in a kingdom's armies often exercised power over free people and could acquire property. Also, the slaves of peasant farmers often had standards of living similar to those of their masters. Slaves who worked under overseers in gangs on large estates were far less fortunate. However, the children and grandchildren of these enslaved agricultural workers gained employment and privileges similar to those of free people. Slaves retained a low social status, but in many respects slavery in West African societies functioned as a means of **assimilation**.

assimilation The process of becoming similar.

Religion

There were two religious traditions in fifteenth-century West Africa: Islamic and indigenous. Islam, which Arab traders introduced into West Africa, took root first in the Sudanese empires and remained prevalent in the cosmopolitan savanna. Even there it was stronger in cities than in rural areas because it was the religion of merchants and bureaucrats. Islam is resolutely monotheistic, asserting that Allah is the only God.

West Africa's indigenous religions remained strongest in the forest region. They were **polytheistic** and **animistic**, recognizing many divinities and spirits. Beneath an all-powerful but remote creator god, lesser gods represented the forces of nature or particular mountains, rivers, trees, and rocks.

polytheistic Many gods.

animistic The belief that inanimate objects have spiritual attributes.

Practitioners of West African indigenous religions believed the spirits of their ancestors could influence their lives. Therefore, ceremonies to sustain ancestral spirits and their power over the earth became central to traditional West African religions. These rituals shaped everyday life, making organized churches and professional clergy rare. Instead, family members with an inclination to do so assumed religious duties.

Art and Music

Religious belief and practice influenced West African art. West Africans, seeking to preserve the images of their ancestors, excelled in woodcarving and sculpture in terra-cotta, bronze, and brass. Throughout the region, artists produced wooden masks representing in highly stylized manners ancestral spirits and gods. Wooden and terra-cotta figurines, sometimes referred to as "**fetishes**," were also common. West Africans used them in funerals, in rituals related to ancestral spirits, in medical practice, and in coming-of-age ceremonies. In contrast to masks and fetishes, the great bronze sculptures of Benin had political functions. They portrayed their subjects, which consisted of kings, warriors, and nobles rather than gods and spirits, realistically.

fetish A natural object or an artifact believed to have magical power. A charm.

 Listen on MyHistoryLab Audio: Ghana: Ewe-Atsiagbekor from Roots of Black Music in America

West African music also served religion. Folk musicians employed such instruments as drums, xylophones, bells, flutes, and mbanzas (predecessor to the banjo) to produce a highly rhythmic accompaniment to the dancing associated with religious rituals. A **call-and-response** style of singing also played a vital role in ritual. Vocal music had polyphonic textures and sophisticated rhythms.

Literature: Oral Histories, Poetry, and Tales

West African literature was part of an oral tradition that passed from generation to generation. At its most formal, trained poets and musicians who served kings and nobles created it. But it was also a folk art that expressed the views of the common people.

At a king's court there could be several poet-musicians who had high status and specialized in poems glorifying rulers and their ancestors. Court poets also used their trained memories to recall historical events and precise genealogies. The self-employed poets, called **griots**, who traveled from place to place were socially inferior to court poets but functioned in a similar manner. Both court poets and griots were men. Women were more involved in folk literature. They joined men in creating and performing work songs. They led in creating and singing dirges, lullabies, and satirical verses.

Just as significant for African-American history were the West African prose tales. Like similar stories in other parts of Africa, these tales took two forms: those with human characters and those with animal characters who represented humans. The tales centered on human characters dealt with such subjects as creation, the origins of death, worldly success, and romantic love.

The animal tales aimed to entertain and to teach lessons. They focused on small creatures, often referred to as "trickster characters," who struggled against larger beasts. Plots centered on the ability of these weak animals to outsmart larger and meaner antagonists.

In West Africa, these tales represented the ability of common people to counteract the power of kings and nobles. When the tales reached America, they became allegories for the struggle between enslaved African Americans and their powerful white masters.

Technology

West African technology was distinctive and important. Although much knowledge about this technology has been lost, iron refining and forging, textile production, architecture, and rice cultivation helped shape life in the region.

As we previously mentioned, iron technology existed in West Africa since ancient times. Blacksmiths produced tools for agriculture, weapons for hunting and war, ceremonial staffs, and religious amulets. These products encouraged the development of cities and kingdoms.

Architecture embodied Islamic and indigenous elements, with the former predominant on the savanna and the latter in the forest region. Building materials consisted of stone, mud, and wood. Public buildings reached large proportions, and some mosques served 3,000 worshippers. Massive stone or mud walls surrounded cities and towns.

Hand looms for household production existed throughout Africa for thousands of years, and cloth made from pounding bark persisted in the forest region into modern times. But trade and Islamic influences led to commercial textile production. By the ninth century CE, large looms, some equipped with pedals, produced narrow strips of wool or cotton. Men, rather than women, made cloth and tailored it into embroidered Islamic robes, shawls, hats, and blankets, which Muslim merchants traded over wide areas.

Of particular importance for African-American history, West Africans living along rivers in coastal regions had produced rice since approximately 1000 BCE. Portuguese who

call-and-response An African-American singing style rooted in Africa. A solo call tells a story to which a group responds, often with repeated lyrics.

griot A West African self-employed poet and oral historian.

1-1

1-2

1-3

1-4

1-5

1-6

arrived during the fifteenth century CE reported large diked rice fields. Deliberate flooding of these fields, transplanting sprouts, and intensive cultivation reemerged as slaves produced rice in the colonial South Carolina low country.

CONCLUSION

Although all of Africa contributed to their background, the history of African Americans begins in West Africa, the region from which the ancestors of most of them unwillingly departed for America. Historians have discovered, as subsequent chapters will show, that West Africans taken to America and their descendants in America preserved much more of their ancestral way of life than scholars once believed possible. West African family organization, work habits, language structures and some words, religious beliefs, legends and stories, pottery styles, art, and music all reached America. These African legacies, although often much modified, influenced the way African Americans and other Americans lived in their new land. They continue to shape American life.

CHAPTER TIMELINE

EVENTS IN AFRICA	WORLD EVENTS

10 million years ago

5–10 million years ago Separation of hominids from apes	**1.6 million years ago** *Homo erectus* beginning to spread through Eurasia
4 million years ago Emergence of *australopithecines*	
2.4 million years ago Emergence of *Homo habilis*	
1.7 million years ago Emergence of *Homo erectus*	

1.5 million years ago

100,000–200,000 years ago Appearance of modern humans	**8000 BCE** Appearance of the first agricultural settlements in southwest Asia
6000 BCE Beginning of Sahara Desert formation	

5000 BCE

5000 BCE First agricultural settlements in Egypt	**3500 BCE** Sumerian civilization in Mesopotamia
3800 BCE Predynastic period in Egypt	
c. 3150 BCE Unification of Egypt	

CHAPTER TIMELINE

EVENTS IN AFRICA   WORLD EVENTS

2500 BCE

2700–2150 BCE
Egypt's Old Kingdom

2300 BCE
Beginning of Indus valley civilization

2100–1650 BCE
Egypt's Middle Kingdom

1500 BCE

1550–700 BCE
Egypt's New Kingdom

1600–1250 BCE
Mycenaean Greek civilization

c. 1500 BCE
Beginning of Shang dynasty in China

1000 BCE

750–670 BCE
Rule of Kushites over Egypt

600–336 BCE
Classical Greek civilization

540 BCE
Founding of Meroë

c. 500 BCE
Beginning of iron smelting in West Africa

50 CE
Destruction of Kush

500 CE

632–750 CE
Islamic conquest
of North Africa

204 BCE–476 CE
Domination of Mediterranean by Roman
Republic and Empire

c. 750–1076 CE
Empire of Ghana; Islam begins to take
root in West Africa

500–1350 CE
European Middle Ages

c. 570 CE
Birth of Muhammad

1200 CE

1230–1468 CE
Empire of Mali

c. 1300 CE
Rise of Yoruba states

CHAPTER TIMELINE

EVENTS IN AFRICA	WORLD EVENTS

1400 CE

1434 CE
Start of Portuguese exploration and establishment of trading outposts on West African coast

c. 1450 CE
Centralization of power in Benin

1464–1591 CE
Empire of Songhai

1492 CE
Christopher Columbus and European encounter of America

1517 CE
Reformation begins in Europe

1600 CE

c. 1650 CE
Rise of Kingdom of Dahomey and the Akan states

1610 CE
Scientific revolution begins in Europe

On MyHistoryLab

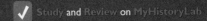 ✓ Study and Review on MyHistoryLab

REVIEW QUESTIONS

1. What was the role of Africa in the evolution of modern humanity?

2. Discuss the controversy concerning the racial identity of the ancient Egyptians. What is the significance of this controversy for the history of African Americans?

3. Compare and contrast the western Sudanese empires with the forest civilizations of the Guinea Coast.

4. Discuss the role of religion in West Africa. What was the African religious heritage of black Americans?

5. Describe West African society on the eve of the expansion of the Atlantic slave trade. What were the society's strengths and weaknesses?

2

Middle Passage CA. 1450–1809

((• Listen to Chapter 2
on MyHistoryLab

The Atlantic slave trade, which lasted for more than three centuries, brought millions of Africans 3,000 miles across the Atlantic Ocean to the Americas. It was the largest forced migration in history. By the eighteenth century, the voyage across the ocean in European ships called "slavers" had become known as the "**Middle Passage**." British sailors coined this phrase to describe the middle leg of a triangular journey first from England to Africa, then from Africa to the Americas, and finally from the Americas back to England.

This chapter describes the Atlantic slave trade and the Middle Passage. It explores their origins both in European colonization of the Americas and in the slave trade that had existed in Africa itself for centuries. It focuses on the experience of the enslaved people whom the trade brought to America. For those who survived, the grueling journey was a prelude to servitude on huge agricultural factories called plantations. Many who became African Americans first experienced plantation life in the West Indies—the Caribbean islands—where a process called "seasoning" prepared them for lives as slaves in the Americas.

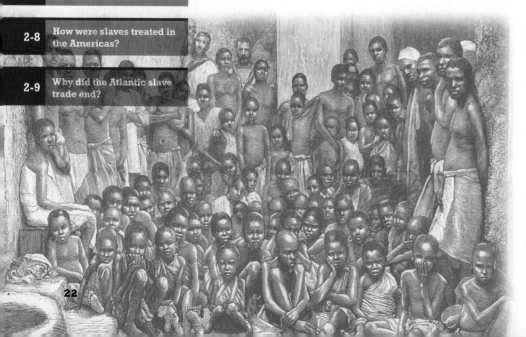

After Great Britain banned the Atlantic slave trade in 1807, British warships enforced the ban. The people portrayed in this early nineteenth-century woodcut were rescued from a slave ship by the H.M.S. *Undine*.

The European Age of Exploration and Colonization

Middle Passage The voyage of slave ships (slavers) across the Atlantic Ocean from Africa to the Americas.

2-1 **How did the arrival of the Europeans affect Africa?**

The origins of the Atlantic slave trade and its long duration were products of Western Europe's expansion of power that began during the fifteenth century and continued into the twentieth century. For a variety of economic, technological, and demographic reasons, Portugal, Spain, the Netherlands, France, England, and other nations sought to explore, conquer, and colonize in Africa, Asia, and the Americas. Their efforts had important consequences for these areas.

Portugal took the lead during the early 1400s when its ships reached Africa's western coast. Portuguese captains hoped to find Christian allies there against the Muslims of North Africa and spread Christianity. But they were more interested in trade with African kingdoms, as were the Spanish, Dutch, English, and French who followed them.

Even more attractive than Africa to the Portuguese and their European successors as sources of trade and wealth were India, China, Japan, and the East Indies (modern Indonesia and Malaysia). In 1487 the Portuguese explorer Bartolomeu Dias discovered the Cape of Good Hope at the southern tip of Africa and thereby established that it was possible to sail around Africa to reach India and regions to its east. Ten years later Vasco da Gama initiated this route on behalf of Portuguese commerce. A similar desire to reach these eastern regions motivated the Spanish monarchy to finance Christopher Columbus's westward voyages that began in 1492.

Columbus, who believed the earth to be much smaller than it is, hoped to reach Japan or India by sailing west, thereby opening a direct trade route between Spain and these eastern countries. Columbus's mistake led to his accidental landfall in the Americas. In turn, that encounter led to the European conquest, settlement, and exploitation of North and South America and the Caribbean islands, where Columbus first landed. Columbus and those who followed him quickly enslaved indigenous Americans (American Indians) as laborers in fields and mines. Almost as quickly, many indigenous peoples either died of European diseases and overwork or escaped beyond the reach of European power. Consequently, European colonizers needed additional laborers. This demand for a workforce in the Americas caused the Atlantic slave trade.

The Slave Trade in Africa

2-2 **How did the slave trade in Africa differ from the Atlantic slave trade?**

Slave labor was not peculiar to the European colonies in the Americas. Slavery and slave trading had existed in all cultures for thousands of years. As Chapter 1 indicates, slave labor was common in West Africa, although it was usually less oppressive than it became in the Americas.

When Portuguese voyagers first arrived at Senegambia, Benin, and Kongo, they found a thriving commerce in slaves. These kingdoms represented the southern extremity of an extensive slave trade conducted by Islamic nations. Although Arabs nurtured antiblack prejudice, race was not the major factor in this Islamic slave trade. Arab merchants and West African kings, for example, imported white slaves from Europe.

In West Africa, Sudanese horsemen conducted the Islamic slave trade. The horsemen invaded the forest region to capture people who could not effectively resist—often

2-1

2-2

2-3

2-4

2-5

2-6

2-7

2-8

2-9

2-1
2-2
2-3
2-4
2-5
2-6
2-7
2-8
2-9

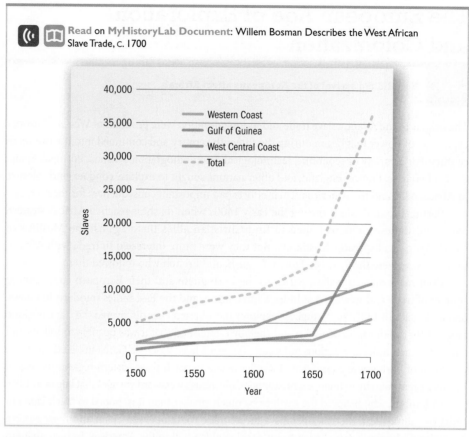

Read on **MyHistoryLab** Document: Willem Bosman Describes the West African Slave Trade, C. 1700

FIGURE 2–1 ESTIMATED ANNUAL EXPORTS OF SLAVES FROM WESTERN AFRICA TO THE AMERICAS, 1500–1700

SOURCE: *John Thornton,* Africa and Africans in the Making of the Atlantic World, 1400–1680 *(New York: Cambridge University Press, 1992), 118.*

they belonged to stateless societies. The trade dealt mainly in women and children who as slaves became concubines and domestic servants in North Africa and southwest Asia. This pattern contrasted with that of the later Atlantic slave trade, which primarily sought young men for agricultural labor in the Americas.

The demand for slaves in Muslim countries remained high from the tenth through the fifteenth centuries because many slaves died from disease or gained freedom and assimilated into Arab society. The trans-Sahara slave trade therefore rivaled the trade in gold across the Sahara. According to historian Roland Oliver, the Atlantic slave trade did not reach the proportions of the trans-Sahara slave trade until 1600 (see Figure 2–1).

The Origins of the Atlantic Slave Trade

2-3   What was the "Middle Passage"?

Guinea Coast The southward-facing coast of West Africa, from which many of the people caught up in the Atlantic slave trade departed for the Americas.

When Portuguese ships first arrived off the **Guinea Coast**, their captains traded chiefly for gold, ivory, and pepper, but they also wanted slaves. During the following decades, Portuguese raiders captured hundreds of Africans to work as domestic servants in

Portugal and Spain. But usually the Portuguese and the other European and white Americans who succeeded them did not themselves capture and enslave people. They instead purchased slaves from African traders. This arrangement began formally in 1472 when the Portuguese merchant Ruy do Siqueira gained permission from the Oba (king) of Benin to trade for slaves within the borders of the Oba's kingdom. Siqueira and other Portuguese found that a commercial infrastructure already existed in West Africa that could distribute European trade goods and procure slaves. The rulers of Benin, Dahomey, and other African kingdoms restricted the Europeans to a few points on the coast, and the kingdoms raided the interior to supply the Europeans with slaves.

Interethnic rivalries in West Africa led to the warfare that produced these slaves during the sixteenth century. Although Africans initially resisted selling members of their own ethnic group to Europeans, they did not at first consider it wrong to sell members of their own race to foreigners. In fact, neither Africans nor Europeans had yet developed a concept of racial solidarity.

Until the early sixteenth century, Portuguese seafarers conducted the Atlantic slave trade on a tiny scale to satisfy a limited market for domestic servants in Portugal and Spain. But the impact of Columbus's voyages drastically changed the slave trade. The Spanish and Portuguese—followed by the Dutch, English, and French—established colonies in the Caribbean, Mexico, Central America, and South America. Because disease and overwork caused the number of American Indians in these regions to decline rapidly, Europeans relied on the Atlantic slave trade to replace them as a source of slave labor (see Map 2–1). As early as 1502, African slaves lived on the island of Hispaniola—modern Haiti and the Dominican Republic. During the sixteenth century, gold and silver mines in Spanish Mexico and Peru, and especially sugar plantations in Portuguese Brazil, produced an enormous demand for labor. Consequently, the Atlantic slave trade grew to huge and tragic proportions to meet that demand.

West African artists recorded the appearance of Europeans who came to trade in gold, ivory, and human beings. This Benin bronze relief sculpture, dating to the late sixteenth or early seventeenth century, portrays two Portuguese men.

Growth of the Atlantic Slave Trade

2-4 What was the relationship between the Atlantic slave trade and the Industrial Revolution?

Because Europe provided an insatiable market for sugar, cultivation of this crop in the Americas became extremely profitable. Sugar plantations employing slave labor spread from Portuguese-ruled Brazil to the Caribbean islands. Later, the cultivation of coffee in Brazil and of tobacco, rice, and **indigo** in British North America added to the demand for African slaves. By 1510 Spain had joined Portugal in the enlarged Atlantic slave trade, and a new, harsher form of slavery appeared in the Americas. Unlike slavery in Africa, Asia, and Europe, slavery in the Americas was based on race, as only Africans and American Indians were enslaved. Most of the slaves were men or boys who served as agricultural laborers.

indigo A bluish-violet dye produced from the indigo plant.

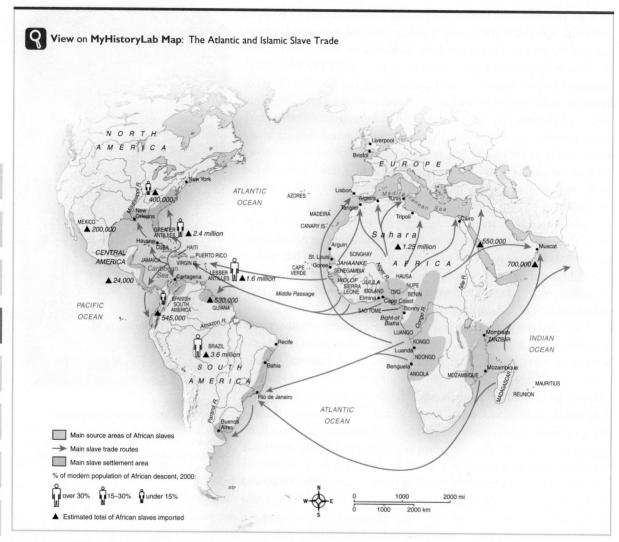

View on MyHistoryLab Map: The Atlantic and Islamic Slave Trade

MAP 2–1 THE ATLANTIC AND ISLAMIC SLAVE TRADES
Not until 1600 did the Atlantic slave trade reach the proportions of the Islamic slave
trade. The map shows the principal sources of slaves, primary routes, and major destinations.

**According to this map, which region in the Americas imported
the most slaves?**

chattel Enslaved
people who were
treated legally as
property.

They became **chattel**—meaning personal property—of their masters and lost their customary human rights.

Portugal and Spain dominated the Atlantic slave trade during the sixteenth century.
They shipped about 2,000 Africans per year to their American colonies, with most by far
going to Brazil. From the beginning of the trade until its nineteenth-century abolition,
about 6,500,000 of the approximately 11,328,000 Africans taken to the Americas went
to Brazil and Spain's colonies. Both the Portuguese and the Spanish monarchies granted
monopolies over the trade to private companies. In Spain this monopoly became known
in 1518 as the *Asiento* (meaning "contract"). The profits from the slave trade were so great

Asiento The monopoly
over the slave trade
from Africa to Spain's
American colonies.

that by 1550 the Dutch, French, and English were becoming involved. During the early seventeenth century, the Dutch drove the Portuguese from the West African coast and became the principal European slave-trading nation.

The Dutch also shifted the center of sugar production to the West Indies. England and France followed, with the former taking control of Barbados and Jamaica and the latter taking Saint Domingue (Haiti), Guadeloupe, and Martinique. With the development of to-bacco as a **cash crop** in Virginia and Maryland during the 1620s and with the expansion of sugar production in the West Indies, the demand for African slaves continued to grow. The result was that England and France competed with the Dutch to control the Atlantic slave trade. After a series of wars, England emerged supreme. It had driven the Dutch out of the trade by 1674. Victories over France and Spain led in 1713 to English control of the *Asiento*, which allowed English traders the exclusive right to supply slaves to all of Spain's American colonies. After 1713, English ships dominated the slave trade, carrying about 20,000 slaves per year from Africa to the Americas. At the peak of the trade during the 1790s, they transported 50,000 per year.

The profits from the Atlantic slave trade, together with those from the sugar and to-bacco produced in the Americas by slave labor, were invested in England and helped fund the **Industrial Revolution** during the eighteenth century. In turn, Africa became a market for cheap English manufactured goods (see Map 2–2). Eventually, two triangular trade

cash crop A crop grown for sale rather than subsistence.

 Watch on MyHistoryLab Video: England Enters the Atlantic Slave Trade

Industrial Revolution An economic change that began in England during the early eighteenth century and spread to Continental Europe and the United States. Industry rather than agriculture became the dominant form of enterprise.

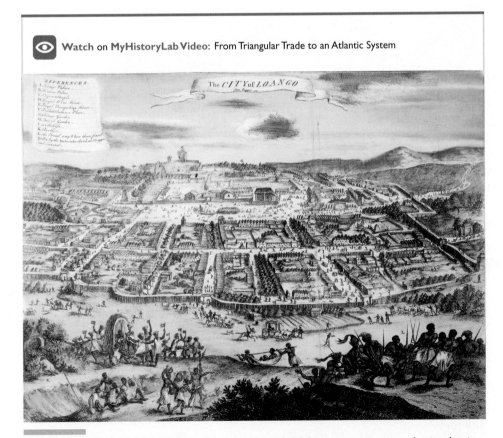

Watch on **MyHistoryLab** Video: From Triangular Trade to an Atlantic System

The Portuguese established the city of Luanda in 1575. This eighteenth-century print portrays the city when it was at its height as a center for the shipment of enslaved Africans to Brazil. *The Granger Collection, New York.*

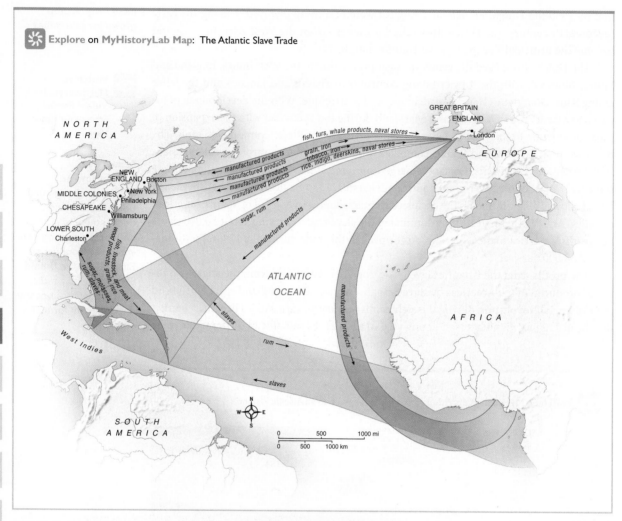

Explore on **MyHistoryLab Map:** The Atlantic Slave Trade

MAP 2–2 ATLANTIC TRADE AMONG THE AMERICAS, GREAT BRITAIN, AND WEST AFRICA DURING THE SEVENTEENTH AND EIGHTEENTH CENTURIES
Often referred to as a triangular trade, this map shows the complexity of early modern Atlantic commerce, of which the slave trade was a major part.

What does this map suggest about the economy of the Atlantic world between 1600 and 1800?

systems developed. In one, traders carried English goods to West Africa and exchanged the goods for slaves. Then the traders carried the slaves to the West Indies and exchanged them for sugar, which they took back to England on the third leg of the triangle. In the other triangular trade, white Americans from Britain's New England colonies carried rum to West Africa to trade for slaves. From Africa they took the slaves to the West Indies to exchange for sugar or molasses—sugar syrup—which they then took home to distill into rum.

✸ EXPLORE ON MYHISTORYLAB
The Atlantic Slave Trade

In what ways was British North America involved in the Atlantic slave trade?

The Atlantic slave trade, over a period of three centuries, brought more than 10 million enslaved Africans to the shores of the Americas. The great majority of them lived in Brazil and the Caribbean islands. A significant minority came to the British North American colonies. In the southern British colonies, they produced tobacco, rice, and other staple crops. In the northern colonies, slaves worked on farms and in shops. White colonists bought slaves and participated in the slave trade as sailors, ship builders, traders, and financiers. Slavery influenced the economy, politics, and society that provided the foundations for the United States.

The slave deck of the bark "Wildfire," brought into Key West on April 30, 1860.

✸ Explore the Topic on MyHistoryLab

1. **Comparison** *Which colonies, and later states, imported the most slaves?* Map the differences among the regions of North America.
2. **Analysis** *How did the ratio of male to female slaves differ across the Thirteen Colonies?* Hypothesize the explanations for this distribution.
3. **Consequence** *What were the major economic activities for different regions of mainland British America and the early United States?* Consider the connections between slavery and regional economic production.

ORIGINS OF AFRICANS IN NORTH AMERICA, 1700–1800	NATIONS PARTICIPATING IN THE SLAVE TRADE, 1700–1800
Region	**Nation***
Angola	Britain
Bight of Benin	Portugal
Bight of Biafra	France
Gold Coast	The Netherlands
Senegambia	Denmark
Sierra Leone	British Colonies/North America

*In order of most to fewest number of slaves traded

2-1
2-2
2-3
2-4
2-5
2-6
2-7
2-8
2-9

The African-American Ordeal from Capture to Destination

2-5 **What happened to Africans after they crossed the Atlantic?**

Watch on
MyHistoryLab
Video: African
Enslavement:
The Terrible
Transformation—
Overview

Read on MyHistoryLab
Document:
A Slave Tells of His Capture
in Africa in 1798

factories
Headquarters for a
European company
that traded for slaves
or engaged in other
commercial enterprises
on the West African
coast.

The availability of large numbers of slaves in West Africa resulted from the wars that accompanied the formation of states in that region. Captives suitable for enslavement were a by-product of these wars. Senegambia and nearby Sierra Leone, then Oyo, Dahomey, and Benin, became, in turn, centers of the trade. Meanwhile, on the west coast of Central Africa, slaves became available as a result of the conflict between the expanding Kingdom of Kongo and its neighbors.

Sometimes African armies enslaved the inhabitants of conquered towns and villages. At other times, raiding parties captured isolated families or kidnapped individuals. As warfare spread to the interior, captives had to march for hundreds of miles to the coast where European traders awaited them.

Once the captives reached the coast, those destined for the Atlantic trade went to fortified structures called **factories**. Such factories contained the headquarters of the traders, warehouses for their trade goods and supplies, and dungeons or outdoor holding pens for the captives. In these pens, slave traders divided families and—as much as possible—ethnic groups to prevent rebellion. The traders stripped captives naked and inspected them for disease and physical defects. Those considered fit for purchase were branded like cattle with a hot iron bearing the symbol of a trading company.

View on **MyHistoryLab Closer Look**: The Voyage to Slavery

In this nineteenth century engraving, African slave traders conduct a group of bound captives from the interior of Africa toward European trading posts.

The Crossing

After being held in a factory for weeks or months, captives faced the frightening prospect of leaving their native land for a voyage across an ocean that many of them had never before seen. Sailors rowed them out in large canoes to slave ships offshore. Once at sea, the slave ships followed the route Columbus had established during his voyages to the Americas: from the Canary Islands off West Africa to the Windward Islands in the Caribbean. The passage normally lasted between two and three months. But the time required for the crossing varied widely. The larger ships usually reached the Caribbean in 40 days, but some voyages took six months.

Both human and natural causes accounted for such delays. During the three centuries that the Atlantic slave trade endured, Western European nations often fought each other, and slave ships became prized targets. As early as the 1580s, English "sea dogs," such as John Hawkins and Sir Francis Drake, attacked Spanish ships to steal their human cargoes. Outright piracy peaked between 1650 and 1725 when demand for slaves in the West Indies increased. There were also such potentially disastrous natural forces as doldrums—long windless spells at sea—and hurricanes, which could destroy ships, crews, and cargoes.

The Slavers and Their Technology

Slave ships (called **slavers**) varied in size but grew larger over the centuries. A ship's tonnage determined how many slaves it could carry, with the formula being two slaves per ton. A ship of 200 tons might therefore carry 400 slaves. But captains often ignored the formula. Some kept their human cargo light, calculating that smaller loads lowered mortality and made revolt less likely. But most captains were "tight packers" who squeezed human beings together hoping that large numbers would offset increased deaths.

slaver A ship used to transport slaves from Africa to the Americas.

The slavers' cargo space was generally only five feet high. Ships' carpenters halved this vertical space by building shelves, so slaves might be packed above and below on planks that measured only 5.5 feet long and 1.3 feet wide. Consequently, slaves had only about 20 to 25 inches of headroom. To add to the discomfort, the crews chained male slaves together in pairs to help prevent rebellion and lodged them away from women and children.

The most frequently reproduced illustration of a slaver's capacity for human cargo comes from the *Brookes*, which sailed from Liverpool, England, during the 1780s. At 300 tons, the *Brookes* was an exceptionally large ship for its time, and the diagrams show how tightly packed the slaves were that it transported. The precise, unemotional renderings of the *Brookes*'s geometrically conceived design scarcely indicate the physical suffering it caused. The renderings do not show the constant shifting, crushing, and chafing among the human cargo caused by the movement of the ship at sea. Also, during storms the crew often neglected to feed the slaves, empty the tubs used for excrement, take slaves on deck for exercise, tend to the sick, or remove the dead.

Mortality rates were high because the crowded, unsanitary conditions encouraged seaboard epidemics. Overall, one-third of the Africans subjected to the trade perished between their capture and embarkation on a slave ship. Another third died during the Middle Passage or during "seasoning" on a Caribbean island.

A Slave's Story

In his book *The Interesting Narrative of the Life of Olaudah Equiano or Gustavus Vassa, the African, Written by Himself,* published in 1789, former slave Olaudah Equiano provides a vivid account of a West African's capture, sale to traders, and voyage to America in 1755. Although recent evidence suggests Equiano *may* have been born in South Carolina rather

2-1
2-2
2-3
2-4
2-5
2-6
2-7
2-8
2-9

View on **MyHistoryLab Closer Look**: Plan and Sections of a Slave Ship and an Illustration of a Slave Camp

Plan of the British slave ship *Brookes*, 1788. This plan, which may undercount the human cargo the *Brookes* carried, shows how tightly Africans were packed aboard slave ships.

than West Africa, scholars respect the accuracy of his account. He tells the story of a young Igbo, the dominant ethnic group in what is today southern Nigeria. African slave raiders capture the boy when he is 10 years old and force him to march along with other captives to the Niger River or one of its tributaries, where they trade him to other Africans. His new captors take him to the coast and sell him to European slave traders whose ships sail to the West Indies.

The boy's experience at the coastal slave factory convinces him he has entered a hell, peopled by evil spirits. The stench caused by forcing many people to live in close confinement makes him nauseated and emotionally agitated. When the sailors lodge him with others below deck on the ship, he is so sick that he loses his appetite and hopes to die. Instead, because he refuses to eat, the sailors take him on deck and whip him.

During the time the ship is in port awaiting a full cargo of slaves, the boy spends much time on deck. After putting to sea, however, he usually remains below deck with the other slaves where "each had scarcely room to turn himself." There, the smells of unwashed bodies and of the toilet tubs, "into which the children often fell and were almost suffocated," create a loathsome atmosphere. The darkness, the chafing of chains on flesh, and the shrieks and groans of the sick and disoriented provide "a scene of horror almost inconceivable."

When slaves are allowed to get fresh air and exercise on deck, the crew strings up nets to prevent them from jumping overboard. Even so, two Africans who are chained together evade the nets and jump into the ocean, preferring drowning to staying on board. The boy shares their desperation. As the ship goes beyond sight of land, he and the other captives believe they lose "even the least glimpse of hope of [re]gaining the shore" and returning to their country.

Attempts to keep the slaves entertained and in good humor seldom succeeded. Crews sometimes forced the slaves to dance and sing, but their songs, as slave-ship surgeon Alexander Falconbridge testified, were "melancholy lamentations, of their exile from their native country." Depression among the Africans led to a catatonia that contemporary observers called melancholy or extreme nostalgia. Falconbridge noted that the slaves had "a strong attachment to their native country" and a "just sense of the value of liberty."

Although the traders, seeking to lessen the possibility of shipboard conspiracy and rebellion, separated individuals who spoke the same language, the boy described by Equiano manages to find adults who speak Igbo. They explain to him the purpose of the voyage, which he learns is to go to the white people's country to labor for them rather than to be eaten by them. He does not realize that work on a West Indian island could be a death sentence.

A Captain's Story

indentured servant
An individual who sells or loses his or her freedom for a specified number of years.

John Newton, a white captain of a slave ship, who was born in London in 1725, provides another perspective on the Middle Passage. In 1745 Newton, as an **indentured servant**, joined the crew of a slaver bound for Sierra Leone. Indentured servants lost their freedom for a specified number of years either because they sold it or because they were being punished for debt or crime. In 1748, on the return voyage to England, Newton survived a fierce Atlantic storm and, thanking God, became an evangelical Christian. Like most people of his era, Newton saw no contradiction between his newfound faith and his participation in the enslavement and ill treatment of men, women, and children.

Newton was 25 when he became captain of the *Duke of Argyle*, a 140-ton vessel he had converted into a slaver. On October 23 the *Duke of Argyle* reached Frenchman's Bay, Sierra Leone, where Newton observed other ships from England, France, and New England anchored offshore. Two days later, Newton purchased two men and a woman from traders at the port, but he had to sail to several other ports to accumulate a full cargo. Leaving West Africa for the open sea on May 23, 1751, the ship delivered its slaves to Antigua in the West Indies on July 3.

Poor health forced Newton to retire from the slave trade in 1754. Ten years later he became an Anglican priest. By the late 1770s, he had repented his involvement in the slave trade and had become one of its leading opponents. Together with William Cowper—a renowned poet—Newton published the *Olney Hymns* in 1779. Among the selections in this volume was "Amazing Grace," which Newton wrote as a reflection on divine forgiveness for his sins. For several reasons, Newton and other religious Britons had begun to perceive an evil in the slave trade that, despite their piety, they had failed to see earlier.

Provisions for the Middle Passage

Slave ships left Liverpool and other European ports provisioned with food supplies for their crews. These included beans, cheese, beef, flour, and grog—a mixture of rum and water. When the ships reached the Guinea Coast in West Africa, their captains purchased pepper, palm oil, lemons, limes, yams, plantains, and coconuts. Because slaves were not accustomed to European foods, the ships needed these staples of the African diet.

Although slaver captains realized it was in their interest to feed their human cargoes well, they often skimped on supplies to save money and make room for more slaves. Therefore, the food on a slave ship was often insufficient to prevent malnutrition and weakened immune systems among people already traumatized by separation from their families and homelands. As a result, many Africans died during the Middle Passage from diseases amid the horrid conditions that were normal aboard the slave ships. Others died from depression: they refused to eat despite the crew's efforts to force food down their throats.

Sanitation, Disease, and Death

Diseases such as malaria, yellow fever, measles, smallpox, hookworm, scurvy, and dysentery constantly threatened African cargoes and European crews during the Middle Passage. Astronomical death rates prevailed on board the slave ships before 1750. Mortality dropped after that date because ships became faster and ships' surgeons knew more about hygiene and diet. There were also early forms of vaccinations against smallpox, which may have been the worst killer of slaves on ships. But, even after 1750, poor sanitation led to many deaths.

Usually slavers provided only three or four toilet tubs below deck for enslaved Africans to use during the Middle Passage. They had to struggle among themselves to get to the tubs, and children had a particularly difficult time. Those too ill to reach the tubs excreted where they lay, and diseases such as dysentery, which are spread by human waste, thrived.

2-1
2-2
2-3
2-4
2-5
2-6
2-7
2-8
2-9

2-1

2-2

2-3

2-4

2-5

2-6

2-7

2-8

2-9

((•)) 📖 **Read** on **MyHistoryLab Document:** Olaudah Equiano Describes the Middle Passage, 1789

Portrait of a Negro Man, Olaudah Equiano, *1780s.*

SOURCE: *EX 17082 Portrait of a Negro Man, Olaudah Equiano, 1780s (previously attributed to Joshua Reynolds), by English School (18th century) Royal Albert Memorial Museum, Exeter, Devon, UK/Bridgeman Art Library.*

Dysentery, known by contemporaries as "the bloody flux," vied with smallpox to kill the most slaves aboard ships.

What role ships' surgeons—general practitioners in modern terminology—played in preventing or inadvertently encouraging deaths aboard slave ships is difficult to determine. Some of them were frauds. The era's primitive medical knowledge limited the best of the surgeons. Captains rewarded them with "head money" for the number of healthy slaves who arrived in the Americas. But they could also be blamed for deaths at sea that reduced the value of the human cargo.

Many surgeons recognized that African remedies worked better than European medications in alleviating the slaves' symptoms. Therefore, the surgeons collected herbs and foods along the Guinea Coast. They learned African nursing techniques, which they found more effective in treating onboard diseases than European procedures. What the surgeons did not understand and regarded as superstition was the holistic nature of African medicine. African healers maintained that body, mind, and spirit were interconnected elements of the totality of a person's well-being.

The enslaved Africans were often just as dumbfounded by the beliefs and actions of their captors. They thought they had entered a world of bad spirits when they boarded a slaver, and they attempted to counteract the spirits with rituals from their homeland. John Newton noted that during one voyage he feared slaves had tried to poison the ship's drinking water. He was relieved to discover that they were only putting what he called "charms" in the water supply. Such fetishes, representing the power of spirits, were important in West African religions. But Newton held such beliefs in contempt.

Resistance and Revolt at Sea

Because many enslaved Africans refused to accept their fate, slaver captains had to be vigilant. Uprisings occurred often, and Newton himself put down a potentially serious one aboard the *Duke of Argyle.* Twenty men had broken their chains below deck but were apprehended before they could assault the crew.

Most such rebellions took place while a ship prepared to set sail. The African coast was in sight, and the slaves could still hope to return home. But some revolts occurred on the open sea, where it was unlikely the Africans, even if their revolt succeeded, could return to their homes or regain their freedom. Both sorts of revolt indicate that not even capture, forced march to the coast, imprisonment, branding, and sale could break the spirit of many captives. These Africans preferred to face death rather than accept bondage.

Other slaves resisted their captors by drowning or starving themselves. As we previously indicated, captains used nets to prevent suicide by drowning. To deal with self-imposed starvation, they used hot coals or a metal device called a *speculum oris* to force individuals to open their mouths for feeding.

VOICES   The Journal of a Dutch Slaver

The following account of slave trading on the West African coast is from a journal kept on the Dutch slaver St. Jan *between March and November 1659. Although written from a European point of view, it describes the conditions Africans faced on such ships.*

We weighed anchor, by the order of the Hon'ble Director, Johan Valckenborch, and the Hon'ble Director, Jasper van Heussen to proceed on our voyage to Rio Reael [on the Guinea Coast] to trade for slaves for the hon'ble company.

March 8. Saturday. Arrived with our ship before Ardra, to take on board the surgeon's mate and a supply of tamarinds for refreshment for the slaves; sailed again next day on our voyage to Rio Reael.

17. Arrived at Rio Reael in front of a village called Bany, where we found the company's yacht, named the *Vrede*, which was sent out to assist us to trade for slaves.

In April. Nothing was done except to trade for slaves.

May 6. One of our seamen died. . . .

22. Again weighed anchor and ran out of Rio Reael accompanied by the yacht *Vrede*; purchased there two hundred and nineteen head of slaves, men, women, boys and girls, and set our course for the high land of Ambosius, for the purpose of procuring food there for the slaves, as nothing was to be had at Rio Reael.

June 29. Sunday. Again resolved to proceed on our voyage, as there also but little food was to be had for the slaves in consequence of the great rains which fell every day, and because many of the slaves were suffering from the bloody flux in consequence of the bad provisions we were supplied with at El Mina. . . .

July 27. Our surgeon, named Martyn de Lanoy, died of the bloody flux.

Aug. 11. Again resolved to pursue our voyage towards the island of Annebo, in order to purchase there some refreshments for the slaves. . . .

Aug. 15. Arrived at the island Annebo, where we purchased for the slaves one hundred half tierces of beans, twelve hogs, five thousand coconuts, five thousand sweet oranges, besides some other stores.

Sept. 21. The skipper called the ships officers aft, and resolved to run for the island of Tobago and to procure water there; otherwise we should have perished for want of water, as many of our water casks had leaked dry.

24. Friday. Arrived at the island of Tobago and hauled water there, also purchased some bread, as our hands had had no ration for three weeks.

Nov. 1. Lost our ship on the Reef of Rocus [north of Caracas], and all hands immediately took to the boat, as there was no prospect of saving the slaves, for we must abandon the ship in consequence of the heavy surf.

4. Arrived with the boat at the island of Curaco; the Hon'ble Governor Beck ordered two sloops to take the slaves off the wreck, one of which sloops with eighty four slaves on board, was captured by a privateer [pirate vessel].

1. **What dangers did the slaves and crew on board the *St. Jan* face?**
2. **What is the attitude of the author of the journal toward slaves?**

SOURCE: Elizabeth Donnan, ed., *Documents Illustrative of the History of the Slave Trade to America*, 4 vols. (Washington, DC: Carnegie Institute, 1930–35), 1: 141–45. Reprinted with permission.

2-1
2-2
2-3
2-4
2-5
2-6
2-7
2-8
2-9

2-1

2-2

2-3

2-4

2-5

2-6

2-7

2-8

2-9

Cruelty

The Atlantic slave trade required more capital than any other maritime commerce during the seventeenth and eighteenth centuries. The investments for the ships, the exceptionally large crews they employed, the navigational equipment, the armaments, the purchase of slaves in Africa, and the supplies of food and water needed to feed hundreds of passengers were phenomenal. The aim was to carry as many Africans in healthy condition to the Americas as possible in order to make the large profits that justified such expenditures. Yet, as we have indicated, conditions aboard the vessels were abysmal.

Scholars have debated how much deliberate cruelty the enslaved Africans suffered from ships' crews. The West Indian historian Eric Williams asserts that the horrors of the Middle Passage have been exaggerated. Many writers, Williams contends, are led astray by the writings of those who, during the late eighteenth and early nineteenth centuries, sought to abolish the slave trade. In his view—and that of other historians—the difficulties of the Middle Passage were similar to those of European indentured servants who suffered high mortality rates on the voyage to America.

From this perspective the primary cause of death at sea on all ships carrying passengers across the Atlantic to the Americas was epidemic disease, against which medical practitioners had few tools before the twentieth century. Contributing factors included inadequate means of preserving food from spoilage and failure to prevent freshwater from becoming contaminated during the long ocean crossing. According to Williams, overcrowding by slavers was only a secondary cause for the high mortality rates.

Such observations help place conditions aboard the slave ships in a broader perspective. Cruelty and suffering are, to some degree, historically relative in that practices acceptable in the past are now considered inhumane. Yet cruelty aboard slavers must also be placed in a cultural context. Cultures distinguish between what constitutes acceptable behavior toward their own people on the one hand and toward strangers on the other. For Europeans, Africans were cultural strangers, and what became normal in the Atlantic slave trade was in fact exceptionally cruel compared to how Europeans treated each other. Slaves below deck received only one-half the space allocated on board to European soldiers, free emigrants, indentured servants, and convicts. Europeans regarded slavery itself as a condition suitable only for non-Christians. And, as strangers, Africans faced brutalization by European crew members who often cared little about the physical and emotional damage they inflicted.

African Women on Slave Ships

For similar reasons, African women did not enjoy the same protection against unwanted sexual attention from European men that European women received. Consequently, sailors during long voyages attempted to sate their sexual appetites with enslaved women. African women caught in the Atlantic slave trade were worth half the price of African men in Caribbean markets, and as a result, captains took fewer of them on board their vessels. Perhaps because the women were less valuable commodities, crew members felt they had license to abuse them sexually. As historian Marcus Rediker points out, because women and children appeared less likely to revolt, they often had "more freedom of movement on slave ships." But that very ability to move about made them more vulnerable to sexual assault. The separate below-deck compartments for women on slave ships also made them easier targets than they otherwise might have been.

Historian Barbara Bush speculates that the horrid experience of the Middle Passage may have influenced black women's attitudes toward sexuality and procreation. This, in turn, may help explain why slave populations in the Caribbean and Latin America failed to reproduce themselves: exhaustion, terror, and disgust can depress sex drives.

VOICES   Dysentery (or the Bloody Flux)

Alexander Falconbridge (d. 1792) served as ship's surgeon on four British slavers between 1780 and 1787. In 1788 he became an opponent of the trade and published An Account of the Slave Trade on the Coast of Africa. *Here he describes in gruesome detail conditions in slave quarters during a dysentery epidemic that he mistakenly attributes to stale air and heat.*

Some wet and blowing weather having occasioned the port-holes to be shut, and the grating to be covered, fluxes and fevers among the Negroes ensued. While they were in this situation, my profession requiring it, I frequently went down among them, till at length their apartments became so extremely hot, as to be only sufferable for a very short time. . . . It is not in the power of the human imagination, to picture to itself a situation more dreadful or disgusting. Numbers of the slaves having fainted, they were carried upon deck, where several of them died, and the rest were, with great difficulty, restored. It had nearly proved fatal to me also. The climate was too warm to admit the wearing of any clothing but a shirt, and that I had pulled off before I went down; notwithstanding which, by only continuing among them for about a quarter of an hour, I was so overcome with the heat, stench, and foul air, that I had nearly fainted; and it was not without assistance, that I could get upon deck. The consequence was, that I soon after fell sick of the same disorder, from which I did not recover for several months. . . .

The place allotted for the sick Negroes is under the half deck, where they lie on the bare planks. By this means, those who are emaciated, frequently have their skin, and even their flesh, entirely rubbed off, by the motion of the ship, from the prominent parts of the shoulders, elbows, and hips, so as to render the bones in those parts quite bare. And some of them, by constantly lying in the blood and mucus, that had flowed from those afflicted with the flux, and which . . . is generally so violent as to prevent their being kept clean, have their flesh much sooner rubbed off, than those who have only to contend with the mere friction of the ship. The excruciating pain which the poor sufferers feel from being obliged to continue in such a dreadful situation, frequently for several weeks, in case they happen to live so long, is not to be conceived or described. Few, indeed, are ever able to withstand the fatal effects of it. The utmost skill of the surgeon is here ineffectual. . . .

The surgeon, upon going between decks, in the morning, to examine the situation of the slaves, frequently finds several dead; and among the men, sometimes a dead and living Negroe fastened by their irons together. When this is the case, they are brought upon the deck, and being laid on the grating, the living Negroe is disengaged, and the dead one thrown overboard. . . .

1. **Could slave traders have avoided the suffering described in this passage?**
2. **What impact would such suffering have had on those who survived it?**

SOURCE: Alexander Falconbridge, *An Account of the Slave Trade on the Coast of Africa* (London: privately printed, 1788), in John H. Bracey Jr. and Manisha Sinha, *African American Mosaic: A Documentary History from the Slave Trade to the Twenty-first Century* (Upper Saddle River, NJ: Prentice Hall, 2004), 1: 24.

2-1 2-2 2-3 2-4 2-5 2-6 2-7 2-8 2-9

Landing and Sale in the West Indies

2-6   **How did Africans adapt to conditions in the Americas?**

As a slaver neared the West Indies, the crew prepared its human cargo for landing and sale. Those bound for the larger Caribbean islands or for the British colonies of southern North America often received some weeks of rest in the easternmost islands of the West Indies.

French slave traders typically rested their slave passengers on Martinique. The English preferred Barbados. Sale to white plantation owners followed.

The process of landing and sale that ended the Middle Passage was often as protracted as the events that began it in Africa. After anchoring at one of the Lesser Antilles Islands—Barbados, St. Kitts, or Antigua—English slaver captains haggled with the agents of local planters over numbers and prices. They then determined whether to sell all their slaves at their first port of call, sell some of them, sail to another island, or sail to a North American port. If the market looked good in the first port, the captain might still take a week or more to sell his cargo.

Often, captains and crew had to do more to prepare slaves for sale than allow them to clean themselves and exercise. The ravages of cruelty, confinement, and disease could not be easily remedied. Slaves were required to oil their bodies to conceal blemishes, rashes, and bruises. Ships' surgeons used hemp to plug the anuses of those suffering from dysentery to block the bloody discharge the disease caused.

Humiliation continued as the slaves went to market. Once again they suffered close physical inspection from potential buyers. Unless a single purchaser agreed to buy an entire cargo of slaves, auctions took place either on deck or in sale yards on shore. However, some captains employed "the scramble." In these barbaric spectacles, the captain established standard prices for men, women, and children; herded the Africans together in a corral; and then allowed buyers to rush pell-mell among them to grab and rope together the slaves they desired.

((•)) 📖 **Read** on **MyHistoryLab Document:** Bryan Edwards Describes the "Maroon Negroes of the Island of Jamaica," 1807

This nineteenth-century engraving suggests the humiliation Africans endured as they were subjected to physical inspections before being sold.

Seasoning

2-7 **What was "seasoning"?**

Seasoning followed sale. This term referred to a period of up to two years of **acculturating** slaves and breaking them in to plantation routines. On Barbados, Jamaica, and other Caribbean islands, planters divided slaves into three categories: **Creoles** (slaves born in the Americas), old Africans (those who had lived in the Americas for some time), and new Africans (those who had just survived the Middle Passage). Creole slaves were worth three times the value of unseasoned new Africans. Seasoning began the process of making new Africans more like Creoles.

In the West Indies, this process involved more than an apprenticeship in the work routines of the sugar plantations. It also prepared many new arrivals for resale to North American planters, who preferred "seasoned" slaves to "unbroken" ones who came directly from Africa. In fact, before 1720 most of the Africans who ended up in the British colonies of North America had gone first to the West Indies. After that date, the demand for slave labor in the islands had become so great that they could spare fewer slaves for resale to the North American market. As a result, henceforth most slave imports into the tobacco-, rice-, and later cotton-growing regions of the American South came directly from Africa and had to be seasoned by their American masters. But many slaves still came to North America from the Caribbean, to which they had been brought from Africa or where they had been born.

In either case, seasoning was a disciplinary process intended to modify the behavior and attitude of slaves and make them effective laborers. As part of this process, the slaves' new masters gave them new names: Christian names, generic African names, or names from classical Greece and Rome (such as Jupiter, Achilles, or Plato).

The seasoning process also involved learning European languages. Masters in the Spanish Caribbean were especially thorough teachers. Consequently, although Spanish-speaking African slaves and their descendants retained African words, they could be easily understood by any Spanish-speaking person. In the French and English Caribbean islands and in parts of North America, however, slave society produced Creole dialects that in grammar, vocabulary, and intonation had distinctive African linguistic features. These Africanized versions of French and English could not be easily understood by those who spoke more standard dialects.

During seasoning, masters or overseers broke slaves into plantation work by assigning them to one of several work gangs. The strongest men joined the first or "great gang," which did the heavy fieldwork of planting and harvesting. The second gang, including women and older men, did lighter fieldwork, such as weeding. The third gang, composed of children, worked shorter hours and performed such tasks as bringing food and water to the field gangs. Other slaves became domestic servants. New Africans served apprenticeships with old Africans from their same ethnic group or with Creoles.

Planters had to rely on old Africans and Creoles to train new recruits because white people were a minority in the Caribbean. Later, a similar demographic pattern developed in parts of the cotton-producing American South. In both regions, therefore, African custom shaped the cooperative labor of slaves in gangs. But the use of old Africans and Creoles as instructors and the appropriation of African styles of labor should not suggest leniency. Although plantation overseers, who ran day-to-day operations, could be white, of mixed race, or black, they invariably imposed strict discipline. Drivers, who directed the work gangs, were almost

seasoning The process by which newly arrived Africans were broken in to slavery in the Americas.

acculturating Change in individuals who are introduced to a new culture.

Creoles Persons of African and/or European descent born in the Americas.

Watch on MyHistoryLab Video: Survival in a Strange New Land

always black. But they carried whips and punished those who worked too slowly or showed disrespect. Planters assigned recalcitrant new Africans to the strictest overseers and drivers.

Planters housed slaves undergoing seasoning with the old Africans and Creoles who instructed them. The instructors regarded such additions to their households as economic opportunities because the new Africans provided extra labor on the small plots of land that West Indian planters often allocated to slaves. Slaves could sell surplus root vegetables, peas, and fruit from their gardens and save to purchase freedom for themselves or others. Additional workers helped produce larger surpluses to sell at local markets, thereby reducing the time required to accumulate a purchase price.

New Africans also benefited from this arrangement. They learned how to build houses in their new land and how to cultivate vegetables to supplement the food the planter provided. Even though many Africans brought building skills and agricultural knowledge with them to the Americas, old Africans and Creoles helped teach them how to adapt their skills and knowledge to a new climate, topography, building materials, and social organization.

The End of the Journey: Masters and Slaves in the Americas

2-8   How were slaves treated in the Americas?

By what criteria did planters assess the successful seasoning of new Africans? The first criterion was survival. Already weakened and traumatized by the Middle Passage, many Africans did not survive seasoning. Historian James Walvin estimates that one-third died during their first three years in the West Indies. African men died at a greater rate than African women, perhaps because they did the more arduous fieldwork.

A second criterion was that the Africans had to adapt to new foods and a new climate. The foods included salted codfish traded to the West Indies by New England merchants, Indian corn (maize), and varieties of squash not available in West Africa. The Caribbean islands, like West Africa, were tropical, but North America was much cooler. Even within the West Indies, an African was unlikely to find a climate exactly like the one he or she had left behind.

A third criterion was learning a new language. Planters did not require slaves to speak the local language, which could be English, French, Spanish, Danish, or Dutch, fluently. But slaves had to speak a creole dialect well enough to obey commands. A final criterion was psychological. When new Africans ceased to be suicidal, planters assumed they had accepted their status and their separation from their homeland.

It would have suited the planters if their slaves had met all these criteria. Yet that would have required the Africans to have been thoroughly desocialized by the Middle Passage, and they were not. As traumatic as that voyage was, most Africans who entered plantation society in the Americas had not been stripped of their memories or their culture. When their ties to their villages and families were broken, they created bonds with shipmates that simulated blood relationships. Such social bonds became the basis of new extended families. So similar were these new synthetic families to those that had existed in West Africa that slaves considered sexual relations among shipmates and former shipmates incestuous.

As this suggests, African slaves did not lose all their culture during the Middle Passage and seasoning in the Americas. Their value system never totally replicated that of the plantation.

Despite their ordeal, the Africans who survived the Atlantic slave trade and slavery in the Americas were resilient. Seasoning did modify their behavior. Yet the claim that it obliterated African Americans' cultural roots is incorrect.

The Ending of the Atlantic Slave Trade

2-9 **Why did the Atlantic slave trade end?**

The cruelties associated with the Atlantic slave trade contributed to its abolition in the early nineteenth century. During the late 1700s, English abolitionists led by Thomas Clarkson, William Wilberforce, and Granville Sharp began a religiously oriented moral crusade against slavery and the slave trade. Because the English had dominated the Atlantic trade since 1713, Britain's growing antipathy became crucial to the trade's destruction. But it is debatable whether moral outrage alone prompted this humanitarian effort. By the late 1700s, England's industrializing economy was less dependent on the slave trade and the entire plantation system than it had been previously. To maintain its prosperity, England needed raw materials and markets for its manufactured goods. Slowly but surely its ruling classes realized more profits lay in industry and other forms of trade, while leaving Africans in Africa.

So morals and economic self-interest combined when Britain abolished the Atlantic slave trade in 1807 and tried to enforce that abolition on other nations through a naval patrol off the African coast. The following year, the U.S. Congress joined in outlawing the Atlantic trade. Although American, Brazilian, and Spanish slavers defied these prohibitions for years, the forced migration from Africa to the Americas dropped to a tiny percentage of what it had been at its peak. Ironically, the coastal kingdoms of Guinea and western Central Africa fought most fiercely to keep the trade going because their economies had become dependent on it. This persistence gave the English, French, Belgians, and Portuguese an excuse to establish colonial empires in Africa during the nineteenth century in the name of suppressing the slave trade.

Read on
MyHistoryLab
Document: Congress
Prohibits Importation
of Slaves (1807)

CONCLUSION

Over more than three centuries, the Atlantic slave trade brought more than 11 million Africans to the Americas. Several million died in transit. Of those who survived, most came between 1701 and 1810, when more Africans than Europeans reached the New World. Most Africans went to the sugar plantations of the Caribbean and Brazil. Only 500,000 went to the British colonies of North America, either directly or after seasoning in the West Indies. From them have come the nearly 40 million African Americans alive today.

This chapter has described the great forced migration across the Atlantic that brought Africans into slavery in the Americas. We still have much to learn about the origins of the trade, its relationship to the earlier trans-Sahara trade, and its involvement with state formation in West and western Central Africa. Historians continue to debate how cruel the trade was, the ability of transplanted Africans to preserve their cultural heritage, and why Britain abolished the trade in the early nineteenth century.

We are fortunate that a few Africans who experienced the Middle Passage recorded their testimony. Otherwise, we would not appreciate how horrible it was. Even more important, however, is that so many survived the terror of the Atlantic slave trade and carried on. Their struggle testifies to the human spirit that is at the center of the African-American experience.

2-1
2-2
2-3
2-4
2-5
2-6
2-7
2-8
2-9

CHAPTER TIMELINE

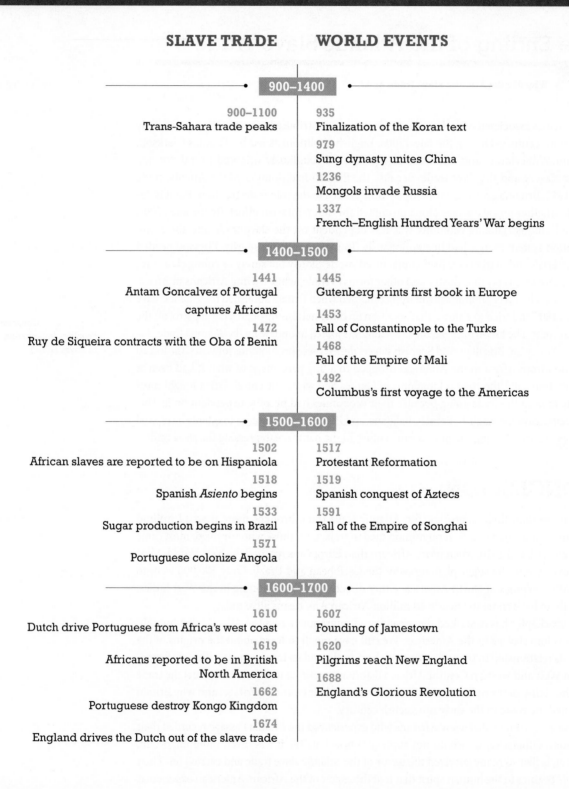

SLAVE TRADE   **WORLD EVENTS**

900–1400

900–1100
Trans-Sahara trade peaks

935
Finalization of the Koran text

979
Sung dynasty unites China

1236
Mongols invade Russia

1337
French–English Hundred Years' War begins

1400–1500

1441
Antam Goncalvez of Portugal captures Africans

1472
Ruy de Siqueira contracts with the Oba of Benin

1445
Gutenberg prints first book in Europe

1453
Fall of Constantinople to the Turks

1468
Fall of the Empire of Mali

1492
Columbus's first voyage to the Americas

1500–1600

1502
African slaves are reported to be on Hispaniola

1518
Spanish *Asiento* begins

1533
Sugar production begins in Brazil

1571
Portuguese colonize Angola

1517
Protestant Reformation

1519
Spanish conquest of Aztecs

1591
Fall of the Empire of Songhai

1600–1700

1610
Dutch drive Portuguese from Africa's west coast

1619
Africans reported to be in British North America

1662
Portuguese destroy Kongo Kingdom

1674
England drives the Dutch out of the slave trade

1607
Founding of Jamestown

1620
Pilgrims reach New England

1688
England's Glorious Revolution

CHAPTER TIMELINE

SLAVE TRADE	WORLD EVENTS

1700–1800

1713 England begins its domination of the slave trade	**1728** Russian exploration of Alaska begins
c. 1745 Olaudah Equiano born	**1776** American Declaration of Independence
1752 British Royal African Company disbands	**1789** United States Constitution ratified
1807 Great Britain abolishes the Atlantic slave trade	**1815** Napoleon defeated at the Battle of Waterloo
1808 United States abolishes the Atlantic slave trade	

On MyHistoryLab

 Study and Review on MyHistoryLab

REVIEW QUESTIONS

1. How did the Atlantic slave trade reflect the times during which it existed?

2. Think about the experience Olaudah Equiano described of a young boy captured by traders and brought to a slave ship. What new and strange things did the boy encounter? How did he explain these things to himself? What kept him from descending into despair?

3. How could John Newton reconcile his Christian faith with his career as a slave-ship captain?

4. What human and natural variables could prolong the Middle Passage across the Atlantic? How could delay make the voyage more dangerous for slaves and crew?

5. How could Africans resist the dehumanizing forces of the Middle Passage and seasoning and use their African cultures to build black cultures in the New World?

Black People in Colonial North America 1526–1763

African Americans lived in North America for nearly three centuries before the United States gained independence from Great Britain in 1783. During that long time period, most of them were slaves in British, French, and Spanish colonies. As a result, they left scant written testimony about their lives. Their history, therefore, must be learned through archaeology and the writings of the white settlers who enslaved and oppressed them.

British Carolinians believed they needed the labor of enslaved Africans for their colony to prosper. The colonial British feared Africans and their African-American descendants. This ambivalence among white Americans concerning African Americans shaped life in colonial South Carolina and in other British colonies in North America. The dichotomy of white economic dependence on black people and fear of black revolt was a central fact of American history and provided a rationale for racial oppression.

British and other European settlers in North America were willing to brand Africans and their American descendants as "barbarous, wild, [and] savage." Although real cultural differences underlay such negative perceptions, white people used them to justify oppressing black people.

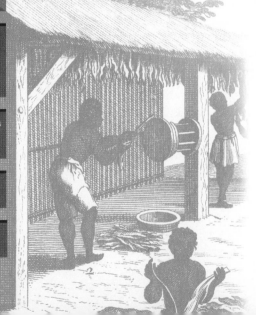

This eighteenth-century woodcut shows enslaved black men, women, and children engaged in the steps involved in the curing of tobacco.

Courtesy of the Library of Congress.

This chapter describes the history of African-American life in colonial North America from the early sixteenth century to the end of the **French and Indian War** in 1763. It concentrates on the British colonies that stretched along the eastern coast of the continent, but also briefly covers the black experience in Spanish Florida, in New Spain's southwestern borderlands, and in French Louisiana. During the seventeenth century, the plantation system that became a central part of black life in America for nearly two centuries took shape in the Chesapeake tobacco country and in the low country of South Carolina and Georgia. Unfree labor, which in the Chesapeake had originally involved both white and black people, solidified into a system of slavery based on race. Although the plantation system did not develop in Britain's northern colonies, race-based slavery existed in them as well. African Americans responded to these conditions by interacting with other groups, preserving parts of their African culture, seeking strength through religion, and resisting and rebelling against enslavement.

French and Indian War
A war between Great Britain and its American Indian allies and France and its American Indian allies, fought between 1754 and 1763 for control of the eastern portion of North America.

The Peoples of North America

3-1 | **Who were the peoples of colonial North America?**

In the North American colonies during the seventeenth and eighteenth centuries, African immigrants gave birth to a new African-American people. Born in North America, they preserved a surprisingly large core of their African cultural heritage. Meanwhile, a new natural environment and contacts with people of American Indian and European descent helped African Americans shape a way of life within the circumstances that slavery forced on them. To understand the early history of African Americans, we must first briefly discuss the other peoples of colonial North America.

American Indians

Historians and anthropologists group the original inhabitants of North America together as American Indians. But when the British began to colonize the Atlantic coastal portion of this huge region during the early seventeenth century, the indigenous peoples who lived there had no such all-inclusive name. They spoke many different languages, lived in diverse environments, and considered themselves distinct from one another. Like other Indian peoples of the Western Hemisphere, they descended from Asians who, at least 15,000 years ago, had migrated eastward by coastal waterways and across a land bridge connecting Siberia and Alaska. Europeans called them Indians as a result of Christopher Columbus's mistaken assumption in 1492 that he had landed on islands near the "Indies," by which he meant near Southeast Asia.

In Mexico, Central America, and Peru, American Indian peoples developed complex, densely populated civilizations with hereditary monarchies, formal religions, armies, and social classes. Cultural developments in Mexico and the northward spread of the cultivation of maize (corn) influenced the indigenous peoples of what is today the United States. In the Southwest, the Anasazi and later Pueblo peoples developed farming communities. Beginning around 900 CE, they produced pottery, studied astronomy, and built large adobe towns. Farther east in what is known as the Woodlands region, the Adena culture flourished in the Ohio River valley as early as 1000 BCE and attained the social organization required

3-1
3-2
3-3
3-4
3-5
3-6
3-7
3-8
3-9
3-10
3-11

to construct large burial mounds. Between the tenth and fourteenth centuries CE, what is known as the Mississippian culture established a civilization, marked by extensive trade routes, division of labor, and urban centers.

Climate change and warfare destroyed the Mississippian culture during the fourteenth century, and only remnants of it existed when Europeans and Africans arrived in North America. By that time, a diverse variety of American Indian cultures existed in what is today the eastern portion of the United States. People resided in towns and villages, supplementing their agricultural economies with fishing and hunting. Gravely weakened by diseases that settlers unwittingly brought from Europe, the woodlands Indians of North America's coastal regions could not effectively resist British settlers during the seventeenth century. Particularly in the Southeast, the British developed an extensive trade in Indian slaves.

The relationships between black people and American Indians during colonial times were complex. Although Indian nations often provided refuge to escaping black slaves, Indians sometimes became slaveholders and on occasion helped crush black revolts. Some black men assisted in the Indian slave trade and sometimes helped defend European colonists against Indian attacks. Meanwhile people of African and Indian descent frequently found themselves in similarly oppressive circumstances in Britain's American colonies. Although white officials attempted to keep them apart, social and sexual contacts between the two groups were frequent.

The Spanish, French, and Dutch

With one exception, European nations sent relatively few settlers to North America. Following Christopher Columbus's voyage in 1492, they recognized the great possibilities for gaining wealth and territory in the Americas. The Spanish, French, and Dutch thought in terms of trade with American Indians and expropriation of Indian labor.

Spain led the way. Beginning shortly after Columbus's first voyage, Spanish adventurers rapidly built a colonial empire in the Americas. Mining of gold and silver, as well as the production of sugar, tobacco, and leather goods, provided a firm economic foundation. But, because few Spanish came to the Western Hemisphere, Spain's colonial economy rested first on the forced labor of the Indian population and then increasingly on enslaved Africans when the Indian population declined from disease and overwork. African slaves arrived in the Spanish colonies as early as 1526. Later overseers in mines and fields often brutally worked Africans and Indians to death. Yet, once again because there were few Spanish in the colonies, some Africans and Indians who survived gained freedom. They became tradesmen, small landholders, and militiamen. Often they were of mixed race and identified with their former masters rather than with the oppressed people beneath them in society. African, Indian, and Spanish customs intermingled in what became a multicultural colonial society.

In part because of Spain's predominance and in part because of domestic religious strife, France did not establish a settlement in the Americas until 1604. That settlement centered on the St. Lawrence River and grew into what was known as either New France or Canada. It became a trading colony, economically based on acquiring beaver pelts and other furs from American Indians. The result was that throughout its existence New France's small French population depended on good commercial and military relations with Indian nations. There never were more than a few thousand slaves in New France, and most of them were Indian war captives. In the huge region of Louisiana, which France claimed from 1699 to 1763 and which stretched from the Gulf of Mexico to the Great

Lakes, there were considerably larger numbers of Indian and African slaves. As in the Spanish colonies, although the death toll was extremely high for both groups of slaves, routes to freedom remained open.

Because the Netherlands—the Dutch homeland—spent much of the late sixteenth century in a struggle for independence from Spain, it, like France, did not succeed in establishing a colony in North America until the early seventeenth century. This colony, New Netherlands, centered on the Hudson River. Its chief settlement, New Amsterdam, located on Manhattan Island, later became New York City after the British conquered it in 1664. Like the French, the Dutch focused on the fur trade and attracted few European settlers. In the region near New Amsterdam, the Dutch West Indian Company established African slavery in 1625. Under Dutch law, slaves retained basic human rights. Those rights and opportunities to work for wages led, as in the Spanish and French colonies, to the early appearance of a free black class.

Spanish Armada A fleet that unsuccessfully attempted to carry out an invasion of England in 1588.

joint-stock companies Primitive corporations that carried out British and Dutch colonization in the Americas during the seventeenth century.

3-1
3-2
3-3
3-4
3-5
3-6
3-7
3-8
3-9
3-10
3-11

The British and Jamestown

Britain's claim to the east coast of North America rested on the voyage of John Cabot, who sailed in 1497, just five years after Columbus's first westward voyage. But, unlike the Spanish who rapidly created an empire in the Americas, the British (also known as the English) were slow to establish themselves in the region Cabot had reached. This was partly due to the harsher North American climate, with winters much colder than in Britain. In addition, the British monarchy was too poor to finance colonizing expeditions, and social turmoil associated with the Protestant Reformation absorbed its energies.

During the 1580s, British aristocrats attempted but failed to colonize Newfoundland, a large island off the east coast of what is today Canada, and Roanoke Island, a small island off the coast of what is today North Carolina. It took the English naval victory over the **Spanish Armada** in 1588 and money raised by **joint-stock companies** to produce at Jamestown in 1607 the first successful British colony in North America. This settlement, established by the Virginia Company of London, was located in the Chesapeake region, which the British called Virginia—after Queen Elizabeth I (r. 1558–1603), the so-called Virgin Queen. The company hoped to make a profit at Jamestown by finding gold, trading with Indians, cutting lumber, or raising crops that could not be produced in Britain.

None of these schemes succeeded. Because of disease, hostility with the Indians, and especially economic failure, the settlement barely survived into the 1620s. By then, however, British settler John Rolfe's experiments, begun in 1612 to cultivate a mild strain of tobacco that could be grown on the

Read on MyHistoryLab Document: Exploring America: Jamestown

Black slavery began in the American colonies at Jamestown, Virginia, in August 1619, when a Dutch ship arrived from Guinea carrying 20 African men and women.

Illustration by Howard Pyle. The Granger Collection, New York.

3-1

3-2

3-3

3-4

3-5

3-6

3-7

3-8

3-9

3-10

3-11

North American mainland, began to pay off. Smoking tobacco had become popular in Europe, and demand for it constantly increased. As a result, growing tobacco soon became the economic mainstay of Virginia and the neighboring colony of Maryland.

Sowing, cultivating, harvesting, and curing tobacco required considerable labor. Yet colonists in the Chesapeake could not follow the Spanish example of enslaving Indians to produce the crop. Disease had reduced the local Indian population, and those who survived eluded British conquest by retreating west.

Unlike the West Indian sugar planters, however, the North American tobacco planters did not immediately turn to Africa for laborers. British advocates of colonizing North America had always promoted it as a means to reduce unemployment, poverty, and crime in England. The idea was to send England's undesirables to America, where they could provide the cheap labor tobacco planters needed. Consequently, until 1700, white labor produced most of the tobacco in the Chesapeake colonies.

Africans Arrive in the Chesapeake

By early 1619, there were, nevertheless, 32 people of African descent living at Jamestown. Nothing is known about when they arrived or from where they came. They were all "in the service of sev[er]all planters." The following August a Dutch warship, carrying 17 African men and three African women, moored at the mouth of the James River. They were part of a group of over 300 who had been taken from Angola by a Portuguese slaver. The Dutch warship had attacked the slaver, taken most of its human cargo, and brought the 20 Angolans to Jamestown. The Dutch captain traded them to local officials for provisions.

The Angolans became servants to Jamestown's officials and favored planters. For two reasons, the colony's inhabitants regarded both the new arrivals and those black people who had been in Jamestown earlier to be *unfree* but not slaves. First, unlike the Portuguese and the Spanish, the British had no law for slavery. Second, at least those Angolans who bore such names as Pedro, Isabella, Antoney, and Angelo were Christians, and—according to British custom and morality in 1619—Christians could not be enslaved. So, once these individuals worked off their purchase price, they regained their freedom. In 1623, Antoney and Isabella married. The next year they became parents of William, whom their master had baptized in the local **Church of England**.

During the following years, people of African descent remained a small minority in the expanding Virginia colony. In 1649 the total Virginia population of about 18,500 included only 300 black people. In neighboring Maryland, the black population also remained small. In 1658 people of African descent accounted for only 3 percent of Maryland's population.

Church of England
A protestant church established in the sixteenth century as the English national or Anglican church with the English monarch as its head. After the American Revolution, its American branch became the Episcopal Church.

Black Servitude in the Chesapeake

3-2 How did black servitude develop in the Chesapeake?

As these statistics suggest, during the early years of the Chesapeake colonies, black people represented a small part of a labor force composed mainly of white people. From the 1620s to the 1670s, black and white people worked in the tobacco fields together, lived together, and slept together. They were all unfree indentured servants.

Indentured servitude had existed in Europe for centuries. In England, parents indentured—or, in other words, apprenticed—their children to "masters," who then controlled their lives and had the right to their labor for a set number of years. In return, the masters supported the children and taught them a trade or profession.

As the demand for labor to produce tobacco in the Chesapeake expanded, indentured servitude came to include adults who sold their freedom for two to seven years in return for the cost of their voyage to North America. Instead of training in a profession, the servants could improve their economic standing by remaining as free persons in America after completing their period of servitude.

When Africans first arrived in Virginia and Maryland, they entered into similar contracts. Indentured servitude could be harsh in the tobacco colonies because masters sought to get as much labor as they could from their servants before the indenture ended. Most indentured servants died from overwork or disease before regaining their freedom. But those who survived, black people as well as white people, could expect eventually to leave their masters and seek their fortunes as free persons.

The foremost example in early Virginia of a black man who emerged from servitude to become a tobacco planter himself is Anthony Johnson, who came to Jamestown from Britain in 1621 and probably was born in Angola. But Johnson was not the only person of African descent who became a free property owner during the first half of the seventeenth century. Here and there, black men seemed to enjoy a status similar to their white counterparts. Free black men in the Chesapeake participated fully in the commercial and legal life of the colonies. They owned land, farmed, lent money, sued in the courts, served as jurors and minor officials, and at times voted.

This suggests that before the 1670s the English in the Chesapeake did not draw a strict line between white freedom and black slavery. Yet, since the early 1600s, the ruling elite had treated black servants differently than white servants. Over the decades, the region's British population gradually came to assume that persons of African descent were inalterably alien. This sentiment provided a foundation for what historian Winthrop D. Jordan calls the "unthinking decision" among the British to establish **chattel slavery**. In this form of slavery, Africans and people of African descent became their master's private property on a level with livestock.

chattel slavery A form of slavery in which the enslaved are treated legally as property.

Race and the Origins of Black Slavery

Between 1640 and 1700, the British tobacco-producing colonies stretching from Delaware to northern Carolina underwent a social and demographic revolution. An economy once based primarily on the labor of white indentured servants became an economy based on the labor of black slaves.

 Watch on MyHistoryLab Video: The Descent into Race Slavery

Although historians debate how this extraordinary change occurred, several interrelated factors brought it about. Some of these factors are easily understood. Others are more complicated and profound because they involve basic assumptions about the American nation.

Several economic and demographic developments led to the mass enslavement of people of African descent in the tobacco colonies. First, during the second quarter of the seventeenth century, Britain's Caribbean sugar colonies set a precedent for enslaving Africans. Second, fewer poor white people came to the tobacco colonies as they found better opportunities for themselves in other regions of British North America. Third, as Britain gained increased control over the Atlantic slave trade, African slaves became less costly.

These changing circumstances provide the context for the beginnings of black slavery as a major phenomenon in British North America. Yet race and class were crucial in shaping

House of Burgesses
A representative body established at Jamestown, Virginia, in 1619.

Read on MyHistoryLab Document: Maryland Addresses the Status of Slaves in 1644

slave codes Sometimes known as "black codes," a series of laws passed to define slaves as property and specify the legal powers of masters over slaves.

the *character* of slavery in the British mainland colonies. From the first arrival of Africans in the Chesapeake, those British who exercised authority made decisions that qualified the apparent social mobility the Africans enjoyed. The British had historically distinguished between how they treated each other and how they treated those who were physically and culturally different from them. Such discrimination had been the basis of British colonial policies toward the Irish—whom England had been trying to conquer for centuries—and the American Indians. Because the English considered Africans even more different from themselves than either the Irish or the Indians, they assumed from the beginning that Africans were generally inferior.

Therefore, although black and white servants residing in the Chesapeake during the early seventeenth century had much in common, their masters made distinctions between them based on race. Unlike white servants, black servants usually did not have surnames, and early census reports listed them separately from white people. By the 1640s, black people could not bear arms, and local Anglican priests maintained that persons of African descent could not become Christians. Although sexual contacts among blacks, whites, and Indians were common, colonial authorities soon discouraged them. In 1662 Virginia's **House of Burgesses** (the colony's legislature) declared that "any christian [white person]" who committed "Fornication with a negro man or woman, he or shee soe offending" would pay double the fine set for committing the same offense with a white person.

These distinctions suggest that the status of black servants had never been the same as that of white servants. But only starting in the 1640s do records indicate a predilection toward making black people slaves rather than servants. During that decade, courts in Virginia and Maryland began to reflect an assumption that it was permissible for persons of African descent to serve their master for life rather than a set term.

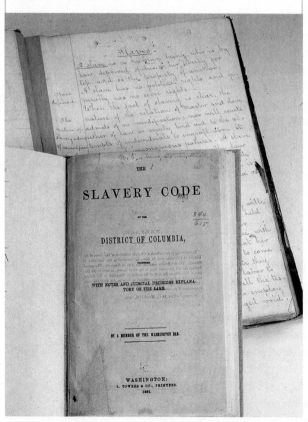

Read on MyHistoryLab Document: The Colony of Virginia Defines Slavery, 1661–1705

Slave codes regulated slaves and asserted the rights of slave owners.

The Emergence of Chattel Slavery

Legal documents and statute books reveal that, during the 1660s, other aspects of chattel slavery emerged in the Chesapeake colonies. Bills of sale began to stipulate that the children of black female servants would also be servants for life. In 1662 the House of Burgesses decreed that a child's condition—free or unfree—followed that of the mother. Just as significant, by the mid-1660s statutes in the Chesapeake colonies assumed servitude to be the natural condition of black people.

With these laws, slavery in British North America emerged in the form it retained until the American Civil War: a racially defined system of perpetual involuntary servitude that compelled almost all black people to work as agricultural laborers. **Slave codes** enacted between 1660 and 1710 further defined American slavery as a system that sought as much to control persons of African descent as to exploit their labor. Slaves could not testify against white people in court, own property, leave their master's estate without a pass, congregate in groups larger than three or four, enter into contracts, or marry. Profession of Christianity no longer protected a black person from enslavement, nor was conversion a cause for **manumission**. In 1669 the House of Burgesses exempted from felony charges masters who killed a slave while administering punishment.

By 1700, just as the slave system began to expand in the southern colonies, enslaved Africans and African Americans had been reduced legally to the status of domestic animals. The only major exception was that, unlike animals (or masters who abused slaves), the law held slaves strictly accountable for crimes they committed.

manumission The act of freeing a slave by the slave's master.

Bacon's Rebellion and American Slavery

The series of events that led to the enslavement of black people in the Chesapeake tobacco colonies preceded their emergence as the great majority of laborers in those colonies. The dwindling supply of white indentured servants, the growing availability of Africans, and preexisting white racial biases affected this transformation. But the key event in bringing it about was the rebellion led by Nathaniel Bacon in 1676.

Bacon's followers were mainly white indentured servants and former indentured servants who resented the control the tobacco-planting elite exercised over the colony's resources and government. But Bacon also appealed to black slaves to join his rebellion. This suggests that poor white and black people had a chance to unite against the **planter elite**.

Before such a class-based, biracial alliance could be realized, Bacon died of dysentery, and his rebellion collapsed. His uprising nevertheless convinced the colony's elite that continued reliance on white agricultural laborers, who could become free and get guns, was dangerous. By switching from indentured white servants to an enslaved black labor force that the planters assumed would never become free or have firearms, the planters hoped to avoid class conflict among white people. Increasingly thereafter, white Americans perceived that both their freedom from class conflict and their prosperity rested on denying freedom to black Americans.

planter elite Those who owned the largest tobacco plantations.

Plantation Slavery, 1700–1750

3-3 | What were the characteristics of plantation slavery from 1700 to 1750?

The reliance of Chesapeake planters on slavery to meet their labor needs resulted from racial prejudice, the declining availability of white indentured servants, the increasing availability of Africans, and fear of white class conflict. When, following the shift from white indentured to enslaved black labor, the demand for tobacco in Europe increased sharply, the newly dominant slave labor system expanded rapidly.

Tobacco Colonies

Between 1700 and 1770, some 80,000 Africans arrived in the tobacco colonies, and even more African Americans were born into slavery there (see Figure 3–1). Tobacco planting spread from Virginia and Maryland to Delaware and North Carolina and from the coastal plain to the foothills of the Appalachian Mountains. In the process, American slavery assumed the form it kept for the next 165 years.

By 1750, 144,872 slaves lived in Virginia and Maryland, accounting for 61 percent of all the slaves in British North America. Another 40,000 slaves lived in the rice-producing regions of South Carolina and Georgia, accounting for 17 percent. It is important to note

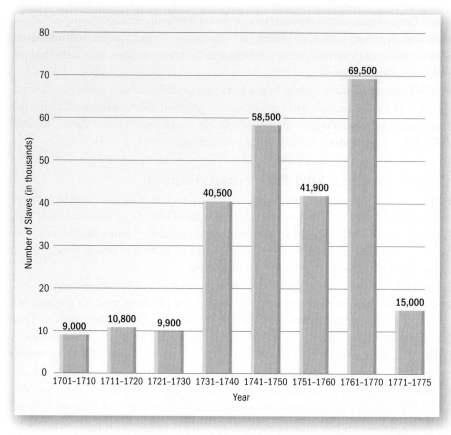

FIGURE 3–1 AFRICANS BROUGHT AS SLAVES TO BRITISH NORTH AMERICA, 1701–1775

The rise in the number of captive Africans shipped to British North America during the early eighteenth century reflects the increasing dependence of British planters on African slave labor. The declines in slave imports during the periods 1751 to 1760 and 1771 to 1775 resulted from disruptions to commerce associated with the French and Indian War (or Seven Years' War) and the struggle between the colonies and Great Britain that preceded the American War for Independence.

SOURCE: *From* The American Colonies: From Settlement of Independence, *by R. C. Simmons (© R. C. Simmons, 1976) is reproduced by permission of PFD (www.pfd.co.uk) on behalf of R. C. Simmons.*

that, unlike in the sugar colonies of the Caribbean where white people were a tiny minority, they constituted a majority in the tobacco colonies and a large minority in the rice colonies. Also, most white southerners did not own slaves. Nevertheless, the economic development of the region depended on black slaves.

The conditions under which slaves lived varied. Most slaveholders farmed small tracts of land and owned fewer than five slaves. These masters and their slaves worked together and developed close relationships. Other masters owned thousands of acres of land and rarely saw most of their slaves.

Before the mid-eighteenth century, nearly all slaves—both men and women—worked in the fields. On the smaller farms, they worked with their master. On larger estates, they worked for an overseer, who was usually white. Like other agricultural workers, enslaved African Americans normally worked from sunup to sundown with breaks for food and rest. Even during colonial times, they usually had Sunday off.

After 1750 some black men began to hold such skilled occupations on plantations as carpenter, smith, carter, cooper, miller, potter, sawyer, tanner, shoemaker, and weaver.

Black women had, with the exception of weaving, less access to skilled occupations. When they did not work in the fields, they worked as domestic servants in the homes of their masters, cooking, washing, cleaning, and caring for children.

Low-Country Slavery

South of the tobacco colonies, on the coastal plain or **low country** of Carolina and Georgia, a distinctive slave society developed (see Map 3–1). The West Indian plantation system had much more influence here than in the Chesapeake, and rice, not tobacco, became the staple crop.

low country The coastal regions of South Carolina and Georgia.

The first British settlers who arrived in 1670 at Charleston (in what would later become South Carolina) came mainly from Barbados, a sugar-producing island in the West Indies. Many of them had been slaveholders on that island and brought slaves with them. Therefore, in the low country, black people were chattel from the start. The region's subtropical climate discouraged white settlement and encouraged dependence on black labor the way it did in the sugar islands. During the early years, nearly one-third of the settlers were African, most of them male. By the early eighteenth century, more Africans had arrived than white people. Carolina also became the center of the Indian slave trade, and during the early 1700s, Indians accounted for approximately one-quarter of the colony's slave population.

By 1740 the Carolina low country had 40,000 slaves, who constituted 90 percent of the population in the region around Charleston. In all, 94,000 Africans arrived at Charleston between 1706 and 1776, which made it North America's leading port of entry for Africans during the eighteenth century.

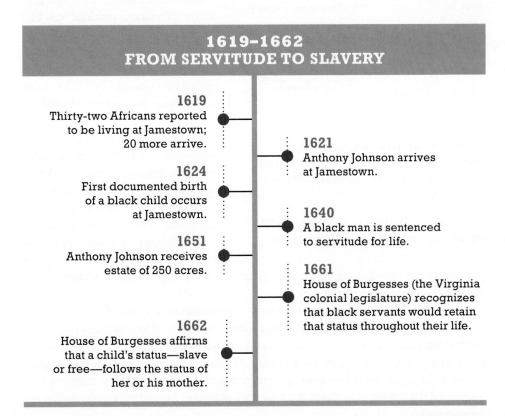

1619–1662
FROM SERVITUDE TO SLAVERY

1619
Thirty-two Africans reported to be living at Jamestown; 20 more arrive.

1621
Anthony Johnson arrives at Jamestown.

1624
First documented birth of a black child occurs at Jamestown.

1640
A black man is sentenced to servitude for life.

1651
Anthony Johnson receives estate of 250 acres.

1661
House of Burgesses (the Virginia colonial legislature) recognizes that black servants would retain that status throughout their life.

1662
House of Burgesses affirms that a child's status—slave or free—follows the status of her or his mother.

3-1

3-2

3-3

3-4

3-5

3-6

3-7

3-8

3-9

3-10

3-11

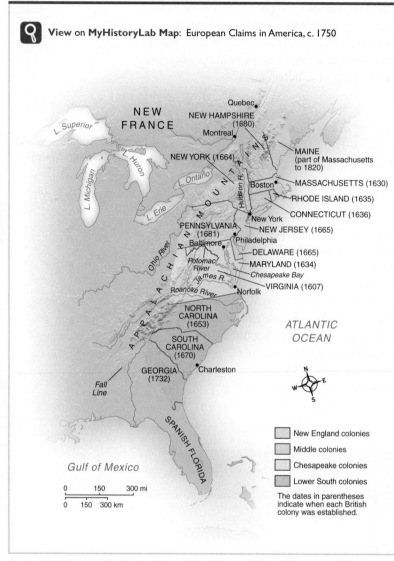

View on **MyHistoryLab Map**: European Claims in America, c. 1750

New England colonies

Middle colonies

Chesapeake colonies

Lower South colonies

The dates in parentheses indicate when each British colony was established.

MAP 3–1 REGIONS OF COLONIAL NORTH AMERICA, 1683–1763
The British colonies on the North American mainland were divided into four regions. They were bordered on the south by Spanish Florida and to the west by regions claimed by France.

How did African Americans in the British colonies benefit from the close proximity of regions controlled by France and Spain?

Starting around 1700, when the low-country planters began concentrating on growing rice, they sought slaves skilled in growing that crop, which had been grown in West Africa for thousands of years. Economies of scale, in which an industry becomes more efficient as it grows larger, were more important in the production of rice than tobacco. Although tobacco could be profitably produced on small farms, rice required large acreages. Therefore, large plantations similar to those on the sugar islands of the West Indies became the rule in the low country.

In 1732 King George II of England chartered the colony of Georgia to serve as a buffer between South Carolina and Spanish Florida. James Oglethorpe, who received the royal charter, wanted to establish a refuge for England's poor, who were expected to become virtuous through their labor. Consequently in 1734 Oglethorpe and the colony's other trustees banned slavery in Georgia. Economic difficulties, combined with land hunger among white South Carolinians, soon led to the ban's repeal. During the 1750s, rice cultivation and slavery spread into Georgia. By 1773 Georgia had as many black people—15,000—as white people.

Enslaved Africans on low-country plantations suffered a high mortality rate from diseases, overwork, and poor treatment, just as their counterparts did on Barbados and other sugar islands. Therefore, unlike the slave population in the Chesapeake colonies, the slave population in the low country did not grow by natural reproduction. Instead, until shortly before the American Revolution, it grew through continued arrivals from Africa.

Low-country slave society developed striking paradoxes in race relations. As the region's black population grew, white people became fearful of revolt, and by 1698 Carolina had the strictest slave code in North America. Yet, as the passage that begins this chapter indicates, black people in Carolina faced the quandary of being both feared and needed by white people. Even as persons of European descent grew fearful of black revolt, the colony in 1704 authorized the arming of enslaved black men when needed for defense against Indian and Spanish raids.

VOICES   A Description of an Eighteenth-Century Virginia Plantation

The following eyewitness account of a large Virginia plantation in Fairfax County indicates the sorts of skilled labor slaves performed by the mid-eighteenth century. George Mason, one of Virginia's leading statesmen during the Revolutionary War era, owned this plantation, which he named Gunston Hall in 1758. The account is by one of Mason's sons.

My father had among his slaves carpenters, coopers, sawyers, blacksmiths, tanners, curriers, shoemakers, spinners, weavers and knitters, and even a distiller. His woods furnished timber and plank for the carpenters and coopers, and charcoal for the blacksmith, his cattle killed for his own consumption and for sale supplied skins for tanners, curriers, and shoemakers, and his sheep gave wool and his fields produced cotton and flax for the weavers and spinners, and his orchards fruit for the distiller. His carpenters and sawyers built and kept in repair all the dwelling-houses, barns, stables, ploughs, harrows, gates, &c., on the plantations and the outhouses at the home house. His coopers made the hogsheads the tobacco was prized in and the tight casks to hold the cider and other liquors. The tanners and curriers with the proper vats &c., tanned and dressed the skins as well for upper as for lower leather to the full amount of the consumption of the estate, and shoemakers made them into shoes for the negroes. . . . The blacksmith did all the iron work required by the establishment, as making and repairing ploughs, harrows, teeth chains, bolts, &c., &c. The spinners, weavers and knitters made all the coarse cloths and stockings used by the negroes, and nearly all worn by the children of it. The distiller made every fall a good deal of apple, peach and persimmon brandy. . . . Moreover, all the beeves and hogs for consumption or sale were driven up and slaughtered there at the proper seasons, and whatever was to be preserved was salted and packed away for after distribution.

1. **What does this passage indicate about plantation life in mid-eighteenth-century Virginia?**
2. **How does the description of black people presented here compare to the passage from the South Carolina statute book that begins this chapter?**

SOURCE: Edmond S. Morgan, *Virginians at Home: Family Life in the Eighteenth Century* (Williamsburg, VA: Colonial Williamsburg, 1952), 53–54. Reprinted with permission.

Of equal significance was the appearance in Carolina, and to some extent in Georgia, of distinct classes among people of color. A Creole population that had absorbed European values lived alongside white people in Charleston and Savannah. Members of this Creole population were frequently mixed-race relatives of their masters and enjoyed social and economic privileges denied to slaves who labored on the nearby rice plantations. Yet this urban mixed-race class was under constant white supervision.

In contrast, slaves who lived in the country retained considerable autonomy in their daily routines. The intense cultivation required to produce rice encouraged the evolution of a "task system" of labor on the low-country plantations. Rather than working in gangs as in the tobacco colonies, slaves on rice plantations had daily tasks. When they completed these tasks, they could work on plots of land assigned to them or do what they pleased without white supervision. Because black people were the great majority in the low-country plantations, they also preserved more of their African heritage than did black people who lived in the region's cities or in the more northerly British mainland colonies.

3-1

3-2

3-3

3-4

3-5

3-6

3-7

3-8

3-9

3-10

3-11

Plantation Technology

During the American colonial era, most people of African descent living on southern plantations employed technologies associated with raising and processing crops for distant markets. A minority gained technical skills associated with a variety of trades.

On low-country rice plantations, slaves built, operated, and maintained irrigation systems. They threshed, winnowed, and pounded rice to remove the husks. At first they performed these labor-intensive operations by hand. By the mid-eighteenth century, however, masters introduced "winnowing fans and pounding mills" powered by draft animals. Also, during the eighteenth century, low-country slave artisans built the vats, pumps, and structures required for turning indigo plants into a blue dye that was popular in Europe.

Enslaved carpenters used a variety of hand tools to construct the buildings required for all these processes. They also built other plantation buildings. Slave sawyers operated water-powered mills to cut lumber. Other slaves made barrels. Plantation blacksmiths used charcoal-burning hearths and billows to form the hoops from iron ingots and—using tongs and hammers—pounded the hoops into shape on anvils. They used a similar process to fashion nails, axe and hammer heads, hooks, horse shoes, hinges, and locks.

Like carpentry, tanning was essential. But, like indigo production, it was a laborious, smelly, and extended operation. Slaves cooked deer and cow hides in lime to remove fur and then washed off the lime with a mixture of animal dung, salt, and water. After drying, softening, stretching, and trimming, slave craftsmen used the leather to make shoes, boots, garments, and other articles.

Slave Life in Early America

3-4   **What factors affected the way slaves lived in early America?**

Little evidence survives of the individual lives of enslaved black people in colonial North America. This is because they, along with American Indians and most white people of that era, were poor, illiterate, and kept no records. Yet recent studies provide a glimpse of their material culture.

Eighteenth-century housing for slaves was minimal and often temporary. In the Chesapeake, small log cabins predominated. They had dirt floors, brick fireplaces, wooden chimneys, and few, if any, windows. African styles of architecture were more common in coastal South Carolina and Georgia. In these regions, slaves built the walls of their houses with tabby—a mixture of lime, oyster shells, and sand—or, occasionally, mud. In either case, the houses had thatched roofs.

The amount of furniture and cooking utensils the cabins contained varied from place to place and according to how long the cabins were occupied. In some cabins, the only furniture consisted of wooden boxes for both storage and seating and planks for beds. But a 1697 inventory of items contained in a slave cabin in Virginia lists chairs, a bed, a large iron kettle, a brass kettle, an iron pot, a frying pan, and a "beer barrel." As the eighteenth century progressed, slave housing on large plantations became more substantial, and slaves acquired tables, linens, chamber pots, and oil lamps. Yet primitive, poorly furnished log cabins persisted in many regions even after the abolition of slavery in 1865.

At first, slaves wore minimal clothing during summer. Men had breechcloths; women had skirts, leaving their upper bodies bare; and children went naked until puberty. Later men wore shirts, trousers, and hats while working in the fields. Women wore shifts (loose, simple dresses) and covered their heads with handkerchiefs. In winter, masters provided heavier cotton and woolen clothing and cheap leather shoes. From the seventeenth century onward, slave women brightened clothing with dyes made from bark, decorated clothing with ornaments, and created African-style head wraps, hats, and hairstyles. In this manner, African Americans retained a sense of personal style compatible with West African culture.

Food consisted of corn, yams, salt pork, and occasionally salt beef and salt fish. Slaves caught fish and raised chickens and rabbits. When, during the eighteenth century, farmers in the Chesapeake began planting wheat, slaves baked biscuits. In the South Carolina low country, rice became an important part of African-American diets, but even there corn was the staple. During colonial times, slaves occasionally supplemented this limited diet with vegetables they raised in their gardens.

Miscegenation and Creolization

3-5   **What role did miscegenation and creolization have in early African-American history?**

When Africans first arrived in the Chesapeake during the early seventeenth century, they interacted culturally and physically with white indentured servants and with American Indians. This mixing of peoples changed all three groups. Interracial sexual contacts—miscegenation—produced people of mixed race. Meanwhile, cultural exchanges became an essential part of the process of creolization that led African parents to produce African-American children. When, as often happened, miscegenation and creolization occurred together, the result was both physical and cultural. However, the dominant British minority in North America during the colonial period defined persons of mixed race as black. Although enslaved mulattoes—those of mixed African and European ancestry—enjoyed some advantages over slaves who had a purely African ancestry, mulattoes as a group did not receive enhanced legal status.

Miscegenation between black people and white people, and black people and Indians, took place throughout British North America during the seventeenth and eighteenth centuries. But it was less extensive and accepted than in sugar colonies in the Caribbean, Latin America, or French Canada. British North America was exceptional because many more white women migrated there than to Canada, Latin America, or the Caribbean. Therefore, in British North America white men were far less likely to take black or Indian wives and concubines. Sexual relations between Africans and Indians were also more limited than they were elsewhere. This was because the coastal Indian population had drastically declined before large numbers of Africans arrived.

Yet miscegenation between black people and the remaining Indians certainly was extensive in British North America. There were also striking examples of black-white intermarriage. In 1656 in Northumberland County, Virginia, a mulatto woman named Elizabeth Kay successfully sued for her freedom and immediately thereafter married her white lawyer. In Norfolk County, Virginia, in 1671, Francis Skiper had to pay a tax on his wife Anne because she was black.

Colonial assemblies banned such interracial marriages mainly to keep white women from bearing mulatto children. The assemblies feared that having free white mothers might allow persons of mixed race to sue and gain their freedom, thereby creating a legally

3-1
3-2
3-3
3-4
3-5
3-6
3-7
3-8
3-9
3-10
3-11

recognized free mixed-race class. Such a class, wealthy white people feared, would blur the distinction between the dominant and subordinate races and weaken white supremacy. The assemblies did far less to prevent white male masters from sexually exploiting their black female slaves—although they considered such exploitation immoral—because the children of such liaisons would be slaves.

The Origins of African-American Culture

3-6 **How did African-American culture originate?**

Creolization and miscegenation transformed the descendants of the Africans who arrived in North America into African Americans. Historians once believed that in this process the Creoles lost their African heritage. But contemporary scholars have found many African legacies not only in African-American culture but in American culture in general.

The second generation of people of African descent in North America did lose their parents' native languages and their ethnic identities. But they retained a generalized West African heritage and passed it on to their descendants. Among the major elements of that heritage were family structure and notions of kinship, religious concepts and practices, African words and modes of expression, musical style and instruments, cooking methods and foods, folk literature, and folk arts.

The preservation of the West African extended family formed the basis for African-American culture. Because most Africans imported into the British colonies during the late seventeenth and early eighteenth centuries were males, most black men of that era could not have wives and children. It was not until the Atlantic slave trade declined briefly during the 1750s that sex ratios became more balanced and African-American family life began to flourish. Without that family life, black people could not have maintained as much of Africa as they did.

By the mid-eighteenth century, extended black families based on biological relationships dominated. Black people retained knowledge of these relationships to second and third cousins over several generations and wide stretches of territory. These extended families had roots in Africa but were also a result of—and a reaction to—slavery. West African **incest taboos** encouraged slaves to pick mates who lived on plantations other than their own. The sale of slaves away from their immediate families tended to extend families over wide areas. Once established, such far-flung kinship ties helped others, who had been forced to leave home, to adapt to new conditions under a new master. And kinfolk sheltered escapees.

incest taboos
Customary rules against sexual relations and marriage within family and kinship groups.

Extended families also influenced African-American naming practices, which in turn reinforced family ties. Africans named male children after close relatives. This custom survived in America because boys were more likely to be separated from their parents by being sold than girls were. Having the name of one's father or grandfather preserved one's family identity. Also, early in the eighteenth century, when more African Americans began to use surnames, they clung to the name of their original master. This reflected a West African predisposition to link a family name with a certain location. Like taking a parent's name, it helped maintain family relationships despite repeated scatterings.

Bible names did not become common among African Americans until the mid-eighteenth century. This was because before that time masters often refused to allow slaves to be converted to Christianity. As a result, African religions—both indigenous and

((• 🕮 Read on **MyHistoryLab Document**: An Architect Describes African-American Music and Instruments in 1818

This eighteenth-century painting of slaves on a South Carolina plantation provides graphic proof of the continuities between West African culture and the emerging culture of African Americans. The religious dance, the drum and banjo, and elements of the participants' clothing are all West African in origin.

Abby Aldrich, Rockefeller Folk Art Museum, Colonial Williamsburg Foundation, VA.

Islamic—persisted in parts of America well into the nineteenth century. Black Americans continued to perform an African circle dance known as the "ring shout" at funerals, and they decorated graves with shells and pottery in the West African manner. They looked to recently arrived Africans for religious guidance, held bodies of water to be sacred, remained in daily contact with their ancestors through **spirit possession**, and practiced **divination** and magic. When they became ill, they turned to "herb doctors" and "root workers." Even when many African Americans began to convert to Christianity, West African religious thought and practice shaped their lives.

The Great Awakening

The major turning point in African-American religion came in conjunction with the religious revival known as the Great Awakening. This social movement of the mid- to late-eighteenth century grew out of growing dissatisfaction among white Americans with a deterministic and increasingly formalistic style of Protestantism that seemed to deny most people a chance for salvation. During the early 1730s in western Massachusetts, a Congregationalist minister named Jonathan Edwards began an emotional and participatory ministry aimed at bringing more people into the church. Later that decade, George Whitefield, an Englishman who along with John Wesley founded the Methodist Church, carried a similarly evangelical style of Christianity to the other mainland colonies. In his sermons, Whitefield appealed to emotions, offered salvation to all who believed in Christ, and preached to black people as well as white people.

spirit possession
A belief rooted in West African religions that spirits may possess human souls.

divination A form of magic aimed at telling the future by interpreting a variety of signs.

 Watch on **MyHistoryLab Video**: The Great Awakening

Some people of African descent had converted to Christianity before Whitefield's arrival in North America. But two factors had prevented widespread black conversion. First, most masters feared that converted slaves would interpret their new religious status as a step toward freedom and equality. Second, many slaves remained so devoted to their ancestral religions that Christianity did not attract them.

With the Great Awakening, however, a process of general conversion began. African Americans did indeed link the spiritual equality preached by evangelical ministers with a hope for earthly equality. They tied salvation for the soul with liberation for the body. They recognized that the preaching style Whitefield and other evangelicals adopted had much in common with West African "spirit possession." As in West African religion, eighteenth-century revivalism in North America emphasized personal rebirth, singing, movement, and emotion. The practice of total body immersion during baptism in rivers, ponds, and lakes that gave the Baptist church its name paralleled West African water rites.

Because it drew African Americans into an evangelical movement that helped shape American society, the Great Awakening increased mutual black-white acculturation. Revivalists appealed to the poor of all races and emphasized spiritual equality. Evangelical Anglican, Baptist, Methodist, and Presbyterian churches welcomed black people. Members of these biracial churches addressed each other as *brother* and *sister*. Black members took communion with white members and served as church officers. The same church discipline applied to both races. By the late eighteenth century, a few black men gained ordination as priests and ministers and—often while still enslaved—preached to white congregations. They thereby influenced white people's perception of how services should be conducted.

Other factors, however, favored the development of a distinct African-American church. From the start, white churches seated black people apart from white people, belying claims to spiritual equality. Black members took communion *after* white members. Masters also tried to use religion to instill in their chattels such self-serving Christian virtues as meekness, humility, and obedience. Consequently, when they could, African Americans established their own churches. Dancing, shouting, clapping, and singing became especially characteristic of their religious meetings. Black spirituals probably date from the eighteenth century, and like African-American Christianity itself, they blended West African and European elements.

African Americans also retained the West African assumption that the souls of the dead returned to their homeland and rejoined their ancestors. Reflecting this family-oriented view of death, African-American funerals were often loud and joyous occasions with dancing, laughing, and drinking. Perhaps most important, the emerging black church reinforced black people's collective identity and helped them persevere in slavery.

Language, Music, and Folk Literature

Although African Americans did not retain their ancestral languages, those languages contributed to the **pidgins** and creolized languages that became **Black English** by the nineteenth century. It was in the low country, with its large and isolated black populations, that African-English creoles lasted the longest. In other regions, where black people were less numerous, creole languages did not last so long. Nevertheless, they contributed many words to American—particularly southern—English.

Music was another essential part of West African life, and it remained so among African Americans, who preserved an antiphonal, call-and-response style of singing with an emphasis on improvisation, complex rhythms, and a strong beat. They sang while working and during religious ceremonies. Early on, masters banned drums and horns because of their potential for long-distance communication among slaves. But the African banjo

---

Read on MyHistoryLab Document: Exploring America: The Great Awakening

3-1

3-2

3-3

3-4

3-5

3-6

3-7

3-8

3-9

3-10

3-11

pidgin A simplified mixture of two or more languages used to communicate between people who speak different languages.

Black English A variety of American English that is influenced by West African grammar, vocabulary, and pronunciation.

VOICES   A Poem by Jupiter Hammon

Jupiter Hammon (1711–1806?) was a favored slave living in Long Island, New York, when on Christmas Day 1760 he composed "An Evening Thought: Salvation by Christ, with Penitential Cries," an excerpt of which appears here. A Calvinist preacher and America's first published black poet, Hammon was deeply influenced by the Great Awakening's emphasis on repentance and Christ's spiritual sovereignty.

Salvation comes by Jesus Christ alone,
The only Son of God;
Redemption now to every one,
That love his holy Word.
Dear Jesus we would fly to Thee,
And leave off every Sin,
Thy tender Mercy well agree;
Salvation from our King.
Salvation comes from God we know,
The true and only One;
It's well agreed and certain true,
He gave his only Son.

Lord hear our penitential Cry:
Salvation from above
It is the Lord that doth supply,
With his Redeeming Love.
Dear Jesus let the Nations cry,
And all the People say,
Salvation comes from Christ on high,
Haste on Tribunal Day.
We cry as Sinners to the Lord,
Salvation to obtain;
It is firmly fixt his holy Word,
Ye shall not cry in vain.,

1. **What elements in Hammond's poem might have appealed to African Americans of his time?**
2. **Does Hammond suggest a relationship between Christ and social justice?**

SOURCE: Dorothy Porter, ed., *Early Negro Writing, 1760–1837* (1971; reprint, Baltimore: Black Classic Press, 1995).

3-1
3-2
3-3
3-4
3-5
3-6
3-7
3-8
3-9
3-10
3-11

survived in America, and African Americans quickly adopted the violin and guitar. Aside from family and religion, music may have been the most important aspect of African culture in the lives of American slaves. Eventually, African-American music influenced all forms of American popular music.

West African folk literature also survived in North America. African tales, proverbs, and riddles—with accretions from American Indian and European stories—entertained, instructed, and united African Americans. Just as the black people on the sea islands of South Carolina and Georgia were most able to retain elements of African language, so did their folk literature remain closest to its African counterpart. Africans used tales of how weak animals like rabbits outsmarted stronger animals like hyenas and lions to symbolize the power of the common people over unjust rulers (see Chapter 1). African Americans used similar tales to portray the ability of slaves to outsmart and ridicule their masters.

The African-American Impact on Colonial Culture

African Americans also influenced the development of white culture. The African-American imprint on southern diction and phraseology is especially clear. Because black women often raised their master's children, generations of white children acquired African-American speech patterns and intonations. Black people also influenced white notions about portents, spirits, and folk remedies. Seventeenth- and eighteenth-century English lore about such things was not that different from West African lore, and white Americans consulted black conjurers and "herb doctors." Black cooks in early America influenced white southern eating habits. Preferences for barbecued pork, fried chicken, black-eyed peas, okra, and collard and mustard greens owed much to West African culinary traditions.

African Americans also used West African culture and skills to shape work habits in the American South during and after colonial times. Africans accustomed to collective agricultural labor imposed the "**gang system**" on most American plantations. Masters learned that their slaves worked harder and longer in groups. Their work songs were also an African legacy, as was the slow, deliberate pace of their labor. By the mid-eighteenth century, masters often employed slaves as builders. As a result, African styles and decorative techniques influenced southern colonial architecture. Black builders introduced African-style high-peaked roofs, front porches, wood carvings, and elaborate ironwork.

gang system A mode of organizing labor that had West African antecedents. In this system American slaves worked in groups under the direction of a slave driver.

Slavery in the Northern Colonies

3-7 How did slavery in the northern colonies differ from slavery in the southern colonies?

The British mainland colonies north of the Chesapeake had histories, cultures, demographics, and economies that differed considerably from those of the southern colonies. Organized religion played a much more important role in the foundation of most of the northern colonies than it did in those of the South (except for Maryland). In New England, where the Pilgrims settled in 1620 and the Puritans in 1630, religious utopianism shaped colonial life. The same was true in the West Jersey portion of New Jersey, where members of the English pietist Society of Friends (Quakers) settled during the 1670s, and in Pennsylvania, which William Penn founded in 1682 as a Quaker colony. Quakers, like other pietists, emphasized nonviolence and a divine spirit within all humans. These beliefs disposed some Quakers to become early opponents of slavery.

Even more important than religion in shaping life in northern British North America were a cooler climate, sufficient numbers of white laborers, lack of a staple crop, and a diversified economy. All these circumstances made black slavery in the colonial North less extensive than, and different from, its southern counterparts. By the end of the colonial period during the 1770s, only 50,000 African Americans lived in the northern colonies in comparison to 400,000 in the southern colonies. But, as in the South, the northern black population varied in size from place to place (see Figure 3–2).

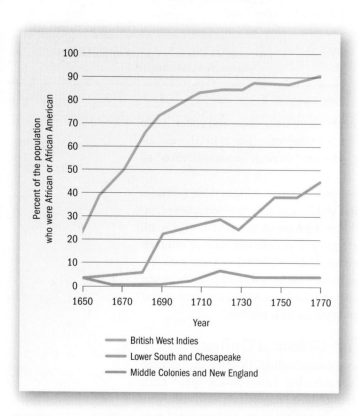

FIGURE 3–2 AFRICANS AS A PERCENTAGE OF THE TOTAL POPULATION OF THE BRITISH AMERICAN COLONIES 1650–1770

SOURCE: *Time on the Cross: The Economics of Negro Slavery* by *Robert W. Fogel and Stanley L. Engerman. Copyright © 1974. Reprinted by permission of W. W. Norton & Company, Inc.*

New York City had a particularly large black population. This dated to 1626 when the city bore the name New Amsterdam and served as the main port of New Netherlands. By 1638, free and enslaved Africans had become a large part of the city's cosmopolitan population. They spoke a variety of European languages and converted to a variety of Christian churches. By 1750, black residents constituted 20 percent of the city's population.

Like all Americans during the colonial era, most northern slaves performed agricultural labor. But, in contrast to those in the South, slaves in the North typically lived in their master's house. They worked with their master, his family, and one or two other slaves on a small farm. In northern cities, which were often home ports for slave traders, enslaved people of African descent worked as artisans, shopkeepers, messengers, domestic servants, and general laborers.

Consequently, most northern African Americans led lives that differed from their counterparts in the South. Mainly because New England had so few slaves, but also because of Puritan religious principles, slavery there was least oppressive. The local slave codes were milder than in the South and, except for the ban on miscegenation, not rigidly enforced. New England slaves could legally own, transfer, and inherit property. From the early seventeenth century onward, Puritans converted Africans and African Americans who came among them to Christianity, recognizing their spiritual equality before God.

In the middle colonies of New York, New Jersey, and Pennsylvania, where black populations were larger and hence perceived by white people to be more threatening, slave codes were stricter and penalties harsher. But, even in these colonies, the curfews imposed on Africans and African Americans, as well as the restrictions on their ability to gather together, were less well enforced than they were farther south.

These conditions encouraged rapid assimilation. Because of their small numbers, frequent isolation from others of African descent, and close association with their masters, northern slaves usually had fewer opportunities to preserve an African heritage. However, there was an increase in African customs among black northerners between 1740 and 1770. Before that time, most northern slaves had been born or "seasoned" in the South or the West Indies. Then, during the mid-eighteenth century, direct imports of African slaves into the North temporarily increased. With that increase came knowledge of African life. But overall, the less harsh and more peripheral nature of slavery in this region limited the retention of African perspectives, just as it allowed the slaves more freedom than most of their southern counterparts enjoyed.

Slavery in Spanish Florida and French Louisiana

3-8 | **How did the experience of African Americans under French and Spanish rule in North America compare to that in the British colonies?**

Just as slavery in Britain's northern colonies differed from slavery in its southern colonies, slavery in Spanish Florida and French Louisiana—areas that later became parts of the United States—had distinctive characteristics.

In 1565 Africans helped construct the Spanish settlement of St. Augustine in Florida, which is now the oldest city in the United States. But the Spanish monarchy regarded the settlement as primarily a military outpost, and plantation agriculture was not significant in Florida under Spanish rule. Therefore, the number of slaves in Florida remained small, and black men served more frequently as soldiers than as fieldworkers. As militiamen, they

3-1
3-2
3-3
3-4
3-5
3-6
3-7
3-8
3-9
3-10
3-11

gained power that eluded slaves in most of the British colonies. As members of the Catholic Church, they acquired social status. When the British took control of Florida in 1763, these local people of African descent retreated along with the city's white inhabitants to Cuba. Only with the British takeover did plantation slavery begin to grow in Florida.

When the French in 1699 established their Louisiana colony in the lower Mississippi River valley, their objective, like that of the Spanish in Florida, was primarily military. In 1720 few black people (either slave or free) lived in the colony. Then, during the following decade, Louisiana imported about 6,000 slaves. By 1731 black people outnumbered white people in the colony. Some of the Africans worked on plantations growing tobacco and indigo. But most lived in the port city of New Orleans, where many became skilled artisans, lived away from their masters, became Roman Catholics, and gained freedom. Unfortunately, early in its history, New Orleans also became a place where white men exploited black women sexually with impunity. This custom eventually created a sizable mixed-race population with elaborate social gradations based on the amount of white ancestry a person had and the lightness of his or her skin.

African Americans in New Spain's Northern Borderlands

3-9   What was African-American life like in New Spain's northern borderlands?

What is today the southwestern United States was from the sixteenth century until 1821 the northernmost part of New Spain. Centered in Mexico, this Spanish colony reached into Texas, California, New Mexico, Colorado, and Arizona. The first people of African descent who entered this huge region were members of early Spanish exploratory expeditions. During the seventeenth century, black soldiers participated in the Spanish conquest of Pueblo Indians. Some black and mulatto women also joined in Spanish military expeditions.

During the colonial era, however, New Spain's North American borderlands had far fewer black people than there were in the British colonies. In part this was because the total non-Indian population in the borderlands was extremely small. As late as 1792, only around 3,000 colonists lived in Texas, including about 450 described as black or mulatto. There were even fewer colonists in New Mexico and California, where people of mixed African, Indian, and Spanish descent were common. Black men in the borderlands gained employment as sailors, soldiers, tradesmen, cattle herders, and day laborers. Some of them were slaves, but others had limited freedom. In contrast to the British colonies, in New Spain's borderlands most slaves were Indians. They worked as domestics and as agricultural laborers or were marched south to Mexico, where they labored in gold and silver mines.

Also in contrast to the British mainland colonies, where no formal aristocracy existed but where white insistence on racial separation gradually grew in strength, both hereditary rank and racial fluidity existed in New Spain's borderlands. In theory, throughout the Spanish empire in the Americas, "racial purity" determined social status, with Spaniards of "pure blood" at the top and Africans and Indians at the bottom. In Texas free black people and Indians suffered legal disabilities. But almost all of the Spaniards who moved north from Mexico were themselves of mixed race, and people of African and Indian descent could more easily acquire status than they could in the British colonies. In the borderlands black men held responsible positions at Roman Catholic missions. A few acquired large landholdings called *ranchos*.

Black Women in Colonial America

3-10   **How did slavery affect black women in colonial America?**

The lives of black women in early North America varied according to the colony in which they lived. The differences between Britain's New England colonies and its southern colonies are particularly clear. In New England religion and demographics made the boundary between slavery and freedom permeable. There black women distinguished themselves in a variety of ways. The thoroughly acculturated Lucy Terry Prince of Deerfield, Massachusetts, published poetry in the 1740s and gained her freedom in 1756. Other black women succeeded as bakers and weavers. But in the South, where most black women of the time lived, they had few opportunities for work beyond tobacco and rice fields and the homes of their masters.

During the late seventeenth and the eighteenth centuries, approximately 90 percent of southern black women worked in the fields. Black women also mothered their children and cooked for their families, a chore that involved lugging firewood and water and tending fires as well as preparing meals. Like other women of their time, colonial black women suffered from inadequate medical attention while giving birth. But because black women worked until the moment they delivered, they were more likely than white women to experience complications in giving birth and to bear low-weight babies.

As the eighteenth century passed, more black women became house servants. Yet most jobs as maids, cooks, and body servants went to the young, the old, or the infirm. Black women also wet-nursed their master's children. None of this was easy work. Those who did it faced constant white supervision and were particularly subject to the sexual exploitation that characterized chattel slavery.

European captains and crews molested and raped black women during the Middle Passage. Masters and overseers similarly used their power to force themselves on female

Read on MyHistoryLab
Document:
Lucy Terry Prince, "Bars Fight" (1746)

3-1

3-2

3-3

3-4

3-5

3-6

3-7

3-8

3-9

3-10

3-11

In this painting African Americans await sale to slave traders, who stand at the doorway on the left.

3-1
3-2
3-3
3-4
3-5
3-6
3-7
3-8
3-9
3-10
3-11

slaves. The results were evident in the large mixed-race populations in the colonies and in the psychological damage it inflicted on African-American women and their mates. In particular, the sexual abuse of black women by white men disrupted the emerging black families in North America because black men usually could not protect their wives from it.

Black Resistance and Rebellion

3-11   **How did African Americans resist slavery?**

That masters regularly used their authority to abuse black women sexually and thereby humiliate black men dramatizes the oppressiveness of a slave system based on race and physical force. Masters often rewarded black women who became their mistresses, just as masters and overseers used incentives to get more labor from field hands. But slaves who did not comply in either case faced a beating. Slavery in America was always a system that relied ultimately on physical force to deny freedom to African Americans. From its start, black men and women responded by resisting their masters as well as they could.

Such resistance ranged from shirking assigned work to sabotage, escape, and rebellion. Before the late eighteenth century, however, resistance and rebellion were not part of a coherent antislavery effort. Before the spread of ideas about natural human rights and universal liberty associated with the American and French revolutions, slave resistance and revolt did not aim to destroy slavery as a social system. Africans and African Americans resisted, escaped, and rebelled but not as part of an effort to free all slaves. Instead, they resisted to force masters to make concessions within the framework of slavery.

African men and women newly arrived in North America openly defied their masters. They frequently refused to work and often could not be persuaded by punishment to change their behavior. Africans tended to escape in groups of individuals who shared a common homeland and language. When they succeeded, they usually became "outliers," living nearby and stealing from their master's estate. Less frequently, they headed west, where they found some safety among white frontiersmen, Indians, or interracial banditti. In 1672 Virginia's colonial government began paying bounties to anyone who killed outliers. Six decades later, the governor of South Carolina offered similar rewards. In some instances, escaped slaves, known as *maroons*—a term derived from the Spanish word *cimarron*, meaning wild—established their own settlements in inaccessible regions.

The most durable of such maroon communities in North America existed in the Spanish colony of Florida. In 1693 the Spanish king officially made this colony a refuge for slaves escaping from the British colonies, although he did not free slaves who were already there. Many such escapees joined the Seminole Indian nation and thereby gained protection between 1763 and 1783, when the British ruled Florida, and after 1821 when the United States took control. It was in part to destroy this refuge for former slaves that the United States fought the Seminole War from 1835 to 1842. Other maroon settlements existed in the South Carolina and Georgia backcountry and the **Great Dismal Swamp** of southern Virginia.

As slaves became acculturated, forms of slave resistance changed. To avoid punishment, African Americans replaced open defiance with more subtle day-to-day obstructionism. They malingered, broke tools, mistreated domestic animals, destroyed crops, poisoned their masters, and stole. Acculturation also brought different escape patterns. Increasingly, the more assimilated slaves predominated among escapees. Most of them were young men who left on their own and relied on their knowledge of American society to pass as free. Although some continued to head for maroon settlements, most sought safety among relatives, in towns, or in the North Carolina piedmont, where there were few slaves.

Great Dismal Swamp
A heavily forested area on the Virginia–North Carolina border that served as a refuge for fugitive slaves during the eighteenth and nineteenth centuries.

In colonial North America, rebellions occurred far more rarely than resistance and escape. More and larger rebellions broke out during the early eighteenth century in Jamaica and Brazil. This discrepancy resulted mainly from demographics: in the sugar-producing colonies, black people outnumbered white people by six or eight to one, but in British North America black people were a majority only in the low country. The larger the proportion of slaves in a population, the more likely they were to rebel. Also, by the mid-eighteenth century, most male slaves in the British mainland colonies were Creoles with families. They had more to lose from a failed rebellion than did the single African men who made up the bulk of the slave population farther south.

Nevertheless there were waves of rebellion in British North America from 1710 to 1722 and 1730 to 1741. Men born in Africa took the lead in these revolts, and the two most notable of them occurred in New York City in 1712 and near Charleston, South Carolina, in 1739. In New York, 27 Africans, taking revenge for "hard usage," set fire to an outbuilding. When white men arrived to put out the blaze, the rebels attacked them with muskets, hatchets, and swords. They killed nine of the white men and wounded six. Shortly thereafter, local militia units captured the rebels. Six of the rebels killed themselves; the other 21 were executed— some brutally. In 1741 another revolt conspiracy in New York led to another mass execution. Authorities put to death 30 black people and four white people convicted of helping them.

Even more frightening for most white people was the rebellion that began at Stono Bridge within 20 miles of Charleston in September 1739. Under the leadership of a man named Jemmy or Tommy, 20 slaves who had recently arrived from Angola broke into a "weare-house, & then plundered it of guns & ammunition." They killed the warehousemen, left their severed heads on the building's steps, and fled toward Florida. Other slaves joined the Angolans until their numbers reached one hundred. They sacked plantations and killed approximately 30 more white people. But when they stopped to celebrate their victories and beat drums to attract other slaves, planters on horseback aided by Indians routed them, killing 44 and dispersing the rest. Many of the rebels, including their leader, remained at large for up to three years, as did the spirit of insurrection. In 1740 Charleston authorities arrested 150 slaves and hanged 10 daily to quell that spirit.

In South Carolina and other southern colonies, white people never entirely lost their fear of slave revolt. Whenever slaves rebelled or were rumored to rebel, the fear became intense. As the quotation that begins this chapter indicates, the unwillingness of many Africans and African Americans to submit to enslavement pushed white southerners into a siege mentality that became a determining factor in American history.

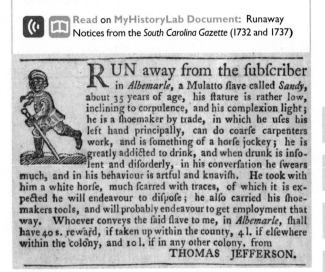

Read on **MyHistoryLab** Document: Runaway Notices from the *South Carolina Gazette* (1732 and 1737**)**

RUN away from the subscriber in *Albemarle*, a Mulatto slave called *Sandy*, about 35 years of age, his stature is rather low, inclining to corpulence, and his complexion light; he is a shoemaker by trade, in which he uses his left hand principally, can do coarse carpenters work, and is something of a horse jockey; he is greatly addicted to drink, and when drunk is insolent and disorderly, in his conversation he swears much, and in his behaviour is artful and knavish. He took with him a white horse, much scarred with traces, of which it is expected he will endeavour to dispose; he also carried his shoemakers tools, and will probably endeavour to get employment that way. Whoever conveys the said slave to me, in *Albemarle*, shall have 40 s. reward, if taken up within the county, 4 l. if elsewhere within the colony, and 10 l. if in any other colony, from

THOMAS JEFFERSON.

Announcement issued by Thomas Jefferson for a reward for a runaway slave, 14 September 1769.

Read on **MyHistoryLab** Document: James Oglethorpe, The Stono Rebellion, 1739

CONCLUSION

Studying the history of black people in early America is both painful and exhilarating. It is painful to learn of their enslavement, the emergence of racism in its modern form, and the loss of so much of the African heritage. But it is exhilarating to learn how much of that heritage Africans and African Americans preserved, how they resisted their oppressors and forged strong family bonds, and how an emerging African-American culture began to influence all aspects of American society.

The varieties of black life during the colonial period also help us understand the complexity of African-American society later in American history. Although they had much in common, black people in the Chesapeake, in the low country, in Britain's northern colonies, in Spanish Florida, in French Louisiana, and in New Spain's borderlands had different experiences, different relationships with white people and Indians, and different prospects. Those who lived in the fledgling colonial towns and cities differed from those who were agricultural laborers. The lives of those who worked on small farms differed from the lives of those who served on large plantations.

Finally, African-American history during the colonial era raises fundamental issues about contingency and determinism in human events. Did economic necessity, racism, and class interest make the development of chattel slavery in the Chesapeake inevitable? Or, had things gone otherwise (e.g., if Bacon's Rebellion had not occurred or had turned out differently), might African Americans in that region have retained more rights and access to freedom? What would have been the impact of that freedom on the colonies to the north and south of the Chesapeake?

CHAPTER TIMELINE

AFRICAN-AMERICAN EVENTS

NATIONAL EVENTS

1450

1492
Columbus reaches the West Indies
1497
John Cabot's voyage to North America for England

1500

1526
One hundred African slaves arrive at failed Spanish colony in present-day South Carolina
1529
Esteban shipwrecked on Texas coast

1519
Spanish conquest of Aztecs
1532
Spanish conquest of Incas

1550

1565
Africans help establish St. Augustine

1565
St. Augustine established
1587
Roanoke colony established

1600

1619
Thirty-two Africans reported to be living in Jamestown; 20 more arrive
1624
First documented African-American child born at Jamestown

1607
Jamestown established
1612
Tobacco cultivated in Virginia by John Rolfe

CHAPTER TIMELINE

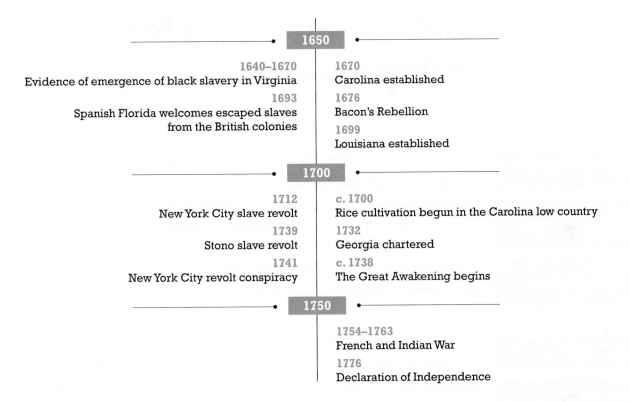

AFRICAN-AMERICAN EVENTS

NATIONAL EVENTS

1650

1640–1670
Evidence of emergence of black slavery in Virginia

1693
Spanish Florida welcomes escaped slaves from the British colonies

1670
Carolina established

1676
Bacon's Rebellion

1699
Louisiana established

1700

1712
New York City slave revolt

1739
Stono slave revolt

1741
New York City revolt conspiracy

c. 1700
Rice cultivation begun in the Carolina low country

1732
Georgia chartered

c. 1738
The Great Awakening begins

1750

1754–1763
French and Indian War

1776
Declaration of Independence

On MyHistoryLab

 Study and Review on MyHistoryLab

REVIEW QUESTIONS

1. Based on your reading of this chapter, do you believe racial prejudice among British settlers in the Chesapeake led them to enslave Africans? Or did the unfree condition of the first Africans to arrive at Jamestown lead to racial prejudice among the settlers?

2. Why did vestiges of African culture survive in British North America? Did these vestiges help or hinder African Americans in dealing with enslavement?

3. Compare and contrast eighteenth-century slavery as it existed in the Chesapeake, in the low country of South Carolina and Georgia, and in the northern colonies.

4. What were the strengths and weaknesses of the black family in the eighteenth century?

5. How did enslaved Africans and African Americans preserve a sense of their own humanity?

((Listen to Chapter 4
on MyHistoryLab

Rising Expectations: African Americans and the Struggle for Independence 1763–1783

LEARNING OBJECTIVES

4-1 What was the crisis in the British Empire?

4-2 What did the Declaration of Independence mean to African Americans?

4-3 How did African Americans contribute to the Enlightenment?

4-4 What roles did African Americans play in the War for Independence?

4-5 How did the American Revolution weaken slavery?

African Americans of the 1770s understood the revolutionary thought of their time. When a large minority of America's white population demanded independence from Britain on the basis of a natural human right to freedom, many black Americans asserted their right to be liberated from slavery. It took a momentous change in outlook from that of earlier ages for either group to perceive freedom as a right. Just as momentous was the dawning awareness among white people of the contradiction between claiming freedom for themselves and denying it to others.

The Great Awakening had nurtured humanitarian opposition to slavery. But secular thought, rooted in the European Enlightenment, shaped a revolutionary ethos in America. According to the precepts of the Enlightenment, all humans had natural, God-given rights that could not be taken from them without their consent. In 1777, the African-American petitioners in Massachusetts alluded to these precepts.

African Americans fought on both sides in the American War for Independence. In this nineteenth-century painting, a black Patriot aims his pistol at a British officer during the Battle of Cowpens, fought in South Carolina in 1781.

William Ranney, "The Battle of Cowpens." Oil on Canvas. Photo by Sam Holland. Courtesy of South Carolina State House.

If the Enlightenment shaped the revolutionary discourse of the late eighteenth century, the French and Indian War, fought between 1754 and 1763, made the American struggle for independence possible. The outcome of that war, which pitted the British, Americans, and their American Indian allies against the French and their Indian allies, created a volatile situation in the Thirteen Colonies. That situation, in turn, produced the American War for Independence and efforts by many enslaved African Americans to gain their freedom.

In this chapter we explore the African-American quest for liberty during the 20 years between 1763, when the French and Indian War ended, and 1783, when Britain recognized the independence of the United States. During this period, African Americans exercised an intellectual and political leadership that had far-ranging implications. A few black writers and scientists emerged, black soldiers fought in battle, black artisans proliferated, and—particularly in the North—black activists publicly argued against enslavement. Most important, many African Americans used the War for Independence to gain their freedom. Some were Patriots fighting for American independence. Others were Loyalists fighting for the British. Still others simply used the dislocations war caused to escape their masters.

The Crisis of the British Empire

4-1   **What was the crisis in the British Empire?**

A great struggle for empire between Great Britain and France created the circumstances within which an independence movement and rising black hopes for freedom developed in America. Starting in 1689, the British and French fought a series of wars in Europe, India, North America, Africa, and the Caribbean. This conflict climaxed in the French and Indian War that began in North America in 1754, spread to Europe in 1756 (where it was called the Seven Years' War), and from there extended to other parts of the world.

The war sprang from competing British and French efforts to control the Ohio River valley and its lucrative **fur trade**. In 1754 and 1755, the French and their Indian allies defeated Virginian and British troops in this region and then attacked the western frontier of the British colonies. Not until 1758 did Britain undertake the vigorous and expensive military effort that by 1763 had forced France to withdraw from North America. Britain took Canada from France and Florida from France's ally Spain. In compensation, Spain received New Orleans and the huge French province of Louisiana in central North America (see Map 4–1).

These changes had momentous consequences. Deprived of their ability to play off Britain against France and Spain, American Indian nations east of the Mississippi River had great difficulty resisting white encroachment. Meanwhile, fugitive slaves escaping into Florida swamps lost their Spanish protection. Americans no longer had to face French and Spanish threats on their frontiers. The bonds between Britain and the Thirteen Colonies rapidly weakened.

The last two of these consequences were closely linked. After the war ended, British officials decided that Americans should be taxed to pay their share of the costs of empire and that their commerce should be more closely regulated. In England it seemed entirely reasonable that the government should proceed in this manner. But white Americans had

fur trade A North American colonial industry involving American Indians trapping fur-bearing animals (chiefly beavers) and exchanging their pelts for European products.

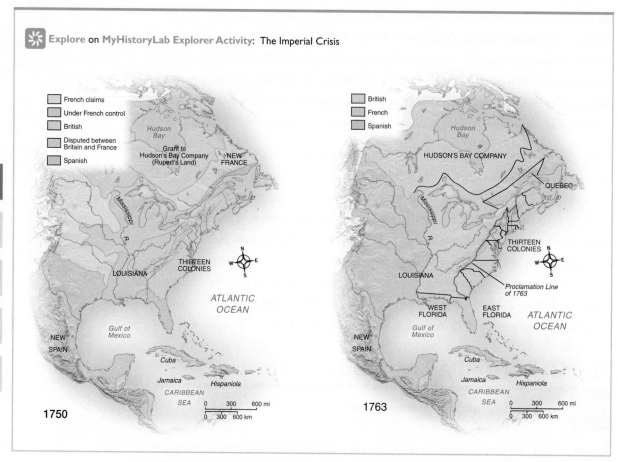

Explore on MyHistoryLab Explorer Activity: The Imperial Crisis

MAP 4–1 EUROPEAN CLAIMS IN NORTH AMERICA, 1750 (LEFT) AND 1763 (RIGHT)
These maps illustrate the dramatic change in the political geography of North America that resulted from the British victory in the French and Indian War (1754–1763). It eliminated France as a North American power. France surrendered Canada and the Ohio River valley to Britain. Spain ceded Florida to Britain and, as compensation, received Louisiana from France.

What was the significance for African Americans of these political changes and, in particular, of Great Britain's acquisition of Florida?

become accustomed to governing themselves, trading with whom they pleased, and paying only local taxes. They were well aware that with the French and Spanish gone, they no longer needed British protection. Therefore, many resisted when the British Parliament asserted its power to tax and govern them.

During the 1760s Parliament passed laws that many Americans considered oppressive. The Proclamation Line of 1763 aimed to placate Britain's Indian allies by forbidding American settlement west of the crest of the Appalachian Mountains. The Sugar Act of 1764 levied **import duties** designed to raise revenue for Britain rather than simply to regulate American trade. In 1765 the Stamp Act, also passed to raise revenue, heavily taxed printed materials.

In response, Americans at the Stamp Act Congress held in New York City in October 1765 took a first step toward united resistance. By agreeing not to import British goods, the

import duties Taxes on goods brought into a country or colony.

congress forced Parliament in 1766 to repeal the Stamp Act. But the Sugar Act and Proc-lamation Line remained in force, and Parliament remained determined to exercise greater control in America.

In 1767 Parliament forced the New York assembly to provide quarters for British troops and enacted the Townshend Acts (named after the British finance minister), which taxed glass, lead, paint, paper, and tea imported into the colonies from Britain. Resistance to these taxes in Boston led the British government to station two regiments of troops there in 1768. The volatile situation this deployment created led in 1770 to the Boston Massacre, when a small detachment of British troops fired into an angry crowd, killing five Bostonians. Among the dead was a black sailor named Crispus Attucks, who had taken the lead in accosting the soldiers. He soon became a martyr among those Americans dissatisfied with British rule, and who called themselves **Patriots**.

As it turned out, Parliament had repealed the Townshend duties, except the one on tea, before the massacre. This parliamentary retreat and reaction against the bloodshed in Boston reduced tension between the colonies and Britain. A period of calm lasted until May 1773, when Parliament passed the Tea Act.

The Tea Act gave the British East India Company a monopoly over all tea sold in the American colonies. American merchants regarded the act as the first step in a plot to bank-rupt them. Because the East India Company had huge tea reserves, it could sell tea much more cheaply than colonial merchants could. Other Americans believed the Tea Act was a trick to get them to pay the tea tax by lowering the price of tea. They feared that once Ameri-cans paid the tax on tea, British leaders would use it as a precedent to raise additional taxes.

To prevent this, Boston's radical **Sons of Liberty** in December 1773 dumped a shipload of tea into the harbor. In response, Britain in early 1774 sent more troops to Boston and pun-ished the city economically, sparking resistance throughout the colonies that eventually led to American independence. Patriot leaders organized the **Continental Congress**, which met in Philadelphia in September 1774 and demanded the repeal of all "oppressive" legislation. By November, Massachusetts Minutemen—members of an irregular militia—had begun to stockpile arms in the villages surrounding Boston.

In April 1775 Minutemen clashed with British troops at Lexington and Concord near Boston. Shortly thereafter, Congress appointed George Washington commander in chief of the Continental Army. After a year during which other armed clashes occurred and the Brit-ish rejected a compromise, Congress in July 1776 declared the colonies to be independent states, and the war became a revolution.

The Declaration of Independence and African Americans

4-2 **What did the Declaration of Independence mean to African Americans?**

The Continental Congress adopted the Declaration of Independence on July 4, 1776. Its principal author was Thomas Jefferson, a Virginia slaveholder who regarded African Americans as an inferior people. Therefore, when Jefferson wrote "that all men are created equal; that they are endowed by their Creator with certain unalienable rights; that among these are life, liberty, and the pursuit of happiness," he did not mean to support black claims for freedom. Similarly John Adams, a Massachusetts nonslaveholder who helped Jefferson

---

Patriots Those Americans who, during the Revolutionary War, favored independence.

Sons of Liberty A secret American organization formed in the Northeast during the summer of 1765 and committed to forcible opposition to the Stamp Act.

Continental Congress A representative assembly that first met in October 1775 and served as the de facto central government of the United States during the Revolutionary War.

 Watch on MyHistoryLab Video: The Limits of Imperial Control, 1763–1775

 Watch on MyHistoryLab Video: Declaring Independence

draft the Declaration, distinguished between the rights of white men of British descent and lack of rights for people of color. In 1765 Adams had written that God had "never intended the American colonists 'for Negroes . . . and therefore never intended us for slaves.'" Jefferson, Adams, and other Patriot leaders were so convinced that black people could not claim the same rights as white people, they felt no need to qualify their words proclaiming universal liberty.

The draft declaration that Jefferson, Adams, and Benjamin Franklin submitted to Congress for approval did denounce the Atlantic slave trade as a "cruel war against human nature itself, violating its most sacred rights of life and liberty in the persons of a distant [African] people." But Congress deleted this passage because delegates from South Carolina and Georgia objected to it. The final version of the Declaration referred to slavery only to accuse the British of arousing African Americans to revolt against their masters.

Yet, although Jefferson and the other delegates did not mean to encourage African Americans to hope the American War for Independence could become a war against slavery, that is what African Americans believed it could be. Black people heard Patriot speakers make unqualified claims for human equality and natural rights. They read accounts of such speeches and listened as white people discussed them. In response, African Americans began to assert that such principles logically applied as much to them as to the white population. They forced white people to confront the contradiction between the new nation's professed ideals and its reality.

The Impact of the Enlightenment

At the center of revolutionary ideology was the European Enlightenment. The roots of this intellectual movement lay in Renaissance secularism and humanism dating back to the fifteenth century. But it was Isaac Newton's *Principia Mathematica*, published in England in 1687, that shaped a new way of perceiving human beings and their universe.

Age of Revolution
A period in Atlantic history that began with the American Revolution in 1776 and ended with the defeat of Napoleonic France in 1815.

Newton used mathematics to portray an orderly, balanced universe that ran according to natural laws that humans could discover through reason. What made Newton's ideas of particular relevance to the **Age of Revolution** was John Locke's application of them to politics.

In his essay "Concerning Human Understanding," published in 1690, Locke maintained that human society—like the physical universe—ran according to natural laws. He contended that at the base of human laws were natural rights all people shared. Human beings, according to Locke, created governments to protect their natural individual rights to life, liberty, and private property. If a government failed to perform this basic duty and became oppressive, he insisted, the people had the right to overthrow it. Locke also maintained that the human mind at birth was a *tabula rasa* (i.e., knowledge and wisdom were not inherited but were acquired through experience). This suggested that with education *all* people could learn and advance.

Most Americans became acquainted with Locke's ideas through pamphlets that a radical English political minority produced during the early eighteenth century. This literature portrayed the British government of the day as a conspiracy aimed at depriving British subjects of their natural rights, reducing them to slaves, and establishing tyranny. After the French and Indian War, Americans, both black and white, interpreted British policies and actions from this same perspective.

The influence of such pamphlets is clear between 1763 and 1776 when white Patriot leaders charged that the British government sought to enslave them by depriving them of their rights as Englishmen. When they made these charges, they had difficulty denying that they themselves deprived African Americans of their natural rights. George Washington, for example, declared in 1774 that "the crisis is arrived when we must assert our rights, or submit to every imposition, that can be heaped upon us, till custom and use shall make us tame and abject, as the blacks we rule over with such arbitrary sway."

African Americans in the Revolutionary Debate

During the 1760s and 1770s, when powerful slave-holders such as George Washington talked of liberty, natural rights, and hatred of enslavement, African Americans listened. Most of them had been born in America, they had absorbed English culture, they were united as a people, and they knew their way in colonial society. Those who lived in or near towns and cities had access to public meetings and news-papers. They were aware of the disputes with Great Britain and the contradictions between demanding liberty for oneself and denying it to others. They understood that the ferment of the 1760s had shaken traditional assumptions about government, and many of them hoped for more changes.

This drawing depicts James Armistead (1760–1831) who, as an enslaved young man, served as a Patriot spy during the War for Independence. Under the command of the Marquis de Lafayette, whose name Armistead later added to his own, he infiltrated British camps in Virginia. He provided information that helped George Washington force the British surrender at Yorktown in 1781.

The greatest source of optimism for African Americans was the expectation that white Patriot leaders would realize that their revolutionary principles were incompatible with slavery. Those in England who believed that white Americans must submit to British authority pointed out the contradiction. Samuel Johnson, London's most famous writer, asked, "How is it that we hear the loudest yelps for liberty among the drivers of negroes?" But white Americans made similar comments. As early as 1763, James Otis of Massachusetts warned, "Those who every day barter away other mens['] liberty, will soon care little for their own."

Such principled misgivings among white people about slavery helped improve the situation for black people in the North and upper South during the war. But African Americans acting on their own behalf played a key role. In January 1766 slaves marched through Charleston, South Carolina, shouting "Liberty!" In the South Carolina and Georgia low country and in the Chesapeake, slaves escaped in massive numbers throughout the revolutionary era.

Rumors of slave uprisings spread throughout the southern colonies. However, it was in New England—the heartland of anti-British radicalism—that African Americans formally made their case for freedom. As early as 1701, a Massachusetts slave won his liberty in court, and there were 11 similar suits before 1750. As the revolutionary era began, such cases multiplied. In addition, although slaves during the seventeenth and early eighteenth centuries had based their

Read on MyHistoryLab Document: Exploring America: The Stamp Act

The drawing portrays a black youngster joining in a Boston demonstration against the Stamp Act of 1765.

freedom suits Legal cases in which slaves sued their master or master's heirs for freedom.

Read on **MyHistoryLab**
Document: Slaves Petition the Governor of Massachusetts to End Slavery, 1774

4-1

4-2

4-3

4-4

4-5

freedom suits on contractual technicalities, during the revolutionary period they increasingly sued on the basis of principles of universal liberty. They did not always win their cases, but they set precedents.

African Americans in Massachusetts, New Hampshire, and Connecticut also petitioned their colonial or state legislatures for gradual emancipation. These petitions, worded like the one at the start of this chapter, indicate that the black men who signed them adopted revolutionary rhetoric to their own cause. It was a rhetoric they had learned as they joined white radicals to confront British authority.

In 1765 black men in Boston demonstrated against the Stamp Act. They rioted against British troops there in 1768 and joined Crispus Attucks in 1770. Black Minutemen stood with their white comrades at Lexington and Concord. In 1773 black petitioners from Boston told a delegate to the colonial assembly, "We expect great things from men who have made such a noble stand against the designs of their *fellow-men* to enslave them. . . . The divine spirit of *freedom*, seems to fire every human breast."

The Black Enlightenment

4-3   **How did African Americans contribute to the Enlightenment?**

Besides influencing radical political discourse during the revolutionary era, the Enlightenment also shaped the careers of America's first black intellectuals. Because it emphasized human reason, the Enlightenment led to the establishment of colleges, academies, and libraries in Europe and America. These institutions usually served a tiny elite, but newspapers and pamphlets made science and literature available to the masses. The eighteenth century was also an era in which amateurs could make serious contributions to human knowledge. Some of these amateurs, such as Thomas Jefferson and Benjamin Franklin, were rich and well educated. What is striking is that some African Americans, with far more limited resources, also became scientists and authors.

Because they had easier access to evangelical Protestantism than to secular learning, most African Americans who gained intellectual distinction during the late eighteenth century owed more to the Great Awakening than to the Enlightenment. The best known of these is Jupiter Hammon, a Long Island slave who published religious poetry in the 1760s. There were also Josiah Bishop and Lemuel Haynes, black ministers to white church congregations in Virginia and New England. But Phillis Wheatley and Benjamin Banneker, who were directly influenced by the Enlightenment, became the most famous black intellectuals of their time.

Phillis Wheatley and Poetry

Listen on MyHistoryLab
Audio: "On Being Brought from Africa to America" poem by Phillis Wheatley; read by Jean Brannon

Wheatley was seven or eight years old when she came to Boston from Africa in 1761 aboard a slaver. John Wheatley, a wealthy merchant, purchased her as a servant for his wife. Although Phillis spoke no English when she arrived, she was soon reading and writing in that language and studying Latin. She pored over the Bible and became a fervent Christian. She also read the fashionable poetry of British author Alexander Pope and became, by age 13, a poet herself.

For the rest of her short life, Wheatley wrote poems to celebrate important events. Like Pope's, Wheatley's poetry reflected the values of the Enlightenment. In 1773 the

VOICES Boston's Slaves Link Their Freedom to American Liberty

In April 1773 a committee of slaves from Boston submitted this petition to the delegate to the Massachusetts General Court from the town of Thompson. The petition, which overflows with sarcasm, demonstrates African-American familiarity with the principles of the Enlightenment and the irony of white Americans' contention that Britain aimed to enslave them. Its authors are of two minds about their society. They see both the potential for black freedom and the entrenched prejudice of white Americans. Note that the authors propose to go to Africa if they gain their freedom.

Boston, April 20th, 1773

Sir,

The efforts made by the legislative of this province in their last sessions to free themselves from slavery, gave us, who are in that deplorable state, a high degree of satisfaction. We expect great things from men who have made such a noble stand against the designs of their *fellow-men* to enslave them. We cannot but wish and hope Sir, that you will have the same grand object, we mean civil and religious liberty, in view in your next session. The divine spirit of *freedom*, seems to fire every humane breast on this continent, except such as are bribed to assist in executing the execrable plan.

We are very sensible that it would be highly detrimental to our present masters, if we were allowed to demand all that of *right* belongs to us for past services; this we disclaim. Even the *Spaniards*, who have not those sublime ideas of freedom that English men have, are conscious that they have no right to all the services of their fellow-men, we mean the *Africans*, whom they have purchased with their money; therefore they allow them one day in a week to work for themselves, to enable them to earn money to purchase the residue of their time. . . . We do not pretend to dictate to you Sir, or to the Honorable Assembly, of which you are a member. We acknowledge our obligations to you for what you have already done, but as the people of this province seem to be actuated by the principles of equity and justice, we cannot but expect your house will again take our deplorable case into serious consideration, and give us that ample relief which, *as men*, we have a natural right to.

But since the wise and righteous governor of the universe, has permitted our fellow men to make us slaves, we bow in submission to him, and determine to behave in such a manner as that we can have reason to expect the divine approbation of, and assistance in, our peaceable and lawful attempts to gain our freedom.

We are willing to submit to such regulations and laws, as may be made relative to us, until we leave the province, which we determine to do as soon as we can, from our joynt labours procure money to transport ourselves to some part of the Coast of *Africa*, where we propose settlement. We are very desirous that you should have instructions relative to us, from your town, therefore we pray you to communicate this letter to them, and ask this favor for us.

In behalf of our fellow slaves in this province, and by order of their Committee.

Peter Bestes,
Sambo Freeman,
Felix Holbrook,
Chester Joie.

For the Representative of the town of Thompson.

---

1. **What is the object of this petition?**
2. **What Enlightenment principles does the petition invoke?**
3. **What is the significance of the slaves' vow to go to Africa if freed?**

SOURCE: Gary B. Nash, *Race and Revolution* (Madison, WI: Madison House, 1990), 173–74.

((•)) 📖 Read on MyHistoryLab Document: Phillis Wheatley Publishes Her Poems, 1773

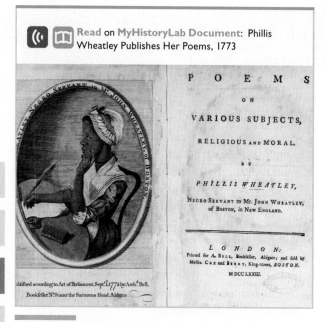

A frontispiece portrait of Phillis Wheatley precedes the title page of her first book of poetry, which was published in 1773. The portrait suggests Wheatley's small physique and studious manner.

Wheatleys sent her to London where her first book of poems—the first book ever by an African-American woman and the second by any American woman—was published under the title *Poems on Various Subjects, Religious and Moral.* The Wheatleys freed Phillis after her return to Boston, although she continued to live in their house until both of them died. In 1778 she married John Peters, a black grocer, and was soon mired in illness and poverty. Two of her children died in infancy, and she died in December 1784 giving birth to her third child, who died with her.

In her writing Wheatley called on black people to adopt white culture. Before her marriage, she lived almost exclusively among white people and absorbed their values. Although she lamented the sorrow her capture had caused her parents, she was grateful to have been brought to America where she could become a Christian. Wheatley did not simply copy her masters' views. Although the Wheatleys were loyal to Britain, she became a fervent Patriot and wrote poems supporting the Patriot cause.

Wheatley also became an advocate and symbol of John Locke's ideas concerning the influence of environment on human beings. White leaders of the Revolution and intellectuals debated whether black people were inherently inferior in intellect to white people or whether this perceived black inferiority was the result of enslavement. Some slaveholders, such as Thomas Jefferson—who held racist assumptions about innate black inferiority—dismissed Wheatley's work as "below the dignity of criticism." But those who favored an environmental perspective considered Wheatley an example of what people of African descent could achieve if freed from oppression.

Benjamin Banneker and Science

In the breadth of his achievement, Benjamin Banneker is even more representative of the Enlightenment than Phillis Wheatley. Like hers, his life epitomizes a flexibility concerning race that the revolutionary era briefly promised to expand.

Banneker was born free in Maryland in 1731. The son of a mixed-race mother and an African father, he inherited a farm near Baltimore from his white grandmother. As a child, Banneker attended a racially integrated school. Later his farm gave him a steady income and the leisure to study literature and science.

With access to the library of his white neighbor George Ellicott, Banneker "mastered Latin and Greek and had a good working knowledge of German and French." Like Jefferson, Franklin, and others of his time, Banneker was fascinated with mechanics and in 1770 constructed a clock. He also wrote a treatise on bees. However, he gained international fame as a mathematician and astronomer. Because of his knowledge in these disciplines, he became a member of the survey commission for Washington, DC. This made him the first black civilian employee of the U.S. government. Between 1791

VOICES   Phillis Wheatley on Liberty and Natural Rights

Phillis Wheatley wrote the following letter to Samson Occom, an American-Indian minister, in 1774, after her return from England and as tensions between Britain and its American colonies intensified. In it, she links divine order, natural rights, and an inner desire for personal liberty. She expresses optimism that Christianity and the emergence of order in Africa will lead to the end of the Atlantic slave trade. And she hopes that God will ultimately overcome the avarice of American slaveholders ("our modern Egyptians") and let them see the contradiction between their words and deeds.

February 11, 1774

Rev'd and honor'd Sir,

I have this Day received your obliging kind Epistle, and am greatly satisfied with your Reasons respecting the Negroes, and think highly reasonable what you offer in Vindication of their natural Rights. Those that invade them cannot be insensible that the divine Light is chasing away the thick Darkness which broods over the Land of Africa; and the Chaos which has reign'd so long, is converting into beautiful Order, and reveals more and more clearly, the glorious Dispensation of civil and religious Liberty, which are so inseparably united, that there is little or no Enjoyment of one without the other. Otherwise, perhaps, the Israelites had been less solicitous for their Freedom from Egyptian Slavery; I don't say they would have been contented without it. By no Means, for in every human Breast, God has implanted a Principle, which we call Love of Freedom; it is impatient of Oppression, and pants for Deliverance. And by the leave of our modern Egyptians, I will assert that the same principle lives in us. God grant Deliverance in his own Way and Time, and get him honor upon all those whose Avarice impels them to countenance and help forward the Calamities of their fellow Creatures. This I desire not for their Hurt, but to convince them of the strange Absurdity of their Conduct whose Words and Actions are so diametrically opposite. How well the cry for Liberty, and the reverse Disposition for the exercise of oppressive Power over others agree, I humbly think it does not require the Penetration of a Philosopher to determine.

Phillis Wheatley

1. **How does this letter reflect principles associated with the Enlightenment?**
2. **What insights does this letter provide into Wheatley's views on slavery and its abolition?**

SOURCE: Roy Finkenbine, ed., *Sources of the African-American Past: Primary Sources in American History* (New York: Longman, 1997), 22–23.

---

and 1796, he used his astronomical observations and mathematical calculations to publish an almanac predicting the positions in the earth's night sky of the sun, moon, and constellations.

Like Wheatley, Banneker thoroughly assimilated white culture and well understood the fundamental issues of human equality raised by the American Revolution. In 1791 he sent Thomas Jefferson, who was then U.S. secretary of state, a copy of his almanac to refute Jefferson's claim in *Notes on the State of Virginia* that black people were inherently inferior intellectually to white people.

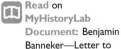

Read on
MyHistoryLab
Document: Benjamin Banneker—Letter to Thomas Jefferson (1791)

African Americans in the War for Independence

4-4   What roles did African Americans play in the War for Independence?

4-1

4-2

4-3

4-4

4-5

Loyalists Those Americans who, during the Revolutionary War, wished to remain within the British Empire.

Continental Army The army created by the Continental Congress in June 1775 to fight British troops. George Washington was its commander in chief.

When it came to fighting between Patriots on one side and the British and their **Loyalist** American allies on the other, African Americans joined the side that offered freedom. In the South, where the British held out the promise of freedom in exchange for military service, black men eagerly fought on the British side as Loyalists. In the North, where white Patriots were more consistently committed to human liberty than in the South, black men just as eagerly fought on the Patriot side (see Map 4–2).

The war began in earnest in August 1776 when the British landed a large army at Brooklyn, New York, and drove Washington's **Continental Army** across New Jersey into Pennsylvania. The military and diplomatic turning point in the war came the following year at Saratoga, New York, when a poorly executed British strategy to take control of the Hudson River resulted in British general John Burgoyne's surrender of his entire army to Patriot forces. This victory led France and other European powers to enter the war against Britain. Significant fighting ended in October 1781 when Washington and the French forced Lord Cornwallis to surrender another British army at Yorktown, Virginia.

When Washington had organized the Continental Army in July 1775, he forbade the enlistment of new black troops and the reenlistment of black men who had served in the early battles of the war. Shortly thereafter, all 13 states followed Washington's example. Several reasons account for Washington's decision and its ratification by the Continental Congress. Although several black men had served during the French and Indian War, the colonies had traditionally excluded African Americans from militia service. Like others before them, Patriot leaders feared that if they enlisted African-American soldiers, it would encourage slaves to leave their masters without permission. White people—especially in the South—also feared that armed black men would endanger the social order. Paradoxically, white people simultaneously believed black men were too cowardly to be effective soldiers.

Black Loyalists

Because so many Patriot leaders resisted employing black troops, by mid-1775 the British had taken the initiative in recruiting African Americans. During the spring of that year, from Maryland southward, rumors circulated among Americans that the British would instigate slave revolt. However, no such uprisings occurred.

Instead, many slaves escaped and sought British protection as Loyalists. The British employed most black men who escaped to their lines as laborers and foragers. During the siege at Yorktown in 1781, the British used the bodies of black laborers who had died of smallpox in a primitive form of biological warfare to try to infect the Patriot army. Even so, many black refugees fought for British or Loyalist units.

Black Loyalists were most numerous in the low country of South Carolina and Georgia. At the end of the war in 1783, approximately 20,000 African Americans left with the British forces as they evacuated Savannah and Charleston. A few who remained became known as "the plunderers of Georgia." They carried out guerrilla warfare there until 1786.

The most famous British appeal to African Americans to fight for the empire in return for freedom came in Virginia. On November 7, 1775, Lord Dunmore, the last royal

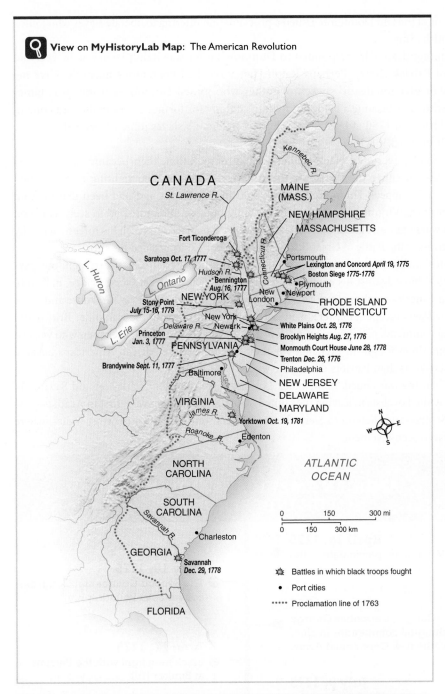

View on MyHistoryLab Map: The American Revolution

MAP 4–2 MAJOR BATTLES OF THE AMERICAN WAR FOR INDEPENDENCE, INDICATING THOSE IN WHICH BLACK TROOPS PARTICIPATED
Black troops fought on both sides during the American War for Independence and participated in most of the major battles.

SOURCE: *Adapted from* The Atlas of African-American History and Politics, *1/e, by A. Smallwood and J. Elliot, © 1998, The McGraw-Hill Companies. Reproduced with permission of The McGraw-Hill Companies.*

Why is it significant that most of these battles were in the North?

governor of the Old Dominion, issued a proclamation offering to liberate slaves who joined the British army.

Among those who responded to Dunmore's offer was Ralph Henry, a 26-year-old slave of Patrick Henry. Perhaps Ralph Henry recalled his famous master's "Give me liberty or give me death" speech. Another who joined Dunmore's troops was James Reid, who later became a leader of Britain's colony for former slaves in Sierra Leone in West Africa. In 1780 at least 20 of Thomas Jefferson's slaves joined Cornwallis's army when it invaded Virginia.

Dunmore recruited black soldiers out of desperation, then became the strongest advocate—on either the British or the American side—of their fighting ability. When he issued his appeal, Dunmore had only 300 British troops and had been driven from Williamsburg, Virginia's colonial capital. Mainly because Dunmore had to seek refuge on British warships, only about 800 African Americans managed to reach his forces. Defeat by the Patriots at the Battle of Great Bridge in December 1775 curtailed his efforts.

Read on MyHistoryLab Document: Lord Dunmore's Proclamation, 1775

But Dunmore's proclamation and the black response to it struck a tremendous psychological blow against his enemies. Of Dunmore's 600 troops at Great Bridge, half were African Americans whose uniforms bore the motto "Liberty to Slaves." As more and more Virginia slaves escaped, masters blamed Dunmore. Throughout the war, other British and Loyalist commanders followed his example, recruiting thousands of black men who worked and sometimes fought in exchange for their freedom. More African Americans became active Loyalists than Patriots during the war.

When the war ended, many black Loyalists, like those in Charleston and Savannah, joined white Loyalists in leaving the United States. Some of them went first to Acadia—now Nova Scotia—and then on to Sierra Leone. Others went to the British West Indies, where some faced reenslavement.

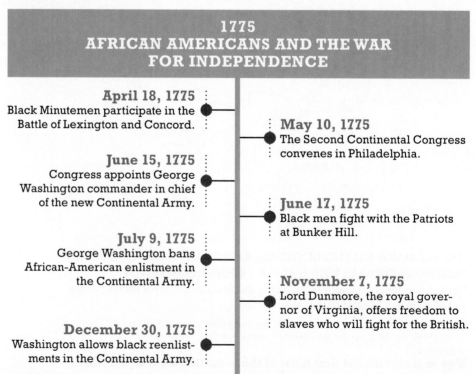

1775
AFRICAN AMERICANS AND THE WAR FOR INDEPENDENCE

April 18, 1775
Black Minutemen participate in the Battle of Lexington and Concord.

May 10, 1775
The Second Continental Congress convenes in Philadelphia.

June 15, 1775
Congress appoints George Washington commander in chief of the new Continental Army.

June 17, 1775
Black men fight with the Patriots at Bunker Hill.

July 9, 1775
George Washington bans African-American enlistment in the Continental Army.

November 7, 1775
Lord Dunmore, the royal governor of Virginia, offers freedom to slaves who will fight for the British.

December 30, 1775
Washington allows black reenlistments in the Continental Army.

Black Patriots

Washington's July 1775 policy to the contrary, black men fought on the Patriot side from the beginning of the Revolutionary War to its conclusion. Before Washington's arrival in Massachusetts, there were black Minutemen at Lexington and Concord, and some of the same men distinguished themselves at Bunker Hill. Among them were Peter Salem, Caesar Dickerson, Pomp Fisk, Prince Hall, Cuff Hayes, Barzillai Lew, Salem Poor, Caesar Weatherbee, and Cuff Whittemore. Lew was a veteran of the French and Indian War. Hall became a prominent black leader. Poor, who wintered with Washington's army at Valley Forge in Pennsylvania in 1777–1778, received a commendation for bravery at Bunker Hill.

Dunmore's use of African-American soldiers prompted Washington to reconsider his ban on black enlistment. "If that man, Dunmore," he wrote in late 1775, "is not crushed before the Spring he will become the most dangerous man in America. His strength will increase like a snowball running down hill. Success will depend on which side can arm the Negro faster." After receiving encouragement from black veterans, Washington, on December 30, 1775, allowed African-American reenlistment in the Continental Army. Congress, fearful of alienating slaveholders, initially would not allow him to go further. By the end of 1776, however, troop shortages forced Congress and the state governments to recruit black soldiers in earnest for the Continental Army and state militias.

For many years, historians presumed that Peter Salem was the black soldier portrayed in this detail from John Trumbull's contemporary oil painting *The Battle of Bunker Hill*. Instead, the soldier was Asaba Grosvenor, a slave who accompanied his master in the fighting.

The Patriot recruitment policy changed most quickly in New England. In early 1777 Massachusetts opened its militia to black men, and Rhode Island formed a black regiment. Connecticut enabled masters to free their slaves to serve as substitutes for the masters or their sons in the militia or Continental Army. New York and New Jersey adopted similar statutes.

Also in 1777, when Congress set state enlistment quotas for the Continental Army, state recruitment officers began to fill those quotas with black men so that white men might serve closer to home in the militia. Meanwhile the southern states of Delaware, Maryland, Virginia, and North Carolina reluctantly began enlisting free black men. Of these states, only Maryland allowed slaves to serve in return for freedom, but the others sometimes allowed slaves to enlist as substitutes for their masters, which usually led to freedom. Except for Rhode Island's black regiment and some companies in Massachusetts, black Patriots served in integrated military units. Enrollment officers often did not specify a man's race when he enlisted, so it is difficult to know precisely how many black men were involved. The figure usually given is 5,000 black soldiers out of a total Patriot force of 300,000.

Black men fought on the Patriot side in nearly every major battle of the war (see Map 4–2). Prince Whipple and Oliver Cromwell crossed the Delaware River with Washington on Christmas night 1776 to surprise Hessian mercenaries (German troops hired to fight on the British side) at Trenton, New Jersey. Others fought at Monmouth, Saratoga, Savannah, Princeton, and Yorktown. In 1777 a Hessian officer reported, "No [Patriot] regiment is to be seen in which there are not Negroes in abundance, and among them are able bodied, strong and brave fellows."

Black women also supported the Patriot cause. Like white women, black women sometimes accompanied their soldier husbands into army camps, if not into battle. A few black women also demonstrated their sympathy for the Patriots in defiance of British authority. When the British occupied Philadelphia in 1777, they put Patriot prisoners of war in the city jail. The following year, a local Patriot correspondent reported that a free black woman, "having received two hard dollars for washing, and hearing of the distress of our prisoners in the goal, went to market and bought some neck beef and two heads, with some green[s], and made a pot of as good broth as she could; but having no more money to buy bread, she got credit of a baker for six loaves of bread, all of which she carried to our unfortunate prisoners."

The Revolution and Emancipation

4-5 How did the American Revolution weaken slavery?

The willingness of African Americans to risk their lives in the Patriot cause encouraged northern legislatures to emancipate slaves within their borders. By the late 1770s, most of these legislatures were debating abolition. Petitions and lawsuits initiated by black people in Massachusetts, Connecticut, New Hampshire, and elsewhere encouraged such consideration. But it had been an emerging market economy, the Great Awakening, and the Enlightenment that established the context in which people who believed deeply in the sanctity of private property could consider such a momentous change. Economic, religious, and intellectual change had convinced many white Americans that slavery should be abolished.

Enlightenment rationalism was a powerful antislavery force. In the light of reason, slavery appeared to be inefficient, barbaric, and oppressive. But rationalism alone could not convince white Americans that black people should be released from slavery. White people also had to believe general emancipation was in their self-interest and their Christian duty.

In the North, where all these forces operated and the economic stake in slave labor was relatively small, emancipation made steady progress. In the Chesapeake, where some of these forces operated, emancipationist sentiment grew, and many masters manumitted their slaves; however, there was no serious threat to the slave system. In the low country of South Carolina and Georgia, where economic interests and white solidarity against large black populations outweighed intellectual and religious considerations, white commitment to black bondage remained absolute.

The movement among white people to abolish slavery began within the Society of Friends. This religious group, whose members were known as Quakers, had always emphasized conscience, human brotherhood, and nonviolence. Also, many leading Quaker families engaged in international business ventures that required educated, efficient, and moral workers. This predisposed such Quakers against a system that forced workers to be uneducated, recalcitrant, and often ignorant of Christian religion. Although members of the Society of Friends had owned and traded slaves for generations, growing numbers of Quakers concluded that slaveholding was sinful.

During the 1730s Benjamin Lay, a former slaveholder, began to exhort his fellow Friends to disassociate themselves from owning and buying slaves. A decade later John Woolman, from southern New Jersey, urged northeastern and Chesapeake Quakers to emancipate their slaves. With assistance from British Quakers, Woolman and Anthony Benezet, a Philadelphia teacher, convinced the Society's 1758 annual meeting to condemn slavery and the slave trade.

Watch on MyHistoryLab
Video: People of Color: New Freedoms, New Struggles

Read on MyHistoryLab
Document: An Early Abolitionist Speaks Out against Slavery in 1757

4-1

4-2

4-3

4-4

4-5

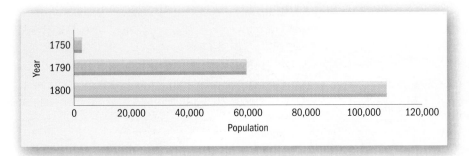

FIGURE 4-1 THE FREE BLACK POPULATION OF THE BRITISH NORTH AMERICAN COLONIES IN 1750 AND OF THE UNITED STATES IN 1790 AND 1800
The impact of revolutionary ideology and a changing economy led to a great increase in the free black population during the 1780s and 1790s.

SOURCE: A Century of Population Growth in the United States, 1790–1900 *(1909), 80. Data for 1750 estimated.*

When the conflict with Britain made human rights a political as well as a religious issue, Woolman and Benezet carried their abolitionist message beyond the Society of Friends. They thereby merged their sectarian crusade with the rationalist efforts of such northern white revolutionary leaders as former slaveholder Benjamin Franklin of Philadelphia and John Jay and Alexander Hamilton—who continued to own slaves—of New York. Under Quaker leadership, antislavery societies organized in the North and the Chesapeake. The societies joined African Americans in petitioning northern legislatures and, in one instance, the Continental Congress to act against slavery or the slave trade.

The Revolutionary Impact

In calling for emancipation, the antislavery societies emphasized black service in the war against British rule and the religious and economic progress of northern African Americans. They also contended that emancipation would prevent black rebellions. As a result, by 1784 all the northern states except New Jersey and New York had undertaken either immediate or gradual abolition of slavery. Delaware, Maryland, and Virginia made manumission easier. Even South Carolina and Georgia undertook to mitigate the most brutal excesses that slavery encouraged among masters. Many observers believed the Revolution had profoundly improved the prospects for African Americans.

In fact, the War for Independence dealt a heavy, although not mortal, blow to slavery (see Figure 4–1). While northern states prepared to abolish involuntary servitude, an estimated 100,000 slaves escaped from their masters in the South. Twenty thousand black people left with the British at the end of the war (see Map 4–3). Meanwhile, numerous escapees found their way to southern cities or to the North, where they joined an expanding free black class.

In the Chesapeake, as well as in the North, individual slaves gained freedom either in return for service in the war or because their masters had embraced Enlightenment principles. Philip Graham of Maryland freed his slaves, commenting that slavery was repugnant to every principle of the late glorious revolution which has taken place in America." The Virginia legislature ordered masters to free slaves who had fought for American independence.

Those Chesapeake slaves who did not become free also made gains during the Revolution because the war hastened the decline of tobacco raising. As planters switched to wheat and corn, they required fewer year-round, full-time workers. This encouraged the planters to free their excess labor force or to negotiate contracts that let slaves serve for a term of years rather than for life. Another alternative was for masters to allow slaves—primarily

4-1

4-2

4-3

4-4

4-5

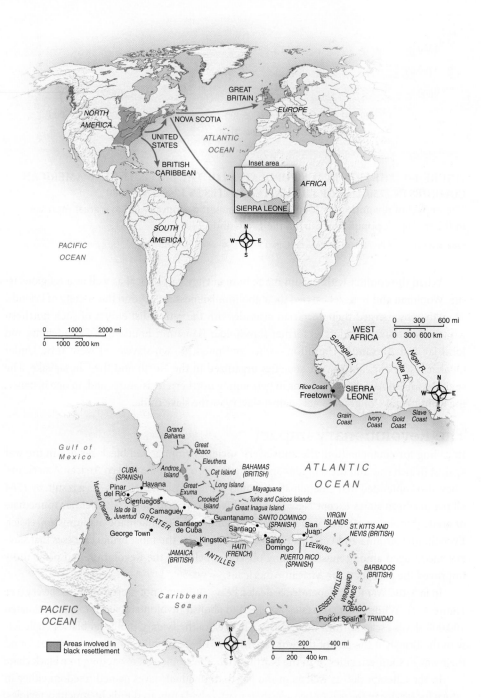

MAP 4–3 THE RESETTLEMENT OF BLACK LOYALISTS AFTER THE AMERICAN WAR FOR INDEPENDENCE

Like their white Loyalist counterparts, many black Loyalists left with the British following the Patriot victory. Most of those who settled in Nova Scotia soon moved on to Great Britain or the British free black colony of Sierra Leone. Some black migrants to the British Caribbean were reenslaved.

SOURCE: Adapted from The Atlas of African-American History and Politics, 1/e, by A. Smallwood and J. Elliot, © 1998, The McGraw-Hill Companies. Reproduced with permission of The McGraw-Hill Companies.

What does the arrival of some black Loyalists in Sierra Leone indicate about Great Britain's changing attitudes toward slavery?

males—to practice skilled trades instead of doing fieldwork. Such slaves often **"hired their own time"** in return for giving their masters a large percentage of their wages.

Even those slaves who remained agricultural workers had more time to garden, hunt, and fish to supply themselves and their families with food and income. They gained more freedom to visit relatives who lived on other plantations, attend religious meetings, and interact with white people. Masters tended to refrain from the barbaric punishments used in the past, to improve slave housing, and to allow slaves more access to religion.

In South Carolina and Georgia, greater autonomy for slaves during the revolutionary era took a different form. The war increased absenteeism among masters and reduced contacts between the black and white populations. The black majorities in rice-producing regions grew larger, more isolated, and more African in culture as the two states imported more slaves from Africa. The increase in master absenteeism also permitted the task system of labor to expand.

hired their own time Refers to a practice in which a master allowed slaves to work for wages paid by someone other than the master himself.

The Revolutionary Promise

Even though the northern states moved toward general emancipation during the revolutionary era, most newly free African Americans lived in the Chesapeake. They gained their freedom by serving in the war or escaping or because of economic and ideological change. As a result, a substantial free black population emerged in the Chesapeake after the war. But in South Carolina and Georgia, the free black class remained tiny. Most low-country free black people were the children of white slave owners. They tended to be less independent of their former masters than their Chesapeake counterparts and lighter complexioned because their freedom was often a result of a family relationship to their masters.

Watch on MyHistoryLab
Video: The American Revolution as Different Americans Saw It

In the North and the Chesapeake, free African Americans frequently moved to cities. Boston, New York, Philadelphia, Baltimore, Richmond, and Norfolk gained substantial free black populations after the Revolution. Black women predominated in this migration because they could more easily find jobs as domestics in the cities than in rural areas. Cities also offered free black people opportunities for community development that did not exist in thinly settled farm country. Although African Americans often used their new mobility to reunite families disrupted by slavery, relocating to a city could disrupt families that had survived enslavement. It took about a generation for stable, urban, two-parent households to emerge.

Newly freed black people also faced economic difficulty, and their occupational status often declined. Frequently they emerged from slavery without the economic resources needed to become independent farmers, shopkeepers, or tradespeople. In the North such economic restraints sometimes forced them to remain with their former masters long after formal emancipation. To make matters worse, white artisans used legal and extralegal means to protect themselves from black competition. Therefore, African Americans who had learned trades as slaves had difficulty employing their skills in freedom.

Yet, in the North and Chesapeake, most African Americans refused to work for their old masters and left the site of their enslavement. Those who had escaped had to leave. For others, leaving indicated a desire to put the stigma of servitude behind and embrace, despite the risks, the opportunities freedom offered. Many former masters did not understand this desire and criticized their former chattels for not staying on as hired hands.

Read on MyHistoryLab
Document: Free African Americans Petition Massachusetts for the Emancipation of All Slaves, 1777

Many African Americans took new names to signify their freedom. They adopted surnames such as *Freedom*, *Liberty*, or *Justice* and dropped classical given names such as *Pompey* and *Caesar*. Some paid homage to their African ancestry and complexion by taking surnames such as *Africa*, *Guinea*, *Brown*, and *Coal*. Others, however, expressed their aspirations in a racially stratified society by replacing African given names, such as *Cuffee* and *Quash*, with Anglicized biblical names and the surnames of famous white people.

CONCLUSION

In the Peace of Paris signed in September 1783, Britain recognized the independence of the United States, acquiesced in American control of the territory between the Appalachian Mountains and the Mississippi River, and returned Florida to Spain. Both sides promised to return confiscated property—including slaves—to their owners, but neither side complied. As the United States gained recognition of its independence, African Americans could claim they had helped secure it. As soldiers in the Continental Army or in Patriot state militias, many black men fought and died for the revolutionary cause. Others supported the British. African Americans, like white Americans, had been divided over the War for Independence. Yet those black men and women who chose the Patriot side, as well as those who became Loyalists, had freedom as their goal.

This chapter has sought to place the African-American experience during the struggle for independence in the broad context of revolutionary ideology derived from the Enlightenment. Black men and women, such as Benjamin Banneker and Phillis Wheatley, exemplified the intellectually liberating impact of eighteenth-century rationalism and recognized its application to black freedom.

During the war, and with the assistance of white opponents of slavery, African Americans combined arguments for natural rights with action to gain freedom. The American Revolution seemed about to fulfill its promise of freedom to a minority of African Americans, and they were ready to embrace the opportunities it offered. By the war's end in 1783, slavery was dying in the North and seemed to be on the wane in the Chesapeake. The first steps toward forming free black communities had been taken. Black leaders and intellectuals had emerged. Although most of their brothers and sisters remained in slavery, although the slave system began to expand again during the 1790s, and although free black people achieved *at best* second-class citizenship, they had made undeniable progress. Yet African Americans were also learning how difficult freedom could be despite the new republic's embrace of revolutionary ideals.

CHAPTER TIMELINE

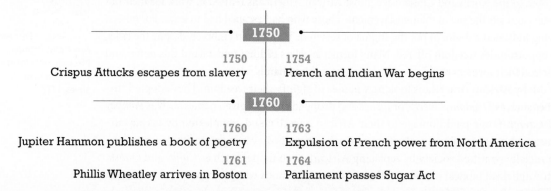

AFRICAN-AMERICAN EVENTS   **NATIONAL EVENTS**

1750

1750
Crispus Attucks escapes from slavery

1754
French and Indian War begins

1760

1760
Jupiter Hammon publishes a book of poetry

1763
Expulsion of French power from North America

1761
Phillis Wheatley arrives in Boston

1764
Parliament passes Sugar Act

CHAPTER TIMELINE

AFRICAN-AMERICAN EVENTS

NATIONAL EVENTS

1765

1765
African Americans in Boston join protests against Stamp Act

1766
Slaves in Charleston, South Carolina, demand "liberty"

1765
Stamp Act Congress

1770

1770
Crispus Attucks is killed during Boston Massacre

1773
Phillis Wheatley publishes a book of poetry
Black Bostonians petition for freedom

1770
Boston Massacre

1773
Boston Tea Party

1775

1775
Black Minutemen fight at Lexington and Concord

1776
Lord Dunmore recruits black soldiers in Virginia

1777
Emancipation begins in the North

1775
Battles of Lexington and Concord

1776
Declaration of Independence

1777
British general John Burgoyne surrenders at Saratoga

1780

1781–1783
20,000 black Loyalists depart with the British troops

1781
Cornwallis surrenders at Yorktown

1783
Britain recognizes U.S. independence

On MyHistoryLab

 Study and Review on MyHistoryLab

REVIEW QUESTIONS

1. How did the Enlightenment affect African Americans during the revolutionary era?

2. What was the relationship between the American Revolution and black freedom?

3. What was the role of African Americans in the War for Independence? How did their choices in this conflict affect how the war was fought?

4. How did the American Revolution encourage assimilation among African Americans? How did it discourage assimilation?

5. Why did a substantial class of free African Americans emerge from the revolutionary era?

African Americans in the New Nation 1783–1820

Except that they were all born slaves in eighteenth-century America, Elizabeth Freeman, Jupiter Hammon, and Gabriel had little in common. Freeman was an illiterate domestic servant when, in 1781, she sued for her freedom in Massachusetts. Hammon, who lived in Long Island, New York, was a poet and orthodox Calvinist preacher who enjoyed the support of his master and never sought his freedom. Gabriel was a literate, skilled slave who in 1800 masterminded a conspiracy to overthrow slavery in Virginia.

In this chapter, we explore how African Americans as diverse as Freeman, Hammon, and Gabriel helped shape the lives of black people during America's early years as an independent republic. We also examine how between 1783 and 1820 the forces for black liberty vied with the forces for slavery and inequality. The end of the War for Independence created great expectations among African Americans. But by 1820, when the Missouri Compromise confirmed the power of slaveholders in national affairs, black people in the North and the South had long known that the struggle for freedom was far from over.

This recent photograph portrays one of several buildings used as slave quarters on Hermitage, Savannah, Georgia. Built during the mid-seventeenth century, the small brick building housed two African-American families into the Civil War years.

That struggle took place at the state and local, as well as regional and national, levels. The forces involved in it were often impersonal. They included the emergence of a market economy in the North, based on wage, and an economy in the South, based on the production of cotton by slave labor. In addition, a revolutionary ideology encouraged African Americans to seek freedom, by force if necessary.

Meanwhile economic self-interest encouraged white northerners to limit black freedom, and fear of race war caused white southerners to strengthen the slave system.

Yet individual and group action also shaped African-American life in the new nation. As urban, church-centered black communities arose, men and women—both slave and free—influenced culture, politics, economics, and perceptions of race. This was particularly true in the North and the Chesapeake but also to a lesser degree in the Deep South. These were years of considerable progress for African Americans, although they ended with free black people facing deteriorating conditions in the North and with slavery spreading westward across the South.

Forces for Freedom

5-1 **What forces worked for black freedom after the Revolution?**

After the War for Independence ended in 1783, a strong trend in the North and the Chesapeake favored emancipation. It had roots in economic change, evangelical Christianity, and a revolutionary ethos based on the Enlightenment's natural rights doctrines. African Americans took advantage of these forces to escape from slavery, purchase the freedom of their families and themselves, sue for freedom in court, and petition state legislatures to grant them equal rights.

In the postrevolutionary North, slavery, although widespread, was not economically essential. Farmers could hire hands during the labor-intensive seasons of planting and harvesting more efficiently than they could maintain a year-round slave labor force. In addition, transatlantic immigration brought to the North plenty of white laborers, who worked cheaply and resented slave competition. As the Great Awakening initiated a new religious morality, as natural rights doctrines flourished, and as a market economy based on wage labor emerged, northern slaveholders had difficulty defending perpetual black slavery.

In Chapter 4, we saw that emancipation in the North was a direct result of the War for Independence. But the *process* of doing away with slavery unfolded in these states only after the war. Meanwhile Congress set a precedent in discouraging the expansion of slavery, and antislavery societies proliferated in the North and Upper South.

Northern Emancipation

Emancipation in the North did not follow a single pattern. Instead, the New England states of Massachusetts (which included Maine until it became a separate state in 1820), Connecticut, Rhode Island, New Hampshire, and Vermont moved more quickly than did the mid-Atlantic states of Pennsylvania, New York, and New Jersey (see Map 5–1). Slavery

5-1
5-2
5-3
5-4
5-5
5-6

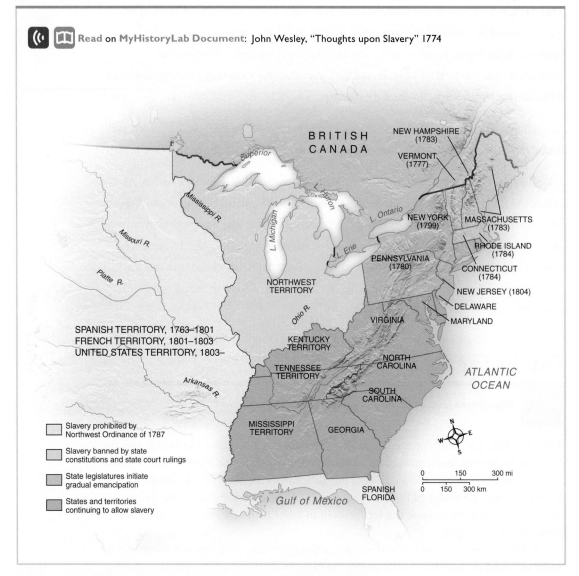

Read on **MyHistoryLab** Document: John Wesley, "Thoughts upon Slavery" 1774

MAP 5–1 EMANCIPATION AND SLAVERY IN THE EARLY REPUBLIC
This map indicates the abolition policies adopted by the states of the Northeast between 1777 and 1804, the antislavery impact of the Northwest Ordinance of 1787, and the extent of slavery in the South during the early republic.

Why did the states and territories shown in this map adopt different policies toward African Americans?

collapsed in the New England states because African Americans who lived there refused to remain in servitude and because most white New Englanders acquiesced. The struggle against slavery in the Mid-Atlantic states was longer and harder because more white people living there had a vested interest in maintaining it.

Vermont and Massachusetts—certainly—and New Hampshire—probably—abolished slavery immediately during the 1770s and 1780s. Vermont, where there had never been more than a few slaves, prohibited slavery in the constitution it adopted in 1777. Massachusetts, in its constitution of 1780, declared "that all men are born free and equal; and that every subject is entitled to liberty." Although this constitution did not specifically ban slavery, within a year Elizabeth Freeman had sued under it for their freedom.

Another Massachusetts slave, Quok Walker, left his master and began living as a free person. In response, Walker's master sought a court order forcing Walker to return to slavery. This case led in 1783 to a Massachusetts Supreme Court ruling that "slavery is . . . as effectively abolished as it can be by the granting of rights and privileges wholly incompatible and repugnant to its existence." Another judge used similar logic to grant Freeman her liberty. These decisions encouraged other Massachusetts slaves to sue for their freedom or simply to leave their masters because the courts had ruled unconstitutional the master's claim to his human chattel.

As a result, the first U.S. census in 1790 found no slaves in Massachusetts. Even before then, black men in the state had gained the right to vote. In 1780 Paul and John Cuffe, free black brothers who lived in Dartmouth, had protested with five other free black men to the state legislature that they were being taxed without representation. By 1783 the courts had decided that African-American men who paid taxes in Massachusetts could vote there.

New Hampshire's record on emancipation is less clear than that of Vermont and Massachusetts. In 1779 black residents petitioned the New Hampshire legislature for freedom. A few years later, several New Hampshire court rulings based on that state's 1783 constitution, which was similar to Massachusetts's, refused to recognize human property. Nevertheless New Hampshire still had about 150 slaves in 1792. Slavery may have withered away there rather than having been abolished by the courts.

In Connecticut and Rhode Island, the state legislatures, rather than individual African Americans, took the initiative against slavery. In 1784 these states adopted gradual abolition plans, which left adult slaves in bondage but proposed to free their children over a period of years. By 1800 only 1,339 slaves remained in New England, and by 1810 only 418—108 in Rhode Island and 310 in Connecticut.

In New Jersey, New York, and Pennsylvania, the investment in slaves was much greater than in New England. After considerable debate, the Pennsylvania legislature in 1780 voted that the children of enslaved mothers would be free at age 28. Under this scheme, Pennsylvania still had 403 slaves in 1830. Emancipation came even more slowly in New York and New Jersey. In 1785 their legislatures *defeated* proposals for gradual abolition. These states had relatively large slave populations, powerful slaveholders, and white workforces fearful of free black competition.

In 1799 the New York legislature finally agreed that male slaves born after July 4 of that year were to be free at age 28 and females at age 25. In 1804 New Jersey adopted a similar law that freed male slaves born after July 4 of that year at age 25 and females at age 21. Under this plan, New Jersey still had 18 slaves in 1860.

Read on **MyHistoryLab**
Document: Two Slaves
Call on Connecticut to End
Slavery, 1779

5-1
5-2
5-3
5-4
5-5
5-6

Table 5–1 SLAVE POPULATIONS IN THE MID-ATLANTIC STATES, 1790–1860								
	1790	**1800**	**1810**	**1820**	**1830**	**1840**	**1850**	**1860**
New York	21,324	20,343	15,017	10,888	75	4		
New Jersey	11,432	12,343	19,851	7,557	2,243	674	236	18
Pennsylvania	3,737	1,706	795	211	403	64		

SOURCE: Philip S. Foner, *History of Black Americans, from Africa to the Emergence of the Cotton Kingdom*, vol. 1 (Westport, CT: Greenwood, 1975), 374.

5-1

5-2

5-3

5-4

5-5

5-6

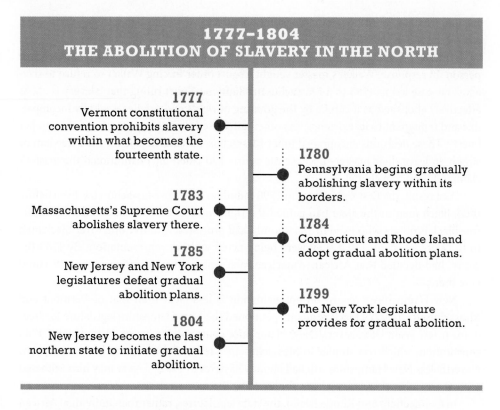

1777–1804
THE ABOLITION OF SLAVERY IN THE NORTH

1777
Vermont constitutional convention prohibits slavery within what becomes the fourteenth state.

1780
Pennsylvania begins gradually abolishing slavery within its borders.

1783
Massachusetts's Supreme Court abolishes slavery there.

1784
Connecticut and Rhode Island adopt gradual abolition plans.

1785
New Jersey and New York legislatures defeat gradual abolition plans.

1799
The New York legislature provides for gradual abolition.

1804
New Jersey becomes the last northern state to initiate gradual abolition.

Explore on MyHistoryLab Activity: The Northwest Territory

Northwest Ordinance Based on earlier legislation drafted by Thomas Jefferson, this 1787 ordinance organized the Northwest Territory, providing for orderly land sales, public education, government, the creation of five to seven states out of the territory, and the prohibition of slavery within the territory.

The Northwest Ordinance of 1787

Nearly as significant as the actions of northern states against slavery was Congress's decision to limit slavery's expansion. During the 1780s, the national government acquired jurisdiction over the region west of the Appalachian Mountains and east of the Mississippi River, north of Spanish Florida and south of Canada. In the process, the government eclipsed several states' conflicting land claims.

During the War for Independence, increasing numbers of white Americans had migrated into this huge region. The migrants—some of whom brought slaves with them—provoked hostilities with American Indian nations. Those who moved into the region's northern portion also faced British opposition, and those who moved into the region's southern portion contested for control against Spanish forces. In response to these circumstances, Congress formulated policies to protect the migrants and provide for their government. The new nation's leaders also disparaged the westward expansion of slavery, and Thomas Jefferson sought to deal with both issues. First, he suggested that the western region be divided into separate territories and prepared for statehood. Second, he proposed that after 1800 slavery be banned from the entire region.

In 1784 Jefferson's antislavery proposal failed by a single vote to pass Congress. Three years later, Congress adopted the **Northwest Ordinance**. This legislation applied the essence of Jefferson's plan to the region north of the Ohio River—what historians call the Old Northwest. Unlike Jefferson's plan, the ordinance banned slavery immediately. But, because it applied only to the Northwest Territory, the ordinance left the huge region south of the Ohio River open to slavery expansion.

Yet, by preventing slaveholders from taking slaves legally into areas north of the Ohio River, the ordinance set a precedent for excluding slavery from U.S. territories. Whether Congress had the power to do this became a contentious issue after President Jefferson annexed the huge Louisiana Territory in 1803 (see p. 98). The issue divided northern and southern politicians until the Civil War.

Antislavery Societies in the North and the Upper South

While African Americans helped destroy slavery in the northeastern states and Congress blocked its advance into the Old Northwest, a few white people organized to spread antislavery sentiment. In 1775 Quaker abolitionist Anthony Benezet organized the first antislavery society in the world. In 1787 it became the Pennsylvania Society for Promoting the Abolition of Slavery, and Benjamin Franklin became its president. By 1800, there were abolition societies in Delaware, Maryland, New Jersey, Connecticut, and Virginia. Organized antislavery sentiment also arose in the new slave states of Kentucky and Tennessee. But such societies never appeared in the Deep South.

From 1794 to 1832, antislavery societies cooperated within the loose framework of the American Convention for Promoting the Abolition of Slavery and Improving the Condition of the African Race. Only white people participated in these Quaker-dominated organizations, although members often cooperated with black leaders. As the northern states adopted abolition plans, the societies focused their attention on Delaware, Maryland, and Virginia. They aimed at gradual, compensated emancipation.

Experience with emancipation in the northern states encouraged the emphasis on gradual abolition. So did the reluctance of white abolitionists to challenge the property rights of masters. Abolitionists also feared that immediate emancipation might lead masters to abandon elderly slaves and assumed that African Americans would require long training before they could be free.

The antislavery societies of the Upper South tended to be small and short lived. A Wilmington, Delaware, society, established in 1788, peaked at 50 members and ceased to exist in 1800. The Maryland society organized in 1781 with six members, grew to 250 in 1797, and disbanded in 1798. African Americans and their white friends, nevertheless, hoped that antislavery sentiment was advancing southward.

Manumission and Self-Purchase

Another hopeful sign for African Americans was that after the Revolution most southern states liberalized their **manumission** laws. This meant that masters could free individual slaves by deed or will. Masters no longer had to go to court or petition a state legislature to prove that an individual they desired to free had performed a "meritorious service."

manumission The act of freeing a slave by the slave's master.

As a result, hundreds of slaveholders in the Upper South freed slaves individually. Religious sentiment and natural rights principles motivated many of these masters. Most of them considered the slave system immoral but opposed general emancipation. And their motives were not always noble. Masters often profited from self-purchase agreements they negotiated with their slaves. Slaves raised money by marketing farm produce or hiring themselves out for wages and then paid their master in installments for their eventual freedom.

Masters also sometimes manumitted slaves who were no longer profitable investments. A master might be switching from tobacco to wheat or corn—crops that did not need a year-round workforce. Or a master might manumit older slaves whose best years as workers were behind them. Frequently, however, slaves—usually young men—presented their masters with the choice of either manumitting them after a term of years or having them escape immediately.

Self-purchase often left African Americans in precarious financial condition. Sometimes they used up their savings to buy their freedom. In other instances, they went into

5-1

5-2

5-3

5-4

5-5

5-6

debt to their former masters, to white lawyers who acted as their agents, or to other white people who had loaned them money to cover their purchase price. After receiving money from a slave, some masters reneged on their agreement to manumit. Many of the freedom suits that became common in the Upper South during this period resulted from such un-ethical behavior by masters.

The Emergence of a Free Black Class in the South

As a result of manumission, self-purchase, and freedom suits, the free black population of the Upper South blossomed. By 1820 the Upper South (Delaware, Maryland, Virginia, District of Columbia, Kentucky, Missouri, North Carolina, and Tennessee) had a free black population of 114,070, compared with a northern free black population of 99,281. However, most of the Upper South's black population remained in slavery while the North's was on the way to general emancipation. In the North, 83.9 percent of African Americans were free in 1820, compared with 10.6 percent of those in the Upper South.

In the Deep South (South Carolina, Georgia, Florida, Louisiana, Alabama, and Mississippi), both the percentage and the absolute numbers of free black people remained much smaller. Generally, masters in the Deep South freed only their illegitimate slave children, other favorites, or those unable to work. Only 20,153 free black people lived in the Deep South in 1820.

The emergence of a free black class in the South, especially in the Deep South, produced social strata more similar to those in Latin America than was the case in the North. As in the Caribbean, South America, and portions of Mexico, there were dominant white people, free people of color, and slaves. In southern cities, such as Charleston, Savannah, and New Orleans, some free African Americans not only identified economically and culturally with their former masters but also acquired slaves.

Forces for Slavery

5-2 **Why did slavery survive in the new United States?**

The forces for black freedom in the new republic rested on widespread African-American dissatisfaction with slavery, economic change, Christian morality, and revolutionary pre-cepts. Yet for the nation as a whole and for the mass of African Americans, the forces favor-ing slavery proved to be stronger. Abolition took place in the North, where slavery was weak. In the South, where it was strong, slavery thrived and the number of slaves grew. At the same time, slavery expanded westward.

The U.S. Constitution

Watch on
MyHistoryLab
Video: Slavery and the
Constitution

The U.S. Constitution, which went into effect in 1789, became a major force in favor of the continued enslavement of African Americans. During the War for Independence, the Con-tinental Congress had provided a weak central government for the United States, as each of the 13 states retained control over its own internal affairs. The Articles of Confederation, which served as the American constitution from 1781 to 1789, formalized this system of divided sovereignty.

However, by the mid-1780s, wealthy and powerful men perceived that the Confedera-tion Congress was too weak to protect their interests. Democratic movements in the states threatened property rights. Congress's inability to regulate commerce led to trade disputes among the states. Congress's inability to tax prevented it from maintaining an army and navy. This meant it could not control the western territories, and, most frightening to the wealthy, it could not help states suppress popular uprisings, such as that led by Daniel Shays in western Massachusetts in 1786.

The fears Shays' Rebellion caused led directly to the Constitutional Convention in Philadelphia that in 1787 produced the Constitution under which the United States is still governed. But the convention could not create a more powerful central government without first making important concessions to southern slaveholders.

Humanitarian opposition to the Atlantic slave trade had mounted during the revolutionary era. Under pressure from black activists—such as Prince Hall of Boston—and Quakers, northern state legislatures during the 1780s forbade their citizens to engage in the slave trade. Economic change in the Upper South also prompted opposition to the trade. Virginia, for example, banned the importation of slaves from abroad nearly a decade before Rhode Island.

Yet convention delegates from South Carolina and Georgia maintained that their states had an acute labor shortage. They threatened to oppose a central government that could stop their citizens from importing slaves. Torn between these conflicting perspectives, the convention compromised by including a provision in the Constitution that prohibited Congress from abolishing the slave trade until 1808. During the 20 years before 1808, when Congress banned the trade, thousands of Africans came unwillingly into southern states. Overall, more slaves entered the United States between 1787 and 1808 than during any other 20-year period in American history. Such huge numbers helped fuel westward expansion of the slave system.

Other proslavery clauses of the Constitution aimed to counteract slave rebellion and escape. The Constitution gave Congress power to put down "insurrections" and "domestic violence." It provided that persons "held to service or labour in one State, escaping into another . . . shall be delivered up on claim of the party to whom such service or labour may be due." This clause was the basis for the **Fugitive Slave Act of 1793**, which allowed masters or their agents to pursue slaves across state lines, capture them, and take them before a magistrate. There, on presentation of satisfactory evidence, masters could regain legal custody of the person they claimed.

Finally the Constitution strengthened the political power of slaveholders through the **Three-Fifths Clause**. This clause resulted from another compromise between northern and southern delegates. Southern delegates wanted slaves to be counted toward representation in the national government but not counted for purposes of taxation. Northern delegates wanted just the opposite. The Three-Fifths Clause split the difference by providing that a slave be counted as three-fifths of a free person in determining a state's representation in the House of Representatives and in the Electoral College. Slaves would be counted similarly if and when Congress instituted a per capita tax.

This gave slaveholders increased representation on the basis of the number of slaves they owned. As a result, the South gained enormous political advantage. For many years, this clause contributed to the domination of the U.S. government by slaveholding southerners, even though the South's population steadily fell behind the North's. That Congress never instituted a per capita tax made this victory for slaveholders all the more remarkable.

Four other factors, however, were more important than constitutional provisions in fostering the continued enslavement of African Americans in the new republic. They

Fugitive Slave Act of 1793 An act of Congress permitting masters to recapture escaped slaves who had reached the free states and, with the authorization of local courts, return with the slave or slaves to their home state.

Three-Fifths Clause A clause in the U.S. Constitution providing that a slave be counted as three-fifths of a free person in determining a state's representation in Congress and the Electoral College and three-fifths of a free person in regard to per capita taxes levied by Congress on the states.

5-1

5-2

5-3

5-4

5-5

5-6

THE FIRST COTTON-GIN.—DRAWN BY WILLIAM L. SHEPPARD.—(SEE PAGE 814.)

Harpers Weekly printed this "conjectural work" in 1869. Although the clothing worn by the men and women shown reflects styles of a later era, the machine suggests how slaves used the gin Eli Whitney invented in 1793.

cotton gin A simple machine invented by Eli Whitney in 1793 to separate cotton seeds from cotton fiber. It greatly speeded this task and encouraged the westward expansion of cotton-growing in the United States.

domestic slave trade A trade dating from the first decade of the nineteenth century in American-born slaves purchased primarily in the border South and sent overland or by sea to the cotton-growing regions of the Old Southwest.

🔍 **View on MyHistoryLab Map:** The Louisiana Purchase

included increased cultivation of cotton, the Louisiana Purchase, declining revolutionary fervor, and intensified white racism.

Cotton

The most obvious of the four factors was the increase in cotton production. By the late eighteenth century, Britain led the world in textile manufacturing. As mechanization made the spinning of cotton cloth more economical, Britain's demand for raw cotton increased dramatically. The United States led in filling that demand as a result of Eli Whitney's invention of the **cotton gin** in 1793. Seeds in cotton bolls had prevented commercial use of the type of cotton most easily grown in the South. Whitney's simple machine provided an easy and quick way to remove them.

Consequently, cotton production in the United States rose from 3,000 bales in 1790 to 178,000 bales in 1810. Cotton became by far the most lucrative U.S. export. Southern cotton production also encouraged the development of textile mills in New England, thereby creating a proslavery alliance between the "lords of the lash and the lords of the loom."

Cotton reinvigorated the slave-labor system, which spread rapidly across Georgia and later into Alabama, Mississippi, Louisiana, and eastern Texas. To make matters worse for African Americans, the westward expansion of cotton production encouraged a **domestic slave trade**. Masters in the old tobacco-growing regions of Maryland, Virginia, and other states began to support themselves by selling their slaves to the new cotton-growing regions (see Figure 5–1).

The Louisiana Purchase and African Americans in the Lower Mississippi Valley

The Jefferson administration's purchase of Louisiana from France in 1803 accelerated the westward expansion of slavery and the domestic slave trade, as the purchase nearly doubled the area of the United States. The purchase also brought under American sovereignty those black people, both free and slave, who lived in the portion of the territory that centered on the city of New Orleans. As Chapter 3 indicates, black life in the New Orleans area had developed a distinctive pattern. Although people of African descent were a majority of the area's population, they consisted of two distinct groups. First were the free people of color who called themselves Creoles. They were usually craftsmen and shopkeepers, spoke French, belonged to the Roman Catholic Church, and aspired to equal rights with other free inhabitants. Some of them bought and sold slaves.

The second black group grew more rapidly. It consisted of slaves, most of whom had come directly from Africa and worked on Louisiana plantations. At first the slaves produced tobacco and indigo, but by the 1790s sugar and cotton had emerged as the crops of the future. As demand for these crops grew, conditions for slaves in Louisiana became increasingly harsh, especially after the region became part of the United States. The slaves' rural location, their predominantly African culture, and, eventually, their Protestant religion cut them off from free people of color. In 1770 the region that later became the state of Louisiana had a slave population of 5,600. By 1810 it had 34,660, and by 1820 the slave population numbered 149,654. This tremendous growth, involving an extremely harsh form of slavery in a huge region, constituted a warning to all opponents of that institution. With the termination of the external slave trade, the notorious slave markets of New Orleans became the dreaded destination of thousands of African Americans "sold south" by their masters in the domestic slave trade.

Conservatism and Racism

The waning of revolutionary humanitarianism and the rise of a more intense racism among white people were less tangible forces than cotton production and the Louisiana Purchase, but they were just as important in strengthening slavery. They also made life more difficult for free African Americans.

By the 1790s white Americans had begun a long retreat from the egalitarianism of the revolutionary era. In the North and the Chesapeake, most white people became less willing to challenge the prerogatives of slaveholders and more willing to accept slavery as suitable for African Americans. This shift strengthened the slaveholders and their nonslaveholding white supporters in the Deep South who had never embraced the humanitarian precepts of the Enlightenment and Great Awakening.

Increasing proslavery sentiment among white Americans stemmed, in part, from revulsion against the radicalism of the French Revolution that had begun in 1789. Reports from France of bloody class and religious warfare, disruption of the social order, and redistribution of property led most Americans to value property rights—including rights to human property—and order above equal rights. In addition, as cotton production spread westward and the value of slaves soared, rationalist and evangelical criticism of human bondage withered.

Using race to justify slavery was an important component of this conservative trend. Unlike white people, the argument went, black people were unsuited for freedom or citizenship. A new scientific racism supported this outlook. As early as the 1770s, some American intellectuals challenged the Enlightenment theory that perceived racial differences were not essential or inherent but results of the different environments in which Africans and Europeans originated. These intellectuals instead proposed that God had created a great chain of being from lesser creatures to higher creatures. In this chain, black people constituted a separate species as close to the great apes as to white people.

Such views became common among white northerners and southerners—and they had practical results. During the 1790s Congress expressed its determination to exclude African Americans from the benefits of citizenship in "a white man's country." A 1790 law limited

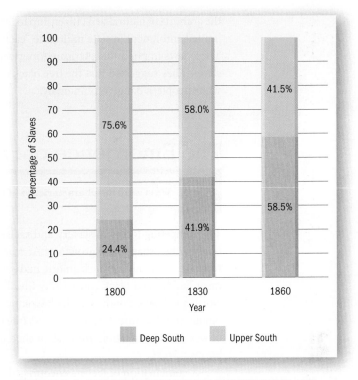

FIGURE 5–1 DISTRIBUTION OF THE SOUTHERN SLAVE POPULATION, 1800–1860
The demand for slaves in the cotton-growing Deep South produced a major shift in the distribution of the slave population.

Read on MyHistoryLab
Document: Exploring America: Racism in American History

the granting of naturalized citizenship to "any alien, being a white person." In 1792 Congress limited enrollment in state militias to "each and every free, able-bodied white male citizen." These laws implied that African Americans had no place in the United States except as slaves. They suggested that the free black class was an anomaly and, in the opinion of most white people, a dangerous anomaly.

The Emergence of Free Black Communities

5-3   **What were the characteristics of early free black communities?**

The competing forces of slavery and racism, on one hand, and freedom and opportunity, on the other, shaped the growth of African-American communities in the early American republic. A distinctive black culture had existed since the early colonial period. But enslavement had limited black community life. The advent of large free black populations in the North and Upper South after the Revolution allowed African Americans to establish autonomous and dynamic communities. As free black people in these cities acquired a modicum of wealth and education, they established institutions that have shaped African-American life ever since.

A combination of factors encouraged African Americans to form these distinctive institutions. First, as they emerged from slavery, they realized they would have inferior status in white-dominated organizations or not be allowed to participate in them at all. Second, black people valued the African heritage they had preserved over generations in slavery. They wanted institutions that would perpetuate that heritage.

The earliest black community institutions were mutual aid societies. Patterned on similar white organizations, these societies were like modern insurance companies and benevolent organizations. They provided for their members' medical and burial expenses and helped support widows and children. African Americans in Newport, Rhode Island, organized the first black mutual aid society in 1780. Seven years later, Richard Allen and Absalom Jones established the more famous Free African Society in Philadelphia. Most early free black societies admitted only men, but similar organizations for women appeared during the 1790s.

These ostensibly secular societies maintained a decidedly Christian moral character. They insisted that their members meet standards of middle-class propriety and, in effect, became self-improvement as well as mutual aid societies. By the early 1800s, such societies also organized resistance to kidnappers who sought to recapture fugitive slaves or enslave free African Americans.

Of particular importance were the black Freemasons because, unlike other free black organizations, the Masons united black men from several northern cities. Combining rationalism with secrecy and obscure ritual, Freemasonry was a major movement among European and American men during the late eighteenth and early nineteenth centuries. Opportunities for male bonding, wearing fancy regalia, and achieving prestige in a supposedly ancient hierarchy attracted both black and white men.

The most famous black Mason of his time was Prince Hall, the Revolutionary War veteran and abolitionist. During the 1770s he began in Boston what became known as the **Prince Hall Masons**. Hall's relationship to Masonry epitomizes the free black predicament in America.

Read on **MyHistoryLab** Document: Preamble of the Free African Society (1787)

Prince Hall Masons
A black Masonic order formed in 1791 in Boston under the leadership of Prince Hall. He became its first Grand Master and promoted its expansion to other cities.

In 1775 the local white Masonic lodge in Boston rejected Hall's application for membership because of his black ancestry. Therefore Hall, who was a Patriot, organized African Lodge No. 1 on the basis of a limited license he secured from a British Masonic lodge associated with the British army that then occupied Boston. The irony of this situation compounded when, after the War for Independence, American Masonry refused to grant the African Lodge a full charter. Hall again had to turn to the British Masons, who approved his application in 1787. Under this British charter, Hall in 1791 organized the African Grand Lodge of North America—later renamed the Prince Hall Grand Lodge—and became its first grand master. Even before this he had begun authorizing black lodges in other cities, including Philadelphia and Providence, Rhode Island.

The Origins of Independent Black Churches

Although black churches emerged at least a decade later than black benevolent associations, the churches quickly became the core of African-American communities. Not only did these churches attend to the spiritual needs of free black people and—in some southern cities—slaves, but their pastors also became the primary African-American leaders. Black church buildings housed schools, social organizations, and antislavery meetings.

During the late eighteenth century, as the egalitarian spirit of the Great Awakening waned among white Baptists, Methodists, and Episcopalians, separate but not independent black churches appeared in the South. The biracial churches the Awakening spawned had never embraced African Americans on an equal basis with white people, and as time passed, white people denied black people significant influence in church governance. White parishioners also subjected African Americans to segregated seating, communion services, Sunday schools, and cemeteries. In response, African Americans formed separate black congregations, usually headed by black ministers but subordinate to white church hierarchies. The first such congregations appeared during the 1770s in South Carolina and Georgia.

In contrast to these subordinate churches, a truly independent black church emerged gradually in Philadelphia between the 1780s and the early 1800s. The movement for such a church began within the city's white-controlled St. George's Methodist Church. Richard Allen and Absalom Jones, who led the movement, could rely for help on the Free African Society they established in 1787.

Allen in 1780 and Jones in 1783 had purchased their freedom. In 1786 Allen, a fervent Methodist since the 1770s, received permission from St. George's white leadership to use the church in the evenings to preach to black people. Jones joined Allen's congregation. Soon they and other black members of St. George's chafed under policies they considered un-Christian and insulting.

The break came in 1792 when St. George's white leaders grievously insulted the church's black members. An attempt by white trustees to prevent Jones from praying in what the trustees considered the white section of the church led black members to walk out. "We all went out of the church in a body," recalled Allen, "and they were no more plagued with us in the church."

BROTHER PRINCE HALL
WARRANTEE WORSHIPFUL MASTER, AFRICAN LODGE 459, A. L. 5784, A. D. 1784
FOUNDER OF COLORED FRATERNITY OF FREE AND ACCEPTED MASONS.
BOSTON, MASS.
COPYRIGHT 1924 BY W. H. COSTON

RAISED TO MASTER MASON

This late eighteenth-century portrait of Prince Hall (1735?–1807) dressed as a gentleman places him among Masonic symbols. A former slave, a skilled craftsman and entrepreneur, an abolitionist, and an advocate of black education, Hall is best remembered as the founder of the African Lodge of North America, popularly known as the Prince Hall Masons.

5-1
5-2
5-3
5-4
5-5
5-6

VOICES   Richard Allen on the Break with St. George's Church

It took an emotionally wrenching experience to convince Richard Allen, Absalom Jones, and other black Methodists that they must break their association with St. George's Church. Allen published posthumously the following account in 1833 as part of his autobiography, The Life Experiences and Gospel Labors of the Rt. Rev. Richard Allen. *Although many years had passed since the incident, Allen's account retains a strong emotional immediacy.*

A number of us usually attended St. George's church in Fourth street; and when the colored people began to get numerous in attending the church, they moved us from the seats we usually sat on, and placed us around the wall, and on Sabbath morning, we went to the church and the sexton stood at the door, and told us to go in the gallery. He told us to go, and we would see where to sit. We expected to take the seats over the ones we formerly occupied below, not knowing any better. We took those seats. Meeting had begun and they were nearly done singing, and just as we got to the seats, the elder said, "Let us pray." We had not been long upon our knees before I heard considerable scuffling and low talking. I raised my head up and saw one of the trustees, H M, having hold of the Rev. Absalom Jones, pulling him up off his knees, and saying, "You must get up—you must not

kneel here." Mr. Jones replied, "Wait until prayer is over." Mr. H M said, "No, you must get up now, or I will call for aid and force you away." Mr. Jones said, "Wait until prayer is over, and I will get up and trouble you no more." With that he [H M] beckoned to one of the other trustees, Mr. L S to come to his assistance. He came, and went to William White to pull him up. By this time prayer was over, and we all went out of the church in a body, and they were no more plagued with us in the church. . . . We then hired a storeroom, and held worship by ourselves. Here we were pursued with threats of being disowned, and read publicly out of meeting if we did continue worship in the place we had hired; but we believed the Lord would be our friend. We got subscription papers out to raise money to build the house of the Lord.

1. **What sparked the confrontation Allen describes?**
2. **How did white leaders respond to the withdrawal of the church's black members?**

SOURCE: *The Life Experiences and Gospel Labors of Rt. Rev. Richard Allen, 1833.*

  Read on **MyHistoryLab Document:** Address to the Free People of Colour of these United States, 1830

St. George's white leaders fought hard and long to control the expanding and economically valuable black congregation. Yet other white Philadelphians, led by abolitionist Benjamin Rush, applauded the concept of an independent "African church." Rush and other sympathetic white residents contributed to the new church's building fund. When construction began in 1793, Rush and at least one hundred other white people joined with African Americans at a banquet to celebrate the occasion.

However, the black congregation soon split. When the majority determined that the new church would be Episcopalian rather than Methodist, Allen and a few others refused to join. The result was *two* black churches in Philadelphia. St. Thomas's Episcopal Church, with Jones as priest, opened in July 1794 as an African-American congregation within the white-led national Episcopal Church. Then Allen's Mother Bethel congregation became the first truly independent black church. The white leaders of St. George's tried to control Mother Bethel until 1816. That year Mother Bethel became the birthplace of the **African Methodist Episcopal (AME) Church**. Allen became the first bishop of this

African Methodist Episcopal (AME) Church Founded in Philadelphia in 1816, it was the first (and became the largest) independent black church.

5-1
5-2
5-3
5-4
5-5
5-6

organization, which spread to other cities in the North and the South.

The First Black Schools

Schools for African-American children, slave and free, date to the early 1700s. In both North and South, white clergy ran the schools. So did Quakers, early abolition societies, and missionaries acting for the Anglican Society for the Propagation of the Gospel in Foreign Parts. But the first schools established by African Americans to instruct African-American children arose after the Revolution. The new black mutual aid societies and churches created and sustained them.

Schools for black people organized or taught by white people continued to flourish. Black people founded their own schools because local white authorities regularly refused either to admit black children to public schools or to maintain adequate separate black schools.

Free black people in Baltimore supported schools during the 1790s, and during the early 1800s similar schools opened in Washington, DC. Such schools frequently employed white teachers. Not until Philadelphia's Mother Bethel Church established the Augustine School in 1818 did a school for black children exist that was entirely administered and taught by African Americans.

These schools faced great difficulties. Because many black families could not afford the fees, the schools strained their meager resources by accepting charity cases. In addition, some black parents believed education was pointless when African Americans often could not get skilled jobs. And white people feared competition from skilled black workers, believed black schools attracted undesirable populations, and—particularly in the South—feared that educated free African Americans would encourage slaves to revolt. Threats of violence against black schools and efforts to suppress them were common. Nevertheless, such schools continued to operate in the North and Upper South, producing a growing class of literate African Americans.

Read on **MyHistoryLab** Document: Absalom Jones Delivers a Sermon on the Occasion of the Abolition of the International Slave Trade, 1808

Raphaelle Peale, the son of famous Philadelphia portraitist Charles Wilson Peale, completed this oil portrait of the Reverend Absalom Jones (1746–1818) in 1810. Reverend Jones is shown in his ecclesiastical robes holding a Bible in his hand.

5-1

5-2

5-3

5-4

5-5

5-6

Black Leaders and Choices

5-4   Who were the early black leaders in America, and what were their varying ideas, tactics, and solutions for the problems faced by blacks?

By the 1790s an educated black elite existed in the North and the Chesapeake. It provided leadership for African Americans in religion, economic advancement, and racial politics. Experience had driven members of this elite to a contradictory perception of themselves and of America. On the one hand, they were acculturated, patriotic Americans who had achieved some personal well-being and security. On the other hand, they knew that American society had not lived up to its revolutionary principles.

VOICES Absalom Jones Petitions Congress on Behalf of Fugitives Facing Reenslavement

Absalom Jones wrote his petition to Congress on behalf of four black men who had been manumitted in North Carolina. Because they were in danger of being reenslaved, they had taken refuge in Philadelphia. The men, under whose names the petition appears in the Annals of Congress, were Jupiter Nicholson, Jacob Nicholson, Joe Albert, and Thomas Pritchet. Jones provided brief accounts of their troubles. Here we include only the important general principles that Jones invoked. Southern representatives argued that accepting a petition from alleged slaves would set a dangerous precedent, and Congress refused to accept the petition.

To the President, Senate, and House of Representatives,

The Petition and Representation of the under-named Freemen, respectfully showeth:

That, being of African descent, the late inhabitants and natives of North Carolina, to you only, under God, can we apply with any hope of effect, for redress of our grievances, having been compelled to leave the State wherein we had a right of residence, as freemen liberated under the hand and seal of humane and conscientious masters, the validity of which act of justice in restoring us to our native right of freedom, was confirmed by judgment of the Superior Court of North Carolina . . . yet, not long after this decision, a law of that State was enacted, under which men of cruel disposition, and void of just principle, received countenance and authority in violently seizing, imprisoning, and selling into slavery, such as had been so emancipated; whereby we were reduced to the necessity of separating from some of our nearest and most tender connections, and seeking refuge in such parts of the Union where more regard is paid to the public declaration in favor of liberty and the common right of man, several hundreds, under our circumstances, having, in consequence of the said law, been hunted day and night, like beasts of the forest,

by armed men with dogs, and made a prey of as free and lawful plunder . . .

We beseech your impartial attention to our hard condition, not only with respect to our personal sufferings, as freemen, but as a class of that people who, distinguished by color, are therefore with a degrading partiality, considered by many, even of those in eminent stations, as unentitled to that public justice and protection which is the great object of Government. . . .

If, notwithstanding all that has been publicly avowed as essential principles respecting the extent of human right to freedom; notwithstanding we have had that right restored to us, so far as was in the power of those by whom we were held as slaves, we cannot claim the privilege of representation in your councils, yet we trust we may address you as fellow-men, who, under God, the sovereign Ruler of the Universe, are entrusted with the distribution of justice, for the terror of evil-doers, the encouragement of protection of the innocent, not doubting that you are men of liberal minds, susceptible of benevolent feelings and clear conception of rectitude to a catholic extent, who can admit that black people . . . have natural affections, social and domestic attachments and sensibilities; and that, therefore, we may hope for a share in your sympathetic attention while we represent that the unconstitutional bondage in which multitudes of our fellows in complexion are held, is to us a subject sorrowfully affecting; for we cannot conceive their condition (more especially those who have been emancipated and tasted the sweets of liberty, and again reduced to slavery by kidnappers and man-stealers) to be less afflicting or deplorable than the situation of citizens of the United States, captured and enslaved through the unrighteous policy prevalent in Algiers . . . may we not be allowed to consider this stretch of power, morally and politically, a Governmental defect, if not a direct violation of the declared fundamental principles of the Constitution; and finally, is not some remedy for an evil of such magnitude highly worthy of the deep inquiry and unfeigned zeal of the supreme Legislative body of a free and enlightened people?

> 1. On what principles does Jones believe the U.S. government is bound to act?
> 2. What does Jones's petition indicate concerning the legal status of African Americans?

SOURCE: *Annals of Congress*, 4 Cong., 2 sess. (January 23, 1797), 2015–18.

Prominent among these leaders were members of the clergy. Two of the most important of them were Richard Allen and Absalom Jones. Besides organizing his church, Allen opened a school in Philadelphia for black children, wrote against slavery and racial prejudice, and made his home a refuge for fugitive slaves. A year before his death in 1831, Allen presided over the first national black convention.

Jones, too, was an early abolitionist. In 1797 his concern for fugitives facing reenslavement led him to become the first African American to petition Congress. His petition anticipated later abolitionists in suggesting that slavery violated the spirit of the U.S. Constitution and that Congress could abolish it.

Other influential black ministers of the late eighteenth and early nineteenth centuries were Jupiter Hammon of Long Island, Daniel Coker of Baltimore, John Chavis of Virginia, and Lemuel Haynes of New England. Hammon became a well-known poet. Coker, who was of mixed race, conducted a school, cofounded the AME Church, and advocated black migration to Africa. Chavis also combined preaching and teaching and gained a wide reputation as a biblical scholar. Haynes was perhaps even better known for his intellectual accomplishments. The son of a white mother and black father, Haynes served with the Minutemen and Continental Army, spoke against slavery, and in 1780 became the first ordained black Congregationalist minister serving as pastor to white congregations.

African-American entrepreneurs vied with black clergy for influence. Prince Hall owned leather dressing and catering businesses in Boston. Peter Williams, principal founder of New York's AME Zion Church, prospered as a tobacco merchant. Another prominent black businessman was James Forten of Philadelphia, described as "probably the most noteworthy free African-American entrepreneur in the early nineteenth century." Born to free parents in 1766, Forten was a Patriot during the War for Independence and became the owner of his own business in 1798. For the rest of his life, he advocated equal rights and abolition.

American patriotism, religious conviction, organizational skill, intellectual inquisitiveness, and antislavery activism delineate the lives of most free black leaders in this era. Yet these leaders often were torn in their perceptions of what was best for African Americans. Hammon and Chavis accommodated slavery and racial oppression. They condemned slavery and lauded human liberty, but they were not activists. They maintained that God would eventually end injustice. As late as 1836, Chavis wrote, "Slavery is a national evil no one doubts, but what is to be done? . . . All that can be done, is to make the best of a bad bargain. . . . I am clearly of the opinion that immediate emancipation would be to entail the greatest earthly curse upon my brethren according to the flesh."

James Forten, portrait by an unknown artist.

Allen, Jones, Hall, and Forten were more optimistic than Hammon and Chavis about the ability of African Americans to mold their destiny in the United States. Although they each expressed misgivings, they believed that, despite setbacks, the egalitarian principles of the American Revolution would prevail if black people insisted on liberty. Forten never despaired that African Americans would be integrated into the larger American society on the basis of their individual talent and enterprise. Although he was often frustrated, Hall pursued for four decades a strategy based on the assumption that white authority would reward black protest and patriotism.

Migration

African Americans, however, had another alternative: migration from the United States to establish their own society free from white prejudices. In 1787 British philanthropists, including Olaudah Equiano, had established Freetown in Sierra Leone on the West African coast as a refuge for former slaves. As we mentioned in Chapter 4, some African Americans who had been Loyalists during the American Revolution settled there. Other black and white Americans proposed that free black people should settle in western North America or the Caribbean islands. There were great practical obstacles to mass black migration to each of these regions. Migration was expensive, difficult to organize, and involved long, often fruitless negotiations with foreign governments. But no black leader during the early national period was immune to the appeal of such proposals.

In 1787 Hall petitioned the Massachusetts legislature to support efforts by black Bostonians to establish a colony in Africa. Although he recognized black progress in Massachusetts, Hall maintained that he and others found themselves "in many respects, in very disagreeable and disadvantageous circumstances; most of which must attend us so long as we and our children live in America." By the mid-1810s, a few influential white Americans had also decided that there was no place in the United States for free African Americans. In 1816 they organized the **American Colonization Society**. Under its auspices, Coker in 1820 led the first party of 86 African Americans to the new colony of Liberia on the West African coast.

The major black advocate of migration to Africa during this period, however, was Paul Cuffe, a prosperous New England sea captain who cooperated with British humanitarians and entrepreneurs to promote migration. He saw African-American colonization in West Africa as a way to end the Atlantic slave trade, spread Christianity, create a refuge for free black people, and make profits. Before his death in 1817, Cuffe had influenced not only Coker but also—at least temporarily—Forten, Allen, and Jones to consider colonization as a viable alternative for African Americans.

Slave Uprisings

While, after the Revolution, black northerners grew increasingly aware of the limits to their freedom, black southerners faced perpetual slavery. As cotton production expanded westward, as new slave states entered the Union, and as masters in the Upper South turned away from the revolutionary commitment to gradual emancipation, slaves pursued several strategies.

Some lowered their expectations and loyally served their masters. Most continued patterns of day-to-day resistance. Many escaped. A few risked their lives to join forceful revolutionary movements to destroy slavery. When hundreds of slaves rallied behind Gabriel in 1800 near Richmond or behind Charles Deslondes in 1811 near New Orleans, they frightened white southerners. But they raised hopes for freedom among countless African Americans.

The egalitarian principles of the American and French revolutions influenced Gabriel and Deslondes. Unlike earlier slave rebels, they acted not to revenge personal grievances or

American Colonization Society (ACS, 1816–1912) An organization founded in Washington, DC, by prominent slaveholders. It claimed to encourage the ultimate abolition of slavery by sending free African Americans to its West African colony of Liberia.

to establish maroon communities but to destroy slavery because it denied natural human rights to its victims. The American Declaration of Independence and the legend of Haiti's Toussaint Louverture provided the intellectual foundations for their efforts. Louverture, against great odds, had led the enslaved black people of the French sugar colony of Saint Domingue—modern Haiti—to freedom and independence. This bitter and bloody struggle lasted from 1791 to 1804. Many white planters fled the island with their slaves to take refuge in Cuba, Jamaica, South Carolina, Virginia, and, somewhat later, Louisiana. The Haitian slaves carried the spirit of revolution with them to their new homes.

During the early 1790s, black unrest and rumors of revolt mounted in Virginia. The state militia arrested suspected plotters, who got off with whippings. In this revolutionary atmosphere, Gabriel, the human property of Thomas Prosser Sr., prepared to lead a massive slave insurrection. Gabriel, an acculturated and literate blacksmith, well understood the rationalist and revolutionary currents of his time.

While the ideology of the American Revolution shaped Gabriel's actions, he also perceived that white people were politically divided and distracted by an undeclared naval war with France. He enjoyed secret support from a few white people and hoped poor white people would rally to his cause as he and his associates planned to kill those who supported slavery and take control of central Virginia.

But on August 30, 1800—the day set for the uprising—two slaves revealed the plan to white authorities while a tremendous thunderstorm prevented Gabriel's followers from assaulting Richmond. Then Virginia governor—and future U.S. president—James Monroe had suspects arrested. Gabriel, who relied on white allies to get to Norfolk, was among the last captured. In October he and 26 others, convicted of "conspiracy and insurrection," were hanged. Yet by demonstrating that slaves could organize for large-scale rebellion, they left a legacy of fear among slaveholders and hope for liberation among southern African Americans.

The far less famous Louisiana Rebellion took place under similar circumstances. By the early 1800s, white refugees from Haiti had settled with their slaves in what was then known as Orleans Territory. As they arrived, rumors of slave insurrection spread across the territory. The rumors became reality on January 8, 1811, when Deslondes, a Haitian native and slave driver on a plantation north of New Orleans, initiated a massive revolt in cooperation with maroons.

Deslondes's organized at least 180 men and women. They marched south along the Mississippi River toward New Orleans plundering and burning plantations, but killing only two white people and one recalcitrant slave. On January 10 about 700 territorial militia, slaveholding vigilantes, and U.S. troops overwhelmed the rebels. Well-armed white men slaughtered 66 rebels and captured 30. They tried the captives, found 22—including Deslondes—guilty of rebellion, and shot them. Then they

Toussaint Louverture (1744–1803) led the black rebellion in the French colony of St. Domingue on the Caribbean island of Hispaniola that led to the creation of the independent black republic of Haiti in 1804. Louverture became an inspiration for black rebels in the United States.

cut off the heads of the executed men and displayed them on pikes to warn other African Americans of the consequences of revolt.

The White Southern Reaction

Although Deslondes's uprising was one of the few major slave revolts in American history, Gabriel's conspiracy and events in Haiti left the more significant legacy. For generations, enslaved African Americans regarded Louverture as a black George Washington and recalled Gabriel's revolutionary message. The networks among slaves that Gabriel established survived his death, and, as the domestic slave trade carried black Virginians southwestward, they brought his promise of liberation with them. White southerners responded to these black revolutionary currents by rejecting the egalitarian values of the Enlightenment. Because white southerners feared race war and believed emancipation would encourage African Americans to begin such a war, most of them determined to make black bondage stronger, not weaker.

Beginning with South Carolina in December 1800, southern states outlawed assemblies of slaves, placed curfews on slaves and free black people, and made manumissions more difficult. The practice of white men on horseback patrolling slave quarters revived. Assuming that revolutionaries like Gabriel received encouragement from northern white abolitionists, white southerners became suspicious of outsiders. Based on an assumption that local free African Americans were even more involved in slave uprisings than white outsiders, some white southerners advocated forcing them to leave.

The War of 1812

5-5	How did the war of 1812 affect African Americans?

Watch on
MyHistoryLab
Video:
The War of 1812

Many of the themes developed in this chapter—African-American patriotism, opportunities for freedom, migration sentiment, and influences pushing slaves toward revolutionary action—are reflected in the black experience during the American war with Britain that began in 1812 and lasted until early 1815. This conflict, known as the War of 1812, was a late development in a massive military and economic struggle between Britain and France for mastery over the Atlantic world.

British military support for American Indian resistance in the Old Northwest, an American desire to annex Canada, and especially Britain's interference with American ships trading with Europe drew the United States into the Franco-British war. Many Americans regarded the War of 1812 as a second war for independence, and American forces won important victories. But the United States failed to conquer Canada; suffered the burning of Washington, DC; and allowed the war to end in a draw. It was also a war in which black military service, and white fear of slave revolt, had important roles (see Map 5–2).

By 1812 prejudice and fear of revolt had nearly obliterated positive white memories of black Patriot soldiers during the Revolution. Because of the news from Haiti and because of Gabriel's conspiracy, most white southerners joined John Randolph of Virginia in regarding African Americans as "an internal foe." Therefore, when the War of 1812 began, southern states refused to enlist black men for fear they would use their guns to aid slave revolts. Meanwhile a lack of enthusiasm for the war, combined with the absence of a British threat to their part of the country, kept northern states from mobilizing black troops in 1812 and 1813.

Southern fears of slave revolt mounted during the spring of 1813 when the British invaded the Chesapeake. As they had during the Revolution, British generals offered slaves freedom in Canada or the British West Indies in return for help. In response,

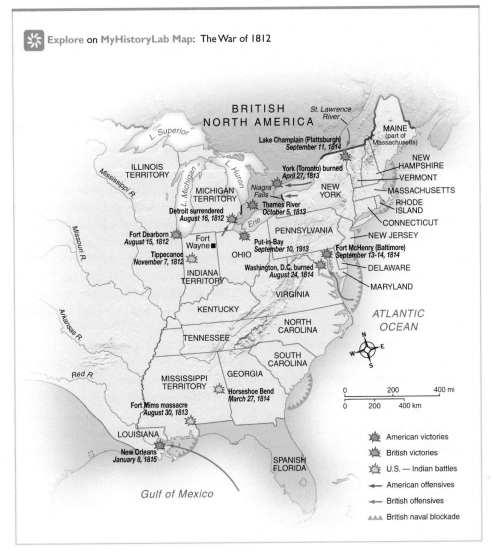

Explore on **MyHistoryLab Map**: The War of 1812

MAP 5–2 THE WAR OF 1812

As during the War for Independence, African Americans fought on both sides during the War of 1812. Some joined the British army that burned Washington, DC. Others helped the United States win control of Lake Erie in 1813 and stop the British invasion of Louisiana at the Battle of New Orleans in 1815.

What was at stake for African Americans in the War of 1812?

African Americans joined the British army that burned Washington, DC, in 1814 and attacked Baltimore.

The threat this British army posed to Philadelphia and New York led to the first active black involvement in the war on the American side. The New York state legislature authorized two black regiments, offered freedom to slaves who enlisted, and promised compensation to their masters. African Americans in Philadelphia and New York City volunteered to help build fortifications. In Philadelphia, James Forten, Richard Allen, and Absalom Jones patriotically raised a "Black Brigade," although it did not engage in battle.

African-American men nevertheless fought at two of the war's most important battles. During the naval engagement at Put-in-Bay on Lake Erie in September 1813, which secured control of the Great Lakes for the United States, one-quarter of Commandant Oliver Hazard Perry's 400 sailors were black. At the Battle of New Orleans—fought in January 1815, about a month after a peace treaty had been negotiated but not ratified—African Americans also fought bravely under the command of General Andrew Jackson.

The Missouri Compromise

5-6 **What impact did the Missouri Compromise have on African Americans?**

Read on MyHistoryLab
Document: Thomas Jefferson Reacts to the "Missouri Question," 1820

Read on MyHistoryLab
Document: Missouri Admitted to Statehood, Slavery at Issue, 1820

After 1815, as the United States emerged from a difficult war, sectional issues between the North and South, which constitutional compromises and the political climate had pushed into the background, revived. The nation's first political parties—the Federalist and the Republican—had failed to confront slavery as a national issue. The northern wing of the modernizing Federalist Party had abolitionist tendencies. But during the 1790s when they controlled the national government, the Federalists did not raise the slavery issue. Then the victory of the agrarian and state-rights-oriented Republican Party in 1800 fatally weakened the Federalists as a national organization. The result was a series of proslavery presidential administrations in Washington.

It took innovations in transportation and production that began during the 1810s, as well as the rapid disappearance of slavery in the northern states, to transform the North into a region consciously at odds with the South's traditional culture and slave-labor economy. The first major expression of intensifying sectional differences over slavery and its expansion came in 1819 when the slaveholding Missouri Territory, which had been carved out of the Louisiana Territory, applied for admission to the Union as a slave state. Northerners expressed deep reservations about the creation of such a new slave state. Many of them feared it would destroy the political balance between the sections and encourage the expansion of slavery elsewhere. The aged Thomas Jefferson called this negative northern reaction a "fire bell in the night." He meant that henceforth slaveholders had to be on guard in national politics to protect their interests.

African Americans also appreciated the significance of the Missouri crisis. Black residents of Washington, DC, crowded into the U.S. Senate gallery as that body debated the issue. Finally Henry Clay of Kentucky, the slaveholding Speaker of the House of Representatives, directed an effort that in 1820 produced a compromise that temporarily quieted North-South discord. Clay's **Missouri Compromise** (see Map 5–3) permitted Missouri to become a slave state; maintained a sectional political balance by admitting Maine, which had been part of Massachusetts, as a free state; and banned slavery north of the 36° 30 line of latitude in the old Louisiana Territory. Yet sectional relations would never be the same, and a new black and white antislavery militancy soon confronted the white South.

Missouri Compromise
Sectional compromise in Congress in 1820 that admitted Missouri to the Union as a slave state and Maine as a free state and prohibited slavery in the Louisiana Purchase territory above 36° 30' north latitude.

CONCLUSION

The period between the War for Independence and the Missouri Compromise was a time of transition for African Americans. On one hand, the legacy of the American Revolution brought emancipation in the North and a promise of equal opportunity with white Americans. On the other hand, during the 1790s slavery and racism had grown stronger. Through a combination of antiblack prejudice among white people and African Americans' desire to preserve their cultural traditions, black urban

Explore on **MyHistoryLab Map:** The Missouri Compromise of 1820

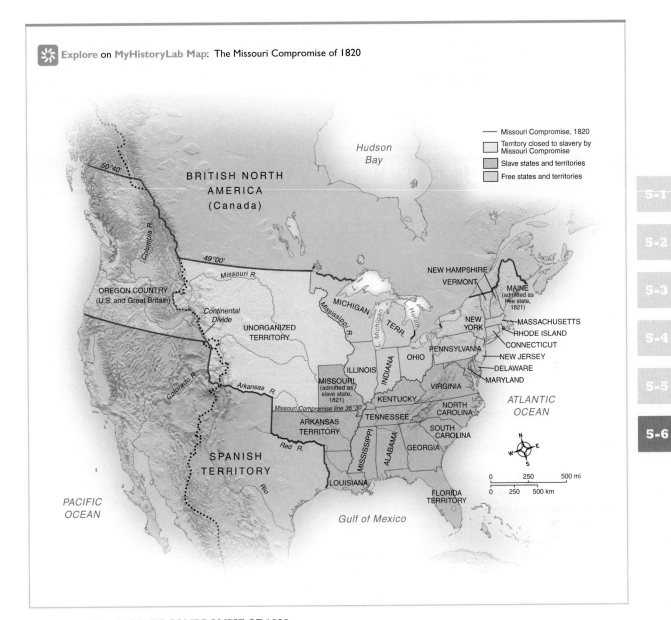

MAP 5–3 THE MISSOURI COMPROMISE OF 1820
Under the Missouri Compromise, Missouri entered the Union as a slave state, Maine entered as a free state, and Congress banned slavery in the huge unorganized portion of the old Louisiana Territory north of the 36° 30 line of latitude.

Which section of the United States did the Missouri Compromise favor?

communities arose in the North, Upper South, and, occasionally—in Charleston and Savannah, for example—in the Deep South.

Spreading freedom in the North and upper South, and the emergence of black communities North and South, were heartening developments. There were new opportunities for education, spiritual expression, and economic growth. But the mass of African Americans remained in slavery. The forces for human bondage became stronger. Freedom for those who had gained it in the Upper South and North was marginal and precarious.

Gabriel's conspiracy in Virginia and Deslondes's rebellion in Louisiana indicated that revolutionary principles persisted among black southerners. But these rebellions and British recruitment of slaves during the War of 1812 convinced most white southerners that black bondage had to be permanent. In these circumstances, African Americans looked to the future with mixed emotions. A few determined that the only hope for real freedom lay in migration from the United States.

CHAPTER TIMELINE

AFRICAN-AMERICAN EVENTS

NATIONAL EVENTS

1775–1780

1775
First antislavery society formed

1777
Vermont bans slavery

1776
Declaration of Independence

1777
Battle of Saratoga

1780–1785

1780
Pennsylvania begins gradual emancipation

1781
Elizabeth Freeman begins her legal suit for freedom

1782
Virginia repeals its ban on manumission

1783
Massachusetts bans slavery and black men gain the right to vote there

1784
Connecticut and Rhode Island begin gradual abolition

1781
Articles of Confederation ratified

1783
Great Britain recognizes independence of the United States

1785–1790

1785
New Jersey and New York defeat gradual emancipation

1787
Northwest Ordinance bans slavery in the territory north of the Ohio River

1786
Shays' Rebellion

1787
Constitutional Convention

1789
Constitution ratified

George Washington becomes president of the United States

1790–1795

1793
Congress passes Fugitive Slave Law

1794
Mother Bethel Church established in Philadelphia

CHAPTER TIMELINE

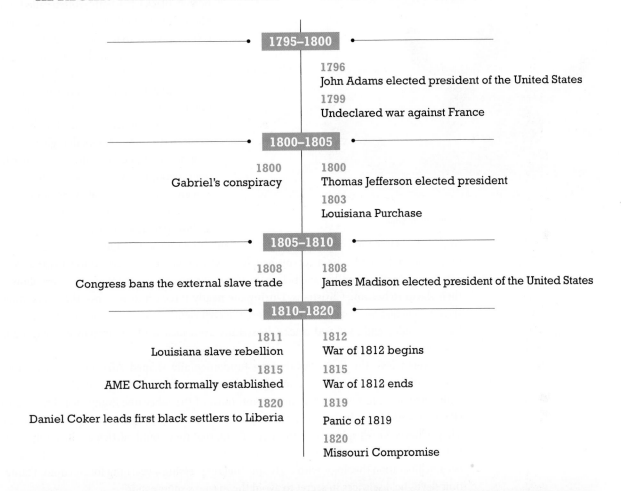

AFRICAN-AMERICAN EVENTS   **NATIONAL EVENTS**

1795–1800

1796
John Adams elected president of the United States

1799
Undeclared war against France

1800–1805

1800
Gabriel's conspiracy

1800
Thomas Jefferson elected president

1803
Louisiana Purchase

1805–1810

1808
Congress bans the external slave trade

1808
James Madison elected president of the United States

1810–1820

1811
Louisiana slave rebellion

1812
War of 1812 begins

1815
AME Church formally established

1815
War of 1812 ends

1820
Daniel Coker leads first black settlers to Liberia

1819
Panic of 1819

1820
Missouri Compromise

On MyHistoryLab

 Study and Review on MyHistoryLab

REVIEW QUESTIONS

1. Which were stronger in the early American republic, the forces in favor of black freedom or those in favor of continued enslavement?

2. How did African Americans achieve emancipation in the North?

3. How was the U.S. Constitution, as it was drafted in 1787, a proslavery document? How was it an antislavery document?

4. Why were separate institutions important in shaping the lives of free black people during the late eighteenth and early nineteenth centuries?

5. Why did Gabriel believe he and his followers could abolish slavery in Virginia through an armed uprising?

CONNECTING THE PAST

The Great Awakening and the Black Church

Preacher meeting in the African Church, Cincinnati, Ohio.

THE GREAT AWAKENING AND AFRICAN-AMERICAN life and culture are closely connected. Black Christianity, often called "the black church," both shaped the huge evangelical revival that flourished in British North America during the mid-eighteenth century—*and* sprang from it. Black Christians, and *especially* black preachers, combined African and Christian religious beliefs and practices. Their churches became community centers that guided and supported families, nurtured resistance to oppression, pointed the way to freedom, and encouraged cultural expression.

No single event or movement, no matter how pervasive, can shape all aspects of something as large and dependent on personal interpretation as religious belief, practice, and organization. In the Virginia colony, people of African descent converted to Christianity as early as the 1620s. After that and before the Great Awakening, some colonial masters allowed their slaves to become Christians. During the nearly three centuries since the Awakening, slavery, segregation, poverty, urbanization, the civil rights movement, and activist theology have expanded and modified black Christianity. New ideas and circumstances continue to change it.

Nevertheless, the Great Awakening fundamentally shaped African-American religious institutions and culture. Under its influence, nearly all African Americans affiliated with Christian churches. Just as important, most of them became evangelical Protestants (Baptists and Methodists) rather than Episcopalians, Presbyterians, or Roman Catholics. They believed God's spirit dwelt in each human, that they could participate in a holy community, achieve brotherhood, gain salvation, and bring on the millennium. Black theology became liberation theology, with early spirituals expressing a yearning for freedom. Plantation slaves held services in secret to avoid the master's suppression.

The Great Awakening also initiated the chain of events that produced separate black congregations and independent black churches. Separate black congregations within larger white church organizations date to the 1770s. Independent churches, such as the African Methodist Episcopal (AME) Church and African Methodist Episcopal Zion (AME Zion) Church, arose between 1790 and 1822. Racial discrimination and segregation among white Methodists (and later Baptists) helped shape these developments. Yet the creation of separate congregations and independent churches freed black Christians to preserve African beliefs and rituals that contributed so much to their religious sensibilities. Separation also allowed black church buildings to become centers of antislavery activism, powerbases for abolitionist ministers, and venues for abolitionist meetings that white churches often barred.

During the Civil War, black churches supported the Union cause, encouraged black men to enlist in Union armies, and urged emancipation as a war aim. During Reconstruction, black northern churches (along with many of their white coun-terparts) sent missionaries and teachers south to serve the freed people. As a result, the black churches expanded southward during the late nineteenth century. In the South, as earlier in the North, the churches housed schools, com-munity organizations, mutual aid societies, benevolent groups, women's clubs, and fraternal societies. Black min-isters provided political leadership. After Reconstruction, black churches helped their communities endure decades of oppression. By the mid-twentieth century, they had be-come centers for and leaders of the civil rights movement. Throughout these years, the black experience during the Great Awakening exerted its influence.

Not all black leaders praised the black church. In 1848, Frederick Douglass, who opposed all racial seg-regation, criticized the church as too emotional, too fo-cused on heaven, too expensive, and too conservative. Black ministers, Douglass charged, were often unquali-fied. He preferred a black struggle for equality within white churches.

Other black leaders have also called for a better-educated clergy. But most have been more supportive than Douglass of the black church. In 1903, W. E. B. Du Bois declared, "The Negro church of to-day is the social center of Negro life in the United States, and the most characteristic expression of African character." Du Bois

Richard Allen (1760–1831), American Methodist bishop and founder of the African Methodist Episcopal Church.

also thought the black church influenced "poor whites." Their religion, he claimed, "is a plain copy of Negro thought and methods." He added caustically, "The mass of 'gospel' hymns which has swept through American churches and well-nigh ruined our sense of song consists largely of debased imitations of Negro melodies." More broadly, he asserted, "The study of Negro religion is not only a vital part of the history of the Negro in America, but no uninteresting part of American history."

Du Bois also valued black ministers: "The Preacher is the most unique personality developed by the Negro on American soil. . . . The combination of a certain adroitness with a deep-set earnestness, of tact with consummate ability, gave him his preeminence, and helps him maintain it." By the time Du Bois died in 1963, the leadership such ministers provided to the civil rights movement had borne out this view. That leadership is also a legacy of the Great Awakening.

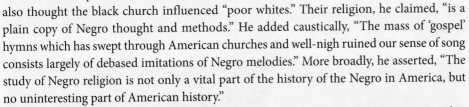

1. **How has the black church changed since the Great Awakening?**

2. **How has the black church remained the same since the Great Awakening?**

6

Life in the Cotton Kingdom 1793–1861

Listen to Chapter 6
on MyHistoryLab

LEARNING OBJECTIVES

6-1 Why was cotton cultivation central to the expansion of slavery?

6-2 How did the cultivation of various crops shape the experience of slavery?

6-3 How did the duties of house slaves and skilled slaves differ from those of urban and agricultural slaves?

6-4 What was the role of punishment in slavery?

6-5 What were the characteristics of the domestic slave trade between 1820 and 1860?

6-6 What were the conditions that shaped family life and the health and welfare of slaves?

6-7 How did African Americans adapt to life under slavery, and what role did religion play?

6-8 How have historians evaluated slavery and slaves?

Solomon Northup, a free black man, had been kidnapped into slavery during the 1840s. After 12 years in bondage, he finally escaped. In his autobiography, he identifies the central cruelty of slavery. It was the nearly absolute power masters had over their slaves. In other words, the root cause of black suffering in slavery lay not in abuses, but in the institution of slavery itself.

In this chapter we describe the life of black people in the slave South from the rise of the Cotton Kingdom during the 1790s to the eve of the Civil War in 1860. During the period this chapter covers, slavery in the South peaked as a productive system and means of white control over black southerners. We describe the extent of that slave system, how it varied across the South, and how it operated. The chapter also investigates the slave communities that African-American men, women, and children built.

In this engraving, which dates to about 1858, slaves harvest cotton on a southern plantation. Note the division of labor with women picking and men packing and carrying.

The Expansion of Slavery

6-1 Why was cotton cultivation central to the expansion of slavery?

Eli Whitney's invention of the cotton gin in 1793 made the cultivation of cotton profitable on the North American mainland (see Chapter 5). It led to the rapid and extensive expansion of slavery from the Atlantic coast to Texas (see Map 6–1). Enslaved black labor cleared forests and drained swamps to make these lands fit for cultivation.

The expansion of the cotton culture led to the removal of the American Indians—some of them slaveholders—who inhabited this vast region. During the 1830s and 1840s, the U.S. Army forced the Cherokee, Chickasaw, Choctaw, Creek, and most Seminole to leave their ancestral lands for Indian Territory in what is now Oklahoma. Many Indians died during this forced migration, and the Cherokee remember it as "The Trail of Tears." Yet the

6-1 6-2 6-3 6-4 6-5 6-6 6-7 6-8

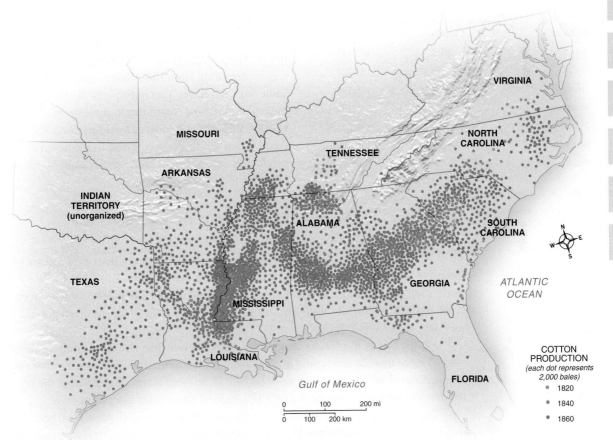

MAP 6-1 COTTON PRODUCTION IN THE SOUTH, 1820–1860
Cotton production expanded westward between 1820 and 1860 into Alabama, Mississippi, Louisiana, Texas, Arkansas, and western Tennessee.

Sam Bowers Hilliard, *Atlas of Antebellum Southern Agriculture* (Louisiana State University Press, 1984), 67–71.

Why did cotton production spread westward?

TABLE 6–1 U.S. SLAVE POPULATION, 1820 AND 1860

	1820	1860
United States	1,538,125	3,953,760
North	19,108	64
South	1,519,017	3,953,696
Upper South	965,514	1,530,229
Delaware	4,509	1,798
Kentucky	127,732	225,483
Maryland	107,397	87,189
Missouri	10,222	114,931
North Carolina	205,017	331,059
Tennessee	80,107	275,719
Virginia	425,153	490,865
Washington, DC	6,377	3,185
Lower South	553,503	2,423,467
Alabama	41,879	435,080
Arkansas	1,617	111,115
Florida	*	61,745
Georgia	149,654	462,198
Louisiana	69,064	331,726
Mississippi	32,814	436,631
South Carolina	258,475	402,406
Texas	*	182,566

*Florida and Texas were not states in 1820.

SOURCE: *Slaves without Masters: The Free Negro in the Antebellum South.* Copyright © 1974 by Ira Berlin. Reprinted by permission of The New Press. www.thenewpress.com.

Cherokees created in Oklahoma an economy dependent on black slave labor. By 1860 there were 7,000 slaves there, which accounted for 14 percent of the population.

Far fewer slaves lived in the other western territories. Kansas never had more than a few dozen slaves during the 1850s and had none after 1858. In New Mexico in 1850, there were about 40 black slaves and 3,000 American Indian slaves. When Utah Territory legalized slavery in 1852, only about 26 enslaved black people were living there, and by 1860 Utah had just 29 black people. Although California entered the Union as a state in 1850 under a constitution that banned slavery, two years later more than 300 illegally held slaves worked there as prospectors or servants.

Slave Population Growth

In contrast to the Far West, during the period of territorial expansion a tremendous increase in the number of African Americans in bondage occurred in the region stretching from the Atlantic coast to Texas (see Table 6–1). But slaves were not equally distributed across the region. Western North Carolina, eastern Tennessee, western Virginia, and most of Missouri never had many slaves. Their numbers grew fastest in the newer cotton-producing states, such as Alabama and Mississippi (see Map 6–2).

Ownership of Slaves in the Old South

Slaveholders were as unevenly distributed across the South as slaves and, unlike slaves, declined in number. In 1830, 1,314,272 white southerners (36 percent of a total white southern population of 3,650,758) owned slaves. In 1860 only 383,673 white southerners (4.7 percent of a total white southern population of 8,097,463) owned slaves.

Almost half of the South's slaveholders owned fewer than five slaves, only 12 percent owned more than 20 slaves, and just 1 percent owned more than 50 slaves. Yet more than half the slaves belonged to masters who had 20 or more slaves. So, although the typical slaveholder owned few slaves, the typical slave lived on a sizable plantation.

Since the time of Anthony Johnson in the mid-1600s, a few black people had been slaveholders, and this class continued to exist. Many of them became slaveholders to protect their families from sale and disruption. This was because, as the nineteenth century progressed, southern states made it more difficult for masters to manumit slaves and for slaves to purchase their freedom. The states also threatened to expel former slaves from their territory. In response, black men and women sometimes purchased relatives who were in danger of sale to traders and who—if legally free—might be forced by white authorities to leave a state. Some African Americans, however, purchased slaves for financial reasons and passed those slaves on to their heirs.

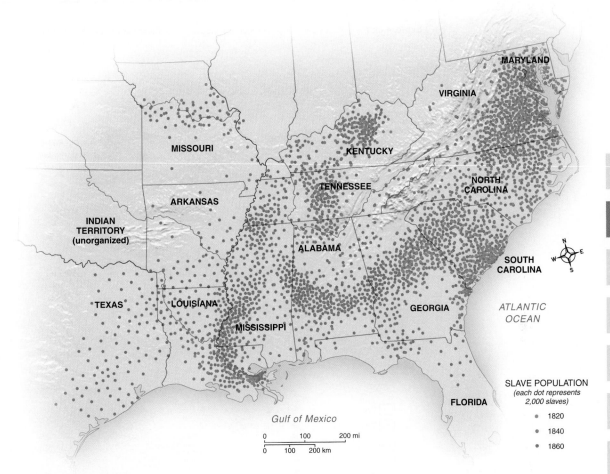

MAP 6–2 SLAVE POPULATION, 1820–1860
Slavery spread southwestward from the Upper South and the eastern seaboard following the spread of cotton cultivation.

Atlas of Antebellum Southern Agriculture, by Sam Bowers Hillard, pp. 67–71, 1984.

What does this map suggest about black life in the South?

Slave Labor in Agriculture

6-2 **How did the cultivation of various crops shape the experience of slavery?**

Agricultural laborers constituted 75 percent of the South's slave population. About 55 percent of the slaves cultivated cotton, 10 percent grew tobacco, and 10 percent produced sugar, rice, or hemp. About 15 percent were domestic servants, and the remaining 10 percent worked in trades and industries.

Tobacco

During the 1800s, tobacco remained important in Virginia, Maryland, Kentucky, and parts of North Carolina and Missouri (see Map 6–3). A difficult crop to produce, tobacco required

6-1

6-2

6-3

6-4

6-5

6-6

6-7

6-8

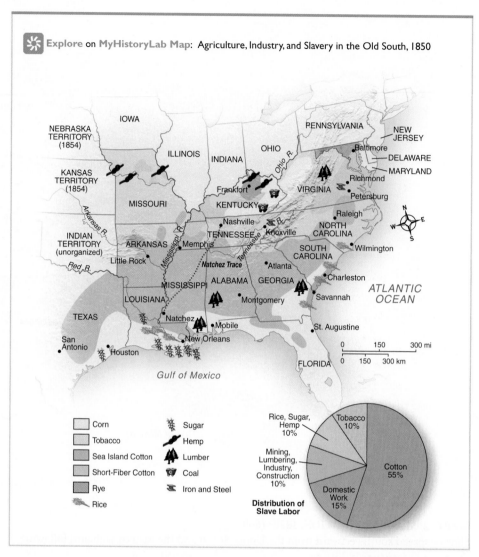

Explore on **MyHistoryLab** Map: Agriculture, Industry, and Slavery in the Old South, 1850

Distribution of Slave Labor

- Tobacco 10%
- Rice, Sugar, Hemp 10%
- Mining, Lumbering, Industry, Construction 10%
- Domestic Work 15%
- Cotton 55%

Legend:
- Corn
- Tobacco
- Sea Island Cotton
- Short-Fiber Cotton
- Rye
- Rice
- Sugar
- Hemp
- Lumber
- Coal
- Iron and Steel

MAP 6–3 AGRICULTURE, INDUSTRY, AND SLAVERY IN THE OLD SOUTH, 1850
The experience of the African American in slavery varied according to their occupation and the region of the South in which they lived.

To what degree did climate affect the type of crop slaves produced?

a long growing season and careful cultivation. Robert Ellett, a former slave, recalled that when he was just eight years old he worked in Virginia "a-worming tobacco." He "examined tobacco leaves, pull[ed] off the worms, if there were any, and killed them." He claimed that if an overseer discovered that slaves had overlooked worms on the tobacco plants, the overseer had the slaves whipped or forced them to eat the worms. Nancy Williams, another Virginia slave, recalled that sometimes as a punishment slaves had to inhale burning tobacco until they became nauseated.

Rice

Unlike the cultivation of tobacco, which spread west and south from Maryland and Virginia, rice production remained confined to the South Carolina and Georgia low country. As they had since colonial times (see Chapter 3), slaves in these coastal regions worked according to task systems that allowed them considerable autonomy. But that did not make their work easy.

Rice cultivation required intensive labor, and rice plantations needed large labor forces to grow and harvest the crop and maintain the fields. By 1860, 20 rice plantations had 300 to 500 slaves each, and eight others had between 500 and 1,000 slaves each. The only American plantation employing more than 1,000 slaves was in the rice-producing region. Such vast plantations represented sizable capital investments, and masters or overseers carefully monitored slave productivity.

Sugar

Another important crop that grew in a restricted region was sugar, which slaves cultivated on plantations along the Mississippi River in southern Louisiana. Commercial production of sugarcane did not begin in Louisiana until the 1790s. It required a consistently warm climate, a long growing season, and at least 60 inches of rain per year.

Raising sugarcane and refining sugar also required constant labor. Together with the great profitability of the sugar crop, these demands encouraged masters to work their slaves hard. Slave life on sugar plantations was harsh, and African Americans across the South feared being sent to labor on them.

Slaves cultivated, harvested, and processed sugar cane in hot and humid conditions, adding to the toll it took on their strength and health. Because cane could not be allowed to stand too long in the fields, harvest time was hectic. As one former slave recalled, "On cane plantations in sugar time, there is no distinction as to the days of the week. They [the slaves] worked on the Sabbath as if it were Monday or Thursday."

Listen on MyHistoryLab Audio: Pick a Bale of Cotton

Cotton

Although tobacco, rice, and sugar were economically significant, cotton was by far the South's and the country's most important staple crop. By 1860 cotton exports amounted to more than 50 percent of the annual dollar value of all U.S. exports (see Figure 6–1).

Cotton as a crop did not require cultivation as intensive as that needed for tobacco, rice, or sugar. However the cotton culture was so extensive that cotton planters as a group employed the most slave labor. By 1860, out of the 2,500,000 slaves employed in agriculture in the United States, 1,815,000 of them produced cotton. Cotton drove the South's economy and its westward expansion.

Demand for cotton fiber in the textile mills of Britain and New England

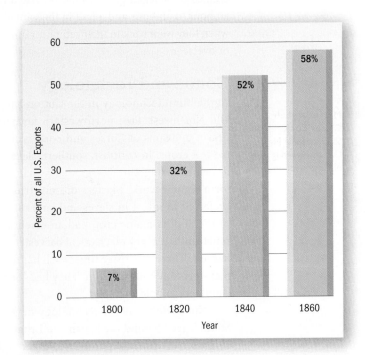

FIGURE 6–1 COTTON EXPORTS AS A PERCENTAGE OF ALL U.S. EXPORTS, 1800–1860
Cotton rapidly emerged as the country's most important export crop after 1800 and was key to its prosperity. Because slave labor produced the cotton, increasing exports strengthened the slave system itself.

stimulated the westward spread of cotton cultivation. Between 1830 and 1860, this demand increased by at least 5 percent per year. In response, American production of cotton rose from 3,000 bales in 1790 to 731,000 in 1830 to 3,837,000 in 1860. The new states of Alabama, Louisiana, and Mississippi led in this mounting production.

During the early nineteenth century, potential profits drew white farmers to the rich Black Belt lands of Mississippi and Alabama. Rapid population growth allowed Mississippi to gain statehood in 1817 and Alabama in 1819. By 1860 these states had become the leading cotton producers. They also had the greatest concentration of plantations with one hundred or more slaves. Twenty-four of Mississippi's slaveholders each owned between 308 and 899 slaves.

As huge agricultural units drew in labor, the price of slaves increased. During the 1830s, a prime male field hand sold in the New Orleans slave market for $1,250 (about $32,000 today). Prices dipped during the hard times of the early 1840s. But, by the 1850s, such slaves cost $1,800 (more than $52,000 today). Young women usually sold for up to $500 less than young men. Elderly slaves, unless they were highly skilled, sold for far less.

The enslaved men and women who worked in the cotton fields rose before dawn when the master or overseer sounded the plantation bell or horn. They ate breakfast and then assembled in work gangs of 20 or 25 under the control of black slave drivers. They plowed and planted in the spring. They weeded with heavy hoes in the summer and harvested in the late fall. During harvest season, adult slaves picked about 200 pounds of cotton per day. Regardless of the season, the work was hard, and white overseers whipped those who seemed to be lagging. Slaves usually had a two-hour break at midday in the summer and an hour to an hour and a half in the winter. Then they returned to the fields until sunset, when they went back to their cabins for dinner and an early bedtime enforced by the master or overseer.

Cotton and Technology

Agricultural technology in the Cotton Kingdom was primitive compared to that in the Old Northwest. Free northwestern farmers by the 1840s used a variety of machines, drawn by teams of horses and constructed of wood and iron, to plant, cultivate, and harvest crops. In contrast, southern slave workers relied on simple plows and harrows, drawn by a single mule—as well as handheld shovels, rakes, and heavy hoes—to perform similar work. Masters did not trust slaves with expensive machinery. They also preferred to invest in slaves and land rather than labor-saving devices. And the nature of the South's major crop had an essential impact. Because cotton ripened unevenly, nineteenth-century mechanical harvesters could not discern which plants were ready for harvest. Therefore, three times each harvest season, enslaved men, women, and children picked cotton bolls by hand. They had long sacks tied to their waists or hung from their shoulders to hold the bolls.

Nineteenth-century technology nevertheless impacted slaves' lives. Although the South lagged behind the North and Britain in applying steam power to transportation, it surpassed continental Europe and other regions of the world. After 1811 the Mississippi River teamed with steamboats. Railroads helped open the Old Southwest to cotton production, which encouraged the growth of the domestic slave trade and the disruption of black families.

In some instances technology improved plantation conditions. Early in the nineteenth century, cotton gins became much larger and more efficient than the ones Eli Whitney designed during the 1790s. Enslaved men operated gins powered by mules attached to long

Read on MyHistoryLab Document: Frederick Law Olmsted, from *A Journey in the Seabord States*, 1856

View on MyHistoryLab Closer Look: Steamboats in New Orleans Awaiting Bales of Cotton for Shipment

"sweeps" walking in circles. Once bolls had been cleaned of their seeds, slaves used presses, driven by huge screws turned by either man or mule power, to form bales. Slaves packaged the bales in cloth bagging and took them by wagon to river steamboat landings for shipment to market.

Other Crops

Besides cotton, sugar, tobacco, and rice, slaves in the Old South produced hemp, corn, wheat, oats, rye, white potatoes, and sweet potatoes. They also raised cattle, hogs, sheep, and horses. The hogs and corn were mainly for consumption on the plantations. But all the hemp and much of the other livestock and wheat went to market. In fact, wheat replaced tobacco as the main cash crop in much of Maryland and Virginia. The transition to wheat encouraged many planters to substitute free labor for slave labor, but slaves continued to grow wheat in the South until the Civil War.

The hemp industry centered in Kentucky. Before the Civil War, planters used hemp, which is closely related to marijuana, to make rope and bagging for cotton bales. This tied Kentucky economically to the Deep South. But, because hemp required much less labor than rice, sugar, or cotton, Kentucky developed a distinctive slave system. Three slaves could tend 50 acres of hemp, so slave labor forces were much smaller there than elsewhere.

House Servants and Skilled Slaves

6-3 How did the duties of house slaves and skilled slaves differ from those of urban and agricultural slaves?

About 75 percent of the slave workforce in the nineteenth century consisted of field hands. But because masters wanted to make their plantations as self-sufficient as possible, they also employed slaves as house servants and skilled craftsmen. Slaves who performed domestic duties, drove carriages, or learned a craft considered themselves privileged. However they were also suspended between two different worlds.

House slaves worked as cooks, maids, butlers, nurses, and gardeners. Their work was less physically demanding than fieldwork, and they often received better food and clothing. Nevertheless nineteenth-century kitchen work was grueling, and maids and butlers were on call at all hours. House servants' jobs were also more stressful than field hands' jobs because the servants were under closer white supervision. In addition, house servants were by necessity cut off from the slave community centered in the slave quarters.

Skilled slaves tended to be even more elite than house servants were. And, as had been true earlier, black men had a decided advantage over black women—apart from those who were seamstresses—in becoming skilled. Slave carpenters, blacksmiths, and millwrights built and maintained plantation houses, slave quarters, and machinery. Because they might need to travel to get tools or spare parts, such skilled slaves gained a more cosmopolitan outlook than field hands or house servants. They got a taste of freedom, which from the masters' point of view was dangerous.

As plantation slavery declined in the Chesapeake, skilled slaves could leave their master's estate to "hire their time." Either they or their masters negotiated labor contracts with employers who needed their expertise. In effect, these slaves worked for money. Although masters often kept all or most of what they earned, some of these skilled slaves merely paid their master a set rate and lived as independent contractors.

6-1
6-2
6-3
6-4
6-5
6-6
6-7
6-8

6-1
6-2
6-3
6-4
6-5
6-6
6-7
6-8

Urban and Industrial Slavery

Most skilled slaves who hired their time lived in the South's towns and cities, where they interacted with free black communities. Many of them resided in Baltimore and New Orleans, which were major ports and the Old South's largest cities. Others lived in smaller southern cities as well.

Slave populations in southern cities were often large, although they tended to decline between 1800 and 1860. In 1840 slaves constituted a majority of Charleston's population of 29,000. They nearly equaled white residents in Memphis and Augusta, which had total populations of 14,700 and 6,000, respectively. Slaves amounted to almost one-quarter of New Orleans's population of 145,000 (see Map 6-4).

When urban slaves were not working for their masters, they could earn money for themselves. As a result, masters had a harder time controlling their lives. Those who contracted to provide their masters with a certain amount of money per year could live on their own, buying their food and clothing.

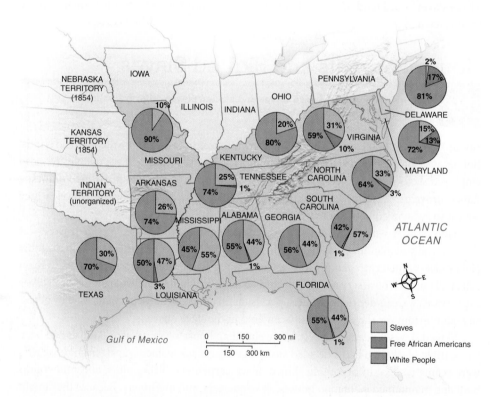

MAP 6–4 POPULATION PERCENTAGES IN THE SOUTHERN STATES, 1850
The percentages of slaves, free African Americans, and white people varied from state to state. In the Upper South, white populations were substantially larger than black populations. In the Deep South, however, the races were more in balance.

Faragher, John Mack; Armitage, Susan H.; Buhle, Mari Jo; Czitrom, Daniel, Out of Many: A History of the American People, Combined Volume, Media and Research Updated, 4th © 2005. Printed and Electronically reproduced by permission of Pearson Education, Inc., Upper Saddle River, New Jersey.

In which two states were there black majorities in 1850, and why?

Urban slaves served as domestics, washwomen, waiters, artisans, stevedores, drayers, hack drivers, and general laborers. In general, they did the urban work that foreign immigrants undertook in northern cities. If urban slaves purchased their freedom, they usually continued in the same work they had done as slaves. Particularly in border cities like Baltimore, Louisville, and Washington, urban slaves increasingly relied on their free black neighbors—and sympathetic white people—to escape north. Urban masters often let slaves purchase their freedom over a term of years to keep them from leaving. In Baltimore, during the early nineteenth century, this "**term slavery**" was gradually replacing slavery for life.

Industrial slavery overlapped with urban slavery, but southern industries that employed slaves were often in rural areas. By 1860 about 5 percent of southern slaves—approximately 200,000 people—worked in industry.

Most southern industrialists did not purchase slaves. Instead, they hired slaves from their masters. The industrial work slaves performed was often dangerous and tiring. But, as historian John B. Boles points out, slaves came to prefer industrial jobs to plantation labor. Like urban slaves, industrial slaves had more opportunities to advance themselves, enjoyed more autonomy, and often received cash incentives. Industrial labor, like urban labor, was a path to freedom for some.

term slavery A type of slavery prevalent in the Chesapeake from the late 1700s to the Civil War in which slaves were able to purchase their freedom from their masters by earning money over a number of years.

Punishment

6-4   What was the role of punishment in slavery?

Those who used slave labor, whether on plantations, on small farms, in urban areas, or in industry, frequently offered incentives to induce slaves to perform well. Yet slave labor by definition is forced labor based on the threat of physical punishment, and White southerners believed that African Americans would not work unless threatened with beatings. Masters denied that this brutal aspect detracted from what they portrayed as the essentially benign and paternalistic character of the South's "peculiar institution."

Nevertheless, fear of the lash drove slaves to work *and* led them to cooperate among themselves for mutual protection. Parents and older relatives taught slave children how to avoid punishment and still resist masters and overseers. They worked slowly—but not too slowly—and feigned illness to maintain their strength. They broke tools and injured mules, oxen, and horses to tacitly protest their condition. This interplay of covert resistance and physical punishment caused anxiety for both masters and slaves. Resistance (described in more detail in Chapter 3) often forced masters to reduce work hours and improve conditions. Yet few slaves escaped being whipped at least once during their lives in bondage.

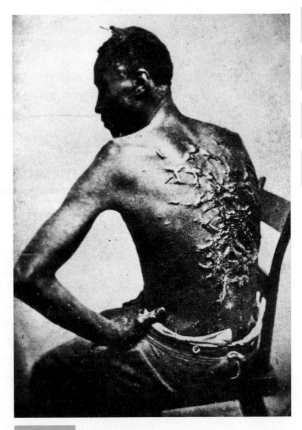

In this 1863 photograph, a former Louisiana slave displays the scars that resulted from repeated whippings. Although this degree of scarring is exceptional, few slaves were able to avoid being whipped at least once in their lives.

6-1
6-2
6-3
6-4
6-5
6-6
6-7
6-8

VOICES   Frederick Douglass on the Readiness of Masters to Use the Whip

This passage from the Narrative of the Life of Frederick Douglass, An American Slave, *published in 1845, suggests the volatile relationship between slaves and masters that could quickly result in violence. As Douglass makes clear, masters and overseers used the whip not just to force slaves to work but also to enforce a distinction between what was proper and even laudable for white men and what was forbidden behavior for slaves.*

It would astonish one, unaccustomed to a slave-holding life, to see with what wonderful ease a slaveholder can find things of which to make occasion to whip a slave. A mere look, word, or motion—a mistake, accident, or want of power—are all matters for which a slave may be whipped at any time. Does a slave look dissatisfied? It is said, he has the devil in him, and it must be whipped out. Does he speak loudly when spoken to by his masters? Then he is getting high-minded, and should be taken down a button-hole lower. Does he forget to pull off his hat at the approach of a white person? Then he is wanting in reverence, and should be whipped for it. Does he ever venture to vindicate his conduct, when censured for it? Then he is guilty of impudence—one of the greatest crimes of which a slave can be guilty. Does he ever venture to suggest a different mode of doing things from that pointed out by his master? He is indeed presumptuous, and getting above himself; and nothing less than a flogging will do for him. Does he, while plowing, break a plough—or, while hoeing, break a hoe? It is owing to his carelessness, and for it a slave must always be whipped.

1. **Why did masters and overseers whip slaves?**
2. **Given the behavior by masters that Douglass describes, how were slaves likely to act around white people?**

SOURCE: Roy Finkenbine, ed., *Sources of the African-American Past* (New York: Longman, 1997), 43–44.

The Domestic Slave Trade

6-5   What were the characteristics of the domestic slave trade between 1820 and 1860?

View on MyHistoryLab
Closer Look: Slave Auction in Richmond, Virginia

The expansion of the Cotton Kingdom south and west combined with the decline of slavery in the Chesapeake to stimulate the domestic slave trade. As masters in Delaware, Maryland, Virginia, North Carolina, and Kentucky trimmed excess slaves from their workforces—or switched entirely from slave to wage labor—they sold men, women, and children to slave traders. The traders in turn shipped these unfortunate people to the slave markets of New Orleans and other cities for resale. Masters also sold slaves as punishment, and fear of being "sold down river" led many slaves in the Chesapeake to escape. A vicious circle resulted: Masters sold slaves south to prevent their escape, and slaves escaped to avoid being sold south.

The number of people traded was huge and, considering that many of them were ripped away from their families, tragic. Starting in the 1820s, about 150,000 slaves per decade moved toward the southwest either with their masters or traders. Between 1820 and 1860, an estimated 50 percent of the slaves of the Upper South moved involuntarily into the Southwest.

Traders operated compounds called slave prisons or slave pens in Baltimore; Washington, DC; Alexandria and Richmond, Virginia; Lexington, Kentucky; Charleston, South Carolina; and in smaller cities. Most of the victims of the trade moved on foot in groups called **coffles**, chained or roped together. There was also a considerable coastal trade in slaves from Chesapeake ports to New Orleans. By the 1840s some traders transported their human cargoes in railroad cars.

The domestic slave trade demonstrated the falseness of slaveholders' portrayals of slavery as a benign institution. Driven by economic necessity, profit, or a desire to frustrate escape plans, masters in the upper South irrevocably separated husbands and wives, mothers and children, and brothers and sisters. Traders sometimes tore babies from their mothers' arms. The journey from the Chesapeake to Mississippi, Alabama, or Louisiana could be long and hard, and some slaves died along the way. A few managed to keep in touch with those they had left behind through letters and travelers, but most could not. After the abolition of slavery in 1865, many African Americans used their new freedom to travel across the South looking for relatives from whom they had been separated long before.

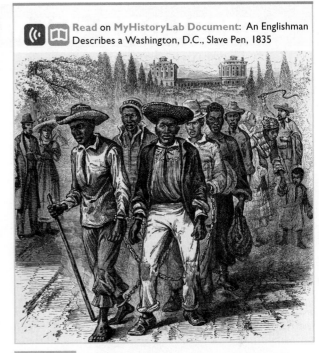

Read on **MyHistoryLab** Document: An Englishman Describes a Washington, D.C., Slave Pen, 1835

A slave-coffle passing the Capitol.

coffle A file of slaves chained together that was typical of the domestic slave trade.

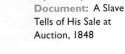

Read on MyHistoryLab Document: A Slave Tells of His Sale at Auction, 1848

Slave Families

6-6 What were the conditions that shaped family life and the health and welfare of slaves?

The families that enslaved African Americans sought to preserve had been developing in America since the seventeenth century. However, such families had no legal standing. Most enslaved men and women could choose their mates, although masters sometimes arranged such things. Masters encouraged pairings among female and male slaves because they assumed correctly that husbands and fathers would be less rebellious than single men. Masters also knew that they would benefit if their human chattel reproduced.

Families were also the core of the African-American community in slavery. Even though no legal sanctions supported slave marriages and the domestic slave trade could sunder them, many such marriages endured. Before they wed, some couples engaged in courting rituals, while others rejected "such foolishness." Similarly, slave weddings ranged from simply "taking up" and living together to religious ceremonies replete with food and frolics.

Read on **MyHistoryLab** Document: Farm Journal Reports on the Care and Feeding of Slaves (1836)

Enslaved couples usually lived together in cabins on their master's property. They had little privacy because nineteenth-century slave cabins were crude, small, one-room dwellings that two families might have to share. But couples who shared cabins were generally better off than husbands and wives who lived on different plantations as the property of different masters. In these cases, children lived with their mother, and their father visited when he could in the evenings. Work patterns that changed with the seasons or with the mood of a master could interfere with such visits. So could the requirement that slaves have passes to leave home.

6-1

6-2

6-3

6-4

6-5

6-6

6-7

6-8

✳ EXPLORE ON MYHISTORYLAB

The Internal Slave Trade

What fueled the domestic slave trade before the Civil War?

In 1808, Congress banned the Atlantic slave trade. But this did not end the slave trade within the United States. Instead the demand for slaves grew as southerners expanded west during the first half of the 1800s. White settlers brought slaves with them or bought them from traders who had acquired the slaves in the East. As this internal slave trade boomed, eastern slaveholders often broke up black families to serve the western market. As the table shows, nearly 73,000 slaves were brought to North America from

SLAVES ARRIVING IN MAINLAND NORTH AMERICA FROM AFRICA, 1776–1807	
State	**Number of Slaves**
Rhode Island	158
Pennsylvania	134
Virginia	30
North Carolina	81
South Carolina	56,406
Georgia	10,269
Florida	1,360
Gulf coast	4,089
Rest of North America	218
Total Number of Slaves, 1776–1807	**72,745**

Africa before 1808. However, the total number of slaves in the United States in 1860 was 3,953,761.

✳ Explore the Topic on MyHistoryLab

1. **Comparison** *How did the size of a slaveholder's farm often relate to the number of enslaved?* Chart this relationship.
2. **Cause** *In what ways did the distribution of U.S. slave population change between 1808 and the 1860s?* Conceptualize the reasons for such trends.
3. **Consequence** *How did the closing of the Trans-Atlantic slave trade affect the price of slaves?* Theorize the resulting impacts on the institution of slavery in the United States.

This woodcut of a black father being sold away from his family appeared in *The Child's Anti-Slavery Book* in 1860. Family ruptures, like the one shown, were among the more common and tragic aspects to slavery, especially in the Upper South, where masters claimed slavery was "mild."

Children

Despite these difficulties, enslaved parents instructed their children in family history, religion, and the skills required to survive in slavery. They sang to their children and told them stories full of folk wisdom. In particular, they impressed on them the importance of extended family relationships. The ability to rely on grandparents, aunts and uncles, cousins, and honorary relatives served as a hedge against the family disruption that the domestic slave trade might inflict. In this manner, too, the extended black family provided slaves with the resources they needed to avoid complete physical, intellectual, cultural, and moral subjugation to their masters.

During an age when infant mortality rates were much higher than they are today, those rates for black southerners were even higher than they were for white people. There were several reasons for this. Enslaved black women usually performed field labor up to the time they delivered a child, and their diets lacked necessary nutrients. Consequently, they tended to have babies whose weights at birth were less than normal. Enslaved infants were also more likely than other children to be subject to such postpartum maladies as rickets, tetany, tetanus, high fevers, intestinal worms, and influenza. More than 50 percent of slave children died before the age of five.

Slaveholders contributed to high infant mortality rates probably more from ignorance than malevolence. It was, after all, in the master's economic self-interest to have slave mothers produce healthy children. Masters often allowed mothers a month to recuperate after giving birth and several months thereafter off from fieldwork to nurse their babies. Although this reduced the mother's productivity, the children's labor might make up the loss when they entered the plantation workforce. Unfortunately, many infants needed more than a few months of breast-feeding to survive.

Black children began doing "light chores" in cotton fields at an early age. These girls are collecting cotton bolls that older workers missed.

The care of slave children varied with the size of a slaveholder's estate, the region it was in, and the mother's work. House servants could carry their babies with them while they worked. On small farms, enslaved women strapped their babies to their backs or left them at the edge of fields, so they could nurse them periodically, although the latter practice risked exposing an infant to ants, flies, or mosquitoes. On larger plantations, mothers could leave a child with an elderly or infirm adult. This encouraged a sense of community and a shared responsibility among the slaves for all black children on a plantation.

As children grew older, they spent much time in unsupervised play, often with white children. Slave childhood was short. Early on, parents and others taught youngsters about the realities of plantation life. As early as age six, children undertook so-called light chores. Work became more taxing as the children grew older, until, between the ages of 8 and 12, they performed adult fieldwork. Sale away from their families, particularly in the Upper South, also accelerated their progress to adulthood.

Sexual Exploitation

As with forced separations, masters' sexual exploitation of black women disrupted enslaved families. Abuse of black women began during the Middle Passage and continued after the abolition of slavery in the United States in 1865.

Read on **MyHistoryLab**
Document: A Slave
Describes the Sexual
Predation of Her
Master, 1861

Long-term relationships between masters and enslaved women were common in the nineteenth-century South. Such continuing relationships rested not on overt coercion but on masters' implicit power and authority. The relationship between Thomas Jefferson and his slave Sally Hemings is the most infamous of these. DNA and circumstantial evidence indicate that Jefferson and Hemings had a long sexual relationship that produced four children who survived to adulthood. It began in 1787 when Hemings served as caretaker

VOICES   A Slaveholder Describes a New Purchase

In this letter to her mother, a white Louisiana woman, Tryphena Blanche Holder Fox, describes her husband's purchase of a slave woman and her children. Several things are apparent in the letter—that investing in slaves was expensive, that the white woman's only concern for the slave woman and her children was their economic value, that it was up to the white woman to supervise the new slaves, and that the slave woman showed her displeasure with her situation.

Hygiene [Jesuit Bend, Louisiana]

Sunday, Dec 27, 1857

Dear Mother,

We are obliged to save every dollar he can "rake & scrape" to pay for a negro woman.... She has two likely children . . . and is soon to have another, and he only pays fourteen hundred for the three. She is considered an excellent bargain . . . he would not sell her and the children for less than $2,000. She came & worked two days, so we could see what she was capable of.... She was sold by a Frenchman.... He has a family of ten & she had all the work to do besides getting her own wood & water from the river. She was not used to do this, and gave them a great deal of trouble.... How much trouble she will give me, I don't know, but I think I can get along with her, passable well any how. Of course it increased my cares, for having invested so much in one purchase, it will be to my interest to see that the children are well taken care of clothed and fed. All of them give more or less trouble....

> 1. **What does Tryphena reveal about the management of slaves?**
> 2. **What does she indicate about the ability of slaves to force concessions from their masters?**

SOURCE: Tryphena Blanche Holder Fox to Anna Rose Holder, December 27, 1857, Mississippi Department of Archives and History, Jackson, Mississippi.

---

to one of Jefferson's daughters at his household in Paris, where he was U.S. ambassador to France. At that time Jefferson was 44 and Hemings about 14.

There is evidence that Hemings and her children enjoyed special privileges on Jefferson's Monticello plantation. But, by modern standards, her relationship to Jefferson began with statutory rape, and Hemings's unfree status and that of her children limited her ability to resist his sexual advances. Even more common than relationships like that of Jefferson and Hemings were instances in which masters, overseers, and their sons forced slave women to have sex against their will. This routine rape caused great distress. Former slave Harriet Jacobs wrote in her autobiography, "I cannot tell how much I suffered in the presence of these wrongs, nor how I am still pained by the retrospect."

White southerners justified sexual abuse of black women in several ways. They maintained that black women were naturally promiscuous and seduced white men. Some pro-slavery apologists argued that the sexual exploitation of black women by white men reduced prostitution and promoted purity among white women. These apologists ignored the devastating emotional impact of sexual exploitation on black women. They failed to note that the rape of black women by white men emphasized in the most degrading manner the inability of black men to protect their wives and daughters.

Diet

The slaves' diet hardly raised the moral issues associated with the sexual exploitation of black women by white men. The typical plantation's weekly ration of one peck of cornmeal (about 14 pounds) and three to four pounds of salt pork or bacon was enough to maintain an adult's body weight and, therefore, appeared to be adequate. But even when black men and women added vegetables, eggs, and poultry that they raised or fish and small game that they caught, this diet was (according to modern medical science) deficient in many nutrients. Because these nutrients are essential to the health of people who perform hard labor in a hot climate, slaves frequently suffered from chronic illnesses.

Yet masters and white southerners generally consumed the same sort of food that slaves ate, and, in comparison to people in other parts of the Atlantic world, enslaved African Americans were not undernourished. Although adult slaves were on average an inch shorter than white northerners, they were three inches taller than new arrivals from Africa, two inches taller than slaves who lived in the West Indies, and one inch taller than British Royal Marines.

African-American cooks, primarily women, developed a distinctive cuisine based on African culinary traditions. They seasoned foods with salt, onions, pepper, and other spices and herbs. They fried meat and fish, served sauce over rice, and flavored vegetables with bits of smoked meat. The availability in the South of such African foods as okra, yams, collard greens, benne seeds, and peanuts strengthened their culinary ties to that continent. Cooking also gave black women the ability to control part of their lives and demonstrate their creativity.

Clothing

Enslaved men and women had less control over what they and their children wore than how they cooked. Although skilled slaves often produced the shoes and clothing plantation workers wore, slaves in general rarely had the time or skill to make their clothes. They went barefoot during the warm months and wore cheap shoes in the winter. Slaveholding women, with the help of trained female house servants, sewed the clothes slaves wore.

This clothing was usually made of homespun cotton or wool. Some slaves also received hand-me-downs from masters and overseers. Although the distribution of clothing varied widely over time and space and according to the generosity of masters, slaves usually received clothing allotments twice a year. At the fall distribution, enslaved men received two outfits for the cold weather along with a jacket and a wool cap. At the spring distribution, they received two cotton outfits. Slave drivers wore garments of finer cloth and greatcoats during the winter. Butlers and carriage drivers wore liveries appropriate to their public duties. Enslaved women received at each distribution two simple dresses of calico or homespun. In the winter they wore capes or cloaks and covered their heads with kerchiefs or bonnets. Because masters gave priority to clothing adult workers, small children often went naked during the warm months.

Although they received standard-issue clothing, black women particularly sought to individualize what they wore. They changed the colors of clothes with dyes they extracted from roots, berries, walnut shells, oak leaves, and indigo. They wove threads of different color into their clothes to make "checkedy" and other patterns.

6-1
6-2
6-3
6-4
6-5
6-6
6-7
6-8

Health

Low birth weight, diet, and clothing all affected the health of slaves. Before the 1830s diseases were endemic among them, and death could come quickly. Much of this ill health resulted from overwork in the South's hot, humid summers; exposure to cold during the winter; and poor hygiene. Slave quarters rarely had privies; human waste could contaminate drinking water; and food was prepared under unsanitary conditions. Dysentery, typhus, food poisoning, diarrhea, hepatitis, tuberculosis, typhoid fever, salmonella, and intestinal worms were common and often fatal maladies.

The South's warm climate encouraged mosquito-borne diseases like yellow fever and malaria, the growth of bacteria, and the spread of viruses. Interaction between people of African and European descent increased the types of illnesses. Smallpox, measles, and gonorrhea were European diseases. Malaria, hookworm, and yellow fever came from Africa. The sickle-cell blood trait protected people of African descent from malaria but could cause sickle-cell anemia, a painful, debilitating, and fatal disease.

African Americans also had greater susceptibility to certain other afflictions than did persons of European descent. Black people suffered from lactose intolerance, which greatly limited the amount of calcium they could absorb from dairy products, and from a limited ability to acquire vitamin D from sunlight in temperate regions. Because many slaves lost calcium through perspiration while working, these tendencies led to a high incidence of debilitating, and sometimes fatal, diseases.

However, black southerners constituted the only New World slave population that grew by natural reproduction. Although slaves had a higher mortality rate than white southerners, it was similar to that of Europeans. Slave health also improved after 1830, when their rising economic value persuaded masters to improve slave quarters, provide warmer winter clothing, reduce overwork, and hire physicians to care for bond people. During the 1840s and 1850s, slaves were more likely than white southerners to be cared for by a physician, although there was often little that nineteenth-century doctors could do to combat disease.

Enslaved African Americans also used traditional remedies—derived from Africa and passed down by generations of women—to treat the sick. Wild cherry bark and herbs like pennyroyal or horehound went into teas to treat colds. Slaves used jimsonweed tea to counter rheumatism and chestnut leaf tea to relieve asthma. One former slave recalled that her grandmother dispensed syrup to treat colic and teas to cure fevers and stomachaches. Some of these folk remedies were more effective than those prescribed by white physicians. This was especially true of kaolin, a white clay that black women used to treat dysentery.

The Socialization of Slaves

6-7 | How did African Americans adapt to life under slavery, and what role did religion play?

African Americans had to acquire the skills needed to protect themselves and their loved ones from a brutal slave system. Folktales, often derived from Africa but on occasion from American Indians, helped pass such skills from generation to generation. Parents, other relatives, and elderly slaves generally told such tales to teach survival, mental agility, and self-confidence.

Children learned to watch what they said to white people, not to talk back, to withhold information about other African Americans, and to dissemble. In particular, they refrained from making antislavery statements and camouflaged their awareness of how masters exploited them. Masters tended to miss the subtlety of the divided consciousness of their bond people. When slaves refused to do simple tasks correctly, masters saw it as black stupidity rather than resistance.

Religion

Along with family and socialization, religion helped African Americans cope with slavery. Some masters denied their slaves access to Christianity, and some slaves ignored the religion. In New Orleans, Baltimore, and a few other locations, there were Roman Catholic slaves, who were usually the human property of Roman Catholic masters. In Maryland during the 1830s, the Jesuits, an order of Roman Catholic priests and brothers, collectively owned approximately 300 slaves. But by the mid-nineteenth century, most American slaves practiced a Protestantism similar but not identical to that of most white southerners.

Biracial Baptist and Methodist congregations persisted in the South longer than they did in northern cities. The southern congregations usually had racially segregated seating, but black and white people joined in communion and church discipline. They shared cemeteries. Many masters during the nineteenth century sponsored plantation churches for slaves, and white missionary organizations also supported such churches.

In the plantation churches, white ministers told their black congregations that Christian slaves must obey their earthly masters as they did God. This was not what slaves wanted to hear. At times slaves walked out on ministers who preached obedience.

Instead of services sponsored by masters, slaves preferred a semisecret black church they conducted themselves under the leadership of self-called, often illiterate black

Read on **MyHistoryLab**
Document: A Catechism
for Slaves, 1854

Read on **MyHistoryLab Document**: Charles C. Jones, *The Religious Instruction of the Negroes in the United States* (1842).

British artist John Antrobus completed this painting in about 1860. It is named *Plantation Burial* and suggests the importance of religion among enslaved African Americans.
John Antrobus, "Negro Burial." Oil painting. The Historic New Orleans Collection. #1960.46.

Listen on **MyHistoryLab**
Audio: Come by Hyar
traditional; sung by Bernice
Reagon

preachers. This church emphasized Moses and deliverance from bondage rather than a consistent theology or Christian meekness. Services involved singing, dancing, shouting, moaning, and clapping. According to historian Peter Kolchin, slaves mixed in African "potions, concoctions, charms, and rituals [used] to ward off evil, cure sickness, harm enemies, and produce amorous behavior." European settlers in America during the previous century had also melded Christian and non-Christian beliefs and practices. So it is not surprising that white as well as black people continued to seek the help of African-American conjurers.

The Character of Slavery and Slaves

6-8   **How have historians evaluated slavery and slaves?**

For over a century, historians have debated the character of the Old South's slave system and the people it held in bondage. During the 1910s southern historian Ulrich B. Phillips portrayed slavery as a benign, paternalistic institution in which Christian slaveholders cared for largely content slaves. Slavery, Phillips argued—as had the slaveholders themselves—rescued members of an inferior race from African barbarism and permitted them to rise as far as they possibly could toward civilization. With different emphasis, historian Eugene D. Genovese has, since the 1960s, also placed paternalism at the heart of southern plantation slavery.

Other historians, however, deny paternalism had much to do with a system that rested on force. Since the 1950s they have contended that slaveholders exploited their bond people in a selfish quest for profits. Although some slaveholders cared about the welfare of their slaves, this brutal portrait of slavery is persuasive in the twenty-first century. Many masters never met their slaves face to face. Most slaves suffered whippings at some point in their lives, and over half the slaves caught up in the domestic slave trade were separated from their families.

Scholars have also compared slavery in the American South with its counterpart in Latin America. Historians note that slaves in Latin American countries influenced by Roman law and the Roman Catholic Church enjoyed more protection from abusive masters than did slaves in the United States, where English law and Protestant Christianity dominated. Routes to freedom, through self-purchase and manumission, were more available in Latin America than in the Old South. More interracial marriage also existed in Latin America. Therefore, some historians maintain, less racism in Latin America than in the United States. Other historians, however, have established that protections offered by law and religion to slaves in Latin America were more theoretical than practical. They argue that racism there merely took a different form than it did in the United States. Certainly the mortality rate among Latin American slaves was far greater than among slaves in the American South. This implies that the conditions under which slaves labored in Latin America were even harsher than the grim conditions slaves often faced in the United States.

Another debate has centered on the character of enslaved African Americans. Historians such as Phillips argued that African Americans were genetically predisposed to being slaves and were therefore usually content. In 1959 Stanley M. Elkins changed the debate by arguing that black people were not inherently inferior or submissive but that concentration-camp-like conditions on plantations made them into childlike "Sambos." They were, according to Elkins, as dependent on their masters as inmates in Nazi extermination camps were on their guards.

A scholarly reaction to Elkins's study led to current understandings of the character of African Americans in slavery. Since the 1960s historians have argued that rather than dehumanizing black people, slavery led them to create institutions that allowed them some control over their lives. Slaves built families, churches, and communities. According to these historians,

6-1
6-2
6-3
6-4
6-5
6-6
6-7
6-8

African-American resistance forced masters to accept African work patterns and black autonomy in the slave quarters. Although these historians may idealize the strength of slave communities within a brutal plantation context, they have enriched our understanding of slave life.

CONCLUSION

African-American life in slavery during the time of the Cotton Kingdom is a vast subject. As slavery expanded westward before 1860, it varied from region to region and according to the crops that slaves cultivated. Although cotton became the South's most important product, many African-American slaves continued to produce tobacco, rice, sugar, and hemp. In the Chesapeake, slaves grew wheat. Others tended livestock or worked in cities and industry. Meanwhile, enslaved African Americans continued to build the community institutions that allowed them to maintain their cultural autonomy and persevere within a brutal system.

The story of African Americans in southern slavery is one of labor, perseverance, and resistance. Black labor was responsible for the growth of a southern economy that helped produce prosperity throughout the United States. Black men and women preserved and expanded an African-American cultural heritage that included African, European, and American Indian roots. They resisted determined efforts to dehumanize them. They developed family relationships, communities, churches, and traditions that helped them preserve their character as a people.

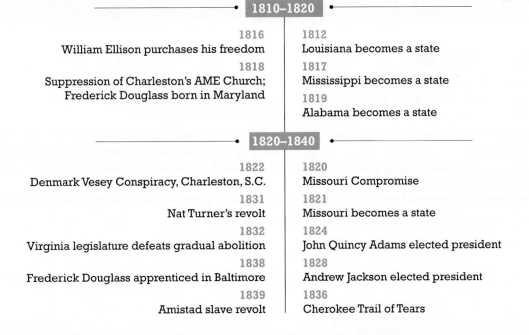

CHAPTER TIMELINE

AFRICAN-AMERICAN EVENTS

NATIONAL EVENTS

1810–1820

1816
William Ellison purchases his freedom

1812
Louisiana becomes a state

1818
Suppression of Charleston's AME Church;
Frederick Douglass born in Maryland

1817
Mississippi becomes a state

1819
Alabama becomes a state

1820–1840

1822
Denmark Vesey Conspiracy, Charleston, S.C.

1820
Missouri Compromise

1831
Nat Turner's revolt

1821
Missouri becomes a state

1832
Virginia legislature defeats gradual abolition

1824
John Quincy Adams elected president

1838
Frederick Douglass apprenticed in Baltimore

1828
Andrew Jackson elected president

1839
Amistad slave revolt

1836
Cherokee Trail of Tears

CHAPTER TIMELINE

AFRICAN-AMERICAN EVENTS	NATIONAL EVENTS

1840–1850

AFRICAN-AMERICAN EVENTS	NATIONAL EVENTS
1841 Solomon Northup kidnapped	1845 Texas annexed as a slave state
1845 Betsy Somayrac's will	1846 War against Mexico begins
	1848 Annexation of New Mexico and California

1850–1860

AFRICAN-AMERICAN EVENTS	NATIONAL EVENTS
1852 Frederick Law Olmsted's first tour of southern states	1850 Compromise of 1850
1853 Solomon Northup publishes *Twelve Years a Slave*	1854 Kansas-Nebraska Act
1855 Celia's trial and execution for killing her master	1856 Republican Party's first presidential election
1857 Supreme Court issues Dred Scott decision	1860 The secession movement begins

On MyHistoryLab

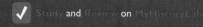
✓ Study and Review on MyHistoryLab

REVIEW QUESTIONS

1. How did the domestic slave trade and the exploitation of black women by white males affect slave families?

2. How significant were black slaveholders in the history of slavery?

3. How did urban and industrial slavery differ from plantation slavery in the Old South?

4. What impact did housing, nutrition, and disease have on the lives of slaves between 1820 and 1860?

5. How did black Christianity differ from white Christianity in the Old South? How did black Christianity in the South differ from black Christianity in the North?

Free Black People in Antebellum America 1820–1861

LEARNING OBJECTIVES

What were the demographics of black freedom?	**7-1**
How did the policies of the Jacksonian Democrats impact African Americans?	**7-2**
What limits were placed on free blacks throughout the North?	**7-3**
What were the characteristics of northern black communities?	**7-4**
What institutions did African Americans rely on most?	**7-5**
How did free African Americans live in the South and the West?	**7-6**

Journalist Samuel Cornish knew that pervasive white prejudice limited the lives of black people. During the 40 years before the Civil War, such prejudice was less rigid but nearly as common in the North as in the South. The northern states had abolished slavery, and free black people living in those states enjoyed more rights than their counterparts in the South. Yet these very rights made many white northerners hostile toward African Americans.

While southern legislatures considered expelling free black people from their states, northern legislatures—particularly in the Old Northwest—restricted black people's ability to move into their states. White workers, North and South, sponsored legislation that limited most free African Americans to menial employment. White people also required most black people to live in segregated areas of cities. Yet such ghettoized African-American communities cultivated a dynamic cultural legacy and built enduring institutions.

This chapter picks up the story of free black communities that began in Chapter 5. It provides a portrait of free African Americans between 1820 and the start of the Civil War. Like the revolutionary era, the antebellum period was a time of hope and fear. The numbers of free African Americans steadily increased. But the number of slaves increased much faster.

Barbering was one of the skilled trades open to black men during the antebellum years. Several wealthy African Americans began their careers as barbers.

Demographics of Freedom

7-1   **What were the demographics of black freedom?**

In 1820 there were 233,504 free African Americans in the United States. In comparison, there were 1,538,125 slaves and 7,861,931 white people. Of the free African Americans, 99,281 lived in the North, 114,070 in the Upper South, and only 20,153 in the Deep South (see Map 7–1).

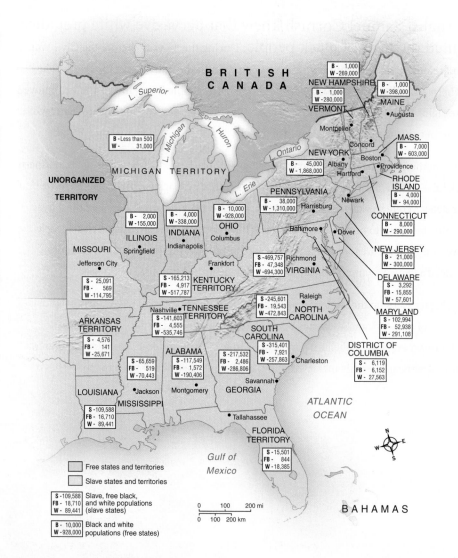

MAP 7–1 THE SLAVE, FREE BLACK, AND WHITE POPULATIONS OF THE UNITED STATES IN 1830
This map does not distinguish the slave from the free black population of the free states, although the process of gradual emancipation in several northeastern states was still under way and some black northerners remained enslaved.

SOURCE: *For slave states, Ira Berlin,* Slaves Without Masters: The Free Negro in the Antebellum South *(New York: New Press, 1971); for free states,* Historical Statistics of the United States *(Washington: GPO, 1960). Note: Figures for free states are rounded to the nearest thousand.*

Which states had the largest and the smallest free black populations in 1830?

As southern states made freedom suits and manumission more difficult, the northern free black population increased more rapidly than the free black populations in either the Upper or the Deep South.

By 1860 the free African-American population had reached 488,070. Of these, 226,152 lived in the North, 224,963 in the Upper South, and 36,955 in the Deep South (see Figures 7–1 and 7–2). A few thousand free black people also lived in the west beyond Missouri, Arkansas, and Texas. Meanwhile, the number of slaves had increased to just under four million, and massive immigration had tripled the white population to 26,957,471.

In 1860, 47.3 percent of the free black population lived in cities, compared with only 32.9 percent of white people. Of urban free African Americans, 62.5 percent lived in cities with populations over 100,000. As a result, free African Americans accounted for a significantly larger percentage of the population of large cities than they did of the total American population. In Baltimore, free black people represented 12 percent of the 212,418 residents. There, as well as in other smaller cities of the Upper South, free African Americans interacted with enslaved populations to create communities embracing both groups. The largest black urban population in the North was in Philadelphia, where 22,185 African Americans made up 4.2 percent of its approximately 533,000 residents. Other important northern cities had much smaller black populations, but they were still large enough to develop dynamic communities.

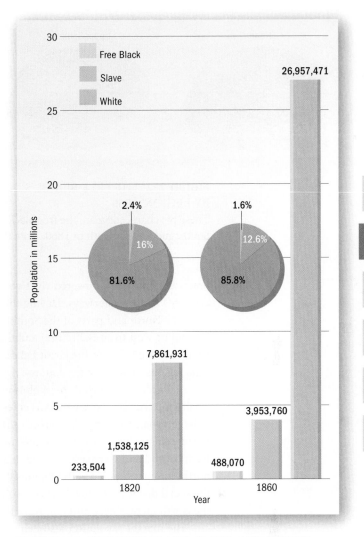

FIGURE 7–1 THE FREE BLACK, SLAVE, AND WHITE POPULATIONS OF THE UNITED STATES IN 1820 AND 1860
The bar graph shows the relationship among the free black, slave, and white populations in the United States in the years 1820 and 1860. The superimposed pie charts illustrate the percentages of these groups in the population in the same years.

The Jacksonian Era

7-2   How did the policies of the Jacksonian Democrats impact African Americans?

After the War of 1812, free African Americans—like other Americans of the time—witnessed rapid economic, social, and political change. Between 1800 and 1860, a **market revolution** transformed the North into a modern industrial society. The Industrial Revolution that began in Britain a century earlier encouraged these changes. But it took improved transportation to bring these changes to America. In 1807, Robert Fulton demonstrated the

market revolution The process between 1800 and 1860 by which an American economy based on subsistence farming, production by skilled artisans, and local markets changed into an economy marked by commercial farming, factory production, and national markets.

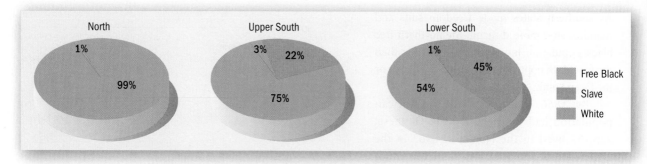

FIGURE 7-2 THE FREE BLACK, SLAVE, AND WHITE POPULATIONS
BY REGION, 1860
These pie charts compare the free black, slave, and white populations of the North, Upper
South, and Lower South in 1860. Note the near balance of the races in the Lower South.

7-1

7-2

7-3

7-4

7-5

7-6

practicality of steam-powered river vessels. Thereafter steamboats speeded travel on the
country's inland waterways. During the 1820s a system of turnpikes and canals began to
unite the North and parts of the South. Of particular importance were the National Road
(extending west from Baltimore) and the Erie Canal, which in 1825 opened a water route
from New York City to the Great Lakes. By the 1830s, railroads linked urban and agricultural regions in much of the country.

As faster transportation revolutionized trade, as a factory system began to replace
small shops run by artisans, and as cities expanded, northern society profoundly changed.
A large urban working class arose. Artisans and small farmers feared for their future.
Entrepreneurs began to replace the traditional social elite. Foreign immigrants, mostly
from Ireland and Germany, poured in as entrepreneurs sought cheap labor. By the 1820s
northern states bristled with religiously inspired reform movements designed to deal with
the social dislocations the market revolution caused. Together these developments made
the North increasingly different from the agrarian South.

The market revolution also helped create mass political parties as communications
improved, populations became more concentrated, and wage workers became more assertive. By 1810 states had begun dropping the property qualifications that had limited citizens' right to vote. One by one, they moved toward universal white manhood suffrage. This
trend doomed the openly elitist Federalist Party and disrupted its foe, the Republican Party.
As the market revolution picked up during the 1820s, unleashing hopes and fears among
Americans, politicians recognized the need for more broadly based political parties.

In the 1824 presidential election all four candidates ran as Republicans, and none received a majority of the popular or electoral vote. War hero Andrew Jackson of Tennessee
led the field, but in early 1825 Congress—exercising its power to decide such elections—
chose Secretary of State John Quincy Adams of Massachusetts to be president. Jackson's supporters claimed that Clay and Adams, by combining their forces in Congress, had cheated
the general out of the presidency. Led by Martin Van Buren of New York, they organized a
new Democratic Party to counter the Adams–Clay program. By appealing to slaveholders,
who believed economic nationalism favored the North over the South, and to "the common
[white] man" throughout the country, the Democrats defeated Adams and elected Jackson
in 1828.

Jackson was a strong but controversial president. In what became known as "Jacksonian
Democracy," he claimed to stand for the people against an anti-democratic wealthy elite.

Read on
MyHistoryLab
Document: Andrew
Jackson's Nullification
Proclamation of 1832

For the most part, Jackson followed a pro-southern agenda. He promoted states' rights, economic localism, and the territorial expansion of slavery. In opposition to Jackson, Clay (a Kentucky slaveholder), Adams, and others formed the Whig Party.

The Whig Party favored a nationalist approach to economic policy, which made it more successful in the North than in the South. It opposed territorial expansion, worried about the growing number of immigrants, and endorsed the moral values of evangelical Protestantism. In contrast to Democratic politicians who increasingly made racist appeals to antiblack prejudices among white voters, Whigs often adopted a more conciliatory tone on race. By the late 1830s, a few northern Whigs claimed their party opposed slavery and racial oppression. They, however, exaggerated. The Whig Party usually nominated slaveholders for the presidency, and few Whig politicians defended black rights.

Limited Freedom in the North

7-3 **What limits were placed on free blacks throughout the North?**

Addressing an interracial audience in Boston in 1846, white abolitionist Joseph C. Lovejoy described the North as a land "partially free." While it was true that slavery had disappeared in the North, white northerners also limited black freedom. They enacted **black laws**. They rarely allowed black men to vote. They often demanded segregated housing, schools, and transportation. And they limited African Americans' employment opportunities.

Black Laws

As indicated in previous chapters, the racially egalitarian impulse of the revolutionary era had by the 1790s begun to wane among white Americans. Meanwhile, the dawning Romantic Age encouraged a general belief that each ethnic and racial group had its own inherent spirit that set it apart from others. As white Americans began to perceive self-reliance, intellectual curiosity, the capacity for self-government, military valor, and an energetic work ethic as inherently "Anglo-Saxon" characteristics, they began to believe other racial groups lacked these virtues.

Most white northerners wanted nothing to do with African Americans. They paradoxically dismissed black people as incapable of honest work and feared black competition for jobs. Contact with African Americans, they believed, had degraded white southerners and would also corrupt white northerners if permitted. Therefore, as historian Leon Litwack puts it, "Nearly every northern state considered, and many adopted, measures to prohibit or restrict the further immigration of Negroes."

Such measures were more prevalent in the Old Northwest than in the Northeast. Ohio, Illinois, Indiana, Michigan, Iowa, and Wisconsin all limited or banned black immigration and discriminated against black residents. Between 1804 and 1849, Ohio's black laws required African Americans entering the state to produce legal evidence that they were free, register with a county clerk, and post a $500 bond "to pay for their support in case of want." State and local authorities rarely enforced these provisions, and by the time the Ohio **Free Soil Party** brought about their repeal in 1849, about 25,000 African Americans lived in the state. But Ohio authorities rigorously enforced other black law provisions. Among them were those prohibiting black testimony against white people in court, black service on juries, and black enlistment in the state militia.

Other governments in the Old Northwest placed even more extreme limits on black freedom than Ohio. In 1813, Illinois Territory threatened African Americans who tried

black laws Laws passed in states of the Old Northwest during the early nineteenth century banning or restricting black settlement and limiting the rights of black residents.

Read on **MyHistoryLab**
Document: North Carolina Codes, 1855

Free Soil Party An almost entirely northern political coalition from 1848 to 1853 opposed to the expansion of slavery into western territories. It included former supporters of the Whig, Democratic, and Liberty parties.

TABLE 7-1 BLACK POPULATION IN THE STATES OF THE OLD NORTHWEST, 1800–1840

	1800	1810	1820	1830	1840
Ohio	337	1,899	4,723	9,574	17,345
Michigan	144	174	293	707	
Illinois		781	1,374	2,384	3,929
Indiana	298	630	1,420	3,632	7,168
Iowa					188

SOURCE: *James Oliver Horton and Lois E. Horton,* In Hope of Liberty: Culture, Community, and Protest among Northern Free Blacks, 1700–1860 *(New York: Oxford University Press, 1997), 104.*

to settle within its borders with repeated whipping until they left. In neighboring Indiana, citizens ratified a state constitution in 1851 that explicitly banned all African Americans from the state, and Michigan, Iowa, and Wisconsin followed Indiana's example. Yet, like Ohio, these states rarely enforced such restrictive laws. As long as northern white people did not feel threatened, they usually tolerated a few black people in their midst (see Table 7–1).

Disfranchisement

Disfranchisement of black voters occurred throughout the North—except in most of New England—during the antebellum decades. The same white antipathy to African Americans that led to exclusionary legislation supported a movement to deny black men the right to vote. At no time before the Civil War could black men vote in the Old-Northwest states of Ohio, Indiana, Illinois, Michigan, and Wisconsin, nor could they ever vote in Iowa. However the northeastern states initially allowed black male suffrage, and efforts to curtail it in that region came as by-products of the Jacksonian Democrats' championing of the common white man.

From the eighteenth century into the early nineteenth, the northeastern elite used property qualifications to prevent the poorest black *and* white men from voting. Because black people were generally less wealthy than white people, these property qualifications gave most white men the right to vote and denied it to most black men. Under such circumstances, white people saw no danger in letting a few relatively well-to-do black men exercise the franchise. It was ironically the Jacksonian movement to end property qualifications that led to the outright disfranchisement of most black voters in the Northeast.

In the political struggle over ending the qualifications, advocates and opponents of universal white male suffrage opposed allowing all black men to vote. They claimed allowing all black men to vote would lead in certain districts to black men being elected to office. That in turn, they maintained, would encourage morally suspect African Americans to corrupt the political process and try to mix socially with white people. Then, they predicted, justifiably angry white people would react violently. In this manner, what had been a class conflict over voting rights became a racial conflict.

Those northeastern states with the larger black populations tended to be most determined to deny black men the right to vote. At one extreme were New Jersey and Connecticut. New Jersey stopped allowing black men to vote in 1807 and in 1844 adopted a white-only suffrage provision in its state constitution. In 1818 Connecticut determined that, although black men who had voted before that date could continue to vote, no new black voters would be allowed. At the other extreme, Maine, New Hampshire, Vermont, and Massachusetts—none of which had a significant African-American population—made no effort to deprive black men of the vote. In the middle were Rhode Island, New York, and Pennsylvania, which had protracted struggles over the issue.

In 1822 Rhode Island denied that black men were eligible to vote in its elections. Then, in 1842, a popular uprising against the state's conservative government extended the franchise to all men, black and white. In New York, an 1821 state constitutional convention defeated an attempt to disfranchise all black men. Instead it raised the property qualification for black voters while eliminating it for white voters. This provision denied the right to vote to nearly all of the 10,000 black men who had previously voted in the state.

A similar protracted struggle in Pennsylvania resulted in a more absolute elimination of black suffrage. In 1838, delegates to a convention to draft a new state constitution voted 77 to 45 to enfranchise all white men and disfranchise all black men. Although African-American leaders organized against the new constitution, Pennsylvanians ratified it by a vote of 113,971 to 112,759.

Segregation

Northern hotels, taverns, and resorts turned black people away unless they were the servants of white guests. Public lecture halls, art exhibits, and religious revivals either banned African Americans or allowed them to attend only at certain times. When they could enter churches and theaters, black people had to sit in segregated sections. Ohio excluded African Americans from state-supported poorhouses and insane asylums.

African Americans faced special difficulty trying to use public transportation. They could ride in a stagecoach only if it had no white passengers. As rail travel became more common during the late 1830s, companies set aside special cars for African Americans. In Massachusetts in 1841, a railroad first used the term **Jim Crow**, which derived from a blackface minstrel act, to describe these cars. Later the term came to define other forms of racial segregation as well. In cities, many omnibus and streetcar companies barred African Americans entirely. Steamboats refused to rent cabins to African Americans. They had to remain on deck at night and during storms. All African Americans, regardless of their wealth or social standing, endured such treatment.

African Americans in northern cities also faced residential segregation. A few wealthy black people lived in white urban neighborhoods, and a few northern cities, such as Cleveland and Detroit, had no patterns of residential segregation. But in most cases, a white

Read on MyHistoryLab Document: Sarah Mapps Douglass, Letter to William Basset, 1837

Jim Crow Term used to describe railroad cars set aside for black people.

7-1
7-2
7-3
7-4
7-5
7-6

This nineteenth-century lithograph depicts a street scene in the notorious Five Points neighborhood of New York City. Amid deteriorating buildings, black people are shown to be victims of poverty, crime, and immorality.

belief that black neighbors led to lowered property values produced such patterns. Neighborhoods existed such as "Nigger Hill" in Boston, "Little Africa" in Cincinnati, "Hayti" in Pittsburgh, and Philadelphia's "Southside." Conditions in these ghettoes were often dreadful. On the other hand, they provided a refuge from constant insult and a place where black institutions could develop.

Because African Americans representing all social and economic classes lived in segregated neighborhoods, the quality of housing in them varied. At its worst, it was bleak and dangerous. People lived in unheated shacks and shanties, in dirt-floored basements, or in houses without doors and windows. These conditions nurtured disease, infant mortality, alcoholism, and crime. Southern visitors to northern cities blamed the victims, insisting that the plight of many urban black northerners proved that African Americans were better off in slavery.

Black Communities in the Urban North

7-4   **What were the characteristics of northern black communities?**

Northern African Americans lived in both rural and urban areas during the antebellum decades, but it was urban black neighborhoods, poor as they might be, that had the concentrated populations required to nurture black community life (see Table 7–2). African-American urban communities of the antebellum period developed from the free black communities that had emerged from slavery in the North during the late eighteenth century (see Chapter 5). The communities varied from city to city and from region to region, yet they had much in common and interacted with each other. Resilient families, poverty, class divisions, active church congregations, the continued development of voluntary organizations, and concern for education characterized them.

The Black Family

By the 1820s, as they became free, northern African Americans left their masters and established their own households. By then the average black family in northern cities had two parents and between two and four children. However, in both the Northeast and Old Northwest, single-parent black families, usually headed by women, became increasingly common during the antebellum period. The difficulty black men had gaining employment may have influenced this trend. It certainly was a function of a high mortality rate among black men, which made many black women widows during their forties.

Meanwhile, financial need and African-American culture encouraged black northerners to take in boarders and create extended families. Economic considerations determined such arrangements, but friendship and family relationships also played a part. Sometimes entire nuclear families boarded, but most boarders were young, single, and male. As historians James Oliver Horton and Lois E. Horton put it, "The opportunity to rely on friends and family for shelter enhanced the mobility of poor people who were often forced to move to find employment. It provided financial assistance when people were unemployed; it provided social supports for people who faced discrimination; and it saved those who had left home or run away from slavery from social isolation."

TABLE 7–2 FREE BLACK POPULATION OF SELECTED CITIES, 1800–1850

City	1800	1850
Baltimore	2,771	25,442
Boston	1,174	1,999
Charleston	951	3,441
New Orleans	800 (estimated)	9,905
New York	3,499	13,815
Philadelphia	4,210	10,736
Washington	123	8,158

SOURCE: *Adapted from "The Free Black in Urban America, 1800–1850: The Shadow of a Dream," by Dr. Leonard P. Curry, p. 250. Copyright © 1981 University of Chicago Press, Chicago, IL. Reprinted by permission of the author.*

Poverty

The rising tide of immigration from Europe hurt northern African Americans economically. Before 1820 black craftsmen had been in demand, but, given the choice, white people preferred to employ other white people, and black people suffered. To make matters worse for African Americans, white workers excluded young black men from apprenticeships, refused to work with black people, and used violence to prevent employers from hiring black workers when white workers were unemployed. By the 1830s these practices had driven African Americans from the skilled trades. For the rest of the antebellum period, most northern black men performed menial day labor. By the 1850s black men were losing (to Irish immigrants) unskilled work as longshoremen, drayers, railroad workers, hod carriers, porters, and shoe shiners, as well as positions in such skilled trades as barbering.

By 1847, 80 percent of employed black men in Philadelphia did unskilled labor. Barbers and shoemakers predominated among those black workers with skills. Among employed black women, 80 percent either washed clothes or worked as domestic servants. Three-quarters of the remaining 20 percent were seamstresses. During the 1850s black women, too, lost work to Irish immigrants.

Unskilled black men often could not find work. When they did work, they received low wages. To escape such conditions in Philadelphia and other ports, they became sailors. By 1850 about 50 percent of the crewmen on American merchant and whaling vessels were black. Not only did these sailors have to leave their families for months at a time and endure brutal conditions at sea, but they also risked imprisonment if their ship anchored at southern ports.

The Northern Black Elite

Despite the poor prospects of most northern African Americans, a northern black elite emerged during the first six decades of the nineteenth century. Membership in this elite could be achieved through talent, wealth, occupation, family connections, complexion, and education. The elite led in the development of black institutions and culture, in the antislavery movement, and in the struggle for racial justice. It also served as the bridge between the black community and sympathetic white people.

Although few African Americans achieved financial security during the antebellum decades, black individuals could become rich. Segregated neighborhoods gave rise to a black professional class of physicians, lawyers, ministers, and undertakers who served an exclusively black clientele. Black merchants gained wealth by selling to black communities. Other relatively well-off African Americans included skilled tradesmen, such as carpenters, barbers, waiters, and coachmen, who generally found employment among white people.

Although less so than in the South, complexion also influenced social standing among African Americans in the North. White people often preferred to hire people of mixed race, successful black men often chose light-complexioned brides, and African Americans generally accepted white notions of human beauty.

By the 1820s the black elite had become better educated and more socially polished than its less wealthy black neighbors, yet it could never disassociate itself from them. Segregation and discriminatory legislation in the North applied to all African Americans regardless of class and complexion, and all African Americans shared a common culture and history.

Conspicuous among the black elite were entrepreneurs who, against considerable odds, gained wealth and influence in the antebellum North. As we noted in Chapter 5, James Forten was one of the first of them, and several other examples indicate the character of

7-1

7-2

7-3

7-4

7-5

7-6

VOICES   Maria W. Stewart on the Condition of Black Workers

7-1
7-2
7-3
7-4
7-5
7-6

Maria W. Stewart (1803–1879) was the first black female public speaker in the United States. She was strong willed and spoke without qualification what she believed to be the truth. At times she angered both black and white people. In the following speech, which she delivered in Boston in September 1831, Stewart criticized the treatment accorded to black workers—especially black female workers—in the North.

Tell us no more of southern slavery; for with few exceptions, although I may be very erroneous in my opinion, yet I consider our condition but little better than that.... After all, methinks there are no chains so galling as those that bind the soul, and exclude it from the vast field of useful and scientific knowledge....

I have asked several [white] individuals of my sex, who transact business for themselves, if providing our girls were to give them the most satisfactory references, they would not be willing to grant them an equal opportunity with others? Their reply has been—for their own part, they had no objection; but as it was not the custom, were they to take them into their employ, they would be in danger of losing the public patronage.

And such is the powerful force of prejudice. Let our girls possess whatever amiable qualities of soul they may; let their characters be fair and spotless as innocence itself; let their natural taste and ingenuity be what they may; it is impossible for scarce an individual of them to rise above the condition of servants....

I observed a piece ... respecting us, asserting that we were lazy and idle. I confute them on that point. Take us generally as a people, we are neither lazy nor idle: and considering how little we have to excite or stimulate us, I am almost astonished that there are so many industrious and ambitious ones to be found....

Again it was asserted that we were "a ragged set, crying for liberty." I reply to it, the whites have so long and so loudly proclaimed the theme of equal rights and privileges, that our souls have caught the flame also, ragged as we are. As far as our merit deserves, we feel a common desire to rise above the condition of servants and drudges. I have learnt, by bitter experience, that the continual hard labor deadens the energies of the soul, and benumbs the faculties of the mind; the ideas become confined, the mind barren, and, like the scorching sands of Arabia, produces nothing: or like the uncultivated soil, brings forth thorns and thistles....

Most of our color have dragged out a miserable existence of servitude from the cradle to the grave.... Do you [women] ask, why are you wretched and miserable? I reply, look at many of the most worthy and most interesting of us doomed to spend our lives in gentlemen's kitchens. Look at our young men, smart, active, and energetic, with souls filled with ambitious fire; if they look forward, alas! What are their prospects? They can be nothing but the humblest laborers, on account of their dark complexions; hence many of them lose their ambition, and become worthless....

---

1. **Is Stewart correct in assuming that conditions for black northerners were little better than those for slaves?**

2. **According to Stewart, what was the impact of northern white prejudice on black workers?**

SOURCE: Maria W. Stewart, "Lecture Delivered at the Franklin Hall, Boston, September 21, 1831," as quoted in Roy Finkenbine, *Sources of the African-American Past: Primary Sources in American History* (New York: Longman, 1997), 30–32.

such people. John Remond and his wife, Nancy Lenox Remond, became prosperous restaurateurs, caterers, and retailers. Their fortune subsidized the abolitionist careers of their son Charles Lenox Remond and daughter Sarah Parker Remond. Louis Hayden, who escaped from slavery in Kentucky in 1845, had by 1849 become a successful Boston haberdasher and abolitionist. Perhaps most successful were Stephen Smith and his partner William Whipper, who had extensive business interests in southeast Pennsylvania.

Inventors

In some cases, members of the black elite owed their success to technological innovations. Some black inventors had been born in slavery; others had not. Some participated in black community life; others did not.

In 1834 Henry Blair of Maryland became the first African American to patent an invention—a horse-drawn mechanized corn seed planter. In 1836 he patented a similar cotton seed planter. Henry Boyd, born in Kentucky in 1802, apprenticed as a cabinetmaker, purchased his freedom in 1826, and moved to Cincinnati. In 1835, as that city's leading bed manufacturer, he patented the "Boyd Bedstead."

Lewis Temple was another prominent black inventor of the period. Born free in Richmond, Virginia, Temple moved to New Bedford, Massachusetts. In 1845, at this whaling port, Temple, a blacksmith, devised the toggle harpoon. Set with a wooden pin, the barbed toggle secured a whale to a harpooner's line on impact. At the same time Temple devised his harpoon, Joseph Hawkins of West Windsor, New Jersey, patented "a gridiron used to broil meat," which preserved juices as the meat cooked.

Professionals

The northern black elite also included physicians and lawyers. Among the physicians, some, such as James McCune Smith and John S. Rock, received medical degrees. Either because they had been forced out of medical school or they chose not to go, other prominent black physicians practiced medicine without having earned a degree. (This was legal in the nineteenth century.) James Still of Medford, New Jersey, had meager formal education but used natural remedies to develop a successful practice among black and white people. The multitalented Martin R. Delany, who had been born free in Charles Town, Virginia, in 1812, practiced medicine in Pittsburgh after having been expelled from Harvard Medical School at the insistence of two white classmates.

Prominent black attorneys included Macon B. Allen, who gained admission to the Maine bar in 1844, and Robert Morris, who qualified to practice law in Massachusetts in 1847. Both Allen and Morris apprenticed with white attorneys, and Morris had a particularly successful and lucrative practice. Yet white residents thwarted his attempt to purchase a mansion in a Boston suburb.

Artists and Musicians

Although they rarely achieved great wealth and have not become famous, black artists and musicians were also part of the northern African-American elite. Among the best-known artists are Robert S. Duncanson, Robert Douglass, Patrick Reason, and Edmonia Lewis. Several of them supported the antislavery movement through their artistic work.

Douglass and Reason created portraits of abolitionists during the 1830s. Reason also produced illustrations of the sufferings of slaves. Duncanson, who

Educated at Oberlin College, Edmonia Lewis (1843–1911?) studied sculpture in Rome and emerged as one of the more prolific American artists of the late nineteenth century.

was born in Cincinnati and worked in Europe between 1843 and 1854, painted landscapes and portraits. Lewis, the daughter of a black man and a Chippewa woman, enrolled with abolitionist help at Oberlin College in Ohio and studied sculpture in Rome. Her works, which emphasized African-American themes, came into wide demand after the Civil War.

In Philadelphia a circle of black musicians wrote and performed a wide variety of music for orchestra, voice, and solo instruments. Similar circles existed in New Orleans, Boston, Cleveland, New York, Baltimore, and St. Louis. The best-known professional black singer of the period was Elizabeth Taylor Greenfield, who was born a slave in Mississippi and raised by Quakers in Philadelphia. Known as the "Black Swan," Taylor gained renown for her vocal range.

Authors

The antebellum era was a golden age of African-American literature. Driven by suffering in slavery and limited freedom in the North, black authors portrayed an America that had not lived up to its revolutionary ideals. Black autobiography recounted life in bondage and dramatic escapes. The best known such narrative is Frederick Douglass's classic *Narrative of the Life of Frederick Douglass, an American Slave,* published in 1845.

African Americans also wrote history, novels, and poetry. In 1855 William C. Nell published *The Colored Patriots of the American Revolution*, which reminded its readers that black men had fought for American freedom. William Wells Brown, who had escaped from slavery in Kentucky, became the first African-American novelist. His *Clotel, or the President's Daughter*, published in 1853, used the affair between Thomas Jefferson and Sally Hemings to explore in fiction the moral ramifications of slaveholders who fathered children with their bondwomen. Another black novelist of the antebellum years was Martin R. Delany. His *Blake, or the Huts of America*, a story of emerging revolutionary consciousness among southern slaves, ran as a serial in the *Weekly Anglo-African* during 1859.

Black poets included George M. Horton, a slave living in North Carolina, who in 1829 published *The Hope of Liberty*, and James W. Whitfield of Buffalo, New York, who in 1853 lampooned the song "My Country 'tis of Thee" when he wrote the following:

America, it is to thee

Thou boasted land of liberty,—

Thou land of blood, and crime, and wrong.

African-American women who published fiction during the period include Frances Ellen Watkins Harper and Harriet E. Wilson. Harper was born free in Baltimore in 1825. Associated with the antislavery cause in Pennsylvania and Maine, she published poems that depicted the sufferings of slaves. Wilson published

Read on **MyHistoryLab Document:** Frances E. W. Harper's "The Slave Auction," 1854

Frances Ellen Watkins Harper (1825–1911) was born free in Baltimore. During the 1850s, she published antislavery poetry and traveled across the North as an antislavery speaker.

Our Nig: Or, Sketches from the Life of a Free Black, in a Two-Story White House, North in 1859. This was the first novel published by a black woman in the United States. In the genre of autobiographical fiction, it compared the lives of black domestic workers in the North with those of southern slaves.

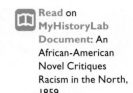

Read on MyHistoryLab Document: An African-American Novel Critiques Racism in the North, 1859

African-American Institutions

7-5 **What institutions did African Americans rely on most?**

In the antebellum decades, the black institutions that had appeared during the revolutionary era in urban areas of the North, Upper South, and—to a lesser extent—the Deep South grew in strength, numbers, and variety. Black institutions of the time included schools, mutual aid organizations, benevolent and fraternal societies, self-improvement and temperance associations, literary groups, newspapers and journals, and theaters. But, aside from families, the most important black community institution remained the church.

Churches

Black church buildings served as community centers. They housed schools and meeting places for other organizations. Antislavery societies often met in churches, and the churches harbored fugitive slaves. All of this went hand in hand with the community leadership black ministers provided. The ministers began schools and voluntary associations. They spoke against slavery, racial oppression, and what they considered weaknesses among African Americans. However, black ministers never spoke with one voice. Throughout the antebellum decades, many followed Jupiter Hammon (see Chapter 5) in admonishing their congregations that preparing one's soul for heaven was more important than gaining equal rights on Earth.

By 1846 the independent African Methodist Episcopal (AME) Church had 296 congregations in the United States and Canada with 17,375 members. The AME Bethel Church, located in Philadelphia, may have had between 2,000 and 3,000 worshippers each Sunday. The AME Zion Church of New York City was probably the second largest black congregation, with about 2,000 members.

Most black Baptist, Presbyterian, Congregationalist, Episcopal, and Roman Catholic congregations remained affiliated with white denominations, although they rarely sent delegates to regional and national church councils. In addition, many northern African Americans continued to attend white churches. To do so, they had to submit to the same second-class status that had driven Richard Allen and Absalom Jones to establish separate black churches in Philadelphia during the 1790s (see Chapter 5). Throughout the antebellum years, northern white churches required their black members to sit in special sections during services, provided separate Sunday schools for black children, and insisted that black people take communion after white people. Even Quakers, who spearheaded white opposition to slavery in the North and South, often provided separate seating for black people at their meetings.

During the 1830s and 1840s, some black leaders criticized the existence of separate black congregations and denominations. Frederick Douglass called them "negro pews, on a higher and larger scale." Such churches, Douglass and others maintained, were part and parcel of a segregationist spirit that divided America according to complexion.

VOICES The Constitution of the Pittsburgh African Education Society

Compared with black southerners, black northerners were fortunate to have access to education, and education societies were prominent among black self-improvement organizations. In January 1832 a group headed by John B. Vashon, a local black barber and philanthropist, met at Pittsburgh's African Church to establish such a society and a school. The following extracts from its constitution indicate the group's motives and plans.

Whereas, ignorance in all ages has been found to debase the human mind, and to subject its votaries to the lowest vices, and most abject depravity—and it must be admitted, that ignorance is the sole cause of the present degradation and bondage of the people of color in these United States—that the intellectual capacity of the black man is equal to that of the white, and that he is equally susceptible of improvement, all ancient history makes manifest; and even modern examples put beyond a single doubt.

We, therefore, the people of color, of the city and vicinity of Pittsburgh, and State of Pennsylvania, for the purpose of dispersing the moral gloom that has so long hung around us, have, under Almighty God, associated ourselves together, which association shall be known by the name of the *Pittsburgh African Education Society. . . .*

It shall be the duty of the Board of Managers . . . to purchase such books and periodicals as the Society may deem it expedient, they shall have power to raise money by subscription or otherwise, to purchase ground, and erect thereon a suitable building or buildings for the accommodation and education of youth, and a hall for the use of the Society. . . .

1. **Why would this group claim that black ignorance was the "sole cause" of black degradation and enslavement?**
2. **Why was the Pittsburgh African Education Society necessary?**

SOURCE: Dorothy Porten, ed., *Early Negro Writing, 1760–1837* (1971; reprint, Baltimore: Black Classics, 1995), 120–22.

Schools

As we noted earlier in this chapter, education, like religion, was racially segregated in the North between 1820 and 1860. Tax-supported compulsory public education for children in the United States began in Massachusetts in 1827 and spread throughout the Northeast and Old Northwest during the 1830s. Some public schools, such as those in Cleveland, Ohio, during the 1850s, admitted black students. But usually, as soon as 20 or more African-American children appeared in a school district, white parents demanded that they attend separate schools.

How to educate African-American children who were not allowed to attend school with white children became a persistent issue in the North. Until 1848 Ohio and the other states of the Old Northwest simply excluded black children from public schools and refused to allocate tax revenues to support separate facilities. The northeastern states were more willing to undertake such expenditures. But, even in these states, white residents resisted using tax dollars to fund education for African Americans. As a result, appropriations for black public schools lagged far behind those for public schools white children attended.

This tendency extended to cities where African-American leaders and white abolitionists had created private schools for black children. In 1812 the African School, established by Prince Hall in 1798, became part of Boston's public school system. As a result, like newly created black public schools in the city, it began to suffer from inadequate funding and a limited curriculum.

Woefully inadequate public funding resulted in poor education or none at all for most black children across the North. The few black schools were dilapidated and overcrowded. White teachers who taught in them received lower pay than those who taught in white schools, and black teachers received even less, so teaching was generally poor. Black parents, however, were often unaware that their children received an inadequate education. Even black and white abolitionists tended to expect less from black students than from white students.

Some black leaders defended segregated schools as better for black children than integrated ones. But, by the 1830s, most northern African Americans favored racially integrated public education, and during the 1840s Frederick Douglass became a leading advocate for such a policy. Douglass, other black leaders, and their white abolitionist allies made the most progress in Massachusetts, where by 1845 all public schools, except those in Boston, had been integrated. After a 10-year struggle, the Massachusetts legislature finally ended segregated schools in that city. This victory encouraged the opponents of segregated public schools across the North. By 1860 integration had advanced among the region's smaller school districts. But, except for those in Boston, urban schools remained segregated on the eve of the Civil War.

In fact, the black elite had more success gaining admission to northern colleges during the antebellum period than most African-American children had in gaining an adequate primary education. Some colleges served African Americans exclusively. In 1854, white Presbyterian minister John Miller Dickey and his Quaker wife Sarah Emlen Cresson established Ashmun Institute in Oxford, Pennsylvania, to educate black missionaries who would go to Africa. In 1855 the AME Church founded Wilberforce University, located near Columbus, Ohio, as another exclusively black college. Earlier some northern previously all white colleges had begun to admit a few black students. They included Bowdoin in Maine, Dartmouth in New Hampshire, Harvard and Mount Pleasant in Massachusetts, Oneida Institute in New York, and Western Reserve University in Ohio. By 1860 many northern colleges, law schools, medical schools, and seminaries admitted black applicants, although not on an equal basis with white applicants.

Voluntary Associations

The African-American mutual aid, benevolent, self-improvement, and fraternal organizations that originated during the late eighteenth century proliferated during the antebellum decades. So did black literary and temperance associations.

Mutual aid societies became especially attractive to black women. In 1830 black women in Philadelphia had 27 such organizations, compared with 16 for black men. By 1855 Philadelphia had 108 black mutual aid societies. Among black benevolent societies, African Dorcas Associations were especially prevalent. Started in 1828 in New York City by black women, these societies distributed used clothing to the poor, especially poor schoolchildren. During the early 1830s, black women also began New York City's Association for the Benefit of Colored Orphans.

During the same period, the Prince Hall Masons created new lodges in the cities of the Northeast and the Chesapeake. Beginning during the 1840s, Black Odd Fellows lodges

7-1

7-2

7-3

7-4

7-5

7-6

also became common. But more prevalent were self-improvement, library, literary, and temperance organizations. These manifested the reform spirit that swept the North and the Upper South during the antebellum decades. Closely linked to evangelical Protestantism, reformers maintained that the moral regeneration of individuals was essential to perfecting society. African Americans shared this belief and formed organizations to put it into practice.

Among the more prestigious of the societies for black men were the Phoenix Literary Society, established in New York City in 1833, and the Philadelphia Library Company of Colored Persons, founded in 1833. Black women formed the Female Literary Society of Philadelphia in 1831, and New York City's Ladies Literary Society in 1834. The Ladies Literary Society of Buffalo emerged in the mid-1830s, and Boston's Afric-American Female Intelligence Society began in 1832.

Black temperance societies spread even more widely than literary and benevolent organizations, although they also tended to be more short-lived. Like their white counterparts, black temperance advocates were middle-class activists who sought to stop those lower on the social ladder from abusing alcoholic beverages.

Free African Americans in the Upper South

7-6 How did free African Americans live in the South and the West?

Life for free black people in the South during the antebellum period differed from that in the North. The free black experience in the Upper South also differed from what it was in the Deep South. In general, free African Americans in the North, despite the limits on their liberty, had opportunities their southern counterparts did not enjoy. Each of the southern regions, nevertheless, offered some advantages to free black residents.

The free black people of the Upper South had much in common with their northern counterparts. In particular, African Americans in the Chesapeake cities of Baltimore, Washington, Richmond, and Norfolk had ties to black northerners, ranging from family and church affiliations to business connections and membership in fraternal organizations. But significant differences that resulted from the South's agricultural economy and slavery set free people of color in the Upper South apart. Although nearly half the free black population in the North lived in cities, only one-third did so in the Upper South, hampering the development there of black communities.

A more important difference was the impact of slavery on the lives of free African Americans in the Upper South. Unlike black northerners, free black people in the Upper South lived alongside slaves. Many had family ties to slaves and were more directly involved than black northerners in the slaves' suffering. Southern white politicians and journalists used the close connection between free black southerners and slaves to justify limiting the freedom of the former group.

free papers Proof of freedom that free black people had to carry at all times in the southern states prior to emancipation. The papers, issued by state governments, identified an individual by name, age, sex, color, height, and so forth.

Free black people of the Upper South were also more at risk of *being* enslaved than were black northerners. Except for Louisiana, with its French and Spanish heritage, all southern states' legal systems assumed African Americans to be slaves unless they could prove otherwise. Free black people had to carry **free papers** and renew them periodically. Free African Americans who got into debt in the South risked being sold into slavery to pay off their creditors.

As the antebellum period progressed, the distinction between free and enslaved African Americans narrowed in the Upper South. Although a few northern states allowed black men to vote, no southern state did after 1835. Free black people of the Upper South also had more difficulty traveling, owning firearms, congregating in groups, and being out after dark than did black northerners. Although residential segregation was less pronounced in southern cities than in the North, African Americans of the Upper South faced a more thorough exclusion from hotels, taverns, trains and coaches, parks, theaters, and hospitals.

Free black people in the Upper South experienced various degrees of hardship in earning a living, although, during the nineteenth century, their employment expanded as slavery declined in Maryland and northern Virginia. Free persons of color in rural areas generally worked as tenant farmers. Rural free African Americans also worked as miners, lumberjacks, and teamsters. In Upper South urban areas, most free black men worked as unskilled day laborers, waiters, whitewashers, and stevedores. Free black women worked as laundresses and domestic servants. As in the North, the most successful African Americans were barbers, butchers, tailors, caterers, merchants, and those teamsters and hack drivers who owned their own horses and vehicles. Before 1850 free black people in the Upper South had less competition from European immigrants for jobs than was the case in northern cities. This changed during the 1850s when Irish and German immigrants competed against free black people in the Upper South just as they did in the North for all types of employment. As in the North, immigrants often used violence to drive African Americans out of skilled trades.

7-1

7-2

7-3

7-4

7-5

7-6

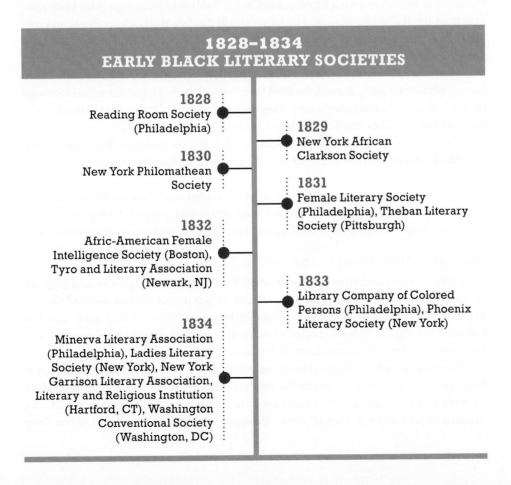

1828–1834
EARLY BLACK LITERARY SOCIETIES

1828
Reading Room Society
(Philadelphia)

1829
New York African
Clarkson Society

1830
New York Philomathean
Society

1831
Female Literary Society
(Philadelphia), Theban Literary
Society (Pittsburgh)

1832
Afric-American Female
Intelligence Society (Boston),
Tyro and Literary Association
(Newark, NJ)

1833
Library Company of Colored
Persons (Philadelphia), Phoenix
Literacy Society (New York)

1834
Minerva Literary Association
(Philadelphia), Ladies Literary
Society (New York), New York
Garrison Literary Association,
Literary and Religious Institution
(Hartford, CT), Washington
Conventional Society
(Washington, DC)

These circumstances made it difficult for free black people in the Upper South to maintain community institutions. In addition, the measures white authorities adopted to prevent slave revolt limited free black autonomy, and such measures became pervasive after the revolt Nat Turner led in southern Virginia in 1831. Many black churches and schools had to close or curtail their activities. Some states required that black churches have white ministers, and some black ministers left for the North. Yet free African Americans persevered. During the late 1830s, new black churches organized in Louisville and Lexington, Kentucky, and in St. Louis, Missouri. By 1860 Baltimore had 15 black churches. Louisville had nine, and Nashville, St. Louis, and Norfolk had four each. Most of these churches ministered to both enslaved and free members.

Black schools and voluntary associations in the Upper South also survived white efforts to suppress them, although the schools faced great challenges. Racially integrated schools and public funding for segregated black schools were out of the question in the South. Most black children received no formal education. Black churches, a few white churches, and a scattering of black and white individuals maintained what educational facilities the Upper South had for black children. The schools met—often sporadically—in churches or private homes. They generally lacked books, chalkboards, and desks. Particularly noteworthy were the efforts of the Oblate Sisters of Providence and John F. Cook. The Oblate Sisters were the first black Roman Catholic religious order in the United States. Cook, for 20 years, conducted a black school in Washington, DC.

Elizabeth Clovis Lange, who was of Haitian descent, established the Oblate Sisters in Baltimore in 1829 to provide a free education to the children of French-speaking black refugees from the Haitian Revolution. The sisters taught English, math, composition, and religion. Cook taught similar subjects at his Union Seminary from 1834 until his death in 1854. Both the sisters and Cook confronted persecution and inadequate funding. Cook had to flee Washington temporarily in 1835 to avoid being killed. Nevertheless, he passed his school on to his son, who kept it going through the Civil War. Meanwhile the Oblate Sisters had increased their influence in the black community. They built a chapel in Baltimore in 1836 that became the first black Catholic church in the United States.

Black voluntary associations, particularly in urban areas of the Upper South, fared better than black schools. By 1838 Baltimore had at least 40 such organizations. As in the North, black women organized their own voluntary associations. Washington's Colored Female Roman Catholic Beneficial Society, for example, provided death benefits for its members. Black benevolent organizations in the Upper South also sought to apprentice orphans to black tradesmen; sponsored fairs, picnics, and parades; and provided protection against kidnappers.

Free African Americans in the Deep South

More than half the South's free black population lived in Maryland, Delaware, and Virginia. To the west and south of these states, the number of free people of color declined sharply. The smaller free black populations in Kentucky, Tennessee, Missouri, and North Carolina had much in common with those in the Chesapeake states. But free African Americans who lived in the Deep South differed from their counterparts in the Upper South.

Free black people in the Deep South were not only far fewer than in either the Upper South or the North but also "largely the product of illicit sexual relations between black slave women and white men." Slaveholder fathers either manumitted their mixed-race children or let them buy their freedom. However, some free black people of the Deep

South traced their ancestry to free mixed-race refugees from Haiti, who sought during the 1790s to avoid that island nation's bloody revolutionary struggle by fleeing to Charleston, Savannah, and New Orleans.

A three-caste system similar to that in Latin America developed in the antebellum Deep South. It included white people, free black people, and slaves. Most free African Americans in the region identified more closely with their former masters than with slaves. To ensure the loyalty of such free people of color, powerful white people provided them with employment, loans, protection, and such special privileges as the ability to vote and to testify against white people. Some states and municipalities formalized this relationship by requiring free African Americans to have white guardians. Free black people in the region were also more likely than those farther north to remain in white churches largely because they identified with the white elite.

In the Deep South, free African Americans—over half of whom lived in cities—were more concentrated in urban areas than were their counterparts in the North and Upper South. Although Deep South cities restricted their employment opportunities, free black people in Charleston, Savannah, Mobile, and New Orleans maintained stronger positions in the skilled trades than free black people in the Upper South or the North. By 1860 in Charleston, three-quarters of the free black men worked in skilled trades. Free African Americans made up only 15 percent of Charleston's male population, yet they constituted 25 percent of its carpenters, 40 percent of its tailors, and 75 percent of its millwrights. In New Orleans, free black men predominated as carpenters, masons, bricklayers, barbers, tailors, cigar makers, and shoemakers. The close ties between free black people and the upper-class white people who did business with them explain much of this success.

Despite these ties, free black communities comparable to those in the Upper South and North arose in the cities of the Deep South. Although they usually lacked separate black churches as community centers, free African Americans in the region created other institutions. In Charleston the Brown Fellowship Society survived throughout the antebellum period. Charleston also had a chapter of the Prince Hall Masons, and free black men and women in the city maintained other fraternal and benevolent associations. In addition to similar sorts of organizations, the free black elite in New Orleans published literary journals and supported an opera house.

Because black churches were rare, wealthy African Americans and black fraternal organizations led in organizing private schools for black children in the cities of the Deep South. In Charleston, the Brown Fellowship Society organized an academy. New Orleans had several schools, most of which were conducted in French—the first or second language for many free black people in the city. Some of the wealthier free black families in these cities sent their children to Europe for education, and the literacy rate among free black people in both Charleston and New Orleans reached markedly high levels for the antebellum period.

In all, free people of color in the Deep South differed substantially from those in the Upper South and the North. Their ties to the white slaveholding class gave them tangible advantages. Yet they were not without sympathy for those who remained in slavery, and white authorities never fully trusted them to be loyal to the slave system. In particular, white people feared contact between free African Americans who lived in the ports of the Deep South and black northerners—especially black sailors. As a new round of slave unrest began in the South and a more militant northern antislavery movement got under way during the 1820s, free black people in the Deep South faced difficult circumstances.

Read on **MyHistoryLab**
Document:
Louisiana State Laws
Governing Slavery, 1825

7-1

7-2

7-3

7-4

7-5

7-6

7-1
7-2
7-3
7-4
7-5
7-6

Painted in 1858 by Thomas Waterman Wood, *Market Woman* portrays a young woman carrying produce she has purchased. There is no indication of her status as either free or enslaved. The portrait provides an example of how black women dressed in antebellum America.

Free African Americans in the Far West

Free black communities in the North, Upper South, and Deep South each had unique features, and all of them had existed for decades by the antebellum period. In the huge region stretching from the Great Plains to the Pacific coast, which had become part of the United States by the late 1840s, free black people were rare. Black communities there were just emerging in a few isolated localities. The prevalence of discriminatory "black laws" in the region's states and territories partially explains the small number of free black westerners. Like similar laws in the Old Northwest, these laws either banned free African Americans or restricted the activities of those allowed to settle. Nevertheless, a few black families sought economic opportunities in the West. During the 1840s they joined white Americans in settling Oregon. The California gold rush of 1849 had by 1852 attracted about 2,000 African Americans, most of whom were men, among hundreds of thousands of white Americans.

Usually these black Californians lived and worked in multicultural communities that also included people of Chinese, Jamaican, Latin American, and white American descent. But in a few localities, African Americans predominated. Some black Californians prospered as gold prospectors. Others worked as steamship stewards, cooks, barbers, laundresses, mechanics, saloonkeepers, whitewashers, porters, and domestics. By the early 1850s, there were black communities centered on churches in San Francisco, Sacramento, and Los Angeles. As in the East, these black communities organized benevolent and self-help societies. Although most African Americans who went west were men, black women sometimes accompanied their husbands and families.

CONCLUSION

During the antebellum period, free African-American communities that had emerged during the revolutionary era grew and fostered black institutions. Particularly in the urban North, life in these segregated communities foreshadowed the pattern of black life from the end of the Civil War into the twentieth century. Although the black elite could gain education, professional expertise, and wealth despite white prejudices, most northern people of color were poor. Extended families, churches, segregation, political marginality, and limited educational opportunities shaped their lives.

Free black people in the Upper South and Deep South faced even more difficulties. Presumed to be slaves if they could not prove otherwise, they confronted more danger of enslavement and harsher restrictive legislation than their counterparts in the North. Even so, energetic black communities existed in the Upper South throughout the antebellum period. In the Deep South, the small free black population was better off economically than were free black people in other regions. But it depended on white slaveholders, who proved to be unreliable allies as sectional controversy mounted. The antislavery movement, secession, and the Civil War would have a more profound impact on the free black communities in the South than in the North. Although it is not wise to generalize about free black people in the trans-Mississippi West, their presence on the Pacific coast in particular demonstrates their involvement in the westward expansion that characterized the United States during the antebellum years. Their West Coast communities indicate the adaptability of black institutions to new circumstances.

CHAPTER TIMELINE

AFRICAN-AMERICAN EVENTS

NATIONAL EVENTS

1800–1810

1807
New Jersey disfranchises black men

1803
Louisiana Purchase

1807
Robert Fulton's steamboat is launched in New York Harbor

1810–1820

1812
African School becomes part of the Boston public school system

1818
Connecticut bars new black voters

1812
War of 1812 begins

1815
War of 1812 ends

1819
Panic of 1819 begins

1820–1830

1821
New York retains property qualification for black voters

1822
Rhode Island disfranchises black voters

1824
Massachusetts defeats attempt to ban black migration to that state

1827
Freedom's Journal begins publication

1828
African Dorcas Association is established

1829
Cincinnati expels black residents

1825
John Quincy Adams becomes president

Erie Canal opens

1827
Massachusetts pioneers compulsory public education

1828
Andrew Jackson is elected president

1830–1940

1831
Maria W. Stewart criticizes treatment of black workers

1834
African Free Schools become part of New York City public school system

1838
Pennsylvania disfranchises black voters

1842
Rhode Island revives black male voting

1843
Edmonia Lewis born

1832
Surge in European immigration begins

1832–1833
Nullification Crisis

1837
Panic of 1837 begins when gold is discovered in California

CHAPTER TIMELINE

AFRICAN-AMERICAN EVENTS

NATIONAL EVENTS

1840–1850

1845
Narrative of the Life of Frederick Douglass is published

1849
Ohio black laws repealed

1846–1848
War against Mexico

1850
Compromise of 1850

On MyHistoryLab

✔ Study and Review on MyHistoryLab

REVIEW QUESTIONS

1. How was black freedom in the North limited in the antebellum decades?

2. How did northern African Americans deal with these limits?

3. What was the relationship of the African-American elite to urban black communities?

4. How did African-American institutions fare between 1820 and 1861?

5. Compare black life in the North to free black life in the Upper South, Deep South, and California.

Opposition to Slavery 1730–1833

LEARNING OBJECTIVES

Why and how did abolitionism begin in America?	8-1
What forces and events fueled the antislavery movement?	8-2
What were the goals of the American Colonization Society?	8-3
What role did black women play in the abolition movement?	8-4
Why was Walker's *Appeal* important?	8-5

In Boston in 1829, black abolitionist David Walker, in harsh language and demands for action, anticipated the militant black and white abolitionists of the 1830s, 1840s, and 1850s. In his *Appeal . . . to the Colored Citizens of the World,* Walker bluntly portrayed the oppression African Americans suffered. He urged black men to redeem themselves by defending their loved ones from abuse. If that led to violence and death, he asked, "Had you not rather be killed than be a slave to a tyrant, who takes the life of your mother, wife and dear little children?"

Walker's *Appeal* was not just a reaction to slavery; it was also a response to a conservative brand of antislavery reform. This chapter explores the emergence, during the eighteenth century, of abolitionism in America; its transformation during the early nineteenth century; and the beginning of a more radical antislavery movement by the late 1820s. Slave revolt conspiracies; political, social, and religious turmoil; and wide-ranging reform shaped this process. Black leaders, including Walker, Denmark Vesey, and Nat Turner, were major contributors. So was white abolitionist William Lloyd Garrison.

This drawing, known as "Nat Turner Preaches Religion," portrays Turner telling "friends and brothers" in August 1831 that God has chosen them to lead a violent "struggle for freedom."

Antislavery Begins in America

8-1   **Why and how did abolitionism begin in America?**

View on
MyHistoryLab
Closer Look:
Speaking Out Against
Slavery

8-1

8-2

8-3

8-4

8-5

The antislavery movement in its broadest context reflected economic, intellectual, and moral changes that affected the Atlantic world during the Age of Revolution that began during the 1760s. In the United States, that age forged *two* antislavery movements that survived until the end of the Civil War. Although separate, the two movements influenced each other. The first movement arose in the South among slaves with the help of free African Americans and a few sympathetic white people.

The second antislavery movement consisted of black and white abolitionists in the North, with outposts in the Upper South. Although abolitionists were always a small minority, far more white people engaged in this movement than in the one southern slaves conducted. In the North, white people controlled the larger antislavery organizations, although African Americans led in direct action against slavery. In the Upper South, African Americans could not openly establish or participate in antislavery organizations, but they cooperated covertly and informally with white abolitionists.

This second antislavery movement began during the 1730s when white Quakers in New Jersey and Pennsylvania realized slaveholding contradicted their belief in spiritual equality. Therefore, they advocated the abolition of slavery—at least among their fellow Quakers—in their home states and in the Chesapeake. As members of a denomination that emphasized nonviolence, Quakers generally expected slavery to be abolished peacefully and gradually.

Quakers remained prominent in the northern antislavery movement for the next 130 years. But the American Revolution, together with the French Revolution that began in 1789 and the Haitian struggle for independence between 1791 and 1804, revitalized the northern and southern antislavery movements and changed their nature. The revolutionary doctrine that all men had a natural right to life, liberty, and property led other northerners besides Quakers and African Americans to endorse the antislavery cause.

In 1775 Philadelphia Quakers organized the first antislavery society in the world. But their organization lapsed during the War for Independence. When they regrouped in 1784 as the Society for the Promotion of the Abolition of Slavery, they attracted non-Quakers. Among the first of these were Benjamin Rush and Benjamin Franklin, both of whom embraced natural rights doctrines. Revolutionary principles also influenced Alexander Hamilton and John Jay, who helped organize New York's first antislavery society. Similarly Prince Hall, the most prominent black abolitionist of his time, based his effort to abolish slavery in Massachusetts on universal rights.

Black and white abolitionists led in abolishing slavery in the North. However, the early northern antislavery movement had several limiting features. First, black and white abolitionists had similar goals but worked in separate organizations. Even white Quaker abolitionists rarely mixed socially with African Americans or welcomed them to their meetings. Second, except in parts of New England, northern abolitionists supported *gradual* emancipation, because they believed they had to protect slaveholders' economic interests. Third, despite natural rights rhetoric, white abolitionists did not advocate equal rights for black people. Fourth, early northern abolitionists did little to bring about abolition in the South, where most slaves lived.

All this indicates that neither Quaker piety nor natural rights principles created a truly egalitarian or sectionally aggressive northern abolitionism. Instead, it took major antislavery efforts carried out by black southerners, widespread religious revivalism, demands for reform, and the growth of northern black institutions to establish a framework for a more biracial and wide-ranging antislavery movement.

From Gabriel to Denmark Vesey

Gabriel's abortive slave revolt conspiracy of 1800 (discussed in Chapter 5) owed as much to revolutionary ideology as did the northern antislavery movement. The arrival of Haitian refugees in Virginia led to slave unrest throughout the 1790s, and Gabriel hoped to attract French revolutionary support. Although he was betrayed and he and 26 of his followers executed, the revolutionary spirit and insurrectionary network he established lived on (see Map 8–1). Virginia authorities had to suppress another slave conspiracy in 1802, and for years sporadic minor revolts erupted.

Read on MyHistoryLab Document: A Virginia Slave Explains Gabriel's Rebellion

8-1

8-2

8-3

8-4

8-5

Gabriel's conspiracy had two other consequences. The first involved the Quaker-led antislavery societies of the Chesapeake. These organizations had always been small and weak compared with antislavery societies in the North. The revelation of Gabriel's plot worsened conditions for these organizations. State and local governments suppressed them, or they withered under negative public opinion. The chance that Maryland, Virginia, and North Carolina would follow the northeastern states' example in abolishing slavery gradually and peacefully all but vanished.

The second consequence was that white southerners and many white northerners became convinced that, so long as African Americans lived among them, a race war like the one in Haiti could erupt in the United States. Slaveholders and their defenders argued that this threat did not result from the oppressiveness of slavery. Instead, they claimed, people of African descent were naturally

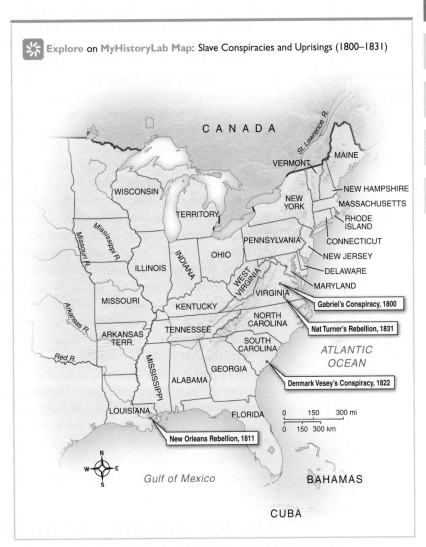

Explore on MyHistoryLab Map: Slave Conspiracies and Uprisings (1800–1831)

MAP 8-1 SLAVE CONSPIRACIES AND UPRISINGS, 1800–1831
Major slave conspiracies and revolts were rare between 1800 and 1860. This was in part because those that took place frightened masters and led them to adopt policies aimed at preventing recurrences.

Does the geographical distribution of slave revolts suggest anything about their nature?

suited for bondage and would be content if a growing class of free black people did not instigate resistance and revolt.

Slavery's defenders contended that free African Americans were a dangerous, criminal, and potentially revolutionary class that had to be regulated, subdued, and ultimately expelled from the country to prevent catastrophe. No system of emancipation that would increase the number of free black people in the United States could be tolerated. Slaveholders who had never shown a willingness to free their slaves began to claim they would favor emancipation if it were not for fear of enlarging such a dangerous group. Without the restrictions slavery placed on African Americans, southern politicians and journalists argued, they would become economic competitors to white workers, a perpetual criminal class, and a revolutionary threat to white rule.

Events in and about Charleston, South Carolina, in 1822 appeared to confirm the threat. In that year black informants revealed that Denmark Vesey, a free black carpenter, had organized a massive slave revolt conspiracy. Like Gabriel before him, Vesey could read and was well aware of the revolutions that had shaken the Atlantic world.

However religion had a more prominent role in Vesey's plot than in Gabriel's. Vesey, a Bible-quoting Methodist who conducted religious classes, resented white authorities' attempts in 1818 to suppress Charleston's African Methodist Episcopal (AME) Church. He believed passages in the Bible about the enslavement of Hebrews in Egypt and their deliverance promised freedom for African Americans. Vesey also relied on aspects of African religion that had survived among low-country slaves to promote his revolutionary efforts. To reach slaves whose Christian convictions blended in with West African spiritualism, he relied on Jack Pritchard—known as Gullah Jack. A "conjure-man" born in East Africa, Pritchard distributed charms and cast spells he claimed would make black revolutionaries invincible.

Vesey and his associates planned to capture arms and ammunition and seize control of Charleston. But about a month before the revolt was to begin, the arrest of one of Vesey's lieutenants put authorities on guard. On June 14, two days before the uprising was to begin, a house servant told his master about the plot, the local government called in the state militia, and arrests followed. Over several weeks, law officers rounded up 131 suspects. The accused received public trials, and juries convicted 76 of them. Thirty-five, including Vesey and Gullah Jack, were hanged.

After the executions, Charleston's city government destroyed what remained of the local AME church, and white churches assumed responsibility for supervising other black congregations. In addition, white South Carolinians sought to make slave patrols more efficient. The state legislature outlawed assemblages of slaves and banned teaching slaves to read. Local authorities jailed black seamen whose ships docked in Charleston until the ships prepared to leave. Assuming that free black and white abolitionists inspired slave unrest, white South Carolinians became more suspicious of local free African Americans and of white Yankees who visited their state.

Read on **MyHistoryLab**
Document:
A Charleston Newspaper Reports on Denmark Vesey's Attempted Uprising, 1822

The Path toward a More Radical Antislavery Movement

8-2 **What forces and events fueled the antislavery movement?**

During the long period from Gabriel's and Vesey's conspiracies, to the year Walker wrote his *Appeal* and beyond, the United States experienced economic, political, and social turmoil. As we described in earlier chapters, the invention of the cotton gin in 1793 led to a vast west-ward expansion of cotton cultivation. Where cotton went, so did slavery. Meanwhile, the states of the Old Northwest passed from frontier conditions to commercial farming, a pro-cess that was facilitated by a revolution in transportation. As steamboats became common and networks of macadam turnpikes (paved with crushed stone and tar), canals, and rail-roads spread, travel time diminished. Americans became more mobile, families scattered, and ties to local communities weakened. For African Americans, subject to the domestic slave trade, mobility came with a high price.

The factory system, which arose in urban areas of the Northeast and spread to parts of the Old Northwest and Upper South, also caused disruption. Cities grew, and increased immigration from Europe meant native black and white people had to compete for em-ployment with foreign-born workers. Farmers became more dependent on urban mar-kets for their crops. The money economy expanded, banks became essential, and private fortunes influenced public policy. Many Americans believed forces beyond their control threatened their way of life and the nation's republican values. They distrusted change and wanted someone to blame for the uncertainties they faced. This outlook encouraged American politics to become paranoid—dominated by fear of hostile conspiracies.

Slavery and Politics

The charge (see Chapter 7) that John Quincy Adams and Henry Clay had cheated Andrew Jackson out of the presidency in early 1825 reflected this fear of conspiracies. What Jackson's supporters called "the corrupt bargain," alongside claims that Adams favored a wealthy and intellectual elite at the expense of the common white man, led to the organization of the Democratic Party and the election of Jackson to the presidency in 1828. The Democrats claimed to stand for the natural rights and economic well-being of American workers and farmers against what they called the "money power," a conspiratorial alliance of bankers and businessmen.

Yet, from its start, the Democratic Party also represented the interests of the South's slaveholding elite. Democratic politicians, North and South, favored a state rights doctrine that protected slavery from interference by the national government. They became the most ardent supporters of expanding slavery into new regions, leading their opponents to claim they were part of a "**slave power**" conspiracy. Although their rhetoric demanded equal rights for all and special privileges for none, they really cared only about the rights of white men.

The Democratic Party's outlook toward American Indians, women, and African Americans demonstrated this. Democratic politicians led in demanding the removal of Indians to the area west of the Mississippi River. This led to the Cherokee "Trail of Tears" in 1838. Democrats also supported patriarchy, a subservient role for women in family life and the church, and their exclusion from the public sphere. Almost all Democratic leaders believed God and nature had designed African Americans to be slaves.

By the mid-1830s, those Americans who favored a more enlightened political program turned—often reluctantly—to the Whig Party, which opposed Jackson and the Democrats. Politicians such as Henry Clay, Daniel Webster, William H. Seward, and John Quincy Adams, who identified with the Whig Party, emphasized Christian morality and an active national government more than the Democrats did. They regarded themselves as conser-vatives, did not seek to end slavery in the South, and included many wealthy slaveholders within their ranks. But in the North, the party's moral orientation and its opposition to territorial expansion by the United States made it attractive to slavery's opponents.

slave power A key concept in abolitionist and northern antislavery propaganda that depicted southern slaveholders as the driving force in a political conspiracy to promote slavery at the expense of white liberties.

The Whig Party also served as the channel through which evangelical Christianity influenced politics. In the North, Whig politicians appealed to evangelical voters. Often evangelicals themselves, some Whig politicians, and journalists defended the human rights of African Americans and American Indians. They criticized the inhumanity of slaveholders and tried to limit federal support for the "peculiar institution." When and where they could, black men voted for Whig candidates.

The Second Great Awakening

Watch on MyHistoryLab Video: The Second Great Awakening

Second Great Awakening A series of religious revivals in the first half of the nineteenth century characterized by great emotionalism in large public meetings.

During the 1730s and 1740s, the revival known as the Great Awakening used emotional preaching and hymn singing to encourage men and women to embrace Jesus and reform their lives. American churches converted black people, and African Americans in turn helped shape the revival. At the end of the eighteenth century, a new, emotional revivalism began. Known as the **Second Great Awakening**, it lasted through the 1830s. It led laymen to replace established clergy as leaders and sought to impose moral order on a turbulent society.

The Second Great Awakening influenced Richard Allen and Absalom Jones's efforts to establish separate black churches in Philadelphia during the 1790s. It helped shape the character of other black churches that emerged during the 1800s and 1810s. These churches became an essential part of the antislavery movement. However more the Second Great Awakening did not peak until the 1820s. During that decade, revivalists helped democratize religion in America. At days-long camp meetings, revivalists preached that all men and women—not just a few—could save their souls. Just as Jacksonian democracy revolutionized politics in America, the Second Great Awakening revolutionized the nation's spiritual life and—especially in the Northeast and Old Northwest—led many Americans, black and white, to join reform movements.

The Benevolent Empire

Benevolent Empire Network of reform associations affiliated with Protestant churches in the early nineteenth century dedicated to the restoration of moral order.

Evangelicals emphasized "practical Christianity." Those who were truly among the saved, they maintained, must through their deeds oppose sin and save others. Black evangelicals, in particular, called for "a *liberating* faith" applied in ways that advanced material and spiritual well-being. This emphasis on action led during the 1810s and 1820s to what became known as the **Benevolent Empire**, a network of church-related organizations. The Benevolent Empire launched what is now known as antebellum or Jacksonian reform.

Centered in the Northeast, this broad social movement flourished through the 1850s. Voluntary associations organized on behalf of a host of causes. Among them were public education, self-improvement, limiting or abolishing alcohol consumption and sales (the temperance movement), prison reform, and aid to the intellectually and physically challenged. Other associations distributed Bibles and religious tracts, funded missionary activities, and discouraged prostitution. Still others sought to improve health, alleviate shipboard conditions for sailors, and—by the 1840s—gain equal rights for women. The self-improvement, temperance, and missionary associations that free black people—and sometimes slaves—formed in urban areas in conjunction with their churches were part of this movement (see Chapter 7). The most important of these reform associations addressed the problem of African-American bondage. Their members were abolitionists, people who favored abolishing slavery in their respective states and throughout the country.

8-1   8-2   8-3   8-4   8-5

✱ EXPLORE ON MYHISTORYLAB

The Second Great Awakening

How did the Second Great Awakening transform the American religious landscape?

The Second Great Awakening was born on the frontier and backcountry. The movement, which emphasized temperance, provided a closer relationship with God than the established conservative churches did. As such, in the western areas of the United States, the Baptist, Methodist, and Presbyterian churches, as well as smaller revivalist churches, expanded.

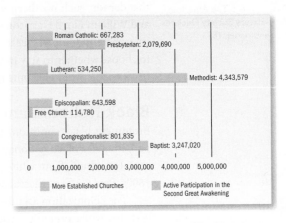

Roman Catholic: 667,283
Presbyterian: 2,079,690
Lutheran: 534,250
Methodist: 4,343,579
Episcopalian: 643,598
Free Church: 114,780
Congregationalist: 801,835
Baptist: 3,247,020

0   1,000,000   2,000,000   3,000,000   4,000,000   5,000,000

☐ More Established Churches   ☐ Active Participation in the Second Great Awakening

This print, published in Harper's Weekly in August 1872, depicts what Harper's calls "A Negro Camp Meeting in the South." Although the print comes from a much later time, it suggests the spirit of revival meetings during the Second Great Awakening.

✱ Explore the Topic on MyHistoryLab

1. **Response** *Which areas were centers of the Second Great Awakening?* Map the strength of the Second Great Awakening in various regions.

2. **Consequence** *What effects did this period of religious fervor have on national politics?* Consider the larger implications of the Second Great Awakening.

3. **Comparison** *How was an area's illiteracy rate linked to the movement's local success?* Consider the reasons for this connection.

8-1

8-2

8-3

8-4

8-5

Colonization

8-3 What were the goals of the American Colonization Society?

The **American Colonization Society (ACS),** founded by white elites, was the most prominent organization of the 1810s and 1820s that *claimed* to be opposed to slavery. However whether it aimed at emancipation is debatable. The ACS had a twofold program. First, it proposed to abolish slavery gradually in the United States, perhaps giving slaveholders financial compensation for giving up their human property. Second, it proposed to send former slaves *and* free African Americans to Africa. To achieve this second goal, the ACS—with the support of the U.S. government—in 1822 formally established the colony of Liberia on the West African coast. The founders of the ACS claimed that free African Americans had to go to Liberia because masters would never emancipate their slaves if they thought

American Colonization Society (ACS) An organization founded in Washington, DC (1816–1912) by prominent slaveholders. It claimed to encourage the ultimate abolition of slavery by sending free African Americans to its West African colony of Liberia.

doing so would increase the size of what they regarded as a shiftless and dangerous free black class. Despite this questionable agenda, the ACS became an integral part of the Benevolent Empire.

The ACS always had its greatest strength in the Upper South and enjoyed the support of slaveholders. But, by the 1820s, the society had branches in every northern state. During that decade, such northern white abolitionists as Arthur and Lewis Tappan, Gerrit Smith, and William Lloyd Garrison supported colonization. They emphasized the ACS's abolitionist aspects and hoped free and soon-to-be-emancipated African Americans would be able to choose whether to stay in the United States or go to Liberia. In either case, they assumed black people would become free.

Read on **MyHistoryLab**
Document: The American Anti-Slavery Society Declares Its Sentiments, 1833

Black Nationalism and Colonization

Prominent black abolitionists initially shared this positive assessment of the ACS. They perpetuated a black nationalist tradition dating back to Prince Hall that, disappointed with repeated rebuffs from white people, endorsed black migration to Africa. During the early 1800s, Paul Cuffe of Massachusetts was the most prominent advocate of this point of view.

black nationalist African Americans who hold the belief that they must seek their racial destiny by establishing separate institutions and, perhaps, migrating as a group to a location (often Africa) outside the United States.

The colonization argument that appealed to Cuffe and many other African Americans was that white prejudice would never allow black people to enjoy full citizenship, equal protection under the law, and economic success in the United States. Black people born in America, this argument held, could enjoy equal rights only in the land of their ancestors. American evangelicalism also led many African Americans to embrace the prospect of bringing Christianity to African nations.

In 1815 Cuffe, who owned and commanded a ship, took 34 African-American settlers to the British free black colony of Sierra Leone, located just north of what became Liberia. Cuffe's death in 1817 prevented him from transporting more settlers to West Africa. Instead, former AME bishop Daniel Coker in 1820 led the first 86 African-American colonists to Liberia. By 1838 approximately 2,500 colonists had made the journey. They lived less than harmoniously with Liberia's 28,000 indigenous inhabitants (see Map 8–2).

In 1847 Liberia became an independent republic. But, despite the efforts of such **black nationalist** advocates as Henry Highland Garnet and Alexander Crummell, only about 10,000 African-American immigrants had gone there by 1860. This number amounted to just 3 percent of the *increase* of America's black population since 1816. Well before 1860, facts demonstrated that African colonization would never fulfill the dreams of its black or white advocates.

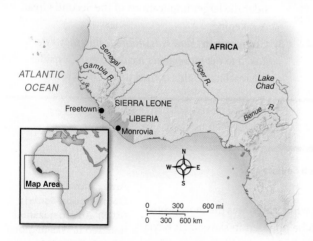

MAP 8–2 THE FOUNDING OF LIBERIA
This map shows the location of Sierra Leone and Liberia in West Africa. British abolitionists established Sierra Leone as a colony for former slaves in 1800. The American Colonization Society established Liberia for the same purpose in 1821.

Why were Sierra Leone and Liberia established in West Africa?

Black Opposition to Colonization

Some African Americans had always opposed overseas colonization, and, as early as 1817, such an influential black leader as James Forten wavered in his support of the ACS. By the mid-1820s, many black abolitionists in cities from Richmond to Boston had criticized colonization in general and the ACS in particular.

Such critics included Samuel Cornish, who in New York City in 1827 began publishing *Freedom's Journal*, the first African-American newspaper. Cornish, a young Presbyterian minister, called for independent black action against slavery. However John Russwurm—the *Journal's* cofounder—was less opposed than Cornish to the ACS. This disagreement contributed to the suspension of the newspaper in 1829. That same year Russwurm, one of the first African Americans to earn a college degree, moved to Liberia.

In contrast to Russwurm, people like Cornish wanted to improve their condition in the United States. They considered Liberia to be foreign and unhealthy. They had no desire to go to Africa or send other African Americans there. They also feared ACS proposals for *voluntary* colonization misled because nearly every southern state required the expulsion of slaves individually freed by their masters. The Maryland and Virginia legislatures were considering legislation designed to require *all* free black people to leave those states or be enslaved. These efforts failed, but they added to African-American fears that colonization would be forced on them.

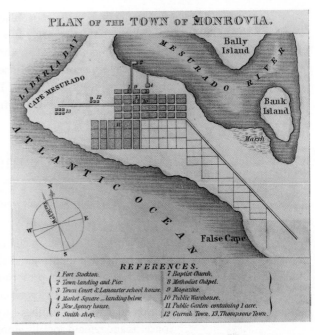

Monrovia, Liberia, c. 1830. This map shows the American Colonization Society's main Liberian settlement as it existed about 10 years after its founding.

8-1

8-2

8-3

8-4

8-5

VOICES   William Watkins Opposes Colonization

In response to a white clergyman who argued that migration to Africa would help alleviate the plight of African Americans, William Watkins stressed black unity, education, and self-improvement in this country.

[The Reverend Mr. Hewitt says] "Let us unite into select societies for the purpose of digesting a plan for raising funds to be appropriated to this grand object" [African colonization]. This we cannot do; we intend to let the burden of this work rest upon the shoulders of those who wish us out of the country. We will, however, compromise the matter with our friend. We are willing and anxious to "unite into select societies for the purpose of digesting a plan": for the improvement of our people in science, morals, domestic economy, &c. We are willing and anxious to form union societies . . . that shall discountenance and destroy, as far as

possible, those unhappy schisms which have too long divided us, though we are brethren. We are willing to unite . . . in the formation of temperance societies . . . that will enable us to exhibit to the world an amount of moral power that would give new impetus to our friends and "strike alarm" into the breasts of our enemies, if not wholly disarm them of the weapons they are hurling against us.

1. **According to Watkins, how will black self-improvement societies help counter colonization?**

2. **What difficulties does Watkins believe African Americans must overcome to make themselves stronger in the United States?**

SOURCE: "A Colored American [Watkins] to Editors," n.d., in *Genius of Universal Emancipation*, December 18, 1829.

8-1

8-2

8-3

8-4

8-5

By the mid-1820s, most black abolitionists had concluded that the ACS represented a proslavery effort to drive free African Americans from the United States. The ACS, they maintained, was not an antislavery organization at all but a proslavery scheme to force free black people to choose between reenslavement or banishment. America, they argued, was their native land. They knew nothing of Africa. Efforts to have them go there rested on a racist assumption that they were not entitled to live in freedom in the land of their birth.

Black Abolitionist Women

8-4   **What role did black women play in the abolition movement?**

Black women joined black men in opposing slavery. In considering their role, it is important to understand that the United States in the early nineteenth century had a rigid gender hierarchy. Law and custom proscribed women from engaging in politics, the professions, and most businesses. In this view, women deemed respectable by black and white Americans—the women of wealthy families—were expected to devote themselves exclusively to domestic concerns and remain socially aloof. Church and benevolent activities constituted their only opportunities for public action. Even in these arenas, custom relegated women to work in auxiliaries to men's organizations.

This was true of the first *formal* abolitionist groups of black women. Among the leaders were Charlotte Forten, the wife of James Forten, and Maria W. Stewart, the widow of a well-to-do Boston ship outfitter. In 1833 Charlotte and her daughters joined other black and white women to found the **Philadelphia Female Anti-Slavery Society**. A year earlier, other black women had established in Salem, Massachusetts, the first women's antislavery society. Women of the black elite also supported the education of black children. They hoped that, as African Americans gained knowledge, white prejudice that supported slavery would diminish.

Stewart's brief career as an antislavery orator provoked far more controversy than those of the Fortens or other early black abolitionist women. Influenced by Walker's *Appeal* and encouraged by William Lloyd Garrison, Stewart in 1831 and 1832 became the first American woman publicly to address male audiences. Stewart pointedly called on black men to act against slavery. "It is true," she told a group assembled at the African Masonic Hall in Boston in 1833, "our fathers bled and died in the revolutionary war, and others fought bravely under the command of [General Andrew] Jackson [at New Orleans in 1815], in defense of liberty. But where is the man that has distinguished himself in these modern days by acting wholly in the defense of African rights and liberty?" Such remarks from a woman cut deeply. Thereafter Stewart met such hostility from the black community that in September 1833 she retired as a public speaker.

Many black women—and white women—did not fit the early nineteenth-century criteria for respectability that applied to the Fortens, Stewart, and others among the African-American elite. Most black women lacked wealth and education. They had to work outside their homes. Particularly in the Upper South, these women became *practical* abolitionists.

From the revolutionary era onward, countless anonymous black women, both slave and free, living in southern border cities risked everything to harbor fugitive slaves. Others saved their meager earnings to purchase freedom for themselves and their loved ones. Among

Read on MyHistoryLab
Document: A Black Feminist Speaks Out in 1851

Philadelphia Female Anti-Slavery Society A biracial abolitionist organization (1833–1870) aligned with the American Anti-Slavery Society. White Quaker women dominated the society, but it included a significant number of black women.

Listen on MyHistoryLab
Audio: What If I Am a Woman? Speech by Maria W. Stewart; read by Ruby Dee

VOICES A Black Woman Speaks Out on the Right to Education

Historians generally believe the antebellum women's rights movement emerged from the antislavery movement during the late 1830s. But as the following letter, published in Freedom's Journal *on August 10, 1827, indicates, some black women advocated equal rights for women much earlier:*

Messrs. Editors,

Will you allow a female to offer a few remarks upon a subject that you must allow to be all-important? I don't know that in any of your papers, you have said sufficient upon the education of females. I hope you are not to be classed with those, who think that our mathematical knowledge should be limited to "fathoming the dish-kettle," and that we have acquired enough of history, if we know that our grandfather's father lived and died. . . . The diffusion of knowledge has destroyed those degraded opinions, and men of the present age, allow, that we have minds that are capable and deserving of culture. There are difficulties . . . in the way of our advancement; but that should

only stir us to greater efforts. We possess not the advantages with those of our sex, whose skins are not coloured like our own, but we can improve what little we have, and make our one talent produce two-fold. . . . Ignorant ourselves, how can we be expected to form the minds of our youth, and conduct them in the paths of knowledge? I would address myself to all mothers. . . . It is their bounden duty to store their daughters' minds with useful learning. They should be made to devote their leisure time to reading books, whence they would derive valuable information, which could never be taken from them . . . Matilda

> 1. **How does Matilda use sarcasm to make her point?**
> 2. **What special difficulties did black women like Matilda face in asserting their rights?**

SOURCE: Herbert Aptheker, ed., *A Documentary History of the Negro People in the United States,* 7 vols. (1951; reprint, New York: Citadel, 1990), 1: 89. Reprinted by permission of Bettina Aptheker, Literary Executer, Herbert Aptheker Estate.

8-1
8-2
8-3
8-4
8-5

them was Alethia Tanner of Washington, who purchased her freedom in 1810 for $1,400 (about $25,600 today). During the 1820s she purchased the freedom of her sister, her sister's 10 children, and her sister's five grandchildren. During the 1830s Tanner purchased the freedom of seven more slaves.

The Baltimore Alliance

Among the stronger black abolitionist opponents of the ACS were William Watkins, Jacob Greener, and Hezekiah Grice. All three worked in Baltimore with Benjamin Lundy, a white Quaker abolitionist who published an antislavery newspaper.

In 1829 Watkins, Greener, and Grice profoundly influenced William Lloyd Garrison, who later became the most influential American antislavery leader. Lundy had convinced Garrison—a young abolitionist and temperance advocate—to leave his native Massachusetts to come to Baltimore as the associate editor of his newspaper. Garrison, a deeply religious product of the Second Great Awakening and a well-schooled journalist, had decided before he came to Baltimore that *gradual* abolition was neither practical nor moral.

Garrison, however, tolerated the ACS until he came under the influence of Watkins, Greener, and Grice. They set him on a course that transformed the abolitionist movement in the United States during the early 1830s. They also initiated a bond between African Americans and Garrison that—although strained at times—shaped the rest of his antislavery career.

In 1831, when he began publishing his abolitionist newspaper, *The Liberator,* in Boston, Garrison led the antislavery movement in a radical direction. It was radical not so much because Garrison rejected gradual abolition and called for immediate emancipation. He had earlier rejected gradualism, and he was not the first to endorse **immediatism**. Instead, the insight he gained from his association with African Americans in Baltimore is what made his brand of abolitionism revolutionary. He learned from Watkins, Greener, and others that immediate emancipation must be combined with a commitment to racial justice in the United States. Immediate emancipation without compensating slaveholders and without expatriating African Americans became the core of Garrison's program for the rest of his long antislavery career.

((•)) Listen on MyHistoryLab
Audio: *The Liberator*

immediatism Refers to an antislavery movement that began in the United States during the late 1820s, which demanded that slavery be abolished immediately rather than gradually.

David Walker and Nat Turner

((•)) ▭ Read on MyHistoryLab Document: David Walker's *Appeal*

8-5 Why was Walker's *Appeal* important?

Two other black abolitionists, David Walker and Nat Turner, helped shape Garrison's brand of abolitionism. Walker and Turner had several things in common. They were from the South and both were deeply religious. They also advocated employing violent means against slavery and had an impact on both the white South and northern abolitionists. Otherwise their circumstances differed, as did the form of their antislavery efforts.

Walker's *Appeal . . . to the Colored Citizens of the World,* was published in Boston in 1829. In it Walker, who in his youth may have been influenced by Denmark Vesey, furiously attacked slavery and white racism. He suggested that slaves use violence to secure their liberty.

The *Appeal* shaped the struggle over slavery in three ways. First, although Garrison advocated only peaceful means, Walker's harsh writing style influenced the tone of Garrison and other advocates of immediate abolition. Second, Walker's effort to instill hope and pride in an oppressed people inspired an increasingly militant black abolitionism. Third, his pamphlet and his ability to have it circulated among free African Americans in the South contributed to white southern fear of encirclement from without and subversion from within. This fear encouraged the section's leaders to make demands on the North that helped bring on the Civil War.

In this last respect, Nat Turner's contribution exceeded Walker's in its impact. Slave conspiracies had not ended with Denmark Vesey's execution in 1822. But in 1831 Turner, a privileged slave from eastern Virginia, became the first to initiate a large-scale slave uprising since Charles Deslondes's revolt in Louisiana in 1811. As a result, Turner inspired far greater fear among white southerners than Walker had.

During the years before Turner's uprising, unrest among slaves in Virginia had increased, and Walker's *Appeal* may have contributed to this.

((•)) ▭ Read on MyHistoryLab Document: William Lloyd Garrison Demands an Immediate End to Slavery, 1831

William Lloyd Garrison (1805–1879) was the leading American abolitionist during the 1830s. He called for immediate emancipation of American slaves, without compensation to their masters, and led the American Anti-Slavery Society.

8-1
8-2
8-3
8-4
8-5

So may have class and regional divisions among white Virginians. In anticipation of a state constitutional convention in 1829, white people in western Virginia, where there were few slaveholders, had called for emancipation. Poorer white men demanded an end to the property qualifications that denied them the vote. As the convention approached, a "spirit of dissatisfaction and insubordination" became manifest among slaves. Some armed themselves and escaped north. As proslavery Virginians grew fearful, they demanded additional restrictions on the ability of local free black people and northern abolitionists to influence slaves.

Yet no evidence indicates that Turner or any of his associates had read Walker's *Appeal*, had contact with northern abolitionists, or knew about divisions among white Virginians. Also, although Turner *did* know about the successful slave revolt in Haiti, he was more a religious visionary than a political revolutionary. As a young man, he spent much of his time studying and memorizing the Bible. He became a lay preacher and a leader among local slaves. By the late 1820s, he had begun to have visions that convinced him God intended him to lead his people to freedom through violence.

After considerable planning, Turner began his uprising on the evening of August 21, 1831. His band, which numbered between 60 and 70, killed 57 white men, women, and children before militia put down the revolt the following morning. That November, Turner and 17 others were executed. In addition, panicked white people in nearby parts of Virginia and North Carolina killed more than 100 African Americans whom they—almost always incorrectly—suspected of being in league with the rebels.

The bloodshed in Virginia inspired general revulsion. White southerners—and some northerners—accused Garrison and other abolitionists of inspiring the revolt. In response, northern abolitionists of both races asserted their commitment to a *peaceful* struggle against slavery. Yet black and white abolitionists respected Turner. Black

Watch on
MyHistoryLab
Video: Nat Turner

Read on **MyHistoryLab**
Document: *Leader of the Slave Rebellion in Southampton, VA*, Told to and Published by Thomas R. Gray, 1831

8-1

8-2

8-3

8-4

8-5

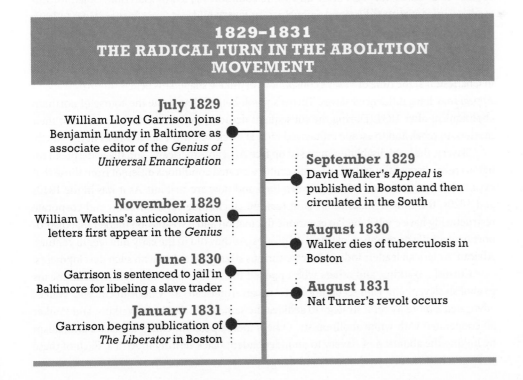

1829–1831
THE RADICAL TURN IN THE ABOLITION MOVEMENT

July 1829
William Lloyd Garrison joins Benjamin Lundy in Baltimore as associate editor of the *Genius of Universal Emancipation*

September 1829
David Walker's *Appeal* is published in Boston and then circulated in the South

November 1829
William Watkins's anticolonization letters first appear in the *Genius*

August 1830
Walker dies of tuberculosis in Boston

June 1830
Garrison is sentenced to jail in Baltimore for libeling a slave trader

August 1831
Nat Turner's revolt occurs

January 1831
Garrison begins publication of *The Liberator* in Boston

Read on **MyHistoryLab Document:** The Confessions of Nat Turner, 1831

This recently colorized drawing of the capture of Nat Turner dates to the 1830s. Turner avoided apprehension for nearly two months following the suppression of his revolt. The artist conveys how Turner maintained his dignity in surrender.

8-1

8-2

8-3

8-4

8-5

abolitionists accorded him the same heroic stature they gave Toussaint Louverture and Gabriel. This tension between lip service to peaceful means and admiration for violence against slavery characterized the antislavery movement for the next 30 years.

CONCLUSION

This chapter has focused on the two principal antislavery movements in the United States before 1833. One movement existed in the South among slaves. The other centered in the North and the Chesapeake among free African Americans and white abolitionists. The two movements shared roots in the age of revolution, and each gained vitality from evangelical Christianity. The Second Great Awakening and the reforming spirit of the Benevolent Empire shaped the northern antislavery effort. The black church, the Bible, and elements of African religion helped inspire slave revolutionaries.

The antislavery movement that existed in the North and portions of the Upper South was always biracial and emphasized peaceful means to end slavery. During the 1810s and for much of the 1820s, many black abolitionists embraced a form of nationalism that encouraged them to cooperate with the conservative white people who led the ACS. As the racist and proslavery nature of that organization became clear, most northern black and white abolitionists, led by Garrison, called for immediate, uncompensated general emancipation that would not force former slaves to leave the United States.

Unlike northern abolitionists, Gabriel, Vesey, and Turner had to rely on violence to fight slavery. However, the two movements had similarities and influenced each other. Walker's life in Charleston at the time of Vesey's conspiracy very likely shaped his beliefs. In turn, Walker's *Appeal* may have influenced slaves. Turner's revolt helped determine the course of northern abolitionism after 1831. During the subsequent decades, the efforts of slaves to resist their masters, to rebel, and to escape influenced radical black and white abolitionists in the North.

Slavery, the legal disabilities imposed on free African Americans, and the widespread religious revivalism of the early nineteenth century created conditions different from those that exist today. But some similarities between then and now are striking. As it was in the 1810s and 1820s, the United States today is in turmoil. Technological innovation and corporate restructuring have contributed to economic fluctuation and a volatile job market that disproportionately affects members of minority groups. As they did in the early nineteenth century, African-American leaders today advocate various strategies to deal with such developments.

Cornish, Watkins, and others who opposed the ACS sought through peaceful means to abolish slavery and gain recognition of African Americans as American citizens. Walker advocated a more forceful strategy to achieve the same ends. Cornish, Watkins, and Walker all cooperated with white abolitionists. Others took a position closer to black nationalism by linking the abolition of slavery to an independent black destiny in Africa. Each of these strategies had virtues, weaknesses, and dangers.

CHAPTER TIMELINE

AFRICAN-AMERICAN EVENTS	NATIONAL AND WORLD EVENTS

1790–1800

1796 or 1797
David Walker born

1791
Haitian Revolution begins

1796
John Adams elected president

1798
Undeclared Franco-American naval war

1800–1810

1800
Gabriel's conspiracy is exposed

1803
Maria W. Stewart born

1805
William Lloyd Garrison born

1800
Thomas Jefferson elected president

1803–1806
Lewis and Clark Expedition

1807
Britain bans Atlantic slave trade

1808
United States bans Atlantic slave trade

1810–1820

1811
Louisiana slave revolt

1815
Paul Cuffe leads African Americans to Sierra Leone

1816
American Colonization Society is formed

1812
War of 1812 begins

1815
War of 1812 ends

1816
James Madison elected president

1820–1830

1822
Denmark Vesey's conspiracy exposed

1824
Benjamin Lundy comes to Baltimore

1827
Freedom's Journal begins publication

1829
William Lloyd Garrison comes to Baltimore;
David Walkers's Appeal

1820
Missouri Compromise passed

1824
John Quincy Adams elected president

1828
Andrew Jackson elected president

1830–1850

1831
Nat Turner's Revolt is suppressed

1832
Great increase in migration to United States begins

1846–1848
Indian Removal Act passed by Congress

On MyHistoryLab

✓ Study and Review on MyHistoryLab

Review Questions

1. What did the program of the ACS mean for African Americans? How did they respond to this program?

2. Analyze the role played in abolitionism (1) by Christianity and (2) by the revolutionary tradition in the Atlantic world. Which was more important in shaping the views of black and white abolitionists?

3. Evaluate the interaction of black and white abolitionists during the early nineteenth century. How did their motives for becoming abolitionists differ?

4. How did Gabriel, Denmark Vesey, and Nat Turner influence the northern abolitionist movement?

5. What risks did Maria W. Stewart take when she called publicly for antislavery action?

Let Your Motto Be Resistance 1833–1850

((Listen to **Chapter 9**
on **MyHistoryLab**

LEARNING OBJECTIVES

How did the racism and violence of the 1830s and 1840s affect the antislavery movement?	**9-1**
What roles did black institutions and moral suasion play in the antislavery movement?	**9-2**
What was the role of black churches and black newspapers in the abolitionist movement?	**9-3**
What were the reasons for the breakup of the American Anti-Slavery Society and what organizations emerged to replace it?	**9-4**
How did abolitionism become more aggressive during the 1840s and 1850s?	**9-5**
How did the views of Frederick Douglass differ from those of Henry Highland Garnet?	**9-6**

When black abolitionist Henry Highland Garnet spoke at the National Convention of Colored Citizens, held in Buffalo, New York, on August 16, 1843, he caused a tremendous stir among those assembled. In 1824, when he was a boy, Garnet had escaped with his family from slavery in Maryland. Thereafter he received an excellent education while growing up in New York. By the 1840s, he had become a powerful speaker. But some of the delegates in his audience pointed out that he was far away from the slaves he claimed to address. Others believed he risked encouraging a potentially disastrous slave revolt. Therefore, by a narrow margin, the convention refused to endorse his speech.

In fact, Garnet had not called for slave revolt but rather for a general strike. This, he contended, would put the onus of initiating violence on masters. Nevertheless, Garnet's speech reflected a new militancy among black and white abolitionists that shaped the antislavery movement during the two decades before the Civil War.

This chapter investigates the causes of that militancy and explores the role of African Americans in the antislavery movement from the establishment of the American Anti-Slavery Society in 1833 to the **Compromise of 1850**. Largely in response to changes in American culture, unrest among slaves, and sectional conflict between North and South, the biracial northern antislavery movement during this period became splintered and diverse. Yet it also became more powerful.

A group of women and children prepare to ford a river as they escape from slavery. Most escapees were young men, but people of both sexes and all age-groups undertook to reach freedom in the North or Canada.

Theodor Kaufmann (1814–1896), "On to Liberty," 1867, Oil on canvas, 36 × 56 in (91.4 × 142.2 cm). The Metropolitan Museum of Art. Gift of Erving and Joyce Wolf, 1982 (1982.443.3). Photograph © The Metropolitan Museum of Art. /Art Resource, NY.

Compromise of 1850 An attempt by the U.S. Congress to settle divisive issues between the North and South, including slavery expansion, apprehension in the North of fugitive slaves, and slavery in the District of Columbia.

Manifest Destiny Doctrine, first expressed in 1845, that the expansion of white Americans across the continent was inevitable and ordained by God.

9-1

9-2

9-3

9-4

9-5

9-6

A Rising Tide of Racism and Violence

9-1 How did the racism and violence of the 1830s and 1840s affect the antislavery movement?

Militancy among abolitionists reflected increasing American racism and violence from the 1830s through the Civil War. White Americans' embrace of an exuberant nationalism called **Manifest Destiny** contributed to this trend. This doctrine, which defined political and economic progress in racial terms, held that God intended the United States to expand its territory, by war if necessary. Another factor was that the American School of Ethnology continued the development of the "scientific" racism that had begun during the late eighteenth century (see Chapter 5). According to these pseudoscientists, white people—particularly white Americans—were a superior race, entitled to rule over other races. As Manifest Destiny gave divine sanction to imperialism, the American School of Ethnology justified white Americans in their continued enslavement of African Americans and extermination of American Indians.

A wave of racially motivated violence, committed by the federal and state governments as well as by white vigilantes, accompanied these developments. Starting in the 1790s, the army waged a systematic campaign to remove American Indians from the states and relocate them west of the Mississippi River (see Chapter 6). During the same decade, antiblack riots became common in northern cities. Wealthy "gentlemen of property and standing," who believed they defended the social order, led the rioters.

Antiblack and Antiabolitionist Riots

Antiblack riots coincided with the start of immediate abolitionism during the late 1820s. The riots became more common as abolitionism gained strength during the 1830s and 1840s (see Figure 9–1 and Map 9–1). Although few northern cities escaped attacks on African Americans and their property, riots in Cincinnati, Providence, New York City, and Philadelphia were infamous.

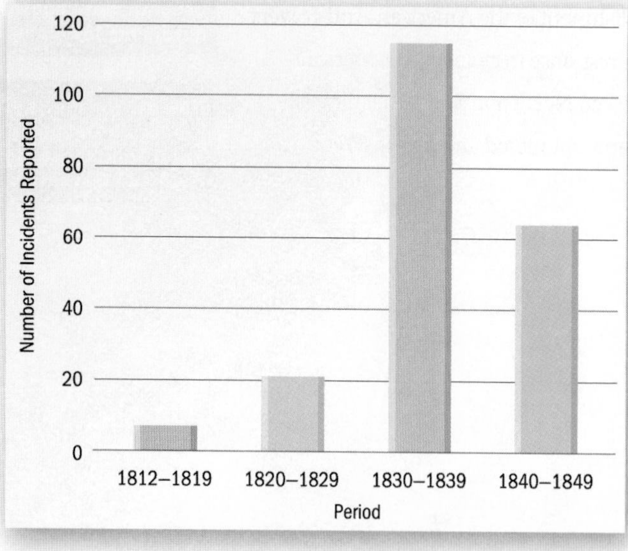

In 1829 a three-day riot instigated by local politicians led many black Cincinnatians to flee to Canada. In 1836 and 1841, mob attacks on the *Philanthropist,* Cincinnati's white-run abolitionist newspaper, expanded into attacks on African-American homes and businesses. During each riot, black residents defended their property with guns. In 1831 white sailors led a mob in Providence that literally tore that city's black neighborhood to pieces. In New York City in 1834, a mob destroyed 12 houses owned by black residents, a black church, a black school, and the home of white abolitionist Lewis Tappan.

No city had more or worse race riots than Philadelphia—the City of Brotherly Love. In 1820, 1829, 1834, 1835, 1838, 1842, and 1849,

FIGURE 9–1 MOB VIOLENCE IN THE UNITED STATES, 1812–1849 This graph illustrates the rise of mob violence in the North in reaction to abolitionist activity. Attacks on abolitionists peaked during the 1830s and then declined as antislavery sentiment spread in the North.

antiblack rampages broke out. In 1838 a white mob burned Pennsylvania Hall, which abolitionists had just built and dedicated to free discussion. The ugliest riot came in 1842 when Irish immigrants led a mob that assaulted members of a black temperance society. When African Americans defended themselves with muskets, the mob responded by looting and burning Philadelphia's principal black neighborhood.

Texas and the War against Mexico

Not only northern cities experienced violence. Under President James K. Polk, the United States adopted a belligerent foreign policy, especially toward the Republic of Mexico, located on its southwestern border. Mexico had gained its independence from Spain in 1822 and in 1829 had abolished slavery within its bounds. Meanwhile, American slaveholders settled in the Mexican province of Texas. At the time, the gigantic regions then known as California and New Mexico (now comprising the states of California, Arizona, New Mexico, Utah, and part of Colorado) also belonged to Mexico. In 1836 Texas won independence and, as a slaveholding republic, applied for annexation to the United States as a slave state. At first Democratic and Whig politicians, who realized that adding a large new slave state to the Union would divide the country along North–South lines, rebuffed the application. But the desire for new territory, encouraged by Manifest Destiny and an expanding slave-labor economy, could not be denied. In 1844 Polk, then the Democratic presidential candidate, called for the annexation of Texas and Oregon, a huge territory in the Pacific Northwest that the United States and Britain had been jointly administering. After Polk defeated Whig candidate Henry Clay, Congress in early 1845 annexed Texas by joint resolution as a slaveholding state.

In early 1846 Polk backed away from confronting Britain over Oregon, agreeing to split its territory along the 49th degree of latitude. Then, a few months later, Polk provoked a war against Mexico that by 1848 forced that country to recognize American sovereignty over Texas and to cede New Mexico and California to the United States (see Map 10-1 on page 198 in Chapter 10). Immediately, the major American political question became: Would

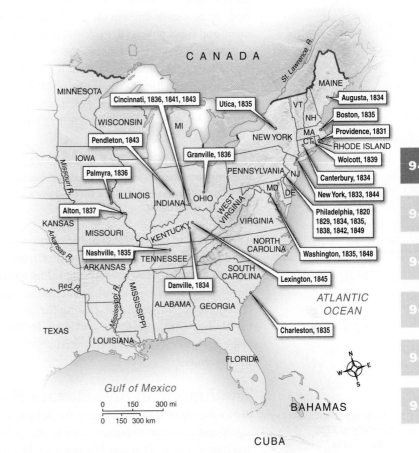

MAP 9-1 ANTIABOLITIONIST AND ANTIBLACK RIOTS DURING THE ANTEBELLUM PERIOD
African Americans faced violent conditions in both the North and South during the antebellum years. Fear among whites of growing free black communities and white antipathy toward spreading abolitionism sparked numerous antiblack and antiabolitionist riots.

Why did most of these riots occur in the Northeast?

View on MyHistoryLab
Closer Look: Texas: From Mexican Province to U.S. State

slavery expand into these territories? If it did, many northerners expected slaveholders to push for new slave states in the Southwest, use their votes to dominate the federal government, and enact policies detrimental to northern workers and farmers.

As such fears spread across the North, slaveholders in turn feared that northerners would seek to exclude slavery from the western lands southerners had helped wrest from Mexico. The resulting Compromise of 1850 (see Chapter 10) attempted to satisfy both sections. But it subjected African Americans to additional violence because part of the Compromise met slaveholders' demands for a stronger fugitive slave law.

The Antislavery Movement

9-2 **What roles did black institutions and moral suasion play in the antislavery movement?**

The increase in race-related violence caused difficulties for an antislavery movement that was itself not free of racial strife and officially limited to peaceful means. Even though African Americans found loyal white allies within the movement, interracial understanding did not come easily. As white abolitionists assumed they should set policy, their black colleagues became resentful. During the same period, abolitionist opposition to achieving abolition through force weakened. By the end of the 1830s, greater autonomy for black abolitionists and peaceful versus violent means became contentious issues within the movement.

The American Anti-Slavery Society

American Anti-Slavery Society (AASS, 1833–1870) The umbrella organization for immediate abolitionists during the 1830s and the main Garrisonian organization after 1840.

Before the era of Manifest Destiny, the **American Anti-Slavery Society (AASS)**—the most significant abolitionist organization of the 1830s—emerged from a turning point in the abolitionist cause. This was William Lloyd Garrison's decision in 1831 to create a movement dedicated to immediate, uncompensated emancipation and to equal rights for African Americans in the United States (see Chapter 8). To reach these goals, abolitionists organized the AASS in December 1833 at Philadelphia's Adelphi Hall.

No white American worked harder than Garrison to bridge racial differences. He spoke to black groups, stayed in the homes of African Americans when he traveled, and welcomed them to his home. Black abolitionists responded with affection and loyalty. But Garrison, like most other white abolitionists, remained stiff and condescending in conversation with black colleagues, and the black experience in the AASS reflected this.

On one hand, it is remarkable that the AASS allowed black men to participate in its meetings without formal restrictions. At the time, no other American organization did so. On the other hand, that black participation was paltry. Three African Americans—James McCrummell, Robert Purvis, and James G. Barbadoes—helped found the AASS, and McCrummell presided at its first meeting. But, among 60 white people attending that meeting, these three were the only African Americans. Throughout the AASS's existence, it rarely allowed black people to hold positions of authority.

As state and local auxiliaries of the AASS organized across the North during the early 1830s, these patterns repeated themselves. Black men participated but did not lead. Black and white women—with some exceptions—could observe the proceedings of these organizations but not participate in them. It took a three-year struggle between 1837 and 1840 over "the woman question" before an AASS annual meeting elected a woman to a leadership position, and that victory helped split the organization.

Read on **MyHistoryLab** Document: The American Anti-Slavery Society Declares Its Sentiments, 1833

Wealthy black abolitionist Robert Purvis is at the very center of this undated photograph of the Philadelphia Anti-Slavery Society. The famous Quaker abolitionist Lucretia Mott and her husband James Mott are seated to Purvis's left. Equally significant as Purvis's central location in the photograph is that he is the *only* African American pictured.

Black and Women's Antislavery Societies

In these circumstances, black men, black women, and white women formed auxiliaries to the AASS. Often African Americans belonged to all-black *and* to integrated, predominantly white auxiliaries. The black organizations arose in part because of racial discord in the predominantly white organizations and because of a black desire for racial solidarity. But, as historian Benjamin Quarles notes, during the 1830s "the founders of Negro societies did not envision their efforts as distinctive or self-contained; rather they viewed their role as that of a true auxiliary—supportive, supplemental, and subsidiary." Despite their differences, black and white abolitionists belonged to a single movement.

All of the women's antislavery societies concentrated on fund-raising. They held bake sales, organized antislavery fairs and bazaars, and sold antislavery memorabilia. The proceeds went to the AASS or to antislavery newspapers. The women's societies also inspired feminism by creating awareness that women had rights and interests that a male-dominated society had to recognize. By writing essays and poems on political subjects and making public speeches, abolitionist women challenged a culture that relegated *respectable* women to domestic duties. During the 1850s famous African-American speaker Sojourner Truth emphasized that all black women, through their physical labor and the pain they suffered in slavery, had earned equal standing with men and their more favored white sisters.

Black men and women also formed auxiliaries during the early 1830s to the Quaker-initiated Free Produce Association, which tried to put economic pressure on slaveholders by boycotting agricultural products produced by slaves. James Cornish led the Colored Free Produce Society of Pennsylvania, which marketed meat, vegetables, cotton, and sugar produced by free labor. With a similar aim, Judith James and Laetitia Rowley organized

 Read on **MyHistoryLab** Document: Elizabeth Margaret Chandler Calls on Women to Become Abolitionists, 1836

 Listen on **MyHistoryLab** Audio: *The Rebirth of Sojourner Truth.* Read by Jean Brannon.

the Colored Female Free Produce Society of Pennsylvania. During the 1850s Frances Ellen Watkins Harper, one of the few prominent black female speakers of the time, always included the free produce movement in her abolitionist lectures and wrote newspaper articles on its behalf.

Moral Suasion

moral suasion
A tactic endorsed by the American Anti-Slavery Society during the 1830s. It appealed to slaveholders and others to support immediate emancipation on the basis of Christian principles.

During the 1830s the AASS adopted a reform strategy based on **moral suasion**—what we would today call moral *persuasion*. This was an appeal to Americans North and South to support abolition and racial justice on the basis of their Christian consciences. Slaveholding, the AASS argued, was a sin and a crime that deprived African Americans of the freedom of conscience they needed to save their souls. Slaveholding led masters to damnation through their indolence, sexual exploitation of black women, and brutality. Abolitionists also argued that slavery was an inefficient labor system that enriched a few masters while impoverishing black and white southerners and hurting the American economy.

Abolitionists did not just criticize white southerners. They noted as well that northern industrialists thrived by manufacturing cloth from cotton produced by slave labor. They pointed out that the U.S. government protected the interests of slaveholders. Northerners who profited from slave-produced cotton and supported the national government with their votes and taxes bore their share of guilt for slavery and faced divine punishment.

The AASS sought to use such arguments to convince masters to free their slaves. They also used them to persuade northerners and nonslaveholding white southerners to put pressure on slaveholders. To reach a white southern audience, the AASS in 1835 launched the Great Postal Campaign to send antislavery literature to southern post offices and individual slaveholders. At about the same time, the AASS organized a petitioning campaign aimed to agitate the slavery issue in Congress. Antislavery women led in circulating and signing the petitions. In 1836 over 30,000 petitions reached Washington.

In the North, AASS agents lectured against slavery and distributed antislavery literature. Often a pair of agents—one black and one white—traveled together. Ideally, the black agent would be a former slave, so he could testify from personal experience to the brutality and immorality of slavery. During the early 1840s, the AASS paired fugitive slave Frederick Douglass with William A. White, a young white Harvard graduate, in a tour through Ohio and Indiana. At first, all the agents were men. Later, abolitionist organizations also employed women.

The reaction to these efforts in the North and the South was not what the leaders of the AASS anticipated. As the story in the Voices box on Frederick Douglass relates, by speaking of racial justice and exemplifying interracial cooperation, abolitionists trod new ground. This created awkward situations that are—in retrospect—humorous. But their audiences often reacted very negatively. Southern postmasters burned antislavery literature, and southern state governments censored the mail. Vigilantes drove off white southerners who openly advocated abolition. Black abolitionists, of course, did not dare denounce slavery when and if they visited the South.

In 1836 southern representatives and their northern allies in Congress passed the Gag Rule forbidding petitions related to slavery from being introduced in the House of Representatives.

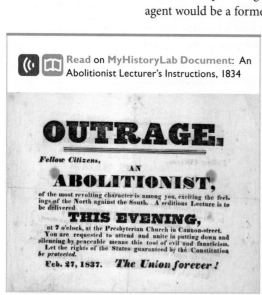

Read on MyHistoryLab Document: An Abolitionist Lecturer's Instructions, 1834

OUTRAGE,

Fellow Citizens,

AN

ABOLITIONIST,

of the most revolting character is among you, exciting the feelings of the North against the South. A seditious Lecture is to be delivered

THIS EVENING,

at 7 o'clock, at the Presbyterian Church in Cannon-street. You are requested to attend and unite in putting down and silencing by peaceable means this tool of evil and fanaticism. Let the rights of the States guaranteed by the Constitution be protected.

Feb. 27, 1837. *The Union forever!*

In an effort to stir antiabolitionist feelings, this broadside announces an upcoming abolitionist lecture at a local New York church.

In response, the AASS sent 415,000 petitions in 1838, and Congressman (and former president) John Quincy Adams began his struggle against the Gag. Adams succeeded in having the Gag repealed in 1844.

Meanwhile, northern mobs continued to assault abolitionist agents, disrupt their meetings, destroy their newspaper presses, and attack black neighborhoods. In 1837 a proslavery mob killed white abolitionist journalist Elijah P. Lovejoy as he defended his printing press in Alton, Illinois. On another occasion, as Douglass, White, and older white abolitionist George Bradburn held an antislavery meeting in the small town of Pendleton, Indiana, an enraged mob attempted to kill Douglass.

Black Community Support

9-3   **What was the role of black churches and black newspapers in the abolitionist movement?**

A maturing African-American community undergirded the antislavery movement and helped it survive violent opposition. The free black population of the United States grew from 59,000 in 1790 to 434,449 in 1850. Gradual emancipation in the northern states, acts of individual manumission in the Upper South, escapes, and a high birthrate accounted for this sevenfold increase. The concentration of a growing black population in such cities as New York, Philadelphia, Baltimore, Boston, and Cincinnati strengthened it. These cities had enough African Americans to support the independent churches, schools, benevolent organizations, and printing presses that self-conscious communities required. These communities became bedrocks of abolitionism.

The Black Convention Movement

The dozens of local, state, and national black conventions held in the North between 1830 and 1864 helped inspire the larger black community. These conventions also manifested the antebellum American reform impulse. Their agenda transcended the antislavery cause. Nevertheless, they provided a setting in which abolitionism could grow and adapt to meet the demands of a sectionally polarized and violent time.

Hezekiah Grice, a young black man who had worked with Benjamin Lundy and William Lloyd Garrison in Baltimore during the 1820s (see Chapter 8), organized the first Black National Convention. The national convention became an annual event for the next five years. During the same period, many state and local black conventions met across the North. All the conventions were small and informal. Still, they were attractive venues for discussing and publicizing black concerns. They called for the abolition of slavery and improving conditions for northern African Americans.

The conventions also stressed black self-help through temperance, sexual morality, education, and thrift. These causes remained important parts of the black agenda throughout the antebellum years. But by the mid-1830s, the national convention movement faltered as black abolitionists placed their hopes in the AASS.

Black Churches in the Antislavery Cause

Black churches were more important than black conventions in the antislavery movement. With few exceptions, leading black abolitionists were ministers. Some of these men led congregations affiliated with African-American churches, such as the African Baptist Church or the African Methodist Episcopal (AME) Church. Others preached to black congregations

VOICES Frederick Douglass Describes an Awkward Situation

Frederick Douglass wrote this passage during the mid-1850s. It is from My Bondage and My Freedom, *the second of his three autobiographies. It relates with humor not only the racial barriers that black and white abolitionists had to break but also primitive conditions they took for granted.*

In the summer of 1843, I was traveling and lecturing in company with William A. White, Esq., through the state of Indiana. Anti-slavery friends were not very abundant in Indiana . . . and beds were not more plentiful than friends. . . . At the close of one of our meetings, we were invited home with a kindly-disposed old farmer, who, in the generous enthusiasm of the moment, seemed to have forgotten that he had but one spare bed, and that his guests were an ill-matched pair. . . . White is remarkably fine looking, and very evidently a born gentleman; the idea of putting us in the same bed was hardly to be tolerated;

and yet there we were, and but the one bed for us, and that, by the way, was in the same room occupied by the other members of the family. . . . After witnessing the confusion as long as I liked, I relieved the kindly-disposed family by playfully saying, "Friend White, having got entirely rid of my prejudice against color, I think, as proof of it, I must allow you to sleep with me to-night." White kept up the joke, by seeming to esteem himself the favored party, and thus the difficulty was removed.

1. **What does this passage reveal about American life during the 1840s?**
2. **What does Douglass tell us about his personality?**

SOURCE: Michael Meyer, ed., *Frederick Douglass: The Narrative and Selected Writings* (New York: Modern Library, 1984), 170–71.

affiliated with predominantly white churches. A few black ministers served white antislavery congregations. In either case, they used their pulpits to attack slavery, racial discrimination, proslavery white churches, and the American Colonization Society (ACS). Black churches also provided forums for abolitionist speakers, such as Frederick Douglass and Garrison, and meeting places for predominantly white antislavery organizations, which frequently could not meet in white churches.

Black Newspapers

Although less influential than black churches, black antislavery newspapers had an important role in the antislavery movement, particularly by the 1840s. Like their white counterparts, they almost always faced financial difficulties, and few survived for long. This was because *reform*—as opposed to *commercial*—newspapers were a luxury that not many subscribers, black or white, could afford. Black newspapers faced added difficulties finding readers because most African Americans were poor, and many were illiterate. Moreover, white abolitionist newspapers, such as *The Liberator,* served a black clientele. They published speeches by black abolitionists and reported black convention proceedings. Some black abolitionists argued, therefore, that a separate black press was unnecessary.

Yet several influential black abolitionist newspapers existed between the late 1820s and the Civil War. The first black newspaper, *Freedom's Journal,* owned and edited by Samuel Cornish and John B. Russwurm, lasted from 1827 to 1829. It proved African Americans could produce interesting, competent journalism that attracted black and white subscribers.

The *Journal* also established a framework for black journalism during the antebellum period by emphasizing opposition to slavery, support for racial justice, and devotion to Christian and democratic values.

Frederick Douglass's **North Star** and its successor *Frederick Douglass' Paper* were the most influential black antislavery newspapers of the late 1840s and the 1850s. Heavily subsidized by Gerrit Smith, a wealthy white abolitionist, and attracting more white than black subscribers, Douglass's weeklies gained the support of many black abolitionist organizations.

North Star A weekly newspaper published and edited by Frederick Douglass from 1847 to 1851. *Fredrick Douglass' Paper* (1851–1860) succeeded it.

The American and Foreign Anti-Slavery Society and the Liberty Party

9-4 | What were the reasons for the breakup of the American Anti-Slavery Society and what organizations emerged to replace it?

In 1840 the AASS splintered. Most of its members left to establish the **American and Foreign Anti-Slavery Society (AFASS)** and the **Liberty Party**, the first antislavery political party. In part, the split resulted from long-standing disagreements about the role of women in abolitionism and William Lloyd Garrison's broadening radicalism. By declaring that slavery had irrevocably corrupted the existing American society, by denouncing organized religion as irrevocably proslavery, by becoming a feminist, and by embracing a form of Christian anarchy that precluded formal involvement in politics, Garrison seemed to have lost sight of abolitionism's main concern. However, the failure of moral suasion to make progress against slavery—particularly in the South—and the question of how abolitionists should respond to slave unrest also helped fracture the AASS.

Garrison and his followers retained control of the AASS, which became known as the "Old Organization." By 1842 they had de-emphasized moral suasion and begun calling for disunion—the separation of the North from the South—as the only means of ending northern support for slavery. The U.S. Constitution, Garrison declared, was a proslavery document that had to be replaced before African Americans could gain freedom.

Those who withdrew from the AASS took a more traditional stand on the role of women, believed the country's churches could be converted to abolitionism, and asserted that the Constitution could be used on behalf of abolitionism. Under the leadership of Lewis Tappan, a wealthy white New York City businessman, some of them formed the church-oriented AFASS. Others created the Liberty Party and nominated James G. Birney, a slaveholder-turned-abolitionist, as their candidate in the 1840 presidential election. Birney received few votes, and William Henry Harrison, the Whig candidate, became president. But Birney's candidacy began an increasingly powerful political crusade against slavery.

Black abolitionists joined in the disruption of the Old Organization. As might be expected, most black clerical abolitionists joined the AFASS. After 1840 African Americans were always more prominent as leaders in the AFASS than the AASS. Only in New England did most of them remain loyal to the AASS.

In addition to the AFASS, the Liberty Party attracted black support, although few black men could vote. The platform of the radical New York wing of the party, led by Gerrit Smith, especially appealed to black abolitionists. Of all the antislavery organizations, the New York party advocated the most aggressive action against slavery in the South and became most involved in helping slaves escape.

American and Foreign Anti-Slavery Society (AFASS, 1840–1855) An organization of church-oriented abolitionists.

Liberty Party (1840–1848) The first antislavery political party. Most of its supporters joined the Free Soil Party in 1848, although its radical New York wing maintained a Liberty organization into the 1850s.

9-1
9-2
9-3
9-4
9-5
9-6

A More Aggressive Abolitionism

9-5   How did abolitionism become more aggressive during the 1840s and 1850s?

The New York Liberty Party maintained that the U.S. Constitution, interpreted in the light of the Bible and natural law, outlawed slavery throughout the country. While other Liberty abolitionists recognized Congress's power over slavery only in the District of Columbia, the territories, and interstate commerce, the New Yorkers held it could also act against slavery in the states. They contended that neither northern state militias nor the U.S. Army should help suppress slave revolts. Most important, they argued that, since masters had no legal right to own human beings, slaves who escaped and those who aided them acted within the law.

This body of thought, which dated to the late 1830s, reflected northern abolitionist empathy with slaves as they struggled for freedom. At that time, the domestic slave trade in the Border South states of Maryland, Virginia, Kentucky, and Missouri tore black families apart to fill the demand for labor in new cotton-producing areas farther south. That some slaves responded by escaping or staging minor rebellions encouraged Garnet to deliver his "Address to the Slaves." Slave actions also inspired the New York Liberty Party's constitutional interpretation, and the party's encouragement of black and white northerners to go south to help escapees. Two major seaborne revolts had a similar impact.

The *Amistad* and the *Creole*

Amistad A Spanish schooner on which West African Joseph Cinque led a successful slave revolt in 1839.

In June 1839, 54 African captives, under the leadership of Joseph Cinque, seized control of the Spanish schooner **Amistad** (meaning "friendship"), which had been carrying them to slavery in Honduras. After the Africans lost their way in an attempt to return to their homeland, a U.S. warship captured them off the coast of Long Island, New York. Imprisoned in New Haven, Connecticut, the Africans soon gained the assistance of Lewis Tappan and other abolitionists. As a result of that aid and arguments presented by Congressman John Quincy Adams, the Supreme Court in November 1841 freed Cinque and the others.

Later that November, Madison Washington led a revolt aboard the brig *Creole* as it transported 135 American slaves from Richmond to New Orleans. Washington and about a dozen other black men seized control and sailed the vessel to the Bahamas, a British colony

This 1840 engraving provides a dramatic portrayal of the successful uprising of African slaves on board the Spanish schooner *Amistad* in 1839. *The Granger Collection.*

where slavery had been abolished. There local black fishermen protected the *Creole* by surrounding it with their boats, and most of those on board immediately gained their freedom under British law. A few days later, so did Washington and the other rebels.

Cinque and Washington inspired others to risk their lives and freedom to help African Americans escape bondage. The New York Liberty Party reinforced this commitment by declaring their revolts divinely ordained and strictly legal.

The Underground Railroad

The famous **underground railroad** must be placed within the context of increasing southern white violence against black families, slave resistance, and aggressive northern abolitionism. Slaves, since colonial times, had escaped from their masters, and free black people and some white people had assisted them. But the organized escape of slaves from the Chesapeake, Kentucky, and Missouri along predetermined routes to Canada became common only after the mid-1830s. A united national underground railroad with a president or unified command never existed. Instead, different organizations separated in time and space from one another operated the network (see Map 9–2). Even during the 1840s and 1850s, most of the slaves who escaped did so on their own.

The best-documented underground railroad organizations centered in Ripley, Ohio, and Washington, DC. In southern Ohio and Indiana, some residents, black and white, had helped fugitive slaves since the 1810s as they headed north from Kentucky. By the late 1820s John Rankin, a white Presbyterian minister, lit a lantern each night at his Ripley, Ohio, home—located on a hill above the north shore of the Ohio River—to serve as a beacon for escaping slaves. By the late 1840s former slave John P. Parker was the most aggressive agent of the Ripley-based underground railroad. With Rankin's support, Parker, who had purchased his freedom in 1845, repeatedly went into Kentucky to lead others north. In Washington, Charles T. Torrey, a white Liberty Party abolitionist from Albany, New York, and Thomas Smallwood, a free black resident of Washington, began in 1842 to help slaves escape along a northward route. Between March and November of that year, they sent at least 150 enslaved men, women, and children to Philadelphia. From there, a local black vigilance committee provided the fugitives with transportation to Albany, where a local, predominantly white, vigilance group helped them get to Canada.

The escapees were by no means passive "passengers" in the underground railroad networks. They raised money to pay for their transportation, recruited and aided other escapees, and helped plan escapes. During the mid-1850s, Arrah Weems of Rockville, Maryland, whose freedom had been recently purchased by black and white abolitionists and whose daughter Ann Maria had been rescued by underground railroad agents, became an agent herself.

Weems and others who helped slaves escape took great risks. In 1843 Smallwood had to flee to Canada as Washington police closed in on his home. In 1846 Torrey died of tuberculosis in a Maryland prison while serving a six-year sentence for helping slaves escape. Parker recalled "real warfare" in southern Ohio between underground railroad operators and slaveholders from Kentucky. "I never thought of going uptown without a pistol in my pocket, a knife in my belt, and a blackjack handy," he later recalled.

During the early 1850s, Harriet Tubman, a fugitive slave, became the most active worker on the eastern branch of the underground railroad. Born in 1820 on a Maryland plantation, she suffered years of abuse at the hands of her master. When in 1849 he threatened to sell her and her family south, she escaped to the North. Then she returned about 13 times to Maryland to help others flee. She had the help of Thomas Garrett, a white Quaker abolitionist who lived

underground railroad Refers to several loosely organized, semi-secret biracial networks that helped slaves escape from the border South to the North and Canada. The earliest networks appeared during the first decade of the nineteenth century; others operated into the Civil War years.

 Watch on **MyHistoryLab** Video: Underground Railroad

9-1
9-2
9-3
9-4
9-5
9-6

 **Read** on **MyHistoryLab** Document: Levi Coffin's Underground Railroad Station, 1826–1827

9-1
9-2
9-3
9-4
9-5
9-6

((📖 Read on MyHistoryLab Document: Two Escaped Slaves Tell Their Stories, 1855

Harriet Tubman, standing at the left, is shown in this undated photograph with a group of people she helped escape from slavery. Because she worked in secret during the 1850s, she was known only to others engaged in the underground railroad, the people she helped, and a few other abolitionists.
Sophia Smith Collection, Smith College.

in Wilmington, Delaware, and William Still, the black leader of the Philadelphia Vigilance Association.

Technology and the Underground Railroad

Historian Fergus M. Bordewich notes that before the late 1830s those who helped slaves escape referred to their networks as "lines of posts" or "chains of friends." Only as railroad mileage expanded in the eastern United States did railroad power, speed, and organization serve as a metaphor for escape networks.

But the link between slave escapes and technology was more than a metaphor. Steam engines, whether used to power locomotives or vessels, promoted northward escapes. By the early 1840s, police in Border South cities patrolled steamboat wharves to prevent fugitive slaves from boarding. As rail lines spread, masters in Maryland and Virginia despaired of recapturing slaves who crossed the Mason-Dixon Line.

Canada West

The ultimate destination for many African Americans on the underground railroad was Canada West (present-day Ontario) between Buffalo and Detroit on the northern shore of Lake Erie. Black Americans began to settle in Canada West as early as the 1820s. When the British Empire prohibited slavery after 1833, fugitive slaves became safer in Canada. When Congress passed a stonger fugitive slave law as part of the Compromise of 1850 (see Chapter 10), Canada became an even more important refuge for African Americans. Between 1850 and

✳ EXPLORE ON MYHISTORYLAB
The Underground Railroad

What was the purpose of the underground railroad?

In the early 1800s, a secret network emerged in the United States as the nation became increasingly divided over the issue of slavery. Opponents of slavery helped organize various secret routes and safe houses to covertly smuggle slaves from the slave states of the South to the free states of the North. "Railroad" came to be the code word for the system. "Conductors" guided and assisted the escaped slaves, who were called the "freight." Canada was often the final destination, especially after the Fugitive Slave Law of 1850. Slaves and those helping them to escape faced significant legal and geographical obstacles; nevertheless, the network of departure points in Border States and southern ports, as well as safe houses ("stations") and routes, increased over the decades prior to the Civil War.

MAP 9-2 THE UNDERGROUND RAILROAD

This map illustrates *approximate* routes traveled by escaping slaves through the North to Canada. Although some slaves escaped from the Deep South, most of those who utilized the underground railroad network came from the border slave states.

✳ Explore the Topic on MyHistoryLab

1. **Cause** *What geographic features made passage on the underground railroad more difficult?* Map major "routes" and obstacles along the way.

2. **Analysis** *Which regions of the South provided the most slaves on the railroad?* Consider the reasons for such patterns.

3. **Consequence** *How did Congress's Fugitive Slave Law of 1850 affect the railroad?* Explore the impact of this on "stations," "routes," and "freight."

9-1
9-2
9-3
9-4
9-5
9-6

This is the only surviving photograph of Mary Ann Shadd Cary (1823–1893). An advocate, during the 1850s, of black migration to Canada, Cary also promoted racial integration.

1860, the number of black people in Canada West rose from approximately 8,000 to at least 20,000.

Mary Ann Shadd Cary became the chief advocate of black migration to Canada West, and she was the only such advocate who supported racial integration. Between 1854 and 1858, she edited the *Provincial Freeman,* an abolitionist paper published in Toronto, and lectured in northern cities promoting emigration to Canada. Cary knew, however, that by the 1850s black people faced the same sort of segregation and discrimination in Canada that existed in the northern United States.

Black Militancy

9-6   **How did the views of Frederick Douglass differ from those of Henry Highland Garnet?**

As we mentioned earlier in this chapter, during the 1840s growing numbers of northern black abolitionists advocated forceful action against slavery. This resolve accompanied a trend toward separate black antislavery action. The black convention movement revived during the 1840s, and well-attended meetings took place in Buffalo in 1843 (where Garnet presented his "Address to the Slaves"); in Troy, New York, in 1844; and in Cleveland in 1848. In addition, more black-owned and edited abolitionist newspapers appeared.

The rise in militancy had several causes. First, the breakup of the AASS weakened abolitionist loyalty to the national antislavery organizations. Second, all abolitionists, black and white, explored new antislavery tactics. Third, many black abolitionists came to believe that most white abolitionists enjoyed antislavery debate and theory more than action.

Influenced by the examples of Cinque, Madison Washington, and other rebellious slaves, many black abolitionists during the 1840s and 1850s wanted to do more to encourage slaves to resist and escape. This outlook inspired Garnet, who, as we have described, supported the radical New York wing of the Liberty Party. That organization's willingness to act rather than just talk attracted other black leaders. However black abolitionists, like white abolitionists, approached the subjects of violence and slave rebellion cautiously. As late as 1857, Garnet and Frederick Douglass described slave revolt as "inexpedient."

The black abolitionist desire to go beyond rhetoric found its best outlet in local vigilance organizations. Such associations appeared during the mid-1830s and often had white as well as black members. As the 1840s progressed, African Americans formed more of them and led those that already existed. In this they reacted against a facet of the growing violence in the United States: the use of force by "slave catchers" to recapture fugitive slaves in northern cities.

Black militancy also encouraged charges that white abolitionists did not live up to their words in favor of racial justice. Economic slights rankled the most. At the annual meeting of the AFASS in 1852, a black delegate demanded to know why Lewis Tappan did not employ a black clerk in his business. In 1855 Samuel Ringgold Ward denounced Garrison and his associates

((• 📖 **Read on MyHistoryLab**
Document: Henry Garnet's "Call to Rebellion," 1843

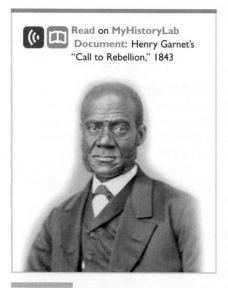

Henry Highland Garnet rivaled Frederick Douglass as a black leader during the antebellum decades. While Douglass emphasized assimilation, Garnet advocated black nationalism. The two men had much in common, however, and by the Civil War their views were almost indistinguishable.

VOICES   Martin R. Delany Describes His Vision of a Black Nation

This excerpt comes from the appendix of Martin R. Delany's The Condition, Elevation, Emigration and Destiny of the Colored People of the United States, Politically Considered, *which he published in 1852. It embodies Delany's black nationalist vision.*

Every people should be the originators of their own designs, the projectors of their own schemes, and creators of the events that lead to their destiny—the consummation of their desires.

Situated as we are in the United States, many, and almost insurmountable obstacles present themselves. We are four-and-a-half millions in numbers, free and bond; six hundred thousand free, and three-and-a-half millions bond.

We have native hearts and virtues, just as other nations; which in their pristine purity are noble, potent, and worthy of example. We are a nation within a nation. . . .

But we have been, by our oppressors, despoiled of our purity, and corrupted in our native characteristics, so that we have inherited their vices, and but few of their virtues, leaving us in character, really a broken people.

Being distinguished by complexion, we are still singled out—although having merged in the habits and customs of our oppressors—as a distinct nation of people. . . . The claims of no people, according to established policy and usage, are respected by any nation, until they are presented in a national capacity.

To accomplish so great and desirable an end, there should be held, a great representative gathering of the colored people of the United States; not what is termed a National Convention, representing en masse, such as have been, for the last few years, held at various times and places; but a true representation of the intelligence and wisdom of the colored freemen. . . . A Confidential Council. . . .

By this Council to be appointed, a Board of Commissioners . . . to go on an expedition to the EASTERN COAST OF AFRICA, to make researches for a suitable location on that section of the coast, for the settlement of colored adventurers from the United States, and elsewhere.

The whole continent is rich in minerals, and the most precious metals, as but a superficial notice of the topographical and geological reports from that country, plainly show. . . . The land is ours—there it lies with inexhaustible resources; let us go and possess it. In Eastern Africa must rise up a nation, to whom all the world must pay commercial tribute.

> 1. **How does this document express black nationalism?**
> 2. **What is Delany's view of Africa?**

SOURCE: *A Documentary History of the Negro People in the United States,* 5th ed. (New York: Citadel, 1968), Volume 1, pp. 327–28. Reprinted by permission from Bettina Aptheker, Literary Executer, Herbert Aptheker Estate.

9-1
9-2
9-3
9-4
9-5
9-6

---

for failing to have an African American "as clerk in an anti-slavery office, or editor, or lecturer to the same extent . . . as white men of the same calibre." These charges reflected factional struggles between the AASS and the AFASS. But they also represented real grievances among black abolitionists and inconsistencies among their white counterparts.

Frederick Douglass

The career of Frederick Douglass illustrates the impact of the failure of some white abolitionists to live up to their egalitarian ideals. Douglass was born a slave in Maryland in 1818. Brilliant, ambitious, and charming, he resisted brutalization, learned to read, and acquired a trade before escaping to New England in 1838. By 1841 he had, with Garrison's encouragement, become an antislavery lecturer, which led to the travels with William White discussed earlier.

But as time passed, Douglass, who had remained loyal to Garrison during the 1840s when most other black abolitionists left the AASS, suspected that his white colleagues

9-1
9-2
9-3
9-4
9-5
9-6

By the mid-1840s, Frederick Douglass had emerged as one of the more powerful speakers of his time. He began publishing his influential newspaper, the *North Star,* in 1847.
Frederick Douglass (1817?–95). Oil on canvas, ©1844, attr. to E. Hammond. The Granger Collection.

wanted him to continue in the role of a fugitive slave even as he became a premier American orator. "People won't believe you ever was a slave, Frederick, if you keep on this way," a white colleague advised him.

Finally Douglass decided he had to free himself from the AASS. In 1847 he asserted his independence by leaving Massachusetts for Rochester, New York, where he began publishing the *North Star*. This decision angered Garrison and his associates but enabled Douglass to chart his course as a black leader. Although Douglass continued to work closely with white abolitionists, he could now do it on his own terms and be more active in the black convention movement, which he considered essential to gaining general emancipation and racial justice.

Revival of Black Nationalism

Douglass always believed black people were part of a larger American nation and that their best prospects for political and economic success lay in the United States. He was, despite his differences with some white abolitionists, an ardent integrationist. He opposed separate black churches and predicted that African Americans would eventually merge into a greater American identity. Most black abolitionists did not go that far, but they believed racial oppression in all its forms could be defeated in the United States.

During the 1840s and 1850s, however, an influential minority of black leaders disagreed with this point of view. Prominent among them were Garnet and Martin R. Delany, Douglass's sometime colleague on the *North Star*. Although they disagreed over important details, Delany and Garnet both favored African-American migration and nationalism as the best means to realize black aspirations.

Since the postrevolutionary days of Prince Hall and Paul Cuffe, some black leaders had believed African Americans could thrive only as a separate nation. They suggested sites in Africa, Latin America, and the American West as possible places to pursue this goal. But it took the rising tide of racism and violence emphasized in this chapter to induce a respectable minority of black abolitionists to reconsider migration. Almost all of them opposed the ACS's African migration scheme, which they regarded as proslavery and racist. Nevertheless Garnet conceded in 1849 that he would "rather see a man free in Liberia [the ACS colony], than a slave in the United States."

Douglass and most black abolitionists rejected this outlook, insisting the aim must be freedom in the United States. Yet emigration plans Garnet and Delany developed during the 1850s became a significant part of African American reform culture. Delany, a physician and novelist, was born free in western Virginia in 1812. He grew up in Pennsylvania and by the late 1840s championed black self-reliance. To further this cause, he promoted mass black migration to Latin America or Africa.

In contrast, Garnet welcomed white assistance for his plan to foster Christianity and economic development in Africa by encouraging *some*—not all—African Americans to migrate there under the patronage of his African Civilization Society. In 1858 he wrote, "Let those who wished to stay, stay here—and those who had enterprise and wished to go, go and found a nation, if possible, of which the colored Americans could be proud."

Little came of these nationalist visions, largely because of the successes of the antislavery movement. Black and white abolitionists, although not perfect allies, awoke many in the North to the brutalities of slavery. They helped convince most white northerners that the slave-labor system and slaveholder control of the national government threatened their

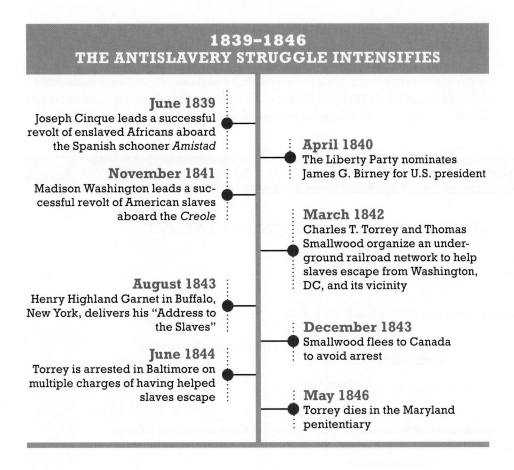

1839–1846
THE ANTISLAVERY STRUGGLE INTENSIFIES

June 1839
Joseph Cinque leads a successful revolt of enslaved Africans aboard the Spanish schooner *Amistad*

April 1840
The Liberty Party nominates James G. Birney for U.S. president

November 1841
Madison Washington leads a successful revolt of American slaves aboard the *Creole*

March 1842
Charles T. Torrey and Thomas Smallwood organize an underground railroad network to help slaves escape from Washington, DC, and its vicinity

August 1843
Henry Highland Garnet in Buffalo, New York, delivers his "Address to the Slaves"

December 1843
Smallwood flees to Canada to avoid arrest

June 1844
Torrey is arrested in Baltimore on multiple charges of having helped slaves escape

May 1846
Torrey dies in the Maryland penitentiary

economic and political interests. At the same time, abolitionist aid to escaping slaves and their defense of fugitive slaves from recapture pushed southern leaders to adopt policies that led to secession and the Civil War. The northern victory in the war, general emancipation, and constitutional protection for black rights made most African Americans—for a time—optimistic about their future in the United States.

CONCLUSION

This chapter has focused on the radical movement for the immediate abolition of slavery. The movement flourished in the United States from 1831, when William Lloyd Garrison began publishing *The Liberator*, through the Civil War. Garrison hoped slavery could be abolished peacefully. But during the 1840s abolitionists adjusted their antislavery tactics to deal with increasing racism and antiblack violence, both of which were related to the existence of slavery. Slave resistance also inspired a more confrontational brand of abolitionism. Many black abolitionists and their white colleagues concluded that the tactic of moral suasion, typical of abolitionism during the 1830s, could not by itself achieve their goals. Most black abolitionists came to believe they needed a combination of moral suasion, political involvement, and direct action to end slavery and improve the lives of African Americans in the United States. By the late 1840s, a minority of black abolitionists contended they had to establish an independent nation beyond the borders of the United States to promote African-American rights, interests, and identity.

Although much has changed since the abolitionist era, these two perspectives remain characteristic of the African-American community. Most African Americans prefer integration within a larger American nation. But black nationalism still has an appeal. Black people often endorse parts of both views, just as Frederick Douglass embraced some facets of black nationalism and Henry Highland Garnet some integrationism. Reformers also still debate whether persuasion is more effective than confrontation.

CHAPTER TIMELINE

AFRICAN-AMERICAN EVENTS

NATIONAL EVENTS

1830–1833

1831
Publication of *The Liberator* begun by William Lloyd Garrison

1833
Formation of AASS

1832
Andrew Jackson reelected president

1833
End of Nullification Controversy

1835–1839

1835
Abolitionist postal campaign

1839
Amistad mutiny

1836
Martin Van Buren elected president; Texas independence from Mexico

1840–1844

1840
Breakup of AASS

1841
Creole revolt

1843
Henry Highland Garnet's "Address to the Slaves"

1840
William H. Harrison elected president

1844
James K. Polk elected president

1845–1849

1847
Publication of the *North Star* begun by Frederick Douglass

1849
Harriet Tubman's career begins

1845
Annexation of Texas

1846
War against Mexico begins

1848
Annexation of Mexico's California and New Mexico provinces

1850–1851

1851
Start of resistance to the Fugitive Slave Act of 1850 Black migration advocated by Martin Delany

1850
Compromise of 1850

On MyHistoryLab

✓ Study and Review on MyHistoryLab

REVIEW QUESTIONS

1. What was the historical significance of Henry Highland Garnet's "Address to the Slaves"? How did Garnet's attitude toward slavery differ from that of William Lloyd Garrison?

2. Evaluate Frederick Douglass's career as an abolitionist. How was he consistent? How was he inconsistent?

3. How did black women contribute to the antislavery movement? How did participation in this movement alter their lives?

4. How did the integrationist views of Frederick Douglass compare with the nationalist views of Martin Delany and Henry Highland Garnet?

5. Why did so many black abolitionists leave the AASS in 1840?

"And Black People Were at the Heart of It": The United States Disunites over Slavery 1846–1861

By the end of the 1840s in the United States, no issue was as controversial as slavery. Slavery or, more accurately, its expansion deeply divided the American people and led to the bloodiest war in American history. Try as they might from 1845 to 1860, political leaders could not solve, evade, or escape slavery, nor could they agree on whether to allow it to expand into the nation's western territories.

Caught in this monumental dispute were the South's nearly four million enslaved men, women, and children. Their future, as well as the fate of the country, was at stake. As many as 750,000 Americans—northern and southern, black and white—would die before a divided nation would be reunified and slavery would be abolished.

Whether slavery should be permitted in the western territories was not a new issue. As early as 1787, Congress had prohibited slavery in the Northwest Territory, the area north of the Ohio River that became the states of Ohio, Indiana, Illinois, Michigan, and Wisconsin. Then in 1819 a major political controversy erupted when Missouri applied for admission to the Union as a slave state. The Missouri Compromise—which admitted Maine as a free state, Missouri as a slave state, and outlawed slavery north of the 36° 30' line of latitude—settled that controversy, but only postponed for 25 years further conflict over the expansion of slavery.

In January 1856, Margaret Garner, her husband Robert, and their four children escaped from Kentucky to Ohio across the frozen Ohio River. They were pursued to the home of a black man by slave owners as well as deputy marshals. The Garners fiercely resisted. Robert Garner shot and wounded one of the deputies. But when it became clear that they were about to be captured, Margaret killed her daughter rather than have the child returned to slavery.

The country's desire to acquire western lands intensified in the 1830s and 1840s. Most white Americans and many free black Americans assumed that the American people should occupy the entire North American continent from the Atlantic to the Pacific. It was their future, their Manifest Destiny (see Chapter 9). In 1846–1847, U.S. troops fought an 18-month conflict that resulted in the acquisition of more than half of Mexico and was a major step toward the fulfillment of Manifest Destiny.

The Lure of the West

10-1 **Why was the expansion of slavery such a divisive issue?**

Even before the war with Mexico, hundreds of Americans made the long journey west, drawn by the opportunity to settle the fertile valleys of California and the Oregon Territory, which included what is today the states of Oregon and Washington. African Americans shared these hopes and dreams. In 1844 a black Missouri farmer with the improbable name of George Washington Bush caught "Oregon fever" and set out with his wife, six children, and four other families on the 1,800-mile trek by wagon train to Oregon. Bush settled north of the Columbia River in what later became the Washington Territory because Oregon's territorial constitution forbade black settlement. Although the law was rarely enforced, black residents were legally subject to whipping every six months until they departed. The statute remained Oregon state law until the 1920s.

Free Labor versus Slave Labor

Westward expansion revived the issue of slavery's future in the territories. Should slavery be legal or prohibited in western lands? Most white Americans held thoroughly ingrained racist beliefs that people of African descent were not and could never be their intellectual, political, or social equals. Yet those same white Americans disagreed vehemently on where those unfree African Americans should be permitted to work and reside.

Most northern white people adamantly opposed allowing southern slaveholders to take their slaves into the former Mexican territories, and they detested the prospect of slavery spreading westward and limiting their opportunities to settle and farm those lands. Except for the increasing number of militant abolitionists, white northerners detested both slavery as a labor system and the black people who were enslaved.

By the mid-nineteenth century, northern black and white people embraced the system of **free labor**—that is, free men and women who worked for compensation to earn a living and improve their lives. If southern slave owners managed to gain a foothold for their unfree labor on the western plains, in the Rocky Mountains, or on the Pacific coast, then the future for free white laborers would be severely restricted, if not destroyed.

The Wilmot Proviso

In 1846, during the Mexican War, a Democratic congressman from Pennsylvania, David Wilmot, introduced a measure in Congress, the so-called Wilmot Proviso, to prohibit slavery in any lands acquired from Mexico. Wilmot later explained that he wanted neither slavery nor black people to taint territory that should be reserved exclusively for whites.

free labor
Mid-nineteenth-century Americans who were free and worked for income or compensation to advance themselves, as opposed to slave labor, which was work done with no financial compensation by people who were not free.

Wilmot Proviso A measure introduced in Congress in 1845 to prohibit slavery in any lands acquired from Mexico. It did not pass.

The **Wilmot Proviso** failed to become law. Nonetheless, white southerners were enraged, and they saw the proviso as a blatant attempt to prevent them from moving west and enjoying the prosperity and way of life that an expanding slave-labor system would create. They considered any attempt to limit the growth of slavery to be the first step toward eliminating it.

White southerners had convinced themselves that black people were a childlike and irresponsible race wholly incapable of surviving as a free people if they were emancipated and compelled to compete with white Americans. Most white people believed the black race would decline and disappear if slaves were freed. Thus, southern white people considered slavery "a positive good"—in the words of Senator John C. Calhoun of South Carolina—that benefited both races and resulted in a society vastly superior to that of the North.

To prevent slavery's expansion, the Free-Soil Party was formed in 1848. It was composed mainly of white people who vigorously opposed slavery's expansion and the supposed desecration that the presence of black men and women might bring to the new western lands. But some black and white abolitionists also supported the Free-Soilers as a way to oppose slavery. They reasoned that even though many Free-Soil supporters were hostile to black people, the party still represented a serious challenge to slavery and its expansion. The Free-Soil candidate for president in 1848 was the former Democratic president Martin Van Buren. He came in a distant third behind the Whig candidate and hero of the Mexican War, Zachary Taylor, who won, and the Democrat Lewis Cass. Nevertheless, 10 Free-Soil congressmen were elected, and the party provided a growing forum to oppose slavery's advance.

African Americans and the Gold Rush

The discovery of gold in California in 1848 sent thousands of Americans hurrying west in 1849. The **Forty-Niners**, as these migrants were called, were almost exclusively male, and most were white Americans. But the desire to get rich had universal appeal, and the gold rush attracted Europeans, Asians (mostly Chinese), and African Americans. By 1850 nearly 900 black men (and fewer than 100 black women) were living in California.

Forty-Niners The men and women who rushed to California in 1849 after gold had been discovered there.

Most of the Forty-Niners—whatever their race or nationality—were placer miners. Using the most basic technology—little more than a pan, a pick, and a shovel—they sought the chips and flakes of gold deposited in the icy streams that flowed down the western slopes of the Sierra Nevada Mountains. Few of these placer miners struck it rich, but many of them made a modest living from the gold they recovered.

The richer veins of the precious metal were deeper underground and required more sophisticated technology and expensive equipment to mine it. Hydraulic mining used high-pressure hoses that sent powerful streams of water into the sides of hills and mountains, scarring the landscape as the sand and soil were ripped away and revealing the rock, stone, and sometimes gold embedded below. A black man known only as Smith worked his mining claim in Amador County with hydraulic equipment.

Quartz mining involved heavy and costly machinery that crushed huge quantities of rock and boulders. Only larger corporations—not individual miners—that had the financial resources to buy and install the machinery and to hire the workers to operate it could employ this technology. Moses L. Rodgers was an ex-slave from Missouri who became knowledgeable and successful in quartz mining operations in the late 1860s. He was both an investor and superintendent of several California gold mines.

California and the Compromise of 1850

With the gold rush, California's population soared to more than 100,000, and its new residents quickly applied for admission to the Union as a free state. White southerners were aghast at the prospect of California prohibiting slavery, and they refused to consider its admission unless slavery was lawful there. Most northerners would not accept this.

Into this dispute stepped Whig Senator Henry Clay, who 30 years earlier had assisted with the Missouri Compromise. In 1850 Clay put together an elaborate piece of legislation, the **Compromise of 1850**, designed not only to settle the controversy over California but also to resolve the issue of slavery's expansion once and for all. To placate northerners, Clay proposed admitting California as a free state and eliminating the slave trade (but not slavery) in the District of Columbia. To satisfy white southerners, he offered a stronger fugitive slave law to make it easier for slave owners to apprehend runaway slaves and return them to slavery. New Mexico and Utah would be organized as territories with no mention of slavery (see Map 10–1).

Clay's measures were hammered into a single bill, but it did not pass. Southern opponents like Senator John C. Calhoun of South Carolina could not tolerate the admission of California without slavery. Northern opponents like Senator William Seward of New York could not tolerate a tougher fugitive slave law. President Zachary Taylor insisted that California should be admitted as a free state and that Clay's compromise was unnecessary. Taylor promised to veto the compromise if Congress passed it.

Clay's effort had failed—or so it seemed. But in the summer of 1850, Taylor died unexpectedly and was succeeded by Millard Fillmore, who was willing to accept the compromise. Senator Stephen Douglas, an ambitious Democrat from Illinois, guided Clay's compromise through Congress by breaking it into separate bills. California entered the Union as a free state, and a stronger fugitive slave law entered the federal legal code.

Fugitive Slave Laws

Those who may have hoped the compromise would forever resolve the dispute over slavery were mistaken. The **Fugitive Slave Law of 1850** created bitter resentment among black and white abolitionists and made slavery a more emotional and personal issue for many white people who had previously considered slavery a remote southern institution.

Had runaway slaves not been an increasingly frustrating problem for slave owners, the federal fugitive slave law would not have needed to be strengthened in 1850. The U.S. Constitution and the fugitive slave law passed in 1793 would seem to have provided ample authority for slave owners to recover runaway slaves.

The Fugitive Slave Law of 1793 permitted slave owners to recover slaves who had escaped to other states. The escaped slave had no rights—no right to a trial, no right to testify, and no guarantee of *habeas corpus* (the legal requirement that a person be brought before a court and not imprisoned illegally).

But by the 1830s and 1840s, hundreds if not thousands of slaves had escaped to freedom by way of the underground railroad, and white southerners increasingly found the 1793 law too weak to overcome the resistance of northern communities to the return of escapees. For example, in January 1847 four Kentuckians and a local law officer attempted to capture Adam Crosswhite, his wife, and their four children after the family had escaped from slavery in Kentucky and settled on a farm near Marshall, Michigan. When the would-be abductors arrived, an old black man mounted a horse and galloped through town ringing a bell warning that the Crosswhites were in danger. About one hundred people helped rescue the family and put them on a railroad train to Canada.

Compromise of 1850 An attempt by the U.S. Congress to settle divisive issues between the North and South, including slavery expansion, apprehension in the North of fugitive slaves, and slavery in the District of Columbia.

Read on MyHistoryLab Document: The Compromise of 1850

Fugitive Slave Law, 1850 Part of the Compromise of 1850. It required law enforcement officials as well as civilians to assist in capturing runaway slaves.

habeas corpus A court order that a person arrested or detained by law enforcement officers must be brought to court and charged with a crime and not held indefinitely.

Read on **MyHistoryLab** Document: The Fugitive Slave Act, 1850

10-1

10-2

10-3

10-4

10-5

10-6

10-7

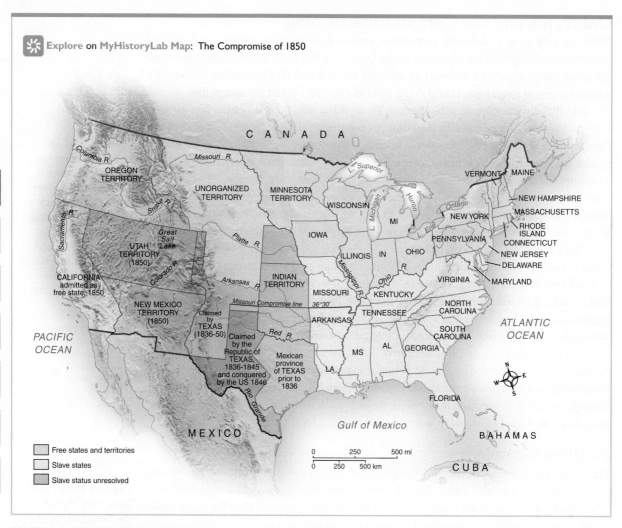

Explore on MyHistoryLab Map: The Compromise of 1850

Free states and territories
Slave states
Slave status unresolved

MAP 10-1 THE COMPROMISE OF 1850
As a result of the war against Mexico, the United States acquired the regions shown on this map as California, Utah Territory, New Mexico Territory, and the portions of Texas not included in the Province of Texas.

With the Compromise of 1850, California entered the Union as a free state. In which remaining western lands would slavery be accepted or rejected?

Northern states had enacted personal liberty laws that made it illegal for state law enforcement officials to help capture runaways. Not only did many northerners refuse to cooperate in returning fugitives to slavery under the 1793 law, but they also encouraged and assisted the fleeing slaves. The local black vigilance committees that were created in many northern communities and discussed in Chapter 9 were especially effective in these efforts. These actions infuriated white southerners and prompted their demand for a stricter fugitive slave law.

The Fugitive Slave Law of 1850 was one of the toughest and harshest measures the U.S. Congress ever passed. Anyone apprehended under the law was almost certain to be sent back to slavery. The law required U.S. marshals, their deputies, and even ordinary citizens to help seize suspected runaways. Those who refused to help apprehend fugitives or who helped the

VOICES African Americans Respond to the Fugitive Slave Law

These two passages reflect the outrage the Fugitive Slave Law of 1850 provoked among black Americans. In the first, John Jacobs, a fugitive slave from South Carolina, urges black people to take up arms to oppose the law. In the second, from a speech he delivered a few days after the passage of the law, Martin Delany defies authorities to search his home for runaway slaves.

> My colored brethren, if you have not swords, I say to you, sell your garments and buy one. . . . They said that they cannot take us back to the South; but I say, under the present law they can; and now they say unto you; let them take only dead bodies. . . . I would, my friends, advise you to show a front to our tyrants and arm yourselves . . . and I would advise the women to have their knives too.

SOURCE: William F. Cheek, *Black Resistance Before the Civil War* (Beverly Hills, CA: Glencoe Press, 1970), 148–49.

> Sir, my house is my castle; in that castle are none but my wife and my children, as free as the angels of heaven, and whose liberty is as sacred as the pillars of God. If any man approaches that house in search of a slave—I care not who he may be, whether the constable, or sheriff, magistrate or even judge of the Supreme Court—nay, let it be he who sanctioned this act to become law [President Millard Fillmore] surrounded by his cabinet as his bodyguard, with the Declaration of Independence waving above his head as his banner, and the constitution of this country upon his breast as his shield—if he crosses the threshold of my door, and I do not lay him a lifeless corpse at my feet, I hope the grave may refuse my body a resting place, and righteous Heaven my spirit a home. O, no! He cannot enter that house and we both live.

SOURCE: Victor Ullman, *Martin R. Delany: The Beginnings of Black Nationalism* (Boston: Beacon Press, 1971), 112.

1. **How and why did these two black men justify the use of violence against those who were enforcing a law passed by Congress?**
2. **Under what circumstances is it permissible to violate the law or threaten to kill another human being?**

10-1

10-2

10-3

10-4

10-5

10-6

10-7

runaways could be fined or imprisoned. The law made it nearly impossible for black people to prove they were free. Slave owners and their agents only had to provide legal documentation from their home state or the testimony of white witnesses before a federal commissioner that the captive was a runaway slave. The federal commissioners were paid $10 for captives returned to bondage but only $5 for those declared free. While the law was in effect, 332 captives were returned to the South and slavery, and only 11 were released as free people.

Fugitive Slaves

10-2 How did African Americans react to the passage of the Fugitive Slave Law of 1850?

The fugitive slave law did more than anger black and white northerners. It exposed them to cruel and heart-wrenching scenes as southern slave owners and slave catchers took advantage of the new law and—with the vigorous assistance of federal authorities—relentlessly pursued runaway slaves. Many white people and virtually all black people felt revulsion over this crackdown on those who had fled from slavery to freedom.

10-1

10-2

10-3

10-4

10-5

10-6

10-7

Leaflets like this reflected the outrage many northerners felt in response to the capture and reenslavement of African Americans that resulted from the passage of a tougher fugitive slave law as part of the Compromise of 1850.

In September 1850 in New York City, federal authorities captured a black porter and returned him to slavery in Baltimore, even though he insisted that because his mother was a free woman he had not been a slave. (In each of the slave states, the law stipulated the status of the mother determined a child's legal status—free or slave.) In Poughkeepsie, New York, slave catchers captured a well-to-do black tailor and returned him to slavery in South Carolina. In Indiana, a black man was apprehended while his wife and children looked on, and he was sent to Kentucky, where his owner claimed he had escaped 19 years earlier.

Even California was not immune to the furor over fugitive slaves. Although the new state prohibited slavery, several hundred black people were illegally held there as slaves in the 1850s. Nevertheless, some slaves ran away to the far West rather than to the North. Black abolitionist Mary Ellen Pleasant hid fugitive Archy Lee in San Francisco in 1858. Other black Californians provided security for runaways from as far east as Maryland.

William and Ellen Craft

Black and white abolitionists had organized vigilance committees to resist the fugitive slave law and to prevent—by force if necessary—the return of fugitives to slavery. In October 1850 slave catchers arrived in Boston prepared to capture and return William and Ellen Craft to slavery in Georgia. In 1848 the Crafts had devised an ingenious escape. Ellen's fair complexion enabled her to disguise herself as a sickly young white man who, accompanied by "his" slave, was traveling north for medical treatment. They journeyed to Boston by railroad and ship and thus escaped from slavery—or so they thought.

Slave catchers vowed to return the Crafts to servitude no matter how long it took. While white abolitionists protected Ellen and black abolitionists hid William, the vigilance committee plastered posters around Boston describing the slave catchers, calling them "man-stealers," and threatening their safety. Within days, the slave catchers left without the Crafts. Soon thereafter, the Crafts sailed to security in England.

Shadrach Minkins

Black and white abolitionists were prepared to use force against the U.S. government and the slave owners and their agents. Sometimes the abolitionists succeeded, sometimes they did not. In early 1851, a few months after the Crafts left Boston, federal marshals apprehended there a black waiter who had escaped from slavery and given himself the name Shadrach Minkins. However, a well-organized band of black men led by Lewis Hayden invaded the courthouse and spirited Minkins to safety in Canada on the underground railroad. Federal authorities brought charges against four black men and four white men who were then indicted by a grand jury for helping Minkins, but local juries refused to convict them.

The Battle at Christiana

In September 1851 a battle erupted in the little town of Christiana, in southern Pennsylvania, when a Maryland slave owner, Edward Gorsuch, arrived to recover two runaway slaves. Accompanied by family members and three deputy U.S. marshals, he confronted a well-armed crowd of at least 25 black men and several white men. Black leader William Parker told Gorsuch to give up any plans to take the runaway slaves. Gorsuch refused, and a battle ensued. Gorsuch was killed, and several black and white men were hurt. The runaway slaves escaped to Canada.

President Fillmore sent U.S. Marines to Pennsylvania, and they helped round up the alleged perpetrators of the violence. Thirty-six black men and five white men were arrested and indicted for treason by a federal grand jury. But after the first trial ended in acquittal, the remaining cases were dropped.

Anthony Burns

Of all the fugitive slave cases, none elicited more support or sorrow than that of Anthony Burns. In 1854 Burns escaped from slavery in Virginia by stowing away on a ship to Boston. After gaining work in a clothing store, he unwisely sent a letter to his brother, who was still a slave. The letter was confiscated, and Burns's former owner set out to

Read on **MyHistoryLab Document:** Anthony Burns Responds to His Excommunication from the Baptist Church, 1855

The "trial" and subsequent return of Anthony Burns to slavery in 1854 resulted in the publication of a popular pamphlet in Boston. Documents like this generated increased support—and funds—for the abolitionist cause.

10-1
10-2
10-3
10-4
10-5
10-6
10-7

10-1

10-2

10-3

10-4

10-5

10-6

10-7

Read on
MyHistoryLab
Exploring America:
Anthony Burns

capture him. Burns was arrested by a deputy marshal who, recalling Shadrach Minkins's escape, placed him under guard in chains in the federal courthouse. Efforts by black and white abolitionists to break into the courthouse with axes, guns, and a battering ram failed, although a deputy U.S. marshal was killed during the assault.

President Franklin Pierce, a northern Democrat who in 1852 had been elected with southern support, sent U.S. troops to Boston—including marines, cavalry, and artillery—to uphold the law and return Burns to Virginia. Black minister Leonard A. Grimes and the vigilance committee tried to purchase Burns's freedom, but the U.S. attorney refused. In June 1854, with church bells tolling and buildings draped in black, thousands of Bostonians watched silently—many in tears—as Anthony Burns was marched through the streets to a ship that would take him to Virginia.

The spectacle of a lone black man, escorted by hundreds of armed troops, as he trudged from freedom to slavery moved even those people who had shown no special interest in or sympathy for fugitives or slaves. One staunchly conservative white man remarked, "When it was all over, and I was left alone in my office, I put my face in my hands and I wept. I could do nothing less."

Yet the government was unrelenting. A federal grand jury indicted seven black men and white men for riot and inciting a riot in their attempt to free Burns. One indictment was set aside on a technicality, and the other charges were then dropped because no Boston jury would convict the accused. Several months later, black Bostonians led by the Rev. Grimes purchased Burns for $1,300. He settled in St. Catherine's, Ontario, in Canada, where he died in 1862.

Margaret Garner

In the winter of 1856, Margaret Garner and seven other slaves escaped from Kentucky across the Ohio River to freedom in Cincinnati. But their owner, Archibald Grimes, pursued them. Grimes, accompanied by a U.S. deputy marshal and several other people, attempted to arrest the fugitives at a small house where they had hidden. Refusing to surrender, the slaves were overpowered and subdued.

Before the fugitives were captured, Garner slit the throat of her daughter with a butcher knife rather than see the child returned to slavery. She was disarmed before she could kill her two sons. Ohio authorities charged her with murder, but by that time she had been returned to Kentucky and then sent to Arkansas with her surviving children to be sold. On the trip down the river, her youngest child and 24 other people drowned in a shipwreck, thereby cruelly fulfilling her wish that the child not grow up to be a slave. Margaret Garner was later sold at a slave market in New Orleans.

The Rochester Convention, 1853

Rochester Convention, 1853 African-American leaders assembled in Rochester, New York, to discuss slavery, abolition, the recently passed fugitive slave law, and their prospects for life in America.

In 1853, while northern communities grappled with the consequences of the fugitive slave law, African-American leaders gathered for a national convention in Rochester, New York. The **Rochester Convention** warned that black Americans were not prepared to submit quietly to a government more concerned about the interests of slave owners than people seeking to free themselves from bondage. The delegates also called for greater unity among black people and to find ways to improve their economic prospects. They asserted their claims to the rights of citizenship and equal protection before the law, and they worried that the wave of European immigrants entering the country would deprive poor black northerners of the menial and unskilled jobs on which they depended. Frederick Douglass spoke of the need for a school to provide training in the skilled trades and manual arts. There was even talk of establishing a Negro museum and library.

Nativism and the Know-Nothings

10-3 Why did many Americans oppose the immigration of Europeans by the 1850s?

Not only did many white Americans look with disfavor and often outright disgust at African Americans, but they were also distressed by and opposed to the increasing numbers of white immigrants coming to the United States. Hundreds of thousands of Europeans arrived in the 1840s and 1850s. In one year—1854—430,000 people arrived on American shores.

The mass starvation that accompanied the potato famine of the 1840s in Ireland drove thousands of Irish people to the United States, where they often encountered intense hostility. Native-born, Protestant, white Americans considered the Catholic Irish crude, ignorant drunks. Irish immigrants also competed with Americans for low-paying unskilled jobs. Anti-Catholic propaganda warned that the influence of the Vatican would weaken American institutions. Mobs attacked Catholic churches and convents.

These anti-immigrant, anti-Catholic, anti-alcohol sentiments helped foster in 1854 the rise of a nativist third political party, the American Party—better known as the "**Know-Nothing Party**." (Its members were supposed to reply "I know nothing" if someone asked if they belonged to the party.) The Know-Nothings attracted considerable support. Feeding on resentment and prejudice, the party grew to one million strong. Most Know-Nothings were in New England, and they even for a short time took political control of Massachusetts, where many of the Irish had settled. The party was also strong in Kentucky, Texas, and elsewhere.

Although Know-Nothings opposed immigrants and Catholics, they disagreed among themselves over slavery and its expansion. As a result, the party soon split into northern and southern factions and collapsed.

Uncle Tom's Cabin

No one contributed more to the growing opposition to slavery among white northerners than Harriet Beecher Stowe. Raised in a religious environment—her father, brothers, and husband were ministers—Stowe developed a hatred of slavery that she converted into a melodramatic but moving novel about slaves and their lives.

Uncle Tom's Cabin, or Life among the Lowly, was first published in installments in the antislavery newspaper *The National Era.* When it appeared as a book in 1852, it sold an astonishing 300,000 copies in a year. In the novel, Stowe depicted slavery's cruelty, inhumanity, and destructive impact on families through characters and a plot that appealed to the sentimentality of nineteenth-century readers.

Uncle Tom's Cabin moved northerners to tears and made slavery more emotional to readers who had previously considered it only a distant system of labor that exploited black people. At the same time, *Uncle Tom's Cabin* infuriated white southerners. They condemned it as a grossly false depiction of slavery and their way of life. They pointed out correctly that Stowe had little firsthand knowledge of slavery and had never even visited the Deep South. But she had lived in Cincinnati for 18 years and witnessed with anguish the desperate attempts of slaves to escape across the Ohio River. In response to her southern critics, Stowe wrote *A Key to Uncle Tom's Cabin,* citing the sources for her novel. Many of those sources were southern newspapers.

10-1

10-2

10-3

10-4

10-5

10-6

10-7

"Know-Nothing Party" This nickname applied to members of the American Party, which opposed immigration in the 1850s.

Read on **MyHistoryLab**
Document: Harriet Beecher Stowe's *Uncle Tom's Cabin,* 1852

Uncle Tom's Cabin This antislavery novel by Harriet Beecher Stowe was a best seller in the 1850s and it helped inflame the controversy over slavery.

Watch on **MyHistoryLab**
Video: Harriet Beecher Stowe and the Making of *Uncle Tom's Cabin*

Read on **MyHistoryLab**
Document: A Southern Scholar Critiques *Uncle Tom's Cabin,* 1852

The Kansas-Nebraska Act

After the Compromise of 1850, the disagreement over slavery's expansion intensified and became violent. In 1854 Senator Stephen Douglas introduced a bill in Congress to organize the Kansas and Nebraska Territories that soon provoked white settlers in Kansas to kill each other over slavery. Douglas's primary concern was to secure the Kansas and Nebraska region for the construction of a transcontinental railroad. To win the support of southern Democrats, who wanted slavery in at least one of the two new territories, Douglas's bill would permit Kansas residents to decide for themselves whether to allow slavery (see Map 10–2).

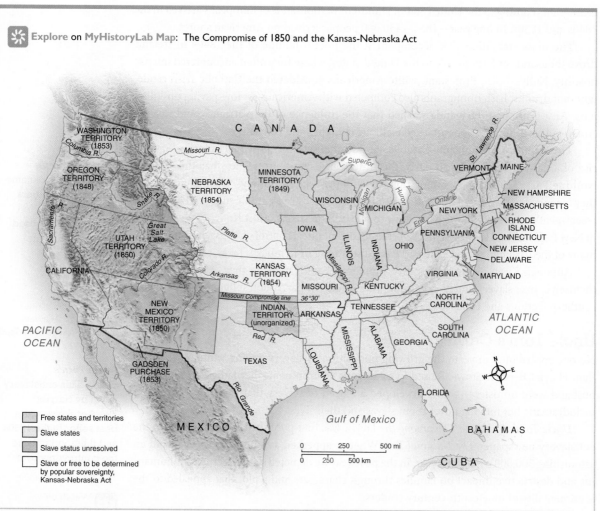

Explore on **MyHistoryLab Map**: The Compromise of 1850 and the Kansas-Nebraska Act

MAP 10–2 THE KANSAS-NEBRASKA ACT

This measure guided through Congress by Democratic Senator Steven A. Douglas opened up the Great Plains to settlement and to railroad development. It also deeply divided the nation by repealing the 1820 Missouri Compromise Line of 36° 30′ and permitting—through popular sovereignty—the people in Kansas to determine slavery's fate in that territory. Eastern Kansas became a bloody battleground between proslavery and antislavery forces.

Where exactly could slavery conceivably exist where it had previously been prohibited?

This proposal—known as "**popular sovereignty**"—angered many northerners because it created the possibility that slavery might expand to areas where it had been prohibited. The Missouri Compromise of 1820 banned slavery north of the 36° 30' line of latitude. Douglas's **Kansas-Nebraska Act** would repeal that limitation and allow settlers in Kansas, which was north of that line, to vote on slavery there.

Douglas managed to muster enough votes in Congress to pass the bill, but its enactment destroyed an already divided Whig Party and drove a wedge between the North and South. The Whig Party disintegrated. Northern Whigs joined supporters of the Free-Soil Party to form the Republican Party, which was organized expressly to oppose the expansion of slavery. Southern Whigs drifted, often without enthusiasm, to the Democrats or Know-Nothings.

Violence soon erupted in Kansas between proslavery and antislavery forces. "**Border ruffians**" from Missouri invaded Kansas to attack antislavery settlers and to vote illegally in Kansas elections. The New England Emigrant Aid Society dispatched people to the territory, and the Rev. Henry Ward Beecher encouraged them to bring firearms. By 1856 Kansas had 8,500 settlers, including 245 slaves, and two rival territorial governments. Civil war had erupted—prompting the press to label the territory "Bleeding Kansas."

More than 200 people died in the escalating violence. Some 500 border ruffians attacked the antislavery town of Lawrence, damaging businesses and killing one person. Abolitionist John Brown and four of his sons sought revenge by hacking five proslavery men to death in Pottawattamie. A proslavery firing squad executed nine Free-Soilers. John Brown reappeared in Missouri, killed a slave owner, and freed 11 slaves. Then he fled to plan an even larger and more dramatic attack on slavery.

Preston Brooks Attacks Charles Sumner

The violence in Kansas spread to Congress. In May 1856, Massachusetts Senator Charles Sumner delivered a tirade in the Senate denouncing the proslavery settlers in Kansas and the southerners who supported them. Speaking of "The Crime against Kansas," Sumner accused South Carolina Senator Andrew P. Butler of keeping slavery as his lover. Butler "has chosen a mistress to whom he has made his vows, and who . . . though polluted in the sight of the world, is chaste in his sight—I mean the harlot slavery." Butler was not present for the speech, but his distant cousin, South Carolina Congressman Preston Brooks, was. Brooks did not appreciate Sumner's verbal assault on a member of his family.

Two days later, Brooks exacted his revenge. Waiting until the Senate adjourned, Brooks strode to the desk where Sumner was seated and attacked him with a cane. The blows rained down until the cane shattered and Sumner tumbled to the floor, bloody and semiconscious. Sumner suffered lingering physical and emotional effects from the beating and did not return to the Senate for almost four years. Brooks resigned from the House of Representatives, paid a $300 fine, and went home to South Carolina a hero. He was easily reelected to his seat.

In the 1856 presidential election, the Democrats—although divided over the debacle in Kansas—nominated James Buchanan of Pennsylvania, another northern Democrat who was acceptable to the South. The Republicans supported a handsome army officer, John C. Fremont. Their slogan was "Free Soil, Free Speech, Free Men, and Fremont." But the Republicans were exclusively a northern party, and, with the demise of the Whigs, the South had become largely a one-party region. Almost no white southerners would support the Republicans, a party whose very existence was based on its opposition to slavery's expansion. Buchanan won the presidency with nearly solid southern support and enough northern votes to carry him to victory, but the Republicans gained enough support and confidence to

popular sovereignty
A proposal in which the residents of a territory (such as Kansas) would vote to legalize or prohibit slavery in that territory.

Kansas-Nebraska Act, 1854 Legislation introduced by Democratic Senator Stephen Douglas to organize the Kansas and Nebraska territories. It provided for "popular sovereignty," whereby settlers would decide whether slavery would be legal or illegal.

Border ruffians Proslavery advocates and vigilantes from Missouri who crossed the border into Kansas in 1855–1857 to support slavery in Kansas by threatening and attacking antislavery settlers.

Read on **MyHistoryLab**
Document: Massachusetts Defies the Fugitive Slave Act, 1855

10-1
10-2
10-3
10-4
10-5
10-6
10-7

Dred Scott v. Sandford
The 1857 U.S. Supreme Court case that ruled against Missouri slave Dred Scott by declaring that black people were not citizens, that they possessed no constitutional rights, and were considered to be property.

10-1

10-2

10-3

10-4

10-5

10-6

10-7

give them hope for the 1860 election. Before then, however, the U.S. Supreme Court intervened in the controversy over slavery.

The *Dred Scott* Decision

10-4   What was the *Dred Scott* case and what was the reaction to the Supreme Court's decision in the case?

When the Supreme Court accepted his case in 1856, Dred Scott was in his fifties and had been entangled in the judicial system for more than a decade. Scott was born in Virginia, but by the 1830s he belonged to John Emerson, an army doctor in Missouri. Emerson took Scott to military posts in Illinois and to Fort Snelling in what is now Minnesota. While at Fort Snelling, Scott married Harriet, a slave woman, and they had a daughter, Eliza, before Emerson returned with the three of them to St. Louis. In 1846, after Emerson's death and with the support of white friends, Scott and his wife filed separate suits for their freedom. By agreement, her suit was set aside pending the outcome of her husband's litigation. Scott and his lawyers contended that because Scott had been taken to territory where slavery was illegal, he had become a free man.

Scott lost his first suit, won his second, but lost again on appeal to the Missouri Supreme Court. His lawyers then appealed to the federal courts where they lost again. The final appeal in **Dred Scott v. Sandford** was to the U.S. Supreme Court.

Questions for the Court

Chief Justice Roger Taney of Maryland framed two questions for the Court to decide in the Scott case: Could Scott, a black man, sue in a federal court? And was Scott free because he had been taken to a state and a territory where slavery was prohibited? In response to the first question, the Court, led by Taney, ruled that Scott—and every other black American—could not sue in a federal court because black people were not citizens. Speaking for the majority (two of the nine justices dissented), Taney emphatically stated that black people had no rights: "They had for more than a century before been regarded as beings of an inferior order; and altogether unfit to associate with the white race, either in social or political relations; and so far inferior that they had no rights which the white man was bound to respect; and that the negro might justly and lawfully be reduced to slavery for his benefit."

A majority of the Court also answered no to the second question. Scott was not a free man, although he had lived in places where slavery was illegal. Scott, Taney

Read on MyHistoryLab Document: The Supreme Court Rules in *Dred Scott v. Sandford*, 1857

The *Dred Scott* case was front-page news on *Frank Leslie's Illustrated Newspaper* in 1857. Harriet and Dred with their two daughters are depicted sympathetically as members of the middle class rather than as abused and mistreated slaves.

maintained, again speaking for the Court, was slave property—and the slave owner's property rights took precedence. To the astonishment of those who opposed slavery's expansion, the Court also ruled that Congress could not pass measures—including the Missouri Compromise or the Kansas-Nebraska Act—that might prevent slave owners from taking their property into any territory. To do so, Taney implied, would violate the Fifth Amendment of the Constitution, which protected people from the loss of their life, liberty, or property without due process of law.

Following the decision, a new owner freed Dred and Harriet Scott. They settled in St. Louis, where he worked as a porter at Barnum's Hotel until he died of tuberculosis in 1858.

Reaction to the *Dred Scott* Decision

The Court had spoken. Would the nation listen? White southerners were delighted with Taney's decision. Republicans were horrified. But instead of earning the acceptance—let alone the approval—of most Americans, the case further inflamed the controversy over slavery. But if white Americans were divided in their reaction to the *Dred Scott* decision, black Americans were discouraged, disgusted, and defiant. Taney's decision delivered another setback to a people—already held in forced labor—who believed that their toil, sweat, and contributions over the previous 250 years to what had become the United States gave them a legitimate role in American society. Now the Supreme Court said they had no rights. They knew better.

At rallies across the North, black people condemned the decision. Black leader H. Ford Douglas vented his rage at an American government and a constitution that could produce such a decision:

> To persist in supporting a government which holds and exercises the power . . . to trample a class under foot as an inferior and degraded race is on the part of the colored man at once the height of folly and the depth of pusillanimity. . . . The only duty the colored man owes to a constitution under which he is declared to be an inferior and degraded being . . . is to denounce and repudiate it, and to do what he can by all proper means to bring it into contempt.

Only Frederick Douglass found a glimmer of hope. He believed—and events proved him right—that the decision was so wrong that it would help destroy slavery.

White Northerners and Black Americans

Many white northerners were genuinely concerned by the struggles of fugitive slaves, moved by *Uncle Tom's Cabin,* and disturbed by the *Dred Scott* decision. Yet as sensitive and sympathetic as some of them were to the plight of black people, most white Americans—including northerners—remained indifferent to, fearful of, or hostile to people of color. By the 1850s, 200,000 black people lived in the northern states, and many white people there were not pleased with their presence. Many white northerners, especially those living in southern Ohio, Indiana, and Illinois, supported the fugitive slave law and were eager to help return runaway slaves to bondage.

The same white northerners who opposed the expansion of slavery to California or Kansas also opposed the migration of free black people to northern states and communities. In 1851 Indiana and Iowa outlawed the emigration of black people, slave or free, to their territory. Illinois did likewise in 1853. White male voters in Michigan in 1850 voted overwhelmingly against permitting black men to vote. Only Ohio was an exception. In 1849 it repealed legislation excluding black people from the state.

These restrictive measures were not new. Most northern states had begun to restrict or deny the rights of black Americans in the early 1800s (see Chapter 7). Although only loosely enforced, the laws reflected the prevailing racial sentiments among many white northerners, as did the widespread antiblack rioting of the 1830s and 1840s.

The Lincoln-Douglas Debates

10-5 What were the positions of Stephen Douglas and Abraham Lincoln on racial equality?

Read on MyHistoryLab
Document: The Lincoln-Douglas Debates, 1858

Watch on MyHistoryLab
Video: The Lincoln-Douglas Debates

10-1

10-2

10-3

10-4

10-5

Lincoln-Douglas debates Abraham Lincoln and Stephen Douglas debated seven times in the 1858 U.S. Senate race in Illinois. They spent most of their time arguing over slavery, its expansion, the *Dred Scott* decision, and the character of African Americans. Douglas won the election.

10-6

10-7

In 1858 Senator Stephen Douglas of Illinois, a Democrat, ran for reelection to the Senate against Republican Abraham Lincoln. The main issues in the campaign were slavery and race, which the two candidates addressed in debates around the state. In carefully reasoned speeches and responses, these experienced and articulate lawyers focused almost exclusively on slavery's expansion and its future in the Union. At Freeport, Illinois, Lincoln, a former Whig congressman, attempted to trap Douglas by asking him if slavery could expand now that the *Dred Scott* decision had ruled slaves were property whom their owners could take into any federal territory. In reply, Douglas, who wanted to be president and had no desire to offend northern or southern voters, cleverly defended "popular sovereignty" and the *Dred Scott* decision. He insisted that slave owners could indeed take their slaves where they pleased. But, he contended, if the people of a territory failed to enact slave codes to protect and control slave property, slave owners were not likely to settle there with their slaves.

Abraham Lincoln and Black People

The **Lincoln-Douglas debates** did not always turn on the fine points of constitutional law or the fate of slavery in the territories. Thanks mainly to Douglas, who accused Lincoln and the Republicans of promoting the interests of black people over those of white people, the debates sometimes degenerated into crude exchanges about which candidate favored white people more and black people less. Douglas proudly advocated white supremacy. "The signers of the Declaration [of Independence] had no reference to the Negro . . . or any other inferior or degraded race when they spoke of the equality of men." He later charged that Lincoln and the Republicans wanted black and white equality. "If you, Black Republicans, think the negro ought to be on social equality with your wives and daughters, . . . you have a perfect right to do so. . . . Those of you who believe the negro is your equal . . . of course will vote for Mr. Lincoln."

Lincoln did not believe in racial equality, and he made that plain. In exasperation, he explained that merely because he opposed slavery did not mean he believed in equality. "I do not understand that because I do not want a negro woman for a slave I must necessarily have her for a wife." He bluntly added,

> I am not, nor ever have been in favor of bringing about in any way the social and political equality of the white and black races . . . ; and I will say in addition to this that there is a physical difference between the races which I believe will forever forbid the two races living together on terms of social and political equality.

But without repudiating these views, Lincoln later tried to transcend this blatant racism. "Let us discard all this quibbling about this man and the other man—this race and that race and the other race being inferior." Instead, he added, let us "unite as one people throughout this land, until we shall once more stand up declaring that all men are created equal." Lincoln stated unequivocally that race had nothing to do with whether a man had the right to be paid for his labor. He pointed out that the black man, "in the right to eat the bread, without leave of anybody else, which his own hand earns, he is my equal and the equal of Judge Douglas, and the equal of every living man."

Lincoln may have won the debate in the minds of many, but Douglas won the election. (State legislators—not voters—elected U.S. senators until the ratification of the Seventeenth Amendment in 1917.) Lincoln, however, made a name for himself that would work to his political advantage in the near future, and Douglas, despite his best efforts, had thoroughly offended many southerners by suggesting that slave owners would not risk taking their human property to a territory that lacked a slave code. Douglas also antagonized white southerners when he opposed the proslavery Kansas Lecompton constitution that he and many others believed had been fraudulently adopted. In two years, these disagreements over slavery would contribute to a decisive split in the Democratic Party.

John Brown and the Raid on Harpers Ferry

10-6 What was the impact of John Brown's raid on Harpers Ferry?

While Lincoln and Douglas were debating, John Brown was plotting. Following his attack on Pottawattamie in Kansas, Brown began to plan the overthrow of slavery in the South itself. In Canada in May 1858, accompanied by 11 white followers, he met 34 black people led by Martin Delany and appealed for their support. Brown was determined to invade the South and end slavery. He hoped to attract legions of slaves as his "army" moved down the Appalachian Mountains into the heart of the plantation system.

Planning the Raid

Only one man at the Canadian gathering agreed to join the raid. Brown returned to the United States and garnered financial support from prosperous white abolitionists. Brown also asked Frederick Douglass and Harriet Tubman to join him. They declined. By the summer of 1859, at a farm in rural Maryland, Brown had assembled an "army" consisting of 17 white men (including three of his adult sons) and five black men. The black men who enlisted were Osborne Anderson; Sheridan Leary, an escaped slave who had become a saddle and harness maker in Oberlin, Ohio; Leary's nephew John A. Copeland, an Oberlin College student; and two escaped slaves, Shields Green and Dangerfield Newby.

The Raid

Brown's invasion began on Sunday night, October 16, 1859, with a raid on Harpers Ferry, Virginia, and the federal arsenal there. Brown hoped to

Read on **MyHistoryLab Document:** William Lloyd Garrison on John Brown's Raid, 1859

John Brown was captured in the Engine House at Harpers Ferry on October 18, 1859. He was quickly tried for treason and convicted. On December 2, 1859, he was hanged. His raid helped catapult the nation toward civil war.

secure weapons and then advance south, but the operation went awry from the start. The dedication and devotion of Brown and his men were not matched by their strategy or his leadership. The first person Brown's band killed was ironically a free black man, Heyward Shepard, who was a baggage handler at the train station. The alarm went out, and opposition gathered.

Although they had lost the initiative, Brown and his men neither advanced nor retreated. Instead, they remained in Harpers Ferry while Virginia and Maryland militia converged on them. Fighting began, and two townspeople, the mayor, and eight of Brown's men, including Sheridan Leary, Dangerfield Newby, and two of Brown's sons, were killed. But Brown managed to seize hostages.

By Tuesday morning, Brown, with his hostages and what remained of his "army," were holed up in an engine house. U.S. Marines under the command of Robert E. Lee arrived, surrounded the building, and demanded Brown's surrender. He refused. The marines broke in. Brown was wounded and captured.

About 150 adult slaves lived near Harpers Ferry. Most of them were aware of the raid, and many of them joined the insurrection. Osborne Anderson provided pikes to slaves. Some of them acquired firearms. Several slaves managed to flee to freedom in the North. Perhaps a dozen black men—in addition to those who accompanied Brown—died during and after the raid.

There was no massive slave uprising. Shields Green and John A. Copeland fled but were caught. Osborne Anderson eluded capture and later fought in the Civil War. Virginia tried Brown, Green, and Copeland for treason. They were found guilty and sentenced to hang. But the violence did not end. In the weeks that followed, the barn of every juror who convicted Brown was burned. Many horses and cattle died. They were apparently poisoned.

The Reaction

John Brown's raid had not proceeded as planned; nonetheless, Brown and his men succeeded in intensifying the deep emotions of those who supported and those who opposed slavery. At first regarded as crazed zealots and insane fanatics, they showed they were willing—even eager—to die for the antislavery cause. The dignity and assurance that Brown, Green, and Copeland displayed as they awaited the gallows impressed many black and white northerners.

For many northerners, the day Brown was executed, December 2, 1859, was a day of mourning. Church bells tolled, and people bowed their heads in prayer. One unnamed black man later solemnly declared, "The memory of John Brown shall be indelibly written upon the tablets of our hearts, and when tyrants cease to oppress the enslaved, we will teach our children to revive his name, and transmit it to the latest posterity, as being the greatest man in the 19th century."

White southerners were traumatized by the raid and outraged that northerners made Brown a hero and a martyr. A wave of hysteria and paranoia swept the South as incredulous white people wondered how northerners could admire a man who sought to kill slave owners and free their slaves.

Brown's raid and the reaction to it further divided a nation already badly split over slavery. Although neither he nor anyone else realized it at the time, Brown and his "army" had propelled the South toward secession from the Union—and thereby moved the nation closer to his goal of destroying slavery.

John Brown's raid Brown's raid on Harpers Ferry, Virginia, in October 1859 failed to lead to a major slave insurrection, but it inflamed the controversy over slavery in the North and South.

Read on **MyHistoryLab**
Document: John Brown Speaks at His Trial, 1859

✳ EXPLORE ON MYHISTORYLAB

The Sectional Crisis

How did the nation increasingly fracture during the Sectional Crisis?

Between 1790 and 1860, the ever-expanding United States saw dramatic changes in its population. The Missouri Compromise of 1820 evaded dealing with the explosive issue of slavery by allowing future southern states to permit slavery and banning its expansion in future northern states. As states were admitted across the South, slavery expanded westward. Enslaved African Americans came to make up significant portions of the total populations of states from the Atlantic coast to Texas. In the North, however, slavery had been gradually banned and industrialization boomed across the region. As the 1860 presidential election neared, the United States found itself ever more divided between North and South, a division centered on slavery.

"Border ruffians" were armed men from Missouri who crossed the border to support proslavery forces in the Kansas territory. These men sought the legalization of slavery in Kansas. They—as well as the opponents of slavery—were willing to resort to violence to achieve their aims.

SLAVES AS A PERCENTAGE OF THE POPULATION IN SLAVEHOLDING STATES	
State	**Percent**
Alabama	45%
Arkansas	26%
Delaware	2%
Florida	44%
Georgia	44%
Kentucky	20%
Louisiana	47%
Maryland	13%
Mississippi	55%
Missouri	10%
North Carolina	33%
South Carolina	57%
Tennessee	25%
Texas	30%
Virginia	31%

SOURCE: *The Civil War Home Page, http://www.civil-war.net/pages/1860_census.html. Created 1997.*

✳ Explore the Topic on MyHistoryLab

1. **Comparison** *How did the demographics of the North differ from the South?* Explore the populations of the two regions based on census results.
2. **Consequence** *What impact did slavery have on immigration to the South?* Map the percentage of foreign-born immigrants in the United States.
3. **Analysis** *In what areas did more people live in towns and cities during this time?* Explain what effects differences in levels of urban population had on area economies.

10-1

10-2

10-3

10-4

10-5

10-6

10-7

The Election of Abraham Lincoln

10-7   How did African Americans and white southerners react to the election of Abraham Lincoln in 1860?

With the country fracturing over slavery, four candidates ran for president in the election of 1860. The Democrats split into a northern faction, which nominated Stephen Douglas, and a southern faction, which nominated John C. Breckenridge of Kentucky. The Constitutional Union Party, a new party formed by former Whigs, nominated John Bell of Tennessee. The breakup of the Democratic Party assured victory for the Republican candidate, Abraham Lincoln (see Map 10–3).

Lincoln's name was not even on the ballot in most southern states because his candidacy was based on the Republican Party's adamant opposition to the expansion of slavery into any western territory. Although Lincoln took pains to reassure white southerners that slavery would continue in states where it already existed, they were not persuaded.

Black People Respond to Lincoln's Election

Although they were less opposed to Lincoln than white southerners, black northerners and white abolitionists were not eager to see Abraham Lincoln become president. Dismayed by his contradictions and racism—he opposed slavery, but he tolerated it; he was against slavery's expansion, but he condemned black Americans as inferiors—many black people refused to support him or did so reluctantly. The New York *Anglo-African* opposed both Republicans and Democrats in the 1860 election, telling its readers to depend on each other. "We have no hope from either [of the] political parties. We must rely on ourselves, the righteousness of our cause, and the advance of just sentiments among the great masses of the . . . people."

Abolitionists such as William Lloyd Garrison and Wendell Phillips believed Lincoln was too willing to tolerate slaveholding interests. But Frederick Douglass wrote, "Lincoln's election will indicate growth in the right direction," and his presidency "must and will be hailed as an anti-slavery triumph."

After Lincoln's election, black leaders almost welcomed the secession of southern states. H. Ford Douglas urged the southern states to leave the Union. "Stand not upon the order of your going, but go at once. . . . There is no union of ideas and interests in this country, and there can be no union between freedom and slavery." Frederick Douglass was convinced that there were men prepared to follow in the footsteps of John Brown's "army" to destroy slavery. "I am for dissolution of the Union—decidedly for a dissolution of the Union! . . . In case of such a dissolution, I believe that men could be found . . . who would venture into those states and raise the standard of liberty there."

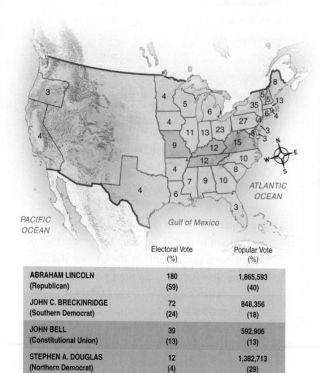

	Electoral Vote (%)	Popular Vote (%)
ABRAHAM LINCOLN (Republican)	180 (59)	1,865,593 (40)
JOHN C. BRECKINRIDGE (Southern Democrat)	72 (24)	848,356 (18)
JOHN BELL (Constitutional Union)	39 (13)	592,906 (13)
STEPHEN A. DOUGLAS (Northern Democrat)	12 (4)	1,382,713 (29)

MAP 10–3 THE ELECTION OF 1860
The results reflect the sectional schism over slavery. Lincoln carried the election, although he won only in northern states. His name did not even appear on the ballot in most southern states.

How was Lincoln able to win without getting any electoral votes from the South?

(((•))) 📖
Read on **MyHistoryLab**
Document: Abraham Lincoln Argues That the United States Cannot Be a "House Divided," 1859

10-1

10-2

10-3

10-4

10-5

10-6

10-7

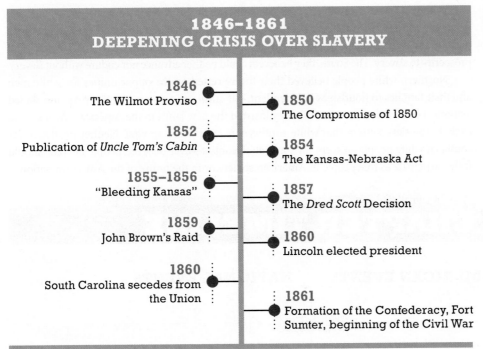

1846–1861
DEEPENING CRISIS OVER SLAVERY

Watch on MyHistoryLab
Video: Dred Scott and the Crises That Led to the Civil War

1846
The Wilmot Proviso

1850
The Compromise of 1850

1852
Publication of *Uncle Tom's Cabin*

1854
The Kansas-Nebraska Act

1855–1856
"Bleeding Kansas"

1857
The *Dred Scott* Decision

1859
John Brown's Raid

1860
Lincoln elected president

1860
South Carolina secedes from the Union

1861
Formation of the Confederacy, Fort Sumter, beginning of the Civil War

10-1
10-2
10-3
10-4
10-5
10-6
10-7

Disunion

When South Carolina seceded on December 20, 1860, it began a procession of southern states out of the Union. By February 1861 seven states—South Carolina, Mississippi, Alabama, Florida, Louisiana, Georgia, and Texas—had seceded and formed the Confederate States of America in Montgomery, Alabama. Before there could be the kind of undertaking against slavery that Douglass had proposed, Abraham Lincoln tried to persuade the seceding states to reconsider. In his inaugural address of March 4, 1861, Lincoln attempted to calm the fears of white southerners but informed them he would not tolerate their withdrawal from the Union. Lincoln repeated his assurance that he would not tamper with slavery in the states where it was already legal.

Lincoln claimed that the "only" dispute between the North and South was over the expansion of slavery. He emphatically warned, however, that he would enforce the Constitution and not permit secession. He pleaded with white southerners to contemplate their actions patiently and thoughtfully, actions that might provoke a civil conflict. Southern whites did not heed him. Slavery was too essential to give up merely to preserve the Union.

Barely a month after Lincoln's inauguration, Confederate leaders demanded that U.S. Army Major Robert Anderson surrender Fort Sumter in the harbor of Charleston, South Carolina. Anderson refused, and on April 12, 1861, Confederate artillery fired on the fort. In the aftermath, Virginia, North Carolina, Tennessee, and Arkansas joined the Confederacy. The Civil War had begun.

CONCLUSION

Virtually every event and episode of major or minor consequence in the United States between 1846 and 1861 involved black people and the expansion of slavery. From the Wilmot Proviso and the Compromise of 1850 to the *Dred Scott* decision and John Brown's raid, white Americans were increasingly perplexed about how the nation could remain half slave and half free. They were unable to resolve the problem of slavery's expansion.

Without the presence of black people in America, neither secession nor civil war would have occurred. Yet the Civil War began because white Americans had developed contradictory visions of the future. White southerners contemplated a future that inextricably linked their security and prosperity to slavery. The South, they believed, could neither advance nor endure without slavery.

Northern white people believed their future rested on the opportunities for white men and their families to flourish as independent, self-sufficient farmers, shopkeepers, and skilled artisans. For their future to prevail, they insisted the new lands in the American West should exclude the slave system that white southerners considered so vital. Neither northern nor southern white people—except for some abolitionists—ever believed people of color should fully participate as free people in American society or in the future of the American nation.

CHAPTER TIMELINE

AFRICAN-AMERICAN EVENTS

NATIONAL EVENTS

1820–1830

1829
David Walker publishes his
Appeal to the Colored Citizens of the World

1820
Missouri Compromise

1830–1840

1831
William Lloyd Garrison begins
publication of *The Liberator*

1833
American Anti-Slavery Society founded

1832
South Carolina nullifies the tariff laws

1836
Texas declares independence from Mexico

1838
Frederick Douglass escapes from slavery

1840–1850

1845
The United States annexes Texas,
and it enters the Union as a slave state

1847
Crosswhite family eludes
capture in Michigan

1848
William and Ellen Craft escape
from slavery in Georgia

1844
James K. Polk elected president

1846–1847
Mexican War

1846
Wilmot Proviso

1847
Mormons begin settlement of Utah

1848
Formation of the Free-Soil Party
Zachary Taylor elected president
Women's rights convention at Seneca Falls, New York

1850–1860

1850
Fugitive Slave Act

1850–1860
Fugitive slaves captured

1850
Compromise of 1850

1852
Publication of *Uncle Tom's Cabin*
Franklin Pierce elected president

CHAPTER TIMELINE

AFRICAN-AMERICAN EVENTS

1851
Shadrach Minkins eludes capture in Boston
Thomas Sims returned to slavery "Battle"
at Christiana

1853
Black convention at Rochester, New York

1854
Anthony Burns returned to slavery in Boston

1856
Margaret Garner kills her daughter
in unsuccessful escape

1857
The *Dred Scott* decision

1859
John Brown's raid on Harpers Ferry

NATIONAL EVENTS

1854
Kansas-Nebraska Act

1855–1856
"Bleeding Kansas"

1856
James Buchanan elected president
Congressman Preston Brooks assaults Senator
Charles Sumner

1858
The Lincoln-Douglas debates

1860–1865

1861
Free black men in Charleston offer
their support to South Carolina

1860
Abraham Lincoln elected president
South Carolina secedes from the Union

1861
Six more southern states secede and form the
Confederacy
Civil War begins after firing on Fort Sumter
Four more southern states join the Confederacy

On MyHistoryLab

 Study and Review on MyHistoryLab

REVIEW QUESTIONS

1. How and why did southern and northern white
people differ over slavery? On what did white people
of both regions agree and disagree about race and
slavery?

2. If you were a northern African American in the
1850s, how would you have responded to the
policies of the U.S. government?

3. If you were a white southerner in the 1850s, would
you have been encouraged or discouraged by U.S.
government policies?

4. Why did seven southern states secede from the
Union within three months after Abraham Lincoln
was elected president in 1860?

5. If you were a black person—either a slave or free—
would you have welcomed the secession of the
southern states? How might secession affect the
future of your people?

Narrative of the Life of Frederick Douglass and Black Autobiography

NARRATIVE

OF THE

LIFE

OF

FREDERICK DOUGLASS,

AN

AMERICAN SLAVE.

WRITTEN BY HIMSELF.

BOSTON:
PUBLISHED AT THE ANTI-SLAVERY OFFICE,
No. 25 CORNHILL.
1845.

Shortly after the *Narrative of the Life of Frederick Douglass, An American Slave, Written by Himself* appeared in 1845, white author and feminist Margaret Fuller reviewed this autobiography in the *New York Tribune*. Comparing Douglass to the famous French novelist Alexandre Dumas, whom Fuller also considered to be black because his grandmother was Haitian, she declared of the *Narrative*, "We have never read one more simple, true, coherent, and warm with genuine feeling. It is an excellent piece of writing, and on that score to be prized as a specimen of the powers of the Black Race, which Prejudice persists in disparaging." Today Douglass's *Narrative* is part of the American literary canon.

Black Americans wrote autobiographies long before 1845. In 1760, Briton Hammon, a Boston slave captured in 1747 by American Indians, published *A Narrative of the Uncommon Suffering, and Surprising Delivery of Briton Hammon, a Negro Man*. In 1798, Venture Smith, a former slave who had purchased his freedom, published *A Narrative of the Life and Adventures of Venture, a Native of Africa, but Resident Above Sixty Years in the United States, Related by Himself*. In 1825, William Grimes published *Life of William Grimes, the Runaway Slave, Written by Himself*. By the 1830s, former slaves' autobiographies were common. Through accounts of suffering in bondage and escape from it, they aimed to reach a white northern audience and gain support for the antislavery movement.

Douglass followed the pattern of these earlier life stories, and like them his *Narrative* sought to increase opposition to slavery. Yet Douglass's is by far the best of the slave narratives. Rather than simple antislavery propaganda, it is a psychological and intellectual portrayal of a slave's struggle for human identity. Douglass's *Narrative* was also immensely successful, selling 30,000 copies within five years of its publication. That number, while not impressive by today's standards, surpassed the *combined* sales of Herman Melville's *Moby-Dick*, Henry Thoreau's *On Walden Pond*, and Walt Whitman's *Leaves of Grass* during a similar period after their publication. Most important, the *Narrative* remains compelling. As Douglass's biographer William S. McFeely observed in 1991, "The person we come to know in these brief pages is unforgettable."

Black leaders have followed Douglass in using autobiography to define themselves and their goals. Douglass himself wrote two more autobiographies: *My Bondage and My Freedom* (1855), and *Life and Times of Frederick Douglass, Written by Himself* (1892). These cover his later career and provide additional information about his life in slavery, but do not match the literary stature of the *Narrative*. In 1868, Elizabeth Keckley, who led the Washington, DC, Contraband Relief Association during the Civil War and worked for Mary Todd Lincoln, published *Behind the Scenes, Or, Thirty Years a Slave and Four Years in the White House*.

Booker T. Washington's *Up from Slavery: An Autobiography* (1901) is organized more like Douglass's *Narrative* than is Keckley's book. Like Douglass, Washington emphasizes education and influencing white opinion. In addition, during the last years of his life, Douglass directly influenced Mary Church Terrell, Washington's young contemporary. Increasingly aware of racism's negative impact, Terrell, like Douglass, became a renowned speaker for civil rights. In 1940, she published her autobiography, *A Colored Woman in a White World*.

Like Douglass, W. E. B. Du Bois, the most influential black activist and intellectual from the 1910s through the 1940s, wrote three autobiographies. He published the first of them, *Darkwater: Voices from within the Veil*, in 1920. Du Bois's themes of the color-line and divided black consciousness are more psychologically sophisticated than Douglass's. Yet Douglass's revelation that in 1841, when he first addressed a white audience, "I felt myself a slave, and the idea of speaking to white people weighed me down," anticipates Du Bois's portrayal of interracial unease.

Martin Luther King Jr. and Malcolm X were less in Douglass's autobiographical tradition. King shared Douglass's commitment to racial integration. Yet *The Autobiography of Martin Luther King* (1998) is not really an autobiography. Instead, it is a selection of King's writings compiled by black historian Clayborne Carson that appeared long after King died. Malcolm was the author of *The Autobiography of Malcolm X* (1965), but black author Alex Haley had a major role in shaping the book. Malcolm's life also differed greatly from Douglass's, although both of their autobiographies stress resistance to conditions white people forced on black people.

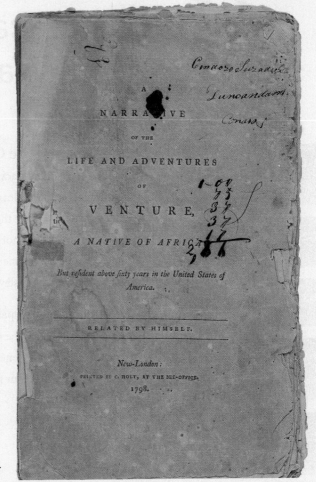

In 1966, the poet Langston Hughes reflected on Douglass's impact: "Douglass was someone who, had he walked with wary foot and frightened tread, from very indecision, might be dead. . . . He is not dead." Neither is his autobiographical legacy among black leaders. In *Dreams of My Father: A Story of Race and Inheritance* (1995), Barack Obama wrote an autobiography in the Douglass manner, as Obama defined himself, despite his biracial and international roots, as a black American.

1. **Does black autobiography have a central historical theme?**

2. **How is *The Narrative of the Life of Frederick Douglass* relevant today?**

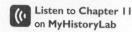
Liberation: African Americans and the Civil War 1861–1865

Slavery caused the Civil War. Yet when the war began in 1861, neither the Union nor the Confederacy entered the conflict with any intention or desire to change the status of black Americans. It was supposed to be a white man's war. White southerners would wage war to make the **Confederacy** a separate and independent nation free to promote slavery. White northerners took up arms to maintain the Union but not to free a single slave. African Americans who wanted to enlist in 1861 were rejected. The Union might be disrupted, but slavery was not going to be disturbed.

Both North and South expected a quick victory. No one anticipated that 48 months of brutal war would rip the nation apart. When the Civil War ended in April 1865, approximately 750,000 Americans were dead—including nearly 50,000 black men. The Union was preserved. Four million people had been freed. Nothing in American history compares with it.

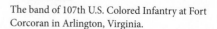
The band of 107th U.S. Colored Infantry at Fort Corcoran in Arlington, Virginia.

Lincoln's Aims

11-1 When the Civil War began, what was Abraham Lincoln's primary objective?

Throughout the war, President Lincoln's unwavering objective was to preserve the Union. Any policies that helped or hindered black people were subordinate to that goal. Following the attack on Fort Sumter in April 1861 and Lincoln's call for state militias to help suppress the rebellion, four more slave states—North Carolina, Virginia, Tennessee, and Arkansas—seceded from the Union and joined the Confederacy. For most of 1861, Lincoln was determined to do nothing that would drive the four remaining slave states—Delaware, Maryland, Kentucky, and Missouri—into the Confederacy. Lincoln feared that if he did or said anything that could be interpreted as interfering with slavery, those four states would leave the Union too.

Meanwhile, Lincoln called for 75,000 men to enlist in the military for 90 days of service to the national government. Many thousands of black and white men, far more than 75,000, responded. White men were accepted. Black men were rejected. Despite being spurned by federal and state authorities, black men remained determined to aid the cause.

Black Men Volunteer and Are Rejected

11-2 How did African Americans respond to the outbreak of the Civil War?

Black people recognized long before most white northerners that the fate of the Union was inextricably tied to the issue of slavery and the future of slavery was tied to the outcome of the war. "Talk as we may," insisted the *Anglo-African*, a black New York newspaper, "we are concerned in this fight and our fate hangs upon its issues."

Black men in New York formed their own military companies and began to drill. In Boston, they drew up a resolution modeled on the Declaration of Independence and appealed for permission to go to war. Black men in Philadelphia volunteered to infiltrate the South to incite slave revolts but were turned down. In Washington, DC, Jacob Dodson, a black employee of the Senate, wrote to Secretary of War Simon Cameron shortly after the fall of Fort Sumter volunteering the services of local black men. Cameron curtly rejected Dodson, "This Department has no intention at the present to call into the service of the government any colored soldiers."

Union Policies toward Confederate Slaves

Slaves started to liberate themselves as soon as the war began, but Union leaders had no coherent policy for dealing with them. To the disappointment of black northerners and white abolitionists, Union military commanders showed more concern for the interests of Confederate slave owners than for the people in bondage.

General Henry Halleck ordered slaves who escaped in the Ohio valley to be returned to their owners, and General Winfield Scott, the army's chief of staff, asked that Confederate slave owners be permitted to recover slaves who crossed the Potomac River. In Tennessee in early 1862, General Ulysses S. Grant returned runaway slaves to their owners if the owners

Confederacy
Association of slave states that left the Union in 1861.

Read on MyHistoryLab
Document: Elizabeth Keckley, *Behind the Scenes: Or, Thirty Years a Slave, and Four Years in the White House*, 1868

11-1

11-2

11-3

11-4

11-5

11-6

11-7

11-8

11-9

These African-American troops served as teamsters for the Union Army in Virginia. Most northern white people—including political leaders—believed that black men lacked the courage and fortitude for combat. They expected black men would do little more as soldiers than haul freight, erect fortifications, serve guard duty, and prepare food.

contraband Slaves who escaped to the Union or were captured by Union troops early in the Civil War; these slaves were considered enemy property.

First Confiscation Act This 1861 Act stated that any slaves used by their masters to benefit the Confederacy would be freed.

supported the Union cause but put them to work on fortifications if their owners favored secession.

"Contraband"

Not all Union commanders were so callous. A month after the war began, three bondmen working on Confederate fortifications in Virginia escaped to the Union's Fortress Monroe on the coast. Their owner, a Confederate colonel, appeared at the fortress the next day under a flag of truce and demanded the return of his slaves under the 1850 Fugitive Slave Act. The incredulous Union commander, General Benjamin Butler, informed him that because Virginia had seceded from the Union, that law was no longer in force. Butler did not free the three slaves, but he did not reenslave them either. He declared them "**contraband**"—enemy property—and put them to work for the Union. Soon, over a thousand slaves fled to Fortress Monroe.

On August 6, 1861, Congress clarified the status of runaway slaves when it passed the **First Confiscation Act**. Through this act, federal forces could seize any property that belonged to Confederates used in the war effort. Any slaves their masters used to benefit the Confederacy—and only those slaves—would be freed. Almost immediately, Union General John C. Fremont (the 1856 Republican presidential candidate) exceeded the strict limits of the act by freeing all the slaves belonging to Confederates in Missouri. President Lincoln countermanded the order and told Fremont that only slaves actively used to aid the Confederate war effort were to be freed. Lincoln worried that Fremont's decision would drive Missouri or Kentucky into the Confederacy.

Black leaders were—to put it mildly—displeased with Lincoln and with federal policies that both prohibited the enlistment of black troops and ignored the plight of the enslaved. As Frederick Douglass stated, "To fight against slaveholders, without fighting against slavery, is but a half-hearted business, and paralyzes the hands engaged in it. . . . Fire must be met with water. . . . War for the destruction of liberty must be met with war for the destruction of slavery." Others were less charitable. Joseph R. Hawley, a white Connecticut Republican, thought Lincoln was foolish to worry about whether the border states might leave the Union: "Permit me to say damn the border states. . . . A thousand Lincolns cannot stop the people from fighting slavery."

Lincoln was unmoved. Union military forces occupied an enclave on South Carolina's southern coast and the sea islands in late 1861, and on May 9, 1862, General David Hunter ordered slavery abolished in South Carolina, Georgia, and Florida. Lincoln revoked Hunter's order and reprimanded him. Nevertheless, thousands of slaves along the South Carolina and Georgia coast threw off their shackles and welcomed Union troops as plantation owners fled to the interior.

Lincoln's Initial Position

11-3 **How did Lincoln's policies on slavery change as the Civil War continued?**

For more than a year, Lincoln remained reluctant to strike decisively against slavery. He believed the long-term solution to slavery and the race problem in the United States was the **compensated emancipation** of slaves followed by their colonization outside the country. That is, slave owners would be paid for their slaves. The slaves would be freed but forced to settle in the Caribbean, Latin America, or West Africa.

In April 1862, at Lincoln's urging, Republicans in Congress (against almost unanimous Democratic opposition) voted to provide funds to "any state which may adopt gradual abolishment of slavery." Lincoln wanted to eliminate slavery from the border states with the approval of slave owners there and thus diminish the likelihood that those states would join the Confederacy.

But leaders in the border states rejected the proposal. Lincoln brought it up again in July. This time he warned congressmen and senators from the border states that if their states opposed compensated emancipation, they might have to accept uncompensated emancipation. They ignored his advice and denounced compensated emancipation as a "radical change in our social system" and an intrusion by the federal government into a state issue.

To many white Americans, Lincoln's support for compensated emancipation and colonization was a misguided attempt to link the war to the issue of slavery. But to black Americans, abolitionists, and an increasing number of Republicans, Lincoln's refusal to abolish slavery immediately was tragic. Antislavery advocates regarded Lincoln's willingness to purchase the freedom of slaves as an admission that he considered those human beings to be property. They deplored his seeming inability to realize the Union would not win the war unless slaves were liberated.

compensated emancipation Emancipation accompanied by the monetary compensation of former slave owners.

Read on **MyHistoryLab** Document: Alexander Hamilton Stephens Declares Slavery and White Supremacy the "Cornerstone" of the Confederacy, 1861

Lincoln Moves toward Emancipation

However, by the summer of 1862, after the border states rejected compensated emancipation, Lincoln concluded that victory and the future of the Union were tied directly to the issue of slavery. Therefore, slavery became the instrument Lincoln would use to hasten the end of the war and restore the Union. He told Secretary of the Navy Gideon Welles, "We must free the slaves or be ourselves subdued. The slaves were undeniably an element of strength to those who had their service, and we must decide whether that element should be with us or against us." Emancipation, Lincoln stressed, would "strike at the heart of the rebellion."

In cabinet meetings in July 1862, Lincoln discussed abolishing slavery. Except for Postmaster General Montgomery Blair, cabinet members supported emancipation. Secretary of State William H. Seward supported abolition but advised Lincoln not to issue a proclamation until the Union Army won a major victory. Otherwise, emancipation might look like the desperate gesture of the leader of a losing cause. Therefore, Lincoln accepted Seward's advice and postponed emancipation.

Lincoln Delays Emancipation

Nevertheless, word circulated that Lincoln intended to abolish slavery. However, weeks passed and slavery did not end. Frustrated abolitionists and Republicans attacked Lincoln.

11-1
11-2
11-3
11-4
11-5
11-6
11-7
11-8
11-9

In his *Prayer of Twenty Millions*, Horace Greeley, editor of the *New York Tribune*, expressed his disappointment that the president had not moved promptly against slavery, the issue that had led the southern states to leave the Union and go to war. Greeley insisted that Lincoln should have long ago warned white southerners that secession would endanger slavery.

On August 22, 1862, Lincoln replied to Greeley and explained his priorities. Placing the preservation of the Union before freedom for the enslaved, Lincoln declared, "My paramount object in this struggle is to save the Union, and is not either to save or destroy slavery. If I could save the Union without freeing any slave I would do it; and if I could save it by freeing all the slaves, I would do it; and if I could do it by freeing some and leaving others alone, I would also do that." He concluded, "I have here stated my purpose according to my view of *official* duty, and I intend no modification of my oft-expressed *personal* wish that all men, everywhere, could be free."

Black People Reject Colonization

Lincoln's policy on emancipation had shifted dramatically, but he remained committed to colonization. On August 14, 1862, Lincoln invited black leaders to the White House and appealed for their support for colonization. After condemning slavery as "the greatest wrong inflicted on any people," he explained that white racism made it unwise for black people to remain in the United States. Lincoln asked the black leaders to begin enlisting volunteers for a colonization project in Central America.

Most black people were unmoved by Lincoln's advice. A black leader from Philadelphia condemned the president. "This is our country as much as it is yours, and we will not leave it." Frederick Douglass accused Lincoln of hypocrisy and claimed that support for colonization would lead white men "to commit all kinds of violence and outrage upon the colored people."

Lincoln would not retreat from his support for colonization. Attempts were already under way to put compensated emancipation and colonization into effect. In April 1862 Congress enacted a bill to pay District of Columbia slave owners up to $300 for each slave they freed and to provide $100,000 to support the voluntary colonization of the freed people in Haiti or Liberia. In 1863 the government tried to settle 453 black American colonists at Ile à Vache, an island near Haiti. The settlers suffered terribly from disease and starvation. This sorry attempt at government-sponsored colonization ended in 1864 when the navy returned 368 survivors to the United States.

The Preliminary Emancipation Proclamation

Preliminary Emancipation Proclamation Proclamation issued on September 22, 1862, declaring that slaves residing in states still in rebellion on January 1, 1863, would be freed.

Finally on September 22, 1862—more than two months after Lincoln first seriously considered freedom for the enslaved—the president issued the **Preliminary Emancipation Proclamation**. It came five days after the Union turned back a Confederate invasion of Maryland at Antietam. This bloody but indecisive victory allowed Lincoln to justify emancipation. But his first proclamation freed no people immediately. Instead it stipulated that anyone in bondage in states or parts of states still in rebellion on January 1, 1863, would be "thenceforward, and forever free." Lincoln's announcement gave the Confederate states one hundred days to return to the Union. If any or all of those states rejoined the Union, the slaves there would remain in bondage. The Union would be preserved, and slavery would be maintained.

Read on MyHistoryLab
Document: Abraham Lincoln Defines His Position on Slavery and the War, 1862

Northern Reaction to Emancipation

In the Union, the Preliminary Emancipation Proclamation was greeted with little enthusiasm. Most black people and abolitionists were, of course, gratified that Lincoln had finally issued the proclamation. But they also worried that—however remote the possibility—some slave states would return to the Union by January 1, denying freedom to those enslaved.

Many white northerners resented emancipation. A northern newspaper editor vilified Lincoln as a "half-witted usurper" and the Proclamation as "monstrous, impudent, and heinous . . . insulting to God as to man, for it declares those 'equal' whom God created unequal."

Even before the announcement of emancipation, antiblack riots flared in the North. In Cincinnati in the summer of 1862, Irish dockworkers invaded black neighborhoods after black men had replaced the striking wharf hands along the city's riverfront. In Brooklyn, New York, Irish Americans burned a tobacco factory that employed black women and children.

Political Opposition to Emancipation

Northern Democrats almost unanimously opposed emancipation. They accused Lincoln and the Republicans of "fanaticism" and regretted that emancipation would liberate "two or three million semi savages" who would "overrun the North" and compete with white working people. The Democratic-controlled lower houses of the legislatures in Indiana and Illinois condemned the Proclamation as "wicked, inhuman, and unholy."

And as some Republicans had predicted and feared, the Democrats capitalized on dissatisfaction with the war's progress and with Republican support for emancipation to make gains in the fall elections. New York and New Jersey elected Democratic governors, and Democrats won 34 more seats in the U.S. House of Representatives, although the Republicans retained a majority.

The Emancipation Proclamation

11-4 **Why did Lincoln issue the Emancipation Proclamation and what was its effect and the reaction to it?**

On January 1, 1863, Abraham Lincoln issued the **Emancipation Proclamation**. It was not the first step toward freedom; since 1861, several thousand slaves had already freed themselves. However, it was the first significant effort by Union authorities to assure freedom to nearly four million people of African descent who, with their ancestors, had been enslaved for 250 years in North America. The Civil War was now a war to make people free.

Black communities and many white people across the North celebrated. Church bells rang. Poems were written, and prayers of thanksgiving offered. Many considered it the most momentous day in American history since July 4, 1776. Frederick Douglass had difficulty describing the emotions of people in Boston when word reached the city late on the night of December 31 that Lincoln would issue the Proclamation the next day. "The effect of this announcement was startling beyond description, and the scene was wild and grand. Joy and gladness exhausted all forms of expression, from shouts of praise to sobs and tears. . . ." Well into the twentieth century, New Year's Day was commemorated as Emancipation Day, a holiday black Americans zealously observed.

Limits of the Proclamation

By limiting emancipation to those states and areas still in rebellion, Lincoln did not include enslaved people in the four border states still in the Union or in areas of Confederate states that Union forces had already occupied. This included 48 counties in western Virginia

Emancipation Proclamation Issued by President Abraham Lincoln on January 1, 1863, the Emancipation Proclamation freed slaves in areas of the Confederate states not under Union control.

Read on **MyHistoryLab**
Document: The Emancipation Proclamation

11-1
11-2
11-3
11-4
11-5
11-6
11-7
11-8
11-9

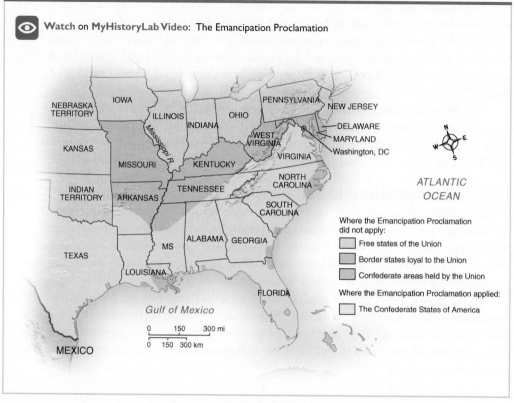

Watch on MyHistoryLab Video: The Emancipation Proclamation

MAP 11-1 EFFECTS OF THE EMANCIPATION PROCLAMATION
When Abraham Lincoln issued the Emancipation Proclamation on January 1, 1863, it applied only to slaves in those portions of the Confederacy not under Union authority. No southern slave owners freed their slaves at Lincoln's command. But many black people already had freed themselves as well as family and friends in the aftermath of Lincoln's order. The Emancipation Proclamation was of extreme importance. It helped the Union win the war. It meant that at long last the U.S. government had joined the abolitionist movement.

Where, according to the map, did slaves reside who were to be freed under the terms of the Proclamation?

that would soon become the state of West Virginia, parts of Tennessee, and 13 parishes (counties) in Louisiana, including New Orleans (see Map 11–1). Thus, thousands of people would remain in bondage despite the Proclamation. Slave owners in the Confederacy did not recognize Lincoln's authority, and they certainly did not free their slaves on January 1 or anytime soon thereafter. Nevertheless, as many as 50,000 slaves liberated themselves in the days and weeks following Lincoln's proclamation. The Emancipation Proclamation remains one of the most important documents in American history. It made the Civil War a war to free people as well as to preserve the Union, and it gave the Union cause moral authority. And as many black people had freed themselves before the Proclamation, many more would liberate themselves after.

Effects of the Proclamation on the South

The Emancipation Proclamation destroyed any chance that Britain or France would offer diplomatic recognition to the Confederate government. Diplomatic recognition

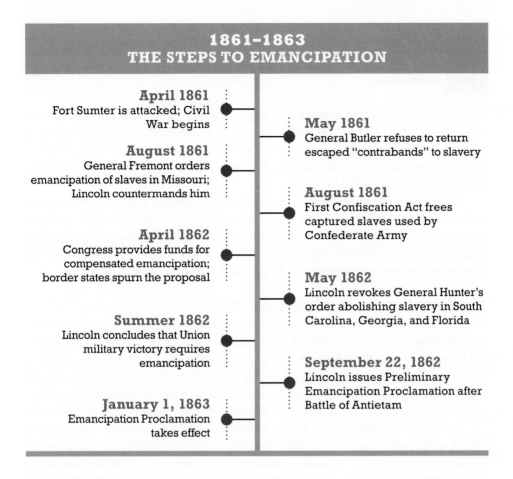

1861–1863
THE STEPS TO EMANCIPATION

April 1861
Fort Sumter is attacked; Civil War begins

May 1861
General Butler refuses to return escaped "contrabands" to slavery

August 1861
General Fremont orders emancipation of slaves in Missouri; Lincoln countermands him

August 1861
First Confiscation Act frees captured slaves used by Confederate Army

April 1862
Congress provides funds for compensated emancipation; border states spurn the proposal

May 1862
Lincoln revokes General Hunter's order abolishing slavery in South Carolina, Georgia, and Florida

Summer 1862
Lincoln concludes that Union military victory requires emancipation

September 22, 1862
Lincoln issues Preliminary Emancipation Proclamation after Battle of Antietam

January 1, 1863
Emancipation Proclamation takes effect

11-1
11-2
11-3
11-4
11-5
11-6
11-7
11-8
11-9

would have meant accepting the Confederacy as a legitimate state equal in international law to the Union, and it would almost surely have led to financial and military assistance for the South. British leaders, who had considered recognizing the Confederacy, now declined to support a "nation" that relied on slavery while its opponent moved to abolish it. In this sense, the Proclamation weakened the Confederacy's ability to prosecute the war.

Even more important, it undermined slavery in the South and contributed directly to the Confederacy's defeat. Black people—aware a Union victory in the war meant freedom—were far less likely to labor for their owners or for the Confederacy. More slaves ran away, especially as Union troops approached. Slave resistance became more likely. The institution of slavery cracked, crumbled, and collapsed after January 1, 1863.

Without emancipation, the United States would not have survived as a unified nation. Abraham Lincoln, after first failing to make the connection between eliminating slavery and preserving the Union, came to understand it fully and grasped what freedom meant to both black and white people. In his annual message to Congress in December 1862, one month before the Proclamation, Lincoln described the importance of emancipation: "We know how to save the Union. The world knows we do know how to save it. We—even we here—hold the power, and bear the responsibility. In giving freedom to the slave, we assure freedom to the free—honorable alike in what we give, and what we preserve."

Black Men Fight for the Union

11-5 | What was the role of black men in the Northern military and what difficulties did they face?

The Emancipation Proclamation not only marked the beginning of the end of slavery but also authorized the enlistment of black troops in the Union Army. Just as white leaders in the North came to realize the preservation of the Union necessitated the abolition of slavery, they also began to understand that black men were needed for the military effort if the Union was to triumph in the Civil War.

Like the decision to free the slaves, the decision to employ black troops proceeded neither smoothly nor logically. The commitment to the Civil War as a white man's war was entrenched, and many white northerners opposed the initial attempts to enlist black troops. As with emancipation, Lincoln moved slowly from outright opposition to cautious acceptance to enthusiastic support for enlisting black men in the Union Army.

The First South Carolina Volunteers

View on MyHistoryLab Closer Look: Black Union Soldiers

Some Union officers recruited black men long before emancipation was proclaimed and before most white northerners were prepared to accept, much less welcome, black troops. In May 1862 General David Hunter began recruiting former slaves along the South Carolina coast and the sea islands, an area Union forces had captured in late 1861. But some black men did not want to enlist, and Hunter used white troops to force black men to "volunteer" for military service. He managed to organize a 500-man regiment—the **First South Carolina Volunteers**.

Through the summer of 1862, Hunter trained and drilled the regiment while awaiting official authorization and funds to pay them. When Congress balked, Hunter disbanded all but one company of the regiment that August. The troops were dispersed, unpaid and disappointed. The surviving company was sent to St. Simon's Island off the Georgia coast to protect former slaves.

Although Congress failed to support Hunter, it did pass the **Second Confiscation Act** and the **Militia Act of 1862**, which authorized President Lincoln to enlist black men. In Louisiana that fall, two regiments of free black men, the Native Guards, were accepted for federal service, and General Benjamin Butler organized them into the Corps d'Afrique. General Rufus Saxton gained the approval of Secretary of War Edwin Stanton to revive Hunter's dispersed regiment and to recall the company that had been sent to St. Simon's Island.

As commander, Saxton appointed Thomas Wentworth Higginson. Higginson was an ardent white abolitionist, one of the Secret Six who had provided financial support for John Brown's raid on Harpers Ferry. He was determined not merely to end slavery but to prove that black people were equal to white people. Higginson set out to mold this regiment of mostly former slaves into an effective fighting force. On Emancipation Day, January 1, 1863, near Beaufort, South Carolina, the First South Carolina Volunteer Regiment was inducted into the U.S. Army.

The Second South Carolina Volunteers

A month later, the Second South Carolina Volunteers began enrolling ex-slaves, many from Georgia and Florida. James Montgomery, another former financial supporter of John Brown, commanded them. But like Hunter, Montgomery found that many former slaves were reluctant to volunteer for military service, so he also used force to recruit them. He concluded that black men responded to the call to arms much the way white men did, except black men were less likely to desert once they joined the army:

First South Carolina Volunteers This black military unit consisted of former slaves recruited in the South Carolina and Georgia low country in 1862 and 1863 for service with Union military forces in the Civil War.

Second Confiscation Act The 1862 Act freeing all slaves of rebel owners.

Militia Act of 1862 The 1862 Act authorizing Lincoln to enlist black soldiers.

Finding it somewhat difficult to induce Negroes to enlist, we resolved to the draft. The negroes reindicate their claim to humanity by shirking the draft in every possible way; acting exactly like white men under similar circumstances. . . . The only difference that I notice is, the negro, after being drafted does not desert; but once dressed in the uniform with arms in his hands he feels himself a man; and acts like one.

The 54th Massachusetts Regiment

While ex-slaves joined the Union ranks in South Carolina, free black men in the North enlisted in what would become the most famous black unit, the **54th Massachusetts Regiment**. In January 1863 Governor John A. Andrew received permission from Secretary of War Stanton to raise a black regiment. Andrew asked prominent black men across the North for help. The **Black Committee**—as it became known—included Frederick Douglass, Martin Delany, Charles Remond, and Henry Highland Garnet. These black leaders were convinced that by serving in the military, black men would prove they deserved to be treated as equals and had earned the right to be citizens.

Poised with their rifles, these African-American soldiers were members of the Twenty-first U.S. Colored Infantry at the battle of Dutch Gap in Virginia in August 1864.

Governor Andrew selected 25-year-old Robert Gould Shaw to command the 54th Massachusetts Regiment. Although not an active abolitionist, he opposed slavery and was determined to prove that black men would fight well. The men the Black Committee recruited came from most of the northern states. As the ranks of the 54th filled, the 55th Massachusetts Regiment and the all-black 5th Massachusetts Cavalry Regiment were also formed.

On May 28, 1863, the 54th paraded through Boston to board a ship for the trip to South Carolina and the war. Thousands turned out to see the black men in blue uniforms. As they passed the home of fiery abolitionist William Lloyd Garrison, he stood erect with a bust of John Brown. As they passed the Old Statehouse where Crispus Attucks and four others had been killed in the Boston Massacre in 1770, the regiment sang "John Brown's Body." The departure of the 54th from the city was perhaps the most emotional event Boston had witnessed since Anthony Burns had been forcibly returned to slavery in 1854.

Black Soldiers Confront Discrimination

However, the enthusiastic departure could not disguise the discrimination and hostility that black troops faced during the war. Many white northerners would accept neither the presence of black troops nor the idea that black men could endure combat. Many white people tolerated black troops only because they preferred that a black man die rather than a white man.

That black troops would serve in separate, all-black units was a matter of course. No one seriously proposed that black men integrate all-white regiments. In 1863 the War Department created the Bureau of Colored Troops, and the Union Army remained segregated throughout the war. The only exceptions were the officers of the black regiments.

Almost all black troops had white officers. Yet many white officers, convinced such service would taint their military record, refused to command black troops. Others believed black men could not be trained for combat. Even those white officers who were willing to command black troops sometimes regarded their men as "niggers" suited only for work or fatigue duty. Some were armed with picks and axes. Others served as hospital guards and teamsters.

Black soldiers were paid less than white soldiers. Based on the assumption that black troops would be used almost exclusively for construction, transportation, cooking, and

54th Massachusetts Regiment This all-black volunteer infantry regiment was recruited in the northern states for service with Union military forces in the Civil War. It was made up almost entirely of black men who had been free. It was commanded by white officers.

Black Committee An organization of prominent black men in the North who assisted in recruiting African Americans to fight for the Union in the Civil War.

11-1
11-2
11-3
11-4
11-5
11-6
11-7
11-8
11-9

Read on MyHistoryLab Document: An African American Soldier Writes to President Lincoln, 1863

Read on MyHistoryLab Document: A Free Black Volunteer Describes His Feelings about Fighting for the Union, 1864

burial details, and not for fighting, the War Department authorized a lower pay scale for them. This demoralized black soldiers, particularly after they had shown they were more than capable of fighting.

The 54th Massachusetts Regiment refused to accept their pay until they received equal pay. To take no compensation was an enormous sacrifice for men who had wives, children, and families to support. For some, however, it was more than a monetary loss. Sergeant William Walker insisted—despite orders—that the men in his company take no pay until they received equal pay. He was charged with mutiny, convicted, and shot.

The pay issue festered for nearly two years. Finally, near the end of the war, Congress enacted a compromise, but many black soldiers remained dissatisfied. The law equalized pay between black and white troops but made it retroactive only to January 1, 1864—except for black men who had never been slaves. Therefore, the thousands of black men who had been slaves and had joined the military before January 1, 1864, would not be entitled to equal pay for the entire period of their service. The War Department compounded the problem with bureaucratic delays.

Black Men in Combat

Once black men put on the Union uniform, they took part in almost every battle that was fought during the rest of the Civil War. Black troops not only faced an enemy dedicated to the belief that black people belonged in slavery but also confronted white northerners' doubts about their fighting abilities. Yet by war's end, black units had suffered disproportionately more casualties than white units.

In October 1862, the first black unit went into combat in Missouri. James H. Lane, a white Free-Soiler, recruited 500 black men in Kansas. Most were runaway slaves from Missouri and Arkansas. After hasty training, they advanced against a Confederate position at Island Mountain. The black troops held off an attack until reinforcements repulsed the Confederates. Soon thereafter, the black unit became the First Kansas Colored Infantry.

On July 17, 1863, at Honey Springs in Indian Territory (now Oklahoma), the Kansas soldiers attacked a Confederate force of white Texans and Cherokee Indians. After a 20-minute battle, the black troops broke through the southern line, won a victory, and captured the flags of a Texas regiment.

In January 1863, Thomas Wentworth Higginson led the First South Carolina Volunteers on raids on the Georgia and Florida coasts. At one point, they were surrounded at night by Confederate cavalry but fought their way out and escaped.

On June 3, 1863, the 54th Massachusetts Regiment arrived in South Carolina and joined the raids in Georgia. Other raids in the Carolina low country devastated rice plantations and liberated hundreds of slaves.

The Assault on Battery Wagner

Since 1861 and the Confederate capture of Fort Sumter in Charleston Harbor, Union leaders had been determined to retake the fort and occupy nearby Charleston—the heart of secession. In 1863 Union commanders began a land and sea offensive to seize the fort. But **Battery Wagner**, a fortified installation on the northern tip of Morris Island, guarded the entrance to the harbor.

Frustrated in their efforts to enter the harbor, Major General Quincy A. Gilmore and Rear Admiral John Dahlgren decided on a full-scale assault on Wagner. After an unsuccessful attack by white troops, Colonel Shaw volunteered to lead the 54th in a second attack on the battery.

At sunset, 650 men of the first brigade of the 54th prepared to lead more than 5,000 Union troops in storming the battery. The regiment was tired and hungry but eager

Battery Wagner This defensive fortification guarded Fort Sumter near the entrance to Charleston Harbor in South Carolina. It was the scene in July 1863 of a major Union assault by the 54th Massachusetts Regiment, a black unit. The assault failed, but the bravery and valor of the black troops earned them fame and glory.

for the assault. Colonel Shaw told his troops, "Now I want you to prove yourselves men."

At 7:45 P.M., the 54th charged and was met by heavy rifle and artillery fire. Within minutes, the sand was littered with injured and dying men. Sergeant Major Lewis Douglass (the son of Frederick Douglass) was among those who took part. The 54th reached the walls, only to be thrown back in hand-to-hand combat. Shaw was killed.

Although white troops supported the 54th, the attack could not be sustained, and the battle was over by 1 A.M. But within days, the courage of the 54th was known across the North, putting to rest—for a time—the myth that black men lacked the nerve to fight.

The day after the attack, Shaw and 20 of his men were buried in a trench outside Wagner. Several wounded men

On the evening of July 18, 1863, more than six hundred black men led by their white commander, Colonel Robert Gould Shaw, attacked the heavily fortified Battery Wagner on Morris Island near the southern approach to Charleston harbor. They made a frontal assault through withering fire and managed to breach the battery before Confederate forces threw them back. Shaw was killed, and the 54th suffered heavy losses. It was a defining moment of the Civil War, demonstrating to skeptical white people the valor and determination of black troops.

had drowned when the tide came in. Altogether 246 black and white men were killed, 890 were wounded, and 391 were taken prisoner. Forty-two percent of the men of the 54th were killed or injured, and 80 men were taken prisoner.

Union forces never took Wagner. The Confederates abandoned Charleston as the war was ending in February 1865. Black Union troops—the 21st U.S. Colored Infantry and the 55th Massachusetts Regiment—occupied the city. Years later Charles Crowley recalled the scene: "Never, while memory holds power to retain anything, shall I forget the thrilling strain of music of the Union, as sung by our sable soldiers when marching up Meeting Street with the battle stained banners flapping in the breeze."

Read on **MyHistoryLab**
Document: Lewis Douglass Describes the Battle of Fort Wagner, 1863

Olustee

On February 20, 1864, the 54th fought again and was joined by two black regiments—the First North Carolina and the Eighth U.S. of Pennsylvania—and six white regiments at the Battle at Olustee in northern Florida. After almost five hours of combat, Confederate forces forced a Union retreat. The 54th had marched 110 miles in 100 hours before entering the engagement.

The Crater

As impressive as black troops often were in battle, northern commanders sometimes hesitated to commit them to combat. In 1864, after Union troops laid siege to Petersburg, Virginia, white soldiers of the 48th Pennsylvania, who had been coal miners before the war, offered to dig a tunnel and set off an explosion under Confederate lines. General Ambrose Burnside assigned black troops to prepare to lead the attack after the blast.

Only hours before the blast was set to go off, Burnside's superior, General George Meade, replaced the black troops with inadequately trained white soldiers. Meade either lacked confidence in the black unit or was worried he would be blamed for using black men as shields for white soldiers if the attack failed.

11-1
11-2
11-3
11-4
11-5
11-6
11-7
11-8
11-9

On July 30, 1864, at 4:45 A.M., what was perhaps the largest man-made explosion in history up to that time buried a Confederate regiment and an artillery battery and created a crater 170 feet long, 60 feet wide, and 30 feet deep. But the white Union troops rushed down into the crater instead of fanning out around it in pursuit of the stunned enemy. While the Union soldiers marveled at the destruction, the Confederates counterattacked and threw back the Union troops, including the black troops, who were finally brought forward. Some black men were murdered after they surrendered. More than 4,000 Union troops, many of them black, were killed or wounded.

The Confederate Reaction to Black Soldiers

11-6   How did Confederate forces deal with black troops during the Civil War?

On June 7, 1863, Confederate forces attempting to relieve the Union siege of Vicksburg attacked black Union troops at Milliken's Bend on the Mississippi River. Although armed with outdated muskets and not fully trained, the defenders fought off the Confederate attack. The southern soldiers who lost at Milliken's Bend, enraged by having to fight black troops, executed several black prisoners and sold others into slavery.

The Abuse and Murder of Black Troops

Confederate leaders and troops refused to recognize black men as legitimate soldiers. Captured black soldiers were abused and even murdered rather than treated as prisoners of war. Confederate Secretary of War James A. Seddon ordered that captured black soldiers be executed: "We ought never to be inconvenienced with such prisoners . . . summary execution must therefore be inflicted on those taken."

Protests erupted across the North after Confederate authorities decided to treat 80 men of the 54th Massachusetts Regiment who had been captured in the attack on Battery Wagner not as prisoners of war but as rebellious slaves. Frederick Douglass refused to recruit any more black men and held Abraham Lincoln personally responsible for tolerating the mistreatment of black prisoners.

Lincoln responded by issuing **General Order 11**, threatening to execute southern troops or confine them to hard labor: "For every soldier of the United States killed in violation of the laws of war a rebel soldier shall be executed, and for every one enslaved by the enemy or sold into slavery a rebel soldier shall be placed at hard labor on the public works, and continued at such labor until the other shall be released and receive the treatment due to a prisoner of war."

Lincoln's order did not prevent the Confederates from sending the men of the 54th to trial by the state of South Carolina. The state regarded the black soldiers as either rebellious slaves or free black men inciting rebellion. Four black soldiers went on trial in Charleston police court, but the court declared it lacked jurisdiction. The black prisoners were eventually sent to prisoner-of-war camps.

The Fort Pillow Massacre

The war's worst atrocity against black troops occurred at **Fort Pillow** in Tennessee on April 12, 1864. Confederates under the command of Nathan Bedford Forrest slaughtered 300 black troops and their white commander, William F. Bradford, after many of them had surrendered. The Fort Pillow Massacre became the subject of an intense debate in Lincoln's

General Order 11 Order threatening retaliation for the mistreatment of black soldiers by Confederate forces.

Fort Pillow This fort on the east bank of the Mississippi River north of Memphis, Tennessee, was the scene of a massacre of black Union troops as well as some white soldiers and officers by Confederate cavalry in April 1864.

VOICES A Black Nurse on the Horrors of War and the Sacrifice of Black Soldiers

Susie King Taylor was born a slave in Georgia and learned to read and write in Savannah. She escaped to Union forces in 1862 and served as a nurse and laundress with the First South Carolina Volunteers. In these passages, written years later, she recalls her service with the black men who went into combat and pays tribute to them.

It seems strange how our aversion to seeing suffering is overcome in war,—how we are able to see the most sickening sights, such as men with their limbs blown off and mangled by the deadly shells, without a shudder; and instead of turning away, how we hurry to assist in alleviating their pain, bind up their wounds, and press the cool water to their parched lips, with feelings only of sympathy and pity. . . .

I look around now and see the comforts that our younger generation enjoy, and think of the blood that was shed to make these comforts possible for them, and see how little some of

them appreciate the old soldiers. My heart burns within me at this want of appreciation. There are only a few of them left now, so let us all, as the ranks close, take a deeper interest in them. Let the younger generation take an interest also, and remember that it was through the efforts of these veterans that we older ones enjoy our liberty today.

1. **How does Taylor describe what men in combat endure?**
2. **Who is the object of Taylor's criticism, and why does she offer it?**

SOURCE: Susie King Taylor, *Reminiscences of My Life in Camp* (Boston: Taylor, 1902), 31–32, 51–52.

  Read on MyHistoryLab Document: An African-American Army Laundress Describes Her Service, 1902

---

cabinet. But rather than retaliate indiscriminately—as General Order 11 required—the cabinet decided to punish only those responsible for the killings, if and when they were apprehended. But no one was punished during or after the war. Instead, black troops exacted revenge themselves. In fighting around Petersburg later that year, black soldiers shouting "Remember Fort Pillow!" reportedly murdered several Confederate prisoners.

On their own, Union commanders in the field also retaliated for the Confederate treatment of captured black troops. When captured black men were virtually enslaved and forced to work at Richmond and Charleston on Confederate fortifications that were under Union attack, Union officers put Confederate prisoners to work on Union installations that were under fire. Aware they were not likely to be treated as well as white soldiers if they were captured, black men often fought desperately.

Read on MyHistoryLab Document Exploring America: Fort Pillow Massacre

Black Men in the Union Navy

11-7 **Besides being soldiers, what other roles did African Americans play in the Union war effort?**

Black men had a tradition of serving at sea and had been in the U.S. Navy almost continuously since its creation in the 1790s. In the early nineteenth century, there were so many black sailors that some white people tried to ban black men from the navy. However, black sailors did not serve in segregated units. Naval crews were integrated. About

17,000, or over 20 percent, of the men who served in the Union Navy during the war were black sailors.

Nonetheless, black sailors encountered rampant discrimination and exploitation during the Civil War. They were paid less than white sailors and assigned the hardest and filthiest tasks. Many were stewards who waited on white officers. White officers and sailors often treated black sailors with contempt. Some white men, however, admired the black sailors. One observed, "We never were betrayed when we trusted one of them, they were always our friends and were ready, if necessary, to lay down their lives for us."

Liberators, Spies, and Guides

Besides serving as soldiers and sailors, black men and women aided themselves and the Union cause as liberators, spies, guides, and messengers. At about 3 A.M. on May 13, 1862, Robert Smalls, a 23-year-old slave, fired the boiler on the *Planter*, a Confederate supply ship moored in Charleston Harbor. With the aid of seven black crewmen, Smalls sailed the *Planter* past Confederate fortifications, including Fort Sumter, to the Union fleet outside the harbor and to freedom. Smalls liberated himself and 15 other slaves, including the families of several crewmen and his own wife, daughter, and son.

In 1863 Harriet Tubman organized a spy ring in the South Carolina low country, and in cooperation with the all-black Second South Carolina Volunteer Regiment, she helped organize an expedition that destroyed plantations and freed nearly 800 slaves, many of whom joined the Union Army.

In Richmond in 1864, slaves helped more than one hundred escaped Union prisoners of war. Other slaves drew sketches and maps of Confederate fortifications and warned Union forces about troop movements. A black couple near Fredericksburg, Virginia, cleverly transmitted military intelligence to Union general Joseph Hooker. The woman washed laundry for a Confederate officer and hung shirts and blankets in patterns that conveyed information to her husband, a cook and groom for Union troops, and he relayed the information to Union officers.

Mary Elizabeth Bowser was a former slave who worked as a servant at the Confederate White House in Richmond. She overheard conversations by President Jefferson Davis and his subordinates, and—because she was literate—she covertly examined Confederate correspondence. She relayed the information to Union agents until the Confederates became suspicious. Bowser and slave Jim Pemberton fled after trying to burn down the mansion to distract their pursuers.

((Listen on
MyHistoryLab
Audio: *Harriet Tubman* read by Jean Brannon

Violent Opposition to Black People

11-8 | **What was the nature of the opposition of northern whites to blacks?**

No matter how well black men fought, no matter how much individual black women contributed, and no matter how many people—black and white—died "to make men free," many white northerners, both civilian and military, remained bitter and often violently hostile to black people. They used intimidation, threats, and terror to injure and kill people of color.

The New York City Draft Riot

Irish Catholic Americans, themselves held in contempt by prosperous white Protestants, indulged in an orgy of violence in New York City in July 1863. The **New York draft riot** arose from racial, religious, and class antagonisms. Democrats, including New York Governor Horatio Seymour, convinced poor, unskilled Irish workers and other white northerners that the war had become a crusade to benefit black people.

The violence began when federal officials prepared to select the first men to be drafted by the Union for military service. An enraged mob of mostly Irish men attacked the draft offices and any black people who were around. Many of the Irish men were angry because black men had replaced striking Irish stevedores on the city's wharves the month before and because rich white northerners could purchase an exemption from the draft.

The riot went on for four days. The police could not control it. Black people were beaten and lynched. The Colored Orphan Asylum was burned to the ground, although the children had already fled. The mob attacked businesses that employed black people. Protestant churches were burned. Rioters set fire to Horace Greeley's *New York Tribune*. The houses of Republicans and abolitionists were destroyed. The violence did not end until the army arrived. Soldiers who had been fighting Confederates at Gettysburg two weeks earlier found themselves firing on New York rioters.

Union Troops and Slaves

White Union troops who brutalized southern freedmen sometimes exceeded the savagery of northern civilians. In November 1861 men from the 47th New York Regiment raped an eight-year-old black girl. On Sherman's march through Georgia in 1864, a drunken Irish soldier from an Ohio regiment shot into a crowd of black children, wounding one youngster. He was tried and convicted but released on a technicality and returned to the army.

However, some Union soldiers wanted to fight for the liberation of black people. One Wisconsin private wrote, "I have no heart in this war if the slaves cannot be free." The desire of slaves for freedom moved many. A Union officer noted that those who believed slaves were satisfied with slavery were wrong. "It is claimed the negroes are so well contented with their slavery; if it ever was so, that day has ceased." Several Union soldiers wept when they witnessed a daughter reunited with her mother 10 years after a slave sale had separated them.

Refugees

Throughout the war, black people freed themselves. It was not easy. Confederate authorities did not hesitate to reenslave or even execute black people who sought freedom. In 1862, six black people were hanged near Georgetown, South Carolina, when they were captured trying to reach Union forces.

As Union armies plunged deep into the Confederacy in 1863 and 1864, thousands of black people liberated themselves and became refugees. When General William Tecumseh Sherman's army of 60,000 troops laid waste to Georgia in 1864, an estimated 10,000 former slaves followed his troops to Savannah, although they lacked adequate food, clothing, and housing. Sherman did not like black people, and his troops tried to discourage the refugees. As one elderly black couple prepared to leave a plantation, Union soldiers as well as their master urged them to remain. They declined: "We must go, freedom is as sweet to us as it is to you."

New York City draft riot In early July 1863 in opposition to the forthcoming military draft, rioting erupted in New York City. Many of the victims were black men, women, and children.

Read on **MyHistoryLab** Document: John Torrey Describes the New York City Draft Riot, 1863

Black People and the Confederacy

> **11-9** What was the role of slaves and blacks for the Confederates?

The Confederacy was based on the defense of slavery, and it benefited from the usually coerced but sometimes willing labor of black people. Slaves toiled in southern fields and factories during the Civil War. The greater the burden of work the slaves took on, the more white men there were who could become soldiers. When the war began, southern whites believed their disadvantage in manpower would be partly offset by the slaves whose presence would free a disproportionately large number of white southerners to go to war. While slaves would tend cotton, corn, and cattle, white southern men would fight.

Skilled and Unskilled Slaves in Southern Industry

Slave labor helped sustain the Confederate war effort. More than 800 slaves and several hundred free black people, for example, worked at the South's largest industrial complex in Richmond, Virginia. The sprawling Tredegar Iron Works along the James River produced half of the 2,200 cannons that Confederate military forces used. It also furnished locomotives, iron plates, boilers, and nails.

As white men departed for military service, the Tredegar operators relied increasingly on slaves for skilled and unskilled labor. By 1864, slaves represented half of the workforce at Tredegar. They toiled in the machine shop, rolling mill, foundry, and as blacksmiths. Most slaves at Tredegar were hired from their owners at $200 per year. Unfortunately for Tredegar and the Confederacy but fortunately for its slave laborers, many of them escaped as Union military forces closed in on Richmond in 1864. Other black men across the South loaded and unloaded ships, worked on the railroads, and labored in salt mines.

The Impressment of Black People

As the war went on, the Confederacy needed more troops and laborers. Slave owners were first asked—and then compelled—to contribute their slave laborers to the war effort. In July 1861, the Confederate Congress required free black people to register and enroll for military labor. In the summer of 1862 the Virginia legislature authorized the **impressment** of 10,000 slaves between the ages of 18 and 45 for up to 60 days. The owners would receive $16 per month per slave. But many slave owners who enjoyed the benefits of forced labor did not want to be forced to turn their slaves over to state authorities.

In South Carolina in 1863, Confederate officials appealed to slave owners for 2,500 slaves to help fortify Charleston. The owners offered fewer than 1,000. During the Union bombardment of Fort Sumter, 500 slaves did the difficult, dirty, and dangerous work of building and rebuilding the fort. Slaves were even forced into combat. Two Virginia slaves who were compelled to load and fire Confederate cannons near Yorktown were shot and killed.

Although many slave owners resisted the impressment of their bondmen, other white southerners who did not own slaves were infuriated when the Confederate **conscription law** in 1862 exempted men who owned 20 or more slaves from military service. One Mississippi soldier deserted the Confederate Army, claiming he "did not propose to fight for the rich men while they were home having a good time." Although the law was widely criticized, planters—always a small percentage of the white southern

impressment During the Civil War, Southern states and the Confederate government required slave owners to provide slaves to work on such public projects as fortifications, roads, and wharves. The owners (not the slaves) were usually compensated for the work.

conscription law The 1862 Confederate law defining who was required to provide military service.

population—dominated the Confederate government and would not permit the repeal of the exemption.

Confederates Enslave Free Black People

After Lincoln's Emancipation Proclamation, Confederate President Jefferson Davis issued a counter proclamation in February 1863 declaring that free black people would be enslaved, "all free negroes within the limits of the Southern Confederacy shall be placed on the slave status, and be deemed to be chattels . . . forever." This directive was not widely enforced. Davis, however, also ordered Confederate armies that invaded Union states to capture free black people in the North and enslave them.

This was done. Several hundred northern black people were taken south after Confederate forces invaded Pennsylvania in 1863 and fought at Gettysburg. Robert E. Lee's Army of Northern Virginia at Greensburg, Pennsylvania, captured at least 50 black people. A southern victory in the Civil War could have led to the enslavement of more than 132,000 free black residents of the Confederate States.

Black Confederates

Most of the labor black people did for the Confederacy was involuntary; however, a few free black men and women offered their services to the southern cause. In Lynchburg, Virginia, in the spring of 1861, 70 free black people volunteered "to act in whatever capacity may be assigned them." In Memphis in the fall, several hundred black residents cheered for Jefferson Davis and sang patriotic songs. These demonstrations of black support were made early in the conflict when the outcome was in doubt and long before the war became a crusade against slavery.

The status of many free black southerners remained precarious. In Virginia in 1861, impressment laws, like those applying to slaves, compelled free black men to work on Confederate defenses around Richmond and Petersburg. Months before the war, South Carolina considered forcing its free black population to choose between enslavement and exile. The legislature rejected the proposal, but it terrified the state's free black people. Many people of color there had been free for generations. Fair in complexion, they had education, skills, homes, and businesses. Some even owned slaves. When the war came, many were willing to demonstrate their devotion to the South in a desperate attempt to gain white acceptance before they lost their freedom and property.

In early 1861, before the formation of the Confederacy but after the secession of South Carolina, 82 free black men in Charleston petitioned Governor Francis W. Pickens "to be assigned any service where we can be useful." White southern leaders generally ignored offers of free black support unless it was for menial labor. But when Charleston was under siege between 1863 and 1865, black and white residents were grateful that volunteer fire brigades composed of free black men turned out to fight fires caused by Union artillery.

Personal Servants

Other black men contributed in different ways to the Confederate military effort. Black musicians in Virginia played for Confederate regiments and received the same pay as white musicians. Wealthy white men often took their slaves—personal servants—with them when they went off to war. The servants cooked, cleaned uniforms, cared for weapons, maintained horses, and even provided entertainment. Some were loyal and devoted. They cared for owners who were wounded or fell sick and accompanied the bodies of dead masters home.

11-1
11-2
11-3
11-4
11-5
11-6
11-7
11-8
11-9

Being the personal servant for a soldier was hard and sometimes dangerous work. Those close to combat could be killed or injured. One white father warned his son not to take Sam, a valuable slave, into battle. "I hear you are likely to have a big battle soon, and I write to tell you not to let Sam go into the fight with you. Keep him in the rear, for that nigger is worth a thousand dollars." The father evidently placed a higher value on the slave than on his son.

Black Men Fighting for the South

Approximately 144,000 black men from the southern states fought with the Union Army. Most had been slaves. Although it was technically not legal until almost the end of the war, a much smaller number of black men also fought for the Confederacy. White New York troops claimed to have encountered about 700 armed black men in late 1861 near Newport News, Virginia. In 1862 a black Confederate sharpshooter positioned himself in a chimney and shot several Union soldiers before he was killed. Fifty black men served as pickets for the Confederates along the Rappahannock River in Virginia in 1863.

John Wilson Buckner, a free black man with a light complexion, enlisted in the First South Carolina Artillery. As a member of the well-regarded free black Ellison family of Stateburg, South Carolina, Buckner was considered an "honorary white man." He fought for the Confederacy in the defense of Charleston at Battery Wagner in July 1863 and was wounded just before the 54th Massachusetts Regiment assaulted the fort.

Some black civilians supported the war effort and stood to profit if the South won. Buckner's uncles grew corn, sweet potatoes, peas, sorghum, and beans on the Ellison family plantation to feed Confederate troops. They also patriotically invested almost $7,000 in Confederate bonds and notes. Like prosperous white families, the Ellisons lost most of this investment with the defeat of the Confederacy.

Other black southerners also suffered economically from the Confederate defeat. Richard Mack, a South Carolina slave, went off to war as a personal servant. After his master died, he became an orderly for another Confederate officer. He worked hard and accumulated a large sum in Confederate currency. He later joked, "If we had won, I would be rich."

In Virginia, free black people and slaves also contributed to the Confederate cause. Pompey Scott of Amelia County gave $20 to the war effort. William, a slave who had amassed $150, invested in Confederate State Loan Bonds. Lewis, a Mecklenburg County slave, was not permitted to join a cavalry unit as a bugler, so he donated his bugle and $20 to the Confederacy.

White southerners praised the few black people who actively supported the South. Several states awarded pensions to black men who served in the war and survived. Henry Clay Lightfoot, a slave in Culpeper, Virginia, went to war as a body servant of Captain William Holcomb. After the war, he bought a house, raised a family, and was elected to the Culpeper town council. He collected a pension from Virginia, and when he died in 1931, the United Daughters of the Confederacy draped his coffin in a Confederate flag.

Black Opposition to the Confederacy

Although many white southerners and some northerners believed most slaves would support their masters, in fact most slaves did not. When a slave named Tom was asked if slaves would fight for their masters, he replied, "I know they say dese tings, but dey lies. Our masters may talk now all dey choose; but one ting's sartin,—dey don't dare to try us. Jess put de guns in our hans, and you'll soon see dat we not only knows how to shoot, but who, to shoot. My master wouldn't be wuff much ef I was a soldier."

The Confederate Debate on Black Troops

By late 1863 and 1864, prospects for the Confederacy had become grim. The Union naval blockade had become increasingly effective, and the likelihood of British aid had all but vanished. Confederate armies suffered crushing defeats at Vicksburg and Gettysburg in 1863 and absorbed terrible losses in Tennessee, Georgia, and Virginia in 1864.

As defeat loomed, white southerners began to discuss the possibility of arming black men. Several newspapers advocated it. In September 1863, the Montgomery (Alabama) *Weekly Mail* admitted it would have been preposterous to contemplate the need for black troops earlier in the war, but it had now become necessary to save the white South.

In early 1864 General Patrick Cleburne recommended enlisting slaves and promising them their freedom if they remained loyal to the Confederacy. Cleburne argued that this policy would gain recognition and aid from Britain and would disrupt Union military efforts to recruit black southerners. Yet the prospect of arming slaves and free black men appalled most white southerners. Jefferson Davis ordered military officers, including Cleburne, to cease discussing it.

> Watch on **MyHistoryLab Video:** The Meaning of the Civil War for Americans

Black troops were among the first Union military forces to "liberate" the devastated city of Charleston, South Carolina, in the waning weeks of the Civil War. On February 21, 1865, the 55th Massachusetts Regiment occupied Charleston. Black residents—many of them former slaves—eagerly welcomed the soldiers. Defeated and discouraged white residents remained secluded indoors.

Most white southerners were convinced that to arm slaves and put black men in gray uniforms defied the assumptions on which southern society was based. Black people were inferior, and their proper status was to be slaves. The *Richmond Whig* declared in 1864 that "servitude is a divinely appointed condition for the highest good of the slave." It was absurd to contemplate black people as soldiers and as free people. Georgia politician Howell Cobb explained that slaves could not be armed. "If slaves will make good soldiers our whole theory of slavery is wrong."

Explore on **MyHistoryLab Activity:** Battles of the Civil War—Gettysburg

The Civil War for white southerners was a war to prevent the abolition of slavery. Now white southern voices were proposing abolition to preserve the southern nation. North Carolina Senator Robert M. T. Hunter opposed any attempt to enlist slaves and free them. "If we are right in passing this measure we were wrong in denying to the old government the right to interfere with the institution of slavery and to emancipate slaves."

Nevertheless, as the military situation deteriorated, the South moved toward employing black troops. In November 1864, Virginia Governor William Smith enthusiastically supported the idea. "There is not a man that would not cheerfully put the negro in the Army rather than become a slave himself. . . . Standing before God and my country, I do not hesitate to say that I would arm such portion of our able-bodied slaves population as may be necessary." In February 1865, Jefferson Davis and the Confederate cabinet conceded, "We are reduced to choosing whether the negroes shall fight for us or against us."

The opinion of General Robert E. Lee was critical to determining whether the Confederacy would decide to arm black men. No southerner was more revered and respected. Lee had freed nearly 200 slaves in keeping with the instructions of his father-in-law George Washington Parke Custis's will in 1862, which provided that the slaves be emancipated within five years of Custis's death in 1857.

With his army struggling to survive a desperate winter around Petersburg and Richmond, Lee announced in February 1865 that he favored both enrolling and emancipating black troops. "My own opinion is that we should employ them without delay." Less than a month later in March 1865, although many white southerners still opposed it, the Confederate Congress voted to enlist 300,000 black men between the ages of 18 and 45. They would receive the same pay, equipment, and supplies as white soldiers. But those who were slaves would not be freed unless their owner consented and the state where they served agreed to their emancipation.

It was a desperate measure by a nearly defeated government and did not affect the outcome of the conflict. Before the war ended in April, authorities in Virginia managed to recruit some black men and send a few into combat. By the end of March, one company of 35 black men—12 free black men and 23 slaves—was organized. On April 4, 1865, Union troops attacked Confederate supply wagons that the black troops were guarding in Amelia County. Less than a week later, Lee surrendered to Grant at Appomattox Court House, and the Civil War ended.

CONCLUSION

The Civil War ended with the decisive defeat of the Confederacy. The Union was preserved. The ordeal of slavery for millions of people of African descent was over. Slavery—having thrived in America for nearly 250 years—was finally abolished by an amendment to the Constitution. Congress passed the Thirteenth Amendment on January 31, 1865. It was ratified by 27 states and declared in effect on December 18, 1865.

Were it not for the presence and labors of more than four million black people, there would have been no Civil War. Had it not been for the presence and contributions of nearly 200,000 black soldiers and sailors, the Union would not have won. Almost 50,000 of those black men died in combat and of disease during the war. Twenty-one black men were awarded the Medal of Honor for heroism.

Abraham Lincoln represented the dramatic shift in attitudes and policies toward African Americans during the Civil War. When the war began, Lincoln insisted it was a white man's conflict to suppress rebellious white southerners. Black people, Lincoln remained convinced, would be better off outside the United States. But the war went on, and thousands of white men died. Lincoln issued the Emancipation Proclamation and welcomed the enlistment of black troops. The president came to appreciate the achievements and devotion of black troops and condemned the mean-spiritedness of white northerners who opposed the war. Lincoln wrote in 1863, "And then there will be some black men who can remember that, with silent tongue, and clenched teeth, and steady eye, and well-poised bayonet, they have helped mankind on to this great consummation; while, I fear, there will be some white ones, unable to forget that, with malignant heart, and deceitful speech, they have strove to hinder it."

CHAPTER TIMELINE

AFRICAN-AMERICAN EVENTS

NATIONAL EVENTS

1860–1861

April–May 1861
Black men volunteer for military service and are rejected

August 1861
First Confiscation Act

November 1860
Abraham Lincoln elected president

December 1860
South Carolina secedes from the Union

February 1861
The Confederate States of America is formed

March 1861
Lincoln inaugurated

April 1861
The firing on Fort Sumter begins the Civil War

November 1861
Union forces capture the sea islands and coastal areas of South Carolina and Georgia

1862–1863

May 1862
Robert Smalls escapes with the *Planter* and 16 slaves

May–August 1862
The First South Carolina Volunteers, an all-black regiment, forms

September 1862
Lincoln announces the Preliminary Emancipation Proclamation

October 1862
Black troops see combat for the first time in Missouri

January 1, 1863
Lincoln issues the Emancipation Proclamation

January–March 1863
Troops recruited for the 54th and the 55th Massachusetts Regiments

June 1863
Battle of Milliken's Bend

July 1863
Assault on Battery Wagner; New York City draft riots

September 1862
Battle of Antietam

March 1863
The U.S. government enacts a Conscription Act

July 1863
Battles of Vicksburg and Gettysburg

CHAPTER TIMELINE

AFRICAN-AMERICAN EVENTS   NATIONAL EVENTS

1864–1965

AFRICAN-AMERICAN EVENTS	NATIONAL EVENTS
February 1864 Battle at Olustee	**November 1864** Lincoln is reelected
April 1864 Fort Pillow Massacre	**November–December 1864** Sherman's march to the sea
February 1865 Black troops lead the occupation of Charleston	**February 1865** Charleston falls
March 1865 Confederate Congress approves the enlistment of black men	**March 1865** Richmond falls
December 1865 Thirteenth Amendment ratified	**April 1865** Lee surrenders at Appomattox Lincoln is assassinated

On MyHistoryLab

 Study and Review on MyHistoryLab

REVIEW QUESTIONS

1. How did the Union's goals in the Civil War change between 1861 and 1865? What accounts for those changes?

2. How did the Confederate government's policies toward slaves change during the Civil War? When and why did those changes occur?

3. When the Civil War began, why did northern black men volunteer to serve in the Union army if the war had not yet become a war to end slavery?

4. How did Abraham Lincoln's policies and attitudes toward black people change during the Civil War? Does Lincoln deserve credit as "the Great Emancipator"? Why or why not?

5. What did the Emancipation Proclamation seek to achieve? Why was it issued? What did it actually accomplish?

6. What did black men and women contribute to the Union war effort? Was it in their interests to participate in the Civil War? Why or why not?

7. Why did some black people support the Confederacy?

8. Was the result of the Civil War worth the loss of 750,000 lives?

The Meaning of Freedom: The Promise of Reconstruction 1865–1868

What did freedom mean to a people who had endured and survived 250 years of enslavement in America? What did the future hold for nearly four million African Americans in 1865? Freedom meant many things to many people. But to most former slaves, it meant that families would stay together. Freedom meant that women would no longer be sexually exploited. Freedom meant learning to read and write. Freedom meant organizing churches. Freedom meant moving around without having to obtain permission. Freedom meant that labor would produce income for the laborer and not the master. Freedom meant working without the whip. Freedom meant land to own, cultivate, and live on. Freedom meant a trial before a jury if charged with a crime. Freedom meant voting. Freedom meant citizenship and having the same rights as white people.

Years after slavery ended, a former Texas slave, Margrett Nillin, was asked if she preferred slavery or freedom. She answered unequivocally, "Well, it's dis way, in slavery I owns nothin' and never owns nothin'. In freedom I's own de home and raise de family. All dat causes me worryment and in slavery I has no worryment, but I takes freedom."

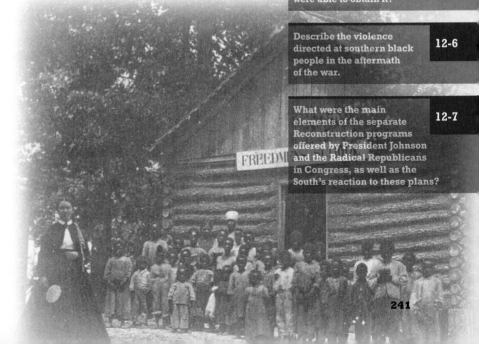

Students assembled in front of James Plantation School in North Carolina shortly after the Civil War ended in 1865. Compared to many such schools, this one was exceptionally well constructed. Notice the students' clothes and lack of shoes.

The End of Slavery

12-1 **What did freedom mean to nearly four million people who had been slaves?**

With the collapse of slavery, many black people were quick to inform white people that whatever loyalty, devotion, and cooperation they might have shown as slaves had never reflected their inner feelings and attitudes. Near Opelousas, Louisiana, a Union officer asked a young black man why he did not love his master, and the youth responded sharply, "When my master begins to lub me, den it'll be time enough for me to lub him. What I wants is to get away. I want to take me off from dis plantation, where I can be free."

In North Carolina, planter Robert P. Howell was disappointed that a loyal slave named Lovet fled at the first opportunity. "He was about my age and I had always treated him more as a companion than a slave. When I left I put everything in his charge, told him that he was free, but to remain on the place and take care of things. He promised me faithfully that he would, but he was the first one to leave . . . and I did not see him for several years."

Emancipation was traumatic for many former masters. Former slave Robert Falls recalled that his master assembled the slaves to inform them they were free. "I hates to do it, but I must. You all ain't my niggers no more. You is free. Just as free as I am. Here I have raised you all to work for me, and now you are going to leave me. I am an old man, and I can't get along without you. I don't know what I am going to do." In less than a year, he was dead. Falls attributed his master's death to the end of slavery: "It killed him."

Differing Reactions of Former Slaves

Other slaves bluntly displayed their reaction to years of bondage. In Goodman, Mississippi, a slave named Caddy learned she was free and rushed from the field to find her owner. "Caddy threw down that hoe, she marched herself up to the big house, then, she looked around and found the mistress. She went over to the mistress, she flipped up her dress and told the white woman to do something. She said it mean and ugly. This is what she said: 'Kiss my ass!'"

In contrast, some slaves, especially elderly ones, were apprehensive about freedom. On a South Carolina plantation, an older black woman refused to accept emancipation. "I ain' no free nigger! I is got a marster and mistiss! Dee right dar in de great house. Ef you don' b'lieve me, you go dar an' see."

Reuniting Black Families

As slavery ended, the most urgent need for many freed people was finding family members who had been sold away from them. Slavery had not destroyed the black family. Husbands, wives, and children went to great lengths to reassemble their families after the Civil War. For years and even decades after the end of slavery, advertisements in black newspapers appealed for information about missing kinfolk. For example, the Colored Tennessean published the following notice on August 5, 1865:

> Saml. Dove wishes to know of the whereabouts of his mother, Areno, his sisters Maria, Neziah and Peggy, and his brother Edmond, who were owned by Geo. Dove of Rockingham County, Shenandoah Valley, Va. Sold in Richmond, after which Saml. and Edmond were taken to Nashville, Tenn., by Joe Mick; Areno was left at the Eagle Tavern, Richmond. Respectfully yours, Saml. Dove, Utica, New York.

In North Carolina a northern journalist met a middle-aged black man "plodding along, staff in hand, and apparently very footsore and tired." The nearly exhausted freedman explained that he had walked almost 600 miles looking for his wife and children, who had been sold four years earlier.

There were emotional reunions as family members found each other after years of separation. Ben and Betty Dodson had been apart for 20 years when Ben found her in a refugee camp after the war. "Glory! glory! hallelujah," he shouted as he hugged his wife. "Dis is my Betty, shuah. I foun' you at las'. I's hunted and hunted till I track you up here. I's boun' to hunt till I fin' you if you's alive."

Other searches had more heart-wrenching results. Husbands and wives sometimes learned that their spouses had remarried during the separation. Believing his wife had died, the husband of Laura Spicer remarried—only to learn after the war that Laura was still alive. Sadly, he wrote to her but refused to meet: "I would come and see you but I know I could not bear it. I want to see you and I don't want to see you. I love you just as well as I did the last day I saw you, and it will not do for you and I to meet."

One freedman testified to the close ties that bound many slave families when he replied bitterly to the claim that he had had a kind master who had fed him and never used the whip: "Kind! yes, he gib men corn enough, and he gib me pork enough, and he neber gib me one lick wid de whip, but whar's my wife?—whar's my chill'en? Take away de pork, I say; take away de corn, I can work and raise dese for myself, but gib me back de wife of my bosom, and gib me back my poor chill'en as was sold away."

Land

12-2 | **How did the government help former slaves acquire land of their own?**

As people embraced freedom and left their masters, they wanted land. Nineteenth-century Americans of virtually every background associated economic security with owning land. Former slaves believed their future as a free people was tied to the possession of land. But just as it had been impossible to abolish slavery without federal intervention, it would not be possible to procure land without the assistance of the U.S. government. At first, federal authorities seemed determined to make land available to freedmen.

Special Field Order #15

Shortly after his army arrived in Savannah—after having devastated Georgia—Union General William T. Sherman announced that freedmen would receive land. On January 16, 1865, he issued **Special Field Order #15**. This military directive set aside a 30-mile-wide tract of land along the Atlantic coast from Charleston, South Carolina, 245 miles south to Jacksonville, Florida. White owners had abandoned the land, and Sherman reserved it for black families. The head of each family would receive "possessory title" to 40 acres of land. Sherman also gave the freedmen the use of army mules—hence the slogan, "Forty acres and a mule."

Within six months, 40,000 freed people were working 400,000 acres in the South Carolina and Georgia low country and on the sea islands. Former slaves generally avoided the slave crops of cotton and rice and instead planted sweet potatoes and corn. They also worked together as families and kinfolk. They avoided the gang labor associated with slavery. Most husbands and fathers preferred that their wives and daughters not work in

Special Field Order #15 General William Tecumseh Sherman issued this military directive in January 1865. It set aside lands along the coast from Charleston, South Carolina, to Jacksonville, Florida, for former slaves. President Andrew Johnson revoked the order six months later.

the fields as slave women had been forced to do. Black women who worked in the homes of white families were increasingly willing to resist what they considered the unreasonable demands of white women.

The Port Royal Experiment

Meanwhile, hundreds of former slaves had been cultivating land for three years. In late 1861 Union military forces carved out an enclave around Beaufort and Port Royal, South Carolina, that remained under federal authority for the rest of the war. White planters fled to the interior, leaving their slaves behind. Under the supervision of U.S. Treasury officials and northern reformers and missionaries who hurried south in 1862, ex-slaves began to work the land in what came to be known as the "**Port Royal Experiment**." When Treasury agents auctioned off portions of the land for nonpayment of taxes, freedmen purchased some of it. But northern businessmen bought most of the real estate and then hired black people to raise cotton.

White owners sometimes returned to their former lands only to find that black families had taken charge. Black farmers told one former owner, "We own this land now, put it out of your head that it will ever be yours again." And on one South Carolina sea island, white men were turned back by armed black men.

The Freedmen's Bureau

12-3 **What was the Freedmen's Bureau, its goals, and how effective was it?**

As the war ended in early 1865, Congress created the Bureau of Refugees, Freedmen, and Abandoned Lands—commonly called the **Freedmen's Bureau**. Created as a temporary agency to assist freedmen to make the transition to freedom, the bureau was placed under the control of the U.S. Army, and General Oliver O. Howard was put in command.

The bureau was given enormous responsibilities. It was designed to help freedmen obtain land, gain an education, negotiate labor contracts with white planters, settle legal and criminal disputes involving black and white people, and provide food, medical care, and transportation for black and white people left destitute by the war. However, Congress never provided sufficient funds or personnel to carry out these tasks.

The Freedmen's Bureau never had more than 900 agents spread across the South from Virginia to Texas. Mississippi, for example, had 12 agents in 1866. One agent often served a county with a population of 10,000 to 20,000 freedmen. Few of the agents were black because few military officers were black. John Mercer Langston of Virginia was an inspector of schools assigned to the bureau's main office in Washington, DC; Major Martin R. Delany worked with freedmen on the South Carolina sea islands. Large portions of the South had been devastated by the war. Richmond, Atlanta, Columbia, South Carolina, and Charleston were in ruins. Railroads had been torn up. Factories were destroyed. Sherman's army laid waste to farms, plantations, and towns in Georgia and the Carolinas. Southern planters lost nearly four million human beings they had owned as property and had controlled as labor.

The need for assistance was desperate as thousands of black and white southerners endured disease and extreme privation as the Civil War ended. A terrible smallpox epidemic swept through the South and killed as many as one million newly freed people. The Bureau was overwhelmed as it tried to provide medical care to freedmen and thousands of white

Port Royal Experiment An effort by northern white missionaries, educators, and businessmen in the Sea Islands near Beaufort, South Carolina, to transform former slaves into educated, reliable, and industrious wage earners. Most of the freedmen did not acquire the land they worked.

Freedmen's Bureau Congress established the Bureau of Refugees, Freedmen, and Abandoned Lands in February 1865 to assist black and white southerners left destitute by the Civil War.

12-1
12-2
12-3
12-4
12-5
12-6
12-7

📖 Read on MyHistoryLab Document: The Freedmen's Bureau Bill (1865)

THE FREEDMEN'S BUREAU.—Drawn by A. R. Waud.—[See Page 467.]

Freedmen's Bureau agents often found themselves in the middle of angry disputes over land and labor that erupted between black and white southerners. Too often the bureau officers sided with the white landowners in these disagreements with former slaves.

Harper's Weekly, July 25, 1868.

people who were suffering and dying from malnutrition, cholera, yellow fever, and pneumonia, as well as smallpox. The bureau established camps for the homeless, fed the hungry, and cared for orphans and the sick as best it could.

In July 1865 the bureau took a first step toward distributing land when General Howard issued Circular 13 ordering agents to "set aside" 40-acre plots for freedmen. But the allocation had hardly begun when the order was revoked, and authorities announced that land already distributed under Sherman's Special Field Order #15 was to be returned to its white owners. The reason for this reversal was that Andrew Johnson, who had become president after Lincoln's assassination in April 1865, began to pardon hundreds and then thousands of former Confederates and restore their lands to them. General Howard had to tell black people that they had to relinquish the land they thought they had acquired. Speaking to some 2,000 freedmen on South Carolina's Edisto Island in October 1865, Howard pleaded with them to "lay aside their bitter feelings, and to become reconciled to their old masters." A black man shouted a response, "Why, General Howard, why do you take away our lands? You take them from us who are true, always true to the Government! You give them to our all-time enemies. This is not right!"

A committee rejected Howard's appeal for reconciliation and forgiveness and an unhappy black man insisted the government provide land:

> You ask us to forgive the landowners of our island. You only lost your right arm in war and
> might forgive them. The man who tied me to a tree and gave me 39 lashes and who stripped

VOICES A Freedmen's Bureau Commissioner Tells Freed People What Freedom Means

In June 1865 Charles Soule, the commissioner of contracts for the Freedmen's Bureau, told freedmen in Orangeburg, South Carolina, what to expect and how to behave in the coming year:

You are now free, but you must know that the only difference you can feel yet, between slavery and freedom, is that neither you nor your children can be bought or sold. You may have a harder time this year than you have ever had before; it will be the price you pay for your freedom. You will have to work hard, and get very little to eat, and very few clothes to wear. If you get through this year alive and well, you should be thankful.... You cannot be paid in money, for there is no good money in the District, nothing but Confederate paper. Then, what can you be paid with? Why, with food, with clothes, with the free use of your little houses and plots. You do not own a cent's worth except yourselves.

You do not understand why some of the white people who used to own you do not have to work in the field. It is because they are rich. If every man were poor, and worked in his own field, there would be no big farms, and very little cotton or corn raised to sell; there would be no money, and nothing to buy. Some people must be rich, to pay the others, and they have

the right to do no work except to look out after their property.

Remember that all of your working time belongs to the man who hires you: therefore you must not leave work without his leave not even to nurse a child, or to go and visit a wife or husband. When you wish to go off the place, get a pass as you used to, and then you will run no danger of being taken up by our soldiers.

In short, do just about as the good men among you have always done. Remember that even if you are badly off, no one can buy and sell you: remember that if you help yourselves, GOD will help you, and trust hopefully that next year and the year after will bring some new blessing to you.

1. **According to Soule, what is the difference between slavery and freedom?**
2. **Does freedom mean that freed people will have economic opportunities equal to those of white people?**
3. **How should freed people have responded to Soule's advice?**

SOURCE: Ira Berlin et al., "The Terrain of Freedom: The Struggle over the Meaning of Free Labor in the U.S. South," *History Workshop* 22 (Autumn 1986): 108–30.

and flogged my mother and my sister and who will not let me stay in his empty hut except I will do his planting and be satisfied with his price and who combines with others to keep away land from me well knowing I would not have anything to do with him if I had land of my own—that man I cannot well forgive.

These appeals moved Howard. He returned to Washington and attempted to persuade Congress to provide land. Congress refused, and President Johnson was determined that white people would get their lands back. It seemed so sensible to most white people. Property that had belonged to white families for generations simply could not be given to freedmen. Freedmen saw it differently. They deserved land that they and their families had worked without compensation for generations. Freedmen believed it was the only way to make freedom meaningful and to gain independence from white people. As it turned out, most freedmen were forced off land they thought should belong to them.

Southern Homestead Act

In early 1866 Congress attempted to provide land for freedmen with the passage of the **Southern Homestead Act**. More than three million acres of public land were set aside for black people and white southerners who had remained loyal to the Union. Much of this land, however, consisted of swampy wetlands or unfertile pinewoods unsuitable for farming. More than 4,000 black families—three-quarters of them in Florida—did claim some of this land, but many lacked the financial resources to cultivate it. Eventually timber companies acquired much of it, and the Southern Homestead Act largely failed.

Sharecropping

To make matters worse, by 1866 bureau officials tried to force freedmen to sign labor contracts with white landowners—returning black people to white authority. Black men who refused to sign contracts could be arrested. Theoretically, these contracts were legal agreements between two equals: landowner and laborer. But they were seldom freely concluded. Bureau agents usually sided with the landowner and pressured freedmen to accept unequal terms.

Occasionally, the landowner would pay wages to the laborer. But because most landowners lacked cash to pay wages, they typically agreed to provide the laborer with part of the crop. The laborer, often grudgingly, agreed to work under the supervision of the landowner. The contracts required labor for a full year, and the laborer could neither quit nor strike. Landowners demanded that the laborers work the fields in gangs. Freedmen, however, resisted this system. They sometimes insisted on making decisions involving planting, fertilizing, and harvesting as they sought to exercise independence (see Map 12–1).

Thus, it took time for a new form of agricultural labor to develop. But by the 1870s, the system of **sharecropping** dominated most of the South. There were no wages. Freedmen worked land as families—not in gangs—and not under direct white supervision. The landowner provided seed, tools, fertilizer, and work animals (mules, horses, oxen), and the black family received one-third of the crop. There were many variations on these arrangements, and black families were often cheated out of their fair share of the crop. Without land of their own, they remained under white authority well into the twentieth century.

Southern Homestead Act Congress passed this measure in 1866 that set aside over three million acres of land for former slaves and loyal white southerners to farm following the Civil War. Most of the land was not fertile or suitable for agriculture, and the act largely failed.

sharecropping The system following the Civil War in which former slaves worked land owned by white people and "paid" for the use of the land and for tools, seeds, fertilizer, and mules by sharing the crop—usually cotton—with the owner.

The Black Church

12-4 **What role did the black church play in African-American life in the post-war decades?**

In the years after slavery, the church became the most important institution among African Americans other than the family. It filled deep spiritual needs, offered enriching music, provided charity and compassion to those in need, developed community and political leaders, and was free of white supervision. Before slavery's demise, free black people and slaves often attended white churches where they participated in religious services conducted by white clergymen and where they were treated as second-class Christians.

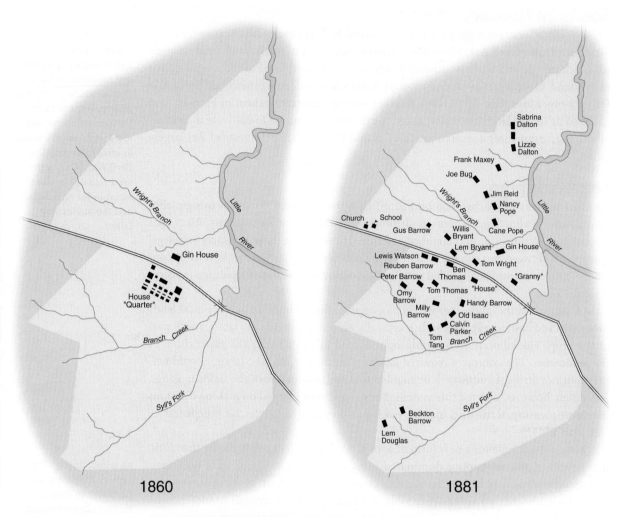

1860

1881

**MAP 12–1 THE EFFECT OF SHARECROPPING ON THE SOUTHERN PLANTATION:
THE BARROW PLANTATION, OGLETHORPE COUNTY, GEORGIA**
With the end of slavery and the advent of sharecropping, black people would no longer
agree to work in fields as gangs. They preferred to have each family cultivate separate
plots of land, thereby distancing themselves as much as possible from slavery and white
supervision.

**Although many freed people worked the same land that they had as
slaves, how does this map suggest the changes experienced by black
people in family life, religion, education, and their relationships with
white people?**

Once liberated, black men and women organized their own churches with their own
ministers. Most black people considered white ministers incapable of delivering a meaningful message. Nancy Williams recalled, "Ole white preachers used to talk wid dey tongues
widdout sayin' nothin', but Jesus told us slaves to talk wid our hearts."
    Northern white missionaries were sometimes appalled by the unlettered and ungram-
matical black preachers who nevertheless communicated effectively and emotionally with

Freedwomen washing laundry along a creek near Circleville, Texas, c. 1866.

their parishioners. A visiting white clergyman was impressed and humbled on hearing a black preacher who lacked education but more than made up for it with his devout faith. "He talked about Christ and his salvation as one who understood what he said.... Here was an unlearned man, one who could not read, telling of the love of Christ, of Christian faith and duty in a way which I have not learned."

Other black and white religious leaders anguished over what they considered moral laxity and displaced values among the freed people. They preached about honesty, thrift, temperance, and elimination of sexual promiscuity. They demanded an end to "rum-suckers, bar-room loafers, whiskey dealers and card players among the men, and to those women who dressed finely on ill gotten gain."

Church members struggled, scrimped, and saved to buy land and build churches. Most former slaves founded Baptist and Methodist churches. These denominations tended to be more autonomous and less subject to outside control. Their doctrine was usually simple and direct without complex theology. Of the Methodist churches, the African Methodist Episcopal (AME) Church made giant strides in the South after the Civil War.

In Charleston the AME Church was resurrected 40 years after it had been forced to disband during the turmoil over the Denmark Vesey plot in 1822 (see Chapter 8). But by the 1870s, three AME congregations were thriving in Charleston. In Wilmington, North Carolina, the 1,600 members of the Front Street Methodist Church decided to join the AME Church soon after the Civil War ended. They replaced the longtime white minister with a black man.

The Presbyterian, Congregational, and Episcopal churches appealed to the more prosperous members of the black community. Their services tended to be more formal and solemn. Black people who had been free before the Civil War were usually affiliated with these congregations and remained so after the conflict. Well-to-do free black people in

12-1

12-2

12-3

12-4

12-5

12-6

12-7

Hundreds of black churches were founded across the South following the Civil War, and they grew spectacularly in the decades that followed. This illustration shows a congregation crowded into Richmond's First African Baptist Church in 1874.

Charleston organized St. Mark's Protestant Episcopal Church when they separated from the white Episcopal Church, but they retained their white minister Joseph Seabrook as rector.

The Roman Catholic Church made modest in-roads among black southerners. There were all-black parishes in St. Augustine, Savannah, Charleston, and Louisville after the Civil War. For generations before the conflict, many well-to-do free people of color in New Orleans had been Catholics, and their descendants remained faithful to the church.

Religious differences notwithstanding, the black churches, their parishioners, and their clergymen would play a vital role in Reconstruction politics. More than one hundred black ministers were elected to political office after the Civil War.

Education

12-5   **Why was education so important to African Americans, and what were the ways in which they were able to obtain it?**

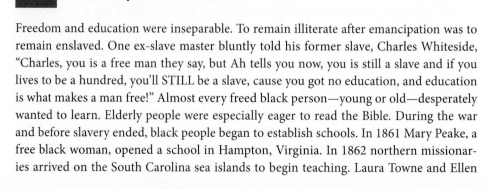

Watch on MyHistoryLab
Video: The Schools that the Civil War and Reconstruction Created

Freedom and education were inseparable. To remain illiterate after emancipation was to remain enslaved. One ex-slave master bluntly told his former slave, Charles Whiteside, "Charles, you is a free man they say, but Ah tells you now, you is still a slave and if you lives to be a hundred, you'll STILL be a slave, cause you got no education, and education is what makes a man free!" Almost every freed black person—young or old—desperately wanted to learn. Elderly people were especially eager to read the Bible. During the war and before slavery ended, black people began to establish schools. In 1861 Mary Peake, a free black woman, opened a school in Hampton, Virginia. In 1862 northern missionaries arrived on the South Carolina sea islands to begin teaching. Laura Towne and Ellen

Murray, two white women, and Charlotte Forten, a black woman, opened Penn School on St. Helena's Island as part of the Port Royal Experiment. They enrolled 138 children and 58 adults. By 1863 there were 1,700 students and 45 teachers at 30 schools in the South Carolina low country.

With the end of the Civil War, northern religious organizations, in cooperation with the Freedmen's Bureau, organized hundreds of schools. Classes were held in stables, homes, former slave cabins, taverns, churches, and even—in Savannah and New Orleans—the old slave markets. Former slaves spent hours in the fields and then trudged to a makeshift school to learn the alphabet and arithmetic.

In 1866 the Freedmen's Bureau set aside $500,000 for education. The Bureau furnished the buildings, while former slaves hired, housed, and fed the teachers. By 1869 the Freedmen's Bureau was involved with 3,000 schools and 150,000 students. Even more impressive, by 1870 black people had contributed $1 million to educate their people.

Black Teachers

Although freedmen appreciated the dedication of the white teachers affiliated with the missionary societies, they usually preferred black teachers and black men and women responded to the call to teach. Virginia C. Green, a northern black woman, felt compelled to go to Mississippi: "Though I have never known servitude they are . . . my people. . . . I look forward with impatience to the time when my people shall be strong, blest with education, purified and made prosperous by virtue and industry." Hezekiah Hunter, a black teacher from New York, commented in 1865 on the need for black teachers: "I believe we best can instruct our own people, knowing our own peculiarities—needs—necessities. Further—I believe we that are competent owe it to our people to teach them our speciality."

In some areas of the South, the sole person available to teach was a poorly educated former slave equipped primarily with a willingness to teach fellow freedmen. One such teacher explained, "I never had the chance of goen to school for I was a slave until freedom. . . . I am the only teacher because we can not doe better now." Many northern teachers, black and white, provided more than the basics of elementary education. Black life and history were occasionally read about and discussed. Abolitionist Lydia Maria Child wrote *The Freedmen's Book,* which offered brief biographies of Benjamin Banneker, Frederick Douglass, and Toussaint Louverture. More often northern teachers, dismayed at the backwardness of the freedmen, struggled to modify behavior and to impart cultural values by teaching piety, thrift, cleanliness, temperance, and timeliness.

((•)) 📖 **Read on MyHistoryLab Document:** Charlotte Forten Describes Life on the Sea Islands, 1864

Charlotte Forten came from a prominent Philadelphia family of color. She joined hundreds of black and white teachers who migrated South during and after the Civil War to instruct the freed people. Some teachers remained for a few months. Others stayed for a lifetime. Charlotte Forten—shown here in an 1866 photograph—taught on the South Carolina sea islands from 1862 to 1864.

12-1

12-2

12-3

12-4

12-5

12-6

12-7

Many former slaves came to resent some of these teachers as condescending, self-righteous, and paternalistic. Sometimes the teachers, especially those who were white, became frustrated with recalcitrant students who did not readily absorb middle-class values. Others, however, derived enormous satisfaction from teaching freedmen. A Virginia teacher commented, "I think I shall stay here as long as I live and teach this people. I have no love or taste for any other work, and I am happy only here with them."

Black Colleges

Northern churches and religious societies established dozens of colleges, universities, academies, and institutes across the South in the late 1860s and the 1870s. Most of these institutions provided elementary and secondary education. Few black students were prepared for actual college or university work. The **American Missionary Association**—an abolitionist and Congregationalist organization—worked with the Freedmen's Bureau to establish Fisk in Tennessee, Hampton in Virginia, Tougaloo in Alabama, and Avery in South Carolina. The primary purpose of these schools was to educate black students to become teachers.

In Missouri, the black enlisted men and white officers of the 62nd and 65th Colored Volunteers raised $6,000 to establish Lincoln Institute in 1866, which would become Lincoln University. The American Baptist Home Mission Society founded Virginia Union, Shaw in North Carolina, Benedict in South Carolina, and Morehouse in Georgia. Northern Methodists helped establish Claflin in South Carolina, Rust in Mississippi, and Bennett in North Carolina. The Episcopalians were responsible for St. Augustine's

American Missionary Association This religious organization sent teachers and clergymen throughout the South following the Civil War to tend to the spiritual and educational needs of former slaves.

12-1
12-2
12-3
12-4
12-5
12-6
12-7

View on **MyHistoryLab Closer Look:** Higher Education for African Americans

Black and white land-grant colleges stressed training in agriculture and industry. In this late nineteenth-century photograph, Hampton Institute students learn milk production. The men are in military uniforms, which was typical for males at these colleges. Military training was a required part of the curriculum.

in North Carolina and St. Paul's in Virginia. These and similar institutions formed the foundation for the historically black colleges and universities.

Response of White Southerners

White southerners considered black people's efforts to learn absurd. For generations, white Americans had considered people of African descent abjectly inferior. When efforts were made to educate former slaves, white southerners reacted with suspicion, contempt, and hostility.

Most white people were well aware that black people could learn. Otherwise, the slave codes that prohibited educating slaves would have been unnecessary. After slavery's end, some white people went out of their way to prevent black people from learning. Countless schools were burned, mostly in rural areas. In Canton, Mississippi, black people collected money to open a school—only to have white residents inform them that the school would be burned and the prospective teacher lynched if it opened. The female teacher at a freedmen's school in Donaldsonville, Louisiana, was shot and killed.

Other white southerners grudgingly tolerated black people's desire to acquire an education. One planter conceded in 1870, "Every little negro in the county is now going to school and the public pays for it. This is one hell of [a] fix but we can't help it, and the best policy is to conform as far as possible to circumstances."

Most white people refused to attend school with black people. No integrated schools were established in the immediate aftermath of emancipation. Most black people were more interested in gaining an education than in whether white students attended school with them. When black youngsters tried to attend a white school in Raleigh, North Carolina, the white students stopped going to it. For a brief time in Charleston, black and white children attended the same school, but they were taught in separate classrooms.

Violence

12-6 **Describe the violence directed at southern black people in the aftermath of the war.**

In the days, weeks, and months after the end of the Civil War, an orgy of brutality and violence swept across the South. White southerners—embittered by their defeat and unable to adjust to the end of slave labor and the loss of millions of dollars worth of slave property—lashed out at black people. There were beatings, murders, rapes, and riots, often with little or no provocation.

Black people who demanded respect, wore better clothing, refused to step aside for white people, or asked to be addressed as "mister" or "missus" were attacked. In South Carolina, a white clergyman shot and killed a black man who protested when another black man was removed from a church service. In Texas, one black man was killed for not removing his hat in the presence of a white man and another for refusing to relinquish a bottle of whiskey. A black woman was beaten for "using insolent language," and a black worker in Alabama was killed for speaking sharply to a white overseer. In Virginia, a black veteran was beaten after announcing he had been proud to serve in the Union Army.

In South Carolina, a white man asked a passing black man whom he belonged to. The black man replied that he no longer belonged to anybody, "I am free now." With that, the white man roared, "Sas me? You black devil!" He then slashed the freedman with a knife.

Watch on MyHistoryLab Video: Reconstruction in Texas

12-1

12-2

12-3

12-4

12-5

12-6

12-7

The sheriff of DeWitt County, Texas, shot a black man who was whistling "Yankee Doodle." A Freedmen's Bureau agent in North Carolina explained the intense white hostility: "The fact is, it's the first notion with a great many of these people, if a Negro says anything or does anything that they don't like, to take a gun and put a bullet into him, or a charge of shot." In Texas another Freedmen's Bureau officer claimed that white people simply killed black people "for the love of killing."

There was also large-scale violence. In 1865 University of North Carolina students twice attacked peaceful meetings of black people. Near Pine Bluff, Arkansas, in 1866, a white mob burned a black settlement and lynched 24 men, women, and children. An estimated 2,000 black people were murdered around Shreveport, Louisiana. In Texas, white people killed 1,000 black people between 1865 and 1868.

In May 1866 white residents of Memphis went on a rampage after black veterans forced police to release a black prisoner. The city was already beset with economic difficulties and racial tensions caused in part by an influx of rural refugees. White people, led by Irish policemen, destroyed hundreds of homes, cabins, shacks, churches, and schools in the black section of Memphis. Altogether, 46 black people and two white men died.

On July 30, 1866, in New Orleans, white people—angered that black men were demanding political rights—assaulted black people on the street and in a convention hall. City policemen, who were mostly Confederate veterans, shot down the black delegates as they fled in panic waving white flags in a futile attempt to surrender. In the assault, 34 black people and three of their white allies died.

Little was done to stem the violence. Most Union troops had been withdrawn from the South and demobilized after the war. The Freedmen's Bureau was usually unwilling and unable to protect the black population. Black people left to defend themselves were usually in no position to retaliate. Instead, they sometimes attempted to bring the perpetrators to justice. In Orangeburg, South Carolina, armed black men brought three white men who had been wreaking violence in the community to the local jail. In Holly Springs, Mississippi, a posse of armed black men apprehended a white man who had murdered a freedwoman.

For black people, the system of justice was thoroughly unjust. Although black people could now testify against white people in court, southern juries remained all white and refused to convict white people charged with harming black people. In Texas during 1865 and 1866, 500 white men were indicted for murdering black people. None were convicted.

The Crusade for Political and Civil Rights

In October 1864 in Syracuse, New York, 145 black leaders gathered in a national convention. Some of the century's most prominent black men and women attended, including Henry Highland Garnet, Frances E. W. Harper, William Wells Brown, Francis L. Cardozo, Richard H. Cain, Jonathan J. Wright, and Jonathan C. Gibbs. They embraced the basic tenets of the American political tradition and proclaimed that they expected to participate fully in it.

Anticipating a future free of slavery, Frederick Douglass optimistically declared "that we hereby assert our full confidence in the fundamental principles of this government . . . the great heart of this nation will ultimately concede us our just claims, accord us our rights, and grant us our full measure of citizenship under the broad shield of the Constitution."

Even before the **Syracuse Convention**, northern Republicans met in Union-controlled territory around Beaufort, South Carolina, and nominated the state's delegates to the 1864 Republican national convention. Among those selected were Robert Smalls and Prince Rivers, former slaves who had exemplary records with the Union Army. The probability of black participation in postwar politics seemed promising.

Syracuse Convention
A meeting of black leaders in Syracuse, New York, to discuss the future of African Americans following the abolition of slavery. They insisted that black people had earned and deserved the same political and legal rights as white Americans.

But northern and southern white leaders who already held power would largely determine whether black Americans would gain political power or acquire the same rights as white people. As the Civil War ended, President Lincoln was more concerned with restoring the seceded states to the Union than in opening political doors for black people. Yet Lincoln suggested that at least some black men deserved the right to vote. On April 11, 1865, he wrote, "I would myself prefer that [the vote] were now conferred on the very intelligent, and on those who serve our cause as soldiers." Three days later he was assassinated.

Presidential Reconstruction under Andrew Johnson

12-7 What were the main elements of the separate Reconstruction programs offered by President Johnson and the Radical Republicans in Congress, as well as the South's reaction to these plans?

Vice President Andrew Johnson became president following Lincoln's assassination and initially seemed inclined to impose stern policies on the white South while befriending the freedmen. He announced that "treason must be made odious, and traitors must be punished and impoverished." In 1864 he had told black people, "I will be your Moses, and lead you through the Red Sea of War and Bondage to a fairer future of Liberty and Peace." Nothing proved to be further from the truth. Andrew Johnson was no friend of black Americans. Born poor in eastern Tennessee and never part of the southern aristocracy, Johnson opposed secession and was the only senator from the seceded states to remain loyal to the Union. He had nonetheless acquired five slaves and the conviction that black people were so inferior that white men must forever govern them. In 1867 Johnson argued that black people could not exercise political power and that they had "less capacity for government than any other race of people. No independent government of any form has ever been successful in their hands. On the contrary, wherever they have been left to their own devices they have shown a constant tendency to relapse into barbarism."

Johnson quickly lost his enthusiasm for punishing traitors. Indeed, he began to placate white southerners. In May 1865 Johnson granted blanket amnesty and pardons to former Confederates willing to swear allegiance to the United States. The main exceptions were high former Confederate officials and those who owned property valued in excess of $20,000, a large sum at the time. Yet even these leaders could appeal for individual pardons. And appeal they did. By 1866 Johnson had pardoned more than 7,000 high-ranking former Confederates and wealthier southerners. Moreover, he had restored land to those white people who had lost it to freedmen.

Johnson's actions encouraged those who had supported secession, owned slaves, and opposed the Union. He permitted longtime southern leaders to regain political influence and authority only months after the end of America's bloodiest conflict. As black people and Radical Republicans watched in disbelief, Johnson appointed provisional governors in the former Confederate states. Leaders in those states then called constitutional conventions, held elections, and prepared to regain their place in the Union. Johnson merely insisted that each former Confederate state formally accept the **Thirteenth Amendment** (ratified in December 1865, it outlawed slavery) and repudiate Confederate war debts.

The southern constitutional conventions excluded black people from the political system and denied them equal rights. As one Mississippi delegate explained, "'Tis nature's law that the superior race must rule and rule they will."

Watch on MyHistoryLab
Video: Presidential Reconstruction

Thirteenth Amendment
This amendment to the U.S. Constitution outlawed slavery and involuntary servitude.

12-1
12-2
12-3
12-4
12-5
12-6
12-7

VOICES   A Northern Black Woman on Teaching Freedmen

Blanche Virginia Harris was born in 1842 in Monroe, Michigan, and graduated from Oberlin College in 1860. She became the principal of a black school in Norfolk, Virginia, attended by 230 students. She organized night classes for adults and a sewing society to provide clothing for impoverished students. Later, she taught in Mississippi, North Carolina, and Tennessee. In the following letter she describes her experiences in Mississippi:

23 January 1866

Natchez, Miss.

I have been in this city now nearly five months. . . . The colored teachers three in number, sent out by the [American Missionary] Association to this city, have been brought down here it is true. And then left to the mercy of the colored people or themselves. The distinction between the two classes of teachers (white and colored) is so marked that it is the topic of conversation among the better class of colored people.

My school is very large, some of them pay and some do not. And from the proceeds I pay the board of my sister and myself, and also for the rent

of two rooms; rent as well as board is very high so I have to work quite hard to meet my expenses. I also furnish lights, wood and coal. I do not write this as fault-finding, far from it. I shall be thankful if I can in any way help. I sometimes get discouraged. . . .

I have become very much attached to my school; the interest they manifest in their studies pleases me. I will now tell you how I employ my time. From 8 A.M. until 2 P.M. I teach the children. At 3 P.M. I have a class of adults and at night I have night school.

One afternoon we have prayer meeting, another sewing school. And another singing school. I hope my next letter may be more interesting to you.

Very Respectfully,
Blanche Harris

1. **Why was the race of the teacher of such concern?**
2. **What did Harris find difficult about teaching, and what did she find rewarding?**

SOURCE: Ellen NicKenzie Lawson, ed., *The Three Sarahs: Documents of Antebellum Black College Women* (New York: Edward Mellon Press, 1984).

Black Codes

After the election of state and local officials, white legislators gathered in state capitals across the South to determine the status and future of the freedmen. With little debate, the legislatures drafted the so-called **black codes**. Southern politicians gave no thought to providing black people with the political and legal rights associated with citizenship.

The black codes sought to ensure the availability of a subservient agricultural labor supply controlled by white people. They imposed severe restrictions on freedmen, who had to sign annual labor contracts with white landowners. In addition, the codes permitted black children ages 2 to 21 to be apprenticed to white people and spelled out their duties and obligations in detail. Corporal punishment was legal. Employers were designated "masters" and employees "servants." The black codes also restricted black people from loitering or vagrancy, using alcohol or firearms, hunting, fishing, and grazing livestock. However, the codes did guarantee rights that slaves had not possessed. Freedmen could marry legally, engage in contracts, purchase property, sue or be sued, and testify in court. But black people could not vote or serve on juries. The black codes conceded—barely—freedom to black people.

black codes Laws that were passed in each of the former Confederate states following the Civil War that applied only to black people. While conceding such rights as the right to marry, to contract a debt, or to own property, the codes severely restricted the rights and opportunities of former slaves in terms of labor and mobility.

Black Conventions

Alarmed by these threats to their freedom, black people met in conventions across the South in 1865 and 1866 to protest, appeal for justice, and chart their future. Men who had been free before the war dominated the conventions. Women and children also attended—as spectators, not delegates—but women were often influential as they offered comments, suggestions, and criticism. These meetings were hardly militant or radical affairs. Delegates respectfully insisted that white people live up to the principles and rights embodied in the Declaration of Independence and the Constitution.

At the AME church in Raleigh, North Carolina, delegates asked for equal rights and the right to vote. At Georgia's convention, they protested against white violence and appealed for leaders who would enforce the law without regard to color: "We ask not for a Black Man's Governor, nor a White Man's Governor, but for a People's Governor, who shall impartially protect the rights of all, and faithfully sustain the Union."

Delegates at the Norfolk meeting reminded white Virginians that black people were patriotic: "We are Americans. We know no other country. We love the land of our birth." But they protested that Virginia's black code caused "invidious political or legal distinctions, on account of color merely." They requested the right to vote and added that they might boycott the businesses of "those who deny to us our equal rights."

Two conventions were held in Charleston, South Carolina—one before and one after the black code was enacted. At the first, delegates stressed the "respect and affection" they felt toward white Charlestonians. The second convention denounced the black code and insisted on its repeal. White authorities ignored the black conventions and their petitions. Instead, they were confident they had relegated the freedmen to a subordinate role.

By late 1865 President Johnson's Reconstruction policies had aroused black people. One black Union veteran summed up the situation: "If you call this Freedom, what do you call Slavery?" Republicans in Congress also opposed Johnson's policies toward the freedmen and the former Confederate states.

The Radical Republicans

Radical Republicans, as the more militant Republicans were called, were especially disturbed that Johnson seemed to have abandoned the ex-slaves to their former masters. They considered white southerners disloyal and unrepentant, despite their military defeat. Moreover, Radical Republicans—unlike moderate Republicans and Democrats—were determined to transform the racial fabric of American society by including black people in the political and economic system.

Among the most influential Radical Republicans were Senators Charles Sumner, Benjamin Wade, and Henry Wilson, as well as Congressmen Thaddeus Stevens, George W. Julian, and James M. Ashley. Few white Americans were as dedicated to the rights of black people as these men. They had fought to abolish slavery and were reluctant to compromise. They were honest, tough, and articulate but also abrasive, difficult, self-righteous, and vain. Black people appreciated them, whereas many white people hated them.

Radical Republicans Members of the Republican Party during Reconstruction who vigorously supported the rights of African Americans to vote, hold political office, and have the same legal and economic opportunities as white people.

Radical Proposals

To provide freedmen with land, Stevens introduced a bill in Congress in late 1865 to confiscate 400 million acres from the wealthiest 10 percent of southerners and distribute it free to freedmen. The remaining land would be auctioned off in plots no larger than 500 acres. Few legislators supported the proposal. Even those who wanted fundamental change considered confiscation a violation of property rights.

Instead, Radical Republicans supported voting rights for black men. They were convinced that black men—to protect themselves and to secure the South for the Republican Party—had to have the right to vote.

Moderate Republicans, however, found the prospect of black voting almost as objectionable as the confiscation of land. They preferred to build the Republican Party in the South by cooperating with President Johnson and attracting loyal white southerners.

The thought of black suffrage appalled northern and southern Democrats. Most white northerners—Republicans and Democrats—favored denying black men the right to vote in their states. After the war, proposals to guarantee the right to vote to black men were defeated in New York, Ohio, Kansas, and the Nebraska Territory. In the District of Columbia, a vote to permit black suffrage lost 6,951 to 35. However, five of the six New England states as well as Iowa, Minnesota, and Wisconsin allowed black men to vote.

As much as they objected to black suffrage, most white northerners objected even more strongly to defiant white southerners. Journalist Charles A. Dana described the attitude of many northerners: "As for negro suffrage, the mass of Union men in the Northwest do not care a great deal. What scares them is the idea that the rebels are all to be let back . . . and made a power in government again, just as though there had been no rebellion."

In December 1865 Congress created the Joint Committee on Reconstruction to determine whether to readmit the southern states to the Union. The committee confirmed reports of widespread mistreatment of black people and white arrogance.

((•)) 📖 **Read** on **MyHistoryLab Document:** The Colored People of South Carolina Protest the "Black Codes," 1865

Bearing a remarkable resemblance to a slave auction, this scene in Monticello, Florida, shows a black man auctioned off to the highest bidder shortly after the Civil War. Under the terms of most southern black codes, black people arrested and fined for vagrancy or loitering could be "sold" if they could not pay the fine. Such spectacles infuriated many northerners and led to demands for more rigid Reconstruction policies.

12-1
12-2
12-3
12-4
12-5
12-6
12-7

The Freedmen's Bureau Bill and the Civil Rights Bill

In early 1866 Senator Lyman Trumbull, a moderate Republican from Illinois, introduced two major bills. The first was to provide more financial support for the Freedmen's Bureau and extend its authority to defend the rights of black people.

The second proposal became the first **Civil Rights Act** in American history. It made any person born in the United States a citizen (except Indians) and entitled them to rights protected by the U.S. government. Black people would possess the same legal rights as white people. The bill was clearly intended to invalidate the black codes.

Johnson's Vetoes

Both measures passed in Congress with nearly unanimous Republican support. President Johnson, however, vetoed them. He claimed that the bill to continue the Freedmen's Bureau would greatly expand the federal bureaucracy and permit too "vast a number of agents" to exercise arbitrary power over the white population. He insisted that the Civil Rights Bill benefited black people at the expense of white people.

The Johnson vetoes stunned Republicans. Although he had not meant to, Johnson drove moderate Republicans into the radical camp and strengthened the Republican Party. The president did not believe Republicans would oppose him to support the freedmen. He was wrong. Congress overrode both vetoes. The Republicans broke with Johnson in 1866, defied him in 1867, and impeached him in 1868 (failing to remove him from office by only one vote in the Senate).

The Fourteenth Amendment

To secure the legal rights of freedmen, Republicans passed the **Fourteenth Amendment**. This amendment fundamentally changed the Constitution by compelling states to accept their residents as citizens and to guarantee that their rights as citizens would be safeguarded.

Its first section guaranteed citizenship to every person born in the United States. This included virtually every black person. In addition, it made each person a citizen of the state in which he or she resided, defined the specific rights of citizens, and protected those rights against the authority of state governments. Citizens had the right to due process (usually a trial) before they could lose their life, liberty, or property:

> All persons born or naturalized in the United States, and subject to the jurisdiction thereof, are citizens of the United States and of the State wherein they reside. No State shall make or enforce any law which shall abridge the privileges or immunities of citizens of the United States; nor shall any State deprive any person of life, liberty, or property, without due process of law; nor deny to any person within its jurisdiction the equal protection of the laws.

Eleven years after Chief Justice Roger Taney declared in the *Dred Scott* decision that black people were "a subordinate and inferior class of beings" who had "no rights that white people were bound to respect," the Fourteenth Amendment vested African Americans with the same rights of citizenship other Americans possessed.

The amendment also threatened to deprive states of representation in Congress if they denied black men the vote. The end of slavery had also made obsolete the Three-Fifths Clause in the Constitution, which had counted slaves as only three-fifths (or 60 percent) of a white person in calculating a state's population and in determining the number of representatives each state was entitled to in the House of Representatives. Republicans feared that southern states would count black people in their populations without permitting them to vote, thereby gaining more representatives than those states had before the Civil War. The amendment mandated that if any state—northern or southern—did not allow adult male

Read on **MyHistoryLab**
Document: The Civil Rights Act of 1866

Civil Rights Act This act nullified the black codes and gave African Americans citizens the basic rights of life, liberty, and due process.

Read on **MyHistoryLab**
Document: President Johnson Vetoes the Civil Rights Act of 1866

Fourteenth Amendment This amendment ratified during Reconstruction made any person born in the United States a citizen of the United States and of the state in which he or she lived.

Read on **MyHistoryLab**
Document: The Thirteenth, Fourteenth, and Fifteenth Amendments to the Constitution, 1865

12-1

12-2

12-3

12-4

12-5

12-6

12-7

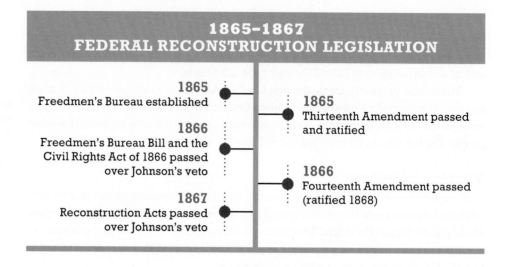

1865–1867
FEDERAL RECONSTRUCTION LEGISLATION

1865
Freedmen's Bureau established

1866
Freedmen's Bureau Bill and the
Civil Rights Act of 1866 passed
over Johnson's veto

1867
Reconstruction Acts passed
over Johnson's veto

1865
Thirteenth Amendment passed
and ratified

1866
Fourteenth Amendment passed
(ratified 1868)

12-1

12-2

12-3

12-4

12-5

12-6

12-7

Reconstruction The
12 years (1865–1877)
following the Civil War,
during which the former
Confederate states
were restored to the
Union and former slaves
became citizens and
gained the right to vote
and hold political office.

**Reconstruction
Acts** Led by Radical
Republicans, Congress
divided the South
into five military
districts. Each former
Confederate state
(except Tennessee)
was to frame a new
state constitution and
establish a new state
government. The first
Reconstruction Act
provided for universal
manhood suffrage,
which granted the right
to vote to all adult males,
including black men.

citizens to vote, then the number of representatives it was entitled to in Congress would be
reduced in proportion to the number of men denied the right to vote.

Democrats almost unanimously opposed the Fourteenth Amendment. Andrew
Johnson denounced it, although he could not prevent its adoption. Except for Tennessee,
southern states refused to ratify it. Women's suffragists felt betrayed because the amendment
limited suffrage to males. Despite this opposition, the amendment was ratified in 1868.

Radical Reconstruction

By 1867 Radical Republicans in Congress had wrested control over **Reconstruction** from
Johnson, and they then imposed policies that brought black men into the political system
as voters and officeholders. It was a dramatic development, second in importance only to
emancipation and the end of slavery.

Republicans swept the 1866 congressional elections despite the belligerent opposition of Johnson and the Democrats. With two-thirds majorities in the House and Senate,
Republicans easily overrode presidential vetoes. Two years after the Civil War, Republicans
dismantled the state governments established in the South under Johnson's authority and
instituted a new Reconstruction policy.

Republicans passed the first of three **Reconstruction Acts** over Johnson's veto in March
1867. It divided the South into five military districts, each under the command of a general
(see Map 12–2). Troops would protect lives and property while new civilian governments were
formed. Elected delegates in each state would draft a new constitution and submit it to the voters.

Universal Manhood Suffrage

The Reconstruction Act stipulated that all adult males in the states of the former Confederacy
were eligible to vote, except for those who had actively supported the Confederacy or were
convicted felons. Once each state had formed a new government and approved the Fourteenth Amendment, it would be readmitted to the Union with representation in Congress.

The advent of Radical Reconstruction was the culmination of the struggle of black people
to gain legal and political rights. Since the 1864 black national convention in Syracuse and the
meetings and conventions in the South in 1865 and 1866, black leaders had argued that one of
the consequences of the Civil War should be the inclusion of black men in the body politic. The
achievement of that goal was due to their persistent and persuasive efforts, the determination of

Radical Republicans, and, ironically, the obstructionism of Andrew Johnson, who had played into their hands.

Black Politics

Full of energy and enthusiasm, black men and women rushed into the political arena in the spring and summer of 1867. Although women could not vote, they joined men at the meetings, rallies, parades, and picnics that accompanied political organizing in the South. For many freed men and women, politics became as important as religious activities. Black people flocked to the Republican Party and the new Union Leagues.

The **Union Leagues** had been established in the North during the Civil War, but they expanded across the South as quasi-political organizations in the late 1860s. The Leagues were social, fraternal, and patriotic groups in which black people often but not always outnumbered white people. League meetings featured ceremonies, rituals, initiation rites, and oaths. They gave people an opportunity to sharpen leadership skills and gain a political education by discussing issues from taxes to schools.

Sit-Ins and Strikes

Political progress did not induce apathy, satisfaction, or contentment among black people. Instead, gaining citizenship, legal rights, and the vote generated more expectations and demands for advancement. For example, black people insisted on equal access to public transportation. In Charleston, South Carolina, black people were permitted to ride only on the outside running boards of the horse- and mule-drawn streetcars. After a Republican rally there in April 1867, black men staged a "sit-in" on one of the vehicles before they were arrested. They wanted to sit on the seats inside. Within a month, after military authorities intervened, the streetcar company gave in. Similar protests occurred in Richmond and New Orleans.

Black workers also struck across the South in 1867. Black longshoremen in New Orleans, Mobile, Savannah, Charleston, and Richmond walked off the job. Black laborers were usually paid less than white men for the same work, which led to labor unrest during the 1860s and 1870s. Sometimes the strikers won, sometimes they lost. In 1869 a black Baltimore longshoreman, Isaac Myers, organized the National Colored Labor Union.

The Reaction of White Southerners

White southerners grimly opposed Radical Reconstruction. They were outraged that black people could claim the same legal and political rights they themselves possessed. Such a possibility seemed preposterous to people convinced of the absolute inferiority of black people.

Explore on **MyHistoryLab Map**: Congressional Reconstruction

MAP 12–2 CONGRESSIONAL RECONSTRUCTION

Under the terms of the First Reconstruction Act of 1867, the former Confederate states (except Tennessee) were divided into five military districts and placed under the authority of military officers. Commanders in each of the five districts were responsible for supervising the reestablishment of civilian governments in each state.

In which states were African Americans a majority of delegates to that state's constitutional convention?

Union League
A social and fraternal organization that stirred political interest and support among black and white Republicans in the South during Reconstruction.

12-1

12-2

12-3

12-4

12-5

12-6

12-7

12-1

12-2

12-3

12-4

12-5

12-6

12-7

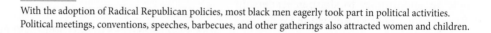

With the adoption of Radical Republican policies, most black men eagerly took part in political activities. Political meetings, conventions, speeches, barbecues, and other gatherings also attracted women and children.

Benjamin F. Perry, whom Johnson had appointed provisional governor of South Carolina in 1865, captures the depth of this racist conviction: "The African," Perry declared, "has been in all ages, a savage or a slave. God created him inferior to the white man in form, color and intellect, and no legislation or culture can make him his equal. . . . His hair, his form and features will not compete with the caucasian race, and it is in vain to think of elevating him to the dignity of the white man. God created differences between the two races, and nothing can make him equal."

Some white people, taking solace in their belief in the innate inferiority of black people, concluded they could turn black suffrage to their advantage. White people, they assumed, should easily be able to control and manipulate black voters just as they had controlled black people during slavery. White southerners who believed this, however, would be disappointed, and their disappointment would turn to fury.

CONCLUSION

Why were black southerners able to gain citizenship and access to the political system by 1868? Most white Americans did not suddenly abandon 250 years of deeply ingrained beliefs that people of African descent were their inferiors. The advances that African Americans achieved fit into a series of complex political developments after the Civil War. Black people themselves had fought and died to preserve the Union, and they had earned the grudging respect of many white people and the open admiration of others. Black leaders in meetings and petitions insisted that their rights be recognized.

White northerners—led by the Radical Republicans—were convinced that President Johnson was wrong to support policies that permitted white southerners to retain pre–Civil

War leaders while the black codes virtually made freedmen slaves again. Republicans were determined that white southerners realize that their defeat had doomed the prewar status quo. Republicans established a Reconstruction program to disfranchise key southern leaders while providing legal rights to freedmen. The right to vote, they reasoned, would enable black people to deal more effectively with white southerners and strengthen the Republican Party in the South.

The result was to make the mid to late 1860s one of the few high points in African-American history. During this period, not only was slavery abolished, but black southerners were able to organize schools and churches, and black people throughout the South acquired legal and political rights that would have been incomprehensible before the war. Yet black people did not stand on the brink of utopia. Most freedmen still lacked land and had no realistic hope of obtaining much, if any, of it. In addition, white violence and cruelty continued almost unabated across much of the South. Still, for millions of African Americans, the future looked more promising than ever before in American history.

CHAPTER TIMELINE

AFRICAN-AMERICAN EVENTS

NATIONAL EVENTS

1862–1864

March 1862
The Port Royal Experiment in South Carolina begins

October 1864
Black national convention in Syracuse, New York

February 1862
Julia Ward Howe publishes the first version of "Battle Hymn of the Republic" in the *Atlantic Monthly*

July 1862
Morrill Land-Grant College Act signed into law

November 1864
President Lincoln reelected

1865–1866

January 1865
General Sherman's Special Field Order #15

March 1865
Freedmen's Bureau established

September–November 1865
Black codes enacted

February 1866
Southern Homestead Act

March 1866
President Johnson vetoes bill to extend the Freedman's Bureau and the Civil Rights Bill

April 1866
Congress overrides Johnson's veto of the Civil Rights Bill

May 1866
Memphis riot

July 1866
Congress enacts new Freedmen's Bureau bill over Johnson's veto; New Orleans riot

April 1865
Lincoln is assassinated; Andrew Johnson succeeds to presidency

May 1865
Johnson begins presidential Reconstruction

June–August 1865
Southern state governments reorganized

December 1865
Thirteenth Amendment to the Constitution ratified

November 1866
Republicans gain greater than two-thirds majorities in House and Senate

CHAPTER TIMELINE

AFRICAN-AMERICAN EVENTS

NATIONAL EVENTS

1867–1969

Spring–Summer 1867
Union Leagues and the Republican Party organized
in southern states

1869
The National Colored Labor Union established
under the leadership of Isaac Myers

March 1867
Congress passes the first Reconstruction Act over
President Johnson's veto
The United States purchases Alaska
from Russia

February 1868
House impeaches President Johnson

May 1868
Senate acquits Johnson by one vote

July 1868
Fourteenth Amendment to the Constitution
ratified

November 1868
Ulysses S. Grant elected president

May 1869
Transcontinental railroad completed

On MyHistoryLab

 ✓ Study and Review on MyHistoryLab

REVIEW QUESTIONS

1. What did freedom mean to ex-slaves? How
did their priorities differ from those of African
Americans who had been free before the Civil War?

2. What did the former slaves and the former
slaveholders want after emancipation? Were these
desires realistic? How did former slaves and former
slaveholders disagree after the end of slavery?

3. Why did African Americans form separate
churches, schools, and social organizations after the
Civil War? What role did the black church play in
the black community?

4. How effective was the Freedmen's Bureau? How
successful was it in assisting ex-slaves to live in
freedom?

5. Why did southern states enact black codes?

6. Why did Radical Republicans object to President
Andrew Johnson's Reconstruction policies? Why
did Congress impose its own Reconstruction
policies?

7. Why were laws passed to enable black men to vote?

8. Why did black men gain the right to vote but not
possession of land?

9. Did congressional Reconstruction secure full equality for African Americans as American citizens?

The Meaning of Freedom: The Failure of Reconstruction 1868–1877

((•)) Listen to Chapter 13 on MyHistoryLab

In 1868, for the first time in American history, thousands of black men would elect hundreds of black and white leaders to state and local offices across the South. Would this newly acquired political influence enable freedmen to complete the transition from slavery to freedom? Would political power propel black people into the mainstream of American society? Equally important, would white southerners and northerners accept black people as fellow citizens?

Events from 1867 to 1877 generated hope that black and white Americans might learn to live together on a compatible and equitable basis. But these developments also raised the possibility that black people's new access to political power would fail to resolve the racial animosity and intolerance that persisted in American life after the Civil War.

LEARNING OBJECTIVES

13-1 What political offices were black men elected to—and not elected to—during Reconstruction?

13-2 What issues were of most concern to black political leaders, and what were the results of their attempts to initiate change in the South?

13-3 Why were so many white southerners opposed to black and white Republicans exercising political power?

13-4 Why was the Ku Klux Klan founded, and how effective was it?

13-5 What were the origins and effects of the Fifteenth Amendment and the Enforcement Acts?

13-6 How and why did black and white Republicans lose control of every southern state by 1877?

13-7 What were the methods used and results of attempts to "redeem" the southern states?

These are the first African Americans to serve in the U.S. Congress. Standing, left to right: Robert C. DeLarge, representative, South Carolina; Jefferson Long, representative, Georgia; Seated, left to right: U.S. Senator Hiram R. Revels, Mississippi; Benjamin S. Turner, representative, Alabama; Josiah T. Walls, representative, Florida; Joseph H. Rainey, representative, South Carolina; Robert B. Elliott, representative, South Carolina.

Constitutional Conventions

13-1 **What political offices were black men elected to—and not elected to—during Reconstruction?**

carpetbagger The derogatory term used during Reconstruction to describe northerners who came South following the Civil War to take advantage of political and economic opportunities. They were labeled "carpetbaggers" because they ostensibly carried all of their possessions in a solitary carpetbag.

13-1
13-2
13-3
13-4
13-5
13-6
13-7

Black men as a group first entered politics as delegates to constitutional conventions in the southern states in 1867 and 1868. Each of the former Confederate states, except Tennessee, which had already been restored to the Union, elected delegates to these conventions. Most southern white men were Democrats. They boycotted these elections to protest Congress's assumption of authority over Reconstruction and the extension of voting privileges to black men. Thus, the delegates to the conventions that met to frame new state constitutions to replace those drawn up in 1865 under President Johnson's authority were mostly Republicans joined by a few conservative southern Democrats. The Republicans represented three constituencies. One group, disparagingly called **carpetbaggers**, consisted of white northern migrants who moved to the South after the war. A second group consisted of native white southerners, mostly small farmers in devastated upland regions of the South who hoped for economic relief from Republican governments. Other southern white people denigrated them as **scalawags**, or scoundrels. African Americans made up the third and largest Republican constituency.

Of the 1,000 men elected as delegates to the 10 state conventions, 265 were black. Black delegates were a majority only in the South Carolina and Louisiana conventions. In most states black men made up 10 to 20 percent of the delegates. At least 107 of the 265 black delegates had been born slaves. Several were well-educated teachers and ministers. Others were tailors, blacksmiths, barbers, and farmers. Most went on to hold other political offices.

These delegates produced impressive constitutions. The new constitutions ensured that all adult males could vote, and except in Mississippi and Virginia, they did not disfranchise many former Confederates. They conferred broad guarantees of civil rights. In several states they provided the first statewide systems of public education. These constitutions were progressive, not radical. Black and white Republicans hoped to attract support from white southerners for the new state governments these documents created by encouraging state support for private businesses, especially railroad construction.

View on **MyHistoryLab** Closer Look: The First Vote

Southern black men cast ballots for the first time in 1867 in the election of delegates to state constitutional conventions. The ballots were provided by the candidates or political parties, not by state or municipal officials. Most nineteenth-century elections were not by secret ballot.

Elections

Elections were held in 1868 to ratify the new constitutions and elect officials. The white Democratic response varied. In some states, Democrats boycotted the elections. In others, they participated but voted against ratification, and in still other states they supported ratification and attempted to elect as many Democrats

TABLE 13-1 AFRICAN-AMERICAN POPULATION AND OFFICEHOLDING DURING RECONSTRUCTION IN THE STATES SUBJECT TO CONGRESSIONAL RECONSTRUCTION

	African-American Population in 1870	African Americans as Percentage of Total Population	Number of African-American Officeholders During Reconstruction
South Carolina	415,814	58.9	314
Mississippi	444,201	53.6	226
Louisiana	364,210	50.1	210
North Carolina	391,650	36.5	180
Alabama	475,510	47.6	167
Georgia	545,142	46.0	108
Virginia	512,841	41.8	85
Florida	91,689	48.7	58
Arkansas	122,169	25.2	46
Texas	253,475	30.9	46
Tennessee	322,331	25.6	20

SOURCE: Eric Foner, *Freedom's Lawmakers: A Directory of Black Officeholders During Reconstruction (New York: Oxford University Press, 1993), xiv; The Statistics of the Population of the United States, Ninth Census (1873), xvii.*

scalawag The derogatory term used during Reconstruction to identify a native white southerner who supported black and white Republicans. They were considered traitors to their people and the Democratic Party.

13-1

13-2

13-3

13-4

13-5

13-6

13-7

as possible. In each state, a majority of those voting eventually voted to ratify, and in each state, black men were elected to office.

Black Political Leaders

Over the next decade, 1,465 black men held political office in the South. Although black leaders individually and collectively enjoyed significant political leverage, white Republicans dominated politics during Reconstruction. In general, the number of black officials in a state reflected the size of that state's African-American population (see Table 13-1).

Initially, black men chose not to run for the most important political offices because they feared their election would further alienate angry white southerners. But as white Republicans swept into office in 1868, black leaders reversed their strategy, and by 1870 black men had been elected to many key positions. No black man was elected governor, but Lieutenant Governor P. B. S. Pinchback served one month (December 1872 to January 1873) as governor in Louisiana after the white governor was removed from office. Blanche K. Bruce and Hiram Revels represented Mississippi in the U.S. Senate. Beginning with Joseph Rainey in 1870 in South Carolina, 14 black men served in the U.S. House of Representatives during Reconstruction. Six black men served as lieutenant governors. In

Hiram R. Revels represented Mississippi in the U.S. Senate from February 1870 until March 1871, completing an unexpired term. He went on to serve as Mississippi's secretary of state. He was born free in Fayetteville, North Carolina, in 1822. He attended Knox College in Illinois before the Civil War. In 1874 he abandoned the Republican Party and became a Democrat. By the 1890s he had acquired a sizable plantation near Natchez.

Mississippi and South Carolina, a majority of the representatives in state houses were black men, and each of these states had two black speakers of the house in the 1870s. Jonathan J. Wright, quoted at the beginning of this chapter, served seven years as a supreme court justice in South Carolina. Four black men served as state superintendents of education, and Francis L. Cardozo served as South Carolina's secretary of state and then treasurer. During Reconstruction, 112 black state senators and 683 black representatives were elected. There were also 41 black sheriffs, five black mayors, and 31 black coroners. Tallahassee, Florida, and Little Rock, Arkansas, had black police chiefs.

Many of these men—by background, experience, and education—were well qualified. However, others were not. Of the 1,465 black officeholders, at least 378 had been free before the Civil War, 933 were literate, and 195 were illiterate (we lack information about the remaining 337). In addition, 64 had attended college or professional school.

Black farmers and artisans—tailors, carpenters, and barbers—were well represented among those who held political office. There were also 237 ministers and 172 teachers. At least 129 had served in the Union Army, and 46 had worked for the Freedmen's Bureau. Several black politicians were wealthy, and a few were former slave owners. Antoine Dubuclet, who became Louisiana's treasurer, had owned more than one hundred slaves and land valued at more than $100,000 before the Civil War. Former slave Ferdinand Havis became a member of the Arkansas House of Representatives. He owned a saloon, a whiskey business, and 2,000 acres near Pine Bluff, where he became known as "the Colored Millionaire."

Although black men did not take over any state politically, a few did dominate districts with sizable black populations. Before he was elected to the U.S. Senate, Blanche K. Bruce all but controlled Bolivar County, Mississippi, where he served as sheriff, tax collector, and superintendent of education. Former slave and Civil War hero Robert Smalls was the political "kingpin" in Beaufort, South Carolina. He served in the South Carolina house and senate and in the U.S. House of Representatives.

The Issues

13-2 **What issues were of most concern to black political leaders, and what were the results of their attempts to initiate change in the South?**

Many but not all black and white Republican leaders favored increasing the authority of state governments to promote the welfare of all the state's citizens. Before the Civil War, most southern states did not provide schools, medical care, assistance for the mentally impaired, or prisons. Such concerns—if attended to at all—were left to local communities or families.

Education and Social Welfare

Black leaders were eager to increase literacy and promote education among black people. Republicans created statewide systems of public education throughout the South. It was a difficult and expensive task, and the results were only a limited success. To pay for it, taxes were increased in states still reeling from the war.

In many rural areas, schools were not built. In other places, teachers were not paid. Some people—black and white—opposed compulsory education laws, preferring to let parents determine whether their children should attend school or work to help the family. Some black leaders favored a poll tax on voting to fund the schools. Thus, although Reconstruction

13-1

13-2

13-3

13-4

13-5

Read on **MyHistoryLab**
Document: An African-American Senator Decries Democratic Political Violence, 1876

13-6

13-7

leaders established a strong commitment to public education, the results they achieved were uneven.

Furthermore, white parents refused to send their children to integrated schools. Although no laws required segregation, public schools during and after Reconstruction were invariably segregated. However, black parents were usually more concerned that their children attend school, and were less concerned that the schools were integrated.

Reconstruction leaders also supported higher education. In 1872 Mississippi legislators took advantage of the 1862 federal Morrill Land-Grant Act, which provided states with funds for agricultural and mechanical colleges, to found the first historically black state university: Alcorn A&M College. The South Carolina legislature created a similar college and attached it to the Methodist-sponsored Claflin University.

Black leaders in the state legislature compelled the University of South Carolina, which had been all white, to admit black students and hire black faculty. As a result, many of the white students and faculty left. Several black politicians enrolled in the law and medical programs at the university.

Despite the costs, Reconstruction leaders also created the first state-supported institutions for the insane, the blind, and the deaf in much of the South. Some southern states during Reconstruction began to offer medical care and public health programs. Some states established orphanages and built prisons. Black leaders also supported revisions to state criminal codes, the elimination of corporal punishment for many crimes, and a reduction in the number of capital crimes.

Civil Rights

Black politicians were often the victims of racial discrimination when they tried to use public transportation and accommodations such as hotels and restaurants. Rather than provide separate arrangements for black customers, white-owned businesses simply excluded black patrons. This was true in the North as well as the South. The Civil War hero Robert Smalls, for example, was ejected from a Philadelphia streetcar in 1864. After protests, the company agreed to accept black riders. In Arkansas, Mifflin Gibbs and W. Hines Furbish successfully sued a local saloon after they had been denied service. In South Carolina, Jonathan J. Wright won $1,200 in a lawsuit against a railroad after he had purchased a first-class ticket but had been forced to ride in the second-class coach.

Black leaders' determination to open public facilities to all people revealed deep divisions between themselves and white Republicans. In several southern states they introduced bills to prevent proprietors from excluding black people from restaurants, barrooms, hotels, concert halls, and auditoriums, as well as railroad coaches, streetcars, and steamboats. Many white Republicans and virtually every Democrat attacked such proposals as efforts to promote social equality and gain access for black people to places where they were not welcome. White politicians blocked these laws in most states. Only South Carolina—with a black majority in the house and many black senators—enacted such a law, but it was not effectively enforced. In Mississippi, the Republican Governor James L. Alcorn vetoed a bill to outlaw racial discrimination by railroads. In Alabama and North Carolina, civil rights bills were defeated, and Georgia and Arkansas enacted measures that encouraged segregation.

Economic Issues

Black politicians sought to promote economic development in general and for black people in particular. For example, white landowners sometimes fired black agricultural laborers near the end of the growing season and then did not pay them. To prevent such abuses, black politicians secured laws that required laborers to be paid before the crop was sold or when it was sold. Some black leaders who had been slaves also wanted to regulate wages, but these proposals failed because most Republicans did not believe states had the authority to regulate wages and prices.

Legislators also enacted measures that protected the land and property of small farmers against seizure for nonpayment of debts. Black and white farmers who lost land, tools, animals, and other property because they could not pay their debts were unlikely to recover financially. "Stay laws" prohibited, or "stayed," authorities from taking property. Besides protecting poor farmers, Republicans hoped these laws would weaken support among white yeomen for the Democratic Party and draw them into the Republican Party.

Land

Black leaders were unable to provide land to landless black and white farmers. Many black and white political leaders believed the state had no right to distribute land. Again, South Carolina was the exception. Its legislature created a state land commission in 1869.

The commission could purchase and distribute land to freedmen. It also gave the freedmen loans on generous terms to pay for the land. Unfortunately, the commission was corrupt and inefficiently managed and had little fertile land to distribute. Yet despite its many difficulties, the commission enabled more than 14,000 black families and a few white families to acquire land in South Carolina. Their descendants still possess some of this land today.

Although some black leaders were reluctant to use the states' power to distribute land, others had no qualms about raising property taxes so high that large landowners would be forced to sell some of their property to pay their taxes. Abraham Galloway of North Carolina explained, "I want to see the man who owns one or two thousand acres of land, taxed a dollar on the acre, and if they can't pay the taxes, sell their property to the highest bidder . . . and then we negroes shall become the land holders."

Business and Industry

Black and white leaders had an easier time enacting legislation to support business and industry. Like most Americans after the Civil War, Republicans believed that expanding the railroad network would stimulate employment, improve transportation, and generate prosperity. State governments approved the sale of state-supported bonds to finance railroad construction. In Georgia, Alabama, Texas, and Arkansas, the railroad network did expand; however, the bonded debt of these states soared, and taxes increased to pay for it. Moreover, railroad financing was often corrupt. Most of the illegal money wound up in the pockets of white businessmen and politicians.

So attractive were business profits that some black political leaders formed corporations. They invested modest sums and believed—like so many capitalists—that the rewards outweighed the risks. In Charleston, 28 black leaders (and two white politicians) formed a horse-drawn streetcar line they called the Enterprise Railroad to carry freight between the city wharves and the railroad terminal. Black leaders in South Carolina also created a fertilizer company. Neither business lasted long. Black men found it far more difficult than white entrepreneurs to finance their corporations.

Black Politicians: An Evaluation

Southern black political leaders on the state level did create the foundation for public education; for state assistance for the blind, deaf, and insane; and for reforming the criminal justice system. They tried (but mostly failed) to outlaw racial discrimination in public facilities and encouraged state support for economic expansion.

But black leaders could not significantly improve the lives of their constituents. Because white Republicans almost always outnumbered them, they could not enact an agenda of their own. Moreover, black leaders often disagreed among themselves about issues and programs. Class and prewar status frequently divided them. Those leaders who had not been slaves and had not been raised in rural isolation were less likely to be concerned with land and agricultural labor. More prosperous black leaders showed more interest in civil rights and encouraging business. Even when they agreed about the need for public education, black leaders often disagreed about how to finance it and whether it should be compulsory.

Republican Factionalism

13-3 Why were so many white southerners opposed to black and white Republicans exercising political power?

Disagreements among black leaders paled compared to the conflicts that divided the Republican Party during Reconstruction. Black and white Republicans often disagreed on political issues and strategy, but the lack of party cohesion and discipline was even more harmful. The Republican Party in the South constantly split into factions as groups fought with each other. Most disagreements were over who should run for and hold political office.

Hundreds of would-be Republican leaders—black and white—sought public offices. If they lost the Republican nomination, they often formed a competing slate of candidates. Then Republicans ran against each other and against the Democrats in the general election. It was not a recipe for political success.

These bitter conflicts were based less on race and issues than on the desperate desire to gain an office that would pay even a modest salary. Most black and white Republicans were not well off. Public office assured them a modicum of economic security.

Ironically, these factional disputes led to a high turnover in political leadership and the loss of that very economic security. It was difficult for black leaders (and white leaders too) to be renominated and reelected to more than one or two terms. This made for inexperienced leadership and added to Republican woes.

Opposition

Even if black and Republican leaders had been less prone to fighting among themselves and more effective in adopting a political platform, they might still have failed to sustain themselves for long. Most white southerners led by conservative Democrats remained absolutely opposed to letting black men vote or hold office. Instead, for most white southerners, the only acceptable political system was one that excluded black men and the Republican Party.

As far as most white people were concerned, the end of slavery and the enfranchisement of black men did not make black people their equals. They did not accept the Fourteenth Amendment, and they attacked Republican governments and their leaders unrelentingly. White southerners blamed the Republicans for an epidemic of waste and corruption in state government. But most of all, they considered it preposterous and outrageous that former slaves could vote and hold office.

13-1
13-2
13-3
13-4
13-5
13-6
13-7

James S. Pike spoke for many white people when he ridiculed black leaders in the South Carolina House of Representatives in 1873:

> The body is almost literally a Black Parliament. . . . The Speaker is black, the Clerk is black, the door-keepers are black, the little pages are black, the chairman of the Ways and Means is black, and the chaplain is coal-black. At some of the desks sit colored men whose types it would be hard to find outside of Congo; whose costume, visages, attitudes, and expression only befit the forecastle of a buccaneer. It must be remembered, also, that these men, with not more than a half a dozen exceptions, have been themselves slaves, and that their ancestors were slaves for generations.

Pike's observations circulated widely in both the North and the South.

White southerners were determined to rid themselves of Republicans and the disgrace of having to live with black men who possessed political rights. White southerners would "redeem" their states by restoring white Democrats to power. This meant not just defeating black and white Republicans in elections but removing them from politics entirely. White southerners believed any means—fair or foul—were justified in exorcising this evil.

The Ku Klux Klan

13-4 **Why was the Ku Klux Klan founded, and how effective was it?**

If the presence of black men in politics was illegitimate—in the eyes of white southerners—then it was acceptable to use violence to remove them. This thinking gave rise to militant terrorist organizations, such as the **Ku Klux Klan**, the Knights of the White Camellia, the White Brotherhood, and the Whitecaps. They were terrorists who resorted to threats, intimidation, beatings, rapes, and murder to restore conservative white Democratic rule and to force black people back into subordination.

The Ku Klux Klan, founded in Pulaski, Tennessee, in 1866, was originally a social club for Confederate veterans who adopted secret oaths and rituals—similar to the Union Leagues but with far more deadly consequences. One of the key figures in the Klan's rapid growth was former Confederate General Nathan Bedford Forrest, who became its leader or grand wizard. The Klan drew its members from all classes of white society, not merely from among the poor. Businessmen, lawyers, physicians, and politicians, as well as farmers and planters, were active in the Klan. The Klan and other armed groups functioned mainly where black people were a large minority and where their votes could affect elections. Klansmen virtually took over areas of western Alabama, northern Georgia, and Florida's panhandle. The Klan controlled the up-country of South Carolina and the area around Mecklenburg County, North Carolina. However, in the Carolina and Georgia low country where there were huge black majorities, the Klan rarely, if ever, appeared.

Although the Klan and similar societies were neither well organized nor unified, they did reduce support for the Republican Party and helped eliminate its leaders. Often wearing hoods and masks to hide their faces, white terrorists embarked on a campaign of violence rarely matched and never exceeded in American history.

Mobs of marauding terrorists beat and killed hundreds of black people—and many white people. Black churches and schools were burned. Republican leaders were threatened or killed. In South Carolina in 1868, the black chairman of the Republican Party,

Ku Klux Klan A secret society founded by former Confederates in Pulaski, Tennessee, in 1866. It transformed itself into a terrorist organization during Reconstruction to drive black and white Republicans from political power in southern states.

Read on MyHistoryLab Document: Organization and Principles of the Ku Klux Klan, 1868

13-1
13-2
13-3
13-4
13-5
13-6
13-7

Read on MyHistoryLab Document: An Ex-Slave Describes a Ku Klux Klan Ride, Late 1860s

The flowing white robes and cone-shaped headgear associated with the Ku Klux Klan today are mostly a twentieth-century phenomenon. The Klansmen of the Reconstruction era, like these two men in Alabama in 1868, were well armed, disguised, and prepared to intimidate black and white Republicans. The note is a Klan death threat directed at Louisiana's first Republican governor, Henry C. Warmoth.

13-1

13-2

13-3

13-4

13-5

13-6

13-7

Benjamin F. Randolph, was murdered as he stepped off a train. Black legislator Lee Nance and white legislator Solomon G. W. Dill were later slain. In 1870 black lawmaker Richard Burke was killed in Sumter County, Alabama, because he was considered too influential among "people of his color."

White men attacked a Republican campaign rally in Eutaw, Alabama, in 1870, killing four black men and wounding 54 other people. After three black leaders were arrested in 1871 in Meridian, Mississippi, for delivering what many white people considered inflammatory speeches, shooting broke out in the courtroom. The Republican judge and two of the defendants were killed, and in a wave of violence, 30 black people were murdered, including every black leader in the small community. In the same year, a mob of 500 men broke into the jail in Union County, South Carolina, and lynched eight black prisoners accused of killing a Confederate veteran.

Nowhere was the Klan more active and violent than in York County, South Carolina. Almost the entire adult white male population joined in threatening, attacking, and murdering the black population. Hundreds were beaten and at least 11 were killed. Terrified

VOICES   An Appeal for Help against the Klan

13-1
13-2
13-3
13-4
13-5
13-6
13-7

H. K. Roberts, a black lieutenant in the South Carolina militia, described Klan terror in York County in late 1870 to Governor Robert K. Scott. Roberts desperately appealed for aid to protect Republicans and defend the black community.

Dec. the 6th 1870.

Antioch P.O.
York County S.C.

To Your Excelency R. K. Scott

Sir I will tell you that on last friday night the 2nd day of this [month] 8 miles from here thier was one of the worst outrages Commited that is on record in the state from 50 to 75 armed men went to the house of Thomas Blacks a colored man fired shots into the house and cald for him he clibed up in the loft of the house they fired up their and he came down jumped out at a window ran about 30 steps was shot down then they shot him after he fell they then draged him about 10 steps and cut his throat from ear to ear their was about 30 bullet holes in his body some 50 to one hundred shots in the house. . . . [They] abused his wife and enquired for one or two more colored men some of the colored people are leaving and a great many lying out in the woods and they reports comes to me evry day that they

Ku Kluxs intend to kill us all out and I heard yesterday that they had 30 stands of arms. . . . I wish you would give me 20 or 25 men or let me enroll that many and I will stop it or catch some of them or send some U S Soldiers on for I tell you their must be something don and that quick to for I do believe that they intend to beat and kill out the Radical party in the upper Counties of the state where the vote is close if we was to have the ellection now the Radicals would turn [out] to vote their ticket I leave the matter with you I hope you will wright back to me by return mail and let me heare what you think you can do for us up here I cant tell whether I can hold my own or not I know some men that stay with us at night for safety but if they come as strong as they were the other night they may kill me and all of my men I remain yours truly as ever.

H.K. Roberts, Lieut.
Commanding Post of State Guards Kings Mountain

> 1. **Why did Roberts write this letter?**
> 2. **Would Roberts have had any reason to exaggerate the violence in York County?**
> 3. **According to Roberts, what motivated white men to attack?**

SOURCE: H. K. Roberts to Governor Robert K. Scott, South Carolina Department of Archives and History.

---

families fled into the woods. Black leaders sent appeals for help to Governor Robert K. Scott (see Voices: An Appeal for Help against the Klan).

But Scott did not send aid. He had already sent the South Carolina militia into areas of Klan activity, and even more violence had resulted. The militia was made up mostly of black men, and white terrorists retaliated by killing militia officers. Scott could not send white men to York County because most of them sympathized with the Klan. Thus, Republican governors like Scott responded ineffectually. Republican-controlled legislatures passed anti-Klan measures and strengthened laws against assault, murder, and conspiracy. Nonetheless, enforcement was weak.

A few Republican leaders did deal harshly and effectively with terrorism. Governors in Tennessee, Texas, and Arkansas declared martial law and sent in hundreds of well-armed white and black men to quell the violence. Hundreds of Klansmen were arrested, many fled, and three were executed in Arkansas. But when Governor William W. Holden of North

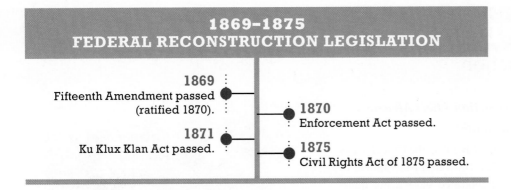

1869–1875
FEDERAL RECONSTRUCTION LEGISLATION

1869
Fifteenth Amendment passed
(ratified 1870).

1870
Enforcement Act passed.

1871
Ku Klux Klan Act passed.

1875
Civil Rights Act of 1875 passed.

Carolina sent the state militia after the Klan, he provoked an angry reaction. Subsequent Klan violence in 10 counties helped Democrats carry the 1870 legislative elections, and the legislature then removed Holden from office.

Outnumbered and outgunned, black people in most areas did not retaliate against the Klan, and the Klan was rarely active where black people were in a majority and prepared to defend themselves. In the cause of white supremacy, the Klan usually attacked those who could not defend themselves.

The West

During the 1830s the U.S. government forced the Five Civilized Tribes—the Cherokee, Chickasaw, Choctaw, Creek, and Seminole—from their southern homelands to Indian Territory in what is now Oklahoma. By 1860 Native Americans there held 7,367 African Americans in slavery. Many of the Indians fought for the Confederacy during the Civil War. Following the war, the former slaves encountered nearly as much violence and hostility from Native Americans as they did from southern white people. Indians were reluctant to share their land with freedmen, and they vigorously opposed policies that favored black voting rights.

Gradually and despite considerable Indian prejudice, some African Americans managed to acquire tribal land. Also, the Creeks and the Seminoles permitted former slaves to take part in tribal government. Black men served in both houses of the Creek legislature—the House of Warriors and the House of Kings. In contrast, the Chickasaw and Choctaw were absolutely opposed to making concessions to freed people.

Elsewhere on the western frontier, black people struggled for legal and political rights and periodically participated in territorial governments. In 1867, 200 black men voted in the Montana territorial election. In the Colorado Territory, William Jefferson Hardin, a barber, campaigned with other black men for the right to vote, a goal that was achieved in 1867. Hardin later moved to Cheyenne and was elected to the Wyoming territorial legislature in 1879.

The Fifteenth Amendment

13-5 What were the origins and effects of the Fifteenth Amendment and the Enforcement Acts?

The federal government under Republican domination tried to protect black voting rights and defend Republican state governments in the South. In 1869 Congress passed the **Fifteenth Amendment**, which was ratified in 1870. It stipulated that a person could not be

Fifteenth Amendment
This constitutional amendment stipulated that the right to vote could not be denied on account of race, color, or because a person had been a slave.

13-1

13-2

13-3

13-4

13-5

13-6

13-7

✳ EXPLORE ON MYHISTORYLAB
Reconstruction

How did Reconstruction Affect African Americans in the South?

In 1865 at the end of the Civil War, the United States was at a crossroads. The Thirteenth Amendment to the Constitution had abolished slavery, but questions remained on what rights—if any—should be granted to the newly liberated African Americans. White political leaders were divided on how to restore the war-torn southern states to the Union. Many white southerners expected to continue their ways of life with freed African Americans regarded as their inferiors. Although the subsequent Fourteenth and Fifteenth Amendments were intended to include African Americans in the legal and political fabric of the nation, most white people in the North and South were unwilling to accept black people as their equals. The early promises of Reconstruction for African Americans went unfulfilled.

✳ Explore the Topic on MyHistoryLab

1. **Analysis** *How did voting patterns for Republicans evolve during the Reconstruction period?* Chart voting patterns to understand reasons behind voting trends.
2. **Comparison** *How did literacy rates differ between African Americans and Euro-Americans in the South?* Theorize how this might affect black disenfranchisement.
3. **Response** *What was the land-holding situation for African Americans at the end of the nineteenth century?* Map land tenure to see discrepancies with whites.

This optimistic 1870 illustration exemplifies the hopes and aspirations generated during Reconstruction as black people gained access to the political system, suggesting that African Americans would soon assume their rightful and equitable role in American society.

RECONSTRUCTION AMENDMENTS TO THE CONSTITUTION

Amendment	Summary	Date
Thirteenth	Abolishes slavery	December 6, 1865
Fourteenth	Ensures equal rights and protections to every person born or naturalized in the United States	July 9, 1868
Fifteenth	Prohibits the denial of the right of vote based on race	February 3, 1870

deprived of the right to vote because of race. "The right of citizens of the United States to vote shall not be denied or abridged by the United States or by any State on account of race, color, or previous condition of servitude." Black people, abolitionists, and reformers hailed the amendment as the culmination of the crusade to end slavery and give black people the same rights as white people.

Northern black men were the amendment's immediate beneficiaries because, before its adoption, black men could vote in only eight northern states. Yet to the disappointment of many, the amendment said nothing about women voting and did not outlaw poll taxes, literacy tests, and property qualifications that could disfranchise citizens.

The Enforcement Acts

In direct response to the terrorism in the South, Congress passed the **Enforcement Acts** in 1870 and 1871; the federal government thereby expanded its authority over the states. The 1870 act outlawed disguises and masks and protected the civil rights of citizens. The 1871 act—known as the Ku Klux Klan Act—made it a federal offense to interfere with a person's right to vote, hold office, serve on a jury, or enjoy equal protection of the law. Those accused of violating the act would be tried in federal court. For extreme violence, the act authorized the president to send in federal troops and suspend the writ of **habeas corpus**. (*Habeas corpus* is the right to be brought before a judge and not be arrested and jailed without cause.)

Black congressmen, who had long advocated federal action against the Klan, endorsed the Enforcement Acts. Representative Joseph Rainey of South Carolina wanted to suspend the Constitution to protect citizens: "I desire that so broad and liberal a construction be placed on its provisions, as will insure protection to the humblest citizen. Tell me nothing of a constitution which fails to shelter beneath its rightful power the people of a country."

Armed with this new legislation, the Justice Department and Attorney General Amos T. Ackerman moved vigorously against the Klan. Hundreds of Klansmen were arrested—700 in Mississippi alone. Faced with a full-scale rebellion in late 1871 in South Carolina's upcountry, President Ulysses S. Grant declared martial law in nine counties, suspended the writ of *habeas corpus*, and sent in the army. Mass arrests and trials followed, but federal authorities permitted many Klansmen to confess and thereby escape prosecution. The government lacked the human and financial resources to bring hundreds of men to court for lengthy trials. Some white men were tried, mostly before black juries, and were imprisoned or fined. Comparatively few Klansmen, however, were punished severely, especially considering the enormity of their crimes.

Enforcement Acts Also known as the Force Acts, these measures were passed by Congress in the early 1870s to undermine the Ku Klux Klan and other terrorist organizations by authorizing the president to use military force and to suspend the writ of *habeas corpus*.

habeas corpus A court order that a person arrested or detained by law enforcement officers must be brought to court and charged with a crime, not just held indefinitely.

The North and Reconstruction

13-6 How and why did black and white Republicans lose control of every southern state by 1877?

Although the federal government did reduce Klan violence for a time, white southerners remained convinced that white supremacy must be restored and Republican governments overturned. Klan violence did not overthrow any state governments, but it undermined freedmen's confidence in the ability of these governments to protect them. Meanwhile, Radical Republicans in Congress grew frustrated that the South and especially black people continued to demand so much of their time and attention year after year. There was less and less sentiment in the North to continue support for the freedmen and involvement in southern affairs.

Many northern Republicans lost interest in civil rights issues and principles and became more concerned with winning elections and the economy. By the mid-1870s, there was more discussion in Congress of political corruption, patronage, veterans' pensions, railroads, taxes, tariffs, the economy, and monetary policy than about rights for black people or the future of the South.

13-1

13-2

13-3

13-4

13-5

13-6

13-7

By the 1870s, the American political system was also awash in corruption, which further detracted from concerns over the South. Although President Grant was a man of integrity, many men in his administration were not. They were implicated in scandals involving the construction of the transcontinental railroad, federal taxes on whiskey, and fraud within the Bureau of Indian Affairs. Nor was the dishonesty limited to Republicans. William Marcy "Boss" Tweed and the Democratic machine that dominated New York City were notoriously corrupt.

Many Republicans began to question the necessity for more moral, military, and political support for African Americans. They were convinced that African Americans had demanded too much for too long from the national government. Former slaves had become citizens and had the right to vote and hold political office. Therefore, they did not need additional help or legislation from the federal government. Equality for black people would come from their labor as free men, which would produce wealth and acceptance by white people. Federal legislation, many northern white people believed, could not create equality.

The Chicago Tribune, a Republican newspaper, had wearied of black agitation by 1874: "Is it not time for the colored race to stop playing baby? The whites of America have done nobly in outgrowing old prejudices against them. They cannot hurry this process by law. Let them obtain social equality as every other man, woman, and child in the world obtain it,—by showing themselves in their lives the social equals of those with whom they wish to consort. If they do this, year by year the prejudices will die away."

Other northern white people, swayed by white southerners' views of black people, began to doubt the wisdom of universal manhood suffrage. Many white people who had nominally supported black suffrage began to believe the exaggerated complaints about corruption among black leaders and the unrelenting claims that freedmen were incapable of self-government. Some white northerners began to conclude that Reconstruction had been a mistake.

Economic conditions contributed to changing attitudes. A financial crisis—the Panic of 1873—sent the economy into a long slump. Businesses and financial institutions failed, unemployment soared, and prices fell. In 1874 the Democrats recaptured a majority in the House of Representatives for the first time since 1860 and also took control of several northern states.

The Freedmen's Bank

Freedmen's Savings Bank A private financial institution chartered by Congress in 1865. Many black people and organizations deposited funds in the bank, which went bankrupt in 1874.

One of the casualties of the financial crisis was the **Freedmen's Savings Bank**, which failed in 1874. Founded in 1865 when hope flourished, the Freedmen's Savings and Trust Company had been chartered by Congress but was not connected to the Freedmen's Bureau. Freedmen and black veterans, churches, fraternal organizations, and benevolent societies opened thousands of accounts in the bank. Most of the deposits totaled under $50, and some amounted to only a few cents.

Although the bank had many black employees, its board of directors consisted of white men. They invested the bank's funds in risky ventures. With the Panic of 1873, the bank lost large sums in unsecured railroad loans. To restore confidence, its directors persuaded Frederick Douglass to serve as president and invest $10,000 of his own money to help shore up the bank. Douglass lost his money, and African Americans across the South lost more than $1 million when the bank closed in June 1874. Eventually about half the depositors received three-fifths of the value of their accounts.

The Civil Rights Act of 1875

Before Reconstruction expired, Congress made one final—some said futile—gesture to protect black people from racial discrimination when it passed the **Civil Rights Act of 1875**. Championed by Senator Charles Sumner of Massachusetts, it was originally intended to open public accommodations—including schools, churches, cemeteries, hotels, and transportation—to all people regardless of race. It passed in the Republican-controlled Senate in 1874, but House Democrats held up passage. It was not enacted until 1875 and then largely as a memorial to Sumner, who had died in 1874. In its final form, the bans on discrimination in churches, cemeteries, and schools were deleted.

The act stipulated "That all persons . . . shall be entitled to the full and equal enjoyment of the accommodations, advantages, facilities, and privileges of inns, public conveyances on land or water, theaters, and other places of public amusement." Even in this weakened form, however, no attempt was made to enforce the act, and in 1883 the Supreme Court declared it unconstitutional. Justice Joseph Bradley wrote that the Fourteenth Amendment protected black people from discrimination by states but not by private businesses. Black newspapers likened the decision to the *Dred Scott* case a quarter century earlier.

> **Civil Rights Act of 1875** This federal legislation outlawed racial discrimination in public accommodations such as hotels and restaurants, and in transportation, including railroad coaches and steamboats. The Supreme Court invalidated it in 1883.

13-1

13-2

13-3

13-4

The End of Reconstruction

13-5

13-7 **What were the methods used and results of attempts to "redeem" the southern states?**

> Watch on MyHistoryLab Video: The Promise and Failure of Reconstruction

13-6

Reconstruction ended as it began—in violence and controversy. Democrats demanded "**redemption**"—a word with biblical and spiritual overtones. They wanted southern states restored to conservative, white political control. By 1875 they had regained authority in all the former Confederate states except Mississippi, Florida, Louisiana, and South Carolina (see Map 13–1). Democrats had redeemed Tennessee in 1870 and Georgia in 1871. Democrats had learned two lessons. First, few black men would vote for the Democratic Party—no matter how much white leaders wanted to believe former slaves were easy to manipulate. Second, intimidation and violence would win elections in areas where the number of black and white voters was nearly equal. The federal government had stymied Klan violence in 1871, but by the mid-1870s the government had become reluctant to send troops to the South to protect black citizens.

> **redemption** The term used for the process, often violent, by which white conservative Democrats regained political control of a southern state from black and white Republicans during Reconstruction.

13-7

Violent Redemption

In Alabama in 1874, black and white Republican leaders were murdered, and white mobs destroyed crops and homes. On election day in Eufaula, white men killed seven and injured nearly 70 unarmed black voters. Black voters were also driven from the polls in Mobile. Democrats won the election and "redeemed" Alabama.

White violence marred every election in Louisiana from 1868 to 1876. After Republicans and Democrats each claimed victory in the 1872 elections, black people seized the small town of Colfax along the Red River to protect themselves against a Democratic takeover. They held out for three weeks. Then on Easter Sunday in 1873, a well-armed white mob attacked the black defenders. At least 105 were killed in the **Colfax Massacre**, the worst single day of bloodshed during Reconstruction. In 1874 the White League almost redeemed Louisiana in a

> **Colfax Massacre** The murder of at least 105 African Americans in 1873 by a white mob, making it the most violent episode of the Reconstruction era.

VOICES   Black Leaders Support the Passage of a Civil Rights Act

Black Congressmen Robert Brown Elliott of South Carolina and James T. Rapier of Alabama spoke passionately in favor of the Sumner civil rights bill in 1874. Both men had been free before the war. Both were also lawyers, and although each accumulated considerable wealth, they died in poverty in the 1880s.

[James T. Rapier]

I must confess it is somewhat embarrassing for a colored man to urge the passage of this bill, because if he exhibit an earnestness in the matter and expresses a desire for its immediate passage, straightaway he is charged with a desire for social equality, as explained by the demagogue and understood by the ignorant white man. But then it is just as embarrassing for him not to do so, for, if he remains silent while the struggle is being carried on around, and for him, he is liable to be charged with a want of interest in a matter that concerns him more than anyone else, which is enough to make his friends desert his cause. So in steering away from Scylla I may run upon Charybdis. But the anomalous, and I may add the supremely ridiculous, position of the Negro at this time, in this country, compel me to say something. Here his condition is without comparison, parallel alone to itself. Just that the law recognizes my right upon this floor as a lawmaker, but that there is no law to secure to me any accommodations whatever while traveling here to discharge my duties as a Representative of a large and wealthy constituency. Here I am

the peer of the proudest, but on a steamboat or car I am not equal to the most degraded. Is not this most anomalous and ridiculous?

[Robert Brown Elliott]

The results of the war, as seen in Reconstruction, have settled forever the political status of my race. The passage of this bill will determine the civil status, not only of the Negro but of any other class of citizens who may feel themselves discriminated against. It will form the capstone of that temple of liberty begun on this continent under discouraging circumstances, carried on in spite of the sneers of monarchists and the cavils of pretended friends of freedom, until at last it stands in all its beautiful symmetry and proportions, a building the grandest which the world has ever seen, realizing the most sanguine expectations and the highest hopes of those who in the name of equal, impartial and universal liberty, laid the foundation stone.

1. **If black men had the right to vote and serve in Congress, why was a civil rights law needed?**
2. **Who would benefit most from the passage of this bill?**
3. **What distinction does the congressmen draw between social discrimination and political rights?**

SOURCE: *Congressional Record*, 43rd Congress, 1st sess., 1874, vol. II, pt. 1, 565–67; Peggy Lamson, *The Glorious Failure* (New York: Norton, 1973), 181.

---

shotgun policy In Mississippi in 1875, white men resorted to violence and intimidation against black and white Republicans to regain political control of the state for conservative Democrats.

wave of violence. Black people were murdered, courts were attacked, and white people refused to pay taxes to the Republican state government. In September, President Grant finally sent federal troops to New Orleans after 3,500 White Leaguers nearly wiped out the black militia and the Metropolitan Police. But the stage had been set for the 1876 campaign.

At least 105 African Americans were murdered on Easter Sunday in 1873 in Colfax, Louisiana, in the single worst episode of racial violence during Reconstruction.

The Shotgun Policy

In 1875 white Mississippians, no longer afraid the national government would intervene in force, declared open warfare on the black majority. The masks and hoods of the Klan

were discarded and white Mississippi unleashed a campaign of violence known as
the "**shotgun policy**" that was extreme
even for Reconstruction. Many Republicans fled, and others were murdered. In
late 1874 an estimated 300 black people
were hunted down outside Vicksburg
after black men armed with inferior
weapons had lost a "battle" with white
men. In 1875, 30 teachers, church leaders, and Republican officials were killed
in Clinton.

Governor Adelbert Ames appealed
for federal help, but President Grant
refused, citing a lack of public support
for intervention. The terrorism intensified, and many black voters went into
hiding on election day, afraid for their
lives and those of their families. Democrats redeemed Mississippi and prided
themselves that they—a superior race
representing the most civilized of all
people—were back in control.

On January 6, 1874, Robert Brown Elliott delivered a ringing speech in the U.S. House of
Representatives in support of the Sumner civil rights bill. Elliott was responding in part
to words uttered the day before by Virginia Congressman John T. Harris, who claimed
that "there is not a gentleman on this floor who can honestly say he really believes that the
colored man is created his equal."

*P.S. Duval and Son, Come and join us brothers; Civil War; Philadelphia, PA; ca. 1863. Chicago Historical
Society ICHi-22051.*

The Hamburg Massacre and the Ellenton Riot

South Carolina Democrats were divided between moderate and extreme factions, but
they united to nominate former Confederate General Wade Hampton for governor after the **Hamburg Massacre**. The prelude to this event occurred on July 4, 1876—the
nation's centennial—when two white men in a buggy confronted the black militia that
was drilling on a town street in Hamburg, a small, mostly black town. Hot words were
exchanged, and days later, Democrats demanded the militia be disarmed. White rifle
club members from around the state arrived in Hamburg and attacked the armory, where
40 black members of the militia defended themselves. The rifle companies brought up a
cannon and reinforcements from Georgia. After the militia ran low on ammunition, white
men captured the armory. One white man was killed, 29 black men were taken prisoner,
and the other 11 fled. Five of the black men identified as leaders were shot down in cold
blood. The rifle companies wrecked the town. Seven white men were indicted for murder. All were acquitted.

Two months after the Hamburg killings, a false allegation that African Americans
had assaulted an elderly white woman gave armed bands of white men the excuse to attack
black people in the rural community of Ellenton about 30 miles south of Hamburg. Between 30 and 100 African Americans were slain in the **Ellenton Massacre**, including state
legislator Simon Coker. Two white men died. No one was charged much less convicted in
the Ellenton affair.

The Hamburg Massacre and Ellenton Riot represented the determined effort of
South Carolina Democrats to imitate Mississippi's "shotgun policy." It also had forced

Hamburg Massacre
White Democrats
attacked black
Republicans in July
1876 in the village
of Hamburg, South
Carolina. Five black
men were murdered as
the Democrats began a
violent effort to redeem
the state.

**Ellenton
Massacre** Between
30 and 100 African
Americans were killed
by marauding white
men in September
1876 in Aiken County,
South Carolina, after
an alleged assault by a
black man on an elderly
white woman.

13-1
13-2
13-3
13-4
13-5
13-6
13-7

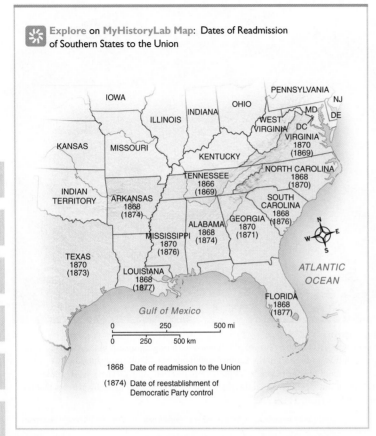

Explore on **MyHistoryLab** Map: Dates of Readmission of Southern States to the Union

1868 Date of readmission to the Union

(1874) Date of reestablishment of Democratic Party control

MAP 13–1 DATES OF READMISSION OF SOUTHERN STATES TO THE UNION AND REESTABLISHMENT OF DEMOCRATIC PARTY CONTROL
Once conservative white Democrats regained political control of a state government from black and white Republicans, they considered that state "redeemed." The first states the Democrats "redeemed" were Georgia, Virginia, and North Carolina. Louisiana, Florida, and South Carolina were the last. (Tennessee was not included in the Reconstruction process under the terms of the 1867 Reconstruction Act.)

In which states did black and white Republicans hold political control for the shortest and longest periods of time?

a reluctant President Grant to send federal troops to South Carolina. In the 1876 election campaign, hundreds of white men in red flannel shirts turned out on mules and horses to support Wade Hampton against incumbent Republican Governor Daniel Chamberlain and his black and white allies.

Democrats beat and killed black people to prevent them from voting. Democratic leaders instructed their followers to treat black voters with contempt: "Treat them so as to show them you are a superior race and that their natural position is that of subordination to the white man."

As the election approached, black people in the up-country of South Carolina knew it would be dangerous if they tried to vote. But in the low country, black people went on the offensive and attacked Democrats. In Charleston, a white man was killed in a racial melee. At a campaign rally at Cainhoy, a few miles outside Charleston, armed black men killed five white men.

A few black men supported Hampton and the Red Shirts. Hampton had a paternalistic view of black people, and, although he considered them inferior, he promised to respect their rights. Martin Delany believed Hampton and the Democrats were more trustworthy than unreliable Republicans; Delany campaigned for Hampton and was later rewarded with an appointment to a minor political post. A few conservative black men during Reconstruction also supported the Democrats and curried their favor and patronage. However, most black people despised them.

The "Compromise" of 1877

Threats, violence, and bloodshed accompanied the elections of 1876 in the South, but the national results were confusing and contradictory. Samuel Tilden, the Democratic presidential candidate, won the popular vote by more than 250,000 and had a large lead—185 to 167—over Republican Rutherford B. Hayes in the electoral vote. The 20 remaining electoral votes were in dispute. Both Democrats and Republicans claimed to have won in Florida, Louisiana, and South Carolina, the last three southern states that had not been redeemed. (There was also one contested vote from Oregon.) Unless Hayes managed to capture all 20 electoral votes of the three con-tested states (and Oregon), Tilden would be the next president (see Map 13–2).

The constitutional crisis over the outcome of the 1876 election was not resolved until shortly before Inauguration Day in March 1877. An informal understanding known as the **Compromise of 1877** ended the dispute. Democrats accepted a Hayes victory, but Hayes let southern Democrats know he would not support Republican governments in Florida, Louisiana, and South Carolina. In 1877 Hayes withdrew the last federal troops from the South, and the Republican administration in those states collapsed. Democrats immediately took control.

Redemption was now complete. White Democrats controlled each of the former Con-federate states. Henry Adams, a black leader from Louisiana, explained what had happened: "The whole South—every state in the South had got into the hands of the very men that held us as slaves."

CONCLUSION

The glorious hopes that emancipation and the Union victory in the Civil War had aroused among African Americans in 1865 appeared forlorn by 1877. To be sure, black people were no longer slave laborers or prop-erty. They lived in tightly knit families that white people no longer controlled. They had established hundreds of schools, churches, and benevolent societies. The Constitution now endowed them with freedom, citizen-ship, and the right to vote. Some black people had even acquired land.

But no one can characterize Reconstruc-tion as a success. The epidemic of terror and violence made it one of the bloodiest eras in American history. Thousands of black people had been beaten, raped, and murdered since 1865 simply because they had acted as free people. Too many white people were determined that black people could not and would not have the same rights that white people enjoyed. White southerners would not tolerate either the presence of black men in politics or white Republicans who accepted black political involvement. Most white northerners and even Radical Republicans grew weary of intervening in southern affairs

Watch on MyHistoryLab Video: The Compromise of 1877

	Precompromise Electoral Vote (%)	Final Electoral Vote (%)	Popular Vote (%)
RUTHERFORD B. HAYES (Republican)	165 (47)	185 (50)	4,034,311 (48)
SAMUEL J. TILDEN (Democrat)	184 (53)	184 (50)	4,288,546 (51)
PETER COOPER (Greenback)	-	-	75,973 (1)
Disputed	20		

MAP 13–2 THE ELECTION OF 1876
Although Democrat Samuel Tilden appeared to have won the election of 1876, Rutherford B. Hayes and the Republicans were able to claim victory after a prolonged political and constitutional controversy involving the disputed Electoral College votes from Louisiana, Florida, and South Carolina (and one from Oregon). In an informal settlement in 1877, Democrats agreed to accept electoral votes for Hayes from those states, and Republicans agreed to permit those states to be "redeemed" by the Democrats. The result was to leave the entire South under the political control of conservative white Democrats. For the first time since 1867, black and white Republicans no longer effectively controlled any former Confederate state.

What factors explain the loss of political power by southern Republicans?

Compromise of 1877 An informal arrangement between national Democrats and Republicans to settle the disputed presidential election of 1876.

and became convinced again that black men and women were their inferiors and were not prepared to participate in government. Reconstruction, they concluded, had been a mistake.

Furthermore, black and white Republicans hurt themselves by indulging in fraud and corruption and by engaging in angry and divisive factionalism. But even if Republicans had been honest and united, white southern Democrats would never have accepted black people as worthy to participate in the political system.

Southern Democrats would accept black people in politics only if Democrats could control black voters. But black voters understood this, rejected control by former slave own-ers, and were loyal to the Republican Party—as flawed as it was.

As grim a turn as life may have taken for black people by 1877, it would get even worse in the decades that followed.

CHAPTER TIMELINE

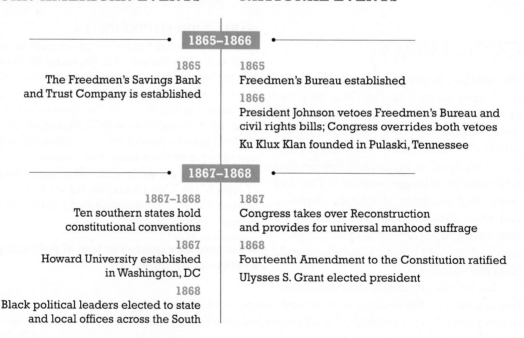

AFRICAN-AMERICAN EVENTS	NATIONAL EVENTS
1865–1866	
1865 The Freedmen's Savings Bank and Trust Company is established	**1865** Freedmen's Bureau established
	1866 President Johnson vetoes Freedmen's Bureau and civil rights bills; Congress overrides both vetoes
	Ku Klux Klan founded in Pulaski, Tennessee
1867–1868	
1867–1868 Ten southern states hold constitutional conventions	**1867** Congress takes over Reconstruction and provides for universal manhood suffrage
1867 Howard University established in Washington, DC	**1868** Fourteenth Amendment to the Constitution ratified
1868 Black political leaders elected to state and local offices across the South	Ulysses S. Grant elected president

CHAPTER TIMELINE

AFRICAN-AMERICAN EVENTS	NATIONAL EVENTS

1869–1870

1870
Hiram R. Revels elected to the U.S. Senate and Joseph H. Rainey to the U.S. House of Representatives

Congress passes the Enforcement Act

1869
Knights of Labor founded in Philadelphia

1870
Fifteenth Amendment to the Constitution ratified

John D. Rockefeller incorporates Standard Oil Co. in Cleveland

1871–1872

1871
Congress passes the Ku Klux Klan Act

1871
William Marcy "Boss" Tweed indicted for fraud in New York City

Chicago Fire

1872
President Grant reelected

Yellowstone National Park established

1873

1873
The Colfax Massacre occurs in Louisiana

1873
Financial panic and economic depression begin

1875–1876

1875
Blanche K. Bruce elected to the U.S. Senate

Congress passes the Civil Rights Act of 1875

Democrats redeem Mississippi with the "shotgun policy"

1876
Hamburg Massacre and Ellenton riot occur in South Carolina

1875
Whiskey Ring exposes corruption in federal liquor tax collections

1876
Disputed presidential election between Samuel J. Tilden and Rutherford B. Hayes

Gen. George A. Custer and U.S. troops defeated by Sioux and Cheyenne in Battle of Little Big Horn

1877

Last federal troops withdrawn from the South

"Compromise of 1877" ends Reconstruction

On MyHistoryLab

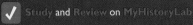 ✓ Study and Review on MyHistoryLab

REVIEW QUESTIONS

1. What issues most concerned black political leaders during Reconstruction?

2. What did black political leaders accomplish and fail to accomplish during Reconstruction? What contributed to their successes and failures?

3. Were black political leaders unqualified to hold office so soon after the end of slavery?

4. To what extent did African Americans dominate southern politics during Reconstruction? Should this era be referred to as "Black Reconstruction"?

5. Why did the Republican Party fail to maintain control of southern state governments during Reconstruction?

6. What was "redemption"? What happened when redemption occurred? What factors contributed to redemption?

7. How and why did Reconstruction end?

8. How effective was Reconstruction in assisting black people to move from slavery to freedom? How effective was it in restoring the southern states to the Union?

Voting and Politics

Entitled "The First Vote," this illustration appeared in *Harper's Weekly*, November 16, 1867. It depicts African Americans casting their votes for the first time.

THE FIFTEENTH AMENDMENT TO THE CONSTITUTION, ratified in 1870, explicitly states that the right "to vote shall not be denied or abridged by the United States or any State on account of race, color, or previous condition of servitude." Why then was it necessary for Congress to pass the Voting Rights Act of 1965?

Race and the right to vote have been volatile issues since the creation of the American republic. The Founding Fathers betrayed a deep mistrust of permitting white men to vote who lacked education and had no stake in society through the possession of property or wealth. Slaves could not vote. Women were disfranchised. But in the late 1700s, a few free black men in the Northeastern states of Pennsylvania, New York, Connecticut, Rhode Island, Massachusetts, New Hampshire, and Vermont did vote. In the early nineteenth century, however, as the political system became more democratic for white men, black men in Pennsylvania and Connecticut—and most black men in New York—lost the right to vote.

Following the Civil War, white southerners and northern Democrats were outraged when Republicans in Congress granted black men the right to vote through Reconstruction legislation and the Fifteenth Amendment. As southern Democrats "redeemed" the former Confederate states, they systematically disfranchised black voters and evaded the Fifteenth Amendment.

To do this, they devised a variety of schemes. Among them were the poll tax, the literacy test, and a requirement that illiterate men could vote only if they could "understand" the Constitution. Several southern states also adopted the grandfather clause, which stipulated that only men who were eligible to vote before 1867 or had fathers or grandfathers who were eligible to vote at that time would be eligible to vote in the late nineteenth century. Violence and intimidation were also used to "persuade" black men and their white allies that they did not want to vote. The U.S. Supreme Court acquiesced in disfranchisement by narrowly defining voting rights for African Americans in a series of cases in the late nineteenth and early twentieth centuries that nullified the Fifteenth Amendment. In tortured logic in one of these cases, Chief Justice Morrison Waite declared that, "The Fifteenth Amendment does not confer the right of suffrage upon anyone." Instead, he claimed, "It prevents the States, or United States, however, from giving preference . . . to one citizen of the United States over another, on account of race, color or previous condition of servitude."

By the early twentieth century, Democrats and Republicans began to hold primary elections to nominate party candidates to run in the general election. Southern Democrats took advantage of this innovation to limit membership in the Democratic Party to white men— and later white women. Only members of the Democratic Party were eligible to vote in the Democratic primary. Because the Republican Party had all but ceased to exist in the South after Reconstruction and rarely ran candidates for statewide offices, victory in the Democratic primary meant victory in the fall election. Black voters who could still vote in the general election found it a meaningless gesture because the "real" election had been the Democratic primary.

As black men and women migrated North and West in the early and mid-twentieth century, they were able to vote in their new communities. Their increasing political strength enabled them to elect black men and women to local and state offices. They also elected black men from northern cities, including Oscar DePriest, Robert Nix, Adam Clayton Powell, and Charles

In the 1960s blacks were still fighting for the voting rights.

Diggs, to serve in the U.S. House of Representatives. With the New Deal in the 1930s, black voters began to support Democratic candidates as they abandoned their longstanding loyalty to the Republican Party. In turn, the Democratic Party increasingly relied on those black voters to support their presidential candidates such as Franklin D. Roosevelt, Harry S Truman, and John F. Kennedy. In the meantime, the Supreme Court declared the grandfather clause unconstitutional in 1915 and outlawed the South's white Democratic primary elections in 1944.

During the Civil Rights movement and with unrelenting pressure from President Lyndon B. Johnson, northern Democrats and Republicans in Congress passed—over the bitter opposition of southern Democrats—the Civil Rights Act of 1964 and the Voting Rights Act of 1965. The Voting Rights Act authorized the U.S. Department of Justice to dispatch federal registrars to states and communities that had a history of suppressing voting rights. As a result, the number of black voters and then black officeholders expanded exponentially across the South.

Yet voting rights still is not a dead issue. In the second decade of the twenty-first century, the Republican Party launched a campaign in 30 states to require voter photo identification at the polls. If implemented, the requirement for government-issued identification will adversely affect poorer voters who lack such documentation—especially African Americans, Hispanics, and Native Americans.

1. Who should be denied the right to vote? Why?

2. To prevent fraud, should voters be required to present photo identification to cast a ballot?

White Supremacy Triumphant: African Americans in the Late Nineteenth Century 1877–1895

Black people struggled against a rising tide of white supremacy in the late nineteenth century. White southerners—and most white northerners—had long been convinced that as a race they were superior to black people intellectually and culturally. They were certain that black people—because of their inferiority—could play only a subservient role in society. During slavery, white southerners had taken that subservience for granted. With slavery's end, black people had allied themselves with radical Republicans during Reconstruction and challenged white supremacy as they became citizens and participated in the political system. The federal government established and enforced—although unevenly—the rights of all citizens to enjoy equal protection of the law and due process of law. But the commitment of the Republicans and the federal government wavered, waned, and then collapsed by the mid-1870s.

Congress, the president, and especially the Supreme Court abandoned the commitment to protect African Americans' civil and legal rights. Political and judicial leaders embraced a laissez-faire approach to social and economic issues. The government would keep its hands off the expanding railroad, steel, and petroleum industries. Neither would government intervene to safeguard the rights of black citizens. The Supreme Court interpreted the Fourteenth Amendment to protect corporations from government regulation, but it failed to protect the basic rights of black people.

LEARNING OBJECTIVES

14-1 How important were African Americans in the political system in the late 1800s after Reconstruction ended?

14-2 What methods were employed to disfranchise black voters?

14-3 How, where, and why did segregation of the races begin?

14-4 What were the rules of "racial etiquette"?

14-5 Why were African Americans the victims of such extensive brutality and violence in the South?

14-6 Why did relatively small numbers of African Americans begin to leave the South?

14-7 What economic situation did large numbers of African Americans find themselves caught up in across the South in the late nineteenth century?

14-8 How just was the legal system for black people in the South?

The Moses Speese family acquired a homestead near Westerville in Custer County, Nebraska. This 1888 photograph shows the extended family assembled in front of their sod house. They have installed a windmill to provide power to pump water from a well. They also possess two teams of horses.

As a result, the conservative white Democrats faced fewer obstacles to the expansion of white authority over the lives of southern African Americans in the late nineteenth century. Between 1875 and 1900, black people in the South were gradually excluded from politics, segregated in public life, and denied equal—even basic—rights. They were forced to behave in a demeaning and deferential manner to white people. Most of them were limited to menial agricultural and domestic jobs that left them poor and dependent on white landowners and merchants. They were often raped, lynched, and beaten. Southern justice was systematically unjust.

Unwilling and unable to tolerate such conditions, some African Americans left the South for Africa or the American West. However, most black people remained in the South, where many acquired a semblance of education, some managed to purchase land, and a few even prospered.

Politics

14-1   **How important were African Americans in the political system in the late 1800s after Reconstruction ended?**

In the late nineteenth century, black people remained important in southern politics. Black men served in Congress, state legislatures, and local governments, and they received federal patronage appointments. But as southern Democrats steadily disfranchised black voters in the 1880s and 1890s, the number of black politicians declined until the political system was virtually all white by 1900 (see Figure 14–1).

For a time, some conservative white Democrats accepted limited black participation in politics as long as no black leader had power over white people and black participation did not challenge white domination. South Carolina's Governor Wade Hampton even assured black people that he respected their rights and would appoint qualified black men to minor offices.

Paternalistic Democrats like Hampton did appoint black men to lower-level positions. Hampton, for example, appointed Richard Gleaves and Martin Delany as trial justices. In turn,

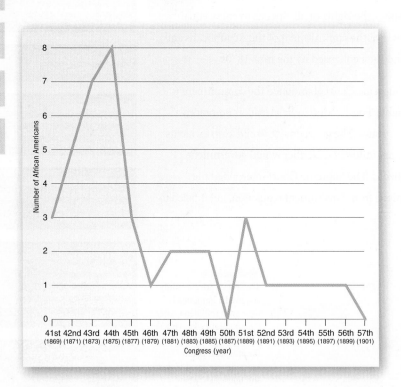

FIGURE 14–1 AFRICAN-AMERICAN REPRESENTATION IN CONGRESS, 1867–1900
Black men served in the U.S. Congress from Joseph Rainey's election in 1870 until George H. White's term concluded in 1901. All were Republicans.

some black men supported the Democrats. A few black Democrats were elected to state legislatures in the 1880s. Some had been Democrats throughout Reconstruction. Others had abandoned the Republicans.

Most black voters, however, remained loyal Republicans even though the party had become a hollow shell of what it had been during Reconstruction. Its few white supporters usually shunned black Republicans. The party rarely fielded candidates for statewide elections, limiting itself to local races in regions where Republicans remained strong.

Black Congressmen

Democrats created oddly shaped congressional districts to confine much of the black population of a state to one district. A black Republican usually represented these districts, while the rest of the state elected white Democrats to Congress. This diluted black voting strength and reduced the number of white people represented by a black congressman. Thus a handful of black Republicans were elected to the House of Representatives long after Reconstruction ended (see Table 14–1).

But these black men wielded only limited power in Washington. They could not persuade their white colleagues to enact significant legislation to benefit their black constituents. They did, however, get Republican presidents to appoint black people to federal positions in

TABLE 14-1 BLACK MEMBERS OF THE U.S. CONGRESS, 1860–1901

Dates	Name	State	Occupation	Prewar Status
1. 1870–1879	Joseph H. Rainey	South Carolina	Barber	Slave, then free
2. 1870–1873	Jefferson Long	Georgia	Tailor, storekeeper	Slave
3. 1870–1873	Hiram Revels*	Mississippi	Barber, minister, teacher, college president	Free
4. 1871–1877	Josiah T. Walls	Florida	Editor, planter, teacher, lawyer	Slave
5. 1871–1873	Benjamin Turner	Alabama	Businessman, farmer, merchant	Slave
6. 1871–1873	Robert C. DeLarge	South Carolina	Tailor	Free
7. 1871–1875	Robert B. Elliott	South Carolina	Lawyer	Free
8. 1873–1879	Richard H. Cain	South Carolina	African Methodist Episcopal minister	Free
9. 1873–1875	Alonzo J. Ransier	South Carolina	Shipping clerk, editor	Free
10. 1873–1875	James T. Rapier	Alabama	Planter, editor, lawyer, teacher	Free
11. 1873–1877, 1882–1883	John R. Lynch	Mississippi	Planter, lawyer, photographer	Slave
12. 1875–1881	Blanche K. Bruce*	Mississippi	Planter, teacher, editor	Slave
13. 1875–1877	Jeremiah Haralson	Alabama	Minister	Slave
14. 1875–1877	John A. Hyman	North Carolina	Storekeeper, farmer	Slave
15. 1875–1877	Charles E. Nash	Louisiana	Mason, cigar maker	Free
16. 1875–1887	Robert Smalls	South Carolina	Ship pilot, editor	Slave
17. 1883–1887	James E. O'Hara	North Carolina	Lawyer	Free
18. 1889–1893	Henry P. Cheatham	North Carolina	Lawyer, teacher	Slave
19. 1889–1891	Thomas E. Miller	South Carolina	Lawyer, college president	Free
20. 1889–1891	John M. Langston	Virginia	Lawyer	Free
21. 1893–1897	George W. Murray	South Carolina	Teacher, farmer	Slave
22. 1897–1901	George H. White	North Carolina	Lawyer	Slave

*Revels and Bruce served in the Senate. The 20 remaining black legislators served in the House.

their districts—including post offices and custom houses—and they denounced the plight of African Americans.

Democrats and Farmer Discontent

Black involvement in southern politics survived Reconstruction, but it did not survive the nineteenth century. Divisions within the Democratic Party and the rise of a new political party—the Populists—accompanied successful efforts to remove black people entirely from southern politics.

Militant Democrats opposed the more paternalistic conservatives who took charge after Reconstruction. For the militants, these redeemers seemed too willing to tolerate limited black participation in politics while showing little interest in the needs of white yeoman farmers. Dissatisfied independents, "readjusters," and other disaffected white people resented the domination of the Democratic Party by former planters, wealthy businessmen, and lawyers who often favored limited government and reduced state support for schools, asylums, orphanages, and prisons while encouraging industry and railroads. Nor did the redeemer and paternalistic Democrats always agree among themselves. Some favored agricultural education, boards of health, and even separate colleges for black students. This disunity permitted insurgent Democrats and even Republicans to exploit economic and racial issues to undermine Democratic solidarity.

Many farmers felt betrayed as the Industrial Revolution transformed society. Wealth was concentrated in the hands of big industrialists and financiers. Farmers were no longer self-sufficient, admired for hard work and self-reliance. They now depended on banks for loans, were exploited when they bought and sold goods, and were at the mercy of railroads when they shipped their commodities. As businessmen got richer, farmers got poorer.

A sharp decline in the price of cotton between 1865 and 1890 hurt small independent (yeomen) farmers in the South. Many lost their land and were forced into tenant farming and sharecropping. By 1890 most farmers in the Deep South, black and white, worked land they did not own.

In response to their woes, farmers organized. In the 1870s they formed the Patrons of Husbandry, or Grange. Initially a fraternal organization, the Grange promoted economic cooperatives and political involvement. Grangers especially favored government regulation of the rates railroads charged to transport crops. By the 1880s, many hard-pressed farmers turned to Farmers' Alliances, which soon spread from the South into the Midwest and Great Plains. These organizations favored railroad regulation, currency inflation (to increase crop prices and reduce debt), and support for agricultural education. By 1888 many of them joined in the National Farmers' Alliance.

The Colored Farmers' Alliance

Colored Farmers' Alliance A large organization of black southern farmers in the 1880s and 1890s that had as many as one million members who agitated for improved conditions and income for black landowners, renters, and sharecroppers.

The alliances, however, were conservative on racial issues and did not challenge the racial status quo. Excluded from the Southern Alliance, black farmers formed their own **Colored Farmers' Alliance**, which expanded across the South and became one of the largest black organizations in American history. The alliances maintained strict racial distinctions but promised to cooperate to resolve their economic woes.

However, black and white alliance members did not always see their economic difficulties from the same perspective. Some white farmers owned the land that the black farmers lived on and worked. Black men saw their alliance as a way of getting a political education. In 1891, 16 black men organized a branch of the Colored Farmers' Alliance in St. Landry

Parish in Louisiana. Their purpose was to help their race and their families and acquire enough information to vote effectively.

But white people were not certain they wanted black men to vote at all—intelligently or otherwise—and they opposed electing black men to office. Paradoxically, they also encouraged black men to vote as long as the black voters supported candidates the alliances backed. By the late 1880s, alliance-backed candidates in the South were elected to state legislatures, to Congress, and to four governorships.

The Populist Party

By 1892 many alliance members threw their political support to a new political party—the People's Party—generally known as the **Populist Party**. Convinced that neither the Democrats nor the Republicans cared about American farmers and industrial workers, the Populists hoped to wrestle control of the economy from bankers, industrialists, and their allies in the traditional parties and let the "people" shape the country's destiny. They urged southern white men to abandon the Democrats and southern black men to reject the Republicans and unite politically to support the Populists.

The foremost proponent of black and white political unity was Thomas Watson of Georgia. He and other Populist leaders believed economic and political cooperation could transcend racial differences. During the 1892 presidential campaign, Watson explained that black and white farmers faced the same economic exploitation, but that they failed to cooperate with each other because of race. At the same time, Watson was not calling for improved race relations. While he opposed economic exploitation that was disguised by race, he was also a staunch supporter of segregation.

Watson eventually became a racial demagogue who thoroughly supported white supremacy. But in 1892 he desperately wanted black and white voters to support Populist candidates. The Populists lost the national election that year and again in 1896, although they did win several congressional and governor's races. Southern Democrats, outraged at the Populist appeal for black votes, resorted again to fraud and terror to prevail. When a biracial coalition of black and white Populists took control of Grimes County in east Texas in 1900, Democrats massacred first the black and then the white leaders.

Nor is it a coincidence that in the election of 1892, when the Democrats carried every southern state, there was an explosion of violence. Democrats were determined to destroy the Populist challenge. That year a record 235 people were lynched in the United States.

The Populist challenge heightened southern Democrats' fears that black voters could decide elections if the white vote split. But many black people were suspicious of the Populists and remained loyal to the Republicans. The Republican Party in the South, however, was much weaker than it had been during Reconstruction because many of its supporters could no longer vote. Years before the alliances and the Populists emerged, southern Democrats had begun to eliminate the black vote.

Populist Party Also known as the Peoples' Party, the Populists supported inflation; the free and unlimited coinage of silver and gold; government ownership of railroads, telephone, and telegraph companies; and an eight-hour workday. They won state and congressional elections but lost the presidential contests in 1892 and 1896.

14-1

14-2

14-3

14-4

14-5

14-6

14-7

14-8

Disfranchisement

14-2   **What methods were employed to disfranchise black voters?**

As early as the late 1870s, southern Democrats worked to undermine black political power. Violence and intimidation, so effective during Reconstruction, continued in the 1880s and 1890s. Frightened, discouraged, or apathetic, many black men stopped voting. White landlords could sometimes intimidate or bribe black sharecroppers and renters not to vote or to vote for the landlord's candidates.

There was also simple injustice. In 1890 black Congressman Thomas E. Miller ran for reelection and won—or so he thought. But he was charged with using illegal ballots and declared the loser. He appealed to the South Carolina Supreme Court, which ruled that although his ballots were printed on the required white paper, it was "of a distinctly yellow tinge." He did not return to Congress.

Evading the Fifteenth Amendment

More militant and determined southern Democrats were unwavering in their efforts to find some "legal" means to prevent black men from voting. However, the Fifteenth Amendment stated that the right to vote could not be denied on "account of race, color, or previous condition of servitude."

White leaders worried that if they imposed what were then legally acceptable barriers to voting—literacy tests, poll taxes, and property qualifications—they would also disfranchise many white voters. But resourceful Democrats found ways around this problem. In 1882, for example, South Carolina passed the Eight Box Law, a primitive literacy test that required voters to deposit separate ballots for separate election races in the proper ballot box. Illiterate voters could not identify the boxes unless white officials assisted them.

Mississippi

Mississippi made the most successful effort to eliminate black voters without openly violating the Fifteenth Amendment. Black men had continued to vote in Mississippi despite intimidation. In 1889 black leaders from 40 Mississippi counties protested the "violent and criminal suppression of the black vote." In response, white men called a constitutional convention to do away with the black vote.

With a single black delegate and 134 white delegates, the convention adopted complex voting requirements that—without mentioning race—disfranchised black voters. Voting required proof of residency and payment of all taxes, including a $2 poll tax. A person convicted of arson, bigamy, or petty theft—crimes the delegates associated with black people—could not vote. People convicted of so-called white crimes—murder, rape, and grand larceny—could vote.

The new Mississippi constitution also required voters to be literate, but illiterate men could still qualify to vote by demonstrating that they understood the constitution if it was read to them. It was taken for granted that white voting registrars would accept almost all white applicants and fail black applicants seeking to register under this provision.

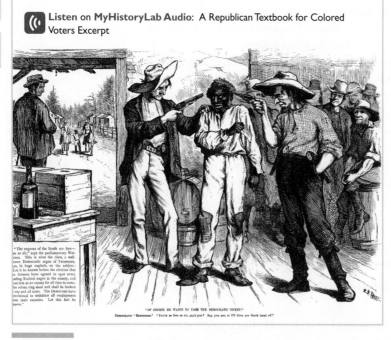

((•)) **Listen on MyHistoryLab Audio:** A Republican Textbook for Colored Voters Excerpt

"OF COURSE HE WANTS TO VOTE THE DEMOCRATIC TICKET!"
Democratic "Reformer." "You're as free as air, ain't you? Say you are, or I'll blow yer black head off!"

A rural black man "freely" exercises his right to vote. Notice the bottle of whiskey next to the ballot box.

South Carolina

Black voting had been declining in South Carolina since the end of Reconstruction. In 1876, 91,870 black men voted. In 1888, only 13,740 did. Unhappy that even so few voters might decide an election, U.S. Senator Benjamin R. Tillman won approval for a constitutional convention in 1895. The convention followed Mississippi's lead and created an "understanding clause," but not without a protest from black leaders.

Six black men and 154 white men were elected to the South Carolina convention. Not surprisingly, as a result of the convention black voters were disfranchised in South Carolina. White delegates did not even pretend that elections should be fair. William Henderson of Berkeley County admitted, "We don't propose to have fair elections. We will get left at that every time. . . . I tell you, gentlemen, if we have fair elections in Berkeley we can't carry it."

The Grandfather Clause

In 1898 Louisiana added a new twist to **disfranchisement**. Its **grandfather clause** stipulated that only men who had been eligible to vote before 1867—or whose father or grandfather had been eligible before that year—would be qualified to vote. Because virtually no black men had been eligible to vote before 1867—most had just emerged from slavery—the law immediately disfranchised almost all black voters.

Except for Kentucky and West Virginia, each southern state had enacted elaborate restrictions on voting by the 1890s. As a result, few black men continued to vote, and none were elected to office.

disfranchisement
White southern Democrats devised a variety of techniques in the late nineteenth and early twentieth centuries to prevent black people from voting. Those techniques included literacy tests, poll taxes, and the grandfather clause as well as intimidation and violence.

grandfather clause
A method southern states used to disfranchise black men. It stipulated that only men whose grandfathers were eligible to vote were themselves eligible to vote. The U.S. Supreme Court invalidated the grandfather clause in 1915.

14-1
14-2
14-3
14-4
14-5
14-6
14-7
14-8

1889–1908
THE SPREAD OF DISFRANCHISEMENT

1889
Florida-Poll tax;
Tennessee-Poll tax

1890
Mississippi-Poll tax, literacy test, understanding clause

1891
Arkansas-Poll tax

1893, 1901
Alabama-Poll tax, literacy test, grandfather clause

1894, 1895
South Carolina-Poll tax, literacy test, understanding clause

1894, 1902
Virginia-Poll tax, literacy test, understanding clause

1897, 1898
Louisiana-Poll tax, literacy test, grandfather clause

1899, 1900
North Carolina-Poll tax, literacy test, grandfather clause

1902
Texas-Poll tax

1908
Georgia-Poll tax, literacy test, understanding clause, grandfather clause

Goldfield et al., *The American Journey* (Upper Saddle River, NJ: Prentice Hall, 2004), 550.

The "Force Bill"

Republicans in Congress in the meantime had made a final, futile attempt to protect black voting rights. In 1890 Massachusetts Congressman Henry Cabot Lodge introduced a bill to require federal supervision of elections in congressional districts where fraud and intimidation were alleged. White southerners were enraged and labeled it the "Force bill" because they believed—incorrectly—that it would force black rule over white people.

This **Federal Elections Bill** easily passed the House, but it failed in the Senate after a 33-day Democratic filibuster. That ended the last significant congressional attempt to protect black voting rights in the South until the passage of the Voting Rights Act in 1965.

Segregation

14-3 How, where, and why did segregation of the races begin?

When black attorney T. McCants Stewart visited Columbia, South Carolina, in 1885, he told readers of the *New York Age* that he had been pleasantly received and had encountered little discrimination. Stewart's visit occurred before most segregation laws had been enacted. In fact, the word **segregation** was almost never used before the twentieth century.

Not that black and white people typically mingled freely in the 1880s and 1890s. They did not. Since Reconstruction, schools, hospitals, asylums, and cemeteries had been segregated. Many restaurants and hotels did not admit black people, and many black people did not venture where they felt unwelcome or were likely to meet hostility. But "Jim Crow" had not yet become legally embedded in southern life.

Jim Crow

The term **Jim Crow** originated with a white performer, Thomas "Daddy" Rice, created in the 1830s and 1840s. Rice blackened his face with charcoal and ridiculed black people. How Rice's character became synonymous with segregation and discrimination is unclear, but by the end of the nineteenth century Jim Crow and segregation were rapidly expanding in the South, greatly restricting the lives of African Americans.

In the decades following slavery's demise, segregation evolved gradually as a way to enforce white domination. If black people were—as white southerners believed—a subordinate race, then their proximity in shops, in parks, and on trains suggested an unacceptable equality in public life.

Moreover, many black people acquiesced in some facets of racial separation. During Reconstruction, people of color formed their own churches and social organizations. Black people were more comfortable around people of their own race than they were among white people. Furthermore, black southerners often accepted separate seating in theaters, concert halls, and other facilities that had been previously closed to them. Segregation, they felt, was better than exclusion.

Segregation on the Railroads

The first segregation laws involved passenger trains. Despite the opposition of black politicians, the Tennessee legislature mandated segregation on railroad coaches in 1881. Florida passed a similar law in 1887. The railroads opposed these laws but not because they wanted to protect the rights of black people. Rather, they were concerned about the expense of maintaining separate cars or sections within cars for black and white people. Whether

---

Federal Elections Bill A measure, also known as the Force bill, to protect the voting rights of black men in the South by providing federal supervision of elections. It passed in the House of Representatives but failed in the Senate.

14-1

14-2

14-3

14-4

segregation The separation of people based on their race in the use of such public facilities as hotels, restaurants, restrooms, drinking fountains, parks, and auditoriums. In many instances segregation meant the exclusion of black people.

14-5

14-6

14-7

Jim Crow "Jump Jim Crow" was a nineteenth-century dance ridiculing black people that was transformed by the twentieth century into a term meaning racial discrimination and segregation.

14-8

they could pay for a first-class ticket or not, most black passengers were confined to grimy second-class cars crowded with smoking and tobacco-chewing black and white men. Hitched just behind the smoke-belching locomotive, these cars were filthy with soot and cinders.

Plessy v. Ferguson

In 1891 the Louisiana legislature required segregated trains within the state, despite opposition from a black organization, the American Citizens' Equal Rights Association of Louisiana, the state's 18 black legislators, and the railroads.

In a test case, black people challenged the law and hoped to demonstrate its absurdity by enlisting the support of a black man who was almost indistinguishable from a white person. In 1892 Homer A. Plessy bought a first-class ticket and attempted to ride on the coach designated for white people. Plessy, who was only one-eighth black, was arrested for violating the new law.

In the case—***Plessy v. Ferguson***—Plessy's lawyers argued that segregation deprived their client of equal protection of the law guaranteed by the Fourteenth Amendment. But in 1896 the Supreme Court, in an 8-to-1 decision, upheld Louisiana's segregation statute. Speaking for the majority, Justice Henry Brown ruled that the law, merely because it required separation of the races, did not deny Plessy his rights, nor did it imply he was inferior. Thus, with the complicity of the Supreme Court, the Fourteenth Amendment no longer afforded black Americans equal treatment under the law. After the *Plessy* decision, southern states and cities created an American apartheid—an elaborate system of racial separation.

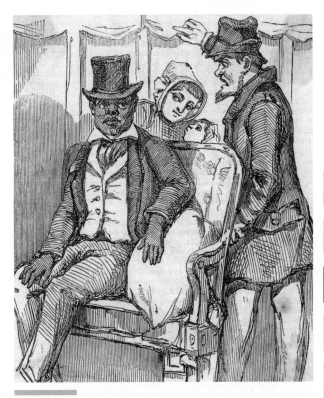

To enforce segregation on a railroad coach, a rather shabbily attired conductor evicts a well-dressed black man from a first-class coach so that he will not pose a danger to a white woman and her child.

 Watch on MyHistoryLab Video: Plessy v. Ferguson

Plessy v. Ferguson In 1896, in an 8-to-1 decision, the U.S. Supreme Court ruled that segregation did not violate the equal protection clause of the Fourteenth Amendment. The "separate but equal" doctrine remained the supreme law of the land until the 1954 *Brown v. Board of Education* decision overturned *Plessy*.

Streetcar Segregation

Before the automobile, the electric streetcar was the primary form of public transportation in American cities and towns. Beginning with Georgia in 1891, states and cities across the South segregated these vehicles. In some communities, the streetcar companies had to operate separate cars for black and white passengers. In others, they designated separate sections within cars. The companies often resisted segregation, citing the expense of duplicating equipment and hiring more employees.

But black people were bitterly opposed to Jim Crow streetcars. During Reconstruction, they had fended off streetcar discrimination with boycotts and sit-ins. Thirty years later, they tried the same techniques. There were boycotts in at least 25 southern cities between 1891 and 1910. Black people refused to ride segregated cars in Atlanta, Augusta, Jacksonville, Montgomery, Mobile, Little Rock, and Columbia. The boycotts seriously hurt the streetcar companies, and segregation was briefly abandoned in Atlanta and Augusta.

Black people also attempted to form alternative transportation companies in Portsmouth and Norfolk, Virginia, and in Chattanooga and Nashville, Tennessee. In 1905 the black community in Nashville organized a black-owned bus company and committed $25,000 to it. They purchased five buses, but the company failed after a few months.

VOICES Majority and Dissenting Opinions on *Plessy v. Ferguson*

The Supreme Court's 8-to-1 decision in Plessy v. Ferguson *sanctioned legal segregation and opened the way for segregation laws throughout the South. The majority opinion ruled that segregation was constitutional so long as both races were provided equal facilities. In practice, of course, the facilities for African Americans were invariably inferior to those for white people.*

From Justice Henry Brown of Michigan's majority opinion:

The object of the [Fourteenth] amendment was undoubtedly to enforce the absolute equality of the two races before the law, but in the nature of things it could not have been intended to abolish distinctions based upon color, or to enforce social, as distinguished from political, equality, or a commingling of the two races upon terms unsatisfactory to either.

We consider the underlying fallacy of the plaintiff's argument to consist in the assumption that the enforced separation of the two races stamps the colored race with a badge of inferiority. If this be so, it is not by the reason of anything found in the act, but solely because the colored race chooses to put that construction upon it. . . . If the two races are to meet on terms of social equality, it must be the result of natural affinities, a mutual appreciation of each other's merits and a voluntary consent of individuals. . . . Legislation is powerless to eradicate racial instincts or to abolish distinctions based upon physical differences. . . . If one race be inferior to the other socially, the Constitution of the United States cannot put them upon the same plane.

From Justice John Marshall Harlan of Kentucky, the lone dissent:

In my opinion, the judgment this day rendered will, in time, prove to be quite as pernicious as the decision made by this tribunal in the Dred Scott Case. . . . But it seems that we have yet, in some of the states, a dominant race, a superior class of citizens, which assumes to regulate the enjoyment of civil rights, common to all citizens, upon the basis of race. The present decision, it may well be apprehended, will not only stimulate aggressions, more or less brutal and irritating, upon the admitted rights of colored citizens, but it will encourage the belief that it is possible, by means of state enactments, to defeat the beneficent purposes which the people of the United States had in view when they adopted the recent amendments of the Constitution, by one which the blacks of this country were made citizens of the United States and of the states in which they respectively reside and whose privileges and immunities, as citizens, the states are forbidden to abridge. . . . What can more certainly arouse race hate, what more certainly create and perpetuate a feeling of distrust between these races, than state enactments which in fact proceed on the ground that the colored citizens are so inferior and degraded that they cannot be allowed to sit in public coaches occupied by white citizens? . . . But in view of the Constitution, in the eyes of the law, there is in this country no superior, dominant, ruling class of citizens. There is no caste here. Our Constitution is color-blind, and neither knows nor tolerates classes among citizens. In respect of civil rights, all citizens are equal before the law.

1. **What does Justice Brown mean when he distinguishes between political and social equality? How does his position compare to that of Congressmen Rapier and Elliott when they argued for civil rights in 1874?** (see p. 329)
2. **How does Justice Harlan counter the majority opinion?**

SOURCE: 163 U.S. 537 United States Reports: *Cases Adjudged in the Supreme Court* (New York: Banks and Brothers, 1896).

Segregation Proliferates

Jim Crow proceeded inexorably. "White" and "colored" signs appeared in railroad stations, theaters, auditoriums, and restrooms, and over drinking fountains. Southern white people went to any length to keep black and white people apart. Courtrooms maintained separate Bibles for black and white witnesses. By 1915 Oklahoma mandated white and colored public telephone booths. New Orleans attempted to segregate customers of black and white prostitutes, but with mixed results.

Although *Plessy v. Ferguson* required "separate but equal" facilities for black and white people, when facilities were made available to black people, they were inferior to those afforded white people. Often, people of color were offered no facilities at all. They were simply excluded.

Read on **MyHistoryLab**
Document: *Plessy v. Ferguson*
Legalizes Segregation, 1896

14-1

Racial Etiquette

14-2

14-4   What were the rules of "racial etiquette"?

14-3

During slavery, white people had insisted that black people act in a subservient manner. Such behavior made white dominance clear. After emancipation, white southerners sought to maintain that dominance through a pattern of racial etiquette that determined how black and white people dealt with each other in their day-to-day affairs.

14-4

Black and white people did not shake hands. Black people did not look white people in the eyes. They were supposed to stare at the ground when addressing white men and women. Black men removed their hats in the presence of white people. White men did not remove their hats in a black home or in the presence of a black woman. Black people went to the back door, not the front door, of a white house. A black man or boy was never to look at a white woman.

14-5

White customers were always served first, even if a black customer had been the first to arrive. Black women could not try on clothing in white businesses. White people did not use titles of respect—Mr., Mrs., Miss—when addressing black adults. They used first names, "boy" or "girl," or sometimes even "nigger." But black people were expected to use Mr., Mrs., or Miss when addressing white people, including adolescents.

14-6

Violence

14-5   Why were African Americans the victims of such extensive brutality and violence in the South?

14-7

The late nineteenth-century South was a violent place. Political and mob violence, so prevalent during Reconstruction, continued unabated into the 1880s and 1890s as Democrats often used force to drive the dwindling number of black and white Republicans out of politics.

14-8

Washington County, Texas

In 1886 in Washington County in Texas, Democrats were determined to keep the control they had won in 1884 through fraud. Masked Democrats tried to seize ballot boxes in a Republican precinct. But armed black men resisted and killed one of the white men. Eight black men were arrested. A mob of white men in disguise broke into the jail and lynched three of the black men. Three white Republicans fled but convinced federal authorities to investigate. The U.S. attorney twice tried to secure convictions for election fraud. The first trial ended in a hung jury, the second in acquittal. The white Democratic sheriff did not investigate the lynching. But the black man charged with the killing of a white man was sentenced to 25 years in prison.

The Phoenix Riot

In the tiny South Carolina community of Phoenix in 1898, a white Republican candidate for Congress urged black men to fill out an affidavit if they were not permitted to vote. This produced a confrontation with Democrats. Words were exchanged, shots were fired, and the Republican candidate was wounded. White men then went on a rampage through rural Greenwood County. Black men were killed—how many is unknown. Others, including Benjamin Mays's father, as related in one of the quotes that opens this chapter—had to humiliate themselves by bowing down and saluting white men.

The Wilmington Riot

While white men roamed Greenwood County for black victims, an even bloodier riot erupted in Wilmington, North Carolina. Black and white men shared power as Republicans and Populists in Wilmington's government, and white Democrats resented it. The Democrats were determined to drive the legitimately elected political leaders from power. Alfred Moore Waddell, a former Confederate and U.S. congressman, vowed in a speech to "choke the Cape Fear [River] with carcasses."

In the midst of this tense situation, Alex Manly, the young editor of a local black newspaper, the *Daily Record,* wrote an editorial condemning white men for the sexual exploitation of black women. Manly also suggested that black men had sexual liaisons with rural white women, which infuriated the white community.

A white mob destroyed the newspaper office. Black and white officials resigned in a vain attempt to prevent further violence, but at least a dozen black men—and perhaps more—were murdered. Some 1,500 black residents of Wilmington fled. White people then bought up black homes and property at bargain rates. Waddell was installed as Wilmington's new mayor. Black Congressman George H. White, who represented Wilmington and North Carolina's second district, served the remainder of his term and then moved north. White was the last black man to serve in Congress from the South until the election of Andrew Young in Atlanta in 1972.

The New Orleans Riot

Robert Charles was a 34-year-old literate laborer who had migrated to New Orleans from rural Mississippi. On July 23, 1900, white New Orleans police officers harassed Charles and a friend. One of the officers attempted to beat Charles with a nightstick. Failing to subdue the large black man, the officer then drew a gun. Charles pulled out his own gun, and each man wounded the other. Charles fled but was tracked down to a rooming house where he had secluded himself with a rifle, with which he proceeded to shoot his tormentors. Eventually, a white mob that numbered as many as 20,000 gathered. In the meantime, Charles methodically shot 27 white people, killing seven, including four policemen. Finally, burned out of the dwelling, Charles was shot, and enraged white people stomped his corpse beyond recognition. Four days of rioting ensued. At least a dozen black people were killed and many more injured.

Lynching

Between 1889 and 1932, 3,745 people were lynched in the United States (see Figure 14–2). Two or three people were lynched, on average, every week for 30 years. Most lynchings

Read on MyHistoryLab
Document: Alex Manly Challenges a White Woman's Call for More Lynchings, 1898

Listen on MyHistoryLab
Audio: Lynch Law in Georgia; by Ida B. Wells Barnett, pamphlet excerpt

happened in the South, and black men were usually the victims. For black southerners, violence was an ever-present possibility. Rarely did a sheriff or police officer protect a potential victim; even if one did, that protection was often not enough.

Lynchers were never apprehended, tried, or convicted. Prominent community members frequently encouraged and even participated in lynch mobs. White politicians, journalists, and clergymen rarely denounced lynching in public. The *Atlanta Constitution* dismissed lynching as relatively inconsequential: "There are places and occasions when the natural fury of men cannot be restrained by all the laws in Christendom."

Lynchings were barbaric, savage, and hideous. Such mob brutality was another manifestation of white supremacy. Black people were murdered, beaten, burned, and mutilated for trivial reasons—or for no reason. Most white southerners justified lynching as a response to the raping of white women by black men. But many lynchings involved no alleged rape. Even in cases when a rape occurred, the person or persons lynched rarely were involved in the crime.

Mobs often attacked black people who had achieved economic success. In Memphis, Thomas Moss with two friends opened the People's Grocery Company in a black neighborhood. The store flourished, but it competed with a white-owned grocery. "They were succeeding too well," one of Moss's friends observed. After the white grocer had the three black men indicted for conspiracy, black people organized a protest, and violence followed. The three black men were jailed. A white mob attacked the jail, lynched them, and looted their store. Ida B. Wells, a newspaper editor and a friend of Moss, was heartbroken: "A finer, cleaner man than he never walked the streets of Memphis." She considered his lynching an "excuse to get rid of Negroes who were acquiring wealth and property and thus keep the race terrorized . . ." In response, she began a lifelong crusade against lynching.

Although less often than men, black women were also lynched. In 1914 in Wagoner County, Oklahoma, 17-year-old Marie Scott was lynched because her brother had killed a white man who had raped her. In Valdosta, Georgia, in 1918, after Mary Turner's husband was lynched, she publicly vowed to bring those responsible to justice. Although she was eight months pregnant, a mob seized her, tied her ankles together, and hanged her upside down from a tree. Someone slit her abdomen, and her nearly full-term child fell to the ground. The mob stomped the infant to death. They then set her clothes on fire and shot her.

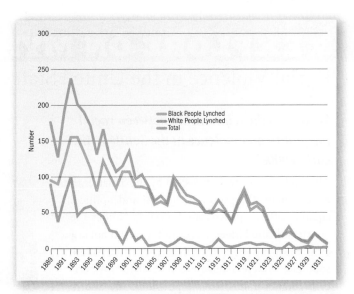

FIGURE 14-2 LYNCHING IN THE UNITED STATES: 1889–1932 Depending on the source, statistics on lynching vary. It was difficult to assemble information on lynching, particularly in the nineteenth century. Not every lynching was recorded.

SOURCE: *The Negro Year Book, 1931–32, 293.*

Read on MyHistoryLab
Document: Ida B. Wells Challenges White Justifications for Lynchings, 1895

Ida Wells Barnett began life as a slave in 1862 and grew up during Reconstruction. As a young woman, she saw the worst indignities and cruelties that the Jim Crow South could inflict, but she fought back as a journalist, agitator, and reformer.

14-1
14-2
14-3
14-4
14-5
14-6
14-7
14-8

✳ EXPLORE ON MYHISTORYLAB

Racial Violence in the United States, 1880–1930

What was the relationship between racial inequality and violence in the South by the early 1900s?

Although slavery was abolished by the Thirteenth Amendment, the promises of legal and political equality offered to African Americans under the Fourteenth and Fifteenth Amendments did not last long following the end of Reconstruction. White southerners were determined that African Americans remain a subordinate people in the South. This system of discrimination included the disfranchisement of African Americans. Widespread violence was also employed to maintain white control. African Americans who threatened the status quo were lynched. Victims were often falsely accused of some crime and subsequently murdered without a trial. Lynching was a tool to maintain the social, political, and economic dominance of white

Lynchings were common and public events in the South. Jesse Washington, a 17-year-old, was accused and found guilty of the murder and rape of a white woman in Waco, Texas, in 1916. Before the sentence could be carried out, he was lynched in front of a crowd of several thousand people.

southerners over African-American people and their communities.

✳ Explore the Topic on MyHistoryLab

1. **Analysis** *In what regions of the South were lynchings most common?* Consider the reasons behind such patterns.
2. **Consequence** *How did white literacy rates correspond to the frequency of lynchings in particular areas?* Explore the relationship between these two elements.
3. **Response** *How did local economic patterns affect the prevalence of lynchings?* Consider connections between land ownership and violence against African Americans.

TOTAL LYNCHINGS IN SELECTED STATES, 1900–1931

State	Total
Alabama	132
Arkansas	127
Florida	170
Georgia	302
Louisiana	172
Mississippi	285
Texas	201

SOURCE: *Lynchings by States and Counties in the United States 1900 to 1931*, Research Department, Tuskegee Institute, http://memory.loc.gov/.

Rape

Although white people often justified lynching as a response to the presumed threat black men posed to the virtue of white women, white men routinely harassed and abused black women. There are no statistics on such abuse, but it surely was more common than lynching. Like lynching, rape demonstrated the power of white men over black men and women.

Black men tried to keep their wives and daughters away from white men. For example, they often refused to permit black women to work as servants in homes where white men were present. One black man commented in 1912, "I believe nearly all white men take, and expect to take, undue liberties with their colored female servants, not only the fathers, but in many cases the sons also." A black man could not easily protect a black woman. He might be killed trying to do so, as an Alabama clergyman pointed out: "White men on the highways and in their stores and on the trains will insult our women and we are powerless to resent it as it would only be an invitation for our lives to be taken."

Many white people believed black women "invited" white males to take advantage of them. Black women were considered inferior, immoral, and lascivious. Therefore, white people reasoned it was impossible to defend the virtue of black women because they had none. Governor Coleman Blease of South Carolina pardoned black and white men found guilty of raping black women. "I am of the opinion," he said in 1913, "as I have always been, and have very serious doubts as to whether the crime of rape can be committed upon a negro."

Migration

14-6 **Why did relatively small numbers of African Americans begin to leave the South?**

14-1
14-2
14-3
14-4
14-5
14-6
14-7
14-8

In 1900 AME Minister Henry McNeal Turner despaired for black people in America: "Every man that has the sense of an animal must see that there is no future in this country for the Negro. [W]e are taken out and burned, shot, hanged, unjointed and murdered in every way. Our civil rights are taken from us by force, our political rights are a farce."

It is therefore surprising that more African Americans did not flee poverty, powerlessness, and brutality in the South. As late as 1910, 90 percent of black Americans still lived in the southern states. And of those who left the South in the 1870s or 1880s, most did not head north. They were more likely to strike out for Africa; move west to Kansas, Oklahoma, and Arkansas; or move from farms to southern towns or cities.

The Liberian Exodus

When in 1875 white Democrats redeemed Mississippi with the "shotgun policy," a group of black people from Winona, Mississippi, wrote to Governor Adelbert Ames "to inquire about the possibility of moving to Africa. [W]e the colored people of Montgomery County are in a bad fix for we have no rights in the county and we want to know of you if there is any way for us to get out of the county. . . ."

Explore on MyHistoryLab Activity: Going Back to Africa

They did not go to Africa, but some black Georgians and South Carolinians did. In 1877 black leaders in South Carolina, including Congressman Richard H. Cain, probate judge Harrison N. Bouey, and Martin Delany, urged black people to migrate to Liberia. Black communities and churches caught "Liberia Fever" while black people in upper South Carolina still felt the trauma of the terror that had ended Reconstruction.

Several black men organized the Liberian Exodus Joint Stock Steamship Company. They raised $6,000 and hired a ship, the *Azor*. The ship left Charleston in April 1878 with 206 migrants aboard, leaving 175 behind because there was not enough room for them. With inadequate food and freshwater and no competent medical care, 23 migrants died at sea. The ship arrived in Liberia on June 3.

In Liberia, several of the migrants prospered. Sam Hill established a 700-acre coffee plantation, and C. L. Parsons became the chief justice of the Liberian Supreme Court. But others did less well, and some returned to the United States. The Liberian Exodus Company experienced financial difficulties and could not pay for further voyages.

The Exodusters

In May 1879 black delegates from 14 states met in a convention in Nashville presided over by Congressman John R. Lynch of Mississippi. The delegates declared that "the colored people should emigrate to those States and Territories where they can enjoy all the rights which are guaranteed by the laws and Constitution of the United States." They also asked Congress—in vain—for $500,000 for this venture.

Nevertheless, black people headed west. Between 1865 and 1880, 40,000 black people known as "**Exodusters**" moved to Kansas. Benjamin "Pap" Singleton, a charismatic ex-slave from Tennessee, persuaded several hundred to migrate. Six black men were instrumental in founding the Kansas town of Nicodemus in 1877. Nicodemus thrived in the 1880s with a hotel, two newspapers, a general store, a drugstore, a school, and three churches.

By 1890, however, Nicodemus went into a decline from which it never recovered. Three railroads were built across Kansas, but each avoided Nicodemus, spelling economic ruin for the community. Eventually more black people settled in Oklahoma than in Kansas. By 1900 African Americans possessed 1.5 million acres in Oklahoma worth $11 million. In 1889 Congress enacted legislation eliminating Indian Territory in Oklahoma, dispossessing the Five Civilized Tribes of their land and dismantling tribal government. More than two dozen black towns were founded in Oklahoma. There were nearly 50 black towns in the West by the early twentieth century (see Map 14–1).

Exodusters Black migrants who left the South during and after Reconstruction and settled in Kansas, often in all-black towns.

With their meager belongings, these African Americans await the arrival of a steamboat in about 1878 to transport them to Kansas or perhaps another western location.

Many people who moved west after the Civil War took advantage of the 1862 Homestead Act, which provided 160 acres of federal land free to those who would settle on it and farm it for at least five years. Life on the frontier was often bleak, dreary, and lonely. People lived in sod houses and relied on cow (or buffalo) chips for heat and cooking fuel as they struggled to endure.

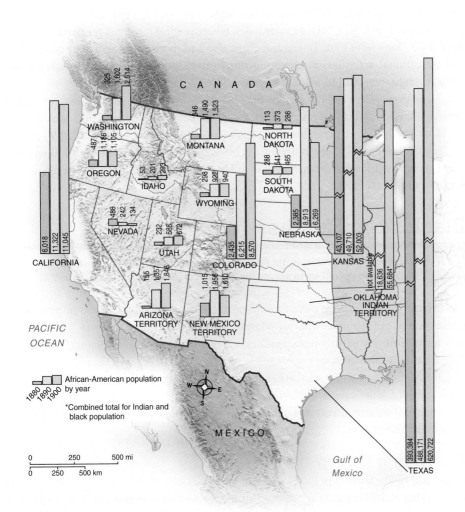

14-1
14-2
14-3
14-4
14-5
14-6
14-7
14-8

MAP 14–1 AFRICAN-AMERICAN POPULATION OF WESTERN TERRITORIES AND STATES, 1880–1900

Although most African Americans remained in the South following the Civil War, thousands of black people moved west and settled on farms and ranches. Others migrated to small towns that were populated mostly by former slaves.

What motivated several thousand African Americans to move to the Great Plains, Rocky Mountains, and West Coast in the late nineteenth century?

Railroads encouraged migration by offering reduced fares. Some western farmers and agents were eager to sell land, but some of it was of little value. Some white residents of Mississippi and South Carolina, which had large black majorities, were glad to see the black people go. However, the loss of cheap black labor alarmed others.

Migration within the South

Many black people left the poverty and isolation of farms and moved to villages and towns in the South. Others went to growing black neighborhoods in larger southern cities like Atlanta, Richmond, and Nashville. Urban areas offered more economic opportunities than rural areas. Although black people were usually confined to menial labor, city work paid cash on a fairly regular basis, whereas rural residents received no money until their crops were sold. Towns and cities also had more entertainment and religious and educational activities. Black youngsters in towns spent more time in school than rural children, who had to work the farms.

Black women had a better chance than black men of finding regular work in a town, although it was usually as a domestic or cleaning woman. This economic situation damaged the black family. Before the increase in migration, a husband and wife headed 90 percent of black families. But with migration, many black men remained in rural areas where they could get farm work, while women went to urban communities. Often these women became single heads of households.

Black Farm Families

14-7   **What economic situation did large numbers of African Americans find themselves caught up in across the South in the late nineteenth century?**

Most black people remained poverty-stricken sharecroppers and renters on impoverished, white-owned land. They were poorly educated. They lacked political power. They were invariably in debt. Many rural black families remained close to involuntary servitude in the decades after Reconstruction.

Many black and white southerners were hardly better off than medieval serfs. They lived in drafty, leaky cabins without electricity or running water. Medical care was often unavailable. Diets were dreary and unbalanced—mostly pork and cornbread—and deficient in vitamins and protein.

Cultivating Cotton

By the late 1800s, farmers in the Midwest and on the Great Plains had access to expensive labor-saving machinery such as reapers, threshers, and combines that enabled them to cultivate hundreds if not thousands of acres of grain. In the South cotton was unaffected by mechanization until the 1930s and 1940s. From the end of slavery into the twentieth century, black farm families annually grew millions of pounds of cotton by spending hundreds of millions of hours in the fields.

Each spring an older youth or adult walked behind a mule and broke the ground with a plow. Men, women, and children then planted cotton seeds and supplied fertilizer to the soil. When the green cotton plants emerged, the weaker plants were removed. From May until July, the field was hoed or chopped repeatedly to remove weeds that competed with the cotton for nutrients.

"Lay-by" time came in July and August as the cotton plants matured and the "fruit" or the cotton bolls grew. There was less work during lay-by time, and children sometimes went to school in July and August. The cotton was then picked by hand beginning in the oppressive heat and humidity of August and continuing into September and October. Because the bolls did not open simultaneously, the fields had to be picked more than once. The larger the family, the larger the labor force, and the more cotton they could harvest.

Picked cotton was stored before it was transported by wagon to the local ginnery. A few cotton gins were still operated with animal or water power; however, by the late nineteenth century steam engines ran the equipment at most ginneries. The modern facility was typically a two-story frame building that featured a large hose-like device that suctioned the cotton from the wagon. A separator then removed debris before a conveyor belt sent the clean cotton to gins that removed the cotton seeds. Then a large hydraulic press compressed the cotton into bales that weighed approximately 500 pounds each. Wagons took the bales to a nearby railroad depot where they were shipped to a textile mill.

Sharecroppers

Most of these black farm families (and many white families) were sharecroppers. Sharecropping had emerged during Reconstruction as landowners allowed the use of their land for a share of the crop. The landlord also usually provided housing, horses or mules, tools, seed, and fertilizer, as well as food and clothing. In return, the landowner received from one-half to three-quarters of the crop.

Sharecropping lent itself to exploitation. By law, verbal agreements were considered contracts. In any case, many sharecroppers were illiterate and could not have read written contracts. The landowner informed the sharecropper of the value of the product raised—typically cotton—and the value of the goods provided to the sharecropping family. Black farmers who disputed white landowners put themselves in peril. Although many sharecroppers knew the proprietor's calculations were wrong, they could do nothing about it. Also, cotton brokers and gin owners routinely paid black farmers less than white farmers per pound for cotton.

Renters

Black farmers preferred renting to sharecropping. As tenants, they paid a flat charge to rent a given number of acres. Payment would be made in either cash—perhaps $5 per acre—or, more typically, in a specified amount of the crop—two bales of cotton per 20 acres. Tenants usually owned their own animals and tools. As Bessie Jones explained, "You see, a sharecropper don't ever have nothing. Before you know it, the man done took it all. But the renter always have something, and then he go to work when he want to go to work. He ain't got to go to work on the man's time. If he didn't make it, he didn't get it."

Crop Liens

Many sharecroppers and renters were also indebted to a merchant for food, clothing, and farm supplies. The merchant advanced the merchandise but took out a **lien** on the crop. If the sharecropper or renter failed to repay the merchant, the merchant was entitled to all or part of the crop once the landowner had received his payment. Merchants tended to charge high prices and interest rates. They usually insisted that farmers plant cotton before they would agree to a lien. Cotton could be sold quickly for cash.

Peonage

Many farmers fell deeply into debt. They were cheated. Bad weather destroyed crops. Crop prices declined. Farmers could not leave the land until their debts were paid. If they tried to depart, the sheriff pursued them. This was **peonage**, and it amounted to enslavement,

Read on MyHistoryLab
Document: A Sharecrop
Contract (1882)

Read on
MyHistoryLab
Document: When
We Worked on
Shares, We Couldn't
Make Nothing

14-1

14-2

14-3

14-4

14-5

14-6

14-7

14-8

lien Black and white farmers purchased goods on credit from local merchants. The merchant demanded collateral in the form of a lien on the crop, typically cotton. If the farmer failed to repay the loan, the merchant had a legal right to seize the crop.

peonage The system that forbade southern farmers, usually sharecroppers and renters, who accumulated debts to leave the land until the debt was repaid—often an impossible task.

VOICES   Cash and Debt for the Black Cotton Farmer

Benjamin E. Mays was born in 1895 in Epworth, South Carolina. He was the youngest and eighth child of parents who had been slaves and whose lives revolved around agriculture. Mays went on to South Carolina State College, to Bates College in Maine, and to the University of Chicago. He became the president of Morehouse College in Atlanta, where he served as a mentor to Martin Luther King, Jr. Mays delivered the eulogy at King's funeral in 1968.

As I recall, Father usually rented forty acres of land for a two-mule farm, or sixty acres if we had three mules. The rent was two bales of cotton weighing 500 pounds each, for every twenty acres rented. So the owner of the land got his two, four, or six bales of cotton out of the first cotton picked and ginned.

To make sixteen bales of cotton on a two-mule farm was considered excellent farming. After four bales were used to pay rent, we would have twelve bales left. The price of cotton fluctuated. If we received ten cents a pound, we would have somewhere between five and six hundred dollars, depending on whether the bales of cotton weighed an average of 450, 475, or 500 pounds. When all of us children were at home we, with our father and mother, were ten. We lived in a four-room house, with no indoor plumbing—no toilet facilities, no running water.

We were never able to clear enough from the crop to carry us from one September to the next. We could usually go on our own from September through February; but every March a lien had to be placed on the crop so that we could get money to buy food and other necessities from March through August, when we would get some relief by selling cotton. Strange as it may seem, neither we nor our neighbors ever raised enough hogs to have meat year round, enough corn and wheat to insure having our daily bread, or cows in sufficient numbers to have enough milk. The curse was cotton. It was difficult to make farmers see that more corn, grain, hogs, and cows meant less cash but more profit in the end. Cotton sold instantly, and that was cash money. Negro farmers wanted to feel the cash—at least for that brief moment as it passed through their hands into the white man's hands!

---

1. **What might have led to greater independence for people like the Mays family?**
2. **Why were southern black and white families so large?**

SOURCE: *Born to Rebel: An Autobiography* (New York: Charles Scribner, 1971), pp. 5–6. Reprinted by permission of the University of Georgia Press, 2001.

---

holding thousands of black people across the South in perpetual bondage. Peonage violated federal law, but the law was rarely enforced. White juries acquitted landowners and merchants who were prosecuted for keeping black people in peonage.

Black Landowners

Considering the incredible obstacles against them, black farm families acquired land at an astonishing rate after the Civil War. Many white people refused to sell land to black buyers, preferring to keep them dependent. Black people also found it difficult to save enough money to purchase land even when they could find a willing seller. Still, they managed to accumulate land.

By 1900 more than 100,000 black families owned their own land in the eight states of the Deep South. Black landownership increased more than 500 percent between 1870 and 1900. Most black people possessed small farms of about 20 acres. These small plots were often subsequently subdivided among sons and grandsons, making it harder for their families to prosper. But some black farmers owned impressive estates. Prince Johnson had 360 acres of excellent Mississippi delta land. Freedman Leon Winter was the richest black man in Tennessee, with real estate worth $70,000 in 1889. In Florida, J. D. McDuffy raised melons, cabbages, and tomatoes on an 800-acre farm near Ocala. Texas freedman Daniel Webster Wallace had a 10,000-acre cattle ranch. Few black people inherited large estates. Most of these landowners had been born into slavery. After emancipation, they managed to accumulate land—usually just a few acres at a time.

White Resentment of Black Success

Many white southerners could not tolerate black economic success and lashed out at those who had achieved it. For example, when one rural black man built an attractive new house, white people told him not to paint it—lest it look better than theirs. He accepted the advice and left the dwelling bare.

In the early twentieth century, Henry Watson, a well-to-do black farmer in Georgia, drove a new car to town. Enraged white people forced Watson and his daughter out at gunpoint and burned the vehicle. Watson was told, "From now on, you niggers walk into town, or use that ole mule if you want to stay in this city."

In 1916 Anthony Crawford, the owner of 427 acres of prime cotton land in Abbeville, South Carolina, was arrested and then released after he quarreled with a local white merchant over the price of cotton seed. But a mob, infuriated that Crawford spoke so bluntly to a white man, went after him. But Crawford resisted and crushed the skull of a white attacker. The mob then stabbed and beat Crawford before the sheriff rescued him and put him in jail. But a second mob broke into the jail and beat him to death. His body was left hanging at the fairgrounds. The coroner's jury ruled that his death had occurred at the hands of persons unknown.

While pursuing a master's degree at the University of Chicago, Benjamin E. Mays briefly taught English at South Carolina State College in Orangeburg. This is a photo taken from the 1926 college yearbook. He met his second wife, Sadie Grey, while teaching in Orangeburg. She was teaching sociology and also working on a graduate degree at the University of Chicago. Mays's first wife, Ellen Harvin, had died from complications due to child birth in 1923.

African Americans and Southern Courts

14-8   How just was the legal system for black people in the South?

The southern criminal justice systems yielded nothing but injustice to black people. Southern lawmakers worried incessantly about what they considered the black crime problem and enacted laws to control the black population. Vagrancy laws made it easy to arrest idle black men or one who was passing through a community. Contract evasion laws ensnared black people who attempted to escape peonage and perpetual servitude.

Segregated Justice

The legal system also became increasingly white after Reconstruction. Black police officers were eliminated, and white policemen acquired a deserved reputation for brutality. Juries were all white by 1900. Judges were white men. Most attorneys were white. The few black lawyers faced daunting hurdles. Some black defendants believed—correctly—that

14-1

14-2

14-3

14-4

14-5

14-6

14-7

14-8

they would be convicted and sentenced to a longer term if they retained a black attorney rather than a white one. Court personnel treated black plaintiffs, defendants, and witnesses with contempt.

A black defendant could not get justice. Black people were more often charged with crimes than white people. They were almost always convicted, regardless of the strength of the evidence or the credibility of witnesses. In one of the few instances when a black man was found not guilty of killing a white man, his attorney advised him to leave town because white people were unlikely to accept the verdict. He fled but returned 20 years later and was castrated by two white men.

Race took precedence in the legal system. Black victims of crime found the law turned against them. In 1897 in Hinds County, Mississippi, a white man beat a black woman with an axe handle. She took him to court, only to have the justice of the peace rule that he knew of "no law to punish a white man for beating a negro woman."

Juries rarely found white people guilty of crimes against black people. In a Georgia case in 1911, the evidence against several white people for holding black families in peonage was so overwhelming that the judge virtually ordered the jury to return a guilty verdict. Nonetheless, after five minutes of deliberation, the jury found the defendants not guilty. Many black and white people were astonished in 1898 in Shreveport, Louisiana, when a jury found a white man guilty of murdering a black man. He was sentenced to five years in prison.

Black people could receive leniency from the judicial system, but it was not justice. They were much less likely to be charged with a crime against another black person, such as raping a black woman, than against a white person. Black people often were not charged with crimes such as adultery and bigamy because white people considered such offenses typical black behavior.

Black defendants who had some personal or economic connection to a prominent white person were less likely to be treated or punished the same way as black people who had no such relationship. In Vicksburg, Mississippi, a black woman watched as the black man who had murdered her husband was acquitted because a white man intervened.

Black people received longer sentences and larger fines than white people. In Georgia, black convicts served much longer sentences than white convicts for the same offense—five times as long for larceny, for example. An 80-year-old black preacher went to prison "for what a white man was fined five dollars." In New Orleans, a black man was sentenced to 90 days in jail for petty theft. A black newspaper said it was "three days for stealing and eighty-seven days for being colored."

The Convict Lease System

convict lease system Southern states and communities leased prisoners to privately operated mines, railroads, and timber companies. These businesses forced the prisoners, who were usually black men, to work in brutal, unhealthy, and dangerous conditions. Many convicts died of abuse and disease.

Conditions in southern prisons were wretched. Black prisoners—many incarcerated for vagrancy, theft, disorderly conduct, and other misdemeanors—spent months and years in oppressive conditions and were unrelentingly abused by white authorities. Nonetheless, conditions got worse.

In the late nineteenth century, southern politicians devised the **convict lease system**. Businesses and planters leased convicts from the state to build railroads, clear swamps, cut timber, tend cotton, and work mines. The company or planter had to feed, clothe, and house the prisoners. Of course, the convicts were not paid. The state and local community were not only freed of the burden of maintaining prisons and jails but also received revenue. For example, the state of South Carolina was paid $3 per month per prisoner. Some states and counties found this so remunerative that law enforcement officials were encouraged to arrest and convict even more black men so that they could contribute to this lucrative enterprise.

Leased convicts endured appalling conditions. They were shackled and beaten, over-worked, and underfed. They slept on vermin-infested straw mattresses and received little or no medical care. They sustained terrible injuries on the job and at the hands of guards. Diseases proliferated in the camps. Hundreds died. They had, in effect, been sentenced to death for petty crimes.

Businessmen and planters found such cheap labor almost irresistible. Black prisoners found it "nine kinds of hell." It was worse than slavery because these black lives had no value to either the government or the businesses involved in this sordid system. As one employer explained in 1883, "But these convicts; we don't own em. One dies, get another." Convict leasing became such a scandal that several states outlawed it by the early twentieth century.

CONCLUSION

With the end of the Civil War and slavery in 1865, more than four million African Americans had looked with hope and anticipation to the future. Four decades later, there were more than nine million African Americans, and more than eight million of them lived in the South. The crushing burden of white supremacy limited their hopes and aspirations. The U.S. government abandoned black people to white southerners and their state and local governments. The federal government that had affirmed their rights as citizens during Reconstruction ignored the legal, political, and economic situation that entrapped most black southerners.

Although the Thirteenth Amendment abolished slavery, thousands of black people were trapped in peonage or labored as sharecroppers and renters, indebted to white landowners and merchants. Yet more than 100,000 black families managed to acquire their own farms by 1900. Many black farmers had also organized and participated in the Colored Farmers' Alliance and the Populist Party, although it brought few tangible benefits.

The Fourteenth Amendment had guaranteed the rights of citizenship that included due process of law. No state could deprive a person of life, liberty, or property without a court proceeding. The amendment also ensured each citizen equal protection of the law. But the Supreme Court had ruled that racial segregation in public places did not infringe on the right to equal protection of the law. And as for the right to life, by the early 1900s, mobs had lynched hundreds of black people.

The Fifteenth Amendment stipulated that race could not be used to deprive a man of the right to vote. But southern states circumvented the amendment with poll taxes, literacy tests, and the grandfather clause. Thus, by 1900, after black men had held political offices across the South for 30 years, no black person served in an elected political position in any southern state.

White people regarded black Americans as an inferior race not entitled to those rights that the Constitution supposedly guaranteed. What could black people do about the discrimination, violence, and powerlessness they had to endure? What strategies, ideas, and leadership could overcome the burdens they were forced to bear? What chances did they have of overcoming white supremacy? How could black people organize to gain fundamental rights that were guaranteed to them?

14-1
14-2
14-3
14-4
14-5
14-6
14-7
14-8

CHAPTER TIMELINE

AFRICAN-AMERICAN EVENTS

NATIONAL EVENTS

1875–1880

1880
Cadet Johnson C. Whittaker
assaulted at West Point

1877
Reconstruction ends

1880
James Garfield elected president

1880–1890

1881
Tennessee segregates passenger trains

Tuskegee Institute founded

1886
Riot in Washington County, Texas

1887
National Colored Farmers' Alliance formed

Florida segregates passenger trains

1889–1890
Southern states disfranchise black voters

1880s
Southern Farmers' Alliance forms

1881
President Garfield assassinated

Clara Barton establishes the Red Cross

1884
Grover Cleveland elected president

1886
Haymarket affair in Chicago

1887
Congress creates the Interstate Commerce
Commission

Dawes Act permits individual Indian families
to own reservation land

1888
Benjamin Harrison elected president

1889
Wall Street Journal established

1890–1895

1891
Georgia segregates streetcars

1892
235 people lynched in the United States,
155 of them African American

1890
Eleven Italians lynched in New Orleans

James A. Naismith invents basketball

1892
Populist Party challenges the Democrats
and Republicans in national elections

Homestead strike at the Carnegie steel
plant near Pittsburgh

Grover Cleveland elected to a second
term as president

1893
Panic of 1893 begins economic depression

CHAPTER TIMELINE

AFRICAN-AMERICAN EVENTS

NATIONAL EVENTS

1895–1900

1896
In *Plessy v. Ferguson,* Supreme Court
upholds legal segregation

1898
Phoenix riot in South Carolina

Wilmington riot in North Carolina

1899–1901
George H. White of North Carolina—the South's last
black congressman until 1972

1900
New Orleans riot

1896
William McKinley elected president
Populist Party's last national campaign

1898
Eugene V. Debs helps found Socialist Party

United States annexes Hawaii

Spanish-American War

1900
William McKinley reelected president

On MyHistoryLab

 Study and Review on MyHistoryLab

REVIEW QUESTIONS

1. How were black people prevented from voting despite the Fifteenth Amendment?

2. How did white Americans justify segregation?

3. Why did the South experience an epidemic of violence and lynching in the late nineteenth century?

4. Why didn't more black people leave the South in this period?

African Americans Challenge White Supremacy 1877–1918

Industrialization and the rise of large, powerful corporations transformed the American economy in the late nineteenth century. As millions of European immigrants crowded into the cities of the North and Midwest to find jobs in the new factories, agricultural production increased and prices declined, impoverishing many rural southerners. Most black people—nearly eight million—remained in the South, where they struggled to confront white supremacy. Living in a society that sought to disregard their rights and exclude them from its institutions and culture, black Americans increasingly relied on their own resources to forge a path into the future.

Some African Americans turned to education to elevate themselves and their people. Some African-American men sought to advance themselves and prove their worth to American society through military service. By the late nineteenth century, however, black Americans mostly relied on each other and their own communities to sustain themselves. They supported churches, schools, and colleges, established businesses, and sometimes formed labor unions and went on strike. They founded their own hospitals. They expressed themselves in music by creating ragtime, jazz, and blues. At times they were allowed to participate with white people in organized sports. More often, they formed their own athletic teams and leagues. African Americans refused to allow white supremacy to prevent them from creating a meaningful place for themselves in American society.

Several hundred African-American cowboys participated in the development of the western cattle empire in the decades after the Civil War. This photo depicts a group of those cowboys near Bonham, Texas, in 1909.

Social Darwinism

15-1 **What scientific and scholarly ideas were developed to support racism during the late nineteenth century?**

Pseudoscientific evidence and academic scholarship bolstered the conviction of many Americans that white people, especially those of English and Germanic descent—Anglo-Saxons—were culturally and racially superior to nonwhites and even other Europeans. Sociologists Herbert Spencer and William Graham Sumner attempted to apply Charles Darwin's theory of evolution to human societies. This theory, called **social Darwinism**, held that through natural selection, the strong would thrive, prosper, and reproduce, while the weak would falter, fail, and die.

Social Darwinism applied to both individuals and "races." It justified great disparities in wealth, suggesting that such men as John D. Rockefeller and Andrew Carnegie were rich because they were "fit," whereas many European immigrants and most African Americans were poor and unlikely to succeed because they were "unfit." The same logic explained why the United States, Britain, and Germany were stronger and more prosperous than countries such as Spain and Italy and why African, Asian, and Latin American societies seemed backward and primitive. In absorbing this ideology of class and race, many Americans and Europeans came to believe they had a responsibility to introduce the benefits and values of Western cultures to the "less advanced" and usually darker peoples of the globe. The English poet Rudyard Kipling called this supposed responsibility "the white man's burden."

Social Darwinism led most Protestant white Americans to believe that other Americans could be ranked from superior to inferior based on their race, nationality, and ethnicity. Black people invariably occupied the bottom of this hierarchy, and the eastern and southern European immigrants who were flooding the country ranked slightly above them. Black people were capable, so the reasoning went, of only a subordinate role in a complex and advanced society. And if their position was biologically ordained, why should society devote substantial resources to educating them?

social Darwinism Derived from Charles Darwin's theory of evolution, Herbert Spencer and William Graham Sumner asserted that life in modern society was competitive and only those individuals who were mentally, emotionally, and physically strong would prevail.

15-1

15-2

15-3

15-4

15-5

15-6

15-7

15-8

Education and Schools

15-2 **What, according to Booker T. Washington, was the chief purpose of education for black people? To what extent did Washington's critics disagree with his position on black education?**

A black youngster who wanted an education in the late nineteenth century faced formidable obstacles. Most black people were poor farmers who had few opportunities for an education and even fewer prospects for a career in business or in a profession. It is a testimony to black perseverance that so many black people did manage to acquire an education and free themselves from illiteracy (see Figure 15–1).

Gaining even a rudimentary education was not easy. Rural schools for black children rarely operated for more than 30 weeks a year. Because of the demands of fieldwork, most black youngsters could not attend school on a regular basis. Brothers and sisters sometimes alternated work and school with each other on a daily basis.

Schools were often dilapidated shacks. They lacked plumbing, electricity, books, and teaching materials. Some schools were in churches and homes. Teachers were poorly paid and often poorly prepared.

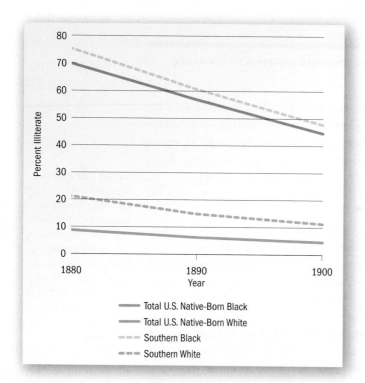

FIGURE 15–1 BLACK AND WHITE ILLITERACY IN THE UNITED STATES AND THE SOUTHERN STATES, 1880–1900
Although more than half of adult black southerners were still illiterate in 1900, black people had made substantial progress in education during the last two decades of the nineteenth century. This progress is especially remarkable considering the difficulties black youngsters and adults faced in acquiring even an elementary education.

Segregated Schools

Although southern states could not afford to support even one first-rate public school system, each of them operated separate schools for black and white children (see Table 15–1). The South had almost no public black high schools. In 1915, not one public black high school existed in 23 southern cities with populations of more than 20,000, including Tampa, New Orleans, Charleston, and Charlotte. But these 23 cities had 36 high schools for white youngsters. Young black people who sought a secondary education often had to travel to a black college or university that offered a high school program.

In many communities, black people, with the assistance of churches and northern philanthropists, operated private academies and high schools to fill the void the lack of public schools created. Typically students were charged a modest tuition and came from more prosperous families. In 1890, 3,106 black youngsters between the ages of 15 and 19 attended black public or private high schools in the South. By 1910, 26,553 did.

The Hampton Model

Some black and many white people regarded education for black youngsters as pointless. Others were convinced the most appropriate education for a black child was industrial or domestic training. Black youngsters, these people maintained, should learn skills they could teach others and use to become productive members of the community.

Hampton Normal and Agricultural Institute was founded in 1868 in Virginia and was dominated for decades by Samuel Chapman Armstrong, a white missionary with paternalistic inclinations. Hampton trained legions of African Americans and Native Americans to teach skills and embrace hard work, diligence, and Christian morality. Armstrong stressed learning trades, such as shoemaking, carpentry, tailoring, and sewing. Hampton placed little emphasis on critical or independent thinking. Instead, students were taught to conform to middle-class values. Armstrong cautioned against black involvement in politics and acquiesced to Jim Crow racial practices.

Booker T. Washington and the Tuskegee Model

Hampton's foremost graduate was Booker T. Washington, who became the nation's leading apostle of industrial training and one of the most remarkable men—black or white—in American history. Washington was born a slave in western Virginia in 1856. His father was an unknown white man. His mother, Jane, raised him in an unimpressive but tidy cabin built of split logs on a small farm. As a child, he worked at a salt works, in coal

Read on MyHistoryLab
Document: Booker T. Washington, The Atlanta Exposition Address (1895)

mines, and as a houseboy for a prominent white family. He learned to read and write at a local school.

Intensely ambitious, Washington set off for Hampton Institute in 1872. While there, he was much affected by Armstrong, his curriculum, and his method of instruction. Washington worked his way through school and taught for two years at Hampton after graduating. In 1881 he accepted an invitation to found a black college in Alabama—Tuskegee Institute. The result was an institution that he forged almost single-handedly and that reflected his experience at Hampton and the influence of Armstrong.

From his arrival at Tuskegee until his death in 1915, Washington worked tirelessly to persuade black and white people that the surest way for black people to advance was by learning skills and demonstrating a willingness to do manual labor. In a famous speech at the Cotton States Exposition in Atlanta in 1895 (see Chapter 16), Washington told his segregated audience, "No race can prosper till it learns that there is as much dignity in tilling a field as in writing a poem. It is at the bottom of life we must begin, and not at the top." He believed that if black people acquired skills and became prosperous small farmers, artisans, and shopkeepers, they would earn the respect and acceptance of white Americans and eradicate the race problem—all without unseemly protest and agitation.

White political leaders and philanthropists, who were more inclined to support the promotion of trades and skills among black people than an academic and liberal education, praised Washington's message. Steel magnate Andrew Carnegie, impressed by Washington, financed the construction of 29 buildings on the campuses of black schools and colleges. Julius Rosenwald, the longtime head of Sears and Roebuck, consulted with Washington and contributed liberally to black education across the South. Disciples of Washington and graduates of Tuskegee fanned out across the South as industrial and agricultural training for black youngsters proliferated.

The Morrill Act, which Congress passed in 1862, entitled each state to the proceeds from the sale of federal land (most of it in the West) for establishing land-grant colleges to provide agricultural and mechanical training. However, southern states did not admit black students to their A&M (Agricultural and Mechanical) schools. In 1890, however, a second Morrill Act permitted states to establish and fund separate black land-grant colleges. By 1915 there were 16 black land-grant colleges.

Most of the institutions were not actually colleges. Few of their students graduated with bachelor's degrees, and many of them were enrolled in primary and secondary programs. Most students at the black land-grant schools had to take courses in trades, agriculture, and domestic sciences. Most of the schools required students to do manual labor for which they were paid small sums. Students built and maintained the campuses and raised the food served in the school cafeteria. Many students were in the "normal" curriculum, which prepared them to teach at a time when most states did not require a college degree for a teaching certificate.

TABLE 15–1 SOUTH CAROLINA'S BLACK AND WHITE PUBLIC SCHOOLS, 1908–1909

Black Schools		White Schools
2,354	Public Schools	2,712
894	Men Teachers	933
1,802	Women Teachers	3,247
181,095	Total Pupils	153,807
123,481	Average Attendance	107,368
77	Pupils per School	55
63	Pupils per Teacher	35
14.7	Average Number of Weeks of School	25.2
$118.17	Average Yearly Salary for Men Teachers	$479.79
$91.45	Average Yearly Salary for Women Teachers	$249.13
$308,153.16	Total Expenditures	$1,590,732.51

SOURCE: *Department of Education Annual Report, South Carolina, 1908–09, 935, 961.*

School for most southern black students and teachers was a part-time activity. Because of the demands of agriculture, few rural students, black or white, attended school more than six months a year. Few teachers were graduates of four-year college programs. In urban communities and the Upper South, the school year lasted longer and education was better financed. But all public southern schools were segregated.

15-1

15-2

15-3

15-4

15-5

15-6

15-7

15-8

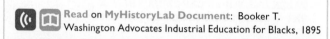

Read on **MyHistoryLab** Document: Booker T. Washington Advocates Industrial Education for Blacks, 1895

Booker T. Washington was by 1900 the most influential black leader in America. White business and political leaders were reassured by his message that black people themselves were responsible for their economic progress and that people of color should avoid a direct challenge to white supremacy. Although W. E. B. Du Bois appreciated Washington's commitment to the advancement of black people, he believed more emphasis should be placed on developing an educated elite who would take the lead in solving the race problem. Washington was a southerner who looked for practical solutions to the problems of everyday life; Du Bois was a northerner who stressed the need for intellectual advancement.

Read on **MyHistoryLab** Document: W. E. B. Du Bois Describes the Role of the "Talented Tenth" in Black Life, 1903

Critics of the Tuskegee Model

Not everyone shared Washington's stress on industrial and agricultural training to the near exclusion of the liberal arts, including literature, history, philosophy, and languages. Washington's program, critics charged, seemed designed to train black people for a subordinate role. Black people, they worried, would continue to labor much as they had in slavery and not far removed from it.

W. E. B. Du Bois, a Fisk- and Harvard-trained scholar, and African Methodist Episcopal (AME) Bishop Henry M. Turner believed education went beyond mere training and the acquisition of skills. It involved intellectual growth. It would confront racial problems, and it would create wise men.

Many of the private black colleges resisted the emphasis on agricultural and mechanical training. They promoted the liberal arts and taught Latin, Greek, mathematics, and natural sciences. Henry L. Morehouse of the American Baptist Home Missionary Society explained that the purpose of education was to develop strong minds. He believed gifted intellectuals—a "talented tenth" as he characterized them in 1896—could lead people forward. Du Bois likewise stressed the need for the best-educated 10 percent of the black population to promote progress and advance the race.

Washington did not deny the importance of a liberal arts education, but he believed industry was the foundation to progress:

On such a foundation as this will grow habits of thrift, a love of work, economy, ownership of property, bank accounts. Out of it in the future will grow practical education, professional education, and positions of public responsibility. Out of it will grow moral and religious strength. Out of it will grow wealth from which alone can come leisure and the opportunity for the enjoyment of literature and the fine arts.

Ultimately, however, Washington was wrong to believe education for black people that focused on economic progress would earn the respect of most white Americans. As Du Bois explained, most white people preferred ignorant and unsuccessful black people to educated and prosperous ones.

As Chapter 16 discusses, the disagreement among black leaders over education would expand by the early twentieth century into a larger controversy. What began as a conversation over the value of practical education became a passionate debate among Washington, Du Bois, and others over the most effective strategy—accommodation or confrontation—for overcoming Jim Crow and white supremacy.

VOICES   Thomas E. Miller and the Mission of the Black Land-Grant College

In 1896 the South Carolina General Assembly established the Colored Normal, Industrial, Agricultural and Mechanical College of South Carolina. It derived funds from the Morrill Acts of 1862 and 1890 and from the state itself. Its first president was former black congressman and lawyer Thomas E. Miller. In an address to the Bamberg County Colored Fair in 1897, Miller embraced the Hampton and Tuskegee models as he described the mission of his institution:

The work of our college is along the industrial line. We are making educated and worthy school teachers, educated and reliable mechanics, educated, reliable and frugal farmers. We teach your sons and daughters how to care for and milk the cows, how to make gilt-edged butter, how to make cheese, what kind of fertilizer each crop needs, the natural strength and productive qualities of the various soils, and last to make a compost heap and how to take care of it. We teach them how to make a wagon, plow and hoe, how to shoe a horse and nurse him when sick. We teach your children how to keep books and typewrite, we teach your girls how to make a dress or undergarment, how to cook, wash and iron. We teach your boys how to make and run an engine, how to make and control electricity, we teach them mechanical and artistic drawing, house and sign painting.

1. **Given the racism of the 1890s, why was or wasn't agricultural and mechanical training the most suitable education for most black youngsters?**
2. **If a young black person did learn the skills Miller mentioned, was he or she educated for an inferior place in society?**

SOURCE: I. A. Newby, *Black Carolinians, A History of Blacks in South Carolina from 1895 to 1968* (Columbia: University of South Carolina Press, 1973), 263.

Church and Religion

15-3   What role did religion play in the lives of African Americans and in their adjustment to discrimination?

In a world in which white people so thoroughly dominated the lives and limited the possibilities of black people, the church had long been the most important institution—after the family—that African Americans controlled for themselves. After the Civil War, black people organized their own churches and religious denominations, which thrived as sources of spiritual comfort and centers of social activity. Black clergymen were often the most influential members of the black community.

The church was integral to the lives of most black people. It fulfilled spiritual needs through sermons and music. It enabled black people, free from white interference, to plan, organize, and lead. It was a sanctuary for black women, who immersed themselves in church activities. Although church members usually had little money to spare, they helped the sick, the bereaved, and those in need. Congregations also helped thousands of youngsters attend school and college.

The church service itself was the most important aspect of religious life for most black congregations. Parishioners were expected to participate and not merely listen quietly to the minister's sermon. In most black churches, members punctuated the minister's call with many an "Amen." They testified, shouted, laughed, cried, and sometimes fainted. Choirs provided joyful music and solemn songs.

Many black ministers had little or no education, a situation that disturbed some black leaders. W. E. B. Du Bois wanted black churches free of "the noisy and unclean leaders of the thoughtless mob" and the clergy replaced by thoughtful "apostles of service and sacrifice." But a black Alabama farmer observed that solemn and erudite preachers would not survive: "You let a man preach de true Gospel and he won't git many nickels in his pocket; but if he hollers and jumps he gits all the nickels he can hold and chickens besides."

A few black women led congregations. Nannie Helen Burroughs established Women's Day in Baptist churches. Women delivered sermons and guided the parishioners. But she complained that Women's Day quickly became more an occasion to raise money than to raise women.

The Church as Solace and Escape

For many black people, the emotional involvement in church services was an escape from their dreary and oppressive daily lives. Growing up in rural South Carolina, Benjamin E. Mays admitted that his Baptist preacher, James F. Marshall, who barely had a fifth-grade education, "emphasized the joys of heaven and the damnation of hell" and that the "trials and tribulations of the world would all be over when one got to heaven." But such messages helped to assuage the impact of white supremacy: "Beaten down at every turn by the white man, as they were, Negroes could perhaps not have survived without this kind of religion."

Clergymen like Marshall refused to challenge white supremacy. Even veiled comments might invite retaliation or lynching. Despite the reluctance of many black clergymen to advocate improvement in race relations, many white people still viewed black religious gatherings as a threat. Black churches were burned and black ministers assaulted and killed with tragic regularity in the late nineteenth-century South.

Black clergymen, like their white counterparts, often stressed middle-class values to their congregations while suggesting that many black people found themselves in shameful situations because of their sinful ways. They urged them to improve their behavior. Black people who had acquired sinful reputations sometimes received funeral sermons that consigned them to eternal damnation.

Some black clergy publicly opposed white supremacy and insisted that black people stand up for their rights. Bishop Henry M. Turner persistently spoke out on racial matters. In 1883, after the Supreme Court declared the 1875 Civil Rights Act unconstitutional, Turner called the Constitution "a dirty rag, a cheat, a libel and ought to be spit upon by every Negro in the land."

The Holiness Movement and the Pentecostal Church

Not all black people belonged to mainline denominations. For example, the Holiness movement and the emergence of Pentecostal churches affected Methodist and Baptist congregations. Partly in reaction to the elite domination and stiff authority of white Methodism, the Holiness movement gained a foothold among white people and spilled over among black southerners. Holiness churches ordained women such as Neely Terry to lead them. Holiness clergy preached that sanctification allowed a Christian to receive a "second blessing" and feel the "perfect love of Christ." Believers thus achieved an emotional reaffirmation and a new state of grace.

The Church of God in Christ (COGIC) became the leading black Holiness church. After successful revivals in Mississippi and Memphis, two black former Baptists—Charles Harrison Mason and C. P. Jones—founded COGIC in 1907. However, Mason was expelled after reporting that he had spoken in tongues. Mason then organized the Pentecostal General Assembly of the Church of God in Christ, and he assigned black men as bishops in Mississippi, Arkansas, Texas, Missouri, and California.

In the meantime, Charles Fox Parham, a white minister, had founded the Pentecostal church in the early twentieth century in Texas. William J. Seymour, who was born a slave in Louisiana, played a key role in the development of the church. After hearing black people speak in tongues in Houston, he went to Los Angeles, where he and others also began to speak in tongues. There he founded what became the Pentecostal church, which grew rapidly.

Charles Harrison Mason joined the Pentecostal movement, and under his leadership the Reorganized COGIC became the leading Pentecostal denomination. It soon spread across the South among black and white people. Although there were tensions between black and white believers, the Pentecostal church was the only significant movement that crossed the racial divide in early twentieth-century America.

Roman Catholics and Episcopalians

Most African Americans belonged to one of the Baptist or Methodist churches. Nevertheless, black people also belonged to other churches and denominations—or to no organized religious group (see Figure 15.2).

About 200,000 African Americans were Roman Catholics in 1890. However, they were rarely fully accepted by the church or white Catholics. In the South, they were segregated in separate churches with separate parish schools.

The most prominent black Catholics came from the Healy family. Eliza Clark was a slave who had nine children by Michael Healy, an Irish-Catholic plantation owner in Georgia. Unlike many white men, Healy genuinely cared for Eliza and their children, although by law he could not marry her. The children were educated in northern schools. James A. Healy graduated from the Jesuit-run Holy Cross College in Massachusetts and was ordained a priest in Paris in 1854. He later became a bishop in Portland, Maine.

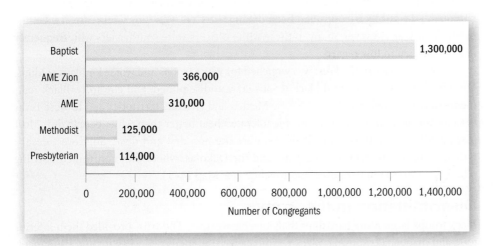

FIGURE 15–2 CHURCH AFFILIATION AMONG SOUTHERN BLACK PEOPLE, 1890
The vast majority of black southerners belonged to Baptist, Methodist, and Presbyterian congregations in the late nineteenth century, although there were about 15,000 black Episcopalians and nationwide perhaps 200,000 black Roman Catholics.

SOURCE: *Edward L. Ayers, The Promise of the New South, 160–61.*

Patrick Healy also attended Holy Cross and became the first black Jesuit priest in the United States. He served eight years as president of Georgetown University in Washington. Eliza Healy took vows as a nun and was the headmistress of a Catholic school in Vermont. Most white people were unaware of the racial ancestry of the Healys, and members of the family did not openly acknowledge being African American even when other black Catholics asked for their support. Bishop James Healy, for example, refused on three occasions to speak to the Congress of Colored Catholics, an association of black Catholics that met at least four times in northern cities between 1889 and 1893. Its members were mainly concerned with the discrimination they faced in the church and with the educational opportunities that were available—or more often not available—to black Catholic children in church schools.

Fairly or not, most African Americans identified black Episcopalians with wealth and privilege. Many black Episcopalians traced their heritage to free black families before the Civil War. By 1903 approximately 15,000 members of black Episcopal parishes worshiped in Richmond, Raleigh, Charleston, and other cities in the North and South.

Red versus Black: The Buffalo Soldiers

15-4 Why did black men in the U.S. Army engage in combat against Native Americans, the Spanish, and Filipinos?

After the Civil War, the U.S. Army was reduced to fewer than 30,000 troops. Congressional Democrats tried to eliminate black soldiers from this small force, but Radical Republicans, led by Massachusetts Senator Henry Wilson, kept the military open to black men. The Army Reorganization Act of 1869 maintained 21 white regiments and four all-black regiments: the 9th and 10th Cavalry Regiments and the 24th and 25th Infantry Regiments. These four regiments spent most of the next three decades on the western frontier. Nearly 12,500 black men served during the late nineteenth century in these segregated units commanded—as black troops had been during the Civil War—by white officers. Unlike in the Civil War, however, many of these white officers were southerners who frequently held black men in low regard.

Military service in the West was wretched for white troops and worse for black soldiers. Too often officers considered black troops lazy, undisciplined, and cowardly. Black regiments were assigned mainly to the New Mexico and Arizona territories and to west Texas because the army thought black people tolerated heat better than white people did. Most black soldiers were thus compelled to endure the hot, dry, and dusty Southwest desert. Others were sent to Kansas, Colorado, and the Dakotas, where they confronted howling blizzards, subzero temperatures, and frostbite (see Map 15–1).

Discrimination in the Army

Black troops faced more hardships than adverse weather. The army provided them inferior food and inadequate housing. Black regiments were allotted used weapons and equipment. The army sent its worst horses—often old and lame—to the black cavalry.

Long stretches of boredom, tedious duty, and loneliness marked army life for black and white men in the West. Months might pass without combat. Desertion and alcoholism were endemic, although black soldiers were less likely to desert or turn to drink than were white troops. Black troops realized that although army life could be harsh and dangerous,

15-1

15-2

15-3

15-4

15-5

15-6

15-7

15-8

MAP 15–1 MILITARY POSTS WHERE BLACK TROOPS SERVED, 1866–1917
Black troops in the 9th and 10th Cavalries and the 24th and 25th Infantries were
assigned almost exclusively to western military posts from the end of the Civil War until
the early twentieth century.

Why were African-American troops assigned largely to isolated posts on the western frontier?

it compared favorably to the civilian world, which held few opportunities for them. Army
food was poor, but the private's pay of $13 per month was regular. Moreover, black troops
developed immense pride as professional soldiers.

How African-American troops came to be identified as buffalo soldiers is uncertain. Comanche and Cheyenne Indians began to refer to black troops as "**buffalo
soldiers**" in the 1870s, perhaps because the Plains Indians associated the hair of black
men with the shaggy coat of the buffalo, a sacred animal. The wife of a white officer on
the western frontier referred to buffalo soldiers in her personal correspondence. Famed
artist and sculptor Frederic Remington described black troops as buffalo soldiers in an
article in *Century Magazine* in 1889. The 10th Cavalry later displayed a buffalo in their
unit emblem.

buffalo soldiers Four
regiments of black
soldiers that served with
the U.S. Army on the
western frontier from
the 1870s to the 1890s.
The Plains Indians
called them the buffalo
soldiers.

15-1

15-2

15-3

15-4

15-5

15-6

15-7

15-8

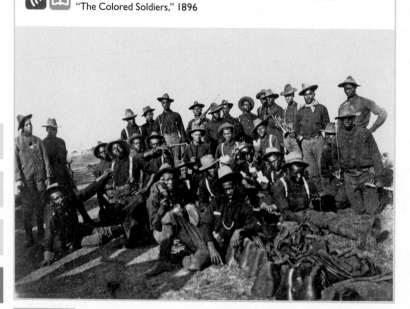

Read on MyHistoryLab Document: Paul Laurence Dunbar, "The Colored Soldiers," 1896

Several black men who were in the 10th Cavalry enjoy some time to themselves near St. Mary's, Montana, in 1894. Within four years they would be in combat against Spanish troops in Cuba during the Spanish-American War.

The Buffalo Soldiers in Combat

From the late 1860s to the early 1890s, the four black regiments repeatedly engaged hostile Indians. In September 1867, 700 Cheyenne attacked 50 Army scouts along a dry riverbed in eastern Colorado. The scouts held out for over a week until the 10th Cavalry rescued them. For more than 12 months in 1879 and 1880, the 9th and 10th Cavalries fought the Apaches under Chief Victorio in New Mexico and Texas in a campaign of raid and counterraid.

In 1879, however, 10th Cavalry troops protected Kiowa women and children from Texas Rangers. Black troops also protected Chickasaw and Cherokee farmers from Kiowa and Comanche bands.

In 1890 the 9th Cavalry was sent to the Pine Ridge Reservation in South Dakota, where Sioux Indians were holding a religious ceremony known as the Ghost Dance. Confined to reservations, some Indians—out of desperation and yearning for the past—believed their participation in the Ghost Dance would bring their ancestors and the almost extinct buffalo back to the Great Plains. White people would vanish, and Indian life would return to what it had been decades earlier. White authorities considered the Ghost Dance an act of defiance.

On December 29, the 7th Cavalry attempted to disarm the Sioux at Wounded Knee on the Pine Ridge Reservation. Shooting erupted, and 146 Indian men, women, and children—along with 26 soldiers—were killed. The 9th Cavalry, 108 miles away, rode the next day through a blizzard and arrived tired and freezing to come to the aid of the 7th Cavalry. The 9th spent the remainder of the winter guarding the Sioux.

Civilian Hostility to Black Soldiers

Despite the gallant performance of the buffalo soldiers, civilians frequently treated them with hostility. In Texas in 1875, Mexicans ambushed five black soldiers, killed two of them, and mutilated their bodies. The next day the infuriated white commander of the 9th Cavalry, Colonel Edward Hatch, rode out with 60 soldiers and apprehended the Mexicans. A local grand jury indicted nine of them for murder, but one was acquitted, and the other eight were released without a trial.

In 1877, 54 black troops from the 9th Cavalry intervened successfully in a political and ethnic dispute between white and Mexican residents of El Paso, Texas. The 9th was also dispatched to police the so-called Johnson County War in Wyoming between big and small ranchers in 1890. One of the state's U.S. senators, who favored the big ranchers, arranged the deployment of black troops; their presence angered the small ranchers, as it was intended to do. Racial violence and bloodshed soon erupted between residents of the town of Suggs, who had run two black soldiers out of town, and several of the soldiers who had disobeyed orders. The troops were withdrawn after the town was shot up and one soldier killed.

Brownsville

One of the worst examples of hostility to black troops, the so-called **Brownsville affair**, also occurred in Texas. In 1906 the 1st Battalion of the 25th Infantry was transferred from Nebraska to Fort Brown in Brownsville, Texas, along the Rio Grande. The black soldiers immediately encountered discrimination from both white people and Mexicans in this border community. Black people were not permitted in public parks, and white businesses refused to serve them. Civilians provoked and attacked black soldiers.

Shortly after midnight on August 14, about 150 shots were fired in Brownsville. One man died, and a Hispanic policeman and the editor of a Spanish-language newspaper were injured. Black troops were blamed for the violence when clips and cartridges from the army's Springfield rifles were found in the street. Two military investigations concluded that black soldiers did the shooting. The army could not identify the specific soldiers responsible because no one would confess or name the alleged perpetrators.

With no hearing or trial, President Theodore Roosevelt dismissed three companies of black men—167 soldiers—from the army. They were barred from rejoining the military and from government employment and were denied veterans' pensions or benefits. The black community, which had supported Roosevelt, reacted angrily. Booker T. Washington, a Roosevelt supporter, wrote, "There is no law, human or divine, which justifies the punishment of an innocent man."

Republican Senator James B. Foraker of Ohio led a Senate investigation that upheld Roosevelt's dismissals. But Foraker, an opponent of Roosevelt, questioned the guilt of the black men. The clips and cartridges that served as evidence were apparently planted. After Roosevelt left office in 1909, the War Department reinstated 14 of the soldiers. In 1972 the Justice Department determined that an injustice had occurred. The black soldiers were posthumously awarded honorable discharges. Congress awarded the only survivor of the Brownsville affair—Dorsie Willis—$25,000 and the right to treatment at veterans' facilities.

Brownsville affair In 1906, a shooting in Brownsville, Texas, was blamed on black soldiers from the 25th Infantry Regiment. President Theodore Roosevelt summarily dismissed 167 black men from the U.S. Army. Later investigations exonerated the men.

African Americans in the Navy

Naval service was even more unappealing than life in the army. In the late nineteenth century approximately one sailor in 10 was a black man. Although warships were technically integrated, in that black and white sailors served on them together, white sailors were often hostile to black sailors. They would not eat or bunk with them or take orders from them. Increasingly, and to enforce a de facto shipboard segregation, black sailors were restricted to stoking boilers and to cooking and serving food to white sailors.

The Black Cowboys

By the 1870s and 1880s, black men joined Mexicans, Native Americans, and white men on the long cattle drives from Texas to Kansas, Nebraska, and Missouri. There were probably no more than a few hundred black cowboys in the late nineteenth and early twentieth centuries.

Tending cattle was monotonous, difficult, and dirty work. Cowboys had to tolerate weather that ranged from incredibly hot to bitter cold. They had to eat unappetizing food. There was no bed to sleep in each night, and their closest companion was often the horse they rode.

Black cowhands sometimes endured discrimination and abuse. They had to tame the toughest horses, work the longest hours, and face hostility in saloons, hotels,

15-1
15-2
15-3
15-4
15-5
15-6
15-7
15-8

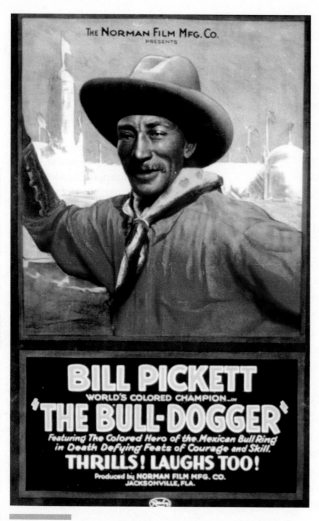

Bill Pickett was an authentic cowboy who became one of the first black movie stars. "The Bull-Dogger" was a 1922 black-and-white silent film aimed at attracting black audiences. (No copies of the film are known to have survived.) Pickett's skill as a bull-dogger was legendary. He would ride alongside a steer, jump off his horse, and grab the animal by the horns. He then wrestled it to the ground by sharply biting the animal's upper lip or nose. Pickett was the hit of the 1904 Cheyenne Frontier Days rodeo in Wyoming.

brothels, and shops in towns like Dodge City, Abilene, or Cheyenne. Still, black cowboys earned the respect of white ranchers and cattle barons.

The Black Cowgirls

Several African-American women were "cowgirls." Johanna "Aunt Chona" was of black and Seminole Indian descent, and she rode side saddle and broke untamed horses in Texas. She called it "gentling" them. Henrietta Williams Foster—"Aunt Rittie"—was born a slave in Mississippi and sold to Texas slave owners. As an ex-slave she became an expert rider who could take control of a herd of cattle. Although lacking formal education, she served as a midwife and also treated injured animals. Small in stature, she could be tough, ornery, and would out-cuss most men.

Mary Fields—otherwise known as "Stagecoach Mary"—operated a stagecoach in Montana for eight years. An imposing woman at six feet tall and 200 pounds, she carried a 38 Smith and Wesson and took part in at least one shooting with an angry cowboy. She lived in Cascade, Montana into the twentieth century.

The Spanish-American War

With the West subdued by 1890, many Americans concluded that the United States should expand overseas. European nations had already carved out colonies in Africa and Asia. Many, but by no means all, Americans favored the extension of U.S. authority to Latin America and the Pacific. In 1893 the navy and American businessmen toppled the monarchy in Hawaii, and the United States annexed those islands in 1898.

The same year, the United States went to war to liberate Cuba from Spain. As in the Civil War, black men enlisted, fought, and died. Many black Americans were convinced, as they had been during previous wars, that their support for the war against Spain would reduce or even eliminate white hostility.

Many black and white Americans, however, questioned the American cause. Some black people saw the war as an effort to extend American racial practices, including Jim Crow, beyond U.S. borders. The Rev. George W. Prioleau, chaplain of the 9th Cavalry, wondered why black Americans supported what he considered a hypocritical war:

> Talk about fighting and freeing poor Cuba and of Spain's brutality. . . . Is America any better than Spain? Has she not subjects in her very midst who are murdered daily without a trial of judge or jury? Has she not subjects in her own borders whose children are half-fed and half-clothed, because their father's skin is black. . . . Yet the Negro is loyal to his country's flag.

Whether or not they harbored doubts, black men by the thousands served in the Spanish-American War and in the Philippine Insurrection that followed it. Shortly before war was declared, the army transferred its four black regiments from the West to Florida to prepare for combat in Cuba. President William McKinley also appealed for volunteers. The War Department designated four of the black volunteer units "immune regiments" because it believed that black men would tolerate the heat and humidity of Cuba better than white troops and that black people were immune or at least less susceptible to yellow fever, which was endemic to Cuba.

State militia (national guard) units were also called into federal service, and several states sent all-black militias, as well as white units. But Georgia's governor refused to permit that state's black militia to serve, and New York would not permit black men to enlist in its militia. The states typically followed the federal example and confined black men to all-black units commanded by white officers, but there were exceptions.

Black Officers

The buffalo soldiers of the 9th and 10th Cavalries and the 24th and 25th Infantries remained under white officers. But the men of several volunteer units insisted they be led by black officers: "No officers, no fight." So for the first time in American history, black men commanded all-black units: the 8th Illinois, the 23rd Kansas, and the 3rd North Carolina. Mindful that many people doubted black men's ability to lead, the colonel of the 8th Illinois cautioned his men, "If we fail, the whole race will have to shoulder the burden." The War Department also permitted black men to serve as lieutenants with other black volunteer units; however, all higher-ranking officers were white men. Charles Young, a black graduate of West Point, was given command of Ohio's 9th Battalion. He served with distinction and was promoted to colonel.

As black and white troops assembled in Georgia and Florida, black men soon realized a U.S. uniform did not lessen white prejudice. White civilians in Georgia killed four black men of the 3rd North Carolina. All-white juries acquitted those who were charged with the murders. After the white proprietor of a drug store in Lakeland, Florida, refused to serve a black soldier at the soda fountain, a mob of black troops gathered. The proprietor was pistol whipped, and a stray bullet killed another white man before the troops were disarmed. In Tampa an all-night riot broke out after drunken white soldiers from Ohio used a black child for target practice. Twenty-seven black soldiers and three white soldiers were seriously wounded.

Most of the black units never saw combat. White military authorities considered black men unreliable and inadequately trained. Black volunteer units stayed behind in Florida when white units embarked for Cuba. However, the buffalo soldiers did go to Cuba, where they performed well despite the doubts and criticism of some white men.

"A Splendid Little War"

In the summer of 1898, U.S. troops arrived in Cuba. Black men of the 10th Cavalry fought alongside Cuban rebels, many of whom were black. Four black American privates earned the Congressional Medal of Honor. Black and white troops were best remembered for their role in the assault on San Juan and Kettle Hills overlooking Santiago in eastern Cuba.

In this assault, black soldiers from the 24th Infantry and the 9th and 10th Cavalries fought alongside white troops including Theodore Roosevelt's volunteer unit, the

Listen on
MyHistoryLab
Audio: The Negro
as Soldier

Rough Riders. In the fiercest fighting of the war, black and white men were thrown together under withering Spanish fire. Although the outcome was in doubt, they took the high ground overlooking Santiago harbor. White soldiers praised the black troops, and in his campaign for vice president in 1900, Theodore Roosevelt stated that black men saved his life during the battle. Later, however, he accused black men of cowardice.

After the War

As hostilities concluded, men of the 24th Infantry agreed to work in yellow fever hospitals after white regiments refused the duty. Some 471 black soldiers contracted yellow fever. Other black troops arrived in Cuba after the war to serve garrison duty. The 8th Illinois and the 23rd Kansas built roads, bridges, schools, and hospitals. The black men were especially pleased at the absence of Jim Crow in Cuba. Some black soldiers considered organizing emigration to Cuba, but nothing came of it. Still other black troops from the 6th Massachusetts joined in the invasion of Puerto Rico as the United States took that island from Spain.

The Philippine Insurrection

With the resounding victory in the war, many Americans decided their nation had an obligation to uplift those less fortunate peoples who had been part of the Spanish empire. Thus, President William McKinley insisted the United States acquire Guam, Puerto Rico, and the Philippines from Spain in the Treaty of Paris that ended the war in December 1898. The Filipinos, like the Cubans, had opposed Spanish rule and expected the American government to support their independence. When they learned that the United States intended to annex the Philippines, the Filipinos, under Emilio Aguinaldo, switched from fighting the Spanish to fighting the occupying U.S. forces.

Would Black Men Fight Brown Men?

Many black and white Americans denounced the effort to take the Philippines. They were unconvinced the Filipinos would benefit from American benevolence. Some wondered how African-American soldiers were helping to lessen racial oppression in the United States by oppressing the Filipinos.

Nonetheless, black soldiers served throughout the campaign in the Pacific islands. The black troops included the regular 25th and 24th Infantries, the 9th Cavalry, and the 48th and 49th Volunteer Regiments. The Filipino rebels attempted to convince black troops to abandon the cause. Posters reminded "The Colored American Soldier" of injustice and lynching in the United States. White troops did not help by calling Filipinos "niggers." Although many black soldiers had reservations about the fighting, they remained loyal. When the conflict ended with an American victory in 1902, only five black men had deserted.

Although black men had served with distinction as professional soldiers for 40 years after the Civil War—on the frontier, in Cuba, and in the Philippines—the army little valued their achievements and sacrifice. White military and political leaders relied on passions and prejudices over evidence of achievement. These circumstances dashed the hopes of those black civilians and soldiers who believed the performance of black troops would demonstrate that black citizens had earned the same rights as other Americans.

VOICES Black Men in Battle in Cuba

On October 1, 1898, a letter appeared in the Illinois Record, *a black newspaper, from one of the men in the 10th Cavalry. The author was probably John E. Lewis, and he wrote the letter from Montauk Point on Long Island in New York, where black and white troops were sent after the war. Lewis described the enthusiastic reaction of the Rough Riders to the 9th and 10th Cavalries, but he complained that the black soldiers' contributions were too often ignored.*

The Rough Riders were mustered out on the 12th and 13th [of September], and when Colonel Roosevelt bade the regiment good-bye he paid a glowing tribute to the 9th and 10th Cavalry, especially in saving them from ambush.

Mr. Editor, if your readers could have heard the Rough Riders yell when the 10th Cav. was mentioned as the 'Smoked Yankees' and that they were of a good breed, they would have been doubly proud of the members of their race who rendered such signal service on the battle field. . . .

When a troop of the 10th made their famous charge of 3,000 yards under the command of Capt. [William J.] Beck, the non-commissioned officers, all colored, distinguished themselves in a manner that will redound to the glory of the race. Among those who distinguished themselves are Carter Smith, acting 1st Sergeant, Sgts. Geo. Taylor, James F. Cole, James H. Williams, Smith Johnson and Corpl. Joseph G. Mitchell who was wounded at San Juan.

All are soldiers whose names should go down in history. They never faltered in the thickest of the battle; they encouraged on in a rain of shot and shell and showed by their actions that they were the leaders. They did not hesitate to take the lead, and when that charge was made it was "save your cartridges, don't waste a shot."

The half will never be told of their deeds upon the battlefield. All deserve praise from the private up, but the praise has been given those who should have been in the lead instead of laying in the rear under cover. And yet they say that the black is not fit to lead.

If our war reports would only give credit where credit is due there would be no need writing these poorly composed lines that your readers might know of the deeds and hardships their dear ones have passed through.

You will read that colored troops, or companies did so and so, but the white papers never mention a name and the world only knows one who has done an act of bravery as a Negro soldier, nameless and friendless. It was never mentioned how, at that famous charge of the 10th Cav. And the rescue of the Rough Riders at San Juan Hill, the yell was started by a single trooper of C Troop, 10th Cav. and was carried down the line.

Brave 1st Sgt. Adam Huston at the head of his troop commanded "forward" which seemed into almost certain death. In him the troop found an able leader; Lieut. [E. D.] Anderson who was in command and fell to the rear and when the command "Forward March," was given, the brave Major [Theodore J.] Wint only smiled, for he admired bravery and did not change the command although he knew that the troops was in a desperate position. The troops were carried safely through. . . .

Will it ever be known how Sgt. Thomas Griffith of Troop C cut the wire fence along the line so that the 10th Cav. and Rough Riders could go through?

Never once did these brave men give thought to danger. . . .

The Spaniard would have sent our army home in disgrace had it not been for the daring and almost reckless charge of the Negro regiments. God was with them in that charge and no man who has ever seen the place will say that it was possible to make the charge without being slaughtered. . . .

[Unsigned]

1. **Why is the author of this letter bitter?**
2. **Why did black men fight in the Spanish-American War?**
3. **Does any of this account seem exaggerated or unreliable? Why or why not?**

SOURCE: Willard B. Gatewood Jr., *Smoked Yankees and the Struggle for Empire: Letters from Negro Soldiers, 1898–1902* (Urbana: University of Illinois Press, 1971), 76–78.

15-1
15-2
15-3
15-4
15-5
15-6
15-7
15-8

15-1

15-2

15-3

15-4

15-5

15-6

15-7

15-8

Black Business People and Entrepreneurs

15-5 What were the major developments among African Americans in businesses and labor unions in the struggle for equality?

As the nineteenth century ended, the American people had become enthralled by their country's scientific, industrial, and agricultural progress. Their enthusiasm for these achievements was exemplified by the fairs and expositions held around the country between 1876 and 1916. Municipal leaders were eager to capitalize on the curiosity of thousands of people who would visit these fairs and leave millions of dollars behind to enrich local businesses.

African Americans and the World's Columbian Exposition

There is no better example of this mania for fairs than the World's Columbian Exposition held in Chicago in 1893 to commemorate the four-hundredth anniversary of Christopher Columbus's first voyage to America. The Chicago fair was spectacular. Located on 600 acres on the city's south side, it featured 200 buildings and exhibits from 46 nations. At the center was the White City, a group of white buildings that were illuminated at night by electric lights. The fair drew 27 million visitors between May and October 1893.

Three black colleges created exhibits that were intended to depict the advances African Americans had achieved since the end of slavery. Wilberforce College won a Columbian Medal and Diploma for its display of academic work by its students that included examples of math, logic, and rhetoric as well as needlecraft and woodwork. The Atlanta University exhibit had photos of the campus with students engaged in nursing, home economics, and crafts. Hampton Institute's display featured dressmaking, tailoring, and woodwork.

Colored American Day at the fair was held on August 25, 1893. Some African Americans, including Ida B. Wells, resented having a separate day for black people, and she criticized Frederick Douglass for agreeing to speak at that day's festivities. But the 75-year-old Douglass delivered a blunt address about race in America. He denounced Americans' commitment to white supremacy and their unjust treatment of people of color: "Men talk of the Negro problem. There is no Negro problem. The problem is whether the American people have honesty enough, loyalty enough, honor enough, patriotism enough to live up to their own Constitution."

Obstacles and Opportunities for Employment among African Americans

During planning for the Chicago fair, African Americans, including Ida B. Wells, complained that black people had been excluded on the committees that organized the exposition. But white people rarely elevated African Americans to positions of authority. Well-educated black men and women stood no chance of gaining employment with any major business or industrial corporation in the 1890s. White males not only monopolized management and supervisory positions, but also took nearly every job that did not involve manual labor.

Although white supremacy and Jim Crow restricted opportunities for educated black people, those same limitations enabled enterprising black men and women to open and operate businesses that served black clientele. By the early twentieth century, black Americans had established banks, newspapers, insurance companies, retail businesses, barbershops, beauty salons, and funeral parlors. Virtually every black community had its own small businesses, markets, street vendors, and other entrepreneurs.

Some black men and women established substantial businesses. In Atlanta, Union Army veteran Alexander Hamilton was a successful building contractor. He supervised construction of the Good Samaritan Building, oversaw the erection of buildings on the Morris Brown College campus, and built many impressive houses on Peachtree Street. Hamilton employed both black and white workmen.

Alonzo Herndon was a former slave who also thrived in Atlanta. His fashionable barbershop on Peachtree Street served well-to-do white men. Herndon opened two other shops, eventually employing 75 men. He also founded the Atlanta Life Insurance Company, the largest black stock company in the world.

In Richmond, Maggie Lena Walker—the secretary-treasurer of the Independent Order of St. Luke, a mutual benefit society, and a founder of the St. Luke's Penny Savings Bank—became the wealthiest black woman in America. Also in Richmond, former slave John Dabney owned a catering business that served wealthy white Virginians. He catered two state dinners for President Grover Cleveland. He purchased houses and invested in real estate.

Madam C. J. Walker may have been the most successful black entrepreneur of them all. Born Sarah Breedlove in 1867 on a Louisiana cotton plantation, she married at age 14 and was a widowed single parent by age 20. She spent the next two decades struggling to make ends meet. In 1905 with $1.50, she developed a formula to nourish and enrich the hair of black women.

The business rapidly became a thriving enterprise that employed hundreds of black women. As she accumulated wealth, she shared it generously with Bethune Cookman College and Tuskegee Institute. She was a major contributor to the NAACP's anti-lynching campaign. When she died at age 51 in 1919, she was reportedly a millionaire.

Despite such successes, most black people who went into business had difficulty surviving. Too often they depended on black customers who were themselves poor. White-owned banks were unlikely to provide credit to black business people. And even the wealthiest black entrepreneurs did not come close to possessing the wealth the richest white Americans accumulated.

African Americans and Labor

Thousands of black southerners worked in factories, mills, and mines. Although most textile mills refused to hire black people except as janitors, many black laborers toiled in tobacco and cigar-making facilities, flour mills, coal mines, sawmills, and turpentine camps, and on railroads. Black women worked for white families as servants. Black workers usually were paid less than white men employed in the same capacity. Conversely, white working people frequently complained they were not hired because employers retained black workers who worked for less pay. Antagonism between black and white laborers was chronic.

In less than two decades in the early twentieth century, Sarah Breedlove rose from abject poverty to become extraordinarily wealthy as Madam C. J. Walker.

15-1

15-2

15-3

15-4

15-5

15-6

15-7

15-8

**View on MyHistoryLab
Map:** Organizing American Labor in the Late Nineteenth Century

15-1

15-2

15-3

15-4

15-5

15-6

15-7

15-8

Unions

When white workers formed labor unions, they usually excluded black workers. The Knights of Labor, however, founded in 1869, was open to all workers (except whiskey salesmen, lawyers, and bankers), and by the mid-1880s counted 50,000 women and 70,000 black workers among its nearly 750,000 members. But by the 1890s, after unsuccessful strikes and a deadly riot in Chicago, the Knights had lost influence to a new organization, the American Federation of Labor (AFL). Founded in 1886, the AFL was ostensibly open to all skilled workers, but most of its local craft unions barred women and black tradesmen. In contrast, the United Mine Workers (UMW), formed in 1890, encouraged black coal miners to join the union rather than serve as strikebreakers. By 1900 approximately 20,000 of the 91,000 members of the UMW were black men. The Industrial Workers of the World, a revolutionary labor organization founded in 1905, brought black and white laborers together.

In 1869 a Baltimore ship caulker, Isaac Myers, organized the National Colored Labor Union, which lasted for seven years. It discouraged strikes and encouraged its members to work hard and be thrifty. However, it lost whatever effectiveness it had when Republican leaders took it over during Reconstruction.

Strikes

During the late nineteenth and early twentieth centuries, most strikes failed because business owners could rely on strikebreakers and the police or national guard to bring the strikes to an often violent end. For a time, black shipyard workers in southern ports achieved success. Black stevedores who loaded and unloaded ships endured oppressive conditions and long hours for low pay. They periodically went on strike in Charleston, Savannah, and New Orleans. The Longshoremen's Protective Union in Charleston won several strikes in the 1870s. In Nashville in 1871 black dockyard workers went on strike, demanding 20 cents an hour. Steamboat owners broke the strike by hiring state convicts for 15 cents an hour.

Black and white laborers who toiled in the Louisiana sugarcane fields earned an average of $13 a week in the 1880s. They were paid in scrip—not cash—that was redeemable only in stores the planters owned, where prices were exorbitant. Workers lived in 12-by-15-foot cabins that they rented from the planters. In some ways, it was worse than slave labor.

Although the state militia had broken previous strikes, 9,000 black and 1,000 white workers responded in 1887 to a call by the Knights of Labor for a new strike. They quit the sugar fields in four parishes (as Louisiana counties are called) to demand more pay. The strike was peaceful, but the governor sent in the militia. The troops fired into a crowd at Pattersonville and killed four people. Local officials killed several strikers who had been taken prisoner. In Thibodaux, "prominent citizens" organized and armed themselves and had martial law declared. More than 35 unarmed black people, including women and children, were killed in their homes and churches. Two black strike leaders were lynched. The strike was broken.

Black washerwomen went on strike in Atlanta in 1881. The strike was well organized through black churches, and it spread to cooks and domestics. A strike committee used persuasion and intimidation to ensure support. Some 3,000 black people joined the strike, and white families went two weeks without clean clothes. However, Atlanta's white community broke the strike. Police arrested strike leaders for disorderly conduct. Black women were fined from $5 to $20. The city council threatened to require each washerwoman to purchase a $25 business license. Although the strike ended without achieving its goal, it demonstrated that poor black women could organize effectively.

Black Professionals

15-6 What opportunities existed for African Americans in the legal and medical professions?

Like business and labor, the medical and legal professions were strictly segregated. Most black physicians, nurses, and lawyers attended all-black professional schools in the late nineteenth century. Black people in need of medical care were either excluded from white hospitals or confined to all-black wards. Since black physicians were denied staff privileges at white hospitals, black people often formed their own hospitals. Most were small with 50 or fewer beds.

Medicine

In 1891 Dr. Daniel Hale Williams established Provident Hospital and Training Institute in Chicago, the first black hospital operated solely by African Americans. In 1894 the Freedmen's Hospital was organized in Washington, DC, and later affiliated with Howard University. Frederick Douglass Memorial Hospital and Training School was founded in Philadelphia in 1895. Dr. Alonzo McClennan and other black physicians established the Hospital and Training School for Nurses in Charleston, South Carolina, in 1897.

By 1890, 909 black (most of whom were male) physicians were practicing in the United States. They served a black population of 7.5 million people. Barred from membership in the American Medical Association, black doctors organized the National Medical Association in Atlanta in 1895.

The number of black women physicians was declining. In 1890, 90 black women were practicing medicine. By 1920 only 65 were. There were fewer medical schools, and most black and white men considered medicine an inappropriate profession for women. But black women also had to contend with the opposition of white women. Isabella Vandervall was a graduate of New York Medical College and Hospital who was accepted for an internship at the Hospital for Women and Children in Syracuse. When she appeared in person, however, the hospital's female administrator rejected Vandervall, declaring, "We can't have you here! You are colored!"

Nursing was different. By 1920 there were 36 black nurse training schools and 2,150 white nursing schools. White nurses resented the competition from black nurses for positions as private duty nurses. In addition, the black physicians who ran nurse training schools exploited their students by hiring them out, as part of their training, for private duty work but requiring them to relinquish their pay to the schools. Moreover, many people—black and white—regarded black nurses more as domestics than as trained professionals. To confront such obstacles, 52 black nurses met in New York City in 1908 and formed the National Association of Colored Graduate Nurses (NACGN). By 1920 the NACGN had 500 members.

Black physicians and nurses struggled to provide medical care to people who were often desperately ill and sought treatment only as a last resort. Disease and sickness flourished among people who were ill nourished, poorly clad, and inadequately housed.

15-1
15-2
15-3
15-4
15-5
15-6
15-7
15-8

15-1
15-2
15-3
15-4
15-5
15-6
15-7
15-8

Lutie A. Lytle graduated from the Central Tennessee College of Law and passed the bar examination. She became a member of the faculty at the same institution, and thus was the first African-American woman to become a professor of law in an American law school.

Tuberculosis, pneumonia, pellagra, hookworm, and syphilis afflicted many poor black people—as they also did poor white people.

The Law

Unlike black physicians and nurses, who were excluded from white hospitals, black lawyers were permitted to practice in what was essentially a white male court system. But white judges and attorneys did not welcome them. Black defendants and plaintiffs often retained white lawyers in the hope that white legal counsel might improve their chances of receiving justice. As a result, many black attorneys had a hard time making a living from the practice of law.

The American Bar Association (ABA) would not admit black attorneys to membership. William H. Lewis, a graduate of Amherst College and the Harvard Law School who was appointed an assistant U.S. attorney general by President William Howard Taft in 1911, was expelled by the ABA in 1912 when its leaders discovered he was black. They defended his expulsion by claiming the association was mainly a social organization. In 1925 black lawyers—led by Howard Law School graduate George H. Woodson—organized the National Bar Association.

Few black women were lawyers. Charlotte Ray was the first (see Chapter 12). In 1900 there were 10 black women practicing law compared to over 700 black men and 112,000 white men. Lutie A. Lytle, who graduated from Central Tennessee Law School in 1897, returned to her alma mater and became the first black woman law professor in the United States.

Music

15-7 **What did African Americans contribute to music in the late nineteenth and early twentieth centuries?**

In the half century after the Civil War, music created and performed by black people evolved into the uniquely American art forms of ragtime, jazz, and blues. The roots of these extraordinary musical innovations are uncertain. Some late nineteenth-century music can be traced to African forms and rhythms. Other sources are slave work songs and spirituals.

Traveling groups of black men, some of them ex-slaves, put on minstrel shows that featured "coon songs" after the Civil War. Many black Americans resented these popular shows as caricatures and exaggerations of black behavior. At least 600 "coon songs" that attracted a predominantly white audience were published by 1900 including "All Coons Look Alike to Me," "Mammy's Little Pickaninny," and "My Coal Black Lady."

Most black people had other forms of musical entertainment. "The Civil Rights Juba," published in 1874, was a precursor to ragtime. In 1871 the Fisk University Jubilee Singers began the first of many fund-raising concert tours that entertained black and white audiences in the United States and Europe for years thereafter with slave songs and spirituals. Other black colleges and universities sent choirs and singers on similar trips.

Ragtime

Ragtime, which emerged in the 1890s, was composed music, written down for performance on the piano. Ragtime pieces were not accompanied by lyrics and not meant to be sung. The creative genius of ragtime, Scott Joplin, was born in Texarkana, Texas, in 1868. He learned to play on a piano his mother bought from her earnings as a maid, and he may have had training in classical music. Joplin learned to transfer complex banjo syncopations to the piano as he fused European harmonies and African rhythms. He played at the World's Columbian Exposition in Chicago in 1893 and soon wrote ragtime sheet music that sold well. In 1899 he composed his best-known tune, the "Maple Leaf Rag," named after a social club (brothel) in Sedalia, Missouri. It sold an astonishing one million copies.

Jazz

Jazz gradually replaced ragtime in popularity in the early twentieth century. Unlike ragtime, jazz was mostly improvised, not composed, and it was not confined to the piano. Jazz incorporated African and European musical elements drawn from such diverse sources as plantation bands, minstrel shows, riverboat ensembles, and Irish and Scottish folk tunes. The first jazz bands emerged around New Orleans where they played at parades, funerals, clubs, and outdoor concerts. Instead of the banjos, pipes, fifes, and violins of earlier black musical groups, these bands relied more on brass, reeds, and drums.

Ferdinand J. La Menthe, regarded as the first prominent jazz musician, was born in 1890 and grew up in a French-speaking family in New Orleans. Young La Menthe played several musical instruments before settling on the piano. He was also a superb composer and arranger. Later he changed his name to Morton and came to be known as Jelly Roll Morton. He played in the "red light" district of New Orleans known as Storyville, where he was also a pool shark and gambler. He moved to Los Angeles in 1917 and to Chicago in 1922, where he led and recorded with "Morton's Red Hot Peppers." He died in 1941.

The Blues

In rural, isolated areas of the South, poor black people composed and sang songs about their lives and experiences. W. C. Handy, the father of the blues, later recalled, "southern Negroes sang about everything. They accompanied themselves on anything from a guitar to a harmonica to a washboard. They played in juke joints (rural nightclubs), at picnics, in lumber camps, and in urban nightclubs."

Handy, who was born in Florence, Alabama, in 1873, took up music despite the opposition of his devoutly Christian parents. He learned to play the guitar and later led his own

Listen on MyHistoryLab Audio: Scott Joplin's Maple Leaf Rag

Scott Joplin (1868–1917) was one of America's most prolific composers, and his name is indelibly linked with ragtime. Although ragtime's popularity faded by the 1920s, Joplin's reputation and compositions were resurrected in 1974 when the Hollywood film *The Sting* relied on Joplin's 1902 rag "The Entertainer" for its soundtrack. In 1976 Scott Joplin was posthumously awarded the Pulitzer Prize for music.

nine-man band. In the Mississippi delta in 1903, Handy encountered "primitive," or "boogie," music unlike anything he had heard before. Handy was not initially impressed by the mostly unskilled and itinerant musicians: "Then I saw the beauty of primitive music. They had the stuff people wanted. It touched the spot. Their music wanted polishing, but it contained the essence. People would pay money for it." Handy composed many tunes, including "Memphis Blues" and "St. Louis Blues."

Handy was not the only musician to "discover" the blues. Gertrude Pridget sang in southern minstrel shows. In 1902 she heard a young black woman in Missouri sing about a lover who had left her. Pridget included the song in her shows. In 1904 she married William "Pa" Rainey and became "Ma" Rainey. She created other "blues" songs based on ballads, hymns, and the experiences of black people. As "Mother of the Blues," Rainey recorded extensively in the 1920s and 1930s.

By 1920 two forms of American music were developing—jazz and the blues. Both drew on African and American musical elements and European styles. But most of all, jazz and the blues represented the experiences of African Americans and the creativity of the musicians who developed and performed the music.

Sports

15-8 **What contributions did African Americans make to athletics in the late nineteenth and early twentieth centuries?**

While talented black musicians were making dramatic innovations, black athletes found that white athletes and sports entrepreneurs increasingly opposed the presence of black men in the boxing ring and on the playing field.

Boxing and Jack Johnson

Black boxers regularly fought white boxers through the end of the nineteenth century, but this offended many white people—especially southerners. In 1892 George Dixon, a black boxer, won the world featherweight title, and some white men cheered his victory, distressing a Chicago journalist: "It was not pleasant to see white men applaud a negro for knocking another white man out." Despite such opinions, there was never any official prohibition of interracial bouts.

The success of another black boxer, heavyweight Jack Johnson, angered many white Americans. Johnson was born in Galveston, Texas, in 1878. Between 1902 and 1907 he won 57 bouts against black and white fighters. In 1908 he beat the white heavyweight champion, Tommy Burns, in Australia. Many white fans were unwilling to accept Johnson as the champion and looked desperately for "a great white hope" who could defeat him. Jim Jeffries, a former champion, came out of retirement to take on Johnson. In a brutal fight in Reno, Nevada, in 1910, Johnson knocked out Jeffries in the fifteenth round.

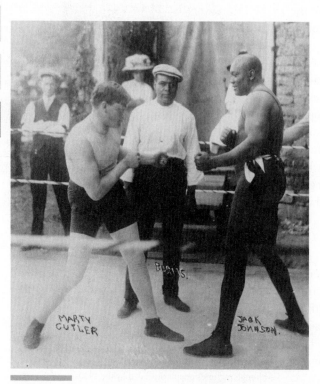

Jack Johnson spars with Marty Cutler in the early twentieth century. Johnson was a superb fighter whose ability to defeat white boxers rankled many white men. But Johnson's involvement with white women infuriated them even more and led to his imprisonment.

Johnson's personal life, as well as his prowess in the ring, provoked white animosity. Having divorced his black wife, he married a white woman in 1911. Several months later, overwhelmed by social ostracism, she committed suicide. After Johnson married a second white woman, he was convicted of violating the Mann Act, which made it illegal to transport a woman across state lines for immoral purposes. The "immorality" was Johnson's marriage to white women. Sentenced to a year in prison and fined $1,000, Johnson fled to Canada and then to France to avoid punishment. He lost his title to Jesse Willard in 1915 in Havana in the twenty-sixth round in a fight many people believe that Johnson threw. He returned to the United States in 1920 and served 10 months in Leavenworth Prison.

Baseball

Baseball became popular after the Civil War. As professional baseball developed in the 1870s and 1880s, both black and white men competed to earn money playing the game. It was not easy. They were the nation's first professional athletes, but professional baseball was unstable. Teams were formed and dissolved with depressing regularity. Players moved from team to team. Some 30 black men played professional baseball in the quarter century after the Civil War.

White players led by A. C. "Cap" Anson of the Chicago White Stockings tried to get club owners to stop signing black men to contracts. Anson, who was from Iowa, resented having to play against black men. In 1887 International League officials rescinded a rule that had permitted them to sign black players. Moses Fleetwood Walker was the last black man to play major league baseball with white men until Jackie Robinson joined the Brooklyn Dodgers in 1947.

In reaction to their exclusion, black men formed their own teams. By 1900 there were five black professional teams including the Norfolk Red Stockings, the Chicago Unions, and the Cuban X Giants of New York. The Negro Leagues would be an integral (but not integrated) part of sports for the next half century.

Basketball and Other Sports

James Naismith invented basketball in 1891 in Springfield, Massachusetts. Black youngsters were playing organized basketball by 1906 in the YMCA in New York City and later in YMCAs in Philadelphia and Washington, DC. By 1910–1911 Howard University and Hampton Institute had basketball teams. In horse racing, black jockeys regularly won major races. Willie Simms won the Kentucky Derby in 1894, 1895, 1896, and 1898. Bicycling and bicycle racing were enormously popular by the 1890s, and in 1899 a black rider, Marshall W. "Major" Taylor, won the world championship.

College Athletics

Generally, white colleges and universities in the North that admitted black students would not let them participate in intercollegiate sports. (Southern colleges and universities did not admit black students.) There were, however, exceptions. In 1889, W. T. S. Jackson and William Henry Lewis played football for Amherst College. Lewis was the captain of the team in 1890. As a law school student, Lewis played for Harvard and was named to the Walter Camp All-American team in 1892. (Lewis was later forced out of the American Bar Association because of his color. See the section "The Law" in this chapter.) White institutions with black players often encountered rampant racism. In 1907 the University of Alabama baseball team canceled a game with the University of Vermont because the

15-1
15-2
15-3
15-4
15-5
15-6
15-7
15-8

Vermont squad had two black infielders. Moreover, opposing teams and their fans frequently abused black players.

White colleges and universities occasionally played black institutions. The Yale Law School baseball team, for example, played Howard in 1898. But black college teams were far more likely to play each other. The first football game between two black colleges took place on December 27, 1892, when Biddle University (today Johnson C. Smith University) defeated Livingston College in Salisbury, North Carolina.

Eventually black athletic conferences were formed. The Central Intercollegiate Athletic Association was organized in 1912 with Hampton, Howard, Virginia Union, and Shaw College in Raleigh among its early members. The Southeastern Conference was established in 1913 and consisted of Morehouse, Fisk, Florida A&M, and Tuskegee, among others. It would become the Southern Intercollegiate Athletic Conference (SIAC). In Texas in 1920, five black colleges founded the Southwestern Athletic Conference: Prairie View A&M, Bishop College, Paul Quinn College, Wiley College, and Sam Houston College.

CONCLUSION

White supremacy was debilitating, discouraging, and dangerous, but black Americans could sometimes turn Jim Crow to their advantage. To combat white racism and improve the economic status of black people, educators like Samuel Chapman Armstrong and Booker T. Washington recommended agricultural and mechanical training for black Americans. But critics such as W. E. B. Du Bois stressed the need to cultivate the minds as well as the hands of black people to develop leaders.

Black men served with distinction in all-black military units in the Indian wars, the Spanish-American War, and the Philippine Insurrection. But no matter how loyal or committed black soldiers were, the white majority never fully trusted or displayed confidence in them. African Americans could only react with outrage when President Theodore Roosevelt dismissed 167 black soldiers in 1906 in the Brownsville affair.

As they tried to shape their own destinies in the late nineteenth century, black Americans organized a variety of institutions. Mostly barred from white schools, churches, hospitals, labor unions, and places of entertainment, they developed businesses and facilities to serve their communities in an environment mostly free from white interference. Black people relied on their own experiences and imaginations to create new music. They occasionally participated in sports with white athletes but more often played separately from them as segregation and white hostility spread.

Although black people recognized their churches, hospitals, schools, and businesses were often inadequately financed and usually less imposing than those of white people, they also knew that at a black school or church, in a black store, or in the care of a black physician or nurse, they would not be abused, mistreated, or ridiculed because of their color.

CHAPTER TIMELINE

AFRICAN-AMERICAN EVENTS

NATIONAL EVENTS

1860–1870

1867
Independent Order of St. Luke founded in Baltimore

1868
Hampton Institute founded

1869–1898
Four regiments of black soldiers serve on the western frontier

1862
Morrill Land-Grant Act is passed to support agricultural and mechanical education

1867
United States purchases Alaska from Russia

1869
Cincinnati "Red Stockings" organized as the first professional baseball team

Rutgers and Princeton play the first college football game

1870–1880

1870
Howard University Law School established

1873
Panic of 1873 is followed by major depression

1880–1890

1881
Tuskegee Institute founded

1887
Black players barred from major league baseball

1881
Clara Barton establishes the Red Cross

1890–1900

1891
Dr. Daniel Hale Williams founds Provident Hospital in Chicago

1892
First black college football game: Biddle vs. Livingstone

1895
Booker T. Washington addresses the Cotton States Exposition in Atlanta

1899
Scott Joplin composes the "Maple Leaf Rag"

1890
Second Morrill Act passed

1891
John D. Rockefeller funds the establishment of the University of Chicago

1892
Grover Cleveland elected to a second term as president

1893
World's Columbian Exposition in Chicago

1895
Sears, Roebuck and Company form a retail mail order business

1896
William McKinley elected president

1898
Spanish-American War

1899
Cumming v. Richmond County [Georgia] Board of Education eliminates Augusta's black high school

CHAPTER TIMELINE

AFRICAN-AMERICAN EVENTS	NATIONAL EVENTS

1900–1910

1903
St. Luke Penny Savings Bank established in Richmond with Maggie Lena Walker as president

1906
Brownsville affair

1908
National Association of Colored Graduate Nurses is founded in New York City; Jack Johnson wins the heavyweight championship in boxing

1900
William McKinley reelected president

1901
President McKinley assassinated; Vice President Theodore Roosevelt becomes president

1903
Henry Ford organizes the Ford Motor Co.

Wilbur and Orville Wright launch the first powered aircraft at Kitty Hawk, North Carolina

1904
Theodore Roosevelt reelected president

1908
William Howard Taft elected president

On MyHistoryLab

 Study and Review on MyHistoryLab

REVIEW QUESTIONS

1. How and why did the agricultural and mechanical training that Hampton Institute and Tuskegee Institute offered gain so much support among both black and white people? Why did black colleges and universities emphasize learning trades and acquiring skills?

2. How compatible was the educational philosophy of the late nineteenth century with the era's racial ideology?

3. Of what value was an education for a black person in the 1890s or early 1900s? To what use could a black person put an education?

4. What purpose did the black church serve? What were the strengths and weaknesses of the black church? What roles did black clergymen play in late nineteenth-century America?

5. How could a black soldier justify participating in wars against Native Americans, the Spanish, and the Filipinos? Why did black soldiers serve? How well did they serve?

6. Did black people derive any benefits from the expansion of segregation and Jim Crow?

7. Why did ragtime, jazz, and the blues emerge and become popular?

8. How did segregation affect amateur and professional athletics in the United States?

Conciliation, Agitation, and Migration: African Americans in the Early Twentieth Century 1895–1928

As the twentieth century dawned, black and white Americans had profoundly different views on the future of black people in America. Most white people believed black Americans were an inferior race capable of little more than manual labor and entitled to only the most basic legal rights. Black Americans rejected those assertions and worked for a more equitable place in society. Black scholar W. E. B. Du Bois announced in 1903 that race would be the century's critical issue: "The problem of the twentieth century is the problem of the color line—the relation of the darker to the lighter races of men in Asia and Africa, in America and the islands of the sea."

LEARNING OBJECTIVES

What advice for advancement did Booker T. Washington offer to African Americans? | 16-1

What were the views of W. E. B. Du Bois on promoting progress among African Americans in early twentieth-century America? | 16-2

What were the origins and goals of the NAACP? | 16-3

What role did black women play in advocating reform and in fostering progress among African Americans? | 16-4

What were the defining characteristics of the black elite? | 16-5

How did African Americans contribute to the U.S. war effort in World War I? | 16-6

What were the causes of racial violence in the early twentieth century and why was that violence so intense? | 16-7

Why did African Americans begin to leave the rural South in the early twentieth century, and what kinds of lives were they able to make for themselves in urban communities? | 16-8

Although Tuskegee Institute stressed agricultural and vocational subjects, students did enroll in math, science, and English courses. Here students in a U.S. history class are involved in a discussion of Virginia's founding in the early seventeenth century. Notice that the male and female students are segregated and that the classroom features portraits of three U.S. presidents and several American flags.

341

16-1

16-2

16-3

16-4

16-5

16-6

16-7

16-8

Refusing to accept the inferiority to which they had been consigned, black people devised strategies and organized institutions to enable them to prosper in a hostile society. However, African Americans and their leaders disagreed about how to secure the constitutional rights and the material comforts that so many white Americans took for granted. Some, following Du Bois, a founder of the Niagara Movement and the National Association for the Advancement of Colored People (NAACP), favored a frontal assault on discrimination, disfranchisement, and Jim Crow. Others, following Booker T. Washington of the Tuskegee Institute, cautioned against the vigorous pursuit of civil rights and political power and insisted that agricultural and industrial training would generate prosperity and self-sufficiency among people of color.

The emergence of the club movement among black women and other self-help organizations enabled more prosperous black people to aid those suffering from poverty and prejudice. The black elite, often reviled for ostentatious social displays, came to be designated the **Talented Tenth**, and many of them took seriously their responsibilities to aid their brethren.

Talented Tenth Term popularized by W. E. B. Du Bois for the educated black elite of the late nineteenth and early twentieth centuries. The upper 10 percent was supposed to assume responsibility for the leadership and advancement of the remaining 90 percent of African Americans.

When the United States entered World War I in 1917, black men responded patriotically, as they had in previous conflicts. They joined a Jim Crow military that was fighting to make the world safe for democracy. But black people in America were not safe, and democracy did not prevail. Racial violence erupted before, during, and after the war.

In the meantime, one of the most important episodes in American history—a vast and prolonged migration of hundreds of thousands of rural black southerners to northern cities—began in earnest after 1910. Drawn mainly by economic opportunities, black people moved to New York, Philadelphia, Cleveland, Chicago, and other urban centers where they became the core of the black working class.

By the 1910s, many Americans were anxious about the rapid economic and social changes that confronted the United States, including industrialization, the rise of powerful corporations, the explosive growth of cities, and the influx of millions of immigrants. Their apprehensions spawned a disparate collection of reform efforts known as the progressive movement. In general, progressives believed America needed a new social awareness to deal with the new social and economic problems. But most of the middle- and upper-class white people who formed the core of the movement showed little interest in white racism and its impact. Indeed, many were racists themselves. They were primarily concerned with the concentration of wealth, with the pervasive political corruption in state and local governments, and with the plight of working-class immigrants in American cities. They cared deeply about the debilitating effects of alcohol, tainted food, and prostitution, but little about the grim impact of white supremacy.

The reforms of the progressive movement nonetheless offered a glimmer of hope that racial advancement was possible. If efforts were made to improve America, was it not possible also to improve the policies and conditions affecting black Americans? But how much militancy or forbearance was necessary to achieve racial progress? Did it even make sense for black people to demand a meaningful role in a nation that despised them? Perhaps it was wiser to rely on each other rather than plead for white recognition and respect.

Booker T. Washington's Approach

16-1 **What advice for advancement did Booker T. Washington offer to African Americans?**

Booker T. Washington's commitment to agricultural and industrial education was the basis for his approach to "the problem of the color line." By 1900, Washington was convinced that black men and women who had mastered skills acquired at institutions like Tuskegee and Hampton would be recognized, if not welcomed, as productive contributors to the southern economy. He believed economic acceptance would lead to political and social acceptance.

The Tuskegee leader eloquently outlined his philosophy in the speech he delivered at the opening ceremonies of the Cotton States Exposition in Atlanta in 1895 (see Chapter 15). Black people, he told his segregated audience, would find genuine opportunities in the South. "When it comes to business, pure and simple, it is in the South that the Negro is given a man's chance in the commercial world." Washington added that black people should not expect too much but should welcome menial labor as a first step in the struggle for progress. He told white listeners that the lives of black and white southerners were historically linked and that black people were far more loyal and steadfast than newly arrived immigrants.

Washington reassured white people that cooperation between the races in the interest of prosperity did not endanger segregation: "In all things that are purely social we can be as separate as the fingers, yet one as the hand in all things essential to mutual progress." Finally, Washington implied that black people need not protest because they were denied rights white men possessed. Instead, he urged his black listeners to struggle steadily rather than make defiant demands: "The wisest among my race understand that the agitation of questions of social equality is the extremest folly, and that progress in the enjoyment of all the privileges that will come to us must be the result of severe and constant struggle rather than of artificial forcing." Washington was convinced that as African Americans became productive and made economic progress, white people would concede them their rights.

The speech was warmly received by both white and black listeners and by those who read it when it was widely reprinted. But not everyone was complimentary. The black editor of the *Washington Bee*, W. Calvin Chase, complained, "He said something that was death to the Afro-American and elevating to white people." Bishop Henry M. Turner added that Washington "will have to live a long time to undo the harm he has done our race."

White people regarded Washington's speech as moderate, sensible, and praiseworthy. Almost overnight he was designated the spokesman for African Americans. Washington took full advantage of the recognition.

16-1
16-2
16-3
16-4
16-5
16-6
16-7
16-8

16-1

16-2

16-3

16-4

16-5

16-6

16-7

16-8

Washington's Influence

Booker T. Washington was a complex man. Many people found him unassertive, dignified, and patient. Yet he was ambitious, aggressive, and opportunistic as well as shrewd, calculating, and devious. He had an uncanny ability to elicit a positive response from other people.

After the Atlanta speech, Washington's influence soared. He received extensive and mostly positive coverage in black newspapers. Some of that popularity stemmed from admiration for his leadership and agreement with his ideas. But Washington also flattered editors, paid for advertisements for Tuskegee, and subsidized struggling African-American journalists.

He was especially effective in dealing with prominent white businessmen and philanthropists. Washington's management of Tuskegee so impressed William H. Baldwin, vice president of the Southern Railroad, that Baldwin agreed to serve as the chairman of Tuskegee's board. Washington developed support among the nation's industrial elite including steel magnate Andrew Carnegie and Julius Rosenwald, the head of Sears, Roebuck and Company. They trusted Washington's judgment and consulted him before contributing to black colleges and universities. Washington assured them of the wisdom of training black men and women in agricultural and mechanical skills. These students, he reminded donors, would be self-sufficient and productive members of southern society.

Tuskegee Machine
As the president of Tuskegee Institute, Booker T. Washington developed an extensive network of contacts that gave him extraordinary influence with white political leaders and philanthropists as well as with black business people, journalists, and college presidents.

The Tuskegee Machine

Washington advised black people to avoid politics, but he ignored his own advice. Although he never ran for office or was appointed to a political position, Washington was a political figure to be reckoned with. His connections to white businesspeople and politicians gave him enormous influence. With his influence, connections, and organizational skills, Washington operated what came to be known as the "**Tuskegee Machine.**" In 1896 he supported winning Republican presidential candidate William McKinley over the Democratic and Populist William Jennings Bryan. Washington got along superbly with McKinley's successor, Theodore Roosevelt. Although Roosevelt subscribed to social Darwinism (see Chapter 15) and regarded black Americans as inferiors, he respected Washington.

In 1901 Roosevelt invited Washington to dinner at the White House, where Roosevelt's family and a Colorado businessman joined them. Black people applauded, but the white South recoiled in disgust from such a flagrant breach of racial etiquette. Under no circumstances did white people and black people dine together at the same table. Roosevelt was unmoved by the complaints of white southerners, and he continued to correspond and meet with Washington, consulting with him on political appointments. Still, Roosevelt never invited Washington for another meal at the Executive Mansion.

Booker T. Washington had access to and influence among the most powerful political and business leaders in the United States. Here he shares the podium with President Theodore Roosevelt. Washington persuaded Republican leaders like Roosevelt to appoint black men to an assortment of federal offices and convinced businessmen to contribute sizable sums to black colleges and universities. Nevertheless, some African Americans criticized the Tuskegee leader for not speaking out more candidly in opposition to white supremacy and Jim Crow.

Most of Washington's political activities were not public. He secretly helped finance an unsuccessful court case against the Louisiana grandfather clause. (The statute disfranchised those voters—black men—whose grandfathers had not possessed the right to vote. See Chapter 14.) Washington funded two cases challenging Alabama's grandfather clause to the Supreme Court, which rejected both on a technicality. He tried to persuade railroad executives to improve the conditions on segregated coaches and in station waiting rooms. He worked covertly with white attorneys to free a black farm laborer imprisoned under Alabama's peonage law.

Washington was a conservative leader who did not directly or publicly challenge white supremacy. He was willing to accept literacy and property qualifications for voting if they were equitably enforced regardless of race. He also opposed women's suffrage. He attacked lynching only occasionally. But he did write an annual letter to white newspapers filled with data on lynchings that had been compiled at Tuskegee. Washington let the grim statistics speak for themselves rather than denounce the injustice himself.

Opposition to Washington

Years before Washington became prominent, there were black leaders who favored a direct challenge to racial oppression. In 1889 delegates from 23 states met to form the Afro-American League in Chicago. Its main purpose was to press for civil and political rights guaranteed by the Constitution. But the league did not flourish, and the Niagara Movement eventually displaced it.

Opposition to Washington's conciliatory stance on racial matters intensified. William Monroe Trotter, the Harvard-educated editor of the *Boston Guardian*, attacked Washington as "the Great Traitor," "the Benedict Arnold of the Negro Race," and "Pope Washington." At a 1903 meeting of the National Negro Business League in Boston, Trotter stood on a chair and interrupted a speech by Washington, defiantly asking, "Are the rope and the torch all the race is to get under your leadership?" Washington ignored him, and the police arrested the editor for disorderly conduct. He spent 30 days in jail for what newspapers labeled "the Boston Riot."

W. E. B. Du Bois

16-2 What were the views of W. E. B. Du Bois on promoting progress among African Americans in early twentieth-century America?

William Edward Burghardt Du Bois, who was 12 years younger than Booker T. Washington, would eventually eclipse Washington's influence and authority. Du Bois became the most significant black leader in America during the first half of the twentieth century. Whereas slavery, poverty, and the industrial work ethic fostered at Hampton Institute had shaped Washington's life, Du Bois was born and raised in the largely white town of Great Barrington, Massachusetts. It was a small community where he encountered little overt racism and developed a passion for knowledge.

Du Bois graduated from Great Barrington High School at a time when few white and still fewer black youngsters attended more than primary school. He went to Fisk University in Nashville and graduated at age 20. He was the first black man to earn a Ph.D. (in history) at Harvard in 1895, and he pursued additional graduate study in Germany.

Du Bois was perhaps the greatest scholar-activist in American history. He was an intellectual, at ease with words and ideas. He wrote 16 nonfiction books, five novels, and two autobiographies. He was a fearless activist determined to confront disfranchisement, Jim Crow, and lynching. Whereas Washington solicited the goodwill of powerful white leaders and was comfortable with a gradual approach to eradicating white supremacy,

16-1
16-2
16-3
16-4
16-5
16-6
16-7
16-8

VOICES W. E. B. Du Bois on Being Black in America

W. E. B. Du Bois's The Souls of Black Folk *(1903) contained perhaps the most eloquent statement ever written on being black in white America. The difficulties of their circumstances, Du Bois believed, create a double consciousness among Americans of African descent.*

After the Egyptian and Indian, the Greek and Roman, the Teuton and Mongolian, the Negro is a sort of seventh son, born with a veil, and gifted with second-sight in this American world,—a world which yields him no true self-consciousness, but only lets him see himself through the revelation of the other world. It is a peculiar sensation, this double-consciousness, this sense of always looking at one's self through the eyes of others, of measuring one's soul by the tape of a world that looks on in an amused contempt and pity. One ever feels his two-ness,—an American, a Negro; two souls, two thoughts, two unreconciled strivings; two warring ideals in one dark body, whose dogged strength alone keeps it from being torn asunder.

The history of the American Negro is the history of this strife,—this longing to attain self-conscious manhood, to merge his double self into a better and truer self. In this merging he wishes neither of the older selves to be lost. He would not Africanize America, for America has too much to teach the world and Africa. He would not bleach his Negro soul in a flood of white Americanism, for he knows that Negro blood has a message for the world. He simply wishes to make it possible for a man to be both a Negro and an American, without being cursed and spit upon by his fellows, without having the doors of Opportunity closed roughly in his face.

1. **Why does Du Bois maintain that a black person cannot be simply an American?**
2. **Would Du Bois agree, based on his concept of double consciousness, that African Americans have a separate identity and culture from other Americans?**

SOURCE: W. E. B. Du Bois, *The Souls of Black Folk* (New York: Library of America, 1903), 8–9.

Du Bois was impatient with white people who accepted or ignored white domination and had little tolerance for black people who were unwilling to demand their civil and political rights.

The Souls of Black Folk

Du Bois was not always critical of Washington. Following Washington's speech at the Cotton States Exposition in 1895, Du Bois, then a young Harvard Ph.D. teaching at Ohio's Wilberforce University, wrote to praise him: "Let me heartily congratulate you upon your phenomenal success at Atlanta—it was a word fitly spoken." But in 1903, Du Bois, by then an Atlanta University professor, published *The Souls of Black Folk*. One of the major literary works of the twentieth century, it contained the first formal attack on Washington and his leadership.

In a provocative essay, "Of Booker T. Washington and Others," Du Bois conceded it was painful to challenge Washington, a man so highly praised and admired: "One hesitates, therefore, to criticise a life which, beginning with so little, has done so much. And yet the time is come when one may speak in all sincerity and utter courtesy of the mistakes and shortcomings of Mr. Washington's career, as well as the triumphs." Du Bois

Read on MyHistoryLab Document:
W. E. B. Du Bois, from "Of Mr. Booker T. Washington and Others," 1903

16-1

16-2

16-3

16-4

16-5

16-6

16-7

16-8

proceeded to attack Washington for failing to stand up for political and civil rights and higher education for black Americans. Du Bois found even more infuriating Washington's willingness to compromise with the white South and Washington's apparent agreement with white southerners that black people were not their equals: "Mr. Washington represents in Negro thought the old attitude of adjustment and submission . . . and Mr. Washington's programme practically accepts the alleged inferiority of the Negro races." Du Bois stressed that he agreed with Washington on some issues, but he so disagreed on other significant issues that it was vital to oppose Washington's positions.

Washington worried that the opposition of Trotter, Du Bois, and others would jeopardize the flow of funds from white philanthropists to black colleges and universities. To reconcile with his opponents, he organized a meeting with them, funded by white philanthropists, at Carnegie Hall in New York City in 1904. But Du Bois and other opponents of Washington came to the gathering determined to adopt a radical agenda. When Washington loyalists monopolized the proceedings, Du Bois quit in disgust.

The Talented Tenth

Du Bois, joined by a small cadre of black intellectuals, set out to organize an aggressive effort to secure the rights of black citizens. He was convinced that the advancement of black people was the responsibility of the black elite, those he called the Talented Tenth, meaning the upper 10 percent of black Americans. Education, he believed, was the key:

> **Read** on **MyHistoryLab** Document: W. E. B. Du Bois Challenges Booker T. Washington, 1903

This early twentieth-century photograph depicts a dapper young W. E. B. Du Bois (1868–1963). He was a key figure in opposing Booker T. Washington's Tuskegee Machine. Du Bois helped found the NAACP and edited its publication, the *Crisis*, for two decades.

> Work alone will not do it unless inspired by the right ideals and guided by intelligence. Education must not simply teach work—it must teach Life. The Talented Tenth of the Negro race must be made leaders of thought and missionaries of culture among people. No others can do this work, and Negro colleges must train men for it. The Negro race, like all other races, is going to be saved by its exceptional men.

 Watch on **MyHistoryLab** Video: The Conflict between Booker T. Washington and W. E. B. Du Bois

The Niagara Movement

In 1905 Du Bois carried the anti-Washington crusade a step further and invited a select group to meet at Niagara Falls in Canada. The 29 delegates to this meeting demanded voting rights and an end to segregation: "All American citizens have the right to equal treatment in places of public entertainment." They appealed for better schools, health care, and housing; protested the discrimination black soldiers endured; and criticized the racial prejudice of most churches. Perhaps most important, the Niagara gathering insisted that white people did not know what was best for black people: "We repudiate the monstrous doctrine that the oppressor should be the sole authority as to the rights of the oppressed."

16-1
16-2
16-3
16-4
16-5
16-6
16-7
16-8

📖 **Read** on **MyHistoryLab Document**: The Niagara Movement, Declaration of Principles, 1905

The founders of the Niagara Movement posed in front of a photograph of the falls when they met at Niagara Falls, Ontario, Canada, in 1905. W. E. B. Du Bois is second from the right in the middle row.
Photographs and Prints Division, Schomburg Center for Research in Black Culture. The New York Public Library, Astor, Lenox, and Tilden Foundations.

The Niagara Movement that emerged from this meeting attracted 400 members and remained active for years. But the Niagara Movement was no match for the powerful, well-financed Tuskegee Machine. Washington used every means at his disposal to undermine the movement. Black newspaper editors were paid to attack Du Bois and praise Washington. Washington dispatched spies to Niagara meetings to report on the organization's activities. He let it be known that black federal employees might be dismissed if they joined the Niagara Movement.

Niagara members also quarreled among themselves. Du Bois was an inexperienced leader, and difficulties developed between him and Trotter. In 1908 the Niagara Movement virtually collapsed. Most black and white Americans would not support an organization that seemed so uncompromising in its demands.

The NAACP

16-3 **What were the origins and goals of the NAACP?**

As the Niagara Movement expired, the National Association for the Advancement of Colored People (NAACP) came to life. There was no direct link between the demise of the Niagara Movement and the rise of the NAACP. However, the relatively few people—black and white—who felt comfortable with the Niagara Movement's assertive stance on race were inclined to support the NAACP. In its early years the NAACP was a militant organization dedicated to racial justice. White leaders dominated it, and white contributors largely financed it.

A few white progressives were concerned about rampant racial prejudice. After a gathering of leaders in January 1909 in New York City, on February 12—Lincoln's birthday—Oswald Garrison Villard called on "all believers in democracy to join a national conference to discuss present evils, the voicing of protests, and the renewal of the struggle for civil and political liberty."

Villard was the president and editor of the *New York Evening Post* and the grandson of abolitionist William Lloyd Garrison. Prominent progressives endorsed the call, including social workers Lillian Wald and Jane Addams, literary scholar Joel E. Spingarn, and respected attorneys Clarence Darrow and Moorfield Storey. Du Bois, Ida Wells Barnett, and Mary Church Terrell were the black leaders most involved in forming the NAACP.

Using the System

The NAACP was determined that black citizens should fully enjoy the civil and political rights the Constitution guaranteed to all citizens. It relied on the judicial and legislative

16-1

16-2

16-3

16-4

16-5

16-6

16-7

16-8

systems in what would be a persistent and decades-long effort to secure those rights. The NAACP won its first major legal victory in 1915 when the Supreme Court overturned Oklahoma's grandfather clause in *Guinn v. United States.*

In 1917, in a case brought by the Louisville NAACP, the Supreme Court struck down a local law that enforced residential segregation by prohibiting black people and white people from selling real estate to people of the other race. The NAACP also tried in 1918 to secure a federal law prohibiting lynching. With the assistance of Congressman Leonidas Dyer, a white St. Louis Republican, the anti-lynching measure—the Dyer bill—passed in the House of Representatives in 1922. But the Senate blocked it, and it never became law.

Du Bois and the *Crisis*

Du Bois was easily the most prominent black figure associated with the NAACP during its first quarter century. He became director of publicity and research and edited the NAACP publication called the *Crisis*, while largely leaving leadership and administrative tasks to others.

With the *Crisis*, Du Bois the scholar became Du Bois the propagandist. He denounced white racism and atrocities and demanded that black people stand up for their rights: "Agitate, then, brother; protest, reveal the truth and refuse to be silenced. . . . A moment's let up, a moment's acquiescence, means a chance for the wolves of prejudice to get at our necks." These were not the even-tempered, cautious words of Booker T. Washington to which so many Americans had grown accustomed. The *Crisis* became required reading in many black homes. By 1913 it had 30,000 subscribers.

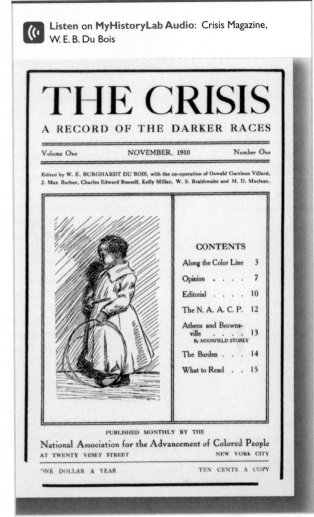

((Listen on **MyHistoryLab Audio:** Crisis Magazine, W. E. B. Du Bois

The first issue of the *Crisis* monthly magazine was published in November 1910.

Washington versus the NAACP

Villard tried to reassure Washington that the NAACP posed no threat and to gain his support for the new association. Many black leaders and members of the NAACP, however, despised Washington and his ideology, and Washington returned the sentiment and worked to subvert the new organization. Washington considered Du Bois little more than the puppet of white people, who dominated the leadership of the NAACP, and the Tuskegee leader declined to debate Du Bois.

Washington became so obsessed with the NAACP that he was not above manipulating white supremacists to damage those connected with it. When he learned that black and white progressives associated with the NAACP were going to gather at the Café Boulevard in New York City in 1911, he allowed Charles Anderson to alert the hostile white press, which described the multiracial dinner in the most inflammatory terms: "Fashionable White

16-1
16-2
16-3
16-4
16-5
16-6
16-7
16-8

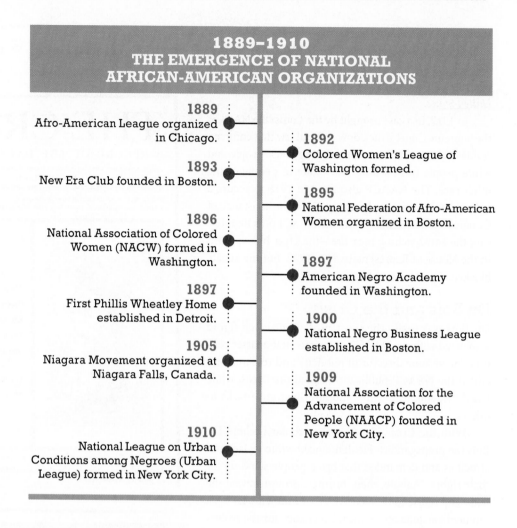

1889–1910
**THE EMERGENCE OF NATIONAL
AFRICAN-AMERICAN ORGANIZATIONS**

1889
Afro-American League organized in Chicago.

1892
Colored Women's League of Washington formed.

1893
New Era Club founded in Boston.

1895
National Federation of Afro-American Women organized in Boston.

1896
National Association of Colored Women (NACW) formed in Washington.

1897
American Negro Academy founded in Washington.

1897
First Phillis Wheatley Home established in Detroit.

1900
National Negro Business League established in Boston.

1905
Niagara Movement organized at Niagara Falls, Canada.

1909
National Association for the Advancement of Colored People (NAACP) founded in New York City.

1910
National League on Urban Conditions among Negroes (Urban League) formed in New York City.

Women Sit at Board with Negroes, Japs and Chinamen to Promote 'Cause' of Miscegenation" proclaimed one headline.

Ultimately, Washington's efforts to ruin the NAACP and reduce its supporters' influence failed. By the time of his death in 1915, the NAACP had 6,000 members and 50 local branches. Its aggressive campaign for civil and political rights replaced Washington's strategy of progress through conciliation and accommodation.

The Urban League

Listen on
MyHistoryLab
Audio: The Progress
of Colored Women;
Mary Church Terrell,
excerpt

In 1910, black and white progressives founded the National League on Urban Conditions among Negroes in New York City. Soon known simply as the Urban League, its goal was to alleviate conditions black people encountered as they moved into large cities in ever-increasing numbers during the early twentieth century. The Urban League worked to improve housing, medical care, and recreational facilities among black residents who lived in segregated neighborhoods in New York, Philadelphia, Atlanta, Nashville, Norfolk, and other cities. The league also assisted youngsters who ran afoul of the law, and it helped establish the Big Brother and Big Sister movements.

Black Women and the Club Movement

16-4 What role did black women play in advocating reform and in fostering progress among African Americans?

Years before the Urban League and the NAACP were founded, black women began creating clubs and organizations. The local groups that began forming in the 1870s and 1880s, such as the Bethel Literary and Historical Association in Washington, DC, were mainly concerned with cultural, religious, and social matters. But many of the mostly middle-class women active in these clubs eventually became more involved with community problems. In 1893 black women in Boston founded the New Era Club.

In 1895 a New Era Club member, Josephine St. Pierre Ruffin, enraged by white journalist James W. Jack's vilification of black women as "prostitutes, thieves, and liars," issued a call to "Let Us Confer Together" that drew 104 black women to a meeting in Boston. The result was the formation of the National Federation of Afro-American Women, which soon included 36 clubs in 12 states. In the meantime, the Colored Women's League of Washington, DC, which had been founded in 1892, appealed for black women to organize a national association at the 1895 meeting of the National Council of Women. At that gathering, representatives from black women's clubs organized the National Colored Woman's League.

The NACW: "Lifting as We Climb"

The two groups—The National Federation of Afro-American Women and the National Colored Woman's League—merged in 1896 to form the National Association of Colored Women (NACW), with Mary Church Terrell elected the first president. The NACW adopted the self-help motto "Lifting as We Climb," and in the reforming spirit of the progressive age they stressed moral, mental, and material advancement. By 1914 the NACW had 50,000 members in 1,000 clubs nationwide.

There were occasionally unpleasant disagreements and conflicts among the club women. More important than these internal struggles were the efforts of black women to confront the problems black people encountered in urban areas as rural southerners migrated to the cities by the thousands in the second and third decades of the twentieth century. The NACW clubs worked to eradicate poverty, end racial discrimination, and promote education. Members cared for older people, especially former slaves. They aided orphans; provided nurseries, health care, and information on child rearing for working mothers; and established homes for delinquent and abandoned girls.

Phillis Wheatley Clubs

Black women also formed Phillis Wheatley clubs and homes across the nation, named in honor of the eighteenth-century African-American poet (see Chapter 4). The residences offered living accommodations for single, black working women in many cities where YWCAs refused to admit them. Some Phillis Wheatley clubs also provided nurseries and classes in domestic skills. In Cleveland, a nurse named Jane Edna Hunter organized a residence for single, black working women who could not find comfortable and affordable housing. In 1911, she formed the Working Girls' Home Association for cleaning women, laundresses, and private duty nurses. With association members contributing five cents a week, Hunter opened a 23-room residence in 1913 that expanded to a 72-room building in 1917.

16-1
16-2
16-3
16-4
16-5
16-6
16-7
16-8

Anna Julia Cooper and Black Feminism

Read on **MyHistoryLab**
Document: Anna Julia
Cooper Describes the
Status of Women in
America, 1892

Anna Julia Cooper was born a slave in Raleigh, North Carolina, in 1858 and graduated from St. Augustine's School. She then earned a bachelor's degree from Oberlin College in 1884. Speaking and writing with increasing confidence and authority, she published *A Voice From the South, by a Black Woman of the South* in 1892. In these essays she stressed the pivotal role that black women would play in the future and chastised white women for their lack of support. In 1900 she addressed the Pan African Conference in London.

Cooper was principal of Washington's famed M Street Colored High School (later Paul Laurence Dunbar High School) from 1901 to 1906. She was forced out in 1906 amid allegations that supporters of the Tuskegee Machine resented her emphasis on academic preparation over vocational training. She went on to teach for four years at Missouri's Lincoln University before returning to M Street High as a teacher. Fluent in French, she earned a Ph.D. at the Sorbonne in Paris.

She was active with the NACW, the NAACP, and the YWCA. Married in 1877, her husband died only two years later. Cooper found time following his death to take in and raise five children. She died in 1964 at age 105.

Women's Suffrage

Historically, many black women had supported women's suffrage. Before the Civil War, many abolitionists, including Mary Ann Shadd Cary, Sojourner Truth, and Frederick Douglass, had also backed women's suffrage. Cary and Truth tried unsuccessfully to vote after the war. Black women, such as Caroline Remond Putnam of Massachusetts, Lottie Rollin of South Carolina, and Frances Ellen Watkins Harper of Pennsylvania, attended conventions of the mostly white American Woman's Suffrage Association in the 1870s.

Black women were also involved in the long struggle for women's suffrage on the state level. Ida Wells Barnett was a leader in the Illinois suffrage effort. By 1900 Wyoming, Utah, Colorado, and Idaho permitted women to vote, and by 1918 women in 17 northern and western states had gained the vote. But as more women won voting rights, women's suffrage became more controversial. The proposed Nineteenth Amendment to the Constitution drove a wedge between black and white advocates of women's political rights. Many opponents of women's suffrage, especially white southerners, warned that granting women the right to vote would increase the number of black voters. Some white women advocated strict literacy and educational requirements for voting to limit the number of black voters, both women and men.

Only two southern states—Kentucky and Tennessee—ratified the Nineteenth Amendment before its adoption in 1920. Black suffragists understood that the right to vote meant political power, and political power could be exercised to acquire civil rights, improve education, and gain respect. White southerners also grasped the importance of voting rights. Thus, despite the Nineteenth Amendment, most black people in the South—both men and women—remained unable to vote.

The Black Elite

16-5 **What were the defining characteristics of the black elite?**

Many of the black leaders described by Du Bois as the Talented Tenth formed protest organizations, joined reform efforts, and organized self-help groups. The leaders were middle- and upper-class black people who were better educated than most Americans—black or white.

The American Negro Academy

In 1897, Episcopal priest Alexander Crummell met with 16 other black men in Washington, DC, to form the American Negro Academy. This scholarly organization was made up of "men of African descent" who assembled periodically to discuss and publish works on history, literature, religion, and science.

The Academy afforded black intellectuals an opportunity to ponder what it meant to be black in America and develop their racial consciousness, thus nurturing ideas and concepts that would mature during the Harlem Renaissance.

Most members of the Academy supported women's rights and women's suffrage. Consequently, it was ironic that black women were not invited to become members of the Academy.

The Upper Class

By the early twentieth century, there were several hundred wealthy African Americans. These black aristocrats distanced themselves from less affluent black and white people and lived in expensive houses. Many of them had fair complexions. They were medical doctors, lawyers, and businessmen.

The black elite formed exclusive organizations that jealously limited membership to the small black upper class. In the 1860s the Ugly Fishing Club was made up of New York City's wealthiest black men. It soon came to be known simply as the Ugly Club, and its membership spread to Newport, Rhode Island; Baltimore; and Philadelphia. In 1904 two wealthy Philadelphia physicians, a dentist, and a pharmacist formed Sigma Pi Phi, better known as Boulé, to provide "inspiration, relaxation, intellectual stimulation, and brotherhood: for male college graduates." Boulé expanded to seven chapters in cities that included Chicago and Memphis.

Organizations like the Diamondback Club and the Cosmos Club in Washington, the Loendi Club in Pittsburgh, and the Bachelor-Benedict Club in New York sponsored luxurious banquets, dances, and debutante balls. Several of these groups owned ornate clubhouses. These elite societies and cliques competed to demonstrate social exclusivity and preeminence.

Fraternities and Sororities

Among the black elite were also the African Americans who established the Greek-letter black fraternities and sororities. In 1906 seven students at Cornell University formed Alpha Phi Alpha, the first college fraternity for black men. The first black sorority, Alpha Kappa Alpha, was founded in 1908 at Howard University. Besides providing college students with an opportunity to enjoy each other's company, the black fraternities and sororities stressed scholarship, social graces, and community involvement.

African-American Inventors

Among the black elite were inventors and innovators who contributed to the technical and industrial transformation of America during the late nineteenth and early twentieth centuries. Like Thomas Edison, Henry Ford, and Harvey Firestone, these African Americans were mostly self-taught and not college educated. But there was an exception. Shelby J. Davidson had graduated from Howard University and was a lawyer.

As a longtime employee of the auditing department of the Post Office Division of the U.S. Treasury, Davidson became an expert on the new and complex adding machines used to maintain post office accounts. In 1908 he received a patent for an electric device that fed paper into the machines.

As prejudice and discrimination against black federal employees intensified, Davidson resigned his auditing position in 1912. He believed that a less qualified white man was promoted while he was not.

16-1
16-2
16-3
16-4
16-5
16-6
16-7
16-8

16-1
16-2
16-3
16-4
16-5
16-6
16-7
16-8

Lewis H. Latimer's *Incandescent Lighting: A Practical Description of the Edison System,* published in 1896, was one of the first books on electric lighting.

Granville Woods was born in Australia in 1856 and grew up in Columbus, Ohio. He developed mechanical skills and became a locomotive engineer. His extensive knowledge of electricity enabled him to win 45 patents. His Synchronous Multiplex Railway Telegraph improved communication among trains and with stations, thereby increasing railroad safety. His invention of an electric railway brake also enhanced safe operations. Thomas Edison challenged Woods's claim to have invented the Multiplex Telegraph, but Woods prevailed. It was one of the rare patent cases that Edison lost.

Lewis Latimer's parents were slaves who had escaped from Virginia to Boston in 1842. Born in 1848, Latimer joined the Union Navy during the Civil War at age 15. After the war he became a skilled draftsman for a patent law firm. In 1874 Latimer received a patent for a flushing mechanism that improved toilets on railway coaches.

He went on to draft diagrams for Alexander Graham Bell's patent application for the telephone. While working for the U.S. Electric Lighting Company, Latimer invented an improved process for manufacturing carbon filaments for light bulbs that he patented in 1882. He went to work for the Edison Electric Light Company in 1883. He served as the chief draftsman for the General Electric/Westinghouse Board of Patent Control after it was formed in 1896.

Presidential Politics

Since Reconstruction, black voters had supported the Republican Party and its presidential candidates. "The Party of Lincoln" welcomed that support and rewarded black men with federal jobs. Republican presidents Theodore Roosevelt (1901–1909) and William Howard Taft (1909–1913) continued that policy.

FRUSTRATED BY THE REPUBLICANS

However, other presidential actions offset whatever goodwill these appointments generated. Roosevelt discharged three companies of black soldiers after the Brownsville incident in 1906, and Taft tolerated restrictions on black voters in the South and encouraged the development of a "lily white" Republican Party, removing black people from federal jobs in the region.

In 1912 the Republican Party split in a bitter feud between President Taft and Theodore Roosevelt, and Roosevelt's supporters formed the Progressive Party, which nominated him to run against Taft and the Democratic candidate, Woodrow Wilson. But as the delegates at the Progressive convention in Chicago sang the "Battle Hymn of the Republic," southern black men who had come to the gathering stood outside the hall, denied admission by white Progressives.

WOODROW WILSON

It was not a complete shock that militant black leaders like William Monroe Trotter and W. E. B. Du Bois urged black voters to break with the Republican Party and support Woodrow Wilson. Wilson was the reform governor of New Jersey and had been president of Princeton

University. Wilson's academic background and his promise to pursue a progressive policy toward black Americans impressed Trotter and Du Bois.

But President Wilson was no friend of black people. Born in Virginia and raised in South Carolina, Wilson had absorbed white southern racial views. Federal agencies and buildings were fully segregated early during Wilson's tenure. In 1914 Trotter and a black delegation met with Wilson to protest segregation in the Treasury Department and the Post Office. Wilson defended separation of the races as a means to avoid friction. Trotter strongly disagreed. Wilson became visibly irritated with Trotter and abruptly ended the meeting.

Black Men and the Military in World War I

16-6 How did African Americans contribute to the U.S. war effort in World War I?

In 1915–1916 Wilson faced more than problems with dissatisfied black people. Relations with Mexico had steadily deteriorated after a revolution and civil war there. War in Europe threatened to draw the United States into conflict with Germany.

The Punitive Expedition to Mexico

In 1914 war almost broke out between the United States and Mexico when U.S. Marines landed at Vera Cruz after an attack on American sailors. Then in March 1916, Francisco "Pancho" Villa, one of the participants in Mexico's civil war, led a force of Mexican rebels across the border into New Mexico in an effort to provoke war with the United States. In response, Wilson dispatched a "punitive expedition" that eventually numbered 15,000 troops under General John J. Pershing.

U.S. forces, including the black 10th Cavalry, spent 10 months in Mexico in 1916–1917 in a futile effort to capture Villa. White officers commanded the 10th Cavalry, as had been the case with black troops since the Civil War. But Lieutenant Colonel Charles Young, an 1889 black graduate of West Point, helped lead the regiment. Young led the black troops against a contingent of Villa's rebels who had ambushed an element of the 13th Cavalry, a white unit, at Santa Cruz de Villegas. As the probability increased that the United States would enter World War I against Germany, U.S. troops were withdrawn from Mexico in 1917.

World War I

When World War I erupted in Europe in August 1914, most Americans had no intention or desire to participate. Wilson issued a proclamation of neutrality and ran for reelection in 1916 on the slogan "He Kept Us Out of War." But German submarine attacks on civilian vessels and the loss of American lives infuriated Wilson and many Americans as a gross violation of U.S. neutrality

Lieutenant Colonel Charles D. Young, an 1889 graduate of the U.S. Military Academy at West Point who served in Cuba, the Philippines, Haiti, and Mexico, was not permitted to command troops during World War I. He returned to military service at the end of the war and was sent to Liberia to help train that country's army. He died while on furlough in Nigeria in 1922.

16-1
16-2
16-3
16-4
16-5
16-6
16-7
16-8

rights. On April 6, 1917, Congress declared war on Germany. Most African Americans supported the war effort. As in previous conflicts, black people sought to demonstrate their loyalty and devotion to the country through military service.

Some white leaders were less enthusiastic about the participation of black men. One southern governor wondered about the wisdom of having the military train and arm thousands of black men at southern camps and posts. General Pershing insisted on white leadership: "Under capable white officers and with sufficient training, Negro soldiers have always acquitted themselves creditably."

Black Troops and Officers

There were about 10,000 black regulars in the U.S. Army in 1917: the 9th and 10th Cavalry Regiments and the 24th and 25th Infantry Regiments. There were more than 5,000 black men in the navy, but virtually all of them were waiters, kitchen attendants, and stokers for the ships' boilers. The Marine Corps did not admit black men. During World War I, the new Selective Service system drafted more than 370,000 black men. Several all-black state National Guard units were also incorporated into federal service.

Although the military remained rigidly segregated, black newspapers and the NAACP campaigned to commission black officers to lead black troops. The War Department created an officer training school at Fort Des Moines, Iowa. Nearly 1,250 black men enrolled—1,000 were civilians, and 250 were enlisted men from the regular regiments—and over 1,000 received commissions. Black officers, however, were confined to the lower ranks, and the overall command of black units remained in white hands.

Discrimination and Its Effects

Most white military leaders, politicians, and journalists embraced racial stereotypes and expected little from black soldiers. As in earlier wars, black troops were discriminated against, abused, and neglected. Some had to drill with picks and shovels rather than rifles. At Camp Hill, Virginia, black troops lived through a cold winter in tents with no floors, no blankets, and no bathing facilities. White men failed to salute black officers, and black officers were denied admission to officers' clubs. Morale among black troops was low, and their performance sometimes reflected it.

Military authorities did not expect to use black troops in combat. The army preferred to employ black troops in labor battalions, as stevedores, in road construction, and as cooks and bakers. Of more than 380,000 black men who served in World War I, only 42,000 went into combat. The army did not prepare black soldiers adequately for combat, but military leaders complained when black soldiers who did face combat performed poorly.

The 368th Infantry Regiment of the 92nd Division came in for especially harsh criticism. Fighting alongside the French in September 1918, the regiment's second and third battalions fell back in disorder. Some men ran. The white regimental commander blamed black officers, and 30 of them were relieved of command. Five officers were court-martialed for cowardice; four were sentenced to death and one to life in prison. All were later freed. But black Lieutenant Howard H. Long argued that the perceptions of white officers caused the poor performance: "Many of the [white] field officers seemed far more concerned with reminding their Negro subordinates that they were Negroes than they were in having an effective unit that would perform well in combat."

White officials stressed the weaknesses of the 368th Infantry Regiment and mostly ignored the commendable records of the 369th, 370th, 371st, and 372nd Regiments.

Read on **MyHistoryLab** Document: French Officers Receive Secret Information Concerning Black American Troops, 1918

African-American troops on the march near Verdun in France in 1918.

16-1

16-2

16-3

16-4

16-5

16-6

16-7

16-8

The 369th compiled an exemplary combat record. Sent to the front for 91 consecutive days, these "Men of Bronze"—as they came to be known—consisted mainly of soldiers from the 15th Regiment of the New York National Guard. They fought alongside the French and lived up to their motto, "Let's Go," as they took part in heavy fighting. They never lost a trench or gave up a prisoner. By June 1918 French commanders were asking for all the black troops the Americans could send.

Most French civilians and troops, unfazed by racist warnings from white American officials about the presumed danger black men posed to white women, praised the conduct of black soldiers and accepted them as equals. Following the triumph of the Allies in World War I, French authorities awarded the Croix de Guerre, France's highest military medal, to the men of the 369th, the 371st, and the 372nd Regiments.

Black troops returned to America on segregated ships. The 15th New York National Guard Unit from the 369th Regiment was not permitted to join the farewell parade in New York City. Even praise from white Americans was riddled with racist stereotypes. The *Milwaukee Sentinel* was typical: "Those two colored regiments fought well, and it calls for special recognition. Is there no way of getting a cargo of watermelons over there?"

Read on **MyHistoryLab** Document: The Reverend F. J. Grimke Speaks to African-American Veterans, 1919

Du Bois's Disappointment

The treatment of black soldiers embittered black leaders who had supported American entry in the war. During the war in 1918, Du Bois appealed to black people in the *Crisis* to "close ranks" and support the war.

Du Bois's unequivocal support may have been connected to his effort to secure an officer's commission in military intelligence through the intervention of Joel E. Spingarn, chairman of the NAACP board of directors. Du Bois did not get his commission; instead, what he got was criticism for his "close ranks" editorial. William Monroe Trotter said that Du Bois had "finally weakened, compromised, deserted the fight, [and] betrayed the cause of his race." To Trotter, Du Bois was "a rank quitter in the cause for equal rights."

By the end of World War I, Du Bois—who had visited black troops in France—could see that black loyalty and sacrifice had not eroded white racism. He wrote defiantly in the *Crisis* that black people were determined to make America yield to its democratic ideals:

> But by the God of heaven, we are cowards and jackasses if now that the war is over, we do not marshal every ounce of our brain and brawn to fight a sterner, longer, more unbending battle against the forces of hell in our own land.
>> We return.
>> We return from fighting.
>> We return fighting.
> Make way for Democracy! We saved it in France, and by the Great Jehovah, we will save it in the United States of America, or know the reason why.

View on
MyHistoryLab
Closer Look: African-
American Soldiers
Return Home

Race Riots

16-7 What were the causes of racial violence in the early twentieth century and why was that violence so intense?

Despite the reformist impulse of the progressive era and the democratic ideals trumpeted as the United States went to war against Germany, most white Americans clung to social Darwinism and white supremacy. White people reacted with contempt and violence to demands by black people for fairer treatment and equal opportunities in American society. The campaigns of the NAACP, the efforts of the black club women, and the services and sacrifices of black men in the war not only failed to alter white racial perceptions but were sometimes accompanied by a backlash against African Americans. Ten black men still in uniform were lynched in 1919.

The racial violence that permeated southern life expanded into northern communities as many white Americans responded with hostility to the arrival of black migrants from the South. Black people defended themselves, and casualties among both races escalated (see Map 16–1).

Atlanta, 1906

In 1906—11 years after Booker T. Washington delivered his Cotton States Exposition address there—white mobs attacked black residents in Atlanta. Several factors aggravated white racial apprehensions in the city. In 1902 four black and four white people had been killed in a riot there. Many rural black people, attracted by economic opportunities, had moved to Atlanta. But white residents considered the newcomers more lawless and immoral than the longtime black residents. The white Atlanta newspapers ran inflammatory accounts about black crime and black men who brutalized white women. However, many

MAP 16-1 MAJOR RACE RIOTS, 1900–1923

In the years between 1900 and 1923, race conflicts and riots occurred in dozens of American communities as black people migrated in increasing numbers to urban areas. The violence reached a peak in the immediate aftermath of World War I during the Red Summer of 1919. White Americans—in the North and South—were determined to keep black people confined to a subordinate role as menial laborers and restricted to well-defined all-black neighborhoods. African Americans who had made significant economic and military contributions to the war effort and who had congregated in large numbers in American cities insisted on participating on a more equitable basis in American society.

Were the causes of each of these riots similar, or were the reasons for the upsurge in racial violence unique to each situation?

of these stories were false or exaggerated. Two white Democrats—Hoke Smith and Clark Howell—were engaged in a divisive campaign for a U.S. Senate seat in 1906, and both candidates stirred up racial animosity. There were also determined and ultimately successful efforts under way to disfranchise black voters in Georgia.

On a warm Saturday night, September 22, 1906, a white man jumped on a box on Decatur Street, one of Atlanta's main thoroughfares, and waved an Atlanta newspaper emblazoned with the headline THIRD ASSAULT. He hollered, "Are white men going to stand for this?" The crowd roared, "No! Save our women!" "Kill the niggers." A five-day orgy of violence followed.

The mayor, police, and fire departments vainly tried to stop the mob. Thousands of white people roamed the streets in search of black victims. Black people were tortured, beaten, and killed. White men pulled black passengers off streetcars. They destroyed black businesses. As white men armed themselves, the police disarmed black men. Black men and women who surrendered to marauding white mobs in hopes of mercy were not spared. Black men who fought back only infuriated the crazed white crowd. Twenty-five black people and one white person died, and hundreds were injured in the riot.

Du Bois hurried home to Atlanta from Alabama to defend his family. He waited on his porch with a shotgun for a mob that never came: "I would without hesitation have sprayed their guts over the grass." In New York, black editor T. Thomas Fortune called for a violent black response: "It makes my blood boil. I would like to be there with a good force of armed men to make Rome howl. I cannot believe that the policy of non-resistance in a situation like that of Atlanta can result in anything but contempt and massacre of the race."

Booker T. Washington looked for a silver lining in the awful affair by noting that "while there is disorder in one community there is peace and harmony in thousands of others." He said that black resistance would merely result in more black fatalities. Washington went to Atlanta and appealed for racial reconciliation.

A Committee of Safety of 10 black and 10 white leaders was formed. Charles T. Hopkins, an influential white Atlantan, warned in strong paternalist terms: "If we let this dependent race be butchered before our eyes, we cannot face God in the judgment day." But little real racial cooperation resulted. Black minister Henry Hugh Proctor worked with white leaders and often seemed to agree with them that Atlanta's main problem was black crime, not white racism.

No members of the white mob were brought to justice. Black Georgia voters were disfranchised. Atlanta's streetcars were segregated. The city had no public high school for black youngsters. The Carnegie Library did not admit black people, and the Atlanta police force had no black officers.

Springfield, 1908

Two years later in August 1908, white citizens of Springfield, Illinois, attacked black residents in an episode that led to the creation of the NAACP in 1909. George Richardson, a black man, was falsely accused of raping a white woman. Although the sheriff got Richardson out of town, a mob tore into Springfield's small black population. Six black people were shot and killed, two were lynched, dozens were injured, and black homes and businesses were wrecked. About 2,000 black people were driven out of Springfield.

Major racial conflicts occurred between 1917 and 1921 in East St. Louis, Illinois; Houston; Chicago; Elaine, Arkansas; and Tulsa. Smaller violent confrontations occurred in Washington, DC; Charleston; Knoxville, Tennessee; Omaha; and Waco and Longview, Texas. Although different incidents sparked each riot, the underlying causes were similar. White residents feared that black migrants would compete for jobs and housing.

East St. Louis, 1917

East St. Louis, Illinois, was a gritty industrial town of nearly 60,000 across the Mississippi River from St. Louis, Missouri. About 10 percent of the inhabitants were black. The town's schools, public facilities, and neighborhoods were segregated. Racial tensions increased in February 1917 after 470 black workers were hired to replace white members of the American Federation of Labor who had gone on strike against the Aluminum Ore Company. On July 1, white people drove through a black neighborhood firing guns. Shortly after, two white plainclothes police officers drove into the same neighborhood and were shot and killed by residents who may have believed the drive-by shooters had returned.

Angry white mobs sought revenge. Black people were mutilated and killed and their bodies thrown into the river. Black homes, many of them little more than cabins and shacks, were burned. Hundreds of black people were left homeless. The police joined the rioters. Thirty-five black people and eight white people died in the violence.

The NAACP sent Du Bois and Martha Gruening to East St. Louis. They compiled a report, "Massacre at East St. Louis," that documented instance after instance of brutality. To protest the riot, the NAACP organized a silent demonstration in New York City, and thousands of well-dressed black people marched to muffled drums down Fifth Avenue.

Houston, 1917

A month after the East St. Louis riot, black soldiers in Houston attacked police officers and civilians. The Third Battalion of the 24th Infantry recently had been transferred from Wyoming and California to Camp Logan near Houston, where the black troops came face-to-face with Jim Crow. Streetcars and public facilities were segregated. White and Hispanic people regularly called the black troops "niggers."

On August 23 a black soldier tried to prevent a police officer, Lee Sparks, from beating a black woman. Sparks clubbed the soldier and hauled him off to jail. Corporal Charles W. Baltimore attempted to determine what had happened, and he was also beaten and incarcerated. Although both soldiers were later released, a rumor circulated that Baltimore had been slain. Led by Sergeant Vida Henry, black men sought revenge.

About one hundred armed black soldiers mounted a two-hour assault on the police station. Fifteen white residents—including five policemen—and one Mexican American, four black soldiers, and two black civilians were killed. The army arrested 118 black soldiers and charged 63 of them with mutiny. Three separate court-martials were held. The NAACP retained the son of Texas legend Sam Houston to help defend them. Eight black men, however, agreed to testify against the defendants. Thirteen black troops were hanged (including Corporal Baltimore) after the first court-martial. Later seven more were executed, seven others were acquitted, and the rest were sentenced to prison terms.

Chicago, 1919

Between 1916 and 1919, the black population of Chicago doubled as migrants from the South moved north in search of jobs, political rights, and humane treatment. Many encountered a violent reception. A housing shortage strained the boundaries between crowded, segregated black neighborhoods and white residential areas. After World War I ended in November 1918, racial tensions increased as black men were hired to replace striking white workers in Chicago.

Read on MyHistoryLab
Document: The *Chicago Defender* Describes a Race Riot, 1919

With summer temperatures rising and racial tensions escalating, Ida B. Wells anticipated a major conflict in the pages of the *Chicago Tribune* in early July. "With one Negro dead as a result of the race riot last week, another one very badly injured in the county hospital; with a half-dozen attacks upon Negro children, and one on the Thirty-fifth street car Tuesday, in which four white men beat one colored man, it looks very much like Chicago is trying to rival the south in its race hatred against the Negro."

The Chicago riot began on Sunday, July 27, 1919—one day after black troops were welcomed home with a parade down the city's Michigan Avenue. Eugene Williams, a young black man, was swimming in Lake Michigan and inadvertently crossed the invisible boundary that separated the black and white beaches and bathing areas. He was stoned by white people and drowned. Instead of arresting the alleged perpetrators, the police arrested a black man who complained about police inaction.

16-1
16-2
16-3
16-4
16-5
16-6
16-7
16-8

Williams's death set off a week of violence that left 23 black people and 15 white people dead. More than 500 were injured, and nearly 1,000 were left homeless after fire raged through a Lithuanian neighborhood. Police often joined white mobs as they attacked black pedestrians and streetcar passengers. Black men formed a barrier along State Street to stop white gangs from the stockyard district. Three regiments of the Illinois National Guard were sent into the streets, but the violence did not end until August 1, when heavy rains kept people indoors.

Elaine, 1919

In 1919, black sharecroppers in and around Elaine, Arkansas, attempted to organize a union and withhold their cotton from the market until they received a higher price. Deputy sheriffs tried to break up a union meeting in a black church, and one of the deputies was killed. In retaliation, white people killed dozens of black people. No white people were prosecuted, but 12 black men were convicted of the deputy's murder. They were sentenced to death, and 67 other black men received prison terms of up to 20 years. Many were tortured and beaten in jail. Ida Wells Barnett and the Equal Rights League generated enormous publicity about the case. The NAACP appealed the convictions, and in 1923 the Supreme Court overturned them.

Tulsa, 1921

Violence erupted in Tulsa on May 31, 1921, after still another black man was accused of rape. Dick Rowland allegedly assaulted a white woman elevator operator, and rumors circulated that white men intended to lynch him. To protect Rowland, who was later found innocent, black men assembled at the jail as white men also gathered there. Angry words were exchanged, and shooting erupted. Several black and white men died in the chaos that ensued.

Black men retreated to their neighborhood, known as Greenwood, to protect their families and homes. The governor dispatched the National Guard, and the sheriff sent Rowland to an unknown location. By the morning of June 1, 500 white men confronted about 1,000 black men across a set of railroad tracks. White men in automobiles were cruising around the black residential area. Approximately 50 armed black people defended themselves in a black church near the edge of Greenwood as white men advanced on them. The attackers set fire to the church. As black people fled the burning building, they were shot. More fires were set. About 2,000 black residents managed to escape to a convention hall. Forty square blocks and more than 1,000 of Greenwood's homes, churches, schools, and businesses went up in flames. White men even used aircraft for reconnaissance and to drop incendiary devices on Greenwood. As many as 300 black people and 20 white people may have perished in what was one of the worst episodes of civilian violence in American history until September 11, 2001.

((• ▢ Read on MyHistoryLab Document: An NAACP Official Investigates the Tulsa Race Riot of 1921

This is the Greenwood neighborhood of Tulsa, Oklahoma, in flames during the riot in June 1921.

In 2001, a biracial commission recommended that the Oklahoma legislature offer restitution. The legislators declined to set aside funds for survivors, but they did appropriate $750,000 to formulate plans for a museum and memorial. They also created a Greenwood Redevelopment Authority and a scholarship program.

Rosewood, 1923

In January 1923, the small town of Rosewood, Florida, was destroyed, and its black residents were driven out or killed. Rosewood was a mostly black community—it had a few white inhabitants—in the pinewoods of west-central Florida not far from the Gulf of Mexico. On New Year's Day, Fannie Taylor, a married white woman from a nearby town, claimed a black man had raped and beaten her. White people assumed Jessie Hunter was responsible. Other white people believed Mrs. Taylor wanted to divert attention away from herself because she had a white lover who was not her husband.

White men sought Hunter and vengeance. Unable to find him, they beat Aaron Carrier, who may have helped Taylor's white lover escape. The mob killed Samuel Carter after mutilating him. Tensions escalated.

On January 4 an angry mob invaded Rosewood, but the black people there were prepared to defend themselves. Led by Sylvester Carrier and his mother Sarah, many townspeople had congregated in the Carrier home. The mob fired on the residence, killing Sarah Carrier. Two white men who attempted to enter the home were killed. Shooting continued until the mob ran out of ammunition on January 5.

The next day a mob of 250, including Ku Klux Klan members from Gainesville, invaded, burned, and destroyed Rosewood. The community's black residents fled to the woods and swamps with little more than the clothes on their backs, never to return. Rosewood was no more.

The precise number of black people who died will never be known. It may have exceeded one hundred. In 1994 the Florida legislature appropriated $2.1 million to survivors of Rosewood and to families who lost property in the assault. Ten survivors were still alive and collected $150,000 each. But many black people could not verify that they had been in Rosewood in 1923 or that they were kin to people who had owned property there. As a result, much of the money was not disbursed.

The Great Migration

16-8 Why did African Americans begin to leave the rural South in the early twentieth century, and what kinds of lives were they able to make for themselves in urban communities?

The Great Migration of African Americans from the rural South to the urban North began as a trickle after the Civil War and became a flood by the second decade of the twentieth century (see Table 16–1). Between 1910 and 1940, 1.75 million black people left the South. As a result, the black population outside the South doubled by 1940. Most of the initial wave of migrants were younger people born in the 1880s and 1890s who had no recollection of slavery but anticipated a better future for themselves and their families in the North.

Why Migrate?

People moved for many reasons. Often they were both pushed from their rural homes and pulled toward urban areas. The push resulted from disasters in southern agriculture

16-1

16-2

16-3

16-4

16-5

16-6

16-7

16-8

TABLE 16-1 BLACK POPULATION GROWTH IN SELECTED NORTHERN CITIES, 1910–1920

	1910		1920		
	Number	**Percentage***	**Number**	**Percentage***	**Percentage Increase**
New York	91,709	1.9%	152,467	2.7%	66.3%
Chicago	44,103	2.0	109,458	4.1	148.2
Philadelphia	84,459	5.5	134,229	7.4	58.9
Detroit	5,741	1.2	40,838	4.1	611.3
St. Louis	43,960	6.4	69,854	9.0	58.9
Cleveland	8,448	1.5	34,451	4.3	307.8
Pittsburgh	25,623	4.8	37,725	6.4	47.2
Cincinnati	19,739	5.4	30,079	7.5	53.2
Indianapolis	21,816	9.3	34,678	11.0	59.0
Newark	9,475	2.7	16,977	4.1	79.2
Kansas City	23,566	9.5	30,719	9.5	30.4
Columbus	12,739	7.0	22,181	9.4	74.1
Gary	383	2.3	5,299	9.6	1,283.6
Youngstown	1,936	2.4	6,662	5.0	244.1
Buffalo	1,773	.4	4,511	.9	154.4
Toledo	1,877	1.1	5,691	2.3	203.2
Akron	657	1.0	5,580	2.7	749.3

*"Percentage" refers to percentage of city's population; "Percentage Increase" refers to growth of the black population.
SOURCE: U.S. Department of Commerce.

in the 1910s. The boll weevil destroyed cotton crops across the South, and floods devastated Mississippi and Alabama in 1915. The pull resulted from labor shortages created by World War I in northern industry and manufacturing. The war interrupted European immigration to the United States, eliminating a main source of cheap labor. At the same time, European governments and the United States placed huge orders for war material with northern factories. Thousands of jobs became available in steel mills, railroads, meatpacking plants, and the automobile industry. Northern businessmen sent labor agents to recruit southern workers.

Many southern white people reacted ambivalently to the loss of black residents. They welcomed the departure of people for whom they had contempt, but they also worried about the loss of tenants and sharecroppers. Southern states and municipalities required labor agents to obtain licenses to recruit workers. Angry white landowners and businessmen forced some of these agents to leave southern towns.

Black newspapers encouraged black southerners to move north. Black railroad porters and dining car employees distributed thousands of copies of the *Chicago Defender* throughout the South. One unnamed black man wrote in the *Defender* that sensible men would leave the poverty, injustice, and violence of the South for the cold weather of the North: "To die from the bite of frost is far more glorious than that of the mob. I beg of you, my brothers, to leave that benighted land. You are free men."

Black people who departed the South (see Table 16–2) escaped the most blatant forms of Jim Crow and the injustice in the judicial system. Black women fled the sexual exploitation of white and black men. Black people in the North could vote. The North also offered better public schools. In the early twentieth century the South had almost no public high schools for black youngsters, and the longer school year in the urban North was not tied to the demands of planting and harvesting crops.

Some black people migrated to escape the dull, bleak, impoverished life and culture of the rural South. The decision to migrate could take years of pondering and planning. To depart was to leave family, friends, and familiar surroundings behind for the uncertainty, confusion, and rapid pace of urban communities. Migrants often first moved to southern towns or cities and then headed for a larger city.

Most migrants maintained a fondness for their southern homes and kinfolk. They returned for holidays, weddings, and funerals. Thousands of black migrants routinely sent money home. Over the years, millions of dollars earned in the North flowed into southern communities.

Destinations

Although many black southerners went to Florida, most migrants from the Carolinas and Virginia settled in Washington, DC, Philadelphia, and New York (see Map 16–2). Black people who left Georgia, Alabama, and Mississippi tended to move to Pittsburgh, Cleveland, and Detroit. Migrants from Louisiana, Mississippi, and Arkansas often rode the Illinois Central Railroad to Chicago. Once they experienced a metropolis, many black people then resettled in smaller communities. Migrants to Philadelphia, for example, moved on to Harrisburg or Altoona, Pennsylvania, or to Wilmington, Delaware.

Few black southerners moved west to California, Oregon, or Washington. California had only 22,000 black residents in 1910. Substantial black migration west did not occur until the 1930s and 1940s. But in 1920 Mallie Robinson made the long trek west. Deserted by her husband, she set out with her five children (including one-year-old Jackie, who would become a baseball legend) and eight other relatives. They boarded a train in Cairo, Georgia; traveled to Los Angeles; and settled in nearby Pasadena. Mallie's half brother, who had already moved west, assured her she would be closer to heaven in California.

However, most black migrants found their destination was near neither heaven nor the Promised Land. Black people congregated in all-black neighborhoods that later would be called ghettoes. White owners resisted selling or renting property to black people outside of these neighborhoods. And many southern black migrants themselves, wary of white hostility, preferred to live among black people, often friends and family who had preceded them north.

Migration from the Caribbean

Many descendants of Africans who had been slaves in the sugarcane fields of the West Indies joined the migration of black southerners to the North. Between 1900 and 1924, 102,000 West Indians came to the United States. Most came from British colonies including Jamaica, Barbados, Montserrat, and Trinidad and Tobago. But black immigrants also arrived from French-held Guadeloupe and Martinique, the Dutch colonies of Aruba and Curacao, and the Danish Virgin Islands (which the United States acquired in 1917). Some of these migrants were middle-class professionals and skilled workers, but many had been employed as laborers building the Panama Canal from 1904 to 1914.

Although white Americans tended to lump all people of color together, regardless of their complexion or origin, the West Indians often did not mix comfortably with African Americans. Some spoke Dutch and French. Those who came from British islands were usually Anglicans (Episcopalians) and not Baptists or Methodists. Almost all of the newcomers sent money home to families in the West Indies. Moreover, many of the Caribbean arrivals were temporary residents; as many as one-third of them would return to the West

TABLE 16–2 AFRICAN-AMERICAN MIGRATION FROM THE SOUTH	
1910s	550,000
1920s	903,000
1930s	480,000
1940s	1,600,000
1950s	1,400,000
1960s	1,000,000
Total	**5,933,000**

SOURCE: *Adapted from Isabel Wilkerson,* The Warmth of Other Suns: The Epic Story of America's Great Migration. *New York: Random House, Vintage Books, 2010, pp. 161, 217, 218.*

Read on **MyHistoryLab**
Document: Letters from the Great Migration, 1917

16-1

16-2

16-3

16-4

16-5

16-6

16-7

16-8

16-1
16-2
16-3
16-4
16-5
16-6
16-7
16-8

MAP 16–2 THE GREAT MIGRATION AND THE DISTRIBUTION OF THE AFRICAN-AMERICAN POPULATION IN 1920
Although several hundred thousand black southerners migrated north during the second and third decades of the twentieth century in the largest internal migration in American history, most African Americans remained in the southern states.

Why did most African Americans stay in the South if so many opportunities beckoned in the North?

Indies. In 1924 Congress restricted immigration to the United States, and migration from the Caribbean dropped drastically.

Northern Communities

Even before the Civil War, most northern cities had small free black populations. By the late nineteenth century, southern migrants began to gravitate to these urban areas and make their presence felt. Black residents established churches, social organizations, businesses, and medical facilities. They gained representation in community and political affairs.

There was less overt segregation in the North. Most northern states and California prohibited racial discrimination in public transportation, hotels, restaurants, theaters, and barbershops. Most of these states also forbade segregated schools. However, enacting such laws and enforcing them were two different matters. Many white businesses and communities

VOICES   A Migrant to the North Writes Home

People who migrated to northern communities often wrote home to describe their new surroundings and experiences and to confess they missed their old homes. One unidentified black man who had moved to Philadelphia made his feelings known to a medical doctor.

Oct. 7, 1919

Philadelphia, Pa.,

Dear Sir:

I take this method of thanking you for yours early responding and the glorious effect of the treatment. Oh. I do feel so fine. Dr. the treatment reach me almost ready to move I am now housekeeping again I like it so much better than rooming. Well Dr. with the aid of God I am making very good I make $75 per month. I am carrying enough insurance to pay me $20 per week if I am not able to be on duty. I don't have to work hard. dont have to mister every little white boy comes along I havent heard a white man call a colored nigger you no now—since I been in the state of Pa. I can ride in the electric street and steam cars any where I get a seat. I dont care to mix with white what I mean

I am not crazy about being with white folks, but if I have to pay the same fare I have learn to want the same accomidation. and if you are the first in a place here shoping you dont have to wait until the white folks get thro tradeing yet amid all this I shall ever love the good old South and I am praying that God may give every well wisher a chance to be a man regardless of his color, and if my going to the front [World War I] would bring about such conditions I am ready any day—well Dr. I dont want to worry you but read between the lines; and maybe you can see a little sense in my weak statement the kids are in school every day I have only two and I guess that all. Dr. when you find time I would be delighted to have word from the good old home state. Wife join me in sending love you and yours.

1. **What is the writer's main reason for having migrated?**
2. **What was more important to this man, better living standards or the sense of liberation he enjoyed in Philadelphia?**

SOURCE: Emmett J. Scott, ed., "Letters of Negro Migrants of 1916–1918," *Journal of Negro History* 4 (July 1, 1919), in Fishel and Quarles, *The Negro American: A Documentary History*, 398–99.

16-1
16-2
16-3
16-4
16-5
16-6
16-7
16-8

---

ignored the statutes and embraced Jim Crow, especially along the Ohio River in southern Ohio, Indiana, and Illinois.

CHICAGO

As early as 1872, Chicago had a black policeman, and in 1876 John W. E. Thomas became the first black man elected to the Illinois Senate. Black physician Daniel Hale Williams established African-American–staffed Provident Hospital on Chicago's South Side in 1891. By 1900 black Chicagoans were the twelfth largest ethnic group in the city, behind such European immigrant groups as the Irish, Poles, and Germans.

Chicago's black population surged from 1900 to 1930 as migrants poured into the city. Black institutions flourished. In 1912 an NAACP branch was established. By 1920 black Chicago had 80 Baptist and 36 Methodist churches. The Olivet Baptist Church grew from 3,500 members in 1916 to 9,000 by 1922. Because the downtown YMCA barred black men, black people raised $50,000 and Julius Rosenwald of Sears, Roebuck and Company contributed $25,000 to build the Wabash YMCA for the black community in 1913. However, many black Chicagoans considered this a surrender to segregation and insisted that they should be admitted to the white YMCA.

The *Chicago Defender* was the city's leading black newspaper. Its founder, Robert S. Abbott, the son of slaves, began publishing the *Defender* in 1905, and by 1920 it had a nationwide circulation of 230,000. Chicago's first black bank, Jesse Binga's State Bank, was established in 1908, and in 1919 Frank L. Gillespie organized the Liberty Insurance Company.

In 1915 black Chicago's political influence expanded when Oscar DePriest was elected second-ward alderman. Two other black men were elected to the city council by 1918. DePriest was then elected to the U.S. House of Representatives as a Republican in 1928, becoming the first black congressman since North Carolina's George White left the House in 1901.

As the number of black Chicagoans swelled, racial tensions exploded in the 1919 race riot. Competition for jobs was a critical issue. White employers, such as the meatpacking companies, regularly replaced white strikers with black workers. Black men took such jobs because most labor unions would not admit them. But a few weeks before the riot in 1919, the Amalgamated Meatcutters Union tried to sponsor a unity parade of black and white stockyard workers. The police prohibited it because, some observers believed, the meatpacking companies feared that black and white working men might unite.

Housing was an even more divisive issue than employment. Chicago's black population was almost entirely confined to an eight-square-mile area on the South Side east of State Street. Prosperous black people who could afford more expensive housing outside the area could not purchase it because of their race. As the black population grew, housing became more congested, and crime and vice increased.

HARLEM

Harlem was a white community in upper Manhattan that had declined by the latter 1800s. It then enjoyed a building boom that occurred in anticipation of the construction of the subway that would link upper Manhattan to downtown New York City by the early twentieth century. But real estate speculators overbuilt and were left with empty houses and apartments. Facing foreclosure, many white property owners sold or rented to black people in Harlem.

As thousands of black people moved to Harlem, many left the "Tenderloin" and "San Juan Hill" areas of Manhattan's West Side, where New York's black residents had lived in the nineteenth century. The construction of Pennsylvania Station forced many to vacate the "Tenderloin." Black churches took the lead in the "On to Harlem" movement as they occupied churches white denominations had formerly used. Some black churches were among the largest property owners in Harlem.

St. Philip's Protestant Episcopal Church, the wealthiest black church in the United States—and noted for its solemn services and elite parishioners—moved in 1910 from West 25th Street in the "Tenderloin" to Harlem. In 1911 St. Philip's purchased 10 apartment houses on West 135th Street between Lennox and Seventh Avenues for $640,000. The Rev. Adam Clayton Powell Sr. and the Abyssinian Baptist Church, St. Mark's Episcopal Church, and the African Methodist Episcopal Zion Church ("Mother Zion") also moved to Harlem and acquired extensive real estate holdings there. The black churches helped make Harlem a black community.

As Harlem's black population increased, large houses and apartments were often subdivided among working families that could not rent or buy in other areas of New York. They paid higher prices for real estate than white people did. The average Harlem family paid $9.50 a room per month. White working families paid $6.50 for similar accommodations elsewhere in New York.

By 1920, 75,000 black people lived in Harlem. Harlem became the "Negro Capital of the World." Black businesses and institutions, including the Odd Fellows, Masons, Elks, Pythians, the NAACP, the Urban League, and the YMCA and YWCA, moved to Harlem. Black newspapers—the *New York News* and *Amsterdam News*—opened in Harlem to compete with the older *New York Age*. One resident exclaimed, "If my race can make Harlem, good lord, what can't it do?"

FAMILIES

Migration placed black families under enormous strains. Relatives frequently moved north separately. Fathers or mothers would leave a spouse and children behind as they sought employment and housing. Children might be left with grandparents. Extended family members—cousins, in-laws, brothers, and sisters—crowded into limited living space.

Men generally found more opportunities for work in northern industries than women did. Unskilled labor during and after World War I was in huge demand. In 1915 Henry Ford astounded industrial America when he began to pay employees of the Ford Motor Company in Detroit the unprecedented sum of $5 per day, and that included black men and occasionally black women. Rarely, however, was a black man promoted beyond menial labor. Except for some opportunities in manufacturing during the war, black women were confined to domestic and janitorial work. Black women employed as domestics lived with white families, worked long hours, and saw more of their white employer's children than they did their own.

Some vulnerable younger women were lured into prostitution in the intimidating urban environment. Black women's organizations worked to prevent newly arrived migrants from being sexually exploited. They did not always succeed. Some women made a calculated decision to turn sex to their economic advantage. Sara Brooks caustically commented, "Some women woulda had a man to come and live in the house and had an outside boyfriend too, in order to get the house paid for and the bills. They meet a man and if he promises 'em four or five dollars to go to bed, they's grab it. That's called sellin' your own body, and I wasn't raised like that."

Despite the stresses and pressures, most black families survived intact. Most northern black families, although hardly well to do, were two-parent households. Women headed comparatively few families. Fathers were present in 7 of 10 black families in New York City in 1925. But the Great Migration transformed southern peasants into an urban proletariat.

CONCLUSION

In 1900 Booker T. Washington was the nation's most influential black leader. He soothed white people and reassured black Americans as he counseled conciliation, patience, and agricultural and mechanical training as the most effective means to bridge the racial divide. His 1895 speech at the Cotton States Exposition in Atlanta elicited praise from both white and black listeners.

Washington had little appreciation for criticism and did not hesitate to attack his opponents, including William Monroe Trotter and W. E. B. Du Bois. He worked to subvert the Niagara Movement and the NAACP. But support for Washington and his conservative strategy diminished as the NAACP openly confronted racial discrimination. Washington died in 1915. By 1920 the NAACP took the lead in the struggle for civil rights as it fought in the courts and legislatures.

16-1
16-2
16-3
16-4
16-5
16-6
16-7
16-8

The Talented Tenth of black Americans, distinguished by their educational and economic resources, promoted "self-help" through a variety of organizations—from women's groups to fraternities and sororities—to enhance their own status and help less affluent black people.

As black men served in World War I and as thousands of black southerners migrated north, many white Americans became alarmed that African Americans were not as content with their subordinate and isolated status as Booker T. Washington had suggested they were. Some white Americans responded with violence in race riots as they attempted to prevent black Americans from assuming a more equitable role in American society. By 1920, despite white opposition, black Americans had demonstrated they would not accept economic subservience and the denial of their rights.

CHAPTER TIMELINE

AFRICAN-AMERICAN EVENTS	NATIONAL EVENTS

1895–1900

1895 Frederick Douglass dies; Booker T. Washington delivers Cotton States Exposition address	**1896** William McKinley is elected president
1896 *Plessy v. Ferguson*	**1898** Spanish-American War
1898 Riot erupts in Wilmington, North Carolina	**1899** Philippine insurrection begins
1900 New Orleans riot	**1900** President McKinley reelected

1900–1905

1903 W. E. B. Du Bois publishes *The Souls of Black Folk*	**1901** McKinley is assassinated; Theodore Roosevelt becomes president
	1904 Theodore Roosevelt elected president

1905–1910

1905 Niagara Movement founded at Niagara Falls, Canada; the *Defender* founded in Chicago	**1905** Thomas Dixon publishes *The Clansman;* the film *Birth of a Nation* is based on the novel
1906 Brownsville affair; Atlanta riot	**1908** William Howard Taft elected president
1908 Springfield riot	
1909 NAACP is founded	

CHAPTER TIMELINE

AFRICAN-AMERICAN EVENTS

NATIONAL EVENTS

1910–1915

1910
Urban League founded in New York City

1912
Du Bois endorses Woodrow Wilson for president

1912
Woodrow Wilson elected president

1914
World War I breaks out in Europe

1915–1923

1915
Guinn v. United States overturns the Oklahoma grandfather clause; Booker T. Washington dies

1917
East St. Louis riot; Houston riot

1919
Chicago riot; Elaine, Arkansas riot

1920
Harlem becomes "The Negro Capital of the World"

1921
Tulsa riot occurs

1923
Rosewood destroyed

1916
President Wilson reelected

1917
United States enters World War I

1918
World War I ends

1919
Treaty of Versailles

1920
Nineteenth Amendment (women's suffrage) ratified; Warren Harding elected president

On MyHistoryLab

 Study and Review on MyHistoryLab

REVIEW QUESTIONS

1. How did the strategies promoted by Booker T. Washington differ from those of W. E. B. Du Bois and the NAACP? Which were more effective?

2. Assess Washington's contributions to the advancement of black people.

3. How did middle-class and prosperous black people try to contribute to progress for their race? Were their efforts effective?

4. Why did most African Americans support U.S. participation in World War I? Was that support justified?

5. What factors contributed to race riots and violence in the World War I era?

6. Why did many black people leave the South in the 1920s? Why didn't this migration begin earlier or later?

7. Why did migrants decide to leave or to stay?

17

African Americans and the 1920s 1918–1929

LEARNING OBJECTIVES

17-1 Why was there an increase in intolerance in the 1920s?

17-2 How did the Ku Klux Klan become so influential in the 1920s?

17-3 How did major black organizations confront racial discrimination and promote progress in the 1920s?

17-4 Why did some black men and women who worked as Pullman Porters form a labor union, and what role did A. Philip Randolph play in those efforts to organize these workers?

17-5 Who were some of the men and women involved in the cultural phenomenon known as the Harlem Renaissance, and what were some of their literary, artistic, dramatic, and musical contributions to that movement?

17-6 What was the role of Harlem and its inhabitants in what popularly came to be known as the Jazz Age?

17-7 What opportunities and obstacles confronted black athletes in the 1920s?

Many Americans had difficulty adjusting to life after World War I. The Allied victory brought little long-term satisfaction or security. The Bolshevik Revolution in Russia in 1917 and labor agitation at home increased anxiety and heightened fears of radicals. Racial and ethnic intolerance escalated as thousands of rural black southerners continued to stream into northern cities, and more than 800,000 immigrants, mostly from Europe, arrived in America in 1920 and 1921.

Americans shunned Europe and its problems and closed their eyes to the imperfections of American society. Enthusiasm for progressive reforms faded as many Americans concluded that government efforts to mitigate poverty, control vice, improve working conditions, and regulate big business had been excessive. Middle-class Americans became preoccupied with making money and acquiring material possessions. They were drawn to newly available technological devices—automobiles, radios, and home appliances—that would revolutionize daily living in the twentieth century. Middle-class black consumers also bought these products, but most African Americans in the 1920s were too poor to afford them.

The fight to stop lynchings was one of the NAACP's most important campaigns in the early twentieth century. In the 1920s the NAACP fought unsuccessfully to secure anti-lynching legislation in Congress. To keep the issue in the public arena, the NAACP persisted with demonstrations and protests like this one at the Crime Conference in Washington, DC.

Many native white Americans, convinced that black people and immigrants threatened their Anglo-Saxon ethnic purity, ever more fervently embraced social Darwinism. Many sought reassurance in organizations that stressed religious, racial, and national pride. Millions of white Americans joined the revived Ku Klux Klan in the 1920s as it promoted white supremacy, American patriotism, and Protestant values.

((· Listen on MyHistoryLab Audio: *I, Too*, reading by Langston Hughes

Led by the NAACP, African Americans denounced injustice and pressed for inclusion in society, the enforcement of civil rights, and economic opportunities. Black workers—notably the members of the **Brotherhood of Sleeping Car Porters**—organized and demanded recognition and improved working conditions, hours, and wages. But the 1920s also saw hundreds of thousands of African Americans enthusiastically support Marcus Garvey and the **Universal Negro Improvement Association (UNIA)**. Garvey celebrated black nationalism and urged his followers to forsake white America, take pride in themselves, and look to Africa. In addition, the 1920s saw black culture blossom and flourish as the artists, writers, musicians, and entertainers of the Harlem Renaissance celebrated black life and society.

Brotherhood of Sleeping Car Porters (BSCP) Black men and women who worked on Pullman passenger coaches on the nation's railroads organized this labor union in 1925 with A. Philip Randolph as its leader.

17-1

17-2

In 1919 and 1920, Americans were bewildered and angered by labor unrest and afraid the communists (or "Reds") in the new Soviet Union would try to incite a revolution in America. There were 3,600 strikes in 1919 as workers who during the war had deferred demands for pay raises and improved working conditions walked off their jobs. Many worried that labor agitation was a prelude to revolution.

Universal Negro Improvement Association (UNIA) Established in 1914 in Jamaica by Marcus Garvey, it fostered racial pride, African heritage, Christian faith, and economic uplift.

17-3

17-4

Political leaders exacerbated these feelings by warning that communists and foreign agents were plotting to overthrow the government. Woodrow Wilson's attorney general, A. Mitchell Palmer, grimly warned Americans of the Red menace and the threat that aliens posed. He ordered 249 aliens deported and some 6,000 arrested and imprisoned, in gross violation of their rights, but it was an action that many Americans approved. Palmer went too far, however, when he predicted the Red revolution would begin in the United States on May 1, 1920. There was no revolution, and confidence in Palmer waned. There were, however, several terrorist bombings, including one on Wall Street in September 1920 that killed 33 people. Moreover, evidence indicates that some business leaders supported the Palmer raids to discourage workers from forming and joining labor unions and participating in strikes. Prompted in part by the **Red Scare**, xenophobia (fear of foreigners) swept the nation in the 1920s.

17-5

17-6

17-7

Varieties of Racism

17-1 Why was there an increase in intolerance in the 1920s?

The entrenched racism of American society found expression in more than one form in the 1920s. There was the sophisticated racism associated with supposedly scholarly studies that

Red Scare The widespread fear among many Americans in the years immediately after World War I, from about 1918 to about 1924, that Russia's 1917 Bolshevik Revolution might result in communists attempting to take over the U.S. government.

reflected the ideology of social Darwinism. There was also the raw bigotry that manifested itself in popular culture and the ideology of the increasingly popular Ku Klux Klan.

Scientific Racism

Many white Americans believed the United States was under siege as European immigrants and black migrants flooded American cities. Pseudoscholars warned about the peril these "inferior" peoples posed. In 1916 Madison Grant published *The Passing of the Great Race*. Grant warned that America was committing "race suicide" because northern Europeans and their descendants—the "Great Race"—were being diluted by inferior people from eastern and southern Europe. Lothrop Stoddard's *The Rising Tide of Color* in 1920 argued that people of color would never be equal to white Americans. In Stoddard's view, there was direct connection between the maintenance of white supremacy and the survival of America as a great nation.

These racist claims were cloaked in the trappings of legitimate scholarship, and they strengthened the cause of white supremacy in the 1920s and helped to "protect" America from the "threat" of immigration. In 1921 and in 1924, Congress severely restricted immigration from southern and eastern Europe, Latin America, and the Caribbean and prohibited it entirely from Asia.

The Birth of a Nation

In 1915 D. W. Griffith released *The Birth of a Nation*, a cinematic masterpiece and historical travesty based on Thomas Dixon's 1905 novel *The Clansman*. Both the book and the film purported to depict Reconstruction in South Carolina. In this epic, immoral and ignorant Negroes joined by shady mulattoes and greedy white Republicans ruthlessly seize control of state government until the heroic and honorable Ku Klux Klan saves the state and rescues its white womanhood. The film was enormously popular. President Wilson had it screened in the White House.

The NAACP was enraged by *The Birth of a Nation* and fought to halt its presentation. The film unleashed racist violence. After seeing it in Lafayette, Indiana, an infuriated white man killed a young black man. In Houston, white theatergoers shouted, "Lynch him!" during a scene in which a white actor in blackface pursued the film's star, Lillian Gish. In front of a St. Louis theater, white real estate agents passed out circulars calling for residential segregation.

Thanks largely to NAACP opposition, the film was banned in Pasadena, California; Wilmington, Delaware; and Boston. With an election looming in Chicago, Republican Mayor "Big Bill" Thompson appointed American Methodist Episcopal Bishop Archibald Carey to the board of censors, which temporarily banned the film there. Ironically, the NAACP campaign may have provided publicity that attracted more viewers to the film. However, the campaign also helped increase NAACP membership.

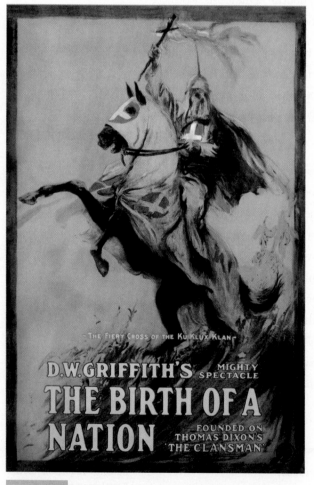

The glorification of the Ku Klux Klan in D. W. Griffith's *The Birth of a Nation,* reflected in this publicity poster, outraged African Americans. The NAACP protested when the silent film was first distributed in 1915 and again when a sound version was released in 1930. The demonstrations attracted publicity to both the film and the NAACP.

The Ku Klux Klan

17-2   How did the Ku Klux Klan become so influential in the 1920s?

The Ku Klux Klan, which had disappeared after Reconstruction, was resurrected a few months after *The Birth of a Nation* was released. On Thanksgiving night in 1915, William J. Simmons and 34 other men gathered at Stone Mountain near Atlanta; in the flickering shadows of a fiery cross, they brought the Klan back to life.

The Ku Klux Klan in the 1920s stood for white supremacy—and more. Klansmen styled themselves as "100 percent Americans" who opposed perceived threats from immigrants as well as black Americans. The Klan claimed to represent white, Anglo-Saxon, Protestant America.

The Klan found enormous support among apprehensive white middle-class Americans in the North and West. Many of them believed the liberal, immoral, and loose lifestyles they associated with urban life, immigrants, and African Americans threatened their religious beliefs and conservative values. The Klan attacked the theory of evolution, fought for the prohibition of alcoholic beverages, and claimed to uphold the "sanctity" of white womanhood. The Ku Klux Klan opposed Jews, Roman Catholics, and black people. Klansmen often used violence. They burned synagogues and Catholic churches. They beat, branded, and lynched opponents.

By 1925 the Klan had an estimated five million members. The Klan attracted small businessmen, shopkeepers, clerks, Protestant clergymen, farmers, and professional people. It was open only to native-born white men, but it also had a Women's Order, a Junior Order for boys, and a Tri K Klub for girls. The Klan was active in Oregon, Colorado, Illinois, and Maine, and it became a potent political force in Indiana, Oklahoma, and Texas, where candidates for office who refused to support or join the Klan stood little chance of election.

The Klan was also a moneymaking machine. Its leaders collected millions of dollars in initiation fees, membership dues, and sales of Klan paraphernalia. But the Klan declined rapidly in the late 1920s when its leaders fought among themselves. Its claim to uphold the purity of white womanhood was damaged when one of its leaders, D. C. Stephenson, was charged in Indiana with raping a young woman who subsequently committed suicide. Stephenson was sentenced to life in prison, and the Klan never fully recovered.

Read on MyHistoryLab
Document: Hiram Evans Links the Klan to Americanism, 1926

17-1

17-2

17-3

17-4

17-5

17-6

17-7

Protest, Pride, and Pan-Africanism: Black Organizations in the 1920s

17-3   How did major black organizations confront racial discrimination and promote progress in the 1920s?

African Americans responded to racism and to cultural and economic developments in the 1920s in several ways. The NAACP continued its efforts to secure constitutional rights and guarantees by advocacy in the political and judicial systems. Many working-class black people who had migrated to northern cities were attracted to the racial pride that Marcus Garvey and the UNIA promoted. There were also attempts to foster racial cooperation among peoples of African descent and to exert diplomatic influence through the

Listen on **MyHistoryLab Audio:** The Creation: A Negro Sermon

17-1

17-2

17-3

17-4

17-5

17-6

17-7

work of Pan-African Congresses that were held during the first three decades of the twentieth century.

The NAACP

During its second decade, the NAACP expanded its influence and increased its membership. In 1916 James Weldon Johnson joined the NAACP as field secretary. He played a pivotal role in the organization's development and in its growth from 9,000 members in 1916 to 90,000 in 1920. Johnson traveled tirelessly, recruiting members and establishing branches.

Johnson impressed both black and white people. Johnson was an excellent diplomat who could negotiate and compromise, but he could also be blunt when necessary. He methodically reported the gruesome details of lynchings, and when some NAACP directors complained in 1921 that these graphic descriptions offended people, Johnson stood his ground: "What we need to do is to root out the thing which makes possible these horrible details. I am of the opinion that this can be done only through the fullest publicity."

Johnson and the NAACP fought hard in Congress to secure passage of the Dyer anti-lynching bill in 1921 and 1922 (see Chapter 16). The legislation ultimately failed, but the NAACP publicized the persistence of barbaric mob behavior in a nation supposedly devoted to fairness and the rule of law.

Johnson blamed the Dyer bill's failure on Republican senators. He charged that the Republican Party took black support for granted because southern Democrats remained committed to white supremacy, and therefore black people had little choice but to vote Republican: "The Republican Party will hold the Negro and do as little for him as possible, and the Democratic Party will have none of him at all." He warned, however, that black voters in the North would abandon the Republicans if this pattern persisted. Johnson pointed out that black voters in Harlem had elected a black Democrat to the state legislature.

The NAACP continued to rely on the judicial system to protect black Americans and enforce their civil rights. By the 1920s the Democratic Party in virtually every southern state barred black people from membership, which excluded them from voting in Democratic primaries. The result was what was known as "white primaries." Because the Republican Party had almost disappeared in most of the South, victory in the Democratic primary led invariably to victory in the general election. In 1924 the NAACP, in cooperation with its El Paso branch, filed suit over the exclusion of black voters from the Democratic primary in Texas. In 1927 the Supreme Court ruled in *Nixon v. Herndon* that the Democratic primary was unconstitutional—the first victory in what would become a 20-year legal struggle to permit black men and women to vote in primary elections across the South.

In Detroit in 1925, black physician Ossian Sweet and his family moved into an all-white neighborhood. For several nights a mob threatened the Sweet family and other people who defended them. One evening, shots fired from the Sweet home killed a white man. As a result, 12 occupants of the house were charged with murder. The NAACP retained Clarence

VOICES The Negro National Anthem: "Lift Every Voice and Sing"

In 1900, to celebrate Abraham Lincoln's birthday, James Weldon Johnson wrote "Lift Every Voice and Sing." His younger brother John Rosamond Johnson composed music to accompany the words. It was published in 1921 and soon thereafter—with the encouragement of the NAACP—the song was embraced as the Negro national anthem.

Lift every voice and sing, 'til earth and
heaven ring,
Ring with the harmonies of liberty
Let our rejoicing rise, high as the list'ning skies,
Let it resound loud as the rolling sea.
Sing a song full of the faith that the dark past
has taught us,
Sing a song full of the hope that the present has
brought us;
Facing the rising sun of our new day begun
Let us march on till victory is won.

Stony the road we trod, bitter the chast'ning rod
Felt in the days when hope unborn had died
Yet with a steady beat, have not our weary feet
Come to the place for which our fathers sighed?
We have come over a way that with tears has
been watered,
We have come, treading our path thro' the blood
of the slaughtered

Out from the gloomy past, 'til now we stand
at last
Where the white gleam of our bright star is cast.

God of our weary years, God of our silent tears
Thou who has brought us thus far on the way
Thou who hast by Thy might, led us into
the light
Keep us forever in the path, we pray.
Lest our feet stray from the places, our God,
where we met Thee
Lest our hearts, drunk with the wine of the
world, we forget Thee
Shadowed beneath Thy hand, may we forever
stand
True to our God, true to our native land.

1. To what native land does Johnson refer in the last line: "True to our God, true to our native land"?
2. Do the lyrics apply to all Americans or only to African Americans? Would the song be appropriate as the American national anthem? Why or why not?

SOURCE: James Weldon Johnson wrote "Lift Every Voice and Sing." His younger brother John Rosamond Johnson composed music to accompany the words.

Darrow and Arthur Garfield Hayes, two of the nation's finest criminal attorneys, to defend the Sweets. The Sweets pleaded self-defense and after two trials were acquitted.

"Up You Mighty Race": Marcus Garvey and the UNIA

With several million enthusiastic followers, Marcus Garvey's UNIA became the largest mass movement of black people in American history. The UNIA enabled black people to celebrate one another and their heritage and to anticipate a glorious future. Garvey was an energetic, charismatic, and flamboyant leader who wove racial pride, Christian faith, and economic cooperation into a black nationalist organization that by the early 1920s had spread throughout the United States.

Garvey was born in 1887 in the British colony of Jamaica. He quit school at age 14 and became a printer in Kingston, the island's capital. He was promoted to foreman before he was fired during a strike in 1907. He traveled to Costa Rica, Panama, Ecuador, and Nicaragua and became disturbed over the conditions black workers endured in fields, factories, and mines. He returned to Jamaica and set out to educate himself. He spent two years in London, where he sharpened his oratorical and debating skills discussing the plight of black people with Africans and people from the Caribbean.

He returned to Jamaica and founded the UNIA in 1914. With the slogan "One God! One Aim! One Destiny!" he stressed the need for black people to organize for their own advancement. Garvey had read Booker T. Washington's *Up From Slavery* and was much impressed with Washington's emphasis on self-help and progress through education and the acquisition of skills.

Garvey came to the United States in 1916 just as thousands of African Americans were migrating to cities. A dynamic speaker whose message resonated among the disaffected urban working class, Garvey built the UNIA into a major movement. He urged his listeners to take pride in themselves as they restored their race to its previous greatness: "We must canonize our own saints, create our own martyrs, and elevate to positions of fame and honor black men and women who have made their distinct contributions to our racial history." He reminded people that Africa had a remarkable past and insisted that his followers change their thinking: "We have outgrown slavery, but our minds are still enslaved to the thinking of the Master Race. Now take these kinks out of your mind, instead of out of your hair."

With the formation of the New York division of the UNIA in Harlem in 1917, Garvey exhorted, "Up you mighty race!" as he commanded black people to take control of their destiny. Still, he blamed them for their predicament: "That the Negro race became a race of slaves was not the fault of God Almighty . . . it was the fault of the race." Their salvation would result from their own exertion and not from concessions by white people.

Garvey's message and the UNIA spread to black communities large and small. He regularly couched his rhetoric in religious terms, and he came to be known as the Black Moses, a messiah.

Garvey and the UNIA also established businesses that employed nearly 1,000 black people. The weekly newspaper, *Negro World,* promoted Garvey's ideology. In New York City, the Negro Factories Corporation operated three grocery stores, two restaurants, a printing plant, a steam laundry, and a factory that turned out clothes for UNIA members. The association also owned property in other cities. Garvey proudly declared to white Americans that the UNIA "employs thousands of black girls and black boys. Girls who could only be washer women in your homes, we made clerks, stenographers. . . . You will see from the start we tried to dignify our race."

Although Garvey and the UNIA are most frequently associated with urban communities in the North, the UNIA also spread rapidly through the rural South in the 1920s. Black farmers and sharecroppers established UNIA chapters from Virginia to Louisiana, and the Garvey movement and the *Negro World* could be found in such remote communities as Kinston, North Carolina; Ty Ty, Georgia; and Cotton Plant, Arkansas.

Read on **MyHistoryLab**
Document: Marcus Garvey Calls for Black Separatism, 1921

17-1
17-2
17-3
17-4
17-5
17-6
17-7

Jamaican-born Marcus Garvey arrived in the United States in 1916 and quickly rose to prominence as the head of the UNIA. Garvey appears here in a 1924 parade in Harlem attired in a uniform similar to those worn by British colonial governors in Jamaica, Trinidad, and elsewhere.

VOICES Marcus Garvey Appeals for a New African Nation

Marcus Garvey and the UNIA offered hope to African Americans in the 1920s. In the following words, Garvey passionately calls for African Americans and West Indians to support the creation of a new African nation:

For five years the Universal Negro Improvement Association has been advocating the cause of Africa for the Africans—that is, that the Negro peoples of the world should concentrate upon the object of building up for themselves a great nation in Africa. . . .

It is only a question of a few more years when Africa will be completely colonized by Negroes, as Europe is by the white race. What we want is an independent African nationality, and if America is to help the Negro peoples of the world establish such a nationality, then we welcome the assistance.

It is hoped that when the time comes for American and West Indian Negroes to settle in Africa, they will realize their responsibilities and duty. It will not be to go to Africa for the purpose of exercising an over-lordship over the natives, . . .

It will be useless, as stated before, for bombastic Negroes to leave America and the West Indies to go to Africa, thinking that they will have privileged positions to inflict upon the race that bastard aristocracy that they have tried to maintain in this Western world at the expense of the masses. Africa shall develop an aristocracy of its own, but it shall be based upon service and loyalty to race. Let all Negroes work toward that end. . . .

The time has really come for the Asiatics to govern themselves in Asia, as the Europeans are in Europe and the Western world, so also is it wise for the Africans to govern themselves at home, and thereby bring peace and satisfaction to the entire human family.

So Negroes, I say, through the Universal Negro Improvement Association, that there is much to live for. I have a vision of the future, and I see before me a picture of a redeemed Africa, with her dotted cities, with her beautiful civilization, with her millions of happy children going to and fro. Why should I lose hope, why should I give up and take a back place in this age of progress? . . .

Africa shall reflect a splendid demonstration of the worth of the Negro, of the determination of the Negro, to set himself free and to establish a government of his own.

1. Why does Garvey call for a black homeland in Africa? How realistic was this call in the 1920s for nationhood in Africa?
2. Who does Garvey believe should lead (or should not lead) the new African nation? What are the qualifications for such leadership?
3. What does Garvey think the globe will look like in the future? How will peoples of various colors coexist?

SOURCE: David Levering Lewis, ed., *The Portable Harlem Renaissance Reader* (New York: Viking Penguin, 1994), 17, 19, 20, 21, 25.

Garvey may be best remembered for his proposal to return black people to Africa on the Black Star Line, a steamship company he founded in 1919. Garvey sold stock in the company for $5 a share, and he hoped to establish a fleet with black officers and crews. Garvey bought three more ships, but he lacked the money to maintain them or transport anyone to Africa.

Moreover, Garvey knew it was unrealistic to expect several million black residents of the Western Hemisphere to join the back-to-Africa enterprise, but he did believe that the UNIA could liberate Africa from European colonial rule. The UNIA adopted a red, green, and black flag for the proposed African republic that represented the blood, land, and race of the African people.

The UNIA attempted to establish a settlement on the Cavalla River in southern Liberia. Garvey also petitioned the League of Nations to permit the UNIA to take over the former German colony of Tanganyika (today's Tanzania) in East Africa. But the major colonial powers in Africa—Britain and France—and the United States thwarted Garvey's plans, and the UNIA never gained a foothold on the continent.

The U.S. government and several black American leaders also worked diligently to undermine Garvey and the UNIA. J. Edgar Hoover and the Bureau of Investigation (the predecessor of the FBI) considered Garvey a threat to the racial status quo. Hoover employed black agents to infiltrate the UNIA and compile information that could be used to deport Garvey, who had never become an American citizen.

Garvey had few friends or admirers among African-American leaders because he and they differed fundamentally on strategy and goals. Garvey deplored efforts to gain legal and political rights within the American system. By appealing to the black masses, he rejected Du Bois's notion that the Talented Tenth would lead the race to liberation. He mocked the NAACP as the "National Association for the Advancement of Certain People." Unlike African-American leaders, Garvey believed black and white people had separate destinies, and he regarded interracial cooperation as absurd.

In 1922 Garvey and three other UNIA leaders were indicted on 12 counts of mail fraud in connection with the sale of stock in the Black Star Line. Eight African-American leaders wrote to the U.S. attorney general to insist on his prosecution. Although Garvey was guilty of no more than mismanagement and incompetence, he was found guilty and sent to prison in 1925. President Calvin Coolidge commuted his sentence in 1927, and he was then deported.

With the loss of its inspirational leader, the UNIA declined steadily in the late 1920s and the 1930s. UNIA businesses closed, and its property—including the *Yarmouth*—was sold. Garvey was never permitted to return to the United States, and he died in London in 1940. However, his legacy persisted. The Rev. Earl Little, a Baptist minister and the father of Malcolm X, belonged to the UNIA and admired Garvey. Malcolm X recalled his father's association with Garvey: "I remember hearing that he had black followers not only in the United States but all around the world, and I remember how the meetings always closed with my father saying, several times, and the people chanting after him, 'Up, you mighty race, you can accomplish what you will!'"

The African Blood Brotherhood

In 1919 black men who had migrated to New York City from the Caribbean formed the African Blood Brotherhood as a radical alternative to Marcus Garvey and the UNIA. Cyril Briggs, who had been born in St. Kitts-Nevis in 1888, was the founder. The brotherhood rejected Garvey's reliance on capitalism and his devotion to Christianity. The brotherhood supported Marxism and had ties to the Communist Party.

Edited by Briggs, the African Blood Brotherhood briefly published the *Crusader* in the early 1920s. Unlike the UNIA, the Brotherhood's rejection of private enterprise and mainstream religion prevented it from becoming a mass movement. It never had more than 3,000 supporters.

Pan-Africanism

While Garvey, Du Bois, and Briggs differed on the most appropriate strategy for advancing African Americans, they shared an abiding interest in Africa. Garvey, Du Bois,

Briggs, and other black leaders believed people of African descent from around the world should come together to share their heritage, discuss their ties to the continent, and explore ways to moderate—if not eliminate—colonial rule in Africa, a concept termed **Pan-Africanism**.

By 1914 Britain, France, Germany, Portugal, Belgium, Spain, and Italy had established colonies across almost all of Africa. Only Liberia and Ethiopia (then called Abyssinia) remained independent. Christian missionaries sought to convert Africans, and European companies exploited Africa's human and natural resources. As they gained control over the continent, the European powers confirmed their conviction that they represented a superior race and culture.

The first Pan-African Congress convened in London in 1900 and was organized principally by Henry Sylvester Williams, a lawyer from Trinidad. Du Bois chaired the Committee on the Address to the Nations of the World. He called for the creation of "a great central Negro state of the world." But Du Bois did not insist on the immediate withdrawal of the European powers from Africa. Instead, he offered a modest recommendation that would provide "as soon as practicable the rights of responsible self-government to the black colonies of Africa and the West Indies."

The second Pan-African Congress met in Paris for three days in February 1919 near Versailles, where the peace conference ending World War I was assembled. There were 58 delegates from 16 nations. Du Bois was among the 16 African Americans in attendance. (None of them had been to Africa.) Marcus Garvey did not attend. The delegates took seriously the Fourteen Points that President Wilson had proposed to create a new postwar world. They were especially interested in Wilson's fifth point, which called for the interests of colonial peoples to be given "equal weight" in the adjustment of colonial claims after the war. The congress recommended that the League of Nations assume authority over the former German colonies in Africa. The League later established mandates over those colonies but delegated authority to administer those mandates to Britain, France, and Belgium. Two more Pan-African Congresses met in Brussels and London in the 1920s but also failed to influence the policies of the colonial powers.

Pan-Africanism
A movement of people of African descent from sub-Saharan Africa in the early twentieth century that emphasized their identity, shared experiences, and the need to liberate Africa from its European colonizers.

Labor

17-4 Why did some black men and women who worked as Pullman Porters form a labor union, and what role did A. Philip Randolph play in those efforts to organize these workers?

The arrival of thousands of black migrants in American cities during and after World War I changed the composition of the industrial workforce and intensified pressure on labor unions to admit black members. By 1916, 12,000 of the nearly 50,000 workers in the Chicago stockyards were black people. In Detroit, black laborers made up nearly 14 percent of the workforce in the automobile industry. The Ford Motor Company employed 50 black people in 1916 and 2,500 by 1920.

Yet even with the Industrial Revolution and the Great Migration, more than two-thirds of black workers in 1920 were employed in agriculture and domestic service (see Figure 17–1). Less than 20 percent were engaged in manufacturing. Many black men and women remained confined to the rural South. Those who were part of industrial America disproportionately worked in the least desirable, lowest paying jobs. Still, work

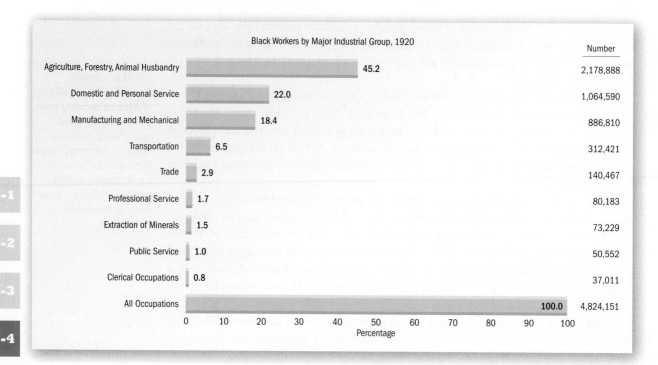

FIGURE 17–1 BLACK WORKERS BY MAJOR INDUSTRIAL GROUP, 1920
By 1920 thousands of African Americans had moved to northern cities and were employed in a variety of mostly unskilled and low-paying industrial jobs that nonetheless paid more than farm labor. Still, agriculture remained the largest single source of employment among black people, and agriculture and domestic service together employed more than two-thirds of African-American men and women. About 5 percent were employed in "white-collar" jobs.

SOURCE: Sterling D. Spero and Abram L. Harris, *The Black Worker: The Negro and the Labor Movement* (1928), 81.

in the factories, mills, and mines paid more than agriculture (Figure 17–2). But even those with skills were usually not admitted to the local craft unions that made up the American Federation of Labor (AFL).

By the World War I years, the NAACP and the Urban League regularly appealed to employers and unions to accept black laborers. The Urban League attempted to convince business owners that black employees would be efficient and reliable. But many employers preferred to divide black and white workers by hiring black men and women as strike-breakers, thereby enraging striking white workers. In 1918 Urban League officials met with Samuel Gompers, the longtime president of the AFL, and he agreed to bring more black people into the federation, but there were few tangible results. The Urban League did persuade the Department of Labor to establish a Division of Negro Economics to advise the secretary of labor on issues involving black workers.

The Brotherhood of Sleeping Car Porters

By the 1920s the Pullman Company, which owned and operated passenger railroad coaches, was the single largest employer of black people in the United States. More than 12,000 black men were porters on Pullman railroad cars.

Pullman porters toiled for upward of 400 hours each month to maintain the coaches and serve the passengers. Porters had to prepare the cars before the train's departure and

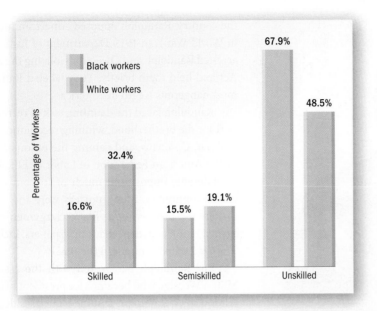

FIGURE 17-2 BLACK AND WHITE WORKERS BY SKILL LEVEL, 1920
Only one-third of black workers, compared to slightly more than one-half of
white workers, found employment in skilled or semiskilled jobs in 1920.

SOURCE: Sterling D. Spero and Abram L. Harris, *The Black Worker: The Negro and the Labor Movement* (1928), 85.

service them after the train arrived at its destination, although they were paid only for the
duration of the trip. They assisted passengers, shined shoes (they had to purchase the pol-
ish themselves), and arranged sleeping compartments. Considered mere servants by most
passengers, porters had little time for rest. To add to the indignity, white travelers invariably
referred to these black men as "George," no matter what their actual name was.

Although strenuous and time consuming, Pullman employment was the most satisfactory work many black men could hope to achieve. Barred from business and industry,
black men with college degrees often worked as sleeping car porters. As poorly paid as
they were compared with many white workers, they still earned more than most black
schoolteachers. Most of these Pullman employees regarded themselves as solid, respectable members of the middle class.

It seemed unlikely that men as subservient and unobtrusive as the Pullman porters
would form a labor union to challenge one of America's most powerful corporations. But
they did. The key figure in this effort was A. Philip Randolph. In 1925 Pullman porters in
Harlem invited Randolph to become their "general organizer" as they formed the Brotherhood of Sleeping Car Porters (BSCP). Randolph accepted.

A. Philip Randolph

Randolph was a socialist with superb oratorical skills who had earned a reputation as a
radical on the streets of Harlem. He was born in 1889 in Crescent City, Florida. He attended high school at Cookman Institute (later Bethune-Cookman College) and migrated
in 1911 to New York City, where he attended City College and joined the Socialist Party.
With Chandler Owen, he founded the *Messenger*, a monthly socialist journal that drew the
attention of federal agents because they regarded it as the only radical Negro magazine in

In this painting by Betsy G. Reyneau, A. Philip Randolph hardly resembles the militant agitator, activist, and labor leader that he was. He became the head of the BSCP, and he eventually rose to power in the AFL. He planned the first March on Washington in 1941 and was responsible for organizing the 1963 March on Washington.

Betsy G. Reyneau, A. Philip Randolph. National Archives.

 Watch on MyHistoryLab Video: The Harlem Renaissance

Harlem Renaissance A large neighborhood in the northern portion of Manhattan Island, which by the 1920s became a center of African-American cultural activities including literature, art, and music.

the country. Randolph opposed American involvement in World War I. In 1919 Department of Justice officials arrested Randolph and Owen for violating the Espionage Act and held them briefly. They labeled Randolph the most dangerous Negro in America.

Randolph faced the daunting task of recruiting support for the brotherhood, winning recognition from the Pullman Company, and gaining the union's acceptance by the American Federation of Labor (AFL). There was considerable opposition, much of it from within the black community. Many porters were too frightened to join the brotherhood. Black clergymen counseled against union activities. Black newspapers, including the *Chicago Defender,* opposed the BSCP.

But Randolph persevered with the assistance of Milton Webster, who became vice president of the brotherhood after Randolph assumed the presidency. With the slogan "Service not servitude," the two men recruited members, organized the brotherhood, and attempted to negotiate with the Pullman Company. Pullman executives ignored Randolph's overtures. They instead fired porters who joined the union, infiltrated union meetings with company agents, and organized the Employees' Representation Plan—an alternative company union that they claimed actually represented the black employees.

Although the NAACP and the Urban League supported the BSCP, progress was slow. In 1928 Randolph threatened to call a strike against the Pullman Company, but he called it off after AFL president William Green promised modest assistance to the as-yet-unrecognized union. Green's offer simply saved face for Randolph. It is unlikely that a strike would have succeeded or that most porters would have followed Randolph's leadership and left the trains. The Great Depression of the 1930s brought layoffs and mass resignations from the brotherhood. The AFL barely responded to repeated charges of discrimination by Randolph, the NAACP, and the Urban League. The BSCP nearly collapsed. Not until the passage of legislation during President Franklin D. Roosevelt's New Deal in the mid-1930s did the BSCP make substantial gains.

The Harlem Renaissance

17-5 Who were some of the men and women involved in the cultural phenomenon known as the Harlem Renaissance, and what were some of their literary, artistic, dramatic, and musical contributions to that movement?

Black intellectuals congregated in Manhattan and gave rise to the creative movement known as the **Harlem Renaissance**. Alain Locke promoted *The New Negro*. Poets, novelists, and painters probed racial themes and grappled with what it meant to be black in America.

This renaissance had no precise beginning. As early as 1920, Du Bois wrote in the *Crisis* that the nation was on the verge of a "renaissance of American Negro literature." In 1925 the *New York Herald Tribune* declared that America was "on the edge, if not already in the midst of, what might not improperly be called a Negro renaissance." No matter when it began, the Harlem Renaissance produced stunning artistic works, especially in creative writing, that continued into the 1930s.

Before Harlem

There had certainly been serious cultural developments among African Americans before the 1920s. From 1897 to 1928, the American Negro Academy was a forum for the Talented Tenth as men such as Alain Locke, Kelly Miller, and Du Bois reflected on race and color.

At the turn of the century, novelist Charles W. Chesnutt depicted a young black woman's attempt to pass for white in *The House Behind the Cedars,* and he wrote about racist violence in the post-Reconstruction South in *The Marrow of Tradition.* Ohio poet Paul Laurence Dunbar wrote evocatively of black life, frequently relying on black dialect. Henry Ossawa Tanner had an illustrious career as a painter. Shortly after he produced "The Banjo Lesson" in 1893, Tanner left for Paris and spent most of the rest of his life in Europe. He died there in 1937.

Carter G. Woodson, the son of Virginia slaves, earned a Ph.D. at Harvard in history and founded in 1915 the Association for the Study of Negro Life and History. He stressed the need for the scholarly examination of Negro history and established the *Journal of Negro History* and the *Negro History Bulletin.* He also founded Associated Publishers to publish books on black history. Woodson wrote several major works, including *The Negro in Our History.* In 1926 he established Negro History Week during February. Not surprisingly, Woodson became known as the "father of Negro history."

During the bloody Red Summer of 1919 when racial violence erupted in Chicago and elsewhere, Claude McKay, a Jamaican who settled—like Marcus Garvey—in New York City, wrote a powerful poem, "If We Must Die," in response to the attacks by white people in Chicago on black residents:

> If we must die, let it not be like hogs
> Hunted and penned in an inglorious spot,
> While round us bark the mad and hungry dogs,
> Making their mock at our accursèd lot.
> If we must die, O let us nobly die,
> So that our precious blood may not be shed
> In vain; then even the monsters we defy
> Shall be constrained to honor us though dead!
> O kinsmen! We must meet the common foe!
> Though far outnumbered let us show us brave,
> And for their thousand blows deal one deathblow!
> What though before us lies the open grave?
> Like men we'll face the murderous, cowardly pack,
> Pressed to the wall, dying, but fighting back!

Listen on
MyHistoryLab
Audio: *If We Must Die;*
poem and reading by
Claude McKay

McKay left the United States for the Soviet Union in 1922 and spent the next 12 years in Europe. In 1928, while in France, he wrote *Home to Harlem,* a novel that depicted life among pimps, prostitutes, loan sharks, and petty criminals.

17-1
17-2
17-3
17-4
17-5
17-6
17-7

Writers and Artists

Few white Americans and still fewer black Americans had access to a college education in the early twentieth century. Only about 2,000 African Americans were pursuing college degrees by 1920. Yet the writers and artists associated with the Harlem Renaissance were the products of some of the nation's finest schools, and, with the exception of Zora Neale Hurston, they did not come from isolated, rural southern communities. Nella Larsen was the only major writer connected to the Harlem Renaissance who did not have a college degree. A native of Chicago, she graduated from the nurse training program at New York City's Lincoln Hospital.

The Harlem Renaissance gradually emerged in the early 1920s and then expanded as more creative figures were drawn to Harlem. In 1923 Jean Toomer published *Cane,* a collection of stories and poetry about southern black life. It sold a mere 500 copies, but it had a major impact on Jessie Fauset and Walter White. Fauset was the literary editor of the *Crisis,* and in 1924 she finished *There Is Confusion,* the first novel published during the renaissance. Her novels explored the manners and color consciousness among well-to-do Negroes. Walter White, who was James Weldon Johnson's assistant at the NAACP, published in 1924 *The Fire in the Flint*, a novel about a black physician who confronted white brutality in Georgia.

In the meantime, the *Crisis,* as well as *Opportunity,* a new publication of the Urban League, published the poetry and short stories of black authors, including Langston Hughes, Countee Cullen, and Zora Neale Hurston. White publishers were also attracted to black literary efforts. In 1925 *Survey Graphic* published a special edition on black life and culture called "Harlem: Mecca of the New Negro." Howard University professor Alain Locke then edited *The New Negro,* which drew much of its material from *Survey Graphic* as well as *Opportunity.* In his opening essay, Locke explained Harlem's literary significance: "Harlem has the same role to play for the new Negro as Dublin has had for the New Ireland or Prague for the New Czechoslovakia."

Disagreements erupted during the Harlem Renaissance over the definition and purpose of black literature. Some, such as Alain Locke, Du Bois, Jessie Fauset, and Benjamin Brawley, wanted black writers to promote positive images of black people in their works. They hoped inspirational literature could help resolve racial conflict in America, and they believed black writers should be included in the larger (and mostly white) American literary tradition. Claude McKay, Langston Hughes, and Zora Neale Hurston disagreed. Their work portrayed the streets and shadows of Harlem and the lives of poor black people. In *The Ways of White Folks,* Hughes ridiculed the notion that writers could promote racial reconciliation.

Du Bois commented caustically after he read McKay's bawdy *Home to Harlem,* "I feel distinctly like taking a bath." Du Bois was less than impressed with Jake, the novel's protagonist, who is intimately involved with the reality of life in Harlem that included opium, alcohol, and sex. Alain Locke dismissed McKay as a mere propagandist, and McKay in turn called Locke "a dyed-in-the-wool pussy-footing professor." Black critic George Schuyler's "The Negro-Art Hokum" in the *Nation* ridiculed black writers who contended that black people even had their own expressive culture that was separate from that of white people.

Read on MyHistoryLab
Document: Alain Locke, from *The New Negro,* 1925

17-1

17-2

17-3

17-4

17-5

17-6

17-7

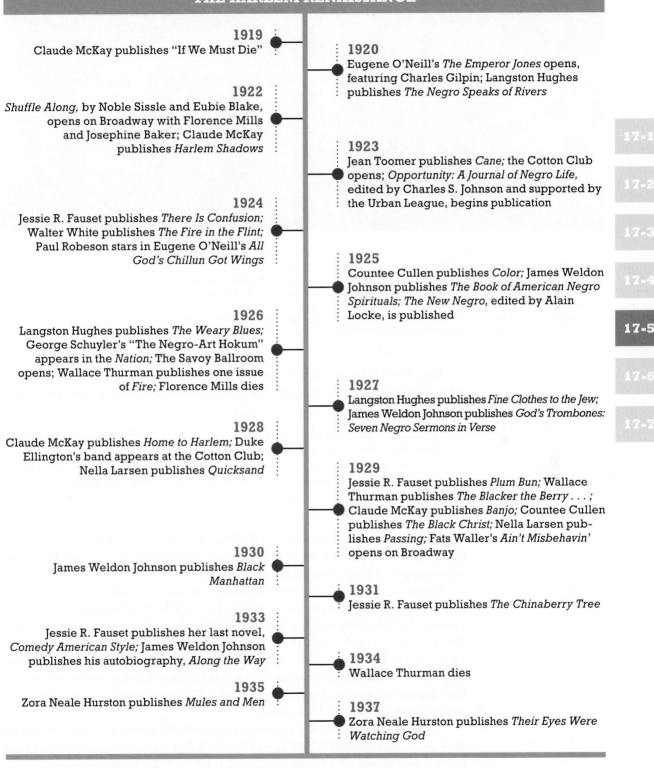

1919–1937
THE HARLEM RENAISSANCE

1919
Claude McKay publishes "If We Must Die"

1920
Eugene O'Neill's *The Emperor Jones* opens, featuring Charles Gilpin; Langston Hughes publishes *The Negro Speaks of Rivers*

1922
Shuffle Along, by Noble Sissle and Eubie Blake, opens on Broadway with Florence Mills and Josephine Baker; Claude McKay publishes *Harlem Shadows*

1923
Jean Toomer publishes *Cane;* the Cotton Club opens; *Opportunity: A Journal of Negro Life,* edited by Charles S. Johnson and supported by the Urban League, begins publication

1924
Jessie R. Fauset publishes *There Is Confusion;* Walter White publishes *The Fire in the Flint;* Paul Robeson stars in Eugene O'Neill's *All God's Chillun Got Wings*

1925
Countee Cullen publishes *Color;* James Weldon Johnson publishes *The Book of American Negro Spirituals; The New Negro,* edited by Alain Locke, is published

1926
Langston Hughes publishes *The Weary Blues;* George Schuyler's "The Negro-Art Hokum" appears in the *Nation;* The Savoy Ballroom opens; Wallace Thurman publishes one issue of *Fire;* Florence Mills dies

1927
Langston Hughes publishes *Fine Clothes to the Jew;* James Weldon Johnson publishes *God's Trombones: Seven Negro Sermons in Verse*

1928
Claude McKay publishes *Home to Harlem;* Duke Ellington's band appears at the Cotton Club; Nella Larsen publishes *Quicksand*

1929
Jessie R. Fauset publishes *Plum Bun;* Wallace Thurman publishes *The Blacker the Berry . . . ;* Claude McKay publishes *Banjo;* Countee Cullen publishes *The Black Christ;* Nella Larsen publishes *Passing;* Fats Waller's *Ain't Misbehavin'* opens on Broadway

1930
James Weldon Johnson publishes *Black Manhattan*

1931
Jessie R. Fauset publishes *The Chinaberry Tree*

1933
Jessie R. Fauset publishes her last novel, *Comedy American Style;* James Weldon Johnson publishes his autobiography, *Along the Way*

1934
Wallace Thurman dies

1935
Zora Neale Hurston publishes *Mules and Men*

1937
Zora Neale Hurston publishes *Their Eyes Were Watching God*

17-1

17-2

17-3

17-4

17-5

17-6

17-7

Artist Aaron Douglas (1899–1979) was born in Topeka, Kansas, and was the sole black student at the University of Nebraska when he graduated in 1922. He moved to Harlem in 1925 and shortly after that visited Paris, where he met celebrated black artist Henry Ossawa Tanner. Douglas returned to Harlem and then taught art at Fisk University in Nashville from 1937 to 1966. His paintings reflected his deep interest in the African-American experience. Notice the Ku Klux Klan as well as black soldiers in this work.

Aaron Douglas, Aspects of Negro Life, *Oil on canvas, 60"×139", Schomburg Center for Research in Black Culture, Art & Artifacts Division, The New York Public Library, Astor, Lenox and Tilden Foundation.*

Langston Hughes, meanwhile, defended the authenticity of black art and literature but insisted the approval or disapproval of white people and black people was of little consequence:

> We younger Negro artists who create now intend to express our individual dark-skinned selves without fear or shame. If white people are pleased, we are glad. If they are not, it doesn't matter. We know we are beautiful. And ugly too. The tom-tom cries and the tom-tom laughs. If colored people are pleased we are glad. If they are not, their displeasure doesn't matter either. We build our temples for tomorrow, strong as we know how, and we stand on top of the mountain, free within ourselves.

Hughes pursued racial themes in *Fine Clothes to the Jew* (1927), which contained "Red Silk Stockings," a poem that depicted young black women who were tempted by liaisons with white men, a subject that offended some readers.

Even more upsetting to those who wanted to safeguard the reputation of black people was Wallace Thurman, who arrived in New York in 1925. In 1926 Thurman published *Fire,* a journal that lasted only one issue but managed to incite enormous controversy and leave Thurman deeply in debt. *Fire* included Thurman's short story "Cordelia the Crude," about a prostitute, and a one-act play by Zora Neale Hurston, *Color Struck.* Hurston replicated the speech of rural black southerners while depicting the jealousy a darker woman feels when a light-skinned rival tries to take her man. Black critic Benjamin Brawley complained that with *Fire* "vulgarity had been mistaken for art."

Thurman, who was a dark black man, antagonized still more people when *The Blacker the Berry . . .* was published in 1929. In it he described the tribulations and sorrows of Emma Lou, a young woman who did not mind being black, "but she did mind being too black."

17-1
17-2
17-3
17-4
17-5
17-6
17-7

The book made it plain that many black people had absorbed a color prejudice that they did not hesitate to inflict on darker members of their own race.

Unlike Thurman, Nella Larsen wrote about black people who were indistinguishable from white people. Her novel *Quicksand* depicted the life of Helga Crane, who, like Larsen herself, had a Danish mother and a black father. In *Passing,* Larsen dealt with a young black woman who passed for white and, indeed, married a white racist.

White People and the Harlem Renaissance

Like many of the writers associated with the Harlem Renaissance, Zora Neale Hurston's pen sliced like a scalpel. She called the white people who took an interest in Harlem "Negrotarians" and her black literary colleagues the "Niggerati." But no matter how they were described, black and white people developed pleasant but often uneasy relationships during the renaissance.

No white man was more attracted to the cultural developments in Harlem than photographer and writer Carl Van Vechten. In 1926 he caused a furor with his novel *Nigger Heaven.* The title, which referred to the balcony where black patrons had to sit in segregated theaters and auditoriums, offended many people. The novel dealt with the coarser aspects of life in Harlem, which irritated Du Bois, Fauset, and Countee Cullen. But Van Vechten wanted a more honest depiction of the black experience, and James Weldon Johnson, Walter White, and Langston Hughes approved of the novel.

Most black writers and artists welcomed the encouragement and financial backing they received from white authors, critics, and publishers. White attention and support were sometimes accompanied by condescension and disdain. Too many "Negrotarians" considered Harlem and its inhabitants exotic, curious, and uncivilized. They found life in Harlem—its clubs, music, and entertainers, as well as its poetry, prose, and painting—more energetic, lively, and sensual than white life and culture. Black culture was also—many white people believed—unsophisticated and primitive, which is what made it so appealing. Black writers like Langston Hughes, Claude McKay, and Countee Cullen wanted to depict black life realistically—from its gangsters to its gamblers. But they resented the notion that black culture was inherently crude and unrefined.

White patrons like Amy Spingarn, whose husband Joel was president of the NAACP board of directors, and Charlotte Osgood "Godmother" Mason supported black writers and artists. Spingarn helped finance Langston Hughes's education at Lincoln University. "Godmother" Mason was a wealthy widow who financially supported black artists. She worked closely with Alain Locke, who helped identify Langston Hughes, Zora Neale Hurston, and Aaron Douglas, among others, who became her "godchildren." Mason wanted no publicity for herself, but her patronage had its costs. In return for financial support, Mason demanded that the black writers keep her informed about their activities, and she did not hesitate to tell them when they were not productive enough. She also tried to influence what they wrote. She preferred that black writers confine themselves to exotic themes. As helpful as Mason's financial assistance and personal encouragement were, she created a system of dependency.

The profusion of literary works associated with the Harlem Renaissance did not so much end as fade away. Black writers remained active into the 1930s. Hurston wrote her two most important works in the 1930s—*Mules and Men* in 1935 and *Their Eyes Were Watching God* in 1937. Although McKay and Hughes continued to have their work published, the Great Depression that began in 1929 devastated book and magazine sales. Subscriptions to the

Crisis and *Opportunity* declined, and both journals published fewer works by creative writers. Many black intellectuals left Harlem. James Weldon Johnson and Aaron Douglas went to Fisk University in Nashville.

Du Bois quarreled with the NAACP and returned to Atlanta University. Alain Locke remained on the faculty at Howard University. Jessie Fauset married an insurance executive and took up housekeeping after her last novel was published in 1931. Nella Larsen was charged unjustly with plagiarism. She quit writing and resumed her career as a nurse. Wallace Thurman died an alcoholic in 1934. Countee Cullen taught French at DeWitt Clinton High School in New York City, where James Baldwin was one of his students in the late 1930s.

Harlem and the Jazz Age

17-6 What was the role of Harlem and its inhabitants in what popularly came to be known as the Jazz Age?

As powerful and important as these black literary voices were, they were less popular than the entertainers, musicians, singers, and dancers who were also part of the Harlem Renaissance. Without Harlem, the 1920s would not have been the Jazz Age. From wailing trumpets, beating drums, dancing feet, and plaintive and mournful songs, Harlem's clubs, cabarets, theaters, and ballrooms echoed with the vibrant and soulful sounds of African Americans. By comparison, white music seemed sedate and bland.

Black and white people flocked to Harlem to enjoy themselves—and to break the law. In 1919–1920, the Eighteenth Amendment and the Volstead Act prohibited the manufacture, distribution, and sale of alcoholic beverages. But liquor flowed freely in Harlem's fancy establishments and smoky dives. Musicians and entertainers, like Harlem's working-class residents, had migrated there. The blues and their sorrowful tales of troubled and broken relationships arrived from the Mississippi delta and rural South. Jazz had its origins in New Orleans, but it drew on ragtime and spirituals as it moved up the Mississippi River to Kansas City and Chicago on its way to Harlem.

The Cotton Club was Harlem's most exclusive and fashionable nightspot. Opened in 1923, it catered to well-to-do white people who regarded a trip to Harlem as a foreign excursion. The club's entertainers and waiters were black, but the customers were white. Black patrons were not admitted. The club featured well-choreographed and fast-paced two-hour revues that included a chorus line of attractive young women—all brown skinned, all under age 21, and all over five feet six inches tall. No dark women appeared.

In 1928 Edward K. "Duke" Ellington and his orchestra began a 12-year association with the Cotton Club. Although Ellington had not yet begun to compose his own music in earnest, his band already had an elegant, sophisticated, and recognizable African-American sound. Another club, Connie's Inn, also served a mostly white clientele. Thomas "Fats" Waller played a rambunctious piano at Connie's. Connie's also put on stunning musical revues, perhaps the best known of which was *Hot Chocolates*. Dancers who performed at Connie's included the legendary Bill "Bojangles" Robinson and Earl "Snakehips" Tucker. A young trumpeter from New Orleans, Louis Armstrong, played briefly at Connie's. Armstrong amazed listeners with his virtuoso trumpet and gravelly voice.

Harlem's black residents were more likely to step into one of Harlem's less pretentious and inexpensive establishments, such as the Sugar Cane. In these places, the beer and liquor were cheap, the food was plentiful, the music was good, and there were no elaborate production numbers. Even less impressive clubs and bars remained open after the legal closing hour of 3 A.M. "Arrangements" were made with the police, who looked the other way as the music and alcohol continued through the night. Musicians from "legal" clubs drifted into the after-hours joints and played until dawn.

Another popular—and sometimes necessary—form of entertainment among Harlemites was the rent party. Housing costs in Harlem were extravagant, and white people and real estate agents refused to rent or sell to black people in most other areas of New York City. To make the steep monthly rent payments, apartment dwellers would push the furniture aside and begin cooking chicken, chitterlings, rice, okra, and sweet potatoes. They would distribute a few flyers and hire a musician or two. Partygoers paid 10 cents to 50 cents for admission. Food and liquor were sold. With a decent crowd, the month's rent was paid.

Song, Dance, and Stage

Black women became popular as singers and dancers in Harlem and then often appeared in Broadway shows and revues. Florence Mills entranced audiences with her diminutive singing voice in several Broadway productions including *Plantation Review, Dixie to Broadway,* and *Blackbirds* before she died of appendicitis in 1927. Adelaide Hall also appeared in *Blackbirds* and later

She was called the "Empress of the Blues," and during the 1920s no singer in America was more popular than Bessie Smith.

opened her own nightclubs in London and Paris. Ethel Waters worked her way up from smoky gin joints in Harlem basements, where she sang risqué and comic songs, to Broadway shows, and then to films. Years later she toured with Billy Graham's religious revivals.

White men wrote many of the popular Broadway productions that starred black entertainers. In 1921, however, Eubie Blake and Noble Sissle put on *Shuffle Along,* which became a major hit. Its most memorable tune was "I'm Just Wild About Harry." Sissle and Blake's *Chocolate Dandies* in 1924 was created especially for a thin, lanky, dark, and funny young lady named Josephine Baker. But in 1925 Baker moved to Paris, where she starred in the *Revue Nègre,* which created a sensation in the French capital. She remained in France for the rest of her life.

White playwright Eugene O'Neill wrote serious drama involving black people. Charles Gilpin and then Paul Robeson appeared in O'Neill's *Emperor Jones.* Robeson—who had an illustrious career—was a graduate of Rutgers University, where he was an all-American football player. He earned a law degree at Columbia University but abandoned the law for the stage. He appeared in numerous productions, including O'Neill's *All God's Chillun Got Wings,* Shakespeare's *Othello,* Gershwin's *Porgy and Bess,* and Kern and Hammerstein's *Showboat.*

17-1

17-2

17-3

17-4

17-5

17-6

17-7

Sports

17-1
17-2
17-3
17-4
17-5
17-6
17-7

17-7 **What opportunities and obstacles confronted black athletes in the 1920s?**

Sports flourished in the 1920s. Americans worshiped their athletic heroes. Babe Ruth and Jack Dempsey were as well known as President Coolidge. Professional athletics, especially baseball and boxing, expanded dramatically. Professional football and basketball emerged later. Black men had been banned from major league baseball in 1887 (see Chapter 15). Nevertheless, in 1901 Baltimore Orioles manager John J. McGraw signed a black man, Charlie Grant, to play second, claiming he was "Chief Tokohoma," a full-blooded Cherokee Indian. Chicago White Sox owner Charles Comiskey knew otherwise, and Grant did not play in the major leagues.

Playing among themselves, black baseball players barely made a living as they moved from team to team in an ever-fluctuating and disorganized system that saw teams come and go with monotonous regularity. No leagues functioned effectively for the black teams and players. Owners of the black teams were sometimes involved in organized crime.

Negro National League A professional baseball league for black players and teams organized in 1912.

Black players crisscrossed the country on trains and in automobiles as they played each other in small towns and large cities for meager money shared from gate receipts. It was an insecure and nomadic life. The black clubs kept few individual or team statistics, and their financial records were frequently in disarray.

Rube Foster

Andrew "Rube" Foster was the father of black baseball in twentieth-century America. In 1911 he founded the Chicago American Giants, and he pitched with them regularly until 1915; after that, he mainly managed the team. A fine athlete, Foster was an even more talented organizer and administrator.

In 1919 in the *Chicago Defender,* he argued for a Negro baseball league. In 1920 he was the catalyst in the formation of the eight-team **Negro National League** and became its president and secretary. It was the first stable black league.

Foster and the new league took advantage of the migration of black people to northern cities. The black ball clubs usually played late in the afternoon or in the early evening so fans could attend after a day's work. (This was before night baseball.) Sunday doubleheaders in Chicago or Kansas City might draw 8,000 to 10,000 people. Players were paid regularly, and athletes on Foster's Giants earned at least $175 a month. The biggest obstacle that black teams faced was the lack of their own fields or stadiums. They were forced to rent, often at exorbitant rates, from major league clubs, which frequently kept the profits from concessions.

Black baseball thrived—more or less—in the 1920s, thanks mostly to Foster's dedication. He was a tireless worker and strict disciplinarian, but the pressure may have been too much. He suffered a mental breakdown in 1926 and died in 1930. The loss of Foster—combined with the Depression—disrupted the league system.

Andrew "Rube" Foster was the father of black baseball. An outstanding pitcher, he reportedly taught major-league-great Christy Mathewson how to throw the screwball. He became the owner and manager of the Chicago American Giants, and he was the founder of the Negro National League. His teams won the pennant in 1920, 1921, and 1922. He was elected to the Baseball Hall of Fame in Cooperstown in 1981.

College Sports

Football, baseball, basketball, and track and field were popular at the collegiate level. Amateur sports were less rigidly segregated than professional baseball. Black men played for white northern universities, although few teams had more than one black player. For example, Paul Robeson was on the Rutgers football team in 1916 that played against Frederick Douglass "Fritz" Pollard and Brown University. Pollard was the first black man to play in the Rose Bowl, where Brown lost to Washington State in 1916.

Pollard played professional football in the 1920s. He played for four early National Football League (NFL) teams, including Milwaukee and Providence. In 1921 he became the first African-American head coach in the league when he took charge of the Akron team. Later he coached an independent all-black team, the Chicago Black Hawks. Pollard, who died in 1986, was inducted into the NFL Hall of Fame in 2005.

Black college players on white teams encountered discrimination when the teams traveled. Spectators taunted and threatened them. The Big Ten had an unwritten agreement that basketball coaches would not accept black players. All-white college teams sometimes refused to play schools with black players.

Sports in black colleges and universities thrived in the 1920s. Baseball and football were the most popular spectator events. Traditional rivalries attracted large crowds. Several schools played baseball religiously each Easter Monday. In 1926 Livingstone College defeated Biddle University (now Johnson C. Smith University) before a crowd of 6,000 in Charlotte, North Carolina. With the migration of black people to the North, black colleges began to play football in northern cities. Howard and Lincoln played to a scoreless tie before 18,000 people in Philadelphia on Thanksgiving in 1925. Hampton and Lincoln played at New York's Polo Grounds on the edge of Harlem in 1929 in a game Lincoln won 13–7 before 10,000 spectators.

CONCLUSION

For African Americans, the 1920s must have seemed little more than a depressing continuation of earlier decades. Little appeared to have changed. Racial violence and lynching persisted. *The Birth of a Nation* mocked black people and inflamed racial animosity. "Experts" offered "proof" that people of color were inferior and threatened America's ethnic purity. The Ku Klux Klan became a formidable organization again. Millions of white men joined the Klan, and millions more supported it.

Nevertheless, positive developments in the 1920s gave hope for a more promising future. The NAACP became an organization to be reckoned with as it fought for anti-lynching legislation in Congress and for civil and political rights in the courts. Its membership exceeded 100,000 during the 1920s. Although many black and white Americans ridiculed Marcus Garvey for his flamboyant style and excessive rhetoric, he offered racial pride and self-respect as he enrolled hundreds of thousands of black people in the UNIA.

Black workers made little progress as they sought concessions from big business and representation within the ranks of organized labor. A. Philip Randolph founded the BSCP and began a struggle with both the Pullman Company and the AFL that would begin to pay off in the 1930s.

The Harlem Renaissance was a cultural awakening in literature and the arts that was unprecedented in African-American history. A torrent of words poured forth from novelists, essayists, and poets. Although they disagreed—sometimes vehemently—on the purposes of black art, the writers and artists who were a part of the renaissance had an enduring

17-1

17-2

17-3

17-4

17-5

17-6

17-7

impact. The renaissance allowed thoughtful and creative men and women to grapple with what it meant to be black in a society in which the white majority had defined the black minority as inferior, incapable, and backward. Hereafter, African Americans were less likely to let other people characterize them in demeaning ways.

Black musicians, dancers, singers, entertainers, and athletes made names for themselves and contributed to popular culture in a mostly urban environment. As the 1930s began, it remained to be seen whether the modest but real progress of the 1920s would be sustained.

CHAPTER TIMELINE

AFRICAN-AMERICAN EVENTS   **NATIONAL EVENTS**

1919

1919
Pan-African Congress meets in Paris
Marcus Garvey founds Black Star Line and the UNIA

1919
Eighteenth Amendment (Prohibition) ratified
Volstead Act passed

1920

1920
Rube Foster organizes the Negro National League in baseball

1920
Nineteenth Amendment gives women the right to vote
Warren Harding elected president

1921

1921
Tulsa, Oklahoma, race riot occurs

1921
Congress establishes immigration quotas

1922

1922
Dyer anti-lynching bill fails in Senate
Marcus Garvey meets with Ku Klux Klan leaders in Atlanta
Ku Klux Klan virtually takes over Oklahoma

1924

1924
Calvin Coolidge elected president
Congress grants citizenship to Native Americans

1925

1925
Ossian Sweet case tried in Detroit
A. Philip Randolph founds the Brotherhood of Sleeping Car Porters

1925
Ku Klux Klan is at peak of prominence

CHAPTER TIMELINE

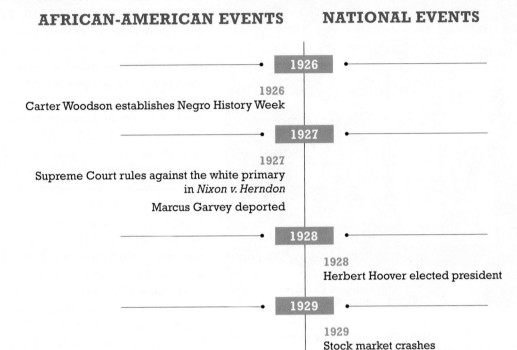

AFRICAN-AMERICAN EVENTS

NATIONAL EVENTS

1926

1926
Carter Woodson establishes Negro History Week

1927

1927
Supreme Court rules against the white primary
in *Nixon v. Herndon*

Marcus Garvey deported

1928

1928
Herbert Hoover elected president

1929

1929
Stock market crashes

On MyHistoryLab

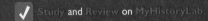

✓ Study and Review on MyHistoryLab

REVIEW QUESTIONS

1. To what extent, if any, had the intensity of white supremacy changed by the 1920s from what it had been two to three decades earlier?

2. What examples of progress could leaders like W. E. B. Du Bois, James Weldon Johnson, A. Philip Randolph, and Marcus Garvey point to in the 1920s?

3. Why did so many African-American leaders reject Marcus Garvey?

4. How did the black nationalism of the Universal Negro Improvement Association differ from the white nationalism of the Ku Klux Klan?

5. What economic opportunities existed for African Americans who had migrated to northern cities?

6. Why did the literary and artistic movement known as the Harlem Renaissance emerge?

7. What was distinctive about black writers, artists, and musicians? Were their creative works essentially a part of American culture or separate from it?

8. Did African Americans have any reason to be optimistic by the late 1920s?

CONNECTING THE PAST

Migration

African-American men, women, and children who participated in the Great Migration to the north, with suitcases and luggage placed in front, Chicago, 1918.

CHICAGO HAD SLIGHTLY MORE THAN 40,000 black residents in 1910. By 2010, more than one million African Americans lived in Chicago and its suburbs. This huge growth in the city's black population was part of the Great Migration, the largest internal movement of people in American history. Yet this massive shift in population was only one of many instances over the long course of history that Africans and their descendants have willingly or unwillingly changed locations.

Early humans roamed from Africa into Asia and Europe as hunters and gatherers about 100,000 years ago. Between the sixteenth and nineteenth centuries, 12 million Africans were forced to endure the horrors of the Middle Passage and the Atlantic slave trade. In the decades before the Civil War, thousands of southern slaves escaped to freedom in the northern states and Canada by way of the underground railroad. In the late 1870s, economic and political oppression led as many as 40,000 former slaves known as Exodusters to leave the South and move west to Kansas and Oklahoma. About the same time a small number of freedmen left the United States and went to Liberia in West Africa.

But it was the twentieth century's Great Migration that prompted recent and profound political and economic changes in American society. Most of these migrants boarded segregated passenger trains in southern towns to travel on the overground railroad to northern and western communities. Unlike the nineteenth century abolitionist movement and the civil rights movement of the 1950s and 1960s, no dynamic organizations or inspirational leaders were involved in this remarkable resettlement. Instead, individuals, husbands, wives, and friends made what was often a heart-wrenching decision to leave the southern communities where they had been born and raised for a strange and distant destination like Chicago, Pittsburgh, or New York City. They did so because, like the slaves who had fled to freedom a century earlier, the migrants wanted a better life. They hoped to liberate themselves from economic dependence, and to escape the segregation and violence that exemplified life in the Jim Crow South.

While life in the North and the West may have been an improvement, black migrants did not suddenly find themselves residing in the Promised Land. White workers resented black competition for unskilled jobs in manufacturing. Labor unions prohibited black membership. White employers' use of black workers as strikebreakers or scabs further alienated white workingmen. Black women were confined to domestic work and denied employment as retail clerks, bank tellers, waitresses, or secretaries. But the "white" and "colored" signs that saturated the South rarely were seen in the North. Buses, streetcars, and passenger trains had open seating. Black people did not have to step aside when white people passed on city sidewalks.

Many myths accompanied the migrants. Black people who already lived in northern cities looked down on the "countrified" ways of the new arrivals and ridiculed the way they talked, dressed, and carried themselves. They disparaged the newcomers' supposed lack of education, low incomes, and inability to maintain stable families. But these perceptions proved to be inaccurate. Migrants had a sense of purpose and commitment. They were better educated than the people they left behind. They had higher incomes and were less likely to be on welfare than African Americans who already resided in the North. They were more likely to be married and remain married. Their children lived in two-parent households.

The development of black political power was one of the unexpected consequences of the Great Migration. Black men and women voted freely in the North and West. Living together in black neighborhoods afforded them the opportunity to elect black city councilmen, aldermen, and congressmen. By the 1950s, black men from Chicago, Detroit, Philadelphia, and Harlem served in the U.S. House of Representatives. In the 1960s and 1970s, black mayors were elected in Cleveland, Newark, Detroit, and Los Angeles. Democratic presidential candidates Harry Truman in 1948 and John F. Kennedy in 1960 relied on black voters in northern cities to provide them with margins of victory.

By the middle of the twentieth century, several million African Americans lived in densely populated urban communities throughout the nation. Here are residents of Harlem on Seventh Avenue on a cold February day in 1956.

The Civil Rights Act of 1964 and the Voting Rights Act of 1965 eradicated Jim Crow in the South. The Great Migration began to reverse itself. Black people who had migrated to northern communities in the 1940s and 1950s began to retire in the 1980s and 1990s to towns and communities they had left as young people. Now, with a shifting racial dynamic in the United States that included the election of an African-American president, there is a new migration. Black people from Africa and the Caribbean increasingly come to America. Between 2000 and 2010, 216,900 Africans moved to the United States. Not all of them will remain, but more will come, attracted to a place where their predecessors were sold and toiled as slaves. Those predecessors and their descendants helped create a vibrant nation that now draws immigrants from nearly every corner of the globe.

1. **What specific factors account for the Great Migration?**

2. **Under what circumstances would you move hundreds of miles from your friends and family?**

CHAPTER

18

Listen to Chapter 18
on MyHistoryLab

Black Protest, the Great Depression, and the New Deal 1929–1940

LEARNING OBJECTIVES

18-1 What caused the Great Depression of the 1930s and what were the economic effects on blacks in the cities and rural areas?

18-2 What were the varieties of protests continued by blacks during the Great Depression to address economic concerns and challenge racial discrimination?

18-3 How did the New Deal affect African Americans?

18-4 What was the "black cabinet," its purpose, and its goals?

18-5 What role did organized labor play in radicalizing black Americans in the 1930s?

18-6 What was the *Scottsboro* case and what were its consequences?

18-7 What was the Tuskegee study and its impact?

For African Americans, the Great Depression was an era of suffering made worse by the horrors and burdens of American racism as well as a time of profound political change, demographic shifts, and social activism that would lay the foundation for the progress of ensuing decades. At the beginning of the economic collapse in late 1929, most African Americans were either trapped in the failing southern agricultural system or eking out a bare existence at the margins of the booming urban economy. The economy's fall pushed many black Americans to the edge of starvation, throwing them off the land and out of the small niches they had carved out in other occupations. Coming out of the southern-dominated Democratic Party, President Franklin Roosevelt's New Deal programs for fighting the Depression might have simply reinforced existing racism, as in fact it did to some extent. But from another perspective,

Photographer Margaret Bourke White may not have intended to contrast the American dream of prosperity—for white families—and the harsh realities of life for black Americans in this Depression photograph, but it has become representative of existing racial disparity. The collapse of the economy spurred the search for radical critiques and solutions to deal with the desperate conditions millions of African Americans endured. Separate economic development and the creation of parallel institutions and organizations was one option. But was it practicable?

the emerging political power of African-American voters in the North, the development of civil rights organizations, and the growth of an antiracist agenda among radicals and labor unions created the preconditions for a profound change in American politics. Amid economic despair, peonage, lynchings, and labor conflicts, black people saw glimmers of hope in protests against racial segregation and radical critiques of capitalist exploitation. Their protests helped shape the policies and programs of the New Deal. The 1930s were thus the dark dawn of a new era that witnessed, among other significant changes, the rise to prominence of a remarkable cadre of black social scientists.

The Cataclysm, 1929–1933

18-1   What caused the Great Depression of the 1930s and what were the economic effects on blacks in the cities and rural areas?

The Great Depression was a cataclysm. National income fell from $81 billion in 1929 to $40 billion in 1932. Overnight millions of Americans lost their life savings in bank closings and home foreclosures. Americans responded by buying fewer consumer goods; in turn, businesses cut back production, investment, and payrolls. The result was a downward spiral of economic activity made worse by increasing numbers of unemployed (see Figure 18–1). The standard of living of nearly everyone, from farmers to small businessmen and entrepreneurs to wage laborers, dropped to a fraction of what it had been before 1929.

Watch on MyHistoryLab Video: The Great Depression

Most people blamed the stock market crash and Republican President Herbert Hoover for the hard times, but the true explanation is more complicated. Although its causes are hotly debated, the Great Depression was probably the result of several factors, including rampant speculation, corporate capitalism's drive for markets and profits unchecked by federal regulation, the failure of those in the government or private sector to understand how the economy worked, a weak international trading system, overproduction of—and low prices for—many agricultural goods and raw materials, and—most important—the great inequality of wealth and income that limited the purchasing power of millions of Americans.

Read on MyHistoryLab Document: Dealing with Hard Times

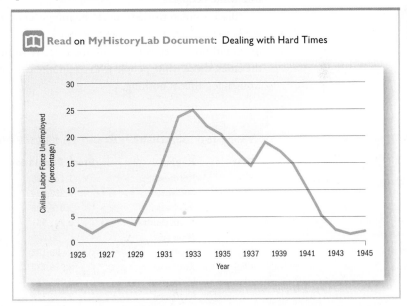

Harder Times for Black America

The economic collapse hit African Americans particularly hard. Most black people remained in the rural South mired in an exploitive agricultural system. Indeed, the Depression worsened the key problems besetting

FIGURE 18–1 UNEMPLOYMENT, 1925–1945
With the collapse of the American economy, unemployment soared in the 1930s. New Deal programs alleviated some of the suffering, but full recovery did not come until the defense industries swung into action with the U.S. entry into World War II.

Explore on
MyHistoryLab
Activity: The Great
Depression

cash-crop production in the 1920s. Consumer demand for cotton and sugar fell with the depressed economy; however, as farmers grew more of these crops to make ends meet, the supply of these staples increased. The result was a catastrophe, with prices for cotton—still the mainstay of the southern economy—plunging from 18 cents a pound in 1929 to six cents in 1933. Black sharecroppers and tenant farmers, nearly powerless in the rural South, were reduced to starvation or thrown off the land.

The hard times also struck those 1.5 million African Americans who had escaped the South for northern urban communities (see Table 18–1). Even during the prosperous 1920s, black Americans had suffered layoffs, and their living standards had steadily fallen. After 1929 the same forces that impoverished rural Americans swept those in urban areas further toward the economic margins as waves of refugees from the farms crowded into the cities and competed for scarce jobs (see Table 18–2). By 1934, when the federal government noted that 17 percent of white citizens could not support themselves, the figure for black Americans had increased to 38 percent overall. In Chicago, 40 percent of African-American men were unemployed; in Pittsburgh, 48 percent; in Harlem, 50 percent; in Philadelphia, 56 percent; and in Detroit, 60 percent. The figures were even more dire for black workers in southern cities. In Atlanta, Georgia, 65 percent of black workers needed public assistance, and in Norfolk, Virginia, a stunning 80 percent had to apply for welfare.

African Americans lost jobs in those parts of the economy where they had gained a tenuous foothold. Before 1929, jobs in low-status or poorly paid occupations, such as garbage collection, foundries, or domestic service, had been regarded as "Negro work" and hence were generally immune from white competition. As desperation set in, however, white southerners not only competed for these jobs but also used the old tactics of terror and intimidation to compel employers to fire black people. Unions, north and south, continued to exclude African Americans from membership and pressured manufacturers to hire white people.

Black women workers, overwhelmingly concentrated in domestic service and laundry work, were affected even more than black men. There were fewer jobs because many families could no longer afford domestic help. With many impoverished women coming into the cities, those white people who could hire help found they could employ these desperate women for almost nothing.

TABLE 18–1 DEMOGRAPHIC SHIFTS: THE SECOND GREAT MIGRATION, 1930–1950

Year	Region	Black Population	Total Population	% Black
1930	Northeast	1,146,985	34,427,091	3.33
	Midwest	1,262,234	38,594,100	3.27
	Southeast	7,079,626	25,680,803	27.57
	South Central	2,281,951	12,176,830	18.74
	Mountain	30,225	3,701,789	0.82
	Pacific	90,122	8,622,047	1.05
1950	Northeast	2,018,182	39,477,986	5.11
	Midwest	2,227,876	44,460,762	5.01
	Southeast	7,793,379	32,659,516	23.86
	South Central	2,432,028	14,517,572	16.73
	Mountain	66,429	5,074,998	1.31
	Pacific	507,043	15,114,964	3.35

SOURCE: U.S. Bureau of the Census Release, *1991*, and Statistical Abstract, *1990*. Also see Schomburg Center, The New York Public Library, African American Desk Reference *(New York: John Wiley & Sons, 1999), 100–101.*

African Americans were no strangers to adversity, and many used the survival strategies developed through centuries of hardship to eke out an existence during the first years of the Great Depression. Survival demanded that black women pool their resources and adhere to a collective spirit that found fertile ground in segregated northern neighborhoods. In Chicago, for example, women and their families lived in crowded tenements in which they shared bathrooms and other facilities including hot plates, stoves, and sinks. They bartered and exchanged goods and services because money was so scarce.

Rural black women, like their urban sisters, had to rely on their individual and collective ingenuity to survive. As one observer of black women household heads in rural Georgia noted, "In their effort to maintain existence, these people are catching and selling fish, reselling vegetables, sewing in exchange for old clothes, letting out sleeping space, and doing odd jobs. They understand how to help each other. Stoves are used in common, wash boilers go their rounds, and garden crops are exchanged and shared." Nonetheless, the depth and duration of this downturn strained these mutual aid strategies to the breaking point. By 1933 the clock seemed to have been turned back to 1865, when many African Americans could claim to own little more than their bodies.

TABLE 18–2 MEDIAN INCOME OF BLACK FAMILIES COMPARED TO THE MEDIAN INCOME OF WHITE FAMILIES FOR SELECTED CITIES, 1935–1936

City and Type of Family	Black	White	Black Income as a Percentage of White Income
Husband–Wife Families			
New York	$980	$1,930	51%
Chicago	$726	$1,687	43%
Columbus	$831	$1,622	51%
Atlanta	$632	$1,876	34%
Columbia	$576	$1,876	31%
Mobile	$481	$1,419	34%
Other Families			
Atlanta	$332	$940	35%
Columbia	$254	$1,403	18%
Mobile	$301	$784	38%

SOURCE: *Median Income of Black Families . . . White Families for Selected Cities, 1935–1936 from An American Dilemma: The Negro Problem and Modern Democracy by Gunnar Myrdal. Copyright © 1944, 1962 by Harper and Row Publishers, Inc. Reprinted by permission of HarperCollins Publishers.*

Black Businesses in the Depression: Collapse and Survival

Black businessmen and professionals also suffered. African Americans who had built successful businesses and professional practices in medicine and law, for example, faced the same Depression-borne problems as other businesses, but they suffered even more because the communities on which they depended were poorer. Two types of black-owned businesses, banks and insurance companies, illustrate how black enterprises stood or fell during the economic crisis.

The Binga Bank, Chicago's first black-owned-and-operated financial institution, had been founded in 1908 by its president, Jesse Binga (1865–1950), a Detroit-born real estate broker who had worked as a barber and a Pullman porter. Binga had managed the bank so effectively that by 1930 its deposits had grown to more than $1.5 million. The Binga Bank was, during its early years, an important symbol of successful black capitalism and as such represented the hopes and aspirations of black Chicagoans. But the bank's assets were too heavily invested in mortgages to black churches and fraternal societies, many of which could not meet their payments after their members lost their jobs. Binga refused to seize the properties of these community institutions, but his restraint, coupled with financial improprieties, led to the bank's failure. Sentenced to prison in 1933, Binga was pardoned by the Governor of Illinois Dwight H. Green on April 12, 1941. He never regained his fortune.

Some black businesses survived the economic cataclysm although often in a much weakened state. Among the businesses still standing when prosperity finally returned in the 1940s were the leading black insurance companies. Atlanta Life Insurance Company, for example—founded in 1905 by a former Georgia slave, Alonzo Franklin Herndon—not only survived the Depression but recorded substantial profit. Between 1931 and 1936, its assets increased by more than $1 million. This was in part because insurance companies such as Atlanta Life provided an essential service for African Americans, particularly in an era before government-provided social security, and could thus depend on a continued flow of premiums. And unlike the Binga Bank, Atlanta Life's officers drastically reduced their investments in mortgages in the black community.

The North Carolina Mutual Life Insurance Company, founded in Durham, weathered the Great Depression under the astute leadership of Charles Clinton Spaulding (1874–1952). In 1899 Spaulding joined with two other African Americans to transform the insurance company into the nation's largest black business. His partners were his uncle, Dr. Aaron McDuffie Moore, Durham's only black physician, and John Merrick, a former slave and leading real estate agent and barbershop owner. Following on the heels of the great migration to the North, Spaulding expanded the company's territory into Virginia, Maryland, and the District of Columbia. It is still one of the three largest black-owned insurance companies in the United States.

Many of the 250 black hospitals, clinics, and nursing training schools that black physicians, such as Dr. Daniel Hale Williams, had launched since the 1890s could not survive the ravages of the Depression. Confronting a diminishing clientele and worsening health among black people, some black physicians began encouraging their patients to demand admission to the segregated, government-operated hospitals and clinics. At the outset of the Depression, Dr. Matilda A. Evans (1872–1935) of Columbia, South Carolina, an 1897 graduate of the Woman's Medical College in Philadelphia, mobilized a diverse constituency of black parents, professionals, and religious and business leaders to persuade the state board of health to provide free inoculations and immunization shots to black schoolchildren. Other healthcare professionals volunteered to conduct free medical and dental examinations. When Evans's Columbia Clinic opened in July 1930, over 700 patients showed up. This short-lived clinic reflected Evans's belief that health care was a state responsibility just as important as the provision of free public education. The deteriorating economic conditions of both the state of South Carolina and its people made it impossible to sustain this effort. But the Columbia Clinic movement taught black people a powerful lesson about how to mobilize to achieve change and thus raised, as Evans anticipated it would, black consciousness about the need to apply pressure on the state for more access to public resources.

The Failure of Relief

Before Franklin Roosevelt's New Deal, private charities or, as a last resort, state and local governments were responsible for providing relief from economic hardships. Even in good times these institutions provided too little for all those in need. Moreover, African Americans had a much harder time getting aid than white people and were given less when they did get it. The Depression made it impossible for the nation's charitable organizations to meet the needs of more than a small portion of the hungry, homeless, and unemployed millions. In turn, state and local governments could not or would not provide unemployment insurance or increased welfare benefits to ease the suffering of those most vulnerable to the economic disaster. Even when these governments wanted to help, the economic collapse so lowered tax receipts that it became nearly impossible for relief agencies to act.

Despite the need to alleviate the economic disaster, President Hoover hesitated to respond. Steeped in the free-market orthodoxy of his time, he believed government should do little to interfere with the workings of the economy. Nevertheless, Hoover did more to counteract a depression than any previous president had done. He tried to convince businesses that if they retained employees and did not cut wages, they would contribute to the health of the general economy and promote their own best interests. The president also approved loans to banks, railroads, and insurance companies by the Reconstruction Finance Corporation, a federal agency created to rescue large corporations. He hoped these businesses would reinvigorate production, create new jobs, and restore consumer spending. His faith was misplaced. Businesses took the government loans and still laid off workers, much the same way many banks behaved in 2009 after receiving government funds to prevent them from failing.

Hoover's reluctance to use the federal government to intervene in the economy extended to the provision of relief. He suggested that local governments and charities should address the needs of the unemployed, the homeless, and the starving masses. Hoover was not a callous person, but he was trapped in a rigid ideology. He watched with dismay the wandering groups of men, women, and children who began settling into what they called, with grim humor, "Hoovervilles"—sordid clusters of shacks made of tin, cardboard, and burlap next to railroad tracks and dumps. Still, he refused to allow the federal government to provide direct relief.

Hoover's inactivity was bad enough, but his politics were as racist as those of the Democratic Party. Wanting to create a white Republican Party in the South, he cultivated white southerners by attempting to appoint to the U.S. Supreme Court Judge John Parker of North Carolina, who believed in "separate but equal," and by displacing black Republican leaders. Hoover's policy was not new. For decades the national Republican Party had treated black voters with contempt and often declined to reward them with patronage appointments. This policy looked even worse during the early 1930s against the backdrop of black suffering.

Black Protest during the Great Depression

18-2   What were the varieties of protests continued by blacks during the Great Depression to address economic concerns and challenge racial discrimination?

During the 1930s African-American men and women initiated their own agenda and determined to use every resource at their disposal to destroy the obstacles to racial justice and barriers to equal opportunity. The NAACP sponsored a legal campaign, led by Charles Houston and Thurgood Marshall, against educational discrimination and political disfranchisement; mobilized black communities; and sustained hope in the struggle. Black people benefited from the New Deal but less than white people did. The disparity between black and white lives was a spur to action. The juxtaposition of black subordination and misery alongside the new forms of federal aid so willingly distributed to white citizens convinced black Americans to intensify their own struggle for their rights as Americans. Many embraced radical critiques of American capitalism, but few ever considered communism a viable alternative to American democracy. Black people would emerge from the Depression more determined than ever to make democracy work for them.

The NAACP and Civil Rights Struggles

During the 1930s the NAACP became a more effective advocate for African-American civil rights. The biracial organization took the lead in pressing the government to protect African-American rights and eliminate the blatant racism in government programs. Part of the reason

18-1
18-2
18-3
18-4
18-5
18-6
18-7

18-1

18-2

18-3

18-4

18-5

18-6

18-7

for this new dynamism was the astute leadership of Walter White. White was an insistent voice of protest, personally investigating 42 lynchings and eight race riots, and he was an ardent lobbyist for civil rights legislation and racial justice.

The NAACP's new dynamism became apparent in 1930 when Walter White took a prominent role in the successful campaign to defeat Hoover's nomination of John J. Parker to the Supreme Court. Parker had openly embraced white supremacy, stating, for example, that the "participation of the Negro in politics is a source of evil and danger to both races." The NAACP formed a coalition with the AFL to persuade the Senate to reject Parker's nomination. It was the first time since 1854 that the Senate had refused to confirm a nominee to the Court. Although the NAACP could take only part of the credit for Parker's defeat, White trumpeted the victory and let it be known that African Americans would not be silent while "the Hoover administration proposed to conciliate southern white sentiment by sacrificing the Negro and his rights."

Du Bois Ignites a Controversy

The NAACP had critics, even within its own ranks. Many younger black people criticized its focus on civil liberties and deplored it for ignoring the economic misery of most African Americans. In 1934 W. E. B. Du Bois, editor of the NAACP's journal, the *Crisis*, joined the chorus. Criticizing what he considered the group's overemphasis on integration, Du Bois advocated a program of self-determination he hoped would permit black people to develop "an economic nation within a nation." Du Bois acknowledged that this internal economy could meet only part of the needs of the African-American community. But he insisted it could be developed and expanded in many ways.

Black intellectuals attacked Du Bois for advocating "voluntary segregation." Sociologist E. Franklin Frazier, for example, called the idea of black businesses succeeding within a segregated economy a black upper-class fantasy and social myth. Nevertheless, Du Bois held fast to his position that, as long as discrimination persisted, the NAACP should combine its opposition to legal segregation with vigorous support to improve segregated institutions. He was eventually forced from the editorship of the *Crisis*, but his resignation did not end the controversy. By the late 1930s the NAACP had developed a greater emphasis on economic policy and stronger ties to the growing labor movement.

Challenging Racial Discrimination in the Courts

A dramatic expansion of its legal campaign against racial discrimination enhanced the NAACP's effectiveness. Central to this project was the hiring of Charles Hamilton Houston, a Harvard-trained African-American lawyer and scholar, to lead it. Houston laid out a plan for a legal program to challenge inequality in education and the exclusion of black people from voting in the South. He used lawsuits to force state and local governments to live up to the Constitution and to inspire community organization.

Houston did not focus directly on eliminating segregation but rather sought to force southern states to equalize their facilities. Studies by the NAACP had revealed great disparities in per capita expenditures for white and black students and huge differences in salaries for white and black teachers. Houston was no supporter of segregation. He hoped to use litigation to secure judgments that would so increase the cost of separate institutions that states would be forced to abandon them.

To execute his agenda, Houston convinced Walter White in 1936 to hire his former student at Howard, Thurgood Marshall. During the 1930s Marshall and Houston focused on bringing greater parity between the pay of black and white teachers, a project they hoped

Thurgood Marshall (1908–1993), Charles Hamilton Houston (1895–1950), and Donald Gaines Murray. In 1935, attorneys Marshall and Houston handled Donald Murray's suit against the University of Maryland Law School. In 1938 Murray became the first African American to graduate from a southern state school. Thus began the relentless black attack against segregated education in America.

18-1
18-2
18-3
18-4
18-5
18-6
18-7

would increase NAACP membership among teachers, their students, and parents. The two men, working with a network of African-American attorneys, also attempted to end discrimination against black students in professional and graduate schools. Inequalities were obvious here because many southern states offered no graduate facilities of any kind to black students. Like other campaigns, this focus on graduate education was intended to establish precedents that might be used to gain equality in other areas and as an organizing tool to strengthen local NAACP branches. The first significant accomplishment in this campaign was the Supreme Court's 1938 decision in *Gaines v. Canada*. The Court ordered the state of Missouri to provide black citizens an opportunity to study law in a state-supported institution. Failure to do so, the Court held, would violate the equal protection of the law clause of the Fourteenth Amendment to the Constitution. In the 1940s several southern states, including North Carolina, Texas, Oklahoma, and South Carolina, also established law schools for their black citizens.

The *Gaines* decision encouraged Marshall and the NAACP to persist in challenging the constitutionality of the "separate but equal" doctrine. The case of *Sipuel v. Board of Regents of the University of Oklahoma* (1947) was another such effort. In this case Ada Lois Sipuel sought admission to the law school of the University of Oklahoma at Norman. In accordance with state statutes, she was refused admission but granted an out-of-state tuition award. Marshall argued that this arrangement failed to meet the needs of the state's black citizens. The Supreme Court declared that Oklahoma was obliged under the equal protection clause of the Fourteenth Amendment to provide a legal education for Sipuel. The case established the principle that the states had to provide a separate law school for African-American students in their home states.

Heman Sweatt, a black mail carrier, tested this principle in a suit against the University of Texas Law School. In *Sweatt v. Painter* (1950), the Supreme Court again sided with the NAACP lawyers. In response to Sweatt's initial challenge, Texas had created a separate law school that had inadequate library facilities, faculty, and support staff. It was separate but hardly equal. Marshall and black lawyers in Texas argued that the legal education offered Sweatt at the black law school was so inferior it violated the equal protection clause of the Fourteenth Amendment. These early legal victories laid the legal foundation for the 1954 *Brown v. Topeka Board of Education* decision.

Terrell law The Terrell law was a Texas law banning African-American participation in the Democratic primary.

The fight against political disfranchisement also helped mobilize local and state communities and NAACP branches. Nowhere was this more apparent than in Texas. In 1923 the Texas legislature enacted the **Terrell law**, which declared, "In no event shall a Negro be eligible to participate in a Democratic primary election . . . in . . . Texas." In the one-party South, the Democratic primaries were more important than the general elections, which usually merely rubber-stamped the choice made in the primary. Thus, to be denied the right to vote in Democratic Party primaries was to be disfranchised. The NAACP developed a case to test the constitutionality of the Terrell law and began a 20-year battle through the courts.

The Texas white primary fight was the most sustained and intense effort that any NAACP chapter undertook during the interwar period. It began in the 1920s and won its first victory when the Supreme Court ruled in 1927 in *Nixon v. Herndon* that the Texas Democratic primary was unconstitutional (see Chapter 17). At the national headquarters, Houston and Marshall orchestrated the assault, and subsequent decisions chipped away at the legal basis for the white primary. Finally, in 1944 the Supreme Court issued a ruling in *Smith v. Allwright* that ended the white primary altogether. It was the NAACP's greatest legal victory to that time. Many more would soon follow.

Black Women and Community Organizing

Black women made exceptional contributions to the NAACP during the 1930s through their fund-raising and membership drives. Three agitators for racial justice were Daisy Adams Lampkin (c. 1884–1965), Juanita Mitchell (1913–1992), and Ella Baker (1903–1986). These women worked closely with White and the NAACP throughout the Depression and World War II. Lampkin, a native of Washington, DC, in 1915, became the president of the Negro Women's Franchise League, a group dedicated to fighting for the vote. In 1930 Walter White enlisted her as regional field secretary of the NAACP, a post she held until she was made national field secretary in 1935.

Juanita E. Jackson was born in Hot Springs, Arkansas, and raised in Baltimore. She earned a degree in education from the University of Pennsylvania in 1931 and then returned to Baltimore, where she helped found the City-Wide Young People's Forum. This organization encouraged young people to combat such scourges as unemployment, segregation, and lynching. The success of the group prompted Walter White to offer her the leadership of the NAACP's new youth program, which she directed from 1935 to 1938. In 1950 she received a law degree from the University of Maryland. As the first black woman admitted to practice law in Maryland, she embarked on a series of cases that helped destroy racial segregation on the state's public beaches and in its public schools.

Ella Baker, who became one of the most important women in the civil rights movement of the 1950s and 1960s, began her life's work during the Depression. Born in Norfolk, Virginia, Baker moved to New York City in 1927 and worked as a waitress and as an organizer in radical politics. Within two years after her arrival, she had co-founded with George Schuyler the Young Negroes' Cooperative League in Harlem. The group practiced collective decision making and attempted to involve all segments of the community in the cooperatives. As she worked with the young men and women, Baker developed a strong belief in grassroots mobilization. She also worked with women's and labor groups, such as the Harlem Housewives Cooperative, the Women's Day Workers and Industrial League, and the YWCA. In 1936 she worked as a teacher with the Works Progress Administration (WPA)—a New Deal organization created to provide jobs for the unemployed—and eventually became one of its assistant supervisors. Walter White was impressed with her relentless organizing and management skills. In 1941, after much persuasion, Baker accepted White's offer to become an assistant field secretary of the NAACP. She traveled across the country and throughout the South, making friendships that would serve her well in the coming decades. From 1943 to 1946, Baker worked as director of NAACP branches and built up the organization's membership.

Other black women organized outside the NAACP. Black women in Detroit provide a potent illustration of this kind of activity. On June 10, 1930, 50 black women responded to a call issued by Fannie B. Peck, wife of Rev. William H. Peck, pastor of the 2,000-member Bethel African Methodist Episcopal Church and the president of the Booker T. Washington Trade Association. Out of this initial meeting emerged the Detroit Housewives' League, an organization that combined economic nationalism and black women's self-determination to help black families and businesses survive the Depression. Peck had been inspired by M. A. L. Holsey, secretary of the National Negro Business League. Holsey described the directed spending campaigns that enabled housewives in Harlem to consolidate their economic power to persuade businesses to hire black women and children. Fannie Peck became convinced that such an organization would also succeed in Detroit.

The Detroit organization grew rapidly. By 1934, 10,000 black women belonged to it. The only requirement for membership was a pledge to support black businesses, buy black products, and patronize black professionals, thereby keeping money in the community. The league quickly spread to other cities. Housewives' leagues in Chicago, Baltimore, Washington, Durham (North Carolina), Harlem, and Cleveland used boycotts of merchants who refused to sell black products and employ black children as clerks or stock persons to secure an estimated 75,000 new jobs for black people.

African Americans and the New Deal

18-3 **How did the New Deal affect African Americans?**

In 1932, the third year of the Great Depression, voters elected New York governor Franklin Delano Roosevelt to the presidency in a landslide. Roosevelt's lopsided victory over Hoover demonstrated the country's loss of faith in the Republican Party and its economic philosophy and heralded the emergence of a new electoral coalition. The new president appealed to the Democratic Party's base of support in the white South, but to this group he added a coalition of western farmers, industrial workers, white ethnic groups in northern cities, and reform-minded intellectuals. For the time being,

18-1

18-2

18-3

18-4

18-5

18-6

18-7

however, black Americans still clung to the Republican banner. But this was the last election in which the party of Lincoln could take them for granted. To counter the Depression, in his first term Roosevelt inaugurated a multitude of programs—collectively known as the New Deal—that would shift the allegiance of African Americans. Initially his programs continued past patterns of discrimination against African Americans, but by 1935 the New Deal was providing more equal benefits and prompting profound social changes. The result was a new political order that ultimately undermined the edifice of American racism.

Roosevelt and the First New Deal, 1933–1935

During his first one hundred days in office, Roosevelt pressed through Congress a profusion of bold new economic initiatives that came to be known as the first New Deal. To combat the Depression, Roosevelt, unlike Hoover, followed no predetermined plan. Instead, he favored experimentation over ideology as the guide to federal action. With little resistance Congress passed the president's sprawling and complex laws aimed at overhauling the nation's financial, agricultural, and industrial systems. Meanwhile, Roosevelt moved to counter the immediate suffering of the unemployed with a massive emergency federal relief effort. Many of the first New Deal's programs benefited both white and black people, but the strength of white southerners in the Democratic Party and the nearly complete lack of African-American political power in the South caused much of this early program to be unfairly administered.

The **Agricultural Adjustment Act (AAA),** designed to protect farmers by giving them subsidies to limit production and thereby stabilize prices, illustrates the key benefits and problems African Americans experienced during the first New Deal. The theory underlying the AAA was that lessening production would increase agricultural prices. Essentially, farmers would be paid to grow less. The program provided for sharecroppers and tenant farmers to get part of the subsidies and allowed new rural relief agencies to dispense supplementary income to off-season wageworkers.

This program helped many African Americans, mainly because it pumped billions of dollars into an economic sector on which over 4.5 million black people relied for their livelihood. Also, the AAA was designed to remedy the problems of those farmers—disproportionately African American—who were overreliant on such cash crops as cotton. The flow of money from the AAA did, for a time, slow the exodus of black people from farming. Fewer left the farms in the first two years of the program than in the two years before it began.

But if the AAA brought real benefits to black farmers, it was often contrary to protections written into the law, administered unfairly and corruptly. Local control of the AAA resided in the hands of the Extension Service and County Agricultural Conservation Committees, which were supposed to represent all farmers. The county agents, however, were often the planters themselves, and the committees mirrored southern politics as a whole by excluding black people. During the first two years of the AAA, black farmers complained bitterly that white landlords simply grabbed and pocketed the millions of dollars of benefit checks they were supposed to forward to tenants. To compound the injury, some planters then evicted the sharecroppers and tenants from the land.

The experience of African Americans with the **National Industrial Recovery Act (NIRA)** mimicked the problems with the AAA. The NIRA was intended to revive manufacturing by allowing industries to cooperate in establishing codes of conduct to govern prices, wage levels, and employment practices, all of which were to

18-1

Watch on MyHistoryLab Video: The New Deal

18-2

18-3

18-4

18-5

Agricultural Adjustment Act (AAA) A federal program that provided subsidies to farmers to grow less to help stabilize prices.

18-6

18-7

Read on MyHistoryLab Document: E. E. Lewis, "Black Cotton Farmers and the AAA," 1935

National Industrial Recovery Act (NIRA) Federal law intended to promote the revival of manufacturing by allowing for cooperation among industries.

VOICES   A Black Sharecropper Details Abuse in the Administration of Agricultural Relief

This is one of many letters black sharecroppers sent to the NAACP for assistance to halt the mass evictions and abuse of New Deal relief efforts.

ALABAMA

June 21, 1934

Dear Sir:—

I am writing you these few lines ask you if it is any possible chance of you fining out just why F.E.R.A. office here in . . . refuse to gave me work when I have six in family to care for and also my wife's mother who is over 65 years old and been under the Doctor care for the past seven years of course my wife has a little job but its not with the relief work which some weeks she makes five dollars and some weeks less with four children to take care off which range in age 8–6–4–3 years old and we have $5 per month rent and also $1.74 per week Insurance which that don't enclude Food and Clothing and Fuel to burn. Now Mr. White in the past two and half months I am being going to the relief office trying to get on the relief work and it seem like it is empossible and also just before the first of April I went up to the relief office and explain my case to Mr . . . , the man that gave out the work cards and he gave me a food order for the amount of $2—two dollars and also I got some work to do. But as soon as I got paid for the 24 hours work he came to me to collect $2 for the food order that he gave me and I refuse to gave him $2 and I havent been able to get any more work to do and I have been going up to the office each day sence. But they tell me at the office that they cant gave me work because my wife is working. Of course if that maybe the case I can gave you the name and the address of at least a hundred families where there is two and three in one family who are working on the relief project and I know of at least twenty single men with no one but theirself to take care of and are working twenty-four hours every week and they got to gave their foreman one dollar each every week if they want to stay on the job.

Now Mr. White the white man who my wife work for and my wife told him that they refuse to gave me work because she was working for me and he went up to relief office to see about it But they told him that they didnt cut me out of work because my wife were working but they cut me off because I were unable to do the work. and of course I know that to be very much untrue. The trouble is I refuse to be a fool like so many of my race here and else where around here to pay for a food order that is supose to be giving to the needy free of charge but lots are paying for them and also paying for their job. Of course Mr. White I am colored and when you go up to the relief office The Colored people is treated just as if they were dogs and not human beings. I have been up in the office and I have seen with my own eyes my color kicked and beaten down a whole flight of stairs. I have seen everything done except been murder. Understand Mr. White the little job that my wife has isn't on the relief is a private and everybody that is head of any thing here in the relief office is kin to one another. Now Mr. White the lady that is head of the relief is Mrs. . . . which I saw here once since I was cut off from work and I explained my case to her and she told that she would send a investigator around to my home the next morning whose name is Miss. el; and she told me that when I gave Mr. . . . the $2 for the food order she would O.K. my work card. Mr. White if possible will you please fine out for me just what is the reason they refuse to gave me work when I have six in family and rent to pay. Insurance, Doctor bill, milk bill, buy food and clothing and with only my wife at work it is impossible Mr. White.

1. **Why did the writer seek help from Walter White and the NAACP?**
2. **What were some of the reasons, both implied and noted, that prevented even more black people from protesting economic inequality?**

SOURCE: Herbert Aptheker, ed., *A Documentary History of the Negro People in the United States, 1933–1945,* Vol. 4, New York: Citadel Press, 1974; 1992, pp. 58–60. Reprinted by permission of Bettina Aptheker, Literary Executer, Herbert Aptheker Estate.

18-1

18-2

18-3

18-4

18-5

18-6

18-7

Read on **MyHistoryLab**
Document: Luther C. Wandall Describes His Experience in the Civilian Conservation Corp (CCC), 1935

18-1

18-2

18-3

18-4

18-5

18-6

Watch on **MyHistoryLab**
Video: Responding to the Great Depression: Whose New Deal?

18-7

be overseen by a National Recovery Administration (NRA). The NRA oversaw the drafting of the codes but faced tremendous resistance from employers and unions in eliminating racial disparities in wage rates and working conditions. Even when African-American advocates did win wage increases for occupations in which black people predominated, the result was often a shift to white labor. To the relief of many African-American advocates and workers, the Supreme Court declared the NIRA unconstitutional in 1935.

The New Deal's national welfare programs included the Federal Emergency Relief Administration (FERA), the Civilian Conservation Corps (CCC), the Public Works Administration, and the Civil Works Administration (CWA). Although inadequate and unfairly administered on local levels, these programs were often the only thing standing between black people and starvation. FERA provided funds for local and state relief operations to restart and expand their programs. The program pulled millions of people back from the brink of starvation. Because African Americans suffered greater economic devastation, they received benefits at a higher rate than white people. However, many in the Roosevelt administration deemed direct welfare to be morally debilitating, so the government emphasized hiring the unemployed for public works projects. The CWA was a temporary agency created to help people through the winter of 1933–1934. The CCC built segregated camps to employ young men and remove them from the poverty and hopelessness of urban areas. Yet despite the segregation, former enrollees conceded that their experience in the CCC helped them secure better jobs and a middle-class life after World War II. By the time the CCC was abolished in 1945, more than 200,000 African-American youth had taken part in it.

These relief programs helped many African Americans through the worst parts of the Depression. However, the programs also tended to be less helpful to black people than they were to white people. For example, in its early days the CCC was a tightly segregated institution, with only about 5 percent of its slots going to black youths during its first year. Likewise, although FERA tended to be administered fairly in northern cities, in the South it reached few of those in need.

Black Officials in the New Deal

The first New Deal was not completely bleak for African Americans. In addition to the benefits—however grudgingly disbursed—that New Deal relief programs provided, African Americans also gained new influence and allies within the Roosevelt administration. Their experience reflected the growing availability of highly trained African Americans for government service and the emerging consciousness among white liberals about the problems—and potential electoral power—of black people.

Black people found a staunch ally in First Lady Eleanor Roosevelt. She was revered for her relentless commitment to racial justice. She arranged meetings at the White House for black leaders. She cajoled her husband to consider legislation for black rights. She defied Jim Crow laws by refusing to sit in a "white only" section while attending a meeting in the South. Moreover, she wrote newspaper columns calling for "fair play and equal opportunity for Negro citizens." Roosevelt further endeared herself to black Americans when she resigned her membership in the Daughters of the American Revolution after that organization refused to allow a young black opera singer, Marian Anderson, to perform at its Constitution Hall in Washington in 1939.

Other liberals joined Eleanor Roosevelt to press for racial justice and seek the appointment of African Americans throughout the government. Early in 1933 President Roosevelt acceded to their request that he appoint someone in his administration to assume responsibility for ensuring that African Americans received fair treatment. He asked Secretary of the Interior Harold Ickes, a former president of the Chicago chapter of the NAACP and a white man whom most black Americans trusted as a friend, to make this happen. Ickes invited Clark Foreman, a young white Georgian who had rejected his region's racism, to handle the assignment. Foreman recognized the irony of a white man representing black people in the government and immediately began to recruit highly trained African Americans. Similar efforts to bring African Americans into government positions were made by Eleanor Roosevelt, Ickes, and other administration officials. The result was that doors to the government began opening in an unprecedented way.

The Rise of Black Social Scientists

18-4 **What was the "black cabinet," its purpose, and its goals?**

The Roosevelt administration employed professional black architects, lawyers, engineers, economists, statisticians, interviewers, office managers, and social workers. The Department of Commerce hired Eugene K. Jones, on leave from the National Urban League. The National Youth Administration brought in Mary McLeod Bethune, and the Department of Interior employed William H. Hastie and Robert Weaver. Ira De A. Reid joined the Social Security Administration, and Lawrence W. Oxley worked for the Department of Labor. Ambrose Caliver served in the WPA and the Office of Education.

A core of highly placed African-American social scientists thus became linked in a network called the Federal Council on Negro Affairs, more loosely known as Roosevelt's "**black cabinet**." Mary McLeod Bethune was a leader of this body, which consisted primarily of "New Deal race specialists." It numbered 27 men and three women working mostly in temporary emergency agencies, and it included such stalwarts as housing administrator Robert Weaver. The group met every Friday in Bethune's Washington home. This cadre of advisers pressured the president and the heads of federal agencies to adopt and support color-blind policies and lobbied to advance the economic, educational, and social status of black Americans.

black cabinet Informal group of highly placed African-American advisers to President Franklin D. Roosevelt.

Social Scientists and the New Deal

Many black intellectuals, scholars, and writers believed the social sciences could be used to adjudicate race relations, and during the New Deal they found greater receptiveness to their work than ever before. In sociology E. Franklin Frazier and Charles S. Johnson took the lead. Frazier's pioneering studies of black families placed him at the forefront of debates on social policy. Throughout the 1930s, as the editor of *Opportunity*, the journal of the Urban League, Johnson published insightful critiques of American racial practices and policies, as well as the work of emerging black novelists, poets, and playwrights.

18-1
18-2
18-3
18-4
18-5
18-6
18-7

Mary McLeod Bethune played a powerful role in Roosevelt's black cabinet. In the 1920s she was the leader of the National Association of Colored Women (NACW) and later founded the National Council of Negro Women (NCNW).

Robert Weaver, along with Mary McLeod Bethune, was a co-leader of Franklin Roosevelt's "black Cabinet." In 1966 Weaver served as secretary of housing and urban development under Lyndon B. Johnson, the first African-American cabinet secretary. He spearheaded the passage of the Housing Act of 1968, which expanded opportunities for black home ownership.

Meanwhile, Ralph Bunche became well known within political science, and Abram Harris and Robert Weaver gained renown in economics.

Historians such as Carter G. Woodson, Lorenzo Greene, Benjamin Quarles, and John Hope Franklin argued that black people had been active agents in the past and not simply the passive objects of white people's actions. Through the Association for the Study of Negro Life and History and Negro History Week, Woodson and his coworkers Lorenzo Greene, Alrutheus Taylor, and Monroe Work deployed their scholarship to dismiss claims of black inferiority. Their scholarly emphasis on racial pride, achievement, and autonomy raised black morale.

The increasing importance of black scholars became apparent late in the 1930s when the Carnegie Corporation, a philanthropic foundation, sponsored a major study of black life. Although Swedish social scientist Gunnar Myrdal led the study, nearly half of the large staff of scholars were African Americans, and several, particularly Bunche, had a major impact on the work. Published in 1944 as *An American Dilemma*, this massive study profoundly affected public understanding of how racism undermined the progress of African Americans, and it helped set the agenda for the civil rights movement.

African Americans and the Second New Deal

By late 1935, after two years marked by a slow recovery, much of the first New Deal lay in shambles. The Supreme Court had invalidated major parts of it, and a conservative backlash was emerging against the Roosevelt administration. In response, Roosevelt pressed for a second burst of legislation marked by the passage of the Social Security Act (SSA), the National Labor Relations Act (NLRA), the creation of the WPA, and other measures considerably more radical than those he had established in 1933. This new set of laws, known as the second New Deal, survived legal challenges and fundamentally changed the United States, particularly by strengthening the role of the federal government.

Roosevelt's leftward political shift helped him win the 1936 presidential election in a landslide. This election cemented a new electoral coalition that yoked the southern wing of the Democratic Party with more liberal farmers and working-class voters who were labor union members in the North and West. The Democratic Party began to win the votes of the large African-American populations in the great cities of the North. The black press fanned the shifting winds, and many more black urban dwellers developed an intense interest in politics. They began to connect political power with the prospect of improving their economic conditions. By the end of the 1930s, black urban voters garnered noteworthy influence in key states such as Illinois, Ohio, Pennsylvania, and New York. This political consciousness led to the election of black state legislators in California, Illinois, Indiana, Kansas, Kentucky, New Jersey, New York, Ohio, Pennsylvania, and West Virginia.

The shift to the Democratic Party did not occur without anxiety. Some black people feared that by joining the party they would open the door for even more white southern Democrats to assume national power and thwart black advancement. But by 1936 most African-American voters were willing to take the risk.

The increased participation of African Americans in the Democratic Party sent chills down the spines of the white southern elite. The tension between black Democrats and white conservative Democrats erupted at the party's 1936 convention in Philadelphia. The seating of 32 black delegates infuriated southern politicians. The selection of a black Baptist minister to open one session with a prayer outraged South Carolina Senator Ellison D. "Cotton Ed" Smith, who, accompanied by Mayor Burnet Maybank of Charleston and other delegates, marched off the floor, proclaiming that they refused to support "any political organization that looks upon the Negro and caters to him as a political and social equal." The next day when Congressman Mitchell of Illinois took to the floor, Smith repeated his walkout. The South Carolina delegation subsequently adopted a protest resolution denouncing the appearance of black men on the convention's program. Southern white protests, however, had no effect on the political decisions of black men and women. Heeding the advice of the NAACP, they voted their personal interests.

Despite the rise of black Democrats, southern congressmen succeeded in excluding many African Americans from key government programs. For example, they insisted on denying the benefits of the NLRA and the SSA to agricultural laborers and domestic servants. These white southerners could not, however, stop the tilt toward fairer administration of programs or the revival of the push for equal rights, which had lain all but dormant since the end of Reconstruction.

The WPA illustrates the changes that the second New Deal and the increasing shift of African Americans to the Democratic Party wrought. The WPA, with Harry Hopkins as its head, was created to employ the unemployed. Under Hopkins's direction and sustained with $1.39 billion in federal funds, the WPA put thousands of men and women to work building new roads, hospitals, city halls, courthouses, and schools. Under the aegis of the WPA, American citizens built bridges, ports, and water systems. Larger-scale infrastructure projects included the Lincoln Tunnel under the Hudson River connecting New York and New Jersey, the Triborough Bridge system linking Manhattan to Long Island, and the Bonneville and Boulder dams.

The WPA was administered far more fairly than were the first New Deal programs. The national government explicitly rejected racial discrimination and made sure local officials complied. Although far from perfect, by 1939 it had provided assistance to one million black families on a far more equitable basis than ever before.

The same pattern prevailed in the WPA's four arts programs—the Federal Art Project, the Federal Music Project, the Federal Theater Project, and the Federal Writers' Project—which employed thousands of musicians, intellectuals, writers, and artists. A fifth program that was

18-1
18-2
18-3
18-4
18-5
18-6
18-7

18-1

18-2

18-3

18-4

18-5

18-6

18-7

One of the most effective New Deal agencies, the WPA offered African Americans numerous opportunities for vocational training. Young men learned from experienced craftsmen. As this 1942 photo illustrates, the intricate lathe operations instruction prepared the trainee with skills that could be used in the defense industries.

created in 1937, the Historical Records Survey, sent teams of writers, including Zora Neale Hurston, to collect folklore and study ethnic groups. One team collected the life histories of 2,000 former slaves.

Between 1935 and 1943, the WPA helped artists display their talents and made their work widely available. Among the black artists hired to adorn government buildings, post offices, and public parks were Aaron Douglas, Charles Alston, Richmond Barthe, Sargent Johnson, Archibald Motley Jr., and Augusta Savage.

The Federal Theater Project established 16 black theater units. Among their most notable productions was a version of *Macbeth* set in Haiti with an all-black cast. White actor John Houseman and black actress Rose McClendon directed the Harlem Federal Theater Project. This project—more than the others—proved controversial due to the fear of communist influence and the leftist political views of some African-American writers and performers.

Organized Labor and Black America

18-5 What role did organized labor play in radicalizing black Americans during the 1930s?

📖 Read the Document: National Labor Relations Act, 1935

The relationship of African Americans to labor unions changed profoundly during the 1930s. Before this time, most local unions affiliated with the national AFL barred black people or restricted them to segregated locals. The railroad unions, which called themselves "brotherhoods," excluded black workers entirely. The New Deal, especially after 1935, did much to transform the labor movement. The NLRA and the militancy of workers provided the opportunity to organize the nation's great mass production industries. Still, leaders of the AFL were unwilling to incorporate into their unions the masses of unskilled workers, many of whom were African American or recent European immigrants. Frustrated by this situation, in 1935 the head of the United Mine Workers, John L. Lewis (1880–1969), and his followers formed the **Committee for Industrial Organization (CIO)** to take on the task.

Committee for Industrial Organization (CIO) Labor organization that was committed to interracial and multiethnic organizing.

Unlike the AFL, the CIO was committed to interracial and multiethnic organizing and so enabled more African Americans to participate in the labor movement. Its leaders knew it was in organized labor's best interest to admit black men and women to membership.

VOICES A. Philip Randolph Inspires a Young Black Activist

In 1928 young E. D. Nixon heard A. Philip Randolph speak, and it changed Nixon's life. He became president of the Montgomery branch of the Brotherhood of Sleeping Car Porters that year and remained in the post until 1964. During that period he played a leading role in mobilizing and organizing the Montgomery bus boycott ignited by Rosa Parks's arrest for refusing to relinquish her seat to a white male passenger. He recalls Randolph's speech in the following passage.

When I heard Randolph speak [in 1928], it was like a light. Most eloquent man I ever heard. He done more to bring me in the fight for civil rights than anybody. Before that time, I figure that a Negro would be kicked around and accept whatever the white man did. I never knew the Negro had a right to enjoy freedom like everyone else. When Randolph stood there and talked that day, it make a different man out of me. From that day on, I was determined that I was gonna fight for freedom until I was able to get some of it for myself.

1. **What does Nixon's reaction to Randolph's speech say about the importance of leadership in the labor movement?**
2. **How did Randolph's speech influence Nixon's later involvement in the struggle for black civil rights?**

SOURCE: Quoted in Studs Turkel, *Hard Times: An Oral History of the Great Depression* (1970; reprint, New York: New Press, pbk ed., 2000), 119.

But it took a massive change in outlook to achieve this unity. By 1940 the CIO had enlisted approximately 210,000 black members.

A. Philip Randolph's Brotherhood of Sleeping Car Porters (BSCP) remained with the AFL, but it also benefited from New Deal legislation. In 1934 Congress had amended the Railway Labor Act in a way that helped the BSCP overcome the opposition of the Pullman Company. The law required that corporations bargain in good faith with unions if the unions could demonstrate through elections monitored by the National Mediation Board that they genuinely represented the corporations' employees. The Pullman Company resisted, but in 1937, long after an election certified the BSCP as the workers' representative, the company finally recognized the brotherhood. Then—and only then—did the AFL grant the BSCP full membership as an international union.

Although most black people in unions were men, some unions also represented and helped improve the lives of black working women. For example, since the early nineteenth century there had been a rigid hierarchy among workers in the tobacco industry, one of the few areas of the economy outside agriculture or domestic service that employed many black women. Jobs were assigned on the basis of race and gender, with black women receiving the most difficult and tedious job, that of "stemmer." In 1939 stemmer Louise "Mama" Harris instigated a series of walkouts at the I. N. Vaughn Company in Richmond. The strikes, which CIO affiliates—including the white women of the International Ladies Garment Workers Union—supported, led to the formation of the Tobacco Workers Organizing Committee, another CIO affiliate. In 1943 black women union leaders and activists, including Theodosia Simpson and Miranda Smith, were involved in a strike against the R. J. Reynolds tobacco company to force it to the negotiating table.

18-1

18-2

18-3

18-4

18-5

18-6

18-7

The Communist Party and African Americans

18-6 What was the *Scottsboro* case and what were its consequences?

Throughout the 1930s the Communist Party intensified its support of African Americans' efforts to address unemployment and job discrimination and to seek social justice. The communists' militant antiracism and determination to be interracial attracted some African Americans. The party expelled members who exhibited racial prejudice and gave black men key leadership positions. James Ford, an African American, ran as the party's vice-presidential candidate in the election of 1932. Although few black men and women actually joined the Communist Party, some became increasingly sympathetic to left-wing ideas and prescriptions as the Depression wore on.

Read on MyHistoryLab
Document: Lester B. Granger Calls on Black Workers to Combat Discrimination in Organized Labor, 1934

Many black workers were drawn to the Communist Party because it criticized the refusal of organized white labor to include them. The communists insisted that "this anti-Negro attitude of the reactionary labor leaders helps to split the ranks of labor, allows the employers to carry out their policy of 'divide and rule,' frustrates the efforts of the working class to emancipate itself from the yoke of capitalism, and dims the class-consciousness of the white workers as well as of the Negro workers." Indeed, much of the push for racial equality within the CIO emanated from those connected with the party.

The International Labor Defense and the "Scottsboro Boys"

The *Scottsboro* case brought the Communist Party to the attention of many African Americans. It began when nine black youths who had caught a ride on a freight train in Alabama were tried, convicted, and sentenced to death for allegedly raping two white women. Their ordeal started on the night of March 25, 1931, when a group of young white hobos accosted them. A fight broke out. The black youths threw the white youths off the train. The losers filed a complaint with the Scottsboro, Alabama, sheriff charging that black hoodlums had assaulted them. The sheriff ordered his deputies to round up every black person on the train. The sweep netted the nine young black men: Ozie Powell, Clarence Norris, Charlie Weems, Olen Montgomery, Willie Robertson, Haywood Patterson, Eugene Williams, Andy Wright, and Roy Wright. The police also discovered two young white women: 19-year-old Victoria Price and 17-year-old Ruby Bates.

Scottsboro Boys Nine young African-American men unjustly accused of raping two white women in Alabama in 1931. The Supreme Court overturned their convictions in 1937.

Afraid of being arrested and perhaps ashamed of being hobos, Price and Bates falsely claimed that the nine black youths had sexually assaulted them. On the basis of that accusation, the "**Scottsboro Boys**" (ranging in age from 13 to 20) were given a hasty trial. They never had a chance. Their white court-appointed attorney came to court drunk each day. Three days after the trial started and 15 days after their arrest, the jurors found them all guilty. Eight received the death sentence, and the youngest was sentenced to life imprisonment, even though medical examinations of Price and Bates proved that neither had been raped.

While other organizations dawdled or refused to intervene, the Communist Party's International Labor Defense (ILD) rushed to help the "boys" by appealing the conviction and death sentence to the Supreme Court. The case produced two important decisions that reaffirmed black people's right to the basic protections that all other American citizens enjoyed. In *Powell v. Alabama* (1932), the Court ruled that the *Scottsboro* defendants had not been given adequate legal counsel and that the trial had taken place in a hostile and volatile atmosphere. Asserting that the youths' right to due process as set forth in the Fourteenth Amendment had been violated, the Court ordered a new trial. Alabama did as

The "Scottsboro Boys," a case of southern justice gone awry, attracted international attention and fueled competition between the NAACP and the Communist Party. In this 1937 photograph the NAACP's Juanita E. Jackson Mitchell visits with the Scottsboro Boys, nine unemployed black young men accused of raping two white women mill workers on a Southern Railroad freight car on March 25, 1931. All were sentenced to death, with one exception. Eugene Williams's life was spared because he was only 13. Victoria Price and Ruby Bates recanted their stories, but it made no difference. The U.S. Supreme Court overturned the death convictions and sentences in two landmark cases, one of which established the right of the accused to competent legal counsel.

18-1
18-2
18-3
18-4
18-5
18-6
18-7

instructed, but the new trial resulted in another guilty verdict and sentences of death or life imprisonment. The ILD promptly appealed, and in *Norris v. Alabama* (1935) the Court decided that all Americans have the right to a trial by a jury of their peers. The systematic exclusion of African Americans from the *Scottsboro* juries, the Court held, denied the defendants equal protection under the law, which the Fourteenth Amendment guaranteed. Chief Justice Charles Evans Hughes pointed out that no black citizens had served on juries in the Alabama counties for decades, even though many were qualified to serve. The Court noted that the exclusion was blatant racial discrimination and called for yet another trial.

Despite these stunning defeats and increasing evidence that the "boys" had been falsely convicted, Alabama still pursued the case. Even when Ruby Bates publicly admitted the rape charge had been a hoax, white Alabamians ignored her. Finally, in 1937 Alabama dropped its charges against five of the nine men, and in the 1940s the state released those still in jail. Altogether, nine innocent black men had collectively served some three-quarters of a century in prison. Clarence Willie Norris, however, escaped and fled to Michigan, returning decades later to receive a ceremonious pardon from Governor George Wallace.

Debating Communist Leadership

Throughout the *Scottsboro* case, the NAACP tried unsuccessfully to wrest control from the Communist Party. Indeed, as the case evolved, tensions and competition between the Communist Party and the NAACP for leadership of black America flared into open hostility. At first, the NAACP had hesitated to defend accused rapists, but it moved more decisively after the Communist Party had taken the lead.

The contest between the NAACP and the communists reveals the differences between the two groups. The party organized protest marches and demonstrations and used its press to denounce more cautious middle-class organizations. In Harlem, for example, the communists staged a 1931 protest march that attracted over 3,000 black men and women. The NAACP countered with a carefully orchestrated campaign that questioned the sincerity and effectiveness of the communists and sought to repair its own reputation as a respectable and effective advocate for African Americans.

Black public opinion divided in its evaluation of the party. Some black men and women applauded the communists. But other African Americans ridiculed the party. George Schuyler, a columnist for the *Pittsburgh Courier*, used his razor-sharp wit to castigate the party and persuade black people that its claim to champion African Americans was a lie.

Although most African Americans applauded the antiracist work that the Communist Party supported and performed, there was no chance they would defect from the traditional American political system, as W. E. B. Du Bois wrote in 1931:

> American Negroes do not propose to be the shock troops of the Communist Revolution, driven out in the front to death, cruelty and humiliation in order to win victories for white workers. . . . Negroes know perfectly well that whenever they try to lead revolution in America, the nation will unite as one fist to crush them and them alone.

The National Negro Congress

National Negro Congress (NNC) Organization founded in 1936 to unite African-American protest groups.

The infighting between the Communist Party and other groups doomed a major attempt to unite all the disparate African-American protest groups into the **National Negro Congress (NNC)**. John P. Davis, a Washington-based economist, organized the NNC, modeling it on his experience as the executive secretary of the Joint Committee on National Recovery, a coalition of black groups that pressed for fairness in the early New Deal. The NNC was to be a federation of organizations on a national scale supported by regional councils. Over 800 delegates representing 585 organizations attended its first meeting, held in Chicago in 1936. However, prominent black activists, leaders, and intellectuals were conspicuously absent, notably those associated with the NAACP. A. Philip Randolph was elected president, and Davis became the executive secretary. The group resolved not to be dominated by any one political faction and to build on the strength of all parts of the black community. Although handicapped by lack of funds, the NNC initially worked effectively at the local or community level. With branches in approximately 70 cities, the organization gained for its members increased employment opportunities, better housing, and adequate relief work. The NNC also prodded labor unions, in particular the CIO, to fight for better conditions and higher wages for black workers.

At the NNC's second meeting in Philadelphia in 1937, a skeptical Davis maintained that the Democratic Party would never allow black people to benefit fairly from the New Deal. Eventually the increasing importance of communists in the NNC alienated most other groups and reduced the organization's ability to speak for most black people. By 1940 it was greatly weakened. Randolph was voted out of office, and the once promising NNC became little more than a front group for the Communist Party.

Misuses of Medical Science: The Tuskegee Study

18-7   What was the Tuskegee study and its impact?

The 1930s marked the rising prominence of black scholars and intellectuals; paradoxically, the decade also witnessed the worst manifestation of racism in American science. This shocking episode of racial mistreatment occurred in Macon County, Alabama, through medical experimentation on impoverished and vulnerable populations. There, in 1932, U.S. Public Health Service (USPHS) officials initiated several major studies of syphilis, a sexually transmitted disease that can cause paralysis, insanity, heart failure, and eventually death. For the subjects of its program—titled the Tuskegee Study of Untreated Syphilis in the Male Negro—the USPHS recruited 622 black men, all of them poor share-croppers and the majority illiterate. Of these men, 431 had advanced cases of syphilis. The rest were free of the disease and served as controls for comparison.

Another experiment decades prior to the one in Tuskegee involved people in Guatemala. As historian Susan Reverby explained, "This experiment is the global, rather than the American South, differed from the Study in Alabama in two major ways: government doctors did infect people with syphilis and then did treat them with penicillin." In 1944 the Public Health Service deliberately injected gonorrhea in "volunteers" who were inmates at the Terre Haute Federal Penitentiary in Indiana but abandoned the study when it proved "difficult to get the men to exhibit infection."

The **Tuskegee Study** was called a treatment program, but it turned out to be an experiment, designed to chart the progression and development of a potentially fatal disease. To gain the men's trust, the government doctors centered their work at Tuskegee Institute and hired a black nurse, Eunice Rivers, who convinced the men they had "bad blood" and needed special treatment. Although penicillin, which can cure the disease, became available in the 1940s, the sharecroppers never received it. Instead, they were given ineffective placebos, which they were told would cure them.

Initially the Tuskegee Study was to last only 6 to 12 months, but it was repeatedly extended. The men received regular physical examinations, which included a painful lumbar puncture. This insertion of a needle into the spinal cord to obtain fluid for diagnosis often caused the men severe headaches, and in a few isolated cases it resulted in paralysis and even death. For almost 40 years, Tuskegee Study doctors observed the men, keeping careful records of their health and performing autopsies on those who died, but they never treated them for syphilis. So little understood was the Tuskegee Study that men not only remained in the program but believed they were fortunate to have the physical examinations, the hot lunches provided on examination days, and the burial allowance the government guaranteed their families. The medical community knew of the Tuskegee experiment, but the general public learned of it only in 1972 when a reporter broke the story. Black attorney Fred D. Gray of Alabama sued the U.S. government on behalf of the participants and their families, but before the case went to trial, the government made a $9 million settlement to the Tuskegee survivors and the descendants of those who had died.

Tuskegee Study A medical study by the U.S. Public Health Service of the effects of syphilis on 622 black men. The study ran from 1932 to the 1970s, and the men were given only placebos and no treatment for the disease.

From 1932 to 1972, the U.S. Public Health Service conducted an experiment on approximately 400 black Alabama sharecroppers to trace the evolution of untreated syphilis. The men were never informed that they had the disease, nor were they given penicillin when it became available. On May 16, 1997, President Bill Clinton on behalf of the U.S. government finally apologized for this cruel and clearly racist experiment on human subjects.

18-1

18-2

18-3

18-4

18-5

18-6

18-7

CONCLUSION

Notable political changes occurred during the early 1930s: the NAACP came of age, black women found their voice, white left-wing leaders joined with black men and women in interracial alliances, organized labor bridged the race chasm, and black voters switched from the Republican to the Democratic Party. The New Deal had stimulated some economic recovery and, more important, laid the basis for a strong national state and a political coalition that, beginning with World War II, would challenge the nation's racial system.

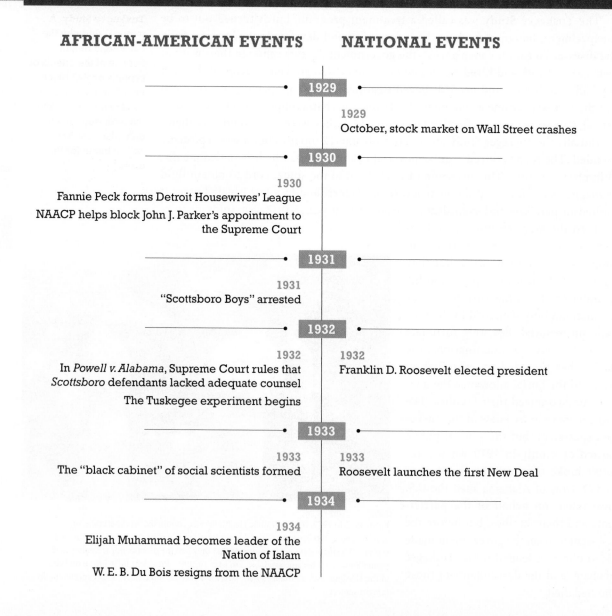

CHAPTER TIMELINE

AFRICAN-AMERICAN EVENTS

NATIONAL EVENTS

1929

1929
October, stock market on Wall Street crashes

1930

1930
Fannie Peck forms Detroit Housewives' League
NAACP helps block John J. Parker's appointment to the Supreme Court

1931

1931
"Scottsboro Boys" arrested

1932

1932
In *Powell v. Alabama*, Supreme Court rules that *Scottsboro* defendants lacked adequate counsel
The Tuskegee experiment begins

1932
Franklin D. Roosevelt elected president

1933

1933
The "black cabinet" of social scientists formed

1933
Roosevelt launches the first New Deal

1934

1934
Elijah Muhammad becomes leader of the Nation of Islam
W. E. B. Du Bois resigns from the NAACP

CHAPTER TIMELINE

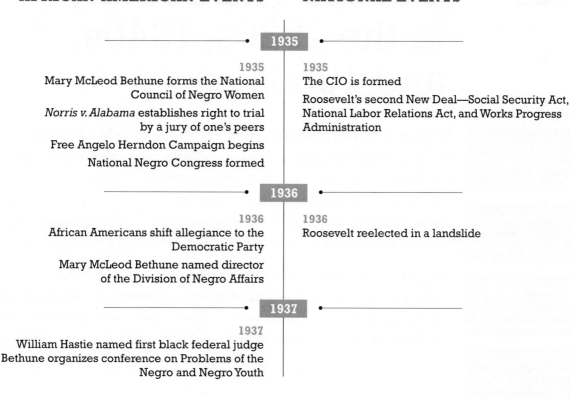

AFRICAN-AMERICAN EVENTS

1935

Mary McLeod Bethune forms the National Council of Negro Women

Norris v. Alabama establishes right to trial by a jury of one's peers

Free Angelo Herndon Campaign begins

National Negro Congress formed

1936

African Americans shift allegiance to the Democratic Party

Mary McLeod Bethune named director of the Division of Negro Affairs

1937

William Hastie named first black federal judge

Bethune organizes conference on Problems of the Negro and Negro Youth

NATIONAL EVENTS

1935

The CIO is formed

Roosevelt's second New Deal—Social Security Act, National Labor Relations Act, and Works Progress Administration

1936

Roosevelt reelected in a landslide

On MyHistoryLab

 Study and Review on MyHistoryLab

REVIEW QUESTIONS

1. Why did African Americans abandon their long association with the Republican Party in favor of the Democratic Party?

2. How did black radicalism influence Roosevelt's New Deal policies and programs?

3. How did black people respond to and survive the Great Depression? How did the experiences of black women during the Depression reflect their race, class, and gender status?

4. How did the New Deal adversely affect black share-croppers, tenants, and farmers? What were the political, social, and economic repercussions of the large-scale migration of African Americans out of the South during the 1930s?

5. What role did racism play in the Tuskegee experiment and the "Scottsboro Boys" case?

6. Why were W. E. B. Du Bois's editorials in the *Crisis* about segregation so divisive and explosive? How did black activists and scholars respond to the idea of voluntary self-segregation?

Meanings of Freedom: Culture and Society in the 1930s, 1940s, and 1950s 1930–1950

LEARNING OBJECTIVES

W. E. B. Du Bois commented often on the gifts black people had given to America. Du Bois had proclaimed, "We are the first fruits of this new nation. . . . We are the people whose subtle sense of song has given America its only American music, its only American fairy tales, its only touch of pathos and humor amid its money-getting plutocracy." African-American "destiny is not a servile imitation of Anglo-Saxon culture, but a stalwart originality which shall unswervingly follow Negro ideals."

A key theme in black life from the 1930s to the early 1950s was the many strategies African Americans devised to protest second-class citizenship, resist negative racial stereotypes, and end white entrepreneurs' appropriation of black culture. At heart, black cultural workers and creative artists sought to shape the representation of black people in American society and

Pitching great Leroy Satchel Paige warms up at New York's Yankee Stadium in 1942.

to sustain a viable black culture for a rapidly urbanizing people. A central issue in this chapter is the extent to which black culture from the 1930s to the 1950s became a source of strength—cultural power—that helped African Americans define and assert themselves within American society.

Cultural power allowed African Americans to craft positive images of black people that challenged negative distortions and helped to build community. As we have seen throughout this book, black people were disfranchised and socially and economically marginalized. But in the arts, black people drove a small wedge into the wall of racial segregation and discrimination. In literature and the visual and performing arts, talented African Americans compelled the attention of white Americans. The 1930s, 1940s, and 1950s—when most black people were suffering from the lingering effects of the Depression and the entrenched Jim Crow regime—were a fertile period in the history of black expressive culture.

Singer and actor Paul Robeson (1898–1976) as "Othello" in 1943. A man of astonishing magnetism and creative power, Paul Robeson became, in 1943, the first black actor to play "Othello" in the United States. He was fluent in many languages, produced over 300 recordings of spiritual and folk music gathered from around the world, and appeared in 11 motion pictures. An unflinching proponent of freedom from racism and want, Robeson received the NAACP's Spingarn Medal in 1945.

19-1
19-2
19-3
19-4
19-5
19-6
19-7
19-8
19-9

Black Culture in a Midwestern City

19-1 How did black institutions support classical music in St. Louis in the 1930s and 1940s?

Beginning in the 1930s, a second wave of black migrants made St. Louis the fifth largest city in the United States. Yet, because of segregation and discrimination, the city's black community developed institutions to address its own educational and cultural needs. Attention has usually focused on St. Louis's contributions to popular culture, but classical music also commanded considerable interest in the city. Black residents struggled to secure training in this genre of music and for opportunities to perform it.

St. Louis is in the heart of a region often considered remote from the nation's cultural centers. Yet it has produced outstanding black jazz musicians. But not all black musicians wanted to play ragtime and jazz, and many of them resented being relegated to these forms. A closer look at black support for classical music in St. Louis during the 1930s and 1940s reveals the diversity of black life—even though white St. Louisianians marginalized or ignored the contributions of black artists.

Schools, churches, labor, and media within the St. Louis black community had to create opportunities for black children to study, appreciate, and perform classical music. The two largest black newspapers, the *St. Louis Argus* and the *St. Louis American*, publicized recitals and concerts. Two all-black institutions supported classical music education: Lincoln University in Jefferson City and Sumner High School.

By the 1940s Lincoln University had become the institution for training St. Louis musicians, and its music instructors were active in the black cultural affairs. Sumner High School had orchestras, bands, choirs, and glee clubs. Many of its music teachers possessed advanced degrees from prestigious music departments. The most influential teacher was Kenneth Billups, an arranger, composer, and founding director of the Legend Singers, a black professional chorus.

Black churches, including Antioch Baptist, Central Baptist, and Berea Presbyterian, sponsored religious programs highlighting the works of both black and white composers. Local 197 of the American Federation of Musicians and the St. Louis Music Association, which was the local branch of the National Association of Negro Musicians, promoted black performing organizations and training. These groups sponsored musical organizations and paid for scholarships and summer choirs for boys and girls.

The Black Culture Industry and American Racism

19-2 How did African Americans merge a distinct aesthetic with a demand for social justice?

Black American artists had to confront discrimination and exploitation in the culture industry. They could rarely afford to produce and disseminate their work. This power often resided in the hands of record companies, publishers, and the owners of radio stations and film studios. Yet black artists in the 1930s and 1940s shaped an emerging consciousness that would erupt in the 1950s and propel a modern movement for civil rights and social justice. Paul Robeson not only won acclaim as a great performing artist, but he became a leading black internationalist and outspoken critic of colonialism and racism. In 1945, the NAACP awarded him its prestigious Spingarn Medal. The U.S. State Department, however, revoked Robeson's passport in 1950 because of his support for radical social and economic reform and his practice of black internationalism.

The political content of black art provoked heated debates among black artists. Many black Americans insisted that music, the visual and performing arts, literature, and oratory serve both a political function and an aesthetic purpose. They expected black artists not only to create beauty but also to use their art to promote freedom. Still, the disparate reasons for white involvement in the marketing and use of black culture created tension among black artists. Although many white Americans had long appreciated black culture, some had also appropriated it for their own profit.

During the late 1930s and 1940s, corporate America recognized the money that could be made from producing and marketing black culture. But black artists had to be made "acceptable" if they were to be successfully marketed to affluent white consumers. These artists had to compromise, mask, and subordinate their true feelings and expressiveness to earn income from their work. Artists who exhibited the right combination of showmanship, charm, and talent could reap some of the financial rewards their creativity generated. The paradox of the black performer—using your art to entertain your oppressor—was most apparent in music.

The Music Culture from Swing to Bebop

19-3   How did swing, big band, and bebop music develop and why were they important for blacks?

Ironically, the very creativity that white Americans valued and often appropriated depended on the artists' ability to preserve some intellectual and emotional autonomy. Black artists had to juxtapose the requirements of earning a living with the need to remain true to their art. Black musicians continuously had to refine, expand, and perfect their art not only for themselves and each other but also for a white-dominated marketplace. In many respects black music is synonymous with black culture; the experience of segregation or self-imposed separation often made possible the creation of new cultural expressions. Music encapsulates and reflects the core values and underlying tensions and anxieties in black communities. In black music we witness cultural producers developing strategies of resistance to white domination.

The Great Depression wrought havoc on the vibrant black culture industry of the 1920s. Record sales in 1932 were only a sixth of those in 1927. Black musicians like Louis Armstrong had enjoyed a golden age of creativity during the 1920s. The record companies had their separate black music labels and sold thousands of records to southern migrants moving to the big cities. New bands sprouted up across the country. The territorial (traveling) bands took the music to the outposts of black America, and the big bands under Fletcher Henderson, Duke Ellington, Count Basie, and Cab Calloway played in white urban dance halls and ballrooms that admitted black people only as staff or entertainers.

New York was where black musicians felt they had to go to prove themselves. After entertaining affluent white people or providing backup music for the Apollo Theater in Harlem, black musicians discarded their masks of docility and deference and made a different sound in their own space and on their own time in late-night jam sessions. In Harlem's small clubs a new kind of jazz was born.

The big band swing style that became popular in the 1930s transformed white American culture. Swing emerged as white bands reduced the music of the more innovative black bandleaders to a broadly appealing formula. The big swing bands of the 1930s played written, arranged music. Swing's popularity helped boost the careers of black and white bandleaders, but it also led to a creative slump that disheartened many younger black musicians. Tired of swing's predictability, they began improvising in the jazz clubs.

In the 1940s at least seven musicians—Charlie Parker, Dizzy Gillespie, Thelonious Monk, Bud Powell, Kenny Clarke, Max Roach, and Ray Brown—were

Charlie "Bird" Parker was one of the most innovative and influential of all American musicians. His playing challenged his contemporaries, influenced generations of jazz musicians, and helped transform jazz from entertainment into one of America's most respected art forms.

among the men most responsible for revolutionizing jazz, ushering in a new sound and dimension that became known as *bebop*. Bebop featured complex rhythms and harmonies and highlighted improvisation. Gillespie (1917–1993) said that Kansas City–born Charlie "Bird" Parker (1920–1955) was "the architect of the style."

White America resisted bebop. The nation was about to enter World War II and was too preoccupied to switch from the big band swing ballroom dancing music to bebop. Moreover, because jazzmen played in small, intimate clubs too small for big bands, they had more freedom from the expectations of white society. Bebop music was of such enduring quality, however, that it shaped American popular culture and style for two generations. Before long, bebop became the principal musical language of jazz musicians around the world.

Bebop was a way of life and had its own attendant styles whose nuances depended on class status and, perhaps, age. Gillespie helped create one side of bebop style in dress, language, and demeanor. He began to wear dark glasses on stage to reduce the glare after he had cataract surgery. He grew a goatee because shaving irritated his bottom lip. He wore pegged pants, jackets with wide lapels, and a beret. Other bebop musicians emulated and modified this attire. Beboppers also created their own slang, hip Black English that mingled colorful and obscene language. They also engaged in a freewheeling lifestyle. But there was a downside to bebop. Some musicians became drug addicts, engaged in parasitical relationships with women, and spent their money recklessly.

Black working-class young men adopted their own style of talking and hip dressing, reflected in their zoot suits and conked hair. Zoot suits featured high-waisted, baggy, pegged pants and long draped coats. A 16-year-old Malcolm Little (who later took the name Malcolm X) plunged into hipster culture when he moved to Boston. His first zoot suit was sky blue with a matching hat, gold watch chain, and monogrammed belt. He then mastered the lindy hop dance style and took to the floor of the Roseland Ballroom, where he shed his life as an un-skilled wageworker and became freer and more empowered.

Bebop was the dominant black music of the war decade, but after 1945 returning vet-erans preferred a slower-paced music, simple love songs, and melodies. This contributed to bebop's waning and led to more transformations. All artistic innovation extracts a high price. Bebop was no exception. Many of the most talented musicians—like Billie Holiday, discussed later in this chapter—paid that price in lives decimated by drugs, poverty, sick-ness, and broken relationships. Few black musicians received the respect, recognition, and financial rewards from white America that their creativity warranted.

Popular Culture for the Masses: Comic Strips, Radio, and Movies

19-4 | **What was the role and presentation of blacks in comic strips, movies, and radio?**

The masses of African Americans participated in more accessible black popular culture outlets. Comic strips, radio programs, and movies were affordable forms of artistic creativ-ity that allowed momentary escape from the bleakness and despair of the Depression years.

The Comics

African Americans quickly noted the difference between the fun that black people made of each other and the mockery white people made of them. These differences were reflected in tone, intent, and sympathetic versus derisive laughter. During the Depression, comic strips in newspapers and comic books featuring superheroes diverted millions of Americans. Comic strips in black newspapers entertained but also affirmed the values and ideals of black people. They portrayed humorous situations and tales of intrigue and action.

The *Philadelphia Independent*, a black paper, ran a serial in the 1930s called "The Jones Family." This strip, drawn by an editorial cartoonist named Branford, was an example of the dual function of entertaining and affirming. The strip centered on the young Jones boy's search for the "good life" of money, success, love, and a happy marriage. But at every turn he confronts a harsh reality. Unable to get a job because of the Depression, he becomes an outlaw and narrowly escapes jail. Constantly "on the run" from oppression, his only consolations are his family and his beautiful, ever-faithful girlfriend.

"The Jones Family" illuminates the gray areas that most African Americans, regardless of their class, faced when attempting to live rational, coherent lives in the northern cities. Although they cherished middle-class values, they often had to live with poverty, crime, and racial oppression. The black comic strips sought to provide entertaining, nonjudgmental prescriptions and blueprints for middle-class life, but to more cynical and alienated black people they seemed to be promoting unattainable values and lifestyles.

Radio and Jazz Musicians and Technological Change

Although there were individual exceptions, African-American jazz musicians embraced the commercial and technological developments that revolutionized the music industry in the 1920s. The phonograph allowed for wide distribution of the music they created, just as the recording studios served as incubators for their creative innovations. By the end of the 1920s, black musicians had embraced electrical recording, and in the 1930s they learned to appreciate microphone amplification—a product of radio technology—which allowed for the dominating rhythmic pulse of electric guitars and bases that would radically change black popular music. By the 1930s jazz musicians were making records that replicated live performances more closely than ever before. Radio and improved record making helped spread black music and ensured its survival.

During the 1930s black musicians, including Duke Ellington, Fats Waller, and Art Tatum, starred in regular radio programs. Many black musicians acquired their first lucrative jobs in radio as full-time staff musicians. Some earned higher salaries than writers, announcers, and white performers. Black musicians succeeded in the radio medium because they were heard and not visible. It was the mastery of their instruments that won audience approval. Perhaps most important, black radio staff musicians could communicate to larger audiences than those who played in clubs and on the traveling circuits. Thus, they enhanced the appeal of their music for a much wider audience.

Radio and Black Disc Jockeys

Chicago was a pioneering center both for recording and performing music. As black music became a commodity, influential black disc jockeys like Al Benson appeared on the radio and attracted a large following in "Bronzeville." Benson, a migrant from Mississippi, was as skilled a businessman as he was a cultural impresario. A determined entrepreneur, Benson arranged "first play rights" with record producers and distributors, catapulting Chicago into a major launch site for new releases. Diverse artists, including bluesman Muddy Waters and gospel singer Mahalia Jackson, benefited from the airplay.

In the post-Depression and pre-modern Civil Rights era, black disc jockeys played the blues, gospel, and jazz and attracted listeners with their sharp banter and fast, smooth-talking

19-1
19-2
19-3
19-4
19-5
19-6
19-7
19-8
19-9

19-1

19-2

19-3

19-4

19-5

19-6

19-7

19-8

19-9

style. The number of black disc jockeys rose from 16 in 1946 to over 500 by 1955. They used their radio shows not only to entertain and to sell records but also to promote the careers of black musicians. As awareness of the buying power of black consumers sank in, both white- and black-owned businesses eagerly sponsored black-appeal radio programs. Black radio stations thus became platforms for independent black music and were essential to the building of black community businesses. Black radio communicated the news, shared announcements, and molded urban black consciousness. Following Benson's lead, a young apprentice, Don Cornelius, would, decades later, launch a legendary music and dance show, "Soul Train." Cornelius explained how his start in radio inspired him: "It was with the advent of black radio that I thought black people would watch music television programs oriented toward themselves."

Radio and Race

During the Depression, black actors in radio and film were frequently marginalized, exploited, or excluded. Commercial radio delivered an audience of white consumers to white advertisers, and it denied black people jobs as announcers, journalists, or technicians. The major labor unions in the entertainment side of the radio industry restricted membership to white people. Still—with its offerings of vaudeville, big bands, drama, and comedy—radio provided relief from the miseries of the Depression to all Americans, black as well as white.

The most popular comedy radio program in the early 1930s—a precursor to the soap operas and sitcoms that were to become staples of radio and television programming—was *The Amos 'n' Andy Show*. The inauguration of this program was a significant moment in radio history. Two white performers, Charles Correll and Freeman Gosden, not only wrote and performed scripts laced with oxymorons and malapropisms but also played the title roles. The show's characters and their humor reinforced unflattering racial and gender stereotypes, but the show was not mean-spirited. Some of the characters conducted themselves with dignity, modeling such positive values as marital fidelity, strong families, hard work, and economic independence. An *Amos 'n' Andy* movie, *Check and Double Check*— released in 1930 when hard times made black entertainers grateful for any employment they could get—featured music by Duke Ellington's orchestra. The movie introduced Ellington to a wider audience of affluent white people and enhanced his reputation.

Black audiences recognized the minstrel stereotyping in *Amos 'n' Andy*, yet many of them still enjoyed the show. A vocal component of the ever more sophisticated and urbanized black population, however, complained that this show and other radio programs reinforced negative images in the nation's consciousness. Educator and activist Nannie Helen Burroughs considered the show demeaning. Robert L. Vann, editor of the *Pittsburgh Courier*, argued that it exploited African Americans for white commercial gain.

The best-known and most successful African-American actor on network radio in the late 1930s was Eddie Anderson, who played Jack Benny's sidekick Rochester in NBC's *The Jack Benny Show*. Like the characters in *Amos 'n' Andy*, Rochester reinforced negative racial stereotypes. Anderson's rationalization of his role suggests his discomfort with it:

> I don't see why certain characters are called stereotypes. The Negro characters being presented are not labeling the Negro race any more than "Luigi" is labeling the Italian people as a whole. The same goes for "Beulah," who is not playing the part of thousands of Negroes, but only the part of one person, "Beulah." They're not saying here is the portrait of the Negro, but here is "Beulah."

Radio and *Destination Freedom*

Between 1948 and 1950, black writers and actors in Chicago produced a unique local radio program about African-American politics, culture, and history for northern urban audiences. According to historian Barbara Diane Savage, this program, called *Destination Freedom,* "provide[d] a glimpse of the politically creative ways African Americans could use the medium of radio when they had freer rein over it. . . . This kind of broadcast was possible because of black migration and the formation of an urban market of working-class and middle-class African Americans." *Destination Freedom* was conceived and written by black journalist and radio scriptwriter Richard Durham. Durham stated his vision of this program with its positive depiction of black lives:

> Somewhere in this ocean of Negro life, with its cross-current and under-currents, lies the very soul of America. . . . It lies there because the real-life story of a single Negro in Alabama walking into a voting booth across a Ku Klux Klan line has more drama and world implications than all the stereotypes Hollywood or radio can turn out in a thousand years."

While Durham enjoyed enormous latitude in developing biographical profiles of black men and women, his power was not absolute. For example, he was not allowed to air a profile of Paul Robeson. In 1950, station WMAQ, despite the success of the program, discontinued it, fearful of the threat of rising anti-communist conservatism.

Richard Durham (1917–1984) migrated to Chicago with his family in the 1920s. From 1948 to 1950 his unique radio series *Destination Freedom* educated the citizens of Bronzeville about the long black struggle for civil rights.

Race, Representation, and the Movies

In the 1930s and 1940s—after the introduction of sound in motion pictures—black and white producers began to make what were known as **race films** for African-American audiences. Except for these race films, white film executives, since the beginning of the film industry, had cast black men and women in roles designed to comfort, reassure, and entertain white audiences. Continuing this trend, African Americans in Hollywood movies of the 1930s were usually cast in servile roles and often portrayed as buffoons.

The film that most firmly cemented the role of black Americans as servants in the American consciousness was *Gone with the Wind* (1939). Hattie McDaniel and Butterfly McQueen were the black "stars" in this epic adaptation of Margaret Mitchell's romantic salute to the Old South. McDaniel had played servant or "Mammy" roles throughout the 1930s. The image of Mammy, the headscarf-wearing, obese, dutiful black woman who preferred nurturing white families to caring for her own children, appealed to white America. But in *Gone with the Wind*, McDaniel gave the performance of a lifetime and in 1940 became the first African American to win an Oscar. Many in the black community criticized her for playing "female Tom" roles. McDaniel retorted she would rather play a maid and earn $700 a week than be one and earn $7 a week. In time, however,

race films Movies made for African-American audiences in the 1930s and 1940s.

Read on **MyHistoryLab Document: Ethel Waters Talks about Blacks in the Movies, 1950**

19-1

19-2

19-3

19-4

19-5

19-6

19-7

19-8

19-9

Fair Play Committee
Organization formed to
promote black actors in
the movie industry and
improve the image of
blacks in film.

Read on
MyHistoryLab
Document: **Paul
Robeson "Welcome
Home Rally," 1949**

19-1

19-2

19-3

19-4

19-5

19-6

19-7

19-8

19-9

McDaniel and other black actors—dismayed by their relegation to demeaning roles—formed the **Fair Play Committee** to lobby the white-dominated movie industry for more substantial roles, to get rid of dialect speech, and to ban the term *nigger* from the screen. But in the *Beulah* radio show, which premiered in 1947, McDaniel again played a wise but subservient maid who provides the family that employs her with advice, guidance, and direction.

Eventually, during and after World War II, Hollywood developed more sophisticated race-directed movies. Of particular significance was the positive, even romanticized, portrayal of black Americans in a movie the War Department financed to gain support among African Americans for the U.S. role in World War II. *The Negro Soldier*, directed by Frank Capra in 1944, played to vast audiences of enthusiastic black people. But even before *The Negro Soldier*, some motion pictures had depicted African Americans positively. Paul Robeson made two movies, *The Emperor Jones* (1933) and *Show Boat* (1936), in which he attempted to change how black men and women were represented on screen. He proclaimed in 1934, "In my music, my plays, my films I want to carry always this central idea: to be African. Multitudes of men have died for less worthy ideals; it is even more eminently worth living for."

To succeed commercially, African-American filmmakers had to disguise their dissent or appeal to an exclusively black audience. One of the most enterprising black filmmakers, Oscar Micheaux (1884–1951), made films aimed primarily at the black public. Unlike the dominant Hollywood stereotypes, the black men and women in Micheaux's films were often educated, cultured, and prosperous. His films featured middle-class or identity issues such as "passing for white."

Micheaux produced more than 30 feature films between 1919 and 1948. In 1932, he released *The Exile*, the first sound motion picture to be made by, with, and for black Americans. The following year he produced *Veiled Aristocrats*, about passing for white among Chicago's black professional class. The plot turns on the revelation that the wealthy "white" heroine is actually "colored," which enables her to marry the talented mulatto hero.

Micheaux tried to transform Hollywood without changing it, much as members of the black bourgeoisie struggled to be included in American society. His films capture the dilemma of black double consciousness. As W. E. B. Du Bois put it, black people always experienced that "peculiar sensation," that "sense of always looking at one's self through the eyes of others, of measuring one's soul by the tape of a world that looks on in amused contempt and pity." Black culture existed within and was shaped by American culture, while simultaneously transforming it. To the degree that black Americans had been assimilated, white American culture was also their culture.

The white immigrants who created Hollywood were determined to help marginal and excluded groups like Jews and Italians assimilate into the American mainstream. Hollywood sought to create the illusion that these groups belonged to the power elite. However, these Hollywood entrepreneurs did not do the same for African Americans. Their films during the Depression represented black people as unassimilable. A small cadre of black filmmakers and actors created independent films and showed them in theaters exclusively for black patrons. Following the lead of pioneers like Micheaux, they created an alternative cinema in which they introduced nuanced and fully human characters.

The Black Chicago Renaissance

19-5 What were the characteristics, developments, artists, and authors of the Chicago Renaissance?

Black culture flourished during the 1930s and 1940s, decades otherwise noted for economic depression and global warfare. African-American musicians thrived in cities as far from Harlem as Kansas City (Missouri), Dallas, Denver, and Oklahoma City. They created a southwestern style of jazz with a blues inflection. The southwestern musical style rivaled the West Coast jazz scene (which often included black and Latino musicians) that radiated from Los Angeles to Portland, Seattle, San Francisco, and Oakland. It even reached as far as Honolulu and found patrons in such Asian cities as Yokohama in Japan, Shanghai and Hong Kong on the coast of China, and Manila in the Philippines.

In many respects, however, Black Chicago became the center of black culture innovation and expressivity during the 1930s and 1940s. In contrast to some of the artists of the "Harlem Renaissance," the leading writers in Chicago harbored no illusions that art would solve the problems caused by white supremacy and black subordination. The Chicago writers of the 1930s and 1940s emphasized the idea that black art had to combine aesthetics and function. It had to be art that served the cause of black freedom.

Arna Bontemps (1902–1973) was to the Black **Chicago Renaissance** what Alain Locke had been to the Harlem Renaissance. Born in Louisiana, Bontemps migrated in 1935 from California to Chicago, where he met Richard Wright and joined the South Side Writers Group, which Wright founded in 1936. The group included poet Margaret Walker and playwright Theodore Ward. It offered criticism and moral support to black writers. Bontemps's association with the group influenced his own writing. After 1935 his novels and short stories reflected a restlessness and revolutionary spirit. In 1936 he published *Black Thunder* about the nineteenth-century slave conspiracy led by Gabriel, and in 1939 he published *Drums at Dusk* about the Haitian Revolution and Toussaint Louverture. Richard Wright's writings also celebrated resistance, but with more nuance. He published *Uncle Tom's Children* in 1938 and his masterpiece, *Native Son*, in 1940.

Among the artists who launched their careers on WPA funds were Margaret Walker and Willard Motley. Walker attracted attention when her collected poems, *For My People*, appeared in the Yale Series of Younger Poets. Willard Motley worked with a radio group while writing his novel *Knock on Any Door* (1947), which depicted the transformation of an Italian-American altar boy into a criminal headed for the electric chair. The novel invited comparisons with Wright's *Native Son*.

Before the 1930s, black intellectuals misjudged Chicago's potential to become a center of black culture. In the late 1920s, black social scientists Charles S. Johnson and E. Franklin Frazier expressed disdain for Black Chicago's artistic and intellectual prospects. Frazier proclaimed that "Chicago has no intelligentsia," and in 1923 Johnson asked rhetorically,

> Who can write of lilies and sunsets in the pungent shadows of the stockyards? . . . the kingdom of the second ward [the black neighborhood] has no self-sustaining intelligentsia, and a miserably poor acquaintance with that of the world surrounding it.

Chicago Renaissance Flourishing of the arts that made Chicago the center of black culture in the 1940s.

19-1

19-2

19-3

19-4

19-5

19-6

19-7

19-8

19-9

VOICES   Margaret Walker on Black Culture

19-1
19-2
19-3
19-4
19-5
19-6
19-7
19-8
19-9

In 1942 Margaret Walker (1915–1998) published For My People, *the most important collection of poetry written by a participant in the Black Chicago Renaissance before Gwendolyn Brooks's* A Street in Bronzeville *(1945). In a 1992 collection of her essays, Walker reflected on the meaning and significance of black culture:*

> Black culture has two main streams: a sociological stream . . . and an artistic stream. . . . In this artistic stream black culture has five branches. These are language, religion, art, music, and literature. . . .
>
> Black music is perhaps the most acceptable of our black culture. The modern world is willing to accept the unique character of African rhythms and the language of the drum. White America, in general, reluctantly admits that black American music is the American music and most indigenous to our culture. In every category or classification of music, moreover, Black America has achieved monumentally. With a broad base of folk music—spirituals and gospel music, seculars (blues, work songs, prison hollers)—individuals have risen in notable achievement in classical, popular, and various forms of jazz. From Black Patti to Marian Anderson and Leontyne Price, the great black American singer has gained worldwide eminence. Roland Hayes, William Warfield, Todd Duncan, the late Ellabelle Davis, Dorothy Maynor, and Mattiwilda Dobbs are notable black artists known the world over. Our blues singers like Bessie Smith, Ma Rainey, and B. B. King; folk singers like Leadbelly, and the greats like Louis Armstrong, Jimmie Lunceford, and Count Basie; great composers like Scott Joplin, Eubie Blake, Charlie Parker, and the incomparable Duke Ellington are significant contributors to the modern world and all represent the undeniable genius of the black American musician.
>
> Individual achievement, while part of our general cultural picture, is not all. It is in language and religion that Black Americans as a group have made a significant contribution to the national fiber of American life and to the modern world. As spiritual creatures we have shown through unmerited suffering that we have a sense of humanity that can enrich the moral fiber and contribute to a new world ethos. Our black culture is aware of human needs and human values. Handicapped as we have been by a racist system of dehumanizing slavery and segregation, our American history of nearly five hundred years reveals that our cultural and spiritual gifts brought from our African past are still intact. It is not only that we are singers and dancers, poets and prophets, great athletes and perceptive politicians—but we are also a body of charismatic and numinous people yet capable of cultic fire as seen in our black churches and still creative enough in intellect to signal the leap forward into a new and humanistic age. We are the authors of the new paradigm. . . .
>
> How then has black culture been disseminated and kept alive? Black culture has survived in the black institutions of Black America. In the black family, the Black Church, the black school, the black press, the black nation, and the black world. This is where our black culture has survived and thrived. This is where it must continue to grow. The ground of common humanity is not yet a reality in the modern world but when it comes as it must in the twenty-first century, Black Africa, and black humanity must be as always the foundation on which it stands and from which it logically proceeds. One world of international brotherhood does not negate the nationalism of black people. It only enforces and re-enforces our common humanity.

1. **According to Walker, what external factors influenced and sustained black culture? What are some of the central themes in black culture?**

2. **What political and symbolic use have African Americans made of black culture?**

SOURCE: *On Being Female, Black, and Free/Essays by Margaret Walker, 1932–1992,* edited by Maryemma Graham. Jackson, University of Mississippi Press, 1997. Reprinted by permission of Maryemma Graham.

Johnson and Frazier were too harsh. Just as Chicago's industrial economy attracted working-class black people, it also nurtured artists who drew inspiration from and reflected this stratum of moving and striving, strolling and styling black people who wanted to transgress class and geographical lines. These working-class people aspired to enjoy the middle-class life of accomplishment and consumption. A critical pulse point on Chicago's South Side came to be known as Bronzeville. It measured and reflected the lives of ordinary working-class people.

Chicago was heir to the Harlem Renaissance. In 1930 Langston Hughes published *Not Without Laughter*, the first major novel about the black experience in Chicago. Hughes moved to the city himself in 1941 and wrote for the *Chicago Defender*. The city had long attracted displaced agricultural workers from the southern cotton fields. By 1930 it had a black population of 233,903. The migrants arrived eager to absorb Chicago's hard-driving blues and jazz culture.

During the 1920s a discernible class structure among African Americans emerged in Chicago, fueled in part by the new migrants. These men and women expanded the consumer base and gave rise to a cadre of educated professionals and entrepreneurs who developed an appreciation for the arts. Black businesses, such as banks and insurance companies, formed the financial foundation. Entrepreneur Walter L. Lee started

((● **Listen** on **MyHistoryLab Audio:** *I've Known Rivers*; poem and reading by Langston Hughes

Langston Hughes identified with poor and working-class black people. He used his poetry, prose, and plays to make the dignity and beauty of black people visible and known.

Your Cab Company and put on the streets each day a half dozen chauffeur-uniformed drivers of vehicles. In the late 1940s, John Johnson would launch a publishing empire with such magazines as *Negro Digest, Jet*, and *Ebony*. These businesses depended less on white patronage than on black support. It was in their best interest to support the arts and provide venues for performances.

Music was the primary inspiration for the creativity of black cultural movements in America. Avant-garde developments in black music preceded black cultural activity in the visual arts, poetry, drama, dance, literature, film, and sports. Cultural creativity was a potent force for raising consciousness and stirring resentment against oppressive living conditions and economic exploitation in different locations in America.

Within the South Side of Chicago, black musical giants, such as trumpeter Louis Armstrong (1898–1971) and his wife, Lillian Hardin Armstrong (1898–1971), a well-known and respected classically trained pianist, nurtured a distinct jazz culture. "Lil" Armstrong led her own band and arranged, composed, and sang. She played with great performers and befriended Louis Armstrong when he arrived in Chicago. They were married in 1924. Lil Armstrong eventually encouraged her husband to leave King Oliver's Creole Jazz Band and join Fletcher Henderson in New York. The Armstrongs were divorced in 1938. She continued her recording career with Decca records under the name Lil Hardin.

The seeds that blossomed into full-bodied jazz culture were planted across America at the turn of the century. The most famous musicians, however, all went to or passed through Chicago. As the Chicago Jazz Age came into its own, "Pretty Baby" became the

19-1
19-2
19-3
19-4
19-5
19-6
19-7
19-8
19-9

city's theme song. It was written by Tony Jackson, whom Jelly Roll Morton (the self-proclaimed "inventor of jazz") called "maybe the best entertainer the world has ever seen." The South Side, specifically along State Street between 31st and 35th, was the beating heart of the city's Jazz Age. Although Chicago did not replace New York as the major location for the aspiring jazz musician, it was the place you went to prove you had what it took to make a name for yourself.

Gospel in Chicago: Thomas Dorsey

The term *gospel* designates the traditional religious music of the black church. It was nurtured and flourished in Chicago's Holiness, Sanctified, Pentecostal, Baptist, and Methodist churches, in storefronts and in large edifices. Gospel music became the backbone of urban and contemporary black religion and is deeply entrenched in worship. The use of instruments—tambourines, drums, pianos, horns, guitars, and Hammond organs—distinguishes gospel from earlier spiritual and black folk music. During the 1930s and 1940s, it developed its own idioms and performance techniques. There were always tensions between genres of black music, and gospel provoked its share of critics. Members of the older generation deemed it too secular and insufficiently spiritual.

The doctrines of black "folk churches" encouraged free expression, group participation, spontaneous testimonies, prayers, witnessing, and music. Singers and choirs rarely performed the same songs in the same way more than once. The performer paid attention to the quality of the sound and to the careful manipulation of timbre, range, and shading. The style of the delivery used the whole body in synchronized movement. The mechanics of the delivery were designed to intensify the performance, giving it added textual variation and melodic improvisation. Performers expanded a melody by a variety of technical devices, including repetition, shouts, slides, slurs, moans, and grunts. The supporting piano and organ frequently engaged in call-and-response interplay.

In Chicago, Thomas Dorsey (1899–1993)—one of the leading composers of the blues since the mid-1920s—was most responsible for developing black urban gospel. Dorsey synthesized elements of the blues with religious hymns to create a gospel blues. His gospel pieces radiated an urban religious spirit. In 1930 Dorsey gained attention when Willie Mae Ford Smith (1904–1994) performed his "If You See My Savior, Tell Him That You Saw Me" at the National Baptist Convention in Chicago. Two years later, in 1932, Dorsey's place in musical history was assured when Theodore Frye, with Dorsey at the piano, performed in the Ebenezer Baptist Church in Chicago his now classic gospel song "Take My Hand, Precious Lord." The song had a profound impact on gospel performers and their audiences. Dorsey's abundant works provided a foundation for shout worship formed in the 1930s and succeeding decades in the urban Protestant churches that transplanted black southerners.

Listen on
MyHistoryLab
Audio: "I Sing
Because I'm Happy";
sung by Mahalia Jackson

One of the greatest gospel singers, Chicago-based Mahalia Jackson (1911–1972), promoted Dorsey's songs all over the country on the church circuit and at religious conventions between 1939 and 1944. Jackson once said of the music, "Gospel songs are the songs of hope. When you sing them you are delivered of your burden." During the Depression and World War II, gospel became big business.

Chicago in Dance and Song: Katherine Dunham and Billie Holiday

The influence of the WPA in Chicago was especially reflected in dance. Dance has always been an integral part of African-American life, and the dances of black people have always been important in the American theater. The first performances by black dancers given within and taken seriously by the concert dance world occurred in the 1930s. The first "Negro Dance Recital in America" was performed in 1931 by the New Negro Art Theater Dance Company. In that same year, Katherine Dunham (1909–2006) founded the Negro Dance Group in Chicago, which survived thanks to WPA support.

Dunham was unique. Trained in anthropology, she studied African-based ritual dance in the Caribbean. In 1938 her troupe stunned an audience with the sexual vitality of its performance of one of her works. When the company, renamed the Katherine Dunham Dance Company, performed in February 1940, audiences and critics were awed.

What kept audiences returning to Dunham dance performances, however, was the dancer's bold sensuality. A reviewer of *Tropical Revue*, for example, wrote that it was "likely to send thermometers soaring to the bursting point. . . . Tempestuous and torrid, raffish and revealing." The *New York Sun* marveled, "Shoulders, midsections and posteriors went round and round. Particularly when the cynosure was Miss Dunham, the vista was full of pulchritude."

Dunham's success in New York led to film offers. The producers of the all-black musical extravaganza *Cabin in the Sky* hired the dance troupe and gave the featured role of Georgia Brown to Dunham. The role gave Dunham, as the *Times* dance critic wrote, the chance "to sizzle." But it also undermined her seriousness, allowing white audiences to view her as the stereotypical sultry black sexpot.

Nevertheless, the profits from the film funded the dancers' stage performances and Dunham's research. In 1943 Dunham moved to New York and opened the Katherine Dunham School of Arts and Research, which trained artists in dance, theater, literature, and world cultures.

Dunham protested racial segregation, even though it hurt her popularity. In the early 1940s she denounced discrimination. In 1944 in Louisville, Kentucky, Dunham announced after a performance, "We are glad we have made you happy. We hope you have enjoyed us. This is the last time I shall play Louisville because the management refuses to let people like us sit by people like you. Maybe after the war we shall have democracy and I can return." Dunham is important because she was a gifted and talented pioneer in dance whose choreography inspired future generations. She also underscored the responsibility that a black artist had to the black community to fight racism.

Billie Holiday (1915–1959), another great performer whose career took shape during the Depression, also used her art to challenge the oppression of black people. Holiday, popularly known as "Lady Day," began singing at age 15 and was discovered three years later by John Hammond, a Chicago jazz producer and promoter. In 1933 Hammond arranged for Holiday's first recording session, and in 1934 she made her debut at the Apollo Theater in Harlem. An incomparable singer known for subtle and artful improvisation, she left a wealth of recordings.

One of America's premier dance artists, the internationally acclaimed Katherine Dunham (1909–2006) performed in the Boboli Gardens in Florence, Italy, in 1950. A talented choreographer, anthropologist, and writer, Dunham founded one of the first black dance companies. She was an outspoken critic of Jim Crow segregation.

19-1
19-2
19-3
19-4
19-5
19-6
19-7
19-8
19-9

Billie Holiday (1915–1959) was one of the greatest jazz singers of all time. Between 1935 and 1938, she released some 80 titles on the Brunswick label for marketing to the black jukebox audience.

Black Visual Art

19-6 How did black graphic artists of the 1930s fuse politics and art in their work?

Chicago artists, such as Charles White, Elizabeth Catlett, and Eldzier Cortor, and Harlem's Jacob Lawrence celebrated working-class black people while implicitly criticizing the racial hierarchy of power and privilege. Their art belonged to the social realist school that flourished in the 1930s. Social realist art was intensely ideological. It strove to fuse propaganda—both left and right wing—to art to make it socially and politically relevant.

As the Depression worsened, black artists became even more determined to portray the crisis in capitalism. This involved depicting social and racial inequality. *Defense Worker*, a painting by Dox Thrash, reflects these concerns. Completed in 1942, just after the United States had entered World War II, it shows a black worker looming over the horizon. The heroic proletarian imagery alludes to the dream of a racially integrated labor force, equal opportunity, and social reform in the wake of the New Deal and the demand for labor triggered by the war.

The Harmon Foundation sponsored five juried exhibitions (1926–1931, 1933) of the work of black artists. The William E. Harmon Awards for Distinguished Achievement among Negroes celebrated black artists in the hope they would serve as role models for others. In the 1930s the WPA established art workshops and art centers in black urban communities to teach art to neighborhood young people and provide work for artists. Sculptor Augusta Savage, as the first director of the Harlem Community Art Center, presided over more than 1,500 students enrolled in day and evening classes in drawing, painting, sculpture, printmaking, and design. Among the teachers was Selma Burke (1900–1995), who sculpted the relief of Franklin D. Roosevelt that appears on the dime coin.

Federal Arts Project New Deal agency formed to promote the creation of public art.

The **Federal Arts Project**, another New Deal agency, sponsored the creation of murals that illustrated American ideals in public buildings, such as post offices and schools. Murals by black artists celebrated the heritage, contributions to society, and struggles of African Americans. Aaron Douglas, a leading painter of such public art, spoke about his work and that of his colleagues in a 1936 essay, "The Negro in American Culture":

> One of our chief concerns has been to establish and maintain recognition of our essential humanity, in other words, complete social and political equality. . . . In this struggle the rest of the proletariat almost invariably has been arrayed against us. . . . But the Negro artist, unlike the white artist, has never known the big house. He is essentially a product of the masses and can never take a position above or beyond their level.

Douglas and other black artists pressed the WPA to appoint more African Americans to its local boards and to hire them for more projects. The Harlem Artists Guild and the Arts and Crafts Guild in Chicago provided forums where black artists could foster the visual arts and support the social and political issues that affected black people.

Black Literature

19-7 What were the themes and impact of the work of Richard Wright and Ralph Ellison?

Black literature, like black art, has been assessed in terms of what it reveals about the social, cultural, and political landscape at a given historical moment. The most distinguishing feature of black literature may be the way that black writers have attempted to create spaces of freedom in their work, to liberate place, a trait that also marks black religious culture and folk cultural practices, such as storytelling. Black literature, like all black cultural production, is valued both for aesthetic reasons on its own and for the way it represents the struggles of black people to attain freedom. Black writers in the 1930s and 1940s felt obliged to address questions of identity and to define and describe urban life to the dispossessed and impoverished black migrants who moved to the cities. They tried to delineate the dimensions of a shared American heritage by portraying the contributions that African Americans had made to American society. Finally, and perhaps most ambitiously, black writers explored the issue of the rights African Americans were entitled to as Americans and the demands they could and should make on the state and society.

Richard Wright's *Native Son*

In 1940 Richard Wright (1908–1960) published *Native Son*, the first of many important novels by Depression-generation black authors. Its tale of the downfall of the young Bigger Thomas could be read as a warning about how economic hardship, segregation, and discrimination could lead young black men to lash out in violence and rage. Setting out for an interview for a job as a chauffeur, Bigger meets with his South Side Chicago neighborhood friends who want him to help them rob a grocery store. Bigger's fear of whites prevents him from going along. Instead, he picks a fight to camouflage his fear and avoid committing the crime. Bigger gets the chauffeur's job, which requires him to drive for the wealthy Dalton family. On his first assignment, he is supposed to drive young Mary Dalton to a university lecture. But she talks him into picking up her boyfriend, Jan—a communist—and taking them to a restaurant in the black neighborhood. Jan and Mary are oblivious to the patronizing way they treat Bigger. After dinner Bigger drives them around the city while they drink and make love in the back seat.

When Jan leaves, Bigger takes an intoxicated Mary home. Because Mary is too drunk to walk, Bigger carries her to her room and is putting her to bed when blind Mrs. Dalton comes to check on her daughter. Bigger panics and covers Mary's head with a pillow to keep her quiet. When Mrs. Dalton leaves, Bigger discovers he has smothered Mary. He burns her body in the basement furnace. Not fully grasping what he has done, Bigger writes a ransom note signed with a phony name to make it seem that Mary has been kidnapped. When Mary's remains are discovered, Bigger flees. Fearing she might betray him, Bigger then murders his girlfriend, Bessie. Bigger is captured, tried, and condemned. The remainder of the novel explores the hysteria and bigotry that envelop the case, the harsh criminal justice system, the insensitivity of the Communist Party—which seeks to exploit Bigger's plight—and the poverty and social ills that plagued Chicago's African-American communities during the Depression.

At the center of the drama is Wright's exploration of how Bigger comes to terms with his murder of Mary and Bessie. In conversations with Max, his communist lawyer, he realizes his irrational fear of white people had caused him to kill the two women and that he was a product of his experiences in the ghetto. At the end of the novel he says, "What I killed for I am."

Wright's novel thrust the impact of urbanization and racism on black men and women into the collective consciousness of the American people. One white critic declared, "[Wright] told us the one thing even the most liberal whites preferred not to hear: that Negroes were far from patient or forgiving, that they were scarred by fear, that they hated every moment of their suppression even when seeming most acquiescent, and that often enough they hated us the decent and cultivated white men who from complicity or neglect shared in the responsibility of their plight."

19-1
19-2
19-3
19-4
19-5
19-6
19-7
19-8
19-9

19-1
19-2
19-3
19-4
19-5
19-6
19-7
19-8
19-9

Richard Wright (1908–1960) was the first black writer to commandeer serious attention in mainstream American literature. In *Native Son* (1940) and *Black Boy* (1945), Wright provided incisive critiques of American racism. He received support from the Federal Writers Project and in his early works he poignantly portrayed the pathos of black southern migrants to the urban industrial North.

Read on
MyHistoryLab
Document: Richard
Wright, "Are We
Solving America's
Race Problem?" 1945

In his closing arguments, the lawyer, Max, describes the psychological conditions that led Bigger to kill and warns of the destructive potential of suppressed black rage:

> The hate and fear which we have inspired in him, woven by our civilization into the very structure of his consciousness and into his blood and bones, into the hourly functioning of his personality, have become the justification of his existence. . . . Kill him and swell the tide of pent up lava that will some day break loose, not in a single, blundering crime, but in a wild cataract of emotion that will brook no control.

Native Son was an immediate success. It became a Book-of-the-Month Club selection and has sold millions of copies.

James Baldwin Challenges Wright

Wright's influence on American literature has been immense. He was the first African-American writer to enjoy an international reputation, and he showed that success and militancy were not mutually exclusive. A younger generation of black writers, however, especially James Baldwin (1924–1987), took issue with Wright. African Americans, they argued, need not be portrayed as hapless victims of racism. In his famous 1949 essay, "Everybody's Protest Novel," Baldwin argued that Bigger's tragedy was not that he was black, poor, and scared but that he had accepted "a theology that denies him life, that he admits the possibility of his being sub-human and feels constrained, therefore, to battle for his humanity according to those brutal criteria bequeathed him at his birth. . . . The failure of the protest novel lies in its rejection of life, the human being, the denial of his beauty, dread, power, in its insistence that it is his categorization alone which is real and which cannot be transcended." In turn, Wright accused Baldwin of trying to destroy his reputation and of betraying all African-American writers who wrote protest literature: "All literature is protest. You can't name a single novel that isn't protest."

Baldwin answered Wright in a second essay in 1951 titled "Many Thousand Gone." "Wright's work," Baldwin declared, "is most clearly committed to the social struggle . . . that artist is strangled who is forced to deal with human beings solely in social terms; and who has, moreover, as Wright had, the necessity thrust on him of being the representative of some thirteen million people. It is a false responsibility (since writers are not congressmen) and impossible, by its nature, of fulfillment."

The controversy ended the friendship between Wright and Baldwin, and Baldwin, whose work would soon include many powerful novels and essays, inherited the mantle of "best-known black American male writer" (see Chapter 22).

Ralph Ellison and *Invisible Man*

The most intricate novel about the black experience in America written during this era was Ralph Ellison's (1914–1994) *Invisible Man*, which won the National Book Award for fiction in 1952. Partially autobiographical, it traces the life of a young black man from his early years in a southern school through his migration to New York City. The novel explores class tensions within American society and the black community. It offers a balanced, incisive perspective on the interaction between white and black Americans.

Echoing Du Bois's classic characterization of the "twoness" of the African-American character, Ellison observed, "[Black people] are an American people who are geared to what is and who yet are driven by a sense of what it is possible for human life to be in this society."

African Americans in Sports

19-8   **How did sports figures contribute to black culture?**

It is in the arena of professional sports that black Americans have demonstrated what human life can achieve when unconstrained by racism. The experiences of black men and women in American sports are a microcosm of their lives in American society. The privileges whites enjoyed in sports in this era paralleled the disadvantages and exclusions that were a constant part of black life. In the 1930s two black athletes, Jesse Owens and Joe Louis, captured the world's attention and inspired African Americans with pride, hope, and pleasure.

Jesse Owens and Joe Louis

Jesse Owens (1913–1980) was born on an Alabama sharecropping farm but grew up in Cleveland. A talented runner, he studied at Ohio State University and prepared for the 1936 Olympics, which were to be held in Berlin, the capital of Nazi Germany. Many African-American leaders objected to participating in the games because they believed this would help legitimate the Nazi myth of the superiority of the so-called Aryan race. Owens debunked that myth, becoming the first Olympian to win four gold medals.

Joe Louis Barrow (1914–1981) was also a son of Alabama sharecroppers. His family migrated to Detroit when he was 12. As a youth, he won a string of local boxing victories. In 1935 he faced former heavyweight champion Primo Carnera. A record crowd of 62,000 attended the fight in New York, which also had political overtones. Louis was fighting an Italian-American when Benito Mussolini, the fascist dictator of Italy, was about to invade Ethiopia. This was the oldest black independent nation in Africa, and many black Americans admired its ruler, Emperor Haile Selassie. Sports writers and police were amazed to observe everyone cheering when Louis beat Carnera in the sixth round.

Louis won the world heavyweight title against James J. Braddock in 1937 and beat the German Max Schmeling in a symbolic victory over Nazism in 1938. Louis retained the world heavyweight title until 1949.

Breaking the Color Barrier in Baseball

Although African Americans were integrated in track and boxing, professional baseball remained segregated until after World War II. Despite the hardships of the Depression, however, virtually every

Jackie Robinson (1919–1972) broke baseball's color barrier when he joined the Brooklyn Dodgers in 1947. He silently endured considerable hostility and threats from angry white citizens.

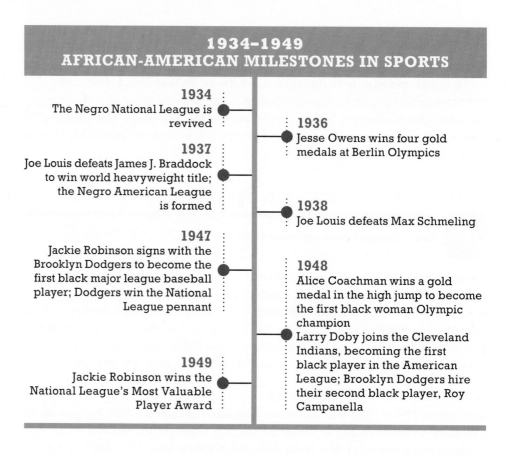

1934–1949
AFRICAN-AMERICAN MILESTONES IN SPORTS

1934
The Negro National League is revived

1936
Jesse Owens wins four gold medals at Berlin Olympics

1937
Joe Louis defeats James J. Braddock to win world heavyweight title; the Negro American League is formed

1938
Joe Louis defeats Max Schmeling

1947
Jackie Robinson signs with the Brooklyn Dodgers to become the first black major league baseball player; Dodgers win the National League pennant

1948
Alice Coachman wins a gold medal in the high jump to become the first black woman Olympic champion
Larry Doby joins the Cleveland Indians, becoming the first black player in the American League; Brooklyn Dodgers hire their second black player, Roy Campanella

1949
Jackie Robinson wins the National League's Most Valuable Player Award

19-1

19-2

19-3

19-4

19-5

19-6

19-7

19-8

19-9

Watch on **MyHistorylab** **Video:** Jackie Robinson and the Integration of Baseball

major black community tried to field its own baseball team. The Negro National League, which had folded in 1932, was revived in 1934, and the Negro American League was formed in 1937. Many of the players in the Negro leagues, including the legendary Josh Gibson, Satchel Paige, Leon Day, and Cool Papa Bell, would have equaled or excelled their white counterparts in the major leagues. Except for Paige, they never had that chance.

In 1947, however, major league baseball, which had had no black players since 1887, became integrated again when Jackie Robinson (1919–1972) signed to play with the Brooklyn Dodgers. In 1945 Branch Rickey, the Dodgers' general manager, decided to sign a black ball player to improve the team's chances of winning the World Series. After scouting the Negro leagues, he signed 26-year-old Jackie Robinson.

Robinson was the ideal choice, a superb athlete and a man of fortitude and determination. Born in Georgia and raised in southern California, he had been an All-American running back in football at UCLA and then had played baseball for the legendary Kansas City Monarchs of the Negro leagues. Robinson broke the color barrier when he opened at first base for the Dodgers in April 1947. Taunted, ridiculed, and threatened by some spectators and players, he responded by playing spectacular baseball. He won the Rookie of the Year honors in 1947, and the Dodgers won the National League pennant. Robinson retired in 1957 but remained outspoken on racial issues until his death from diabetes in 1972.

In July 1947 Larry Doby became the first black player in the American League when he joined the Cleveland Indians. As other major league teams also signed black players, the once popular Negro leagues withered.

Black Religious Culture

19-9 **What were the alternative religious movements and how did they help African Americans?**

Just as black religion was the "invisible institution" that helped African Americans survive slavery, the black church was the visible institution that helped hundreds of thousands of migrants adjust to urban life while affirming a set of core values consisting of freedom, justice, equality, and an African heritage. There was, of course, no single "black church." The term is shorthand for a pluralistic collection of institutions, including most prominently seven independent, historic, and black-controlled denominations: the African Methodist Episcopal Church; the African Methodist Episcopal Zion Church; the Christian Methodist Episcopal Church; the National Baptist Convention, Incorporated; the National Baptist Convention of America, Unincorporated; the Progressive National Baptist Convention; and the Church of God in Christ. Together, these denominations account for more than 80 percent of black Christians.

The black church helped black workers make the transition from being southern peasants to joining a northern urban proletariat. Yet the relationship between black religious tradition and the secular lives of black people was always changing. The blues and jazz performed in nightclubs were transformed into urban gospel music. Many of the nightclub musicians and singers received their training and held their first public performances in their churches. During the Depression, the black church helped black people survive by enabling them to pool their resources and by offering inspiration and spiritual consolation. Here we focus on alternative religious groups that became prominent during the 1930s and 1940s and addressed specific needs growing out of the Depression and the traumatic experience of relocating to alien and often hostile northern cities. Elijah Muhammad's Nation of Islam and Father Divine's Peace Mission Movement combined secular concerns with sacred beliefs. Both strengthened a sense of identity, affirmation, and community among their members.

The Nation of Islam

The **Nation of Islam** emerged in 1929, the year Timothy Drew died. Drew, who took the name Nobel Drew Ali, was founder of the Moorish Science Temple of America, which flourished in Chicago, Detroit, and other cities in the 1920s. After his death, a modified version of the Moorish Science Temple emerged in 1930 in Detroit. It was led by a mysterious door-to-door peddler who was known variously as Wallace D. Fard, Master Farad Muhammad, or Wali Farad. He wrote two manuals of instruction, *The Secret Ritual of the Nation of Islam* and *Teaching for the Lost-Found Nation of Islam in a Mathematical Way.* His teachings that black people were the true Muslims attracted many poor residents in Depression-era Detroit. In addition to the beliefs of Nobel Drew Ali, Fard's Nation of Islam also taught a mixture of Koranic principles, the Christian Bible, his own beliefs, and those of nationalist Marcus Garvey.

Nation of Islam Religious movement that combines Islam with black nationalism.

In 1934, after establishing a Temple of Islam, Fard disappeared, and one of his disciples, Elijah Poole (1897–1975), renamed Elijah Muhammad by Fard, became leader of the Detroit temple and then of a second temple in Chicago. The Nation attracted the attention of federal authorities during World War II when its members refused to serve in the military. Muhammad was arrested in May 1942 on charges of inciting his followers to resist the draft and was imprisoned until 1946. After his release he settled in Chicago and began to expand his movement.

19-1
19-2
19-3
19-4
19-5
19-6
19-7
19-8
19-9

The Nation of Islam taught that black people were the Earth's original human inhabitants who had lived, according to Elijah Muhammad, in the Nile Valley. Approximately 6,000 years ago, a magician named Yakub produced white people. They proved so troublesome that they were banished to Europe, where they began to spread evil. Their worst crime was their enslavement of black people. Elijah Muhammad taught that white supremacy was ending and black people would rediscover their authentic history and culture. To prepare for the coming millennium, he instructed members to adhere to a code of behavior that included abstaining from many traditionally southern black foods, especially pork. Members subscribed to a family-centered culture in which women's role was to produce and rear the next generation. The Nation also demanded part of the South for a black national state.

Father Divine and the Peace Mission Movement

Father Major Jealous Divine (c. 1877–1965) was born George Baker in Savannah. Like Elijah Muhammad, little is known about his early life. He captured attention in 1919 when he settled with 20 followers in Sayville, New York, and began what became known in the 1930s as the **Peace Mission Movement**. Divine secured domestic jobs for many of his followers on the surrounding estates and preached a gospel of hard work, honesty, sobriety, equality, and sexual abstinence. He provided free (or nearly free) meals and shelter for anyone who asked. In 1930 he changed his name to Father Divine. His Peace Movement espoused a racially neutral and economically empowering dogma that appealed to poor and needy black and white urbanites by offering them spiritual guidance and mental and physical healing. The movement embodied ideas from the New Thought, Holiness, Perfectionist, and Adventist religions. Hundreds of people traveled to see Father Divine on weekends, feast at his communal banquet table, and listen to his promises of heaven on Earth. The feasts were symbolic of the early Christian Eucharist and became the defining practices of Divine's religion.

In 1931 the police arrested Divine and 80 followers on charges of being a "public nuisance." Three days after a judge sentenced Divine to a year in jail and a $500 fine, the judge died of a heart attack. Divine was quoted as saying, "I hated to do it." The conviction was reversed, and Divine's reputation as a master of cosmic forces soared. Some of his followers believed he was God. Aside from the belief in the divinity of Father Divine, members of the Peace Movement were drawn to the mission's emphasis on ending racial prejudice and economic inequalities.

In 1933 Divine moved his headquarters to Harlem, where his Peace Mission Movement prospered. He eventually purchased key real-estate and housing projects called "heavens." These acquisitions and other businesses in the Midwest enhanced Divine's ability to provide shelter, jobs, and incomes for his followers. He launched the journal New Day in 1937 to disseminate his teachings. Divine also protested social injustice and encouraged his followers to become politically engaged. Between 1936 and 1940, he lobbied for a federal anti-lynching law. At the time of Divine's death in 1965, the holdings of the Peace Mission were estimated to be worth $10 million. Father Divine's movement echoed the Protestant ethic: work hard, keep both your mind and body healthy, eat right, dress properly, keep good company, and avoid evil and vice.

Peace Mission Movement Religious movement led by Father Major Jealous Divine.

CONCLUSION

The Depression caused intense hardship. It was also a period in which black Americans had an unprecedented impact on American culture. Through the medium of radio, black Americans powerfully helped to change American popular entertainment and gave rise to a new urban consciousness and a sense of belonging. Black people excelled in sports, arts, drama, and music. The Works Projects Administration (WPA) funded artists whose cultural productions were accessible, inclusive, and populist.

The Chicago Black Renaissance reflected the positive impact that the WPA had on the lives of hundreds of artists. A new generation of black jazz musicians transformed black music into an art form that won worldwide admiration and emulation. Black musicians weaned Americans from swing to bebop. Gospel music satisfied the needs of the black urban migrants to express their spiritual and communal feelings. Disc jockeys of black-appeal radio programs helped make black music commercially profitable.

These positive changes occurred against a backdrop of discrimination and segregation. Still, some African Americans found satisfying jobs in film and radio while many others were excluded or relegated to stereotypical roles. Negative typecasting motivated innovative black filmmakers to develop alternative films and artistic institutions that allowed the development of a more balanced representation of black life and culture. However, such creative ventures seldom produced the profits that white entrepreneurs reaped from marketing black cultural productions to white consumers. The mass appeal and unparalleled success of entertainers such as Louis Armstrong and Duke Ellington should not obscure the fate of those artists who refused to entertain white America and instead sought to oppose racism and social and economic injustice.

Black counterculture artists had a lasting impact on America and facilitated the spread of black internationalism and anti-colonialism. Black artists reflected a growing pride and a determination to resist complete assimilation into white culture. Black culture prepared black people for the next level of struggle against the American Jim Crow regime and against ideologies of white supremacy across the black diaspora.

CHAPTER TIMELINE

AFRICAN-AMERICAN EVENTS

NATIONAL EVENTS

1932

1932
Thomas Dorsey's "Take My Hand, Precious Lord"

1932
Franklin D. Roosevelt elected president

1933

1933
Approximately 13 million Americans out of work

1935

1935
Donald Murray and NAACP file suit to integrate University of Maryland School of Law

1935
Committee for Industrial Organization (CIO) established; WPA created; Italy invades Ethiopia

CHAPTER TIMELINE

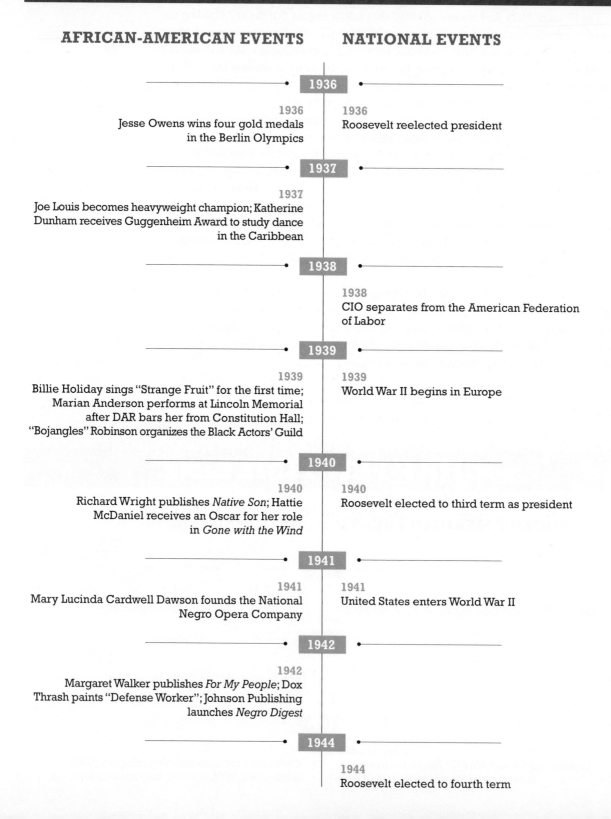

AFRICAN-AMERICAN EVENTS   **NATIONAL EVENTS**

1936

1936
Jesse Owens wins four gold medals
in the Berlin Olympics

1936
Roosevelt reelected president

1937

1937
Joe Louis becomes heavyweight champion; Katherine
Dunham receives Guggenheim Award to study dance
in the Caribbean

1938

1938
CIO separates from the American Federation
of Labor

1939

1939
Billie Holiday sings "Strange Fruit" for the first time;
Marian Anderson performs at Lincoln Memorial
after DAR bars her from Constitution Hall;
"Bojangles" Robinson organizes the Black Actors' Guild

1939
World War II begins in Europe

1940

1940
Richard Wright publishes *Native Son*; Hattie
McDaniel receives an Oscar for her role
in *Gone with the Wind*

1940
Roosevelt elected to third term as president

1941

1941
Mary Lucinda Cardwell Dawson founds the National
Negro Opera Company

1941
United States enters World War II

1942

1942
Margaret Walker publishes *For My People*; Dox
Thrash paints "Defense Worker"; Johnson Publishing
launches *Negro Digest*

1944

1944
Roosevelt elected to fourth term

CHAPTER TIMELINE

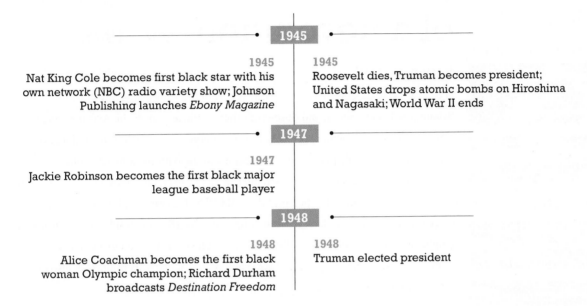

AFRICAN-AMERICAN EVENTS

NATIONAL EVENTS

1945

1945
Nat King Cole becomes first black star with his own network (NBC) radio variety show; Johnson Publishing launches *Ebony Magazine*

1945
Roosevelt dies, Truman becomes president; United States drops atomic bombs on Hiroshima and Nagasaki; World War II ends

1947

1947
Jackie Robinson becomes the first black major league baseball player

1948

1948
Alice Coachman becomes the first black woman Olympic champion; Richard Durham broadcasts *Destination Freedom*

1948
Truman elected president

On MyHistoryLab

✔ Study and Review on MyHistoryLab

REVIEW QUESTIONS

1. How did the Great Depression affect black culture? How did the WPA democratize black culture? How did black religious culture change during this era?

2. How did black artists, musicians, filmmakers, and writers negotiate the dilemma of dual consciousness as articulated by Du Bois? Which parts of black art did white corporate executives find easiest to appropriate and shape for white consumption?

3. How did swing-era big band music lead to bebop? What problems did the bebop musicians encounter? How did black music transform American culture? How did African-American musicians make creative use of radio technology?

4. How did radio broadcasts and Hollywood films portray black Americans during the 1930s and 1940s? How did these images affect white Americans' attitudes and behavior toward black Americans? How did these representations contribute to the emergence of an alternative black radio and/or independent black cinema?

5. How did the Chicago Renaissance compare with the Harlem Renaissance?

6. Why did black athletes become prominent during the 1930s and 1940s? What was their impact on American culture? How did the experiences of black sports figures reflect the status of race relations in the United States?

The World War II Era and the Seeds of a Revolution 1936–1948

Between 1939 and 1954, the U.S. role in the world was transformed. The victory in World War II of the Allies—the Soviet Union, Great Britain, the United States, and dozens of other countries—over the Axis powers of Germany, Italy, and Japan marked America's emergence as the dominant global power. This international role placed new constraints on the nation's domestic policies, particularly when, after the Axis surrender in 1945, suspicions between the United States and the Soviet Union developed into the Cold War. This period also witnessed the rise of black internationalism. Many African Americans forged close bonds with Africans who fought against European colonialism in Africa. The Cold War led to a vast expansion in the size and power of the federal government, particularly its military. It also greatly influenced domestic politics.

Racial segregation as practiced by the U.S. military reminded African Americans of their second-class status in America. The World War II crisis made impossible continued acquiescence to blatant inequalities. The black "Double V" campaign sought victory against racism on the home and fascism on the foreign fronts.

International events replaced the Great Depression as the defining force in the lives of African Americans. In preparing for and fighting World War II, America finally emerged from the Depression and laid the basis for an era of unprecedented prosperity. Industrial and military mobilization resulted in the movement of millions of people from agricultural areas into the cities. This population shift substantially increased black voting strength in the North and West, which—combined with a moral recoil from the savage racial policies of the Nazis—drove the issue of black equality to the forefront of national politics. Moreover, hundreds of thousands of black men and women learned new skills and ideas while serving in the armed forces, and many resolved to claim their rights. Events abroad and in the United States during the 1940s heightened black consciousness and led to a more aggressive militancy among local leaders and black citizens in southern states.

The Cold War also had a tremendous impact on African Americans and their struggle for freedom. The two sides of this global conflict avoided direct confrontation with each other. Instead, they sought to enlist Africans, Asians, and Latin Americans as proxies. American leaders, trying to convince these peoples of America's virtues as a democracy, were pressed to address the segregation and racial discrimination that remained firmly imbedded in American life. At the same time, the advocacy groups and black press that had come of age during the 1930s and 1940s focused attention on fighting racism and demanded the full rights and responsibilities of citizenship for all people. The result was a powerful movement for civil rights that many liberal white Americans and, increasingly, key institutions in the national government supported. Rising opposition to European colonialism in Africa and the development of numerous African independence wars also inspired black American militancy and human rights activism.

These favorable developments, however, provoked strong resistance. White southerners defended segregation with all the power at their command. The emerging conflict with the Soviet Union prompted many white conservatives to charge that all those seeking to fight racial injustice were agents of the communist enemy. These contrary currents—on one hand, the push for a new democracy, and, on the other, the Cold War mentality—would indelibly stamp the emerging civil rights movement.

On the Eve of War, 1936–1941

20-1 | **How did African Americans use the World War II crisis to protest racial discrimination?**

As the world economy wallowed in the Great Depression, the international order collapsed in Europe and Asia. Germany under Adolf Hitler (1889–1945) and Italy under Benito Mussolini (1883–1945) created an alliance, known as the Axis. These fascist dictators advocated a political program based on extreme nationalism that suppressed internal opposition and used violence to gain their will abroad. Germany was the dominant partner in the Axis.

20-1

20-2

20-3

20-4

20-5

Watch on
MyHistoryLab
Video: Origins of
World War II

20-1

20-2

20-3

20-4

20-5

((• Listen on
MyHistoryLab
Audio: Pearl Harbor

Its National Socialist, or Nazi, Party in part blamed communists and foreign powers for the nation's economic depression and loss of power. However, even more than by anticommunism, Hitler was driven by virulent racism and his belief in Anglo-Saxon, or white Aryan, supremacy. Unlike racists in the United States, he blamed Jews for Germany's social and economic problems. The Nazis also despised black people and considered them inferior or subhuman beings. Beginning in the mid-1930s, the Germans and Italians embarked on a series of aggressive confrontations and military campaigns that placed much of Central Europe under their power. In August 1939 Germany signed a nonaggression pact with the Soviet Union, a prelude to its September 1 attack on Poland, which the Soviets joined a few weeks later. Poland's allies, Britain and France, reacted by declaring war on Germany, thus beginning World War II.

As Germany and Italy pursued their aggression in Europe, the empire of Japan sought to dominate East Asia. The Japanese considered themselves the foremost power in the Far East and wanted to drive out or supplant both the European states and the United States, which had extensive economic interests and colonial possessions there. Japan's aggressive expansionist policies also led to conflict in the 1930s with the Soviet Union in Manchuria and to a long and bloody war with the Nationalist regime in China. The United States supported China and encouraged the Europeans to resist Japanese demands for economic and territorial concessions in their Asian colonies. Japan's alliance with Nazi Germany and fascist Italy further aggravated United States–Japanese relations, which deteriorated rapidly after the outbreak of World War II in Europe. These tensions led to war on December 7, 1941, when the Japanese bombed American warships at Pearl Harbor, Hawaii, and launched a massive offensive against British, Dutch, and American territory throughout the Pacific.

President Franklin D. Roosevelt watched the events in Europe and Asia during the 1930s with growing concern, but his ability to react was limited. Roosevelt had trouble convincing Congress to prepare for war because a significant segment of the American population, the isolationists, believed the United States had been hoodwinked into fighting World War I and should avoid becoming entangled in another foreign war. During the late 1930s, the president had managed to overcome some of this opposition and had won the authority to increase the size of the nation's armed forces. By early 1940 the United States had instituted its first peacetime draft to provide men for the army and navy.

African Americans and the Emerging International Crisis

Many African Americans responded to the emerging world crisis with growing activism. When Italy invaded Ethiopia, in 1935, black communities throughout the United States organized to send it aid. Mass meetings to support the Ethiopians were held in New York City under the auspices of the Provisional Committee for the Defense of Ethiopia and the Ethiopian World Federation. Similar rallies occurred in other large cities while reporters from black newspapers, such as J. A. Rogers of the *Pittsburgh Courier*, brought the horror of this war home to their readers. Despite fierce resistance, the Italians won the war in 1936, in part by using poison gas. The conflict alerted many African Americans to the dangers of fascism and fueled even greater interest in and identification with Africa. The flames of black internationalism became even hotter after World War II.

Civil war in Spain stimulated renewed activism among leftist African Americans. In 1936 a fascist-conservative movement led by General Francisco Franco (1892–1975), supported by Germany and Italy, started a civil war to overthrow the left-leaning Spanish Republic. About a hundred African Americans traveled to Spain in 1936–1937 to serve with the Abraham Lincoln Brigade, an integrated fighting force of 3,000 socialist and communist American volunteers. Support of the Abraham Lincoln Brigade reflected a commitment by a few African Americans to the communists' vision of internationalism. Mobilization for war, however, would soon bring most black people and their organizations into the fight against fascism abroad and for equality and justice in the United States (the **"Double V" campaign**).

"Double V" campaign Slogan during World War II that stood for victory over fascism abroad and over racism at home for blacks.

20-1
20-2
20-3
20-4
20-5

A. Philip Randolph and the March on Washington Movement

In 1939 and 1940, the American government spent so much on arms that the U.S. economy was finally lifted out of the Depression. But the United States mobilized its economy for war and rebuilt its military in keeping with past practices of discrimination and exclusion. As unemployed white workers streamed into aircraft factories, shipyards, and other centers of war production, jobless African Americans were left waiting at the gate. Most aircraft manu-facturers, for example, would hire black people only in janitorial positions no matter what their skills were. Many all-white American Federation of Labor (AFL) unions enforced closed-shop agreements that prevented their employers from hiring black workers who were not members of the labor organization. Government-funded training programs regularly rejected black ap-plicants. The United States Employment Service (USES) filled "whites-only" requests for defense workers. The military itself made it clear that although it would accept black men in their proportion to the population, about 11 percent at the time, it would put them in segregated units and assign them to service duties. The navy lim-ited black servicemen to menial positions. The Marine Corps and the Army Air Corps refused to accept them altogether.

When a young African-American man wrote the *Pittsburgh Courier* and suggested a "Double V" cam-paign—victory over fascism abroad and victory over racism at home—the newspaper adopted his words as the battle cry for the entire race. Fighting this struggle in a nation at war would be difficult, but the effort led to the further development of black organizations and transformed the national and international worldviews of many African-Americans. Black internationalism was never a more prominent component of black people's consciousness than during the spirited "Double V" cam-paign. Two months before the 1940 presidential elec-tion, the NAACP, the Urban League, and other groups pressed President Roosevelt to act against discrimina-tion in defense programs. The president listened to their protests, but aside from a few token gestures, he responded with little of substance. As a result, during late 1940 the NAACP and other groups staged mass pro-test rallies around the nation.

((•)) 📖 **Read** on **MyHistoryLab Document:** A. Philip Randolph Calls on Blacks to Support the Fight for Equality at Home and Abroad, 1941

Horace Pippin's (1888–1946) *Mr. Prejudice* (1943) hammers a wedge of racism through a giant V (the sign of victory). It is a powerful expression of black Americans' ongoing struggle against racial discrimination, segregation, and violence even within a nation at war against fascism and Nazism and the spread of communism.
Horace Pippin (1888–1946), "Mr. Prejudice," 1943. Oil on canvas, 18" × 14".
Philadelphia Museum of Art, Gift of Dr. and Mrs. Matthew T. Moore.

March on Washington Movement (MOWM) Movement created by A. Philip Randolph to pressure the federal government to end discrimination in the defense industry and government.

20-1

20-2

20-3

20-4

20-5

In January 1941 A. Philip Randolph, who was president of the Brotherhood of Sleeping Car Porters and who had been working with other groups to get Roosevelt's attention, called on black people to unify their protests and direct them at the national government. He suggested that 10,000 African Americans march on Washington under the slogan "We loyal Negro-American citizens demand the right to work and fight for our country." In the following months, Randolph helped create the **March on Washington Movement (MOWM)**. The MOWM's demands included a presidential order forbidding companies with government contracts from engaging in racial discrimination, eliminating race-based exclusion from defense training courses, and requiring the USES to supply workers on a nonracial basis. Randolph also wanted an order to abolish segregation in the armed forces and the president's support for a law withdrawing the benefits of the National Labor Relations Act from unions that refused to grant membership to black Americans. Unlike the leaders of most other African-American protest groups of the time, Randolph prohibited white involvement and encouraged the black working class to participate.

Many African Americans who had never taken part in the activities of middle-class-dominated groups like the NAACP responded to Randolph's appeal. Soon he alarmed the president by raising the number expected to march to 50,000. Roosevelt, fearing the protest would undermine America's democratic rhetoric and provide grist for the German propaganda mills, dispatched First Lady Eleanor Roosevelt and New York City Mayor Fiorello La Guardia to dissuade Randolph from marching. Their pleas for patience fell on deaf ears, compelling Roosevelt and his top military officials to meet with Randolph and other black leaders. The president offered a set of superficial changes, but the African Americans stood firm in their demands and raised the stakes by increasing their estimate of the number of black marchers coming to Washington to 100,000. By the end of June 1941, the president capitulated and had his aides draft **Executive Order 8802**, prompting Randolph to call off the march.

Executive Order 8802 Order issued by President Franklin D. Roosevelt in 1941 banning discrimination in employment in defense industries and the federal government.

Executive Order 8802

On the surface at least, the president's order marked a significant change in the government's stance. It stated in part,

> I do hereby affirm the policy of the United States that there shall be no discrimination in the employment of workers in the defense industry or government because of race, creed, color, or national origin.

The order instructed all agencies that trained workers to administer such programs without discrimination. To ensure full cooperation with these guidelines, Roosevelt created the **Fair Employment Practices Committee (FEPC)** with the power to investigate complaints of discrimination. The order said nothing about desegregation of the military, but private assurances were made that the barriers to entry in key services would be lowered. Over a dozen African-American scientists would participate in the development of radar and in research projects on other secret defense technologies at Camp Evans in New Jersey.

Fair Employment Practices Committee (FEPC) A committee created by Franklin Roosevelt to investigate complaints of discrimination.

Read on MyHistoryLab
Document: Earl B. Dickerson Talks About the Fair Employment Practices Committee, 1941–1943

Black excitement with the order soon soured as many industries, particularly in the South, made only token hirings of African Americans. What the black community learned in this instance, and what it would witness repeatedly in the decades to come, was that merely articulating antidiscrimination principles and establishing commissions and committees did not eradicate inequalities. Moreover, the order did not mention union discrimination. Nonetheless, the threat of the march, the issuance of the executive order, and the creation of the FEPC marked the formal acknowledgment by the federal government that it bore some responsibility for protecting black and minority rights in employment. Black activists and their allies would have to continue their fight if the order was to have meaning.

Race and the U.S. Armed Forces

20-2 **What role did African-American physicians and nurses play in the struggle to desegregate the military during World War II?**

20-1
20-2
20-3
20-4
20-5

The demands of A. Philip Randolph and other black leaders and healthcare professionals to end segregation in the armed forces initially met stiffer resistance than their pleas for change in the civilian sector. Black men were expected to serve their country; however, at the beginning of the war, most were assigned to segregated service battalions, relegated to noncombat positions, kept out of the more prestigious branches of the service, and confronted by tremendous obstacles to becoming officers.

Institutional Racism in the American Military

Much of the armed forces' racial policy derived from negative attitudes and discriminatory practices common in American society. Reflecting this ingrained racism, a 1925 study by the American War College concluded that African Americans were physically unqualified for combat duty, were by nature subservient and mentally inferior, believed themselves to be inferior to white people, were susceptible to the influence of crowd psychology, could not control themselves in the face of danger, and lacked the initiative and resourcefulness of white people.

Based on this and later studies, the War Department laid out two key policies in 1941 for the use of black soldiers. Although they would be taken into the military at the same rate as white inductees, African Americans would be segregated and would serve primarily in noncombat units.

In creating these policies, the military ignored evidence of the fighting ability that African Americans had shown in previous wars, confirmed by the heroism of Doris "Dorie" Miller during the attack on Pearl Harbor. Like all black sailors in the navy at the time, Miller had been assigned to mess attendant duty. In other words, he was a cook and a waiter. When the Japanese air force attacked the naval base on December 7, 1941, the 22-year-old Miller was below decks on the battleship U.S.S. *West Virginia*. When his captain was wounded, Miller braved bullets to help move him to a more protected area of the deck. He then took charge of

"above and beyond the call of duty"

DORIE MILLER
*Received the Navy Cross
at Pearl Harbor, May 27, 1942*

This World War II War Department recruitment poster recognizes the heroism of Dorie Miller (1919–1943) at Pearl Harbor. His bravery, however, did not alter the navy's policy of restricting black sailors to the kitchens and boiler rooms of navy vessels.

a machine gun, shooting down at least two enemy aircraft before running out of ammunition. On May 27, 1942, the navy awarded him a Navy Cross, the highest medal that the navy could bestow. It then sent Miller back to mess duty without a promotion.

The Costs of Military Discrimination

Although the War and Navy departments held to the fiction of "separate but equal" in their segregation programs, their policies gave black Americans inferior resources or excluded them entirely. Sick and injured black soldiers were treated in segregated wards in military hospitals. Black physicians could treat only black military personnel. At army camps black soldiers were usually placed in the least desirable spots and denied the use of officers' clubs, base stores, and base recreational facilities. Four-fifths of all training camps were located in the South, where black soldiers were harassed and discriminated against off base as well as on. Even on leave, black soldiers were not offered space in the many hotels the government leased and had to make do with the limited accommodations that had been available to black people before the war.

Perhaps most galling was seeing enemy prisoners of war accorded better treatment than African-American soldiers. In 1944 black servicemen stationed at Fort Lawton in Washington State objected to living and working conditions that were inferior to those granted to Italian prisoners of war (POWs). Not only did the Italians receive lighter work assignments than the black Americans, but some Italian POWs were allowed to go to local bars that refused to admit African Americans. The resentment erupted into a riot on August 14, 1944, when black soldiers stoned the barracks housing the Italians. One prisoner was killed, and 24 others were injured. A court-martial convicted 23 black servicemen.

Because of the military's policies, most of the nearly one million African Americans who served during World War II did so in auxiliary units, notably in the transportation and engineering corps. Soldiers in the transportation corps, almost half of whom were black, loaded supplies and drove them in trucks to the front lines. Black engineers built camps and ports, constructed and repaved roads, and performed many other tasks to support frontline troops.

Black soldiers performed well in these tasks but were often subject to unfair military discipline. In Europe, many more black soldiers than white soldiers were executed even though African Americans made up only 10 percent of the total number of soldiers stationed there. One of the most glaring examples of unfair treatment was the navy's handling of a "mutiny" at its Port Chicago base north of San Francisco. On July 17, 1944, an explosion at the base killed 320 sailors, of whom 202 were black ammunition loaders. In the following month, 328 of the surviving ammunition loaders were sent to fill another ship. When 258 of them refused to do so, they were arrested. Eventually the navy charged 50 men with mutiny, convicted them, and sentenced them to terms of imprisonment ranging from 8 to 15 years at Terminal Island in California. The NAACP's Thurgood Marshall filed a brief arguing that the men had been railroaded into prison because of their race, but to no avail.

Soldiers and Civilians Protest Military Discrimination

In military segregation, black American leaders identified a formidable but vulnerable target. Employing a variety of strategies, they mobilized the black civilian workforce, black women's groups, black college students, and an interracial coalition to resist this blatant inequality. They provoked a public dialogue with government and military officials at a

Read on
MyHistoryLab
Document:
Thurgood Marshall,
The Legal Attack to
Secure Civil Rights,
1942

pivotal moment when America's leaders most wanted to present a united democratic front to the world.

Examples of black protest abound. In 1942 the NAACP's journal the *Crisis* and the National Urban League's *Opportunity* published many editorials denouncing military segregation. Walter White traveled across the country and throughout the world visiting camps and making contacts with black soldiers and their white officers. He inundated the War Department and the president with letters citing examples of improper, hostile, and humiliating treatment of black servicemen by military personnel and in the white communities where bases were located.

Black Women in the Struggle to Desegregate the Military

The role of black women in the struggle to desegregate the military has often been overlooked, but their militancy contributed to the effort.

The most prominent example of black women's struggle is found in the history of the National Association of Colored Graduate Nurses. Mabel K. Staupers, its executive director, led an aggressive fight to eliminate quotas in the U.S. Army Nurse Corps. Although many black nurses volunteered during World War II, the navy refused to admit them, and the army allowed few to serve. To draw attention to the unfairness of quotas, Staupers met with First Lady Eleanor Roosevelt in November 1944 and described black nurses' troubled relationship with the armed forces. She told Mrs. Roosevelt that 82 black nurses were serving 150 patients at the all-black hospital at Fort Huachuca, Arizona, at a time when the army was complaining of a nursing shortage and debating the need to draft nurses. Staupers cited the practice of using black women to care for German POWs and asked if this was to be the special role of the black nurse in the war: "When our women hear of the great need for nurses in the Army and when they enter the service it is with the high hopes that they will be used to nurse sick and wounded soldiers who are fighting our country's enemies and not primarily to take care of these enemies."

Soldiers and sailors also resisted segregation and discrimination while in the service. They mounted well-organized

Mabel K. Staupers became the first executive director and later president, of the National Association of Colored Graduate Nurses (NACGN). With verve and perfect timing, she mobilized wide-ranging support to end quotas established by the military to limit the numbers of black nurses in the armed forces nurse corps.

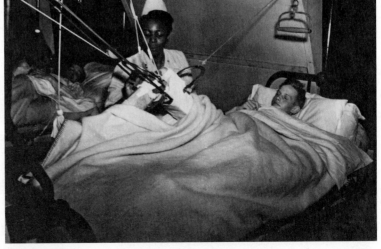

African-American women nurses served at station hospitals at home and abroad. They resented the quotas and discrimination and fought to end segregation in the U.S. military. Still, black nurses such as Lt. Florie E. Grant provided expert care for POWs, as shown in this October 7, 1942, image of her in a hospital ward in England.

VOICES   William H. Hastie Resigns in Protest

20-1
20-2
20-3
20-4
20-5

In January 1943 William H. Hastie, who had been on leave from his post as dean of the Howard University Law School, resigned as civilian aide to Secretary of War Henry L. Stimson to protest the failure to outlaw discrimination in the military. Hastie had taken the position in 1940, but throughout his tenure he had experienced frustration and hostility in attempting to secure equal treatment for black men and women in uniform. In his letter of resignation, which he published in the Chicago Defender, *he explains that the Army Air Forces' reactionary policies and discriminatory practices were the catalyst to his resignation:*

The Army Air Forces are growing in importance and independence. In the post war period they may become the greatest single component of the armed services. Biased policies and harmful practices established in this branch of the army can all too easily infect other branches as well. The situation had become critical. Yet, the whole course of my dealings with the Army Air Forces convinced me that further expression of my views in the form of recommendations within the department would be futile. I, therefore, took the only course which can, I believe, bring results. Public opinion is still the strongest force in American life.

To the Negro soldier and those who influence his thinking, I say with all the force and sincerity at my command that the man in uniform must grit his teeth, square his shoulders and do his best as a soldier, confident that there are millions of Americans outside of the armed services, and more persons than he knows in high places within the military establishment, who will never cease fighting to remove every racial barrier and every humiliating practice which now confront him. But only by being, at all times a first class soldier can the man in uniform help in this battle which shall be fought and won.

When I took office, the Secretary of War directed that all questions of policy and important proposals relating to Negroes should be referred to my office for comment or approval before final action. In December, 1940, the Air Forces referred to me a plan for a segregated training center for Negro pursuit pilots at Tuskegee. I expressed my

entire disagreement with the plan, giving my reasons in detail. My views were disregarded. Since then, the Air Command has never on its own initiative submitted any plan or project to me for comment or recommendation. What information I obtained, I had to seek out. Where I made proposals or recommendations, I volunteered them.

This situation reached its climax in late December, 1942, when I learned through army press releases sent out from St. Louis and from the War Department in Washington that the Air Command was about to establish a segregated officer candidate school at Jefferson Barracks, Mo., to train Negro officers for ground duty with the Army Air Forces. Here was a proposal for a radical departure from present army practice, since the officer candidate-training program is the one large field where the army is eliminating racial segregation.

Moreover, I had actually written to the Air Command several weeks earlier in an attempt to find out what was brewing at Jefferson Barracks. The Air Command replied as late as December 17, 1942, giving not even the slightest hint of any plan for a segregated officer candidate school. It is inconceivable to me that consideration of such a project had not then advanced far enough for my office to have been consulted, even if I had not made specific inquiry. The conclusion is inescapable that the Air Command does not propose to inform, much less counsel with, this office about its plans for Negroes.

1. **Why did African Americans fight so relentlessly to end segregation in the U.S. military? What did the military represent or symbolize to the nation?**

2. **Under what circumstances did African Americans appear to accept segregation and the establishment of separate programs such as the Tuskegee Airmen? Why, then, did African Americans object to the military's efforts to provide equal but separate facilities and educational programs?**

SOURCE: William H. Hastie, "Why I Resigned," *Chicago Defender,* February 6, 1943. Reprinted courtesy of the *Chicago Defender.*

VOICES Separate but Equal Training for Black Army Nurses?

In August 1944 Mabel Staupers received this reply from Under secretary of War Robert Patterson in response to her query about a segregated training center the army had established at Fort Huachuca, Arizona, for black nurses:

AUGUST 7, 1944

Mrs. Mabel K. Staupers R.N.,
Executive Secretary,
National Association of Colored Graduate Nurses, Inc.,
1790 Broadway,
New York 19, N.Y.

Dear Mrs. Staupers:

Thank you for your letter of July 19 with reference to the establishment of the first basic training center for Army Negro nurses at Fort Huachuca.

In establishing the first basic training center for Army Negro nurses at Fort Huachuca, the War Department desired that these nurses receive the best possible training and the most valuable experience for the type of service they would be required to render as Army nurses. It is the policy of the War Department to assign Negro nurses to those hospitals where there is a substantial number of Negro troops in relation to the personnel of the entire installation. The trainee at Fort Huachuca will therefore have the advantage of serving in a facility and under conditions parallel to those under which she will serve as an Army nurse.

You may be assured that the facilities for training afforded Negro nurses at Fort Huachuca will in no way be inferior to those of other similar establishments, and in their subsequent assignments these nurses will have full opportunity to render valuable service to the Army.

Sincerely yours,
(Signed) ROBERT P. PATTERSON
ROBERT P. PATTERSON,
Under Secretary of War

---

1. **How does Patterson's letter reflect the military's position that "separate but equal" did not constitute discrimination against African Americans?**
2. **Why did Mabel Staupers and the National Association of Colored Graduate Nurses object to separate training facilities for black women?**

SOURCE: War Department Files, File #2912, National Archives, Washington, DC.

---

efforts to desegregate officers' clubs. At Freeman Field, Indiana, for example, one hundred black officers refused to back down when their commanders threatened to arrest them for seeking to use the officers' club. In other bases, African-American soldiers responded with violence to violence, intimidation, and threats. Their actions, although quickly suppressed, prompted the army brass to reevaluate their belief in the military efficiency of discrimination.

The Beginning of Military Desegregation

In response to the militancy of black officers, civil rights leaders, and the press, the War Department made changes and began to reeducate soldiers, albeit in a limited fashion. The Advisory Committee on Negro Troop Policies was charged with coordinating the use of black troops and developing policy on social questions and personnel training. In 1943 the War Department also produced its own propaganda film—*The Negro Soldier*, directed by

20-1

20-2

20-3

20-4

20-5

Frank Capra—to alleviate racial tensions. This patronizing film emphasized the contributions black soldiers had made in the nation's wars since the American Revolution and was designed to appeal to both black and white audiences.

Racism remained strong throughout the war, but the persistent push of protest groups and the military's need for soldiers gradually loosened its grip. After the attack on Pearl Harbor, the services had to relax their restrictions on African Americans. The navy, previously the most resistant service, began to accept black men as sailors and noncommissioned officers. By 1943 it allowed African Americans into officer training schools. The Marine Corps began taking African Americans in 1942. Black officers were trained in integrated settings in all services except the Army Air Corps. The War Department even compelled recalcitrant commanding officers to recommend black servicemen for admission to the officer training schools, and soon over 2,000 a year graduated.

Many African Americans also saw combat. Several African-American artillery, tank destroyer, anti-aircraft, and combat engineer battalions fought with distinction in Europe and Asia. Military prejudice seemed to be borne out by the poor showing of the all-black 92nd Combat Division in the Italian campaign in 1944–1945, but investigation revealed that its failure was the result of poor training and leadership by its white commander, General Edward M. Almond, who had no confidence in his men. After the Battle of the Bulge, a massive German counterattack in Belgium in December 1944, 2,500 black volunteers fought in integrated units. Although subject to many of the same kinds of discrimination as African-American men, African-American women also found expanded opportunities in the military. Approximately 4,000 black women served in the Women's Army Auxiliary Corps.

Mabel Staupers's efforts finally bore fruit in 1945. When the War Department claimed there was a shortage of nurses, Staupers mobilized nursing groups of all races to protest the discrimination against black nurses in the Army and Navy Nurse Corps. There was an immediate groundswell of public support to remove quotas. On January 10, 1945, the army opened its Nurse Corps to all applicants without regard to race. The navy followed suit on January 15.

The Tuskegee Airmen

20-3   **How did the Tuskegee Airmen contribute to victory in World War II?**

The most visible group of black soldiers served in the Army Air Force. In January 1941 the War Department announced the formation of an all-black pursuit squadron of fighter planes and the creation of a training program at Tuskegee Army Air Field, Alabama, for black pilots.

Unlike all other units in the army, the 99th Squadron and the 332nd Group, made up of the 100th, 301st, and 302nd Squadrons, had black officers. The 99th went to North Africa in April 1943 and flew its first combat mission against the Italian island of Pantelleria in the Mediterranean on June 2. Later the squadron participated in the air battle over Sicily and supported the invasion of Italy. The squadron regularly engaged German pilots in aerial combat. In July, the 99th was added to the 332nd, and the group participated in campaigns in Italy, France, Germany, and the Balkans.

The **Tuskegee Airmen** gained an impressive record. They flew over 15,500 sorties, completed 1,578 missions, and escorted 200 heavy bombers deep into Germany's

Tuskegee Airmen
All-black combat air unit during World War II.

VOICES A Tuskegee Airman Remembers

Virgil Patterson was a Tuskegee Airman. In an oral history told to historian Ben Vinson III, Patterson recalled both the excitement of being an airman and the racism the Tuskegee Airmen endured:

Between December of 1944 and March of 1945 we saw more action. After having muscled into France, the Allies were preparing to make their final thrust at Hitler. I remember when we flew escort for over 1,000 bombers on their way to Germany. It was an awesome sight, seeing bombers in every direction for a 150-mile stretch. Looking down into the sea we saw still more activity, throngs and throngs of ships. During these months our planes bombarded German factories and troop positions that were preparing to repel the Allied invasion. Thankfully, the Germans didn't have use of the French fleet, which had been scuttled. But the Germans did have friends amongst the French, which made the Allied job more difficult.

Part of our responsibilities included strafing radar installations along the coast of France. On one sortie, I was part of a mission of four planes led by a man named Ballard. My wingman was Jefferson. His wingman was a pilot named Daniels. As we came in towards the ground from an altitude of almost 15,000 feet, I suddenly looked back to find Jefferson and noticed that Daniels, who was flying in front of me, was going up in smoke. I pulled up and started following Ballard, who didn't look back. That's when I noticed that Jefferson was being shot down as well. Ballard and I went in as close

to the coast as we dared and fired furiously at our targets. One, two, three . . . fire! One, two, three . . . fire! That was the interval. I shot short bursts while flying above the ocean at nearly 500 miles an hour.

We lost a number of pilots that day. When I returned to base I learned that Faulkner, our squadron leader, who had been flying at 30,000 feet, turned over and went down. They radioed him, knowing that something must have gone wrong. He was probably unconscious because he didn't respond. A poor oxygen connection apparently caused him to pass out during flight. As for Daniels, I learned many years later that he had survived his ordeal and had become a POW. Ironically, once behind enemy lines, the Germans treated him with proper respect. He was an officer, not a *black* officer. It seemed interesting to me to see how black soldiers had to be in the clutches of the enemy before being bestowed some of the honor that they deserved.

1. **What emotions did combat evoke in Patterson?**
2. **What do his comments about the German treatment of black POWs imply about racism in the U.S. military?**
3. **Do you think Patterson and the other Tuskegee Airmen wanted to be treated as officers or as black officers?**

SOURCE: *Flight: The Story of Virgil Richardson, A Tuskegee Airman in Mexico* (New York: Palgrave, 2004), 66–67.

Rhineland. They accumulated 150 Distinguished Flying Crosses, a Legion of Merit, a Silver Star, 14 Bronze Stars, and 744 Air Medals.

Technology: The Tuskegee Planes

To fly and participate in combat, the Tuskegee Airmen and the black ground troops who looked after their planes had to overcome more than the racism that cast doubt on black soldiers' ability to fight. They also had to master the technology of complex machines. The 332nd Fighter Group flew more different kinds of fighter planes than any other group of pilots during World War II. They were initially equipped with

20-1

20-2

20-3

20-4

20-5

P-40 Warhawks, then with P-39 Airacobras, later with P-47 Thunderbolts, and finally with the P-51 Mustang, the airplane with which they became most identified. Keeping these different kinds of planes in top form placed extreme pressure on the black mechanics who serviced them. The mechanics had to master the schematics of completely different engines and repair them. Despite the challenges this presented, the Tuskegee mechanics acquired the respect of the airmen and were recognized for their exceptional mechanical abilities during the war. They frequently worked round-the-clock, sleeping and eating in shifts in the airplane hangars.

The Transformation of Black Soldiers

A new generation of African Americans became soldiers during World War II, and the experience gave many of them an enhanced sense of themselves and a commitment to the fight for black equality. They returned home with a broader perception of the world and a transformed consciousness. Unlike the black soldiers in World War I, a greater percentage of those drafted at the outset of World War II had attended high school, and more of them were either high school or college graduates. Some black soldiers brought so-called radical ideas with them as they were drafted and sent to segregated installations. The urban and northern black servicemen and women and many of the southern rural recruits had a strong sense of their own self-worth and dignity.

The armed forces first exposed many African Americans to a world outside the segregated South and nurtured a budding international consciousness. Haywood Stephney of Clarksdale, Mississippi, recalled that when he first encountered segregation in the military he simply thought it was supposed to be that way. Like many others, his experiences during the war quickly removed him from "total darkness" and raised fundamental questions about the nation's racial system.

Douglas Conner, another Mississippi veteran, captured the collective understanding of the social and political meaning of the war shared by the men in his unit, the 31st Quartermaster Battalion stationed in Okinawa: ". . . because of the world war, I think many people, especially blacks, got the idea that we're going back, but we're not going back to business as usual. Somehow we're going to change this nation so that there's more equality than there is now." The personal transformation that Conner and others experienced, combined with a number of international, national, and regional forces, laid the foundation for a modern freedom movement.

The distinguished World War II record of the "Tuskegee Airmen," pilots who trained and fought in all-black fighter squadrons, confounded the expectations of white officers who doubted that black men had the ability or nerve to pilot fighter aircraft.

Black People on the Home Front

20-4   How did the war exacerbate tensions and competition over housing and jobs between black and white Americans?

20-1

20-2

20-3

20-4

20-5

Just as they did in the military, African Americans at home fought a dual war against the Axis powers and racism in the United States. Black workers and volunteers helped staff the factories and farms that produced goods for the fight while also purchasing war bonds and participating in other defense activities. The changes the war brought on also created new points of conflict while exacerbating preexisting problems and occasionally igniting full-scale riots. Throughout the war, protest groups and the black press fought employment discrimination and political exclusion.

Black Workers: From Farm to Factory

The war accelerated the migration of African Americans from rural areas to the cities. Even though the farm economy recovered during the war, high-paying defense jobs and other urban occupations tempted many black farmers to abandon the land. By the 1940s the bitter experiences of the previous decades had made it clear there was little future in the cotton fields. Indeed, by the end of the war in 1945, only 28 percent of black men worked on farms, down from 41 percent in 1940. More than 300,000 black men left agricultural labor between 1940 and 1944 alone.

The wartime need for workers, backed by pressure from the government, helped break down some barriers to employing African Americans in industry. During the war the number of black workers in nonfarm employment rose from 2,900,000 to 3,800,000, and thousands moved into previously whites-only jobs.

With so many of their men away at war, black women increasingly found work outside the laundry and domestic service that had previously been their lot. Nationally 600,000 black women—400,000 of them former domestic servants—shifted into industrial jobs. Even those women who stayed in domestic work often saw their wages improve as the supply of competent workers dwindled.

The abundance of industrial jobs helped spur and direct the second phase of the Great Migration, in which some 1.5 million migrants—nearly 15 percent of the population—left the South, swelling the black communities in northern and western cities that had significant war industries. The most dramatic rise in black population was in southern California. Because of its burgeoning aircraft industry and the success of civil rights groups and the federal government in limiting discrimination, Los Angeles saw its relatively small African-American community increase by more than 340,000 during the war.

Many unions became more open to African-American workers as black men and women took jobs in industries. Between 1940 and 1945, black union membership rose from 200,000 to 1.25 million. Those unions connected to the Committee for Industrial Organization (CIO), particularly the United Automobile Workers, were the most open to black membership, whereas AFL affiliates were the most likely to treat African Americans as second-class members or to exclude them altogether. The growth in black membership did not end racism in unions, even in the CIO, but it did provide African Americans with a stronger foundation on which to protest discrimination in employment.

20-1

20-2

20-3

20-4

20-5

Before World War II, few white women and still fewer black women worked in heavy industries, but with so many men in the armed forces, women were recruited for jobs in shipyards and airplane factories, like this aircraft worker. Between 1940 and 1944, the percentage of black women in the industrial workforce increased from 6.8 percent to 18 percent.

The FEPC during the War

After President Roosevelt issued the executive order banning job discrimination in defense industries with government contracts, thousands of impoverished black southerners rushed to cities in the Pacific Northwest, especially to Seattle. Wartime Seattle had offered jobs in its shipyards, in logging-truck manufacturing, and at the Boeing aircraft production plants. By 1945, Boeing employed over 1,200 black workers, approximately 3 percent of its labor force. African Americans also accounted for 7 percent of Seattle's shipyard workers. By 1948 black families in Seattle boasted a median income of $3,314, a mere 10 percent lower than the median for the nation's white families. However, the economic good fortune of black workers on the West Coast was not typical of the rest of the country.

In the Midwest and on the East Coast, many African Americans criticized industry's failure to end economic discrimination. In May 1943 President Roosevelt responded to the ineffectiveness of the FEPC. Executive Order 9346 established a new Committee on Fair Employment Practice, increased its budget, and placed its operation directly under the Executive Office of the President. Roosevelt appointed Malcolm Ross, a combative white liberal, to head the committee. Ross initiated nationwide hearings of cases concerning discrimination in the shipbuilding and railroad industries. These proceedings embarrassed some companies and increased compliance with the FEPC's orders. Resistance, however, was more common. In Mobile, Alabama, for example, the white employees of the Alabama Dry Dock and Shipbuilding Company opposed the FEPC's efforts to pressure the company to promote 12 of the 7,000 African Americans it employed in menial positions to racially mixed welding crews. The white workers went on a rampage, assaulting 50 African Americans. The FEPC thereupon withdrew its plan and acquiesced to the company's discrimination. As a result of this kind of intransigence, the committee failed to redress most of the grievances of black workers. An effort to continue the committee after the war was defeated.

Anatomy of a Race Riot: Detroit, 1943

One of the bloodiest race riots in the nation's history took place in 1943 in Detroit, Michigan, where black and white workers were competing fiercely for jobs and housing. Relations between the two communities had been smoldering for months. The brutality of white police officials was an especially potent factor. Tensions were so palpable that weeks before the riot, the NAACP's Walter White had warned that the city could explode.

The immediate trigger for the riot was a squabble on June 20 between white and black bathers at the segregated city beaches on Belle Isle in the Detroit River. Within hours, 200 white sailors from a nearby base joined the white mob that attacked black men and women. A rumor that white citizens had killed a black woman and thrown her baby over a bridge spread across the city. Soon the riot was in full swing and spread quickly along Woodward Avenue, the city's major thoroughfare, into Paradise Valley. By Monday morning white men in search of more victims had overrun downtown Detroit. The mayor refused to acknowledge that the situation had gotten out of hand, but by Tuesday evening he could no longer deny the crisis.

Six thousand federal troops had to be dispatched to Detroit to restore order. When the violence ended, 34 people had been killed (25 black and nine white people) and more than 700 injured. Of the 25 black people who died, the Detroit police killed 17. However, the police did not kill any of the white men who assaulted African Americans or committed arson.

In the aftermath, the city created the Mayor's Interracial Committee, the first permanent municipal body designed to promote civic harmony and fairness. Despite the efforts of labor and black leaders, many white people in Detroit, including Wayne County prosecutor William E. Dowling, blamed the black press and the NAACP for instigating the riot. Dowling and others accused the city's black citizens of pushing too hard for economic and political equality and insisted that they operated under communist influence.

The G.I. Bill of Rights and Black Veterans

In 1944, President Roosevelt signed the Servicemen's Readjustment Act (known as the "G.I. Bill of Rights"), legislation that would profoundly affect American life and society. It rewarded the sacrifices and accomplishments of black and white veterans in the war with college tuition allowances, stipends for books, and guaranteed loans at low interest rates, with which to purchase homes or launch small businesses.

By 1947, veterans accounted for half of all college students. The G.I. Bill made possible the upward mobility of a generation of American men who entered professions and trades and purchased homes that would become the basis of future wealth. Between 1950 and 1960, Americans built more than 13 million new homes—11 million of them were in the suburbs, where one-quarter of the entire population relocated after the war. The G.I. Bill fueled the boom in higher education, transportation, and the construction industries that undergirded the postwar prosperity America enjoyed.

While many black veterans benefited from the G.I. Bill of Rights, they never received their fair share of funds and assistance. Mississippi Congressman John E. Rankin sabotaged the transformative potential of the G.I. Bill by insisting that state and local veterans' administrators control the distribution of the benefits. The resulting racial disparities were predictable in southern states. In Mississippi, by the summer of 1947, local officials had approved over 3,000 Veterans Administration home loans, but only two went to African-American veterans. In northern urban areas, real estate agencies and banks practiced "redlining" and denied black men mortgages in desirable areas. The denial of loans and the violence that often erupted when black families attempted to move into suburban areas curtailed upward and outward mobility.

Old and New Protest Groups on the Home Front

The NAACP grew tremendously during the war; by the war's end, it stood poised for even greater achievements. During the war, the *Crisis* was one of the most important sources for information about black men and women. The NAACP's membership increased from 50,000 in 1940 to 450,000 at the end of the war. Much of this growth occurred in the South, which by 1945 had more than 150,000 members. Supreme Court victories and especially close monitoring of the "Double V" campaign helped explain these huge increases.

20-1
20-2
20-3
20-4
20-5

Success, however, bred conflict and ambivalence. Leaders split over the value of integration versus self-segregation and questioned the benefit of relying so heavily on legal cases rather than paying more attention to the concerns and needs of working-class black men and women.

Southern Regional Council (SRC)
Organization that conducted research and focused attention on social, political, and educational inequality in the South.

In 1944 southern white liberals joined with African Americans to establish the **Southern Regional Council (SRC)**. This interracial coalition, an important example of the local initiative of private citizens, was devoted to expanding democracy in a region better known for the political and economic oppression and exploitation of its black citizens. The SRC conducted research and focused attention on the political, social, and educational inequalities endemic to black life in the South. Although the events of the 1950s and 1960s would soon overtake its patient, gradualist program, the SRC challenged the facade of southern white supremacy.

Congress of Racial Equality (CORE)
Protest group committed to nonviolent direct action.

In 1942 a far more strident group called the **Congress of Racial Equality (CORE)** was formed. It pursued different tactics from those of the NAACP, Urban League, and other existing civil rights groups. CORE began in Chicago when an interracial group of Christian pacifists gathered to find ways to make America live up to the ideals of equality and justice on which it based its war program. James Farmer and Bayard Rustin were key in getting the group off the ground. Unlike the NAACP, CORE was a decentralized, intensely democratic organization. CORE dedicated itself to the principles of nonviolent direct action as expounded by Indian leader Mohandas Gandhi. During the war CORE expanded to other cities and challenged segregation in the North with sit-ins and other protest tactics that the civil rights movement would later adopt in the South.

African Americans fought discrimination in many ways. Women were central to these efforts. Throughout the 1940s, in countless communities across the South and the Midwest, black women organized women's political councils and other groups to press for integration of public facilities and for the right to pursue collegiate and professional studies. Others were galvanized by the war and took advantage of the limited social and political spaces afforded them to create lasting works in the arts, literature, and popular culture. Women whose names would become virtually synonymous with the modern civil rights movement in the 1950s and 1960s helped lay its foundation in the World War II era. For example, Ella Baker was accumulating contacts and sharpening her organizing skills as she served as the NAACP field secretary. Rosa Parks began resisting segregation laws on Montgomery, Alabama, buses during the 1940s.

Black college students also began protesting segregation in public accommodations. The spark that ignited the Howard University campus civil rights movement came in January 1943. Three sophomore women—Ruth Powell, Marianne Musgrave, and Juanita Morrow sat at a lunch counter near the campus and were refused service. They demanded to see the manager and vowed to wait until he came. Instead, two policemen arrived who instructed the waitress to serve them. When the check arrived, the trio learned they had been charged 25 cents each instead of the customary 10 cents. They placed 35 cents on the counter, turned to leave, and were arrested. Ruth Powell later reported that "the policeman who arrested us told us we were being taken in for investigation because he had no proof that we weren't 'subversive agents.'" In fact, no charges were lodged against the women. The purpose of their arrest had been to intimidate them, but the incident instead fanned the smoldering embers of resentment in the Howard University student body.

The Transition to Peace

After the German surrender in May 1945 and the Japanese surrender in August 1945, the United States began the transition to peace. Many of the gains of black men and women were wiped away as the armed forces demobilized and the factories began reinstituting the discriminatory hiring systems that were in place before the conflict. Access to fair, decent, and affordable housing remained a sore issue, as did the inequalities in educational opportunities and the continuing scourge of police brutality. Thus, as the country tried to regain its prewar footing, it was clear that segregation and discrimination would face a huge challenge in the coming years and that the African-American community was ready, willing, and able to fight in ways undreamed of in earlier eras.

The Cold War and International Politics

20-5 | What were the positive and negative effects of the Cold War on blacks, both in politics and social life?

As the defeat of the Axis powers neared in early 1945, the United Nations began planning for the peace. Within a short time, however, the opposing interests of the Soviet Union and the United States led to a long period of intense hostility that became known as the Cold War. This conflict soon led to a division of Europe into two spheres, with the Soviets dominating part of Germany and the nations to its east and a coalition of democratic capitalist regimes allied with the United States in the west. Thereafter, the overriding goal of the United States and its allies was the "containment" of communism. To this end, the **North Atlantic Treaty Organization (NATO)** was formed in 1949 to provide a military counterforce to Soviet power in Europe while American dollars helped rebuild Western Europe's war-shattered economy. The United States forged a similarly close relationship with Japan. Much of the rest of the world, however, became contested terrain during the Cold War.

North Atlantic Treaty Organization (NATO) Military alliance formed to counter the threat posed by the Soviet Union and its allies.

As the nations of Asia and Africa gained independence from colonial domination over the ensuing decades, the United States struggled to keep them out of the Soviet orbit. It did so through foreign aid, direct military force, and, occasionally, through clandestine operations run by the Central Intelligence Agency. These interventions were matched by a rising diplomatic and propaganda effort to convince the emerging nations that the United States was a model to be emulated and an ally to be trusted.

The Cold War had an enormous influence on American society precisely when the powerful movement for African-American rights was beginning to emerge. The long conflict resulted in the rise of a large permanent military establishment in the United States. The reorganized American military enlisted millions of men and women by the early 1950s and claimed most of the national budget. The federal government also grew in power during the war and provided a check on the control that white southerners had exercised over race relations in their region for so long. American policymakers also became concerned about the nation's ability to win the allegiance of Africans and other nonwhite people in the emerging nations. Soviet propaganda could discredit American sincerity by pointing to the deplorable state of race relations within the United States. Hence, during the Cold War, external pressures reinforced domestic efforts to change American racial policy.

African Americans in World Affairs: W. E. B. Du Bois and Ralph Bunche

The Cold War gave new importance to the voices of African Americans in world affairs. Two men, W. E. B. Du Bois and Ralph Johnson Bunche (1904–1971), represented alternative strategies for responding to this opportunity. Du Bois was highly critical of American policy. For half a century, he had linked the fate of African Americans with that of Africans, and by 1945 was widely hailed as the "Father of Pan-Africanism." In that year he directed the Fifth Pan-African Congress, which met in Manchester, England. Africans who had been radicalized by World War II dominated the conference and encouraged it to denounce Western imperialism. Du Bois considered the United States a protector of the colonial system and opposed its stance in the Cold War.

In contrast to Du Bois, scholar-diplomat Ralph Bunche opted to work within the American system. Bunche held a Harvard doctorate in government and international relations and had spent much of the 1930s studying the problems of African Americans. During World War II, the American government found his expertise on Africa of tremendous value, and Bunche became one of the key policymakers for the region. His analysis of events and changes in Africa and the Far East after World War II led to his appointment as adviser to the U.S. delegation at the San Francisco conference that drafted the United Nations (UN) Charter. In 1948 he served as acting mediator of the UN Special Committee on Palestine, and in 1949 he negotiated an armistice between Egypt and Israel. He received the Spingarn Medal of the NAACP in 1949, and in 1950 he became the first African American to receive the Nobel Peace Prize. Although Bunche worked in concert with national policymakers, he was committed to winning independence for African nations and freedom for his own people.

Anticommunism at Home

The rising tensions with the Soviet Union affected all aspects of domestic life in the United States. Conservatives used fears of communist subversion to attack anyone who advocated change in America. This included people who were or had been members of the Communist Party, union members, liberals, and those who had fought for African-American rights. The Truman administration (1945–1953) responded to fears of subversion by instituting government loyalty programs. Government employees were dismissed for the merest suspicion of disloyalty. Militant American anticommunism reached a feverish peak in the immediate postwar years and ignited an explosion of red-baiting hysteria that led to the rise of Wisconsin Republican Senator Joseph McCarthy (1909–1957) and the **House Un-American Activities Committee (HUAC).** The relentless pursuit of "communist sympathizers" by McCarthy and HUAC ruined many lives. HUAC hounded people in the media and the entertainment industry. Even so prominent a figure as Du Bois was ripe for attack. On February 8, 1951, HUAC indicted him for allegedly serving as an "agent of a foreign principal" in his work with the Peace Information Center. In November a federal judge dismissed the charges.

House Un-American Activities Committee (HUAC) Congressional committee formed to investigate the activities of communists and "communist sympathizers" in America.

Paul Robeson

Paul Robeson (1898–1976) was one of the most tragic victims of these anticommunist witch hunts. This fine scholar and star collegiate athlete, Columbia Law School graduate, consummate performer, and star of stage and screen had always advocated the rights of African Americans and workers. During the 1930s he worked closely with the Communist Party (although he was never a member), becoming one of the most famous defenders of the Soviet Union. Many leftists of the time became disaffected with the Soviet Union after its 1939 pact with Hitler and its brutal repressiveness became clear. Robeson, however, doggedly stuck to his belief in Soviet communism.

In the late 1940s, Robeson's pro-Soviet views and inflammatory statements aroused the ire of the U.S. government and its red hunters. A statement he made at the communist-dominated World Congress of the Defenders of Peace in Paris in 1949 provoked outrage. "It is unthinkable," Robeson said, "that American Negroes would go to war on behalf of those [the United States] who have oppressed us for generations against a country [the Soviet Union] which in one generation has raised our people to full human dignity of mankind." Later in 1949 crowds twice disrupted a Robeson concert in Peekskill, New York, the first time preventing the concert from being held, the second time terrorizing performers and audience members after the concert by throwing rocks at them.

Throughout the 1940s Robeson consistently linked the struggles of black America with the struggles of oppressed peoples around the world. Robeson also refused to sign an affidavit concerning past membership in the Communist Party. In response, the U.S. State Department revoked his passport in 1950. The travel ban remained in effect until the Supreme Court declared it unconstitutional in 1958.

Robeson had combined his art and his politics to attack racial discrimination, segregation, and the ideology of white supremacy and black inferiority in America. During the Cold War the state would tolerate no such dissent even by a world-acclaimed black artist.

Henry Wallace and the 1948 Presidential Election

Robeson's struggles illustrate how conservative attacks choked off left-wing involvement in the struggle for black equality. The attacks destroyed Robeson's brilliant singing career. The increasing importance of black votes to Democrats, however, meant that key elements of the African-American liberation struggle remained at the center of national politics. Nowhere was this more apparent than in the 1948 presidential election.

President Harry S. Truman was not expected to win this election because he faced a strong challenge from Thomas Dewey, the popular and well-financed Republican governor of New York. A challenge from his former secretary of commerce, Henry Wallace, who had been Roosevelt's vice president from 1941 to 1945, compounded Truman's problems. Wallace ran on the ticket of the communist-backed Progressive Party, which sought to take the votes of liberals, leftists, and civil rights advocates disappointed by Truman's moderation. To undercut Wallace's challenge, Truman began to press Congress to pass liberal programs.

Black votes in key northern states were central to Truman's strategy for victory. African Americans in these tightly contested areas could make the difference between victory and defeat, so Truman, to retain their allegiance, sought to demonstrate his administration's support of civil rights. In January 1948 he embraced the findings of his biracial Committee on Civil Rights and called for their enactment into law. The committee's report recommended passage of federal anti-lynching legislation, ending discrimination at the ballot box, abolishing the poll tax, desegregating the military, and many other measures.

The reaction of white southern politicians was swift and threatening, causing Truman to pause. But as the election neared, fear of black disaffection at the polls became so great that the Democratic convention passed a strong pro-civil rights plank. Many white southerners, led by South Carolina's Governor Strom Thurmond, bolted from the convention and formed their own States' Rights, or "Dixiecrat," Party. In the election, the Dixiecrats carried South Carolina, Alabama, Mississippi, and Louisiana. Wallace carried no state. Dewey carried 13 northern and midwestern states, but Truman won a plurality in the popular vote and a majority in the Electoral College. The failure of the bulwark of white supremacy to prevent the Democratic Party from advocating African-American rights, and Truman's victory, despite the defection of hard-line racists, represented a turning point in American politics.

20-1

20-2

20-3

20-4

20-5

Watch on
MyHistoryLab
Video: The Desegre-
gation of the Military
and Blacks in Combat

20-1

20-2

Executive Order 9981
Order issued by
President Harry Truman
in 1948 desegregating
the armed forces.

20-3

20-4

Read on MyHistoryLab
Document: President
Truman Integrates the
Armed Forces, 1948

20-5

Desegregating the Armed Forces

The importance of the black vote, the fight for the allegiance of the emerging nations, and the emerging civil rights movement hastened the desegregation of the military. In February 1948 a communist coup in Czechoslovakia raised the possibility of war between the United States and the Soviet Union and heightened concerns among military leaders about African Americans' willingness to serve yet again in a Jim Crow army. When Congress reinstated the draft in March 1948, A. Philip Randolph, who—in a replay of the March on Washington scenario—had formed the League for Non-Violent Civil Disobedience Against Military Segregation in 1947, warned the nation that black men and women were fed up with segregation and Jim Crow and would not take a Jim Crow draft lying down. On June 24, 1948, the Soviet Union heightened tensions even further when it imposed a blockade on West Berlin.

On July 26, Truman, anticipating war between the superpowers and hoping to shore up his support among black voters for the approaching November elections, issued **Executive Order 9981**, which mandated "equality of treatment and opportunity for all persons in the armed services without regard to race, color, religion, or national origin." After Truman signed the order, leaders of the League for Nonviolent Civil Disobedience Against Military Segregation, disbanded the organization and called off marches planned for Chicago and New York.

Not until 1950 and the outbreak of the Korean War, however, was Truman's order fully implemented. The Korean War reflected the American Cold War policy of containment, which was intended to stop what American leaders believed to be a worldwide conspiracy orchestrated by Moscow to spread communism. In 1950 the North Koreans, allied with the Soviets, attacked the American-supported government in South Korea and launched a "hot war" in the midst of the Cold War. After the North Koreans invaded South Korea, the United States under UN auspices intervened. Heavy casualties early in the war depleted many white combat units. Thus, early in 1951, the army acted on Truman's executive order and authorized the formal integration of its units in Korea. By 1954 the army had disbanded its last all-black units, and the armed forces became one of the first sectors of American society to abandon segregation.

Read on MyHistoryLab Document: Segregation in the Military
During World War II, 1940–1941

African-American civilians demonstrated firm resolve to end racial segregation at home while Americans fought to make the world safe for democracy. The NAACP Detroit branch's 1944 "Parade for Victory" featured pallbearers with caskets as they marched behind a sign that proclaimed "HERE LIES JIM CROW." It conveyed the sentiment, if not the reality. But Jim Crow's days were numbered.

CONCLUSION

The years between 1940 and 1954 were a dynamic period of black activism and witnessed a rising international consciousness among African Americans.

The quest for racial justice in the military and on the home front became an integral part of the ongoing struggle for economic, political, and social progress. President Roosevelt's Executive Order 8802 was a significant victory for A. Philip Randolph's March on Washington Movement and for black workers, who were able to appeal racial discrimination in defense industries to the FEPC. The rise of fascism in Europe alarmed black and white Americans who correctly perceived ideologies based on racial tyranny and state dominance to be hostile to individual freedom and democracy. World War II profoundly transformed black servicemen and servicewomen.

The Cold War created a climate in America that was both hospitable and hostile to the African-American freedom movement. Radicals such as Paul Robeson and W. E. B. Du Bois found no place in this movement or in American society. Instead, more moderate organizations, such as the NAACP's Legal Defense and Educational Fund, pursued their goals within the ideological and legal constraints of the American political system and met with some success. The coming civil rights movement would, however, soon lead to a more varied, vibrant, and successful challenge to racism.

CHAPTER TIMELINE

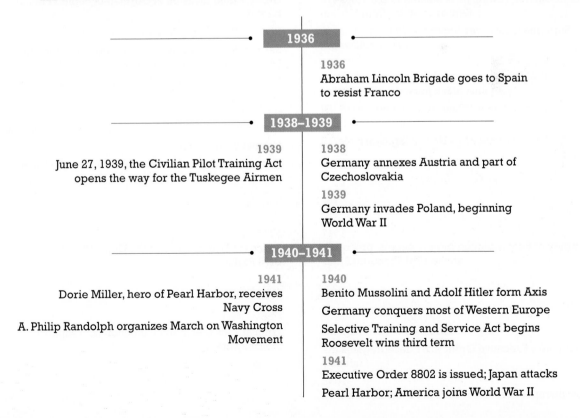

AFRICAN-AMERICAN EVENTS   **NATIONAL AND WORLD EVENTS**

1936

1936
Abraham Lincoln Brigade goes to Spain to resist Franco

1938–1939

1939
June 27, 1939, the Civilian Pilot Training Act opens the way for the Tuskegee Airmen

1938
Germany annexes Austria and part of Czechoslovakia

1939
Germany invades Poland, beginning World War II

1940–1941

1941
Dorie Miller, hero of Pearl Harbor, receives Navy Cross

A. Philip Randolph organizes March on Washington Movement

1940
Benito Mussolini and Adolf Hitler form Axis

Germany conquers most of Western Europe

Selective Training and Service Act begins Roosevelt wins third term

1941
Executive Order 8802 is issued; Japan attacks Pearl Harbor; America joins World War II

CHAPTER TIMELINE

AFRICAN-AMERICAN EVENTS

NATIONAL AND WORLD EVENTS

1942–1943

AFRICAN-AMERICAN EVENTS

1942
Congress of Racial Equality (CORE) founded in Chicago

Charity Adams (Early) becomes first black commissioned officer in the Women's Army Auxiliary Corps

First black cadets graduate from flying school at Tuskegee, Alabama

1943
William H. Hastie resigns in protest from War Department

Race riots in Mobile, Detroit, and Harlem

The black 99th Pursuit Squadron flies its first combat mission

NATIONAL AND WORLD EVENTS

1942
100,000 Japanese Americans interred in camps

1943
Roosevelt signs G.I. Bill

1944–1945

1944
Adam Clayton Powell, Jr., is elected to U.S. House of Representatives from Harlem

Supreme Court overthrows the white primary in *Smith v. Allwright*

1945
Mabel Staupers secures end to discrimination against black nurses in the military

Du Bois, Bethune, White, and Bunche attend UN founding in San Francisco

Paul Robeson receives NAACP Spingarn Medal

1944
D-Day, Allied invasion of German-occupied France, begins

Roosevelt wins fourth term

Servicemen's Readjustment Act provides funds for housing and education after the war

Battle of the Bulge, last major German counteroffensive

1945
United Nations founded
President Roosevelt dies; Truman becomes president

Germany surrenders

United States bombs Hiroshima and Nagasaki; Japan surrenders

1946–1947

1947
Journey of Reconciliation project begins, precursor to the 1961 Freedom Rides

1946
President Truman creates the Committee on Civil Rights

1948–1949

1948
Ada Lois Sipuel v. Board of Regents

Truman's Executive Order 9981 desegregates the military

1949
Riots disrupt Robeson concerts in Peekskill, New York

1948
Truman wins presidential election with support of black voters

On MyHistoryLab

 ✔ Study and Review on MyHistoryLab

REVIEW QUESTIONS

1. How did World War II change the status of African Americans? What were some of the consequences of so many black servicemen fighting in Europe against fascism and Nazism? How did the Tuskegee Airmen contribute to the Allied victory in Europe?

2. How did black women participate in the campaign to desegregate the U.S. military and in the Abraham Lincoln Brigade? How did Mabel Staupers win acceptance of black women into the military nurses corps?

3. What did the "Double V" campaign accomplish? How did African-American civilians support black servicemen? What institutional resources were African Americans able to marshal in their campaign against racism at home?

4. How did World War II affect black workers in America? What was the significance of A. Philip Randolph's March on Washington Movement, and how did President Roosevelt respond to it?

5. Why did the Cold War originate, and what was its significance for black activism? How did the World War II era promote the internationalization of African-American consciousness? How did the State Department attempt to downplay black dissent in America, and why?

6. Why did President Truman decide to desegregate the U.S. military?

The Significance of the Desegregation of the U.S. Military

Howard P. Perry, the first African American to enlist in the Marine Corps.

THROUGH THEIR MILITARY SERVICE AFRICAN AMERICANS have played important roles in the construction and preservation of American democracy. Since their participation in the colonial militia and the Continental Army during the American Revolution, through the recent wars against Iraq and in Afghanistan in the twenty-first century, black Americans have viewed military service as a way to prove their loyalty and bravery, and to show their right to freedom and citizenship.

At the birth of the new nation in 1775–1776, black people composed one-fifth of the population. They fought mostly in integrated colonial militias and army regiments during the American Revolution, but it would take over two centuries and many more wars before military integration became permanent national policy. In the Civil War, the Spanish-American War, World War I, and World War II, black and white servicemen fought in racially segregated units in the Army and Navy. (The Marines did not allow black men to serve until 1942.) The desegregation of the military during the 1950s was thus, in many respects, a monumental and historic achievement. Throughout World War II black communities had waged a "Double V" campaign against Fascism and Nazism abroad and racial segregation and discrimination at home. President Harry Truman's Executive Order 9981 ordering the desegregation of the U.S. military in 1948 helped to set the stage for the emergence of the modern civil rights movement. Desegregation in the military preceded the end of legal segregation and Jim Crow in civilian life by more than a decade. Today, the U.S. military is one of the most racially neutral institutions in America.

The War for Independence (1775–1783) was, as scholars now attest, "the first mass slave rebellion in American history." Enslaved black men fought on both sides of the war. Some fought for the British, but even larger numbers joined the Patriot cause, believing that they would be freed as compensation for their service to the new nation. In 1775, Lord Dunmore, Virginia's last royal governor, promised to free any slave or indentured servant in exchange for their military service to the Crown. In response, George Washington, the Patriot commander, initially vacillated but soon allowed the enlistment of free black men in his army. In both the Battle of Bunker Hill and the Battle of Long Island in 1776, African-American soldiers from the northern states "served in twice the proportion of their numbers in the population." By 1781, at the decisive Battle of Yorktown, which ensured American independence, black troops were estimated to make up one-quarter of the Patriot Army. Despite their military service and contributions, however, the American Revolution would remain the unfinished revolution for African Americans.

Slavery endured and flourished until the 1860s when the election of President Abraham Lincoln, followed by the secession of South Carolina and 10 other southern states, ignited the Civil War. Free African Americans who supported the abolition of slavery pressured an initially reluctant Lincoln to make the destruction of slavery a military objective. When Lincoln issued the Emancipation Proclamation in 1863 and also allowed states to raise black militias, the Civil War became an opportunity for African Americans to fight for their own liberation.

During the Civil War, more than 185,000 African Americans fought in the Union Army and Navy. They provided the crucial margin of manpower that facilitated the North's victory. Approximately 29,000 African American men made up one-fourth of the entire naval enrollment. The recruitment and enlistment of African Americans into the Union Army

Colin Powell (center), Chairman of the Joint Chiefs of Staff, with Former Vice President Richard Cheney and General Norman Schwarzkopf.

was controversial, however. Frederick Douglass, the leading advocate of arming black men, reminded Lincoln that African Americans had fought well enough to help win American independence and insisted that they were eager and more than qualified to fight for their people's freedom and to preserve that independence. On August 25, 1862, the War Department granted General Rufus Saxton, military governor of South Carolina's Sea Islands, the power to raise five regiments of black troops on the islands, albeit under the command of white officers.

The northern victory in the Civil War preserved the Union and ended slavery. But again, black military service failed to end military segregation and discrimination in the military academies at West Point and Annapolis. The closing decades of the nineteenth century simultaneously witnessed the rise of legal segregation and political disfranchisement and helped to fan the Great Migration from the South to northern cities. Still, black people's desire to serve in the military never wavered. Black public protest against military segregation and discrimination continued during World War I and reached a peak in World War II when a nation with a segregated military fought Germany and Japan, nations that embraced a master race ideology.

Black Americans seized the national crisis of World War II to make their demands for civil and human rights heard. In 1949, Wesley A. Brown became the first black midshipman to graduate from the U.S. Naval Academy (founded in 1845). Representative Adam Clayton Powell, Jr., of New York had interceded on his behalf. One of Brown's classmates was future President Jimmy Carter. The desegregation of the military, one of the most significant institutions in American public life, opened opportunities for black men and women. A generation later Colin Luther Powell, born in Harlem, New York to Jamaican-American parents, reached the highest position in the military when he became the twelfth Chairman of the Joint Chief of Staff (1985–1989), after which he was named the Secretary of State in 2001 by President George W. Bush. Today, African Americans constitute almost 20 percent of service men and women in the U.S. armed forces.

The Long Freedom Movement 1950–1965

Between 1954 and 1965, the civil rights movement achieved a revolution, transforming the legal and social status of African Americans. Despite fierce resistance, legally sanctioned segregation, racial discrimination, and disfranchisement fell before a mighty coalition of civil rights groups and their allies. Demonstrations and the pressures of the Cold War compelled high government officials to abandon their early caution. Although racism remained powerful in American life after 1965, and African Americans continued to suffer from severe economic disadvantages, the enlargement of freedom of opportunity and recognition of African Americans' full citizenship rights transformed America and radiated across the globe.

At the height of his moral authority, Martin Luther King, Jr. (1929–1968), delivers the memorable "I Have a Dream" speech at the 1963 March on Washington.

The heart of the story of the modern civil rights movement is the courage and tenacity people showed in their own communities in their determination to attack segregation and exclusion from the political process. Behind the charismatic leaders and the spectacles of the NAACP's Supreme Court victories and the marches and demonstrations captured so dramatically on television were the ordinary citizens who initiated protests, formulated strategies and tactics, and garnered other essential resources that made collective action work. The people's actions were made effective through their families, churches, voluntary associations, political organizations, women's clubs, labor unions, and colleges. The sacrifices and experience gained in the previous one hundred years of struggle had, by the mid-1950s, accumulated sufficiently to permit an all-out attack on white supremacy. The civil rights movement would be long and bloody, and it would not lead to the Promised Land, but it would change America.

The 1950s: Prosperity and Prejudice

21-1 What were the background and conditions of the 1950s that led to the emergence of the national civil rights movement?

For most white Americans, the 1950s were an era of unparalleled prosperity. Affluent white Americans fled to the suburbs; by 1960, 52 percent of Americans owned their own homes. The decade is remembered nostalgically as a time of large, stable nuclear families; wives and mothers who stayed at home; and communities untroubled by drugs, crime, and juvenile delinquency.

For most black Americans, however, the 1950s were less blissful. American society remained rigidly segregated in housing and education. Despite the gains African Americans made during the World War II era, Jim Crow still reigned. Despite legal victories, the threat of white violence kept millions of African Americans from voting in the Deep South and housing integration was a distant dream.

More important, most African Americans did not benefit from the economic boom of the 1950s that allowed so many white Americans to purchase homes in the suburbs. Moving into urban centers, where the number of factories and jobs were just beginning to decline, African Americans suffered a higher unemployment rate than any other segment of the population. White workers, fearing for their jobs, felt threatened by competition from unemployed black workers. As urban neighborhoods deteriorated, conditions ripened for a massive explosion.

The Road to *Brown*

21-2 What events led to *Brown v. Board of Education* (1954), and why was it the most important Supreme Court decision of the twentieth century?

In 1954, with the Supreme Court's decision in *Brown v. Board of Education of Topeka, Kansas*, progress in the desegregation of American society moved into the civilian realm. The *Brown* decision undermined state-sanctioned segregation. The NAACP's legal program of the 1920s and 1930s was largely responsible for this victory. In 1940 the NAACP set up the Legal Defense and Educational Fund (NAACP-LDEF) to attack the legal foundations of race inequality in American education. Thereafter, the NAACP-LDEF fought segregation and discrimination in education, housing, employment, and politics. In the first years of its existence, attorneys for the fund won stunning victories, including a 1944 Supreme Court decision, *Smith v. Allwright*, declaring white primaries unconstitutional, and *Shelley v. Kramer* (1948), outlawing restrictive residential covenants. The life and career of one of the NAACP-LDEF lawyers, Constance Baker Motley, symbolizes the struggle that black professionals, both men and women, waged to overcome racial and gender exclusion as well as the union of disparate forces that planted and nurtured the seeds of the coming revolution. Motley is our guide on the road to *Brown*.

Constance Baker Motley and Black Lawyers in the South

Constance Baker Motley was born in 1921 to immigrant parents from the British West Indies. She grew up in a tightly knit West Indian community in New Haven, Connecticut. The members of New Haven's black community, including Baker's parents, worked as domestics or in service jobs for Yale University. Baker attended integrated schools and experienced episodic racism. In high school, Baker developed a strong racial consciousness.

The most important event in her early life was the lecture that George Crawford, an NAACP lawyer, gave at the local Dixwell Community Center. The talk concerned the Supreme Court decision in *State of Missouri ex rel. Gaines v. Canada*. Crawford explained that the University of Missouri's law school had denied Gaines admission but had offered to pay his tuition expenses to an out-of-state school. The NAACP won a victory when the Supreme Court ruled that the state had violated the Fourteenth Amendment's mandate that state laws provide equal protection regardless of race. After *Gaines*, states had to furnish within their borders facilities for legal education for black people equal to those offered for white citizens.

Baker desperately wanted to go to law school, but her family could not even afford to send her to college. In 1940, however, Baker came to the attention of Clarence Blakeslee, a local white philanthropist who offered to finance her education after hearing her speak at a meeting of black and white community residents. She graduated in 1943 and then went on to become the second black woman ever to attend Columbia University Law School. In 1946 she went to work for the NAACP's LDEF.

In the late 1940s, the NAACP-LDEF's attack on inequality in graduate education provided the basis for a full-scale assault on segregation. No longer would the organization be satisfied only to push for fulfillment of the promise of "separate but equal" facilities. In 1948 the University of Oklahoma Law School denied Ada Lois Sipuel admission because she was black. The Supreme Court, signaling it was willing to take a more activist stance, ordered Oklahoma, in *Sipuel v. Board of Regents of the University of Oklahoma*, to "provide [a legal education] for [Sipuel] in conformity with the equal protection clause of the Fourteenth Amendment and provide it as soon as it does for applicants of any other group."

Another case, *Sweatt v. Painter*, which the Supreme Court decided in 1950, began when the University of Texas at Austin attempted to circumvent court orders to admit Heman Sweatt to its law school by creating a separate facility consisting of three basement rooms, a small library, and a few instructors who would lecture to him alone. The court ruled that the university had deprived Sweatt of intangibles such as "the essential ingredient of a legal education . . . the opportunity for students to discuss the law with their peers and others with whom they would be associated professionally in later life." On the same day the justices

Constance Baker Motley endured many hardships and even assaults as she tried school desegregation cases in the South. Here she leaves the federal court in Birmingham after an unsuccessful attempt to force the University of Alabama to accept a black student.

21-1
21-2
21-3
21-4
21-5
21-6
21-7
21-8

ruled in *Sweatt*, they also declared illegal the University of Oklahoma's segregation of George W. McLaurin from white students attending the Graduate School of Education. In these precedent-setting cases, the Supreme Court signaled a readiness to reconsider the "separate but equal" doctrine of *Plessy* (1896) and to redefine the meaning of the "equal protection of the laws" clause of the Fourteenth Amendment. These cases were important stepping-stones on the road to *Brown*.

Brown and the Coming Revolution

A year after the *Sweatt* and *McLaurin* decisions, black parents and their lawyers filed suits in Kansas, South Carolina, Virginia, Delaware, and the District of Columbia asking the

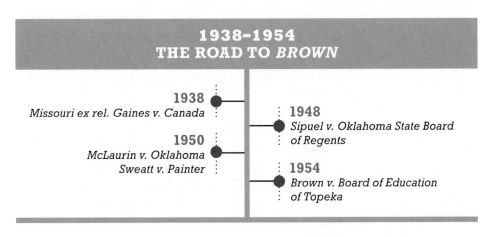

1938–1954
THE ROAD TO *BROWN*

1938
Missouri ex rel. Gaines v. Canada

1948
Sipuel v. Oklahoma State Board of Regents

1950
McLaurin v. Oklahoma
Sweatt v. Painter

1954
Brown v. Board of Education of Topeka

Read on **MyHistoryLab Document:** *McLaurin v. Oklahoma State Regents* Paves the Way for *Brown*, 1950

21-1
21-2
21-3
21-4
21-5
21-6
21-7
21-8

This student at the University of Oklahoma was not allowed to sit in a classroom with white students. It took two Supreme Court decisions to end such segregation at the University of Oklahoma.
Corbis-Bettmann.

courts to apply the qualitative test of the *Sweatt* case to elementary and secondary schools and to declare the "separate but equal" doctrine invalid in public education. Black lawyers in the South handling civil rights cases were frequently assaulted. On February 27, 1942, for example, a former deputy sheriff attacked NAACP attorney Leon A. Ransom in the hall of the Davidson County Courthouse in Nashville, Tennessee.

It was no less difficult for a black woman lawyer to venture into the South in search of justice. Black attorney Derrick Bell, who also worked for the LDEF, said of Motley's work,

> Nothing in the Southern lawyers' background could have prepared them for Connie. To them Negro women were either mammies, maids, or mistresses. None of them had ever dealt with a Negro woman on a peer basis, much less on a level of intellectual equality, which in this case quickly became superiority.

Motley was keenly aware of her precarious situation. "Often a southern judge would refer to men attorneys as Mister, but would make a point of calling me 'Connie,' since traditionally Black women in the South were only called by their first name." Housing was another problem. Motley recalled that when in a southern town for a long trial, "I knew that it was going to be impossible to stay in a decent hotel." These lawyers had to depend on the good graces and courage of local people.

In the late 1940s, the black parents of children attending Scott's Branch School in Clarendon County, South Carolina, approached Roderick W. Elliott, the chairman of the school board, with a modest request. There were 6,531 black students and only 2,375 white students enrolled in the county's schools. Although the county had 30 buses to convey the white students to their schools, no buses were available to black schoolchildren. Some black students had to walk 18 miles round-trip each day. Once they arrived, they entered buildings heated by wood stoves and lit by kerosene lamps. For a drink of water or to go to the toilet they had to go outdoors.

With the encouragement of African Methodist Episcopal pastor and schoolteacher Rev. Joseph Armstrong DeLaine, the parents mustered the courage to petition the school board for buses. Elliott's reply was short: "We ain't got no money to buy a bus for your nigger children." In 1949 DeLaine went to the NAACP officials in Columbia, and Thurgood Marshall was there. On December 20, 1950, Harry Briggs, a navy veteran, and 24 other Clarendon County residents sued the school district. The case, *Briggs v. Elliott*, was the first legal challenge to elementary school segregation to originate in the South. Meanwhile, however, four other cases in different parts of the country were advancing through the federal courts. These would be combined into one case that would decide the fate of the *Plessy* doctrine of "separate but equal."

The years of preparation and hardship paid off. On May 17, 1954, the Court ruled unanimously in favor of the NAACP lawyers and their clients that a classification based solely on race violated the Fourteenth Amendment. The *Brown* decision would eventually lead to the dismantling of the entire structure of Jim Crow laws that regulated important aspects of black life in America: movement, work, marriage, education, housing, and even death and burial. The *Brown* decision, more than any other case, signaled the emerging primacy of equality as a guide to constitutional decisions. This and subsequent decisions helped advance the rights of other minorities and women. As Motley reflected, "In the *Brown* case and in the decisions that followed, we blazed a trail for others by showing the competence of Black lawyers."

Read on MyHistoryLab **Document**: *Brown v. Board of Education of Topeka, Kansas*, 1954

In 1950, when the all-white Sumner School in Topeka, Kansas, refused to admit Linda Brown (1943–), her father, Oliver Brown, filed a lawsuit and testified in court that his daughter had to travel an hour and 20 minutes to attend a black school. The Sumner School was only seven blocks away but practiced racial exclusion. Linda became the "named plaintiff" in the landmark U.S. Supreme Court case *Brown v. Board of Education* (1954), which declared unconstitutional laws mandating public school segregation.

Brown II

21-3 How did white southerners' strategy of massive resistance affect the modern civil rights movement?

A year after the *Brown* decision, in May 1955, the Supreme Court issued a second ruling, commonly known as *Brown II*, which addressed the practical process of desegregation. The Court underscored that the states in the suits should begin prompt compliance with the

1954 ruling and that this should be done with "all deliberate speed." Many black Americans interpreted this to mean "immediately." White southerners hoped it meant a long time or never. Ominously, President Eisenhower seemed displeased with the Court's rulings and refused to put the moral authority of his office behind their enforcement.

Nevertheless, in 1955 and early 1956, desegregation proceeded without hindrance in Maryland, Kentucky, Delaware, Oklahoma, and Missouri. Alabama Governor Jim Folsom declared that his state would obey the courts. Other moderate white southern politicians counseled calm and worked to head off a full-scale conflict with the federal government.

Massive White Resistance

White moderates, however, soon found themselves a shrinking minority, as extremists, determined to maintain white supremacy at any cost, prepared to resist the Court's decisions. The extremists' rhetoric bordered on hysteria but found a receptive audience among many. In 1955 leading businessmen, white-collar professionals, and clergy began organizing, in virtually every southern city, White Citizens' Councils dedicated to preserving "the southern way of life" and the South's "sacred heritage of freedom." The councils used their economic and political power to intimidate African Americans who challenged segregation.

Many white politicians took up the banner of massive resistance. Mississippi Senator James O. Eastland called the *Brown* decision a "monstrous crime." The Virginia legislature closed all public schools in Prince Edward County to thwart integration. On March 12, 1956, 96 southern congressmen led by North Carolina's Senator Sam Ervin, Jr., and South Carolina's Senator Strom Thurmond issued "The Southern Manifesto," vowing to fight to preserve segregation and the southern way of life. The only southern senators who refused to sign the manifesto were Albert Gore, Sr., of Tennessee and Lyndon B. Johnson of Texas.

The NAACP came under siege after the *Brown* decision as southern states tried to destroy it. By 1957 nine southern states had filed suit to eradicate the organization. Some states, alleging the NAACP was linked to a worldwide communist conspiracy, made membership illegal. Membership plummeted from 128,716 to 79,677, and the association lost 246 branches in the South.

Under these pressures, desegregation ground to a halt. By 1958, 13 school systems had been desegregated. By 1960, two years later, the total had risen to only 17. Massive resistance successfully challenged the possibility of achieving change through court action alone.

The Lynching of Emmett Till

White southerners' violent reaction to the growing assertiveness of black people found expression in the summer of 1955 in the lynching of 14-year-old Emmett Till of Chicago, an event that helped galvanize the emerging civil rights movement. Till was visiting relatives in the small town of Money, Mississippi. On a dare from his friends, he entered Bryant's grocery store, bought candy, and said "Bye, baby" to Carolyn Bryant, the wife of the owner, as he left. In the middle of the night a few days after the incident, Bryant's husband and brother-in-law arrived at the small house where Till was staying and kidnapped him at gunpoint. His body was subsequently

In August 1955, 14-year-old Emmett Till was visiting relatives in Money, Mississippi, when he transgressed the line of racial etiquette by speaking to a white woman in a country store. He paid the ultimate price. The lynching of Emmett Till and the subsequent acquittal of his murderers reflected the low regard in which black life was held in the Jim Crow South and the extent to which whites were determined to maintain the racial status quo.

Watch on MyHistoryLab
Video: How Did the Civil Rights Movement Change American Schools?

21-1
21-2
21-3
21-4
21-5
21-6
21-7
21-8

found in the Tallahatchie River tied to a heavy cotton gin fan. Till had a bullet in his head and had been tortured before his murder. Despite overwhelming evidence and the brave testimony of Mose Wright, Till's uncle, and other local black people, an all-white jury acquitted the two men who lynched Till. In early 1956 the murderers sold their confession to *Look* magazine and gloated over their escape from justice. In 2004, new evidence indicated that 10 people may have been involved in the Till lynching.

The Till lynching shaped the consciousness of a generation of young African-American activists. Partly this was due to Till's mother, Mamie Bradley. Unwilling to let America turn away from this crime, she had her son's mangled body displayed in an open casket in Chicago. Thousands of mourners paid their respects, and many committed themselves to fighting the system that made this crime possible. Bradley also traveled around the nation speaking to groups on whom her grief had a profound impact.

New Forms of Protest: The Montgomery Bus Boycott

21-4 | What were the origins and outcome of, and who were the participants in, the Montgomery Bus Boycott?

Strong local communities formed the core of the civil rights movement in the South, and the deeds of brave individuals often sparked them to action. The first and one of the most important expressions of this process occurred in Alabama's capital city. Blessed with well-organized educational, religious, and other institutions, Montgomery's African-American community of 45,000 was poised to make history.

The Roots of Revolution

The movement in Montgomery was the result of years of organization and planning by protest groups. In addition to its numerous churches, two black colleges, and other social organizations, Montgomery had a core of protest groups. One, the Women's Political Council (WPC), had been founded in 1946 by Mary Frances Fair Burks, chair of Alabama State College Department of English, after the all-white League of Women Voters had refused to allow black women to participate in its activities. The WPC was joined by a chapter of the NAACP led by E. D. Nixon, a Pullman train car porter and head of the Alabama chapter of the Brotherhood of Sleeping Car Porters. In 1943 Nixon had founded the Montgomery Voters League, which was dedicated to helping African Americans navigate Alabama's tortuous voter registration process. In the decade after 1945, these groups searched for a way to mobilize the black community to challenge white power.

The 1954 *Brown* decision seemed to provide a means to destroy segregation and discrimination in the city. Four days after it was announced, Jo Ann Robinson wrote to Montgomery's mayor on behalf of the WPC reiterating the complaints of the black community about conditions on the city's buses: "Please consider this plea, for even now plans are being made to ride less, or not at all, on our buses."

Watch on **MyHistoryLab Video:** African-American Women and the Struggle for Civil Rights

Claudette Colvin was a teenager when she refused to obey the transportation segregation laws in Montgomery.

VOICES   Letter of the Montgomery Women's Political Council to Mayor W. A. Gayle

In this letter threatening a boycott of Montgomery's buses, the Women's Political Council politely asks not for the desegregation of the buses but only for new regulations that would prevent black riders from being forced to move to accommodate white riders.

May 21, 1954

Honorable Mayor W. A. Gayle
City Hall
Montgomery, Alabama

Dear Sir:

The Women's Political Council is very grateful to you and the City Commissioners for the hearing you allowed our representative during the month of March, 1954, when the "city-bus-fare-increase case" was being reviewed. There were several things the Council asked for:

1. A city law that would make it possible for Negroes to sit from back toward front, and whites from front toward back until all the seats were taken.
2. That Negroes would not be asked or forced to pay fare at front and go to the rear of the bus to enter.
3. That buses stop at every corner in residential sections occupied by Negroes as they do in communities where whites reside.

We are happy to report that buses have begun stopping at more corners now in some sections where Negroes live than previously. However, the same practices in seating and boarding the bus continue.

Mayor Gayle, three-fourths of the riders of these public conveyances are Negroes. If Negroes did not patronize them, they could not possibly operate.

More and more of our people are already arranging with neighbors and friends to ride to keep from being insulted and humiliated by bus drivers.

There has been talk from twenty-five or more local organizations of planning a city-wide boycott of buses. We, sir, do not feel that forceful measures are necessary in bargaining for a convenience which is right for all bus passengers. We, the Council, believe that when this matter has been put before you and the Commissioners, that agreeable terms can be met in a quiet and in a sensible manner to the satisfaction of all concerned.

Many of our Southern cities in neighboring states have practiced the policies we seek without incident whatsoever. Atlanta, Macon and Savannah in Georgia have done this for years. Even Mobile, in our own state, does this and all the passengers are satisfied.

Please consider this plea, and if possible, act favorably upon it, for even now plans are being made to ride less, or not at all, on our buses. We do not want this.

Respectfully yours,
The Women's Political Council
Jo Ann Robinson, President

1. **What did the Women's Political Council initially hope to accomplish?**
2. **What does this letter suggest about the importance of black women's political organizations in the early years of the civil rights movement?**

SOURCE: Stewart Burns, *Daybreak of Freedom: The Montgomery Bus Boycott* (Chapel Hill: University of North Carolina Press, 1997), 58.

 Read on MyHistoryLab Document: Jo Ann Gibson Robinson Looks Back at the Montgomery Bus Boycott of 1955

The mayor ignored the warning, and the buses remained as segregated as before. All seemed quiet, but Montgomery's black lawyers and NAACP chapter began laying the groundwork for a test case challenging segregation of the city's bus lines.

On March 2, 1955, a 15-year-old Booker T. Washington High School student, Claudette Colvin, was arrested for refusing to give up her seat on a bus to a white woman. The WPC was ready to use this incident to initiate the threatened bus boycott. The Colvins, however, were not members of the black social elite in Montgomery, and for various reasons community leaders decided against protesting Claudette's conviction for allegedly "assaulting" the police officers who had dragged her from the bus. They decided to wait for another opportunity to launch a protest movement.

Rosa Parks

On Thursday, December 1, 1955, Rosa Parks, a 43-year-old department store seamstress and civil rights activist, boarded a city bus and moved to the back where African Americans were required to sit. All seats were taken, so she sat in one toward the middle of the bus. When a white man boarded the bus, the driver ordered Parks to vacate her seat for him. There was nothing unusual in this, but on this fateful day, Parks refused to move. She had not planned to resist on that day, but, as she later said, she had "decided that I would have to know once and for all what rights I had as a human being and a citizen. . . . I was so involved with the attempt to bring about freedom from this kind of thing . . . I felt just resigned to give what I could to protest against the way I was being treated, and felt that all of our meetings, trying to negotiate, bring about petitions before the authorities . . . really hadn't done any good at all." At the time Parks was portrayed as simply tired, but she had been training for just this kind of challenge for years. When her moment came, she seized it; with this act of resistance, she launched the **Montgomery Bus Boycott** and inspired the modern civil rights struggle for freedom and equality.

The plans of the WPC and NAACP came into play after Parks's arrest for violating Montgomery's transportation laws. She was ordered to appear in court on the following Monday. Meanwhile, E. D. Nixon bailed her out of the city jail and began mobilizing the leadership of the black community behind her. Working in tandem with Nixon, Robinson wrote and circulated a flyer calling for a one-day boycott of the buses followed by a mass meeting of the community to discuss the matter. The WPC had planned distribution routes months earlier. Robinson and nearly 200 volunteers distributed 30,000 flyers to beauty parlors and schools, to factories and grocery stores, and to taverns and barbershops throughout the black neighborhoods.

Montgomery Improvement Association

On December 5, 1955, the black community did not ride the buses, and the movement had begun. Nixon and other community leaders, including Jo Ann Gibson Robinson, who would become its chief strategist, formed a new organization, the Montgomery Improvement Association (MIA), to coordinate the boycott. They selected a 26-year-old minister, Martin Luther King, Jr., as its president. That evening there was an overflowing mass meeting of the black community at the Holt Street Baptist Church to decide whether to continue

Rosa Parks, in this 1999 photograph by Paul Richards, is venerated as the mother of the civil rights movement and has remained an important symbol of hope and courage.

Montgomery Bus Boycott Refusal from 1955 to 1957 of African Americans in Montgomery, Alabama, to ride the city's buses until the bus lines were desegregated.

21-1
21-2
21-3
21-4
21-5
21-6
21-7
21-8

the boycott. King, with barely an hour to prepare, defined the goals of the boycott and the civil rights movement that followed. In his dramatic voice, he connected the core values of America and of the Judeo-Christian tradition to the goals of African Americans nationwide as well as in Montgomery.

Martin Luther King, Jr.

Listen on MyHistoryLab Audio: Mass Meeting; speech by Martin Luther King, Jr.

King's speech electrified the meeting, which unanimously decided to boycott the buses until the MIA's demands were met. The speech also marked the beginning of King's role as a leader of the civil rights movement. King had been raised in a prominent ministerial family with a long history of standing up for African-American rights. At age 15, King had entered Morehouse College but did not embrace the ministry as his profession until he came under the influence of its president, Dr. Benjamin E. Mays. By age 25, King had been awarded a Ph.D. in theology from Boston University. He moved to Alabama with his wife, Coretta Scott King, to become pastor of the Dexter Avenue Baptist Church in Montgomery.

In addition to his verbal artistry, King had the ability to inspire moral courage and teach people how to maintain themselves under excruciating pressure. King merged the nonviolence advocated by the Indian nationalist leader Mohandas Gandhi with black Christian faith and church culture to create a unique ideology well suited for the civil rights struggle. King told the Montgomery boycotters, "If we are arrested every day, if we are exploited every day, if we are trampled over every day, don't ever let anyone pull you so low as to hate them. . . . We must realize so many people are taught to hate us that they are not totally responsible for their hate." King's faith was tested. As the boycott proceeded, his home was bombed. Segregationists also bombed Nixon's home and those of two other black clergymen and MIA leaders, Ralph Abernathy and Fred Shuttlesworth, and assaulted other boycott participants.

Walking for Freedom

Although men occupied the top leadership positions in the boycott, women were the key to its effectiveness. The boycott lasted more than a year and over its course nearly all the black women previously dependent on the buses to get to work refused to ride them. Some walked 12 miles a day. Others had the support of their white women employers, who provided transportation. And many helped organize a car pool of 200 vehicles that proved critical to sustaining the boycott. The community held mass meetings nightly in local churches. Robinson edited the MIA newsletter. Other women supported the boycott in dozens of ways. The boycott took 65 percent of the bus company's business, forcing it to cut schedules, lay off drivers, and raise fares. White merchants also suffered. Impressive as it was, the boycott by itself could not end segregation on the buses. Black Montgomery needed a two-pronged strategy of mass local pressure and legal recourse through the courts. The legal backing of the federal government was necessary to end Jim Crow. Thus, NAACP lawyers and MIA's lawyer Fred Gray filed a suit in the names of Claudette Colvin, Mary Louise Smith, and three other women.

Friends in the North

The Montgomery movement was not without allies outside the South. Money poured into the MIA's coffers from concerned Americans. Many northern activists who had long been hoping black southerners would begin just this kind of resistance also swung into action to help. Indeed, black and white activists in many northern cities including New York and Chicago had launched challenges to overthrow housing segregation and promote open access to public beaches and amusement parks. Activist and civil rights groups joined with labor unionists to support issues of economic justice, fair employment, and an end to police corruption and brutality. Two people who were particularly important in the "Long Civil Rights" movement were Bayard Rustin and liberal Jewish lawyer Stanley Levison. Two and a half months into the boycott, Montgomery officials indicted King and one hundred other leaders on charges of conspiracy to disrupt the bus system, and Bayard Rustin arrived in Montgomery. He encouraged the leaders to follow Gandhian practice and submit freely to arrest.

Rustin continued working behind the scenes as one of King's most trusted advisers on nonviolent principles and tactics. Stanley Levison and Ella Baker created a group called In Friendship, which raised money for the boycott. (For more on Ella Baker, see Chapter 18.)

Levison was a wealthy attorney committed to social justice. He had worked with the Communist Party, and Rustin had a long history of association with radical groups. Their influence soon attracted the attention of the FBI, which had long been obsessed with black leaders and organizations. FBI director J. Edgar Hoover called King "the most dangerous man in America," and he pressed his subordinates to prove King was a communist and that the civil rights movement was a Moscow-inspired conspiracy. The FBI began tapping King's telephone and hotel room phones and even threatened to expose his extramarital affairs if he did not commit suicide. By the early 1960s, the FBI had stopped warning King when it uncovered threats to his life.

Victory

As the bus boycott reached the one-year mark, it was obvious that the all-white city government would not budge, no matter how long the boycott lasted. Any white politician who hoped to remain in office had to defend segregation. King and the others who suffered through the ordeal grew discouraged, and in November 1956 their hopes seemed to fade when it became clear the state courts would declare the car pools illegal.

Salvation for the movement came from the cases local women (Claudette Colvin, Aurelia Browder, Susie McDonald, and Mary Louise Smith), Fred Gray, and the NAACP had taken to the federal courts. In keeping with the *Brown* precedent, on November 13, 1956, the Supreme Court in *Browder v. Gayle* ordered an end to Montgomery's bus segregation and overturned the convictions of Colvin and the other women. The bus company agreed not only to end segregation but also to hire African-American drivers and to treat all passengers with equal respect.

The city's black community rejoiced. On December 21, 1956, black citizens of Montgomery boarded the buses and sat wherever they pleased.

No Easy Road to Freedom: 1957–1960

21-5   **What were the goals of the Civil Rights Act of 1957?**

The victory at Montgomery set an example for future protests. It was the result of a highly organized black community led by committed and capable black leaders. These local efforts were bolstered by the advice and involvement of activists from outside the South, the attention of a sympathetic national press, and, crucially, intervention from the federal courts. But local victories could only go so far, particularly as white resistance intensified. In the three years following the boycott, black southerners and their allies across the nation prepared for a broader movement. At the same time, federal officials outside the judiciary found they could

21-1
21-2
21-3
21-4
21-5
21-6
21-7
21-8

not ignore the white South's incipient rebellion without grave consequences for both the nation and their own power.

Martin Luther King, Jr., and the SCLC

By the end of the campaign in Montgomery, Martin Luther King, Jr., had emerged as a moral leader of national stature. On the advice of Levison, Rustin, and Ella Baker, he helped create a new organization, the **Southern Christian Leadership Conference (SCLC)**, to provide an institutional base for continuing the struggle. The SCLC was a federation of civil rights groups, community organizations, and churches that sought to coordinate the burgeoning local movements. Because the ballot was deemed the critical weapon needed to complete school desegregation and secure equal employment opportunity, adequate housing, and equal access to public accommodations, the SCLC focused on securing voting rights for black people. In the three years after the Montgomery Bus Boycott, the SCLC also aided black communities in challenging bus segregation in Tallahassee, Florida, and Atlanta.

The SCLC shared many of the NAACP's goals, but tensions arose between the two organizations. The NAACP's leadership doubted the effectiveness of the protest tactics the SCLC favored. They resented having to divert resources from work on important court cases to defend people arrested in protests and were troubled by the left-wing connections of King's advisers. The fortunes of the NAACP in the South, however, plummeted in the late 1950s as southern states persecuted its members. This left the field to the SCLC. The SCLC and the NAACP worked together, but the tensions over tactics were never far below the surface.

Civil Rights Act of 1957

Despite President Eisenhower's tepid response to *Brown*, Congress proved willing to take a modest step toward ending racial discrimination, passing the Civil Rights Act of 1957, the first such legislation since the end of Reconstruction. It created a commission to monitor violations of black civil rights and to propose remedies for infringements on black voting. It upgraded the Civil Rights Section into a division within the Justice Department and gave it the power to sue states and municipalities that discriminated on the basis of race. Although an important step on the long road toward black enfranchisement, this act disappointed black activists because it was too weak to counter white reaction and because they felt the Eisenhower administration would not enforce it.

Read on **MyHistoryLab Document:** President Eisenhower Uses the National Guard to Desegregate Central High School, 1957

Elizabeth Eckerd, one of nine black students who sought to enroll at Little Rock Central High School in September 1957, endures the taunts of an angry white crowd as she tries to make her way to the school.

Little Rock, Arkansas

Eisenhower may have had little inclination to support the fight for black rights, but the defiance of Arkansas Governor Orville Faubus forced him to. At the beginning of the school year in 1957,

Faubus posted 270 Arkansas national guardsmen outside Little Rock Central High School to prevent nine black youths from entering. When a federal court order forced the governor to allow the children into the school, he simply withdrew the state guard and left the children to face a hate-filled mob.

To defend the sovereignty of the federal courts and the Constitution, Eisenhower had to act. He sent in 1,100 paratroopers from the 101st Airborne Division to Little Rock and put the Arkansas National Guard under federal authority. It was the first time since Reconstruction that troops had been sent to the South to protect the rights of African-American citizens. The troops remained in Little Rock Central High School for the rest of the school year. Governor Faubus closed the Little Rock public schools in 1958–1959. Eight of the nine black students withstood the abuse and curses of segregationists both inside and outside the facility and eventually desegregated the high school. Young African Americans throughout the South would show similar courage.

Black Youth Stand Up by Sitting Down

21-6 | How did the early activism by students differ in tactics and methods from earlier activism?

Beginning in 1960, motivated black college students adapted a strategy that the Congress of Racial Equality (CORE) had used in the 1940s—the "sit-in"—and emerged as the vanguard of the civil rights movement. Their distinctive and independent contributions to the black protest movement accelerated the pace of social change. Before long the movement would inspire more northern black and white students.

Sit-Ins: Greensboro, Nashville, Atlanta

On February 1, 1960, Joseph McNeil, Franklin McCain, David Richmond, and Ezell Blair, Jr., all freshmen at North Carolina Agricultural and Technical College, decided to desegregate local restaurants by sitting at the lunch counter of Greensboro, North Carolina's Woolworth five-and-dime store. At 4:30 in the afternoon the students sat at the counter. They received no service that day but sat quietly doing their schoolwork until the store closed. The action of these four young men electrified their fellow students, and the next day many others joined them. Soon, black women students from Bennett College and a few white students from the University of North Carolina Women's College joined the protest, and by the fifth day hundreds of young, studious, neatly dressed African Americans crowded the downtown store demanding their rights.

Like the black people of Montgomery, the students in Greensboro acted with forethought and with the support of their community. They had long debated how they could best participate in the desegregation movement. All four of the black students had been members of NAACP college or youth groups and were aware of the currents of change flowing through the South. Although they began the sit-in on their own, it quickly gained the support of the black community. Many people in the North and West—both black and white—also joined the campaign by picketing local stores of the national chains that approved of segregation in the South. After facing the collective power of the black community and their allies for months, white businessmen and politicians gave in to the black community's demands.

The students at Greensboro were not alone in their desire to strike out at discrimination. Indeed, at Fisk University in Nashville, Tennessee, students had begun holding

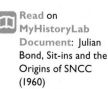

Read on MyHistoryLab Document: Julian Bond, Sit-ins and the Origins of SNCC (1960)

21-1

21-2

21-3

21-4

21-5

21-6

21-7

21-8

View on MyHistoryLab Closer Look: Second Day of Woolworth's Lunch Counter Sit-in

Four students—from the left, Joseph McNeil, Franklin McCain, Billy Smith, and Clarence Henderson—sit patiently at Woolworth's lunch counter on February 2, 1960, the second day of the sit-in in Greensboro, North Carolina. Although not the first sit-in protest against segregated facilities, the Greensboro action triggered a wave of sit-ins by black high school and college students across the South.

nonviolent workshops before the Greensboro sit-in. Even better organized than their comrades in North Carolina, they had been training intensively for a sit-in campaign. Twelve days after the first sit-ins began, the Nashville group swung into action. Hundreds were arrested, and those who sat suffered insults, beatings, arrest, and torture while in jail. Nonetheless, by May 1960 they had compelled major restaurants to desegregate.

Atlanta, Martin Luther King, Jr.'s home base and the site of a large African-American community, spawned an even more dramatic movement. It began after Spelman College freshman Ruby Doris Smith persuaded her friends and classmates to launch sit-ins in the city. On March 15, 1960, two students at Atlanta University, Julian Bond and Lonnie King, executing a carefully orchestrated plan, deployed 200 sit-in students to 10 different eating places. They targeted government-owned property and public places, including bus and train stations and the state capitol, which should have been willing to serve all customers. At the Federal Building, Bond and his classmates attempted to eat in the municipal cafeteria and were arrested. The Atlanta sit-in students broadened their campaign demands to include desegregation of all public facilities, black voting rights, and equal access to educational and employment opportunities. On September 27, 1961, the Atlanta business and political elite gave in.

Just as in Greensboro, the students in Nashville, Atlanta, and other southern cities won the support of local people who had not been previously involved in organized resistance. By April 1960 more than 2,000 students from black high schools and colleges had been arrested in 78 southern towns and cities. Local people demonstrated their allegiance to them in numerous ways, but their most effective tactic was the economic boycott. When business began to suffer, white leaders proved willing to negotiate the racial status quo.

The Student Nonviolent Coordinating Committee

Recognizing the significance of the region-wide student action and fearing it would soon melt away, SCLC's Ella Baker organized a conference for 150 students at her alma mater, Shaw University, in Raleigh, North Carolina. Baker, who managed operations in SCLC's Atlanta headquarters, chafed under the rigid male leadership of the organization. In contrast, she advocated decentralized leadership and celebrated participatory democracy. Her skepticism about SCLC struck a chord with the students.

On April 15–17, 1960, delegates representing over 50 colleges and high schools from 37 communities in 13 states began discussing how to keep the movement going. Baker addressed the group in a speech entitled "More Than a Hamburger" and became the midwife of a new organization named the **Student Nonviolent Coordinating Committee (SNCC)**. The newest addition to the roster of civil rights associations adhered to the ideology of nonviolence, but it also acknowledged the possible need for increased militancy and confrontation. More accommodating black leaders, even some of those in SCLC, objected to the students' use of direct confrontational tactics that disrupted race relations and community peace.

Freedom Rides

The sit-in movement paved the way for the "**Freedom Rides**" of 1961. CORE's James Farmer and Bayard Rustin resolved that it was time for a reprise of their 1947 mission to ride interstate buses and trains in the Upper South. The Freedom Rides tested the Justice Department's willingness to protect the rights of African Americans to use bus terminal facilities on a nonsegregated basis. They also showed the world how far some white southerners would go to preserve segregation.

The first ride ran into trouble on May 4, 1961, when John Lewis, one of the seven black riders, tried to enter the white waiting room of the Greyhound bus terminal in Rock Hill, South Carolina, and was beaten by local white people in full view of the police. The interracial group continued through Alabama toward Jackson, Mississippi, but white violence made escape from Alabama difficult. At Anniston, Alabama, a mob firebombed the bus and beat the escaping riders. Local African Americans led by the Rev. Fred Shuttlesworth took many of the shocked and injured riders to Birmingham.

With the police offering no protection, CORE abandoned the Freedom Rides, and most of the original riders left Alabama. But SNCC activists and students in Nashville refused to let the idea die. At least 20 civil rights workers went to Birmingham, where they vowed on May 20 to ride on to Montgomery. John Lewis remained with the group that arrived in Montgomery. Awaiting them was another angry mob of more than 1,000 white people and not a policeman in sight. This time Lewis was knocked unconscious, and all the riders had to be hospitalized.

News services flashed around the world graphic images of the violence, and the federal government resolved to end the bloodletting. Attorney General Robert Kennedy sent 400 federal marshals to restore law and order. Martin Luther King, Jr., and Ralph Abernathy joined the conflict on May 21, as 1,200 men, women, and children met at Abernathy's church. The federal marshals averted further bloodshed by surrounding the building. Only then did Governor John Patterson order the National Guard and state troopers to protect the protesters. When the group arrived in Jackson, Mississippi, white authorities arrested them. By summer's end, more than 300 Freedom Riders had served time in Mississippi's notorious prisons.

Read on **MyHistoryLab**
Document: Student Nonviolent Coordinating Committee (SNCC) Statement of Purpose, 1960

Student Nonviolent Coordinating Committee (SNCC) Civil rights organization founded by black college students in 1960 at the initiative of Ella Baker.

Freedom Rides Effort in 1961 to desegregate interstate bus and rail travel.

21-1

21-2

21-3

21-4

21-5

21-6

21-7

21-8

Read on **MyHistoryLab Document**: Letters from Mississippi Freedom Summer, 1964

On May 14, in Anniston, Alabama, a white mob firebombed this Freedom Riders' bus and attacked passengers as they escaped the flames.

A Sight to Be Seen: The Movement at High Tide

21-7   Who were the leaders and what were the tactics and effects of their various civil rights activities?

Between 1960 and 1963, the civil rights movement developed the techniques and organization that would finally bring America face-to-face with the conflict between its democratic ideals and the racism of its politics. Day after day the movement squared off against the die-hard resistance of the white South and created a situation that demanded that the president and Congress take action.

The Election of 1960

One of the persistent fears of white southerners was that black Americans, if armed with the ballot, would possess the balance of political power. The presidential election of 1960 proved this to be true. Initially, many African Americans favored the Republican nominee Richard Nixon, who had advocated strong civil rights legislation. The Democratic nominee, Massachusetts Senator John F. Kennedy, in contrast, had done little to distinguish himself to black Americans in the struggles of the 1950s. As the campaign progressed, however,

Kennedy made sympathetic statements in support of black protests. Meanwhile, Nixon attempted to strengthen his position with white southern voters and remained silent about civil rights issues, even though the Republican Party had a strong pro–civil rights record.

Shortly before the election, Martin Luther King, Jr., was sentenced to four months in prison for leading a nonviolent protest march in Atlanta. Kennedy telephoned Coretta Scott King to offer his support, while his brother Robert F. Kennedy used his influence to obtain King's release. These acts impressed African Americans and won their support. African-American voters in key northern cities provided the crucial margin that elected John F. Kennedy.

The Kennedy Administration and the Civil Rights Movement

Early in his administration Kennedy grew concerned about the violence occasioned by the civil rights movement. As the Freedom Rides continued across the Deep South, the activists provoked confrontations and forced the federal government to intervene on their behalf. Kennedy's primary interest at this point was to prevent disorder from getting out of hand and to avoid compromising America's position with the developing nations. But he had little room to maneuver given the power of white southerners in his party and in Congress.

Despite these limitations, Kennedy did aid the cause of civil rights. He issued Executive Order 11063, which required government agencies to discontinue discriminatory policies and practices in federally supported housing, and he named Vice President Lyndon B. Johnson to chair the newly established Committee on Equal Employment Opportunity. Kennedy also nominated Thurgood Marshall to the Second Circuit Court of Appeals. He named journalist Carl Rowan deputy assistant secretary of state. More than 40 African Americans took positions in the new administration. Moreover, Kennedy's brother Robert put muscle into the Civil Rights Division of the Justice Department by hiring an impressive team of lawyers headed by Washington attorney Burke Marshall.

Like Eisenhower, when President Kennedy felt that intractable southern governors were challenging his authority, he acted decisively. On June 25, 1962, one year after James Meredith had filed a complaint of racial discrimination against the University of Mississippi, the U.S. Court of Appeals ruled that the university had to admit him. Governor Ross Barnett vowed to resist, but Kennedy sent 300 federal marshals to uphold the order. Thousands of students rioted at the campus. Two people died, 200 were arrested, and nearly half the marshals were injured. Kennedy did not back down. He federalized the Mississippi National Guard to ensure Meredith's admission. Likewise, in June 1963, the Kennedy administration compelled Governor George Wallace to allow the desegregation of the University of Alabama.

Voter Registration Projects

On June 16, 1961, Robert Kennedy urged student leaders to redirect their energies to voter registration projects and to lessen their concentration on direct-action activities. He and Justice Department aides persuaded the students that the free exercise of the ballot would result in profound and significant social change. James Foreman, SNCC's executive director, followed Kennedy's lead. By October 1962 SNCC had joined forces with the NAACP, SCLC, and CORE in the Voter Education Project funded by major philanthropic foundations and administered by the Southern Regional Council. SNCC was responsible for Alabama and

Mississippi. Drawing on the expertise of Robert Moses and working with a cadre of local leaders like Amzie Moore, head of the NAACP in Mississippi's Cleveland County, and Fannie Lou Hamer of Ruleville, SNCC opened voter registration schools. When the "graduates" attempted to register to vote, it unleashed a wave of white violence and murder across Mississippi.

The Albany Movement

In Albany, Georgia, the civil rights movement met sophisticated resistance and experienced its most profound defeat up to that time. The movement in Albany began in the summer of 1961 when SNCC members moved into the city to register voters. Local groups decided to form a coalition called the Albany Movement. The movement's goal expanded from securing the vote to the total desegregation of the town.

In Laurie Pritchett, Albany's police chief, the movement faced an uncommonly sophisticated opponent. Pritchett studied the past tactics of SNCC and King and resolved not to confront the federal government directly and to avoid the violence that brought negative media attention. When students from a black college decided to desegregate the bus terminal, Pritchett arrested them after they entered the white waiting room and attempted to eat in the bus terminal dining room. Shrewdly, he charged the students with violating a city ordinance for failing to obey a law enforcement officer. The Albany Movement decided to invite King and SCLC to aid them and to overwhelm the police department by filling the jails with protesters. King answered the call. On December 16, 1961, he and more than 250 demonstrators were arrested, joining the 507 people already in jail. Sheriff Pritchett, however, made arrangements to house almost 2,000 people in surrounding jail facilities and trained his deputies in the use of nonviolent techniques. Thus, Pritchett avoided confrontation, violence, and federal intervention.

On December 18, 1961, two days after King's arrest, the city and the Albany Movement announced a truce. King returned to Atlanta, and the city refused to implement the terms of the agreement. When King and Ralph Abernathy returned to Albany in July 1962 for sentencing on their December arrests, they chose 45 days in jail rather than admit guilt by paying a fine. The mass marches resumed, but again Pritchett thwarted King by releasing him from jail to avoid negative publicity. The city's attorney then secured a federal injunction to prevent King and the other leaders from demonstrating. Given his dependence on the federal government, King felt he could not violate the injunction, and he abandoned the protest. For King, the Albany Movement was a failure, his most glaring defeat, and one that called into question the future of the movement.

The Birmingham Confrontation

Watch on MyHistoryLab Video: Photographing the Civil Rights Movement: Birmngham, 1963

By early 1963 the movement appeared to be stalled. Black communities in much of the South were strong and well organized, but their efforts had achieved only modest changes. It was impossible to overcome the power of southern state and local governments without the intervention of the federal government, but national politicians remained reluctant to act unless faced with open defiance by white people or with televised violence against peaceful protesters. King and other black leaders knew that if city governments throughout the South followed the model of Sheriff Pritchett in Albany, the civil rights movement might lose momentum. To rejuvenate the movement, SCLC decided to launch a massive new campaign.

Birmingham, Alabama, a large, tightly segregated industrial city, was chosen as the site for the action. The city was ripe for such a protest, in part because its black community suffered from police brutality and economic, educational, and social discrimination.

The black community had, however, developed a strong phalanx of protest organizations called the Alabama Christian Movement for Human Rights (ACMHR) led by the Rev. Fred Shuttlesworth. The ACMHR and SCLC planned a campaign of boycotts, pickets, and demonstrations code-named "Project C for Confrontation." Their program would be far more extensive than any before, with demands to integrate public facilities, for guarantees of employment opportunities for black workers in downtown businesses, to desegregate the schools, to improve services in black neighborhoods, and to provide low-income housing. Organizers hoped to provoke the city's public safety commissioner Eugene T. "Bull" Connor, who, unlike Sheriff Pritchett, had a reputation for viciousness. Civil rights leaders believed Connor's conduct would horrify the nation and compel Kennedy to act.

Project C began on April 3 with student sit-ins. Days later, marches began, and Connor, following the lead of Pritchett, arrested all who participated but avoided overt violence. When the state courts prohibited further protests, King and Abernathy, among others, violated the ruling. They were arrested and jailed on Good Friday, April 12, 1963.

While in jail, King received a letter from eight local Christian and Jewish clergymen who objected to what they considered the "unwise and untimely" protest activities of black citizens. In response, King wrote an eloquent treatise on the use of direct action. His "Letter From Birmingham City Jail" was widely published in newspapers and magazines. In it, King dismissed those who called for black people to wait.

King's "Letter From Birmingham City Jail" (1963) had a national impact. But the Birmingham movement lost momentum because many of the protesters either were in jail or could not risk new arrests. At this juncture James Bevel of SCLC proposed using schoolchildren to continue the protests. Many observers, and some of those in the movement, criticized this idea; King and other leaders, however, believed it was necessary to risk harm to children to ensure their freedom. Thus, on May 2 and 3, 1963, a "children's crusade" involving thousands of youths, some as young as six, marched. This tactic enraged "Bull" Connor and his officers. The police not only arrested the children but flailed away with nightsticks and set dogs on them. On Connor's order, firefighters aimed their hoses at the youngsters, ripping the clothes from their backs, cutting flesh, and tumbling children down the street. In the ensuing days, many of the children and their parents began to fight back, hurling bottles and rocks at their uniformed tormentors. As the violence escalated, white businessmen became concerned, and the city came to the bargaining table.

President Kennedy deployed Assistant Attorney General for Civil Rights Burke Marshall to negotiate a settlement. On May 10, 1963, white businessmen agreed to integrate downtown facilities and hire black men and women. The following night the KKK bombed the A. G. Gaston Motel, where SCLC had its headquarters, and the house that belonged to King's brother, the Rev. A. D. King. Black citizens in turn burned cars and buildings and attacked the police. Only intervention by King and other leaders prevented a riot. White moderates delivered on the promises, and the agreement stuck.

Although SCLC did not win every demand, Birmingham was a major triumph and a turning point in the movement. The summer of 1963 saw protests across the South, with nearly 800 marches, demonstrations, and sit-ins. Ten civil rights protesters were killed and 20,000 arrested as the white South desperately sought to stem the tide. On June 12, 1963, white extremist Byron de la Beckwith gunned down Medgar Evers in the driveway of his home in Jackson, Mississippi. Evers had been the executive secretary of the NAACP's Mississippi organization and the center of a movement in Jackson. His cold-blooded murder dramatized the hatred some white southerners felt and the lengths to which they would go to prevent change.

Read on MyHistoryLab **Document:** Martin Luther King, Jr., "Letter From Birmingham Jail," 1963

A Hard Victory

21-8   **How did the federal government intermittently support and thwart the long freedom movement?**

The sacrifices in Birmingham and the intensification of the movement throughout the South set the stage for Congress to pass legislation for a Second Reconstruction that would at last fulfill the promise of the first.

The March on Washington

The lingering image of Birmingham and the growing number of demonstrations throughout the South compelled action from President Kennedy. Urging Congressional action, proposed the strongest civil rights bill the country had yet seen. Despite the public's heightened awareness of discrimination, however, he could not muster sufficient support in Congress to counter the southern bloc within his own party.

To demonstrate their support for Kennedy's civil rights legislation, a coalition of civil rights organizations—SCLC, NAACP, CORE, SNCC, and the National Urban League—and their leaders resurrected the idea of organizing a march on Washington that A. Philip Randolph had first proposed in 1941.

On August 28, 1963, nearly 250,000 marchers gathered before the Lincoln Memorial to support the civil rights bill and the movement at large. Throughout the day they sang freedom songs and listened to speeches from civil rights leaders. Finally, late in the afternoon, Martin Luther King, Jr., arose and, casting aside his prepared remarks, delivered an impassioned speech. Most powerfully, King spoke of his vision of the future.

King's words did not still the angry opposition of white southerners. On September 15, 1963, only days after the March on Washington, white racists bombed the 16th St. Baptist Church in Birmingham and killed four girls attending Sunday school: Addie Mae Collins, Denise McNair, Carole Robertson, and Cynthia Wesley. Chris McNair, the father of the youngest victim, pleaded for calm out of the depth of his own pain: "We must not let this change us into something different than who we are. We must be human."

The event shook the nation and, combined with the reaction to Kennedy's assassination on November 22, 1963, set the stage for real change.

The Civil Rights Act of 1964

Kennedy's successor, Lyndon B. Johnson, lobbied hard to pass the landmark Civil Rights Act. Many in the civil rights movement feared that Johnson, a southerner, would back his region's defiance. Nonetheless, only four days after taking the oath of office, Johnson told the nation he planned to support the civil rights bill as a memorial for the slain president. A master politician, Johnson pushed the bill through Congress despite a marathon filibuster by its opponents.

The **Civil Rights Act of 1964** was the culmination of the civil rights movement to that time. The act banned discrimination in places of public accommodation, including restaurants, hotels, gas stations, and entertainment facilities, as well as schools, parks, playgrounds, libraries, and swimming pools. The act also banned discrimination by employers and labor unions on the basis of race, color, religion, national origin, and sex in regard to hiring, promoting, dismissing, or making job referrals. The act had strong provisions for enforcement. Most important, it allowed government agencies to withhold federal money from any program permitting or practicing discrimination.

21-1

Watch on MyHistoryLab Video: Civil Rights March on Washington

21-2

21-3

21-4

Read on MyHistoryLab Document: John Lewis Speaks at the March on Washington, 1963

21-5

Watch on MyHistoryLab Video: Rev. Dr. Martin Luther King Jr.'s Speech

21-6

21-7

21-8

Civil Rights Act of 1964 Federal law banning discrimination in places of public accommodation.

1955–1968
VIOLENCE AND THE CIVIL RIGHTS MOVEMENT

May 7, 1955
Rev. George Lee killed for leading
voter registration drive,
Belzoni, Mississippi

August 13, 1955
Lamar Smith murdered for
organizing black voters,
Brookhaven, Mississippi

August 28, 1955
Emmett Louis Till murdered for
speaking to white woman,
Money, Mississippi

October 22, 1955
John Earl Reese slain by night riders opposed to black school improvements, Mayflower, Texas

January 23, 1957
Willie Edwards, Jr., killed by Klan,
Montgomery, Alabama

September 24, 1957
President Eisenhower orders
federal troops to enforce school
desegregation, Little Rock,
Arkansas

April 27, 1959
Mack Charles Parker taken
from jail and lynched,
Poplarville, Mississippi

May 14, 1961
Freedom Riders attacked in Alabama while testing compliance
with bus desegregation laws

September 25, 1961
Voter registration worker Herbert
Lee killed by a white legislator,
Liberty, Mississippi

April 1, 1962
Civil rights groups launch voter
registration drive

April 9, 1962
Roman Ducksworth, Jr., taken
from bus and killed by police,
Taylorsville, Mississippi

September 30, 1962
Riots erupt when James Meredith,
a black student, enrolls at the
University of Mississippi; Paul
Guihard, European reporter, killed

April 23, 1963
William Lewis Moore slain during
one-man march against segregation, Attalla, Alabama

May 3, 1963
Birmingham police attack
marching children with dogs
and fire hoses

June 12, 1963
Medgar Evers assassinated,
Jackson, Mississippi

September 15, 1963
Schoolgirls Addie Mae Collins,
Denise McNair, Carole Robertson,
and Cynthia Wesley killed in the
bombing of the 16th St. Baptist
Church, Birmingham, Alabama

September 15, 1963
Virgil Lamar Ware killed during
racist violence, Birmingham,
Alabama

January 31, 1964
Louis Allen, witness to the murder
of a civil rights worker, assassinated, Liberty, Mississippi

21-1
21-2
21-3
21-4
21-5
21-6
21-7
21-8

21-1

21-2

21-3

21-4

21-5

21-6

21-7

21-8

1955–1968
VIOLENCE AND THE CIVIL RIGHTS MOVEMENT

April 7, 1964
Rev. Bruce Klunder killed protesting construction of a segregated school, Cleveland, Ohio

May 2, 1964
Henry Hezekiah Dee and Charles Eddie Moore killed by Klan, Meadville, Mississippi

June 21, 1964
Civil rights workers James Chaney, Andrew Goodman, and Michael Schwerner abducted and slain by Klan, Philadelphia, Mississippi

July 11, 1964
Lt. Col. Lemuel Penn killed by Klan, Colbert, Georgia

February 26, 1965
Jimmie Lee Jackson, civil rights marcher, killed by state trooper, Marion, Alabama

March 11, 1965
Selma to Montgomery march volunteer, Rev. James Reeb, beaten to death, Selma, Alabama

March 25, 1965
Viola Gregg Liuzzo killed by Klan while transporting marchers, Selma Highway, Alabama

June 2, 1965
Oneal Moore, black deputy, killed by night riders, Varnado, Louisiana

July 18, 1965
Willie Wallace Brewster killed by night riders, Anniston, Alabama

August 20, 1965
Jonathan Daniels, seminary student, killed by deputy, Hayneville, Alabama

January 3, 1966
Samuel Younge, Jr., student civil rights activist, killed in dispute over whites-only restroom, Tuskegee, Alabama

January 10, 1966
Vernon Dahmer, black community leader, killed in Klan bombing, Hattiesburg, Mississippi

June 10, 1966
Ben Chester White killed by Klan, Natchez, Mississippi

July 30, 1966
Clarence Triggs slain by night riders, Bogalusa, Louisiana

February 2, 1967
Wharlest Jackson, civil rights leader, killed when police fire on protesters, Jackson, Mississippi

February 8, 1968
Students Samuel Hammond, Jr., Delano Middleton, and Henry Smith killed when highway patrolmen fire on protesters, Orangeburg, South Carolina

April 4, 1968
Dr. Martin Luther King, Jr., assassinated, Memphis, Tennessee

This provision had particular importance for the desegregation of schools and colleges across the country. The act also gave the attorney general the power to initiate proceedings against segregated facilities and schools on behalf of people who could not do so on their own. Finally, it created the Equal Employment Opportunity Commission to monitor discrimination in employment.

Mississippi Freedom Summer

While Congress considered the Civil Rights Act, movement activists renewed their focus on voter registration in the Deep South. In the fall of 1963, many CORE and SNCC workers saw segregation crumbling; however, they knew that without the ballot, African Americans could never drive racist politicians from office, gain a fair hearing in court, reduce police and mob violence, or get equal services from state and local governments. CORE took responsibility for running registration campaigns in Louisiana, South Carolina, and Florida, while SNCC took on the two most repressive states, Alabama and Mississippi. By the summer of 1964, national attention had shifted from Alabama to Mississippi, the site of a massive project known as "Freedom Summer."

The voter registration campaign in Mississippi began in late 1963 when Robert "Bob" Moses mobilized the Council of Federated Organizations (COFO), which had been established in 1962 to aid imprisoned Freedom Riders. Moses convinced the members of COFO (CORE, SNCC, SCLC, and the NAACP) to sponsor a mock Freedom Election in Mississippi. On Election Day, 80,000 disfranchised black people voted for COFO candidates. Impressed with the turnout, Moses and other COFO members believed a massive effort to register voters during the summer of 1964 might break the white monopoly on the ballot box.

COFO decided to invite northern white students to participate in the Mississippi project. These students, about 1,000 in all, were to be drawn primarily from the nation's most prestigious universities. This move contradicted the movement's emphasis on black empowerment, but COFO leaders calculated that the presence of elite white students would attract increased media attention and pressure the federal government to provide protection.

Shortly after the project began, three volunteers—two white New Yorkers, 24-year-old Michael Schwerner and 21-year-old Andrew Goodman, and a black Mississippian, 21-year-old James Chaney—disappeared. Unknown at the time, Cecil Price, deputy sheriff of Philadelphia, Mississippi, had arrested the three on a trumped-up speeding charge. That evening the young men were delivered to a deserted road where three carloads of Klansmen waited. Schwerner and Goodman were shot to death. Chaney was beaten with chains and then shot.

While the fate of the three men was at the time unknown, their disappearance focused national attention on white terrorism. During that summer, approximately 30 homes and 37 churches were bombed, 35 civil rights workers were shot at, 80 people were beaten, six were murdered, and more than 1,000 were arrested. In the face of this violence, uncertainty, and fear, many SNCC activists rejected Martin Luther King's commitment to nonviolence, the inclusion of white activists in the movement, and the wisdom of integration. Divisions over these issues increased tensions within the movement.

Despite the problems it encountered, the Freedom Summer organized dozens of Freedom Schools and community centers throughout Mississippi. Its efforts mobilized the state's black people to an extent not seen since the first Reconstruction. Many communities began to develop the rudiments of a political movement, one that would grow in coming years.

21-1
21-2
21-3
21-4
21-5
21-6
21-7
21-8

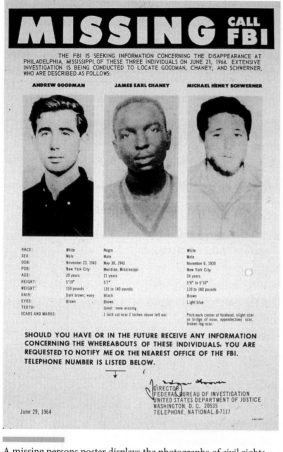

A missing persons poster displays the photographs of civil rights workers Andrew Goodman, James Earl Chaney, and Michael Henry Schwerner after they disappeared in 1964.

Mississippi Freedom Democratic Party (MFDP) Interracial group set up to challenge Mississippi's all-white delegation to the Democratic National Convention in 1964.

The Mississippi Freedom Democratic Party

Freedom Summer intersected with national politics at the Democratic Party National Convention in August 1964 in Atlantic City, New Jersey. White Mississippians routinely excluded African Americans from the political process, and Robert Moses encouraged COFO to set up the **Mississippi Freedom Democratic Party (MFDP)** to challenge the state's regular Democratic delegation at the convention. Under the leadership of veteran activists Fannie Lou Hamer, Victoria Gray, Annie Divine, and Aaron Henry, the MFDP held its first state convention on August 6. Approximately 80,000 citizens put their names on the rolls. The convention elected 64 delegates who traveled to the national convention to present their credentials.

The MFDP challenge caused difficulty for the Democratic Party. Many liberals wanted to seat the civil rights delegation, but President Johnson, who was running for reelection, did not want to alienate white southerners, fearing they would vote for Barry Goldwater, his Republican opponent. Liberal Democratic Senator Hubert H. Humphrey, from Minnesota, worked out a compromise calling for Mississippi regulars to be seated if they swore loyalty to the national party and agreed to cast their 44 votes accordingly. The compromise also created two "at-large" seats for MFDP members Aaron Henry and Ed King. The rest of the Freedom Democrats could attend the convention as nonvoting guests.

Martin Luther King, Jr., Bayard Rustin, and other black leaders counseled acceptance of this compromise. Johnson and the Democrats, they argued, had achieved much of the legislative program the movement favored, and if the party were returned to power, they could do much more. But most of the MFDP delegation, fed up with the violence of Mississippi and unwilling to settle for token representation, rejected the compromise. Many members of SNCC turned their backs on liberalism and cooperation with white people of any political persuasion.

Selma and the Voting Rights Act of 1965

The Civil Rights Act of 1964 contained provisions for helping black voters to register, but white resistance in the Deep South had rendered them ineffective. In Alabama, for example, at least 77 percent of black citizens were unable to vote. Their cause was taken up by businesswoman Amelia P. Boynton, her husband; and the Rev. Frederick Reese, who led the Dallas County Voters League. These three, with others, fought for black enfranchisement and an end to discrimination. Their struggle would help pass the **Voting Rights Act of 1965**, which finally ended the systematic exclusion of African Americans from southern politics.

Selma's sheriff, James G. Clark, worked to block the voter registration activity sponsored by the Boyntons, Reese, and SNCC suffrage workers. By 1964 fewer than 400 of the 15,000 eligible African Americans had registered to vote in Dallas County. President Johnson refused requests to deploy federal marshals to the county to protect voter registration workers. Seeking reinforcements, the workers sent a call to Martin Luther King, Jr., and SCLC. King came and was arrested. In mid-February 1965, during a night march in neighboring Perry County,

Voting Rights Act of 1965 Federal law banning the methods that had systematically excluded African Americans from registering or voting in southern elections.

26-year-old Jimmie Lee Jackson was shot as he tried to shield his mother from a beating by a state trooper. His death and the thrashing of several reporters attracted the national media.

SCLC announced plans for a mass march from Selma to Montgomery to begin on Sunday, March 7, 1965. At the forefront of 600 protesters were King; one of his aides, Hosea Williams; and SCNC's chairman, John Lewis. As the marchers approached the Edmund Pettus Bridge, state troopers and Sheriff Clark's county police tear gassed and beat the retreating marchers while their horses trampled the fallen. Captured in graphic detail by television cameras, this battle became known as "Bloody Sunday." Seizing the moment, King and the activists rescheduled a pilgrimage for March 9. The SCLC leader soon found himself in a dilemma. A federal judge who was normally supportive of civil rights had issued an injunction against the march. Moreover, President Johnson and other key figures in the government urged King not to go through with it. King was reluctant to violate a federal injunction, and he knew he needed Johnson's support to win strong voting rights legislation. But the people of Selma and the hundreds of young SNCC workers would probably march even if King did not.

When the day of the march came, 1,500 protesters marched to the bridge singing. To their surprise, King crossed the Pettus Bridge, prayed briefly, and turned around. He had made a face-saving compromise with the federal authorities. SNCC workers felt betrayed, and King's leadership suffered. That evening local white people clubbed to death James Reeb, a white Unitarian minister from Boston. His martyrdom created a national outcry and prompted Johnson to act. On March 15 the president, in a televised address to Congress, announced he would submit voter registration legislation. He electrified civil rights activists when he invoked the movement's slogan in his Texas drawl, "We shall overcome."

The protests at Selma and the massive white resistance spurred Congress to pass the Voting Rights Act of 1965, which President Johnson signed on August 6. The act outlawed educational requirements for voting in states or counties where less than half the voting-age population had been registered on November 1, 1964, or where less than half had voted in the 1964 presidential election. It also empowered the attorney general to have the Civil Rights Commission assign federal registrars to enroll voters. In Mississippi, black registrants soared from 28,500 in 1964 to 251,000 in 1968 (see Map 21–1).

Gaining voting rights made a tremendous difference. Before passage of the act, Fannie Lou Hamer had unsuccessfully challenged the seating of the Mississippi representatives before the U.S. House of Representatives. In 1968 she was selected as a delegate to the Democratic Party convention. To be sure, southern state legislators resisted the act. They instituted a dazzling array of disfranchisement devices such as gerrymandering, at-large elections, more appointive offices, and higher qualifications for candidates. But the era when white supremacy lay at the core of southern politics was over.

Read on **MyHistoryLab**
Document: Fannie Lou Hamer Fights for Voting Rights in Mississippi, 1964

Fannie Lou Hamer, in words and deeds, refused to compromise with racial injustice. This June 1966 photograph by Flip Schule captures Hamer, a tireless organizer, speaking at an evening rally held at Tougaloo College in Mississippi on the last day of the March Against Fear.

21-1

21-2

21-3

21-4

21-5

21-6

21-7

21-8

CONCLUSION

The two *Brown* decisions ended the legal underpinning of segregation and discrimination and set in motion events that would irrevocably transform the political and social status of African Americans. White southerners resisted the changes *Brown* unleashed, and as their resistance gained momentum, violence against African Americans and their allies exploded.

21-1

21-2

21-3

21-4

21-5

21-6

21-7

21-8

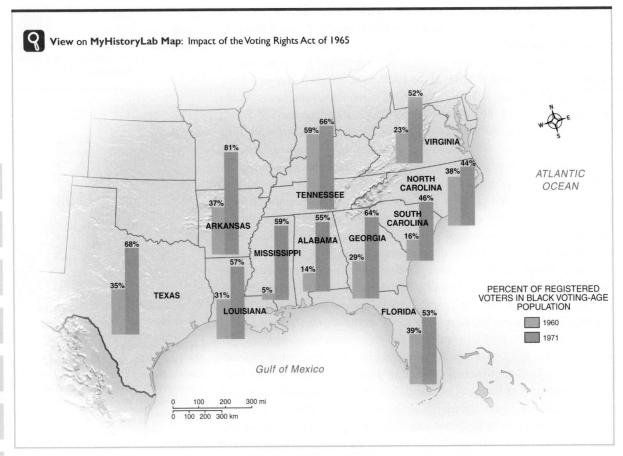

View on **MyHistoryLab Map**: Impact of the Voting Rights Act of 1965

PERCENT OF REGISTERED
VOTERS IN BLACK VOTING-AGE
POPULATION

1960

1971

MAP 21–1 THE EFFECT OF THE VOTING RIGHTS ACT OF 1965
The Voting Rights Act enabled millions of previously disfranchised African Americans in the South to vote.

Why was gaining the right to vote so important for southern African Americans?

The civil rights movement successes depended on many factors. The federal government intervened at crucial moments to enact historic civil rights legislation, issue judgments on behalf of the civil rights protesters, and protect the rule of law with federal marshals and soldiers. Black leaders pursued strategies to provoke confrontations that would ensure federal intervention and garner media coverage. For more than a decade, the victorious freedom fighters of the civil rights movement stormed the legal barricades of segregation. The uncompromising struggle of African Americans, their organizations, and their white allies pressured federal officials in the legislative, executive, and judicial branches of government to enact major civil rights legislation, issue executive orders, and deliver judicial decisions that dismantled segregation in the South.

The victories of this era were far reaching, but as they were achieved, new issues arose that would fracture the movement. Until recently, scholarship concerning the rise and evolution of the civil rights movement focused largely on the South. Impressive new research focuses on the long history of struggles for civil rights and economic justice that occurred during the Great Depression and World War II eras. To be sure, by the advent

❋ EXPLORE ON MYHISTORYLAB
The Civil Rights Movement

How did conditions for African Americans begin to change in the mid-1900s?

Laws in the South known as "Jim Crow laws"—regulations that banned African Americans and whites from, for example, marrying, dining, going to school, or socializing together—ensured racial discrimination. In the North, segregation undergirded the social structure. However, African-American leaders started to make advancements in their fight for equality in the 1950s and 1960s. Civil rights activists protested across the South, making national headlines. In the industrial cities of the North and West, large numbers of African Americans arrived

Young black man drinking from a segregated drinking fountain.

SHIFTS IN AFRICAN-AMERICAN POPULATION IN SELECTED COUNTIES, 1940–1950		
County	Change, in Persons	Percent Change
Columbia County, Georgia	−1,108	−20
Cook County, Illinois	+226,822	+60
Los Angeles County, California	+142,672	+94
Quitman County, Mississippi	−2,416	−9
Wayne County, Michigan	+172,122	+70

SOURCE: *1950 Census, Historic GIS Data: Slavery, Citizenship, & Civil Rights,* Teaching American History Project, *http://www.upa.pdx.edu/ IMS/ currentprojects/TAHv3/Slave_Citizen_GIS.html.*

in the Second Great Migration between 1940 and 1970 as they sought better opportunities than the South afforded them. From these cities, many also began to speak out for an end to racism.

❋ Explore the Topic on MyHistoryLab

1. **Cause** *What challenges did African Americans face during the era of segregation?* Use socioeconomic patterns to consider discrimination.
2. **Comparison** *In what parts of southern cities did African Americans live?* Map segregation in selected urban centers.
3. **Consequence** *What was the demographic impact of the Second Great Migration?* Consider the results of this move to the urban North and West.

21-1

21-2

21-3

21-4

21-5

21-6

21-7

21-8

of the civil rights movement in the South, black residents in northern and western cities, thanks to federal legislation, enjoyed access to public facilities, schools, and jobs in a more diverse economic sector. The civil rights movement has largely been focused on the South because black northerners already had many of the rights granted by the federal legislation of the era. Nonetheless, in all regions, long after the victories of the civil rights movement(s) many black individuals and communities still suffered the negative impact of discrimination and segregation. The future dictated the need for different techniques and new ways of thinking.

CHAPTER TIMELINE

AFRICAN-AMERICAN EVENTS

NATIONAL EVENTS

1954–1958

1954
Supreme Court's *Brown v. Board of Education* decision declares separate but equal education unconstitutional

1955
Supreme Court's *Brown II* decision calls for school districts to desegregate immediately or "with all deliberate speed"

The Interstate Commerce Commission outlaws segregated buses and waiting rooms for interstate passengers

Claudette Colvin arrested for refusing to relinquish her seat to a white woman on a bus in Montgomery

Emmett Till lynched

Rosa Parks arrested for refusing to give up her seat on a city bus, beginning the Montgomery Bus Boycott

1956
The Supreme Court, in *Gayle v. Browder*, bars segregation in intrastate travel

1957
Congress passes the Civil Rights Act of 1957

President Eisenhower enforces integration of Little Rock's Central High School with federal troops

Martin Luther King, Jr., and other religious leaders organize SCLC

1954
First White Citizens Council in Mississippi

1955
The American Federation of Labor and Congress of Industrial Organizations merge to form the AFL-CIO

1956
Segregationists in Congress issue the "Southern Manifesto"

Eisenhower wins second term as president

1960–1965

1960
Black students sit in at Woolworth lunch counter in Greensboro, North Carolina

SNCC founded

Black vote is critical to Kennedy's election

1961
Freedom Riders attacked in Alabama and Mississippi

Kennedy names Thurgood Marshall to the Second Circuit Court of Appeals

Herbert Lee killed in Amite County, Mississippi

1962
COFO is formed

James Meredith desegregates the University of Mississippi with federal support

The Albany Movement fails

Voter Education Project launched

1960
John F. Kennedy elected president

1963
Kennedy is assassinated; Lyndon Johnson succeeds to the presidency

1964
Equal Employment Opportunity Commission established

1965
Johnson outlines the Great Society program to attack poverty

CHAPTER TIMELINE

AFRICAN-AMERICAN EVENTS

1963

Project C highlights racial injustices in Birmingham; King writes his celebrated "Letter From Birmingham Jail"

Federal government compels Governor George C. Wallace to desegregate the University of Alabama

Medgar Evers murdered

W. E. B. Du Bois dies in Ghana, Africa, at age 95

The March on Washington

Martin Luther King, Jr., delivers his "I Have a Dream" speech

Ku Klux Klan bombs the 16th Street Baptist Church in Birmingham, Alabama, killing four girls

Malcolm X breaks with Elijah Muhammad and the Nation of Islam and founds his own movement, Muslim Mosque

1964

SNCC launches the Mississippi Freedom Summer Project to promote voter registration

Twenty-Fourth Amendment to the Constitution outlaws the poll tax

James E. Chaney, Michael Schwerner, and Andrew Goodman murdered in Mississippi

Civil Rights Act of 1964 enacted

The Mississippi Freedom Democratic Party denied seating at the Democratic National Convention

Martin Luther King, Jr., wins the Nobel Peace Prize

1965

Civil rights marchers walk from Selma to Montgomery after violent confrontation in Selma

Voting Rights Act of 1965 enacted

NATIONAL EVENTS

On MyHistoryLab

 Study and Review on MyHistoryLab

REVIEW QUESTIONS

1. What role did "ordinary" or local people play in the civil rights movement? How did children contribute to the struggle for social change?

2. Why did the federal government intervene in the civil rights movement? What were the major pieces of legislation enacted, and how did they dismantle legalized segregation?

3. What were the ideologies, objectives, and tactics of the major civil rights organizations and their leaders?

4. Who were some of the people who lost their lives in the civil rights struggle?

5. What were the major successes and failures of the freedom movement? What intergenerational tensions plagued the movement? How did the movement transform American politics and society?

22 Black Nationalism, Black Power, Black Arts 1965–1980

LEARNING OBJECTIVES

22-1 Why did many African Americans become increasingly militant at the end of the 1960s?

22-2 What factors contributed to and ignited the urban rebellions in the 1960s?

22-3 How did the Vietnam War affect the Great Society and African Americans?

22-4 What was the relationship between the black power movement and black culture?

22-5 What specific policies did President Nixon initiate that affected the civil rights of African Americans?

22-6 What were some of the political accomplishments of the black power movement in the 1970s?

When Lyndon B. Johnson became president in 1963 following John F. Kennedy's assassination, he brought to the position impressive political skills and a willingness to use them to help reconcile the racial, social, and economic disparities in American society. Johnson's escalation of America's involvement in Vietnam, however, undermined his domestic agenda. While Dr. Martin Luther King, Jr., intensified his push for jobs and justice for African Americans, Malcolm X, and others questioned whether American racism could be overcome without violent struggle. A younger generation of freedom fighters lost faith in America's promise of justice and equal opportunity. Rather, some embraced the black radical tradition and a nationalist ideology of community empowerment and mobilization. Some also armed for self-defense again police brutality.

The raised arm with clinched fist symbolizes both black solidarity and the major shift from the passive resistance of the civil rights movement to the militant consciousness of the black power movement generation.

At the same time, a white backlash against the gains of the civil rights movement convinced black leaders and scholars—such as Stokely Carmichael and Charles V. Hamilton—to pursue a black power agenda and mobilize black communities to exercise their recently regained voting rights. They dismissed the inter-racialism of the civil rights movement and found fault with President Johnson's democratic liberalism. Although Martin Luther King was initially ambivalent about black power, it was clear that the winds had shifted direction. The new spirit of change embraced an array of community-level organizers and political figures from Fannie Lou Hamer in Mississippi to Shirley Chisholm in New York, and organizations from the Deacons of Defense in New Orleans to the Black Panther Party in Oakland, California.

Between 1967 and 1980, the dynamics of the civil rights freedom struggle shifted from protest against segregation, disfranchisement, and discrimination to black mobilization for the election of black officials to public office. African-American communities elected an unprecedented number of black politicians as mayors in dozens of America's larger cities. But while witnessing these electoral victories by black officials, the older civil rights movement coalitions fizzled and frayed. Assassins killed Malcolm X in 1965 and both Martin Luther King, Jr., and Robert Kennedy in 1968. Other community organizers and activists were also murdered, including Fred Hampton, deputy chairman of the Illinois Black Panther Party.

The Rise of Black Nationalism

22-1   **Why did many African Americans become increasingly militant at the end of the 1960s?**

President Johnson easily defeated Republican Senator Barry Goldwater in the 1964 election. But his victory proved not to be a mandate for civil rights. In California, for example, voters gave Johnson a decisive win but also approved an amendment to the state constitution that supported the repeal of laws that prohibited housing discrimination. In Alabama, white resentment ran even stronger. It is not a coincidence that Alabama Governor George Wallace became a national political figure who deployed virulent opposition to desegregation at this time. Rewarded by favorable responses from many northern white voters in 1968, Wallace planned a full-scale presidential run in 1972 but was shot and left partially paralyzed by a would-be assassin.

As white Americans support weakened for the goals of the civil rights movement, many black Americans searched for, and some turned completely to, the Black Radical Tradition. They advocated different strategies as white violence escalated. White thugs terrorized the workers in the Council of Federated Organizations in Mississippi. Floyd McKissick of the Congress of Racial Equality (CORE) and Stokely Carmichael of the Student Nonviolent Coordinating Committee (SNCC) became disillusioned and doubted whether King's moderation, nonviolence, and universalism would secure freedom, justice, and civil equality.

Black people in northern and western cities lost patience with the slow pace of racial change. Long into the post-1965 era, African Americans confronted the "invisible" racism embedded in American economic, political, social, and educational institutions and challenged

Watch on MyHistoryLab Video: "The Movement"

22-1

22-2

22-3

22-4

22-5

22-6

the opposition of white people to fair housing, environmental justice, and all policies that required a redistribution of power and resources. In this context, President Lyndon Johnson's "War on Poverty" may be seen as an extension of the black freedom struggle. Black churchmen critiqued racism within white religious groups and even called for black reparations. Black feminists also developed a theology that called for greater gender equality in the leadership of black churches and vehemently denounced sexism in the larger society.

Black power transformed black and white leaders of mainstream religious organizations. In 1946, the Federal Council of Churches, composed of Protestants, Catholics, and Jews, pledged to work for "a non-segregated church and a non-segregated society." Between 1963 and 1965, the National Council of Churches (NCC) gave financial and moral support to the civil rights movement. In 1963, the NCC founded its Commission on Religion and Race to support the black freedom movement. The NCC supported events such as the March on Washington and lobbied for passage of the Civil Rights Act of 1964 and the Voting Rights Act of 1965.

In 1965, the NCC appointed Benjamin Payton as director of the Commission. Payton had his own views about how organized religion could address racial problems. He viewed the economic development of black people and their communities as the critical prerequisite to improving national racial relations. In his first address to the NCC, Payton emphasized the need for "a program of economic development to make civil rights real, in housing, employment, education and health care." In July 1966, he convened a small cadre of men that included Gayraud S. Wilmore, who served as the director of the United Presbyterian's Commission on Religion and Race. Out of this gathering emerged the National Commission of Black Churchmen, which became a key mainstream ecumenical church group advocating black power concepts and strategies for the rest of the 1960s.

The black power movement spurred the creation of black caucuses within predominantly white churches. All these black religious groups pressed for more black leaders within their denominations. The stage was set for James Forman's Black Manifesto.

In April 1969, James Forman, a former Chicago schoolteacher renowned for his work with SNCC, addressed the National Black Economic Development Conference in Detroit, sponsored by the Interreligious Foundation for Community Organizations (which was supported by predominantly white churches). Forman demanded that white churches pay $500 million in reparations for their participation in and benefit from American slavery and racial exploitation. His sharply secular critique of American religion precipitated the withdrawal of mainstream white religious groups from active participation in the civil rights movement. Forman's black power rhetoric and revolutionary ideology offended white groups who recoiled at the idea that black and other minority groups wanted to share real power within the white-dominated churches. Relations between black people and Jews steadily deteriorated as countercharges circulated of "Jewish racism" and "black anti-Semitism."

In ways reminiscent of Marcus Garvey in the 1910s and 1920s, Malcolm X (1925–1965) delineated the critical elements or characteristics of the Black Radical Tradition in three speeches delivered in Detroit between 1963 and 1965. He also advocated unity among black people all over the world.

The son of a Baptist preacher, Malcolm X was born Malcolm Little in Omaha, Nebraska, and grew up in Lansing, Michigan. Klan terrorists burned his family's home, and his father was murdered in 1938 when Malcolm was 13. His mother was subsequently committed to a mental institution, and welfare agencies separated the children. Malcolm was sent to a juvenile detention home, quit school after the eighth grade, and moved to Boston to live with his sister. There he became involved in the street life of gambling, drugs, and burglary. He was arrested and sentenced to a 10-year prison term in 1946. During the six-and-a-half years he spent in prison, he embraced the teachings of Elijah Muhammad of the Nation of Islam, renounced his "slave name," and called himself Malcolm X. In 1954, he became minister of Harlem's Temple Number 7. Articulate, charismatic, and courageous, Malcolm rejected both the tenets of nonviolence and racial integration. His words and thoughts resonated with many black residents in northern urban communities. In 1961, Malcolm began publishing *Muhammad Speaks,* the official newspaper of the Nation. In *The Autobiography of Malcolm X,* published in 1965 by the writer Alex Haley of *Roots* fame, Malcolm declared,

> Few white people realize that many black people today dislike and avoid spending any more time than they must around white people. This "integration" image, as it is popularly interpreted, has millions of vain, self-exalted white people convinced that black people want to sleep in bed with them—and that's a lie! Oh you can't tell the average white man that the Negro man's prime desire isn't to have a white woman—another lie!

Malcolm X attracted the attention of an increasingly disillusioned component of the black population. He dismissed the goal of racial integration and considered King's message of redemption through brotherly love misguided. Malcolm X's voice and critique of capitalism and white supremacy resonated with those who had experienced so much white violence. "The day of nonviolent resistance is over," Malcolm insisted. He declared that "Revolutions are never based upon love-your-enemy, and pray-for-those-who-spitefully-use-you. And revolutions are never waged by singing 'We Shall Overcome.' Revolutions are based on bloodshed."

Malcolm X's New Departure

Malcolm X's popularity created tensions between himself and the leadership of the Nation of Islam. He grew disillusioned when he learned of Elijah Muhammad's adultery. Elijah Muhammad in turn grew jealous of Malcolm's success. When Malcolm described the Kennedy assassination as a case of "the chickens coming home to roost" (meaning Kennedy was a victim of the same kind of violence that afflicted black people), Elijah Muhammad had ordered him to remain silent. He suspended him for this infraction. Malcolm reacted to the suspension by breaking with the Nation of Islam. He founded his own organization, the Muslim Mosque, Inc. That same year he went on a pilgrimage to Mecca. He changed his name to El-Hajj Malik El-Shabazz, founded the Organization for Afro-American Unity (after the Organization of African Unity), repudiated the Nation of Islam's doctrine that all white people are evil, and began lecturing on the connection between the civil rights struggle in the South and the struggle against European colonialism in Africa. On February 14, 1965, assassins associated with the Nation of Islam killed him as he addressed an audience in Harlem.

▶ Watch on MyHistoryLab Video: Malcolm X

Malcolm X (1925–1965) was eloquent, passionate, a courageously outspoken champion of black people, and a critic of American racism. Today he is an iconic figure memorialized in poems, song, films, books, and operas.

22-1

22-2

22-3

22-4

22-5

22-6

Malcolm's militant advocacy of self-defense, of "overturning systems" that deprive African Americans of basic human rights, reflects the long tradition of black radicalism in America dating back to Frederick Douglass and Henry Highland Garnet in the years before the Civil War. The black power movement carried radicalism forward by emphasizing the importance of community-based leaders and of ordinary people mobilizing to secure their best interests through electoral politics.

Stokely Carmichael and Black Power

((• Listen on MyHistoryLab Audio: *Message to the Grassroots* by Malcolm X, excerpt

22-1

22-2

22-3

22-4

22-5

22-6

In 1966 Stokely Carmichael became chairman of SNCC. Later he would abandon the ideal of interracial collaboration and move SNCC toward a stronger embrace of black nationalism. SNCC's few white staffers, including Bob Zellner, who had been with the organization since its inception, left to pursue other activism.

About this time, James Meredith began a one-man "March Against Fear" from Memphis, Tennessee, to Jackson, Mississippi, to encourage black southerners to register and vote. On this march, a white gunman wounded him. SNCC and Carmichael joined with other organizations to complete the march. Carmichael now began to popularize the slogan "black power," which was to become SNCC's rallying cry. Carmichael and SNCC members spent the spring and summer of 1965 in Lowndes County, Alabama where Carmichael suggested that African Americans should found their own political party. Carmichael believed in the right of ordinary citizens to elect their own leaders and devise strategies to achieve the goals they wanted. They renamed this political party the Lowndes County Freedom Party after the November 1966 elections and selected a snarling black panther as the party logo. Ruth Howard, a SNCC field secretary, described the significance of this logo: "The Black Panther is an animal that when it is pressured it moves back until it is cornered, then it comes out fighting for life or death."

((• 📖 Read on MyHistoryLab Document: Stokely Carmichael Calls for a "Black Power" Movement, 1966

Stokely Carmichael (1941–1998) changed his name to Kwame Turé, a combination of the names of two major African leaders, Kwame Nkrumah and Ahmed Sekou Toure. After he settled in Guinea in 1969, he founded the All-African People's Revolutionary Party.

When critics attacked black power as reverse racism, Carmichael rejoined that it promoted positive self-identity, racial pride, and independent political and economic power. As black people became more disillusioned about the slow pace of social change, some questioned whether white people belonged in their organizations. In 1968 CORE followed SNCC's example and ejected its white members, with a resulting loss of financial resources.

In May 1967 Hubert G. Brown became head of SNCC. "H. Rap" Brown, as he became known, raised the militancy of the black power movement's rhetoric, calling white people "honkies" and the police "pigs." In August 1967 Brown told enthusiastic listeners in the black neighborhood of Cambridge, Maryland, that "black folks built America, and if America don't come around, we're going to burn America down." When a fire erupted a few hours later in a dilapidated school in the heart of the city's black community, white firemen refused to fight it. Police charged Brown with inciting a riot and committing arson, but he posted bail and fled. Later he was arrested on other charges.

The Black Panther Party

The most enduring expression of the new black militant political activism was the Black Panther Party for Self-Defense created by Huey P. Newton and Bobby Seale in Oakland, California, in October 1966. Newton and Seale took the name of the party from the black panther symbol of the **Lowndes County Freedom Organization (LCFO)**. The Black Panthers combined black nationalist ideology with Marxist-Leninist doctrines. Working with white radicals, they hoped to fashion the party into a revolutionary vanguard dedicated to ending police brutality. Eldridge Cleaver, the Panthers' minister of education, helped formulate the party's ideology.

> **Lowndes County Freedom Organization (LCFO)** Political organization founded in 1965.

Cleaver began writing the autobiographical essays that appeared as *Soul on Ice* in 1968, the year the party dropped "Self-Defense" from its name. Black people, Cleaver maintained, were victims of colonization. Integrationism could not meet their needs. Instead, like other colonized peoples, they had to be liberated. "To achieve these ends," he wrote, "we believe that political and military machinery that does not exist now and has never existed must be created." Cleaver and other Panther leaders were arrested after a shoot-out with Oakland police in 1968. Cleaver escaped and fled into exile in Algeria and Cuba. Later, he abandoned his radicalism and became involved with the Republican Party and fundamentalist Christianity upon returning to the United States in 1975.

Police Repression and the FBI's COINTELPRO

The Panthers, imposing in appearance in black leather jackets, berets, and "Afro" haircuts, alarmed white policemen, especially when they armed themselves for self-defense and patrolled their neighborhoods to monitor the police. A series of bloody confrontations in Oakland distracted attention from the Panthers' broader political objectives and community service projects. In Oakland and Chicago, the Panthers arranged free breakfast and healthcare programs, worked to instill racial pride, lectured and wrote about black history, and launched some of the earliest drug education programs. These activities won community support and admiration. The Panthers adopted the slogan "Power to the People."

Black Panther Party founders Huey P. Newton and Bobby Seale. The Panthers advocated a radical economic, social, and educational agenda that made it the target of a determined campaign of suppression and elimination by the police and the FBI.

22-1
22-2
22-3
22-4
22-5
22-6

VOICES   The Black Panther Party Platform

22-1

22-2

22-3

22-4

22-5

22-6

Huey Newton and Bobby Seale's Ten-Point Program reflected their determination to move from the pursuit of civil rights to a radical restructuring of American society along socialist lines, with work and rewards equally shared.

October 1966

Black Panther Party Platform and Program: What We Want, What We Believe

1. We want freedom. We want power to determine the destiny of our Black Community . . .
2. We want full employment for our people . . .
3. We want an end to the robbery of the capitalists of our Black Community . . .
4. We want decent housing fit for shelter of human beings . . .
5. We want education for our people that exposes the true nature of this decadent American society. We want education that teaches us our true history and our role in present-day society . . .
6. We want all Black men to be exempt from military service . . .
7. We want an immediate end to POLICE BRUTALITY and MURDER of Black people . . .

8. We want freedom for all Black men held in federal, state, county and city prisons and jails . . .
9. We want all Black people when brought to trial to be tried in court by a jury of their peer group or people from their Black communities, as defined by the Constitution of the United States . . .
10. We want land, bread, housing, education, clothing, justice, and peace. And as our major political objective, a United Nations supervised plebiscite to be held throughout the Black colony in which only Black colonial subjects will be allowed to participate, for the purpose of determining the will of Black people as to their national destiny.

---

1. **How is the Ten-Point Program similar to the Bill of Rights in the U.S. Constitution? How do they differ?**
2. **How did the Panthers propose to achieve black liberation? Why did they emphasize studying history? How did the Panthers' program conflict with or expand upon that of the older civil rights organizations?**

SOURCE: Clayborne Carson et al., eds., *The Eyes on the Prize Civil Rights Reader: Documents, Speeches, and Firsthand Accounts from the Black Freedom Struggle, 1954–1990* (New York: Viking Penguin, 1991), 346–47.

FBI director J. Edgar Hoover hated the Black Panther Party even more than he disliked Martin Luther King, Jr. Under Hoover's direction, the FBI cooperated with local law enforcement officials to ridicule, undermine, and discredit leaders and members of the Black Panther Party. In August 1967 Hoover distributed a memorandum that detailed the FBI's counterintelligence program against black nationalist groups. The purpose, according to the memo, of this new "counterintelligence (COINTELPRO) endeavor is to expose, disrupt, misdirect, discredit, or otherwise neutralize the activities of black nationalist, hate-type organizations and groupings, their leadership, spokesmen, membership, and supporters, and to counter their propensity for violence and civil disorder." Undercover agents infiltrated the Panthers and provoked violence and criminal acts. Not that the Panthers were saints. Huey P. Newton, for example, had a long criminal record. Still, the FBI and its counterintelligence agents provoked much of the mayhem and violence that became associated with the Panthers. Certainly, COINTELPRO helped shape negative public opinion of black nationalist ideology.

In their effort to destroy the party, law enforcement officials killed an estimated 28 Panthers and imprisoned 750 others. In perhaps the worst incident, police in Chicago killed Fred Hampton and Mark Clark in their sleep in a predawn raid on the Illinois Panther headquarters on December 4, 1969. While the police fired hundreds of rounds, only two shots were fired back from within the apartment.

Prisoners' Rights

Despite such repression, black militancy survived in many forms, including the prisoners' rights movement. One of the Panthers' social programs had focused on the conditions of black prisoners. By 1970 more than half the inmates in U.S. prisons were African American. Black activists argued that many African Americans were in jail for political reasons and suffered from unfair sentences and deplorable conditions because of racism and social class bias.

Angela Davis, a philosophy professor at the University of California at Los Angeles, became the first black woman on the FBI's Ten Most Wanted list because of her involvement in prisoners' rights. In 1969 UCLA's board of regents refused to renew her contract, citing her lack of a Ph.D., but in fact they objected to her membership in the Communist Party. During the late 1960s, she had worked on behalf of the Soledad Brothers, three prisoners—George Jackson, John Clutchette, and Fleeta Drumgo—accused of murdering a white guard at Soledad Prison. On August 7, 1970, George Jackson's younger brother, 17-year-old Jonathan Jackson, staged a one-man raid on the San Rafael courthouse in Marin County, California, to try to seize hostages to exchange for the Soledad Brothers. In the ensuing shoot-out, he was killed along with two prisoners and a judge. Angela Davis, accused of supplying the weapons for the raid, was charged with murder, kidnapping, and conspiracy. She escaped and lived as a fugitive, but she was eventually captured and spent over a year in jail. After a long ordeal and a national "Free Angela" campaign, a jury acquitted Davis. On August 21, 1971, George Jackson was shot and killed at San Quentin Prison by guards who claimed he was trying to escape.

Across the country, prisoners at Attica, a maximum-security prison in northern New York State, began a fast in memory of George Jackson that erupted into a full-scale rebellion. On September 9, 1971, 1,200 inmates seized control of half of Attica and took hostages. Four days later, state police and prison guards suppressed the uprising. Tom Wicker, a columnist for the *New York Times,* filed this report:

> A task force consisting of 211 state troopers and corrections officers retook Attica using tear gas, rifles, and shotguns. After the shooting was over, ten hostages and twenty-nine inmates lay dead or dying. At least 450 rounds of ammunition had been discharged. Four hostages and eighty-five inmates suffered gunshot wounds that they survived. After initial reports that several hostages had died at the hands of knife-wielding inmates, pathologists' reports revealed that hostages and inmates all died from gunshot wounds. No guns were found in the possession of inmates.

Listen on
MyHistoryLab
Audio: Angela Davis;
Interview from Prison

A state commission, assembled in October 1971 to reconstruct the events at Attica, concluded, "With the exception of Indian massacres in the late nineteenth-century, the State Police assault which ended the four-day prison uprising was the bloodiest one-day encounter between Americans since the Civil War."

The Inner-City Rebellions

22-2 What factors contributed to and ignited the urban rebellions in the 1960s?

The militant nationalism and growing embrace of black radicalism reflected growing alienation and anger in America's impoverished inner cities. In 1965, 29.1 percent of black households, compared with only 7.8 percent of white households, lived below the poverty line. Almost 50 percent of nonwhite families lived in substandard housing compared with 18 percent of white families. In 1965 the black unemployment rate was 8.5 percent, almost twice the white unemployment rate of 4.3. For black teenagers the unemployment rate was 23 percent compared with 10.8 percent for white teenagers. As psychologist Kenneth Clark declared in 1967, "The masses of Negroes are now starkly aware of the fact that recent civil rights victories benefited a very small percentage of middle-class Negroes while their predicament remained the same or worsened."

The passage of civil rights laws and voting rights legislation did not resolve these social, educational, and economic disparities. This created a fertile environment for the rise in inner-city alienation. As jobs moved to suburbs to which inner-city residents could neither travel nor relocate, inner-city neighborhoods became poorer. School dropout rates reached epidemic proportions, crime and drug use increased, and fragile family structures weakened. These conditions led militants like the Panthers to liken their neighborhoods to exploited colonies kept poor by repressive white political and economic institutions. Few white Americans understood the depths of the black despair that flared into violence each summer between 1965 and 1969, beginning with the Watts rebellion of 1965.

Watts

In the summer of 1965, a section of Los Angeles called Watts exploded. Watts was 98 percent black. Its residents suffered from overcrowding, unemployment, inaccessible healthcare facilities, inadequate public transportation, and crime and drug addiction. Almost 30 percent of Watts' black males were unemployed. The poverty, combined with anger at the often-brutal behavior of Los Angeles' police force in Watts, proved to be an incendiary combination. On August 11, 1965, a policeman pulled over a young black man to check him for drunk driving. The man was arrested, but not before a crowd gathered. The policeman called for reinforcements, and when they arrived, the crowd pelted them with stones, bottles, and other objects. Within hours, Watts was in a total riot.

Governor Pat Brown, a Democrat, sent in the National Guard to restore order, but by the sixth day of the conflagration, Watts had been reduced to rubble and ashes. Thirty-four people had been killed, more than 900 injured, and 4,000 arrested. Total property damage was more than $35 million, equivalent to hundreds of millions of dollars today. The Watts rebellion was the beginning of four summers of uprisings that would engulf cities in the North and Midwest. There were riots in the summer of 1966, but worse ones erupted in Newark and Detroit in 1967.

Newark

Newark, New Jersey, had more than 400,000 inhabitants in 1967. As was true in many other urban areas, white flight to the suburbs in the 1950s and 1960s had made Newark a majority black city; nonetheless, it operated on an inadequate tax base and under white political control. The city could not meet its inhabitants' social needs. The school system

Read on **MyHistoryLab**
Document: Donald
Wheeldin Describes Watts
Two Years After the 1965
Riot, 1967

Watch on
MyHistoryLab
Video: The Los
Angeles Riots

had deteriorated as unemployment increased. In 1967 Newark had the highest unemployment rate among black men in the nation. As tensions flared and police brutality escalated, white officials paid little attention to black people's complaints. On July 12, after a black cab driver in police custody was beaten, protesters gathered at the police station near the Hayes Homes housing project. When a firebomb hit the wall of the station house, the police charged, clubbing the crowd. This triggered one of the most destructive civic rebellions of the period. During four days of rioting, the police and National Guard killed 25 black people—most of them innocent bystanders, including two children. A white policeman and fireman were also killed. Widespread looting and arson caused millions of dollars in property damage.

Detroit

Detroit erupted a few days after Newark. On the night of Saturday, July 23, police raided an after-hours drinking establishment in the black community where more than 80 people were celebrating the return of two veterans from Vietnam. The raid triggered five days of rioting. Of the 59 urban rebellions that occurred in 1967, Detroit's was the deadliest. Forty-three black people died, most of them shot by members of the National Guard, which had been sent in by Republican Governor George Romney. But even the National Guard, combined with 200 state police and 600 Detroit police, could not restore order. President Johnson had to order 4,700 troops of the elite 82nd and 101st Airborne units to Detroit.

The Kerner Commission

On July 29, 1967, after the Newark and Detroit riots, Johnson established the National Advisory Commission on Civil Disorders, headed by Illinois Governor Otto Kerner.

In 1967, Blacks in Detroit expressed their anger and disillusionment about a constellation of social injustices and economic woes.

Read on
MyHistoryLab
Document: Excerpts
from the Kerner
Report, 1968

22-1

22-2

Watch on
MyHistoryLab
Video:
Lyndon Johnson

22-3

22-4

22-5

22-6

**Economic Opportunity
Act of 1964** Federal law
creating the Office of
Economic Opportunity
and a number of
programs aimed at poor
communities.

The commission included two black members, Republican Senator Edward W. Brooke of Massachusetts and Roy Wilkins, executive director of the NAACP.

In its final report, released in 1968, the Kerner Commission indicted white racism as the underlying cause of the riots and warned that America was "moving towards two societies, one white, one black—separate and unequal. . . . Negroes firmly believe that police brutality and harassment occur repeatedly in Negro neighborhoods. This belief is unquestionably one of the major reasons for intense Negro resentment against the police. . . . Physical abuse is only one source of aggravation in the ghetto. In nearly every city surveyed, the Commission heard complaints of harassment of interracial couples, dispersal of social street gatherings and the stopping of Negroes on foot or in cars without objective basis." The report called for massive government aid to the cities, including funds for public housing, better and more integrated schools, two million new jobs, and funding for a "national system of income supplementation." None of its major proposals was enacted.

Difficulties in Creating the Great Society

The urban rebellions of the late 1960s undercut support for the broadest attack the federal government had yet waged on the problems of poor Americans, what President Johnson in his election campaign in 1964 had called "the Great Society." Much of the legislation Johnson pushed through Congress in 1964 and 1965—Medicare, for example, which provided medical care for the elderly and disabled under the Social Security system, or federal aid to education from elementary through graduate schools—remained popular. But the most ambitious Great Society programs—what Johnson called "an unconditional war on poverty"—were controversial and tested the limits of American reform.

Read on **MyHistoryLab Document**: President
Johnson Calls for a "War on Poverty," 1964

One of the most prominent programs of President Johnson's War on Poverty was the Job Corps, which provided occupational training for poor Americans. In this photo, Johnson speaks with James Truesville at a Job Corps center in Camp Catoctin, Maryland.

Lyndon Johnson was a savvy politician. He never lost a deep sympathy for the disadvantaged and the powerless. Entering Congress in 1937, he had been an enthusiastic New Dealer. Elected to the Senate in 1948, he had refused to sign the Southern Manifesto (see Chapter 21) and, as majority leader, had overcome southern filibusters to pass the 1957 and 1960 Civil Rights Acts. As president, he pushed the 1964 Civil Rights Act and the 1965 Voting Rights Act through Congress.

Johnson's concern for the disadvantaged showed itself in the cornerstone of his War on Poverty, the **Economic Opportunity Act of 1964**. This act created an Office of Economic Opportunity that administered programs like Head Start to help disadvantaged preschoolers, Upward Bound to prepare impoverished teenagers for college, and Volunteers in Service to America (or VISTA) to serve as a domestic peace corps to help the poor and undereducated across the country. These programs included community-governing boards on which black men and women gained representation, learning such essential political skills as bargaining and organizing.

The War on Poverty was the first government-sponsored effort to involve poor African Americans directly in designing and implementing programs to serve low-income communities. The program provided meaningful work, access to education, and critical resources to poor people so that they would become leaders in their own communities and run for office. The **Community Action Programs (CAPs)** insisted on "maximum feasible participation" by the poor.

Johnson faced opposition to CAPs and other Great Society programs. Local politicians, fearing the federal government was subsidizing their opponents and undercutting their power, were especially threatened by programs that empowered the previously disfranchised and dispossessed. Others, reflecting persistent white stereotypes of African Americans, complained that Johnson was rewarding lawlessness and laziness with handouts to the undeserving poor. The black residents of America's inner cities, for their part, had their expectations raised by the promises of the Great Society, only to be frustrated by white backlash and minimal gains.

No one will ever know whether Johnson could have won his War on Poverty had he been given the resources to do so. As it turned out, the nation's resources were increasingly diverted into his other war, the war in Vietnam. Statistics tell the story. Government spending, including spending for domestic programs, increased dramatically under Johnson. But most of the money spent on domestic programs during Johnson's presidency, $44.3 billion, went to Social Security benefits, which now included Medicare. Appropriations for the War on Poverty came to only $10 billion. The war in Vietnam, in contrast, consumed $140 billion.

Community Action Programs (CAPs)
Anti-poverty programs involving "maximum feasible participation" by the poor themselves.

22-1

22-2

22-3

22-4

22-5

22-6

Johnson and the War in Vietnam

22-3 **How did the Vietnam War affect the Great Society and African Americans?**

Vietnam was a French colony from the 1860s until the Japanese seized it during World War II. After the war the Vietnamese communists, led by Ho Chi Minh, declared independence, but the French, with massive U.S. financial aid, fought to reassert their control until they were finally defeated in 1954. That same year, with the French pulling out, the Americans arranged a temporary division of the country into a communist-controlled North Vietnam and a U.S.-supported South Vietnam. The United States ignored the possibility that as guarantor of South Vietnam, it would replace the French as targets for those Vietnamese who were determined to end foreign domination and unify their country.

For nine years, under Presidents Eisenhower and Kennedy, American aid and advisers propped up the corrupt and incompetent South Vietnamese government in Saigon. By the time Johnson became president, only the dramatic escalation of American military involvement could keep the South Vietnamese government in power. Johnson himself doubted the advisability of a wholesale American commitment and did not want a foreign war to distract the public's attention or divert resources from the Great Society programs about which he cared so much. Nonetheless, Johnson intervened in Vietnam—gradually, massively, and inexorably.

After the North Vietnamese allegedly attacked U.S. destroyers in the Gulf of Tonkin in August 1964, Johnson pushed a resolution through Congress that gave him authority to escalate American involvement in Vietnam. In the spring of 1965, he authorized the bombing of selected North Vietnamese targets, but that failed to stop the North Vietnamese from

Watch on
MyHistoryLab
Video: Vietnam

22-1
22-2
22-3
22-4
22-5
22-6

❈ EXPLORE ON MYHISTORYLAB
The Vietnam War

What did the war in Vietnam mean for the United States?

Between 1955 and 1975, a civil war raged across Vietnam between the communist government in the north and the weak democracy–dictatorship in the south. In the context of the Cold War, the United States supported the South Vietnamese government, hoping to stop the spread of communism. By the early 1960s, the American government began increasing its troop presence in Vietnam; in 1965, the United States sent its first combat units. American military intervention in Vietnam and the neighboring countries of Southeast Asia grew. As casualties mounted and little military progress was achieved, the intervention became increasingly unpopular at home with the spread of anti-war protests. Some 58,000 American

Troopers of the 327th, Infantry 101st Air Cavalry, Division patrol the Laotian border during 'Operation, Plain' August, 1968.

servicemen and servicewomen died before the United States withdrew in 1975. Soon after, the South Vietnamese government fell as the country was united under a single communist government.

❈ Explore the Topic on MyHistoryLab

1. **Cause** *What geographic challenges did American forces face in Vietnam?* Map the features that hindered the U.S. military effort.
2. **Response** *What was the significance of various U.S. military operations in Vietnam, especially the Tet Offensive?* Explore the unfolding of the war.
3. **Consequence** *What relationships may have existed between war deaths and other socioeconomic factors in an area?* Chart potential correlations and consider underlying reasons.

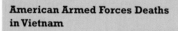

American Armed Forces Deaths in Vietnam	
Year	**Deaths**
1956–1959	4
1960	5
1961	16
1962	53
1963	122
1964	216
1965	1,928
1966	6,350
1967	11,363
1968	16,899
1969	11,780
1970	6,173
1971	2,414
1972	759
1973	68
1974	1
1975	62

SOURCE: *"Statistical Information About Fatal Casualties of the Vietnam War National Archives, National Archives, http://www.archives.gov/research/ military/vietnam-war/casualty-statistics.html#home.*

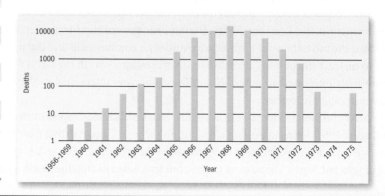

reinforcing their forces in the south. The American military presence in South Vietnam then grew rapidly. By the end of 1966, more than 385,000 U.S. troops were stationed there and by 1968 more than 500,000.

Black Americans and the Vietnam War

In the mid-1960s, black Americans made up 10 percent of the armed forces. This percentage increased during the Vietnam War and by 1969, for example, 18.1 percent of active duty soldiers were black. Black overrepresentation among the U.S. troops in Vietnam resulted, in large part, from draft deferments for college and graduate students who were predominantly white and middle class (such as George W. Bush and Dick Cheney). Black men and women entered the military for many reasons, in addition to the draft. One was patriotism. Another was that the military offered educational and vocational opportunities that the children of the working black poor could not otherwise obtain. Still another was Project 100,000.

Project 100,000

In 1966 the Defense Department launched **Project 100,000** to reduce the military's high rejection rate. The project enabled recruitment officers to accept applicants whom they otherwise would have rejected because of criminal records or lack of skills. It supplied more than 340,000 new recruits for Vietnam, 136,000 of whom were African Americans. As some have argued, this imbalance made the Vietnam War a white man's war but a black man's fight. Although the recruits were promised training and "rehabilitation," they saw more combat duty than regular recruits.

Project 100,000
Military project with the goal of reducing the number of African Americans rejected by the military.

Johnson: Vietnam Destroys the Great Society

By the end of 1967, the nation seemed to be heading toward total racial polarization. In their rage against economic exploitation and police brutality, some inner-city black people had destroyed their own neighborhoods. Frightened white people, unable to comprehend black anger, rallied behind those who promised to restore order by any means. The two men who, only a few years before, had seemed the most effective advocates of racial reconciliation—Lyndon Johnson and Martin Luther King, Jr.,—were both trying to regain the initiative. Each, tragically, alienated the other.

By 1967 Johnson's situation was untenable. He had escalated the war in Vietnam without convincing many Americans it was worth fighting. Misleading claims about the progress of the war had forfeited public trust and opened what journalists called "the credibility gap." Johnson hoped that, with more bombing and more troops, the Vietnamese communists would give up, but he knew that if Congress had to choose between spending on the war and spending on domestic programs, it would choose the war. After Johnson asked for a tax increase, his Great Society programs met increasing resistance.

Despite opposition in Congress, Johnson did not give up on the Great Society. He knew he could initiate no major programs while the Vietnam War lasted, but he continued to push measures, including a law to prohibit discrimination in housing. He also named the architect of the NAACP's attack on segregation, Thurgood Marshall, to the Supreme Court in 1967.

Vietnam trapped Johnson. As the hundreds of thousands of people who demonstrated against the war reminded him, Vietnam was incontestably "Lyndon Johnson's war." It was not, he would have replied, the war he had wanted to fight—that was the war against poverty and discrimination—but he was committed to seeing it through. He believed his and the

22-1

22-2

22-3

22-4

22-5

22-6

Captain Joseph B. Anderson, Jr., of Topeka, Kansas, served as a platoon leader at An Khe, Vietnam, from June 1966 to June 1967, and as company commander in Phouc Vinh, Cambodia, from May 1970 to April 1971. His unit in the 1st Cavalry Division was the subject of The Anderson Platoon, *a 1967 French documentary film.*

Shortly after I got to Vietnam, we got into a real big fight. We were outnumbered at least ten to one. But I didn't know it. I had taken over 1st Platoon of B Company of the 12th Cav. We were up against a Viet Cong battalion. There may have been 300 to 400 of them. And they had just wiped out one of our platoons. At that time in the war, summer of 1966, it was a terrible loss. A bloody massacre.

I was an absolute rarity in Vietnam. A black West Pointer commanding troops. One year after graduation, I was very aggressive about my role and responsibilities as an Army officer serving in Vietnam. I was there to defend the freedom of the South Vietnamese government, stabilize the countryside, and help contain Communism. The Domino Theory was dominant then, predominant as a matter of fact. I was gung ho. And I thought the war would last three years at the most.

There weren't many opportunities for blacks in private industry then. And as a graduate of West Point, I was an officer and a gentleman by act of Congress. Where else could a black go and get that label just like that?

Throughout the Cav, the black representation in the enlisted ranks was heavier than the population as a whole in the United States. One third of my platoon and two of my four squad leaders were black. For many black men, the service, even during a war, was the best of a number of alternatives to staying home and working in the fields or bumming around the streets of Chicago or New York.

There were only a very few incidents of sustained fighting during my tours. Mostly you walked and walked, searched and searched. If you made contact, it would be over in thirty or forty minutes. One burst and then they're gone, because they didn't want to fight or could not stand up against the firepower we could bring with artillery and helicopter gunships.

I had a great deal of respect for the Viet Cong. They were trained and familiar with the jungle. They relied on stealth, on ambush, on their personal skills and wile, as opposed to firepower. They knew it did not pay for them to stand and fight us, so they wouldn't. . . .

What was very clear to me was an awareness among our men that the support for the war was declining in the United States. The gung ho attitude that made our soldiers so effective in 1966, 67, was replaced by the will to survive. They became more security conscious. They would take more defensive measures so they wouldn't get hurt. They were more scared. They wanted to get back home.

Career officers and enlisted men like me did not go back to a hostile environment in America. We went back to bases where we were assimilated and congratulated and decorated for our performance in the conduct of the war.

Personally it was career enhancing. A career Army officer who has not been to war during the war is dead, careerwise. I had done that. I received decorations. Two Silver Stars, five Bronze Stars, eleven Air Medals. . . . But in 1978 I decided I did not want to cool my heels for the next eight to ten years to become a general. . . . I resigned my commission, worked a year as a special assistant to the U.S. Secretary of Commerce, and joined General Motors as a plant manager.

The Anderson Platoon won both an Oscar and an Emmy. As time passes, my memory of Vietnam revolves around the film. I have a print, and I look at it from time to time. And the broadness and scope of my two-year experience narrows down to sixty minutes.

1. **How do the experiences of this Vietnam veteran compare with those of black soldiers in World War II?**
2. **Why were African-American men attracted to military service? What benefits did they derive from the military, and what does their disproportionate representation in it suggest about conditions in black communities?**

SOURCE: "Captain Joseph B. Anderson, Jr., Topeka, Kansas," from *Bloods: An Oral History of the Vietnam War by Black Veterans* by Wallace Terry, copyright © 1984 by Wallace Terry. Used by permission of Random House, Inc.

nation's honor were at stake. Even though objective commentators considered the conflict a stalemate, optimistic reports in 1967, from military commanders and intelligence agents, convinced the president he might yet prevail.

Then, on January 30, 1968, at the start of the Vietnamese New Year (called Tet), communist insurgents attacked 36 of the 44 provincial capitals in South Vietnam as well as its national capital, Saigon, where they penetrated the grounds of the American embassy. Although American and South Vietnamese forces recaptured all the territory that was lost and inflicted massive casualties on the enemy, the Tet Offensive was a major psychological blow for the American public, deepening the suspicion that the administration had not been telling the truth about the war. Washington was forced to reconsider its strategy.

On March 31, 1968, President Johnson told the nation he would halt the bombing of North Vietnam to encourage the start of peace negotiations, which began in Paris in May. Then, as if an afterthought, he added that he would not seek re-nomination as president. Worn out by Vietnam, frustrated in his efforts to achieve the Great Society, the target of bitter criticism, and dispirited by a poor showing in the New Hampshire primary, Lyndon Johnson ended his public career rather than engaging in a potentially bruising re-nomination battle.

King: Searching for a New Strategy

Like Johnson, Martin Luther King, Jr., was attacked on many fronts. Many white people considered him a dangerous radical. Black militants considered him an ineffectual moderate. His first response to the urban rebellions in 1965 and 1966 had been to move his campaign to the North to demonstrate the national range of the civil rights movement. In 1966 King and the SCLC set up operations in Chicago. King was confident he would receive the support of the city's white liberals and the black community. His optimism proved unwarranted.

Chicago's powerful Mayor Richard Daley viewed King suspiciously from the outset, but he treated him with respect and cautioned the police not to use violence against King's civil rights demonstrators. Because King's movement depended on provoking confrontation, not much happened until King attempted to march into the white ethnic enclave of Marquette Park and the all-white suburb of Cicero.

The ensuing violence attracted the nation's television cameras. Chicago's white liberals joined with King and Daley in negotiating the Summit Agreement on housing, which amounted to a hasty retreat by King in the face of virulent white rage and black militancy. The Chicago strategy was a dismal failure.

But Chicago reinforced two important lessons for King. First, racial discrimination was more than a southern problem: in Chicago he witnessed an intensity of hatred and hostility that surpassed even that of Birmingham. Second, racial discrimination was inextricably intertwined with the country's economic structure. And so he began to think more critically about the need not only to eradicate poverty but to end systemic economic inequality. "What good is it to be allowed to eat in a restaurant," he remarked, "if you can't afford a hamburger?" In the fall of 1967, he announced plans for his most ambitious and militant project, an integrated, nonviolent "**Poor People's Campaign**" the following spring. According to the plan, tens of thousands of the nation's dispossessed would descend on Washington to focus attention on the disadvantaged in American society.

Poor People's Campaign Project supported by Martin Luther King involving the march of tens of thousands of poor people on Washington.

King on the Vietnam War

Read on **MyHistoryLab**
Document: Martin Luther
King, Jr., Takes a Stand on the
Vietnam War, 1967

While planning the Poor People's Campaign, King began to attack the war in Vietnam. He rejected what he considered the hypocrisy of the federal government's determination to send black and white men to Vietnam while failing to protect black American civil rights protesters in places like Albany, Birmingham, and Selma. His statements that the president was more concerned about winning in Vietnam than winning the "war against poverty" in America turned Johnson against him and further alienated King from many of Johnson's black supporters, including the more traditional civil rights leaders who supported the war. At the same time, the young militants in SNCC, who had already condemned the war, did not rush to embrace him. But King persisted, and by 1968 he had become one of the war's most trenchant critics.

King's Murder

King's search for a new strategy led him to a closer involvement with labor issues. In February 1968, while attempting to gain union recognition for municipal workers in Memphis, 1,300 members of a virtually all-black sanitation workers local went on strike and, together with the local black community, boycotted downtown merchants. King went to Memphis to address the striking sanitation workers.

The occasion was marked by violence. Nevertheless, King returned to Memphis on April 3 and delivered his last and perhaps most prophetic speech about seeing the promised land. The next day James Earl Ray murdered King as he stood on the balcony of the Lorraine Motel in Memphis. His assassination unleashed a torrent of civic rage in black communities. More than 125 cities experienced uprisings. By April 11, 46 people were dead, 35,000 were injured, and more than 20,000 had been arrested.

Civil Rights Act of 1968
Federal law banning
discrimination in
housing.

In what seemed to many a belated gesture of racial reconciliation, within days of King's assassination, Congress passed the **Civil Rights Act of 1968**. Proposed by Johnson two years before, the act outlawed discrimination in the sale and rental of housing and gave the Justice Department authority to bring suits against such discrimination.

King's assassination also boosted support for the SCLC's faltering Poor People's Campaign. The campaign began in May when more than 2,000 demonstrators settled into a shantytown they called Resurrection City in Washington, DC. For more than a month, they marched daily to federal offices and took part in a mass demonstration on June 19. On June 24, police evicted them, and the campaign ended, leaving an uncertain legacy.

The Black Arts Movement and Black Consciousness

22-4 **What was the relationship between the black power movement and black culture?**

The years between 1967 and 1975 witnessed some of the most intense political and cultural discussions in the history of the black freedom struggle. Black power stimulated debate about both the future of black politics in the post–civil rights era and the role of black art and artists in the quest for black liberation. Creative people revisited the long-standing issue of whether black art is political or aesthetic. For a decade, discussion about black culture and identity focused on the relationship between art, the artist, and the political movement within the black community. This period became known as the "**black arts movement**." Among the outstanding poets who helped shape the revolutionary movement, introducing new forms of black writing and delivering outspoken attacks on "the white aesthetic" while stressing black beauty and pride, were Sonia Sanchez, Nikki Giovanni, and Don L. Lee (Haki Madhubuti). Of equal significance in the development and evolution of this creative flowering was playwright and poet LeRoi Jones.

black arts movement
Artistic movement that seeks to promote black art by black artists for black people.

The formal beginning of the movement was the founding in 1965 of the Black Arts Repertory Theater by Jones, who changed his name to Imamu Amiri Baraka in 1967. Jones was the bridge that linked the political and cultural aspects of black power. He had been associated with the white avant-garde poets in New York in the 1950s and early 1960s, but he began to change in 1965 from an integrationist to a black cultural nationalist.

The guiding ethos of the black arts movement was the determination of black artists to produce black art for black people and thereby to accomplish black liberation. Baraka declared, "The Black man must seek a Black politics, an ordering of the world that is beneficial to his culture, to his interiorization and judgment of the world. The Black Artist . . . is desperately needed to change the images his people identify with, by asserting Black feeling, Black mind, Black judgment." In 1968 he coedited with Larry Neal the anthology *Black Fire,* which revealed the extent to which black writers and thinkers had rejected integration in favor of a new black consciousness and nationalist political engagement.

Listen on **MyHistoryLab**
Audio: *Song of the Front Yard* by Gwendolyn Brooks

The black arts movement was criticized because of its celebration of black maleness, its racial exclusivity, and its homophobia. It was never a unified movement in the sense that all black artists spoke in one voice. There was creative dissent and competing visions of freedom. In 1970 Maya Angelou published an autobiographical novel, *I Know Why the Caged Bird Sings,* which unveiled her experience with sexual abuse and the silencing of black women within black communities. Other black women writers would create a black women's literary renaissance in the 1970s. Still, prominent integrationist writers agreed with some of the black arts movement's tenets and were converted to its principles.

The works of Langston Hughes, Lorraine Hansberry, Gwendolyn Brooks, and James Baldwin linked the black cultural renaissances of the 1930s, 1940s, and 1950s to the black arts movement. Brooks, for example, stressed the commitment of artists to community and the importance of the relationship between the artist and her audience. She had supported community-based arts programs, and it seemed natural that she should "convert" to a black nationalist perspective during the 1960s and join forces with younger artists.

But the most popular black writer of the era was James Baldwin. Baldwin was an integrationist. In his work he had resisted the simple inversion of racial hierarchies that characterized parts of the black power and black arts movements. Yet in many ways, Baldwin was as alienated and angry as some of the artists identified with black arts.

Imamu Amiri Baraka means "spiritual leader, prince, blessed" in Swahili and is the chosen name of LeRoi Jones. The celebrated "father of the black arts movement" remained prolific, influential, and controversial after five decades of creative engagement in America's "culture war."

22-1

22-2

22-3

22-4

22-5

22-6

In *The Fire Next Time* (1963), he concluded with a phrase that echoed years later through discussions of the rebellions in Watts, Newark, and Detroit: "If we do not now dare everything, the fulfillment of that prophecy, recreated from the bible in song by a slave, is upon us: 'God gave Noah the rainbow sign, No more water, the fire next time!'"

Baldwin was also unflinching about white racism and had a major impact on public discourse. At one point he told his white readers, "There appears to be a vast amount of confusion on this point, but I do not know many Negroes who are eager to be 'accepted' by white people, still less to be loved by them; they, the blacks, simply don't wish to be beaten over the head by the whites every instant of our brief passage on this planet." And in *No Name in the Street,* Baldwin declared, "I agree with the Black Panther position concerning black prisoners: not one of them has ever had a fair trial, for not one of them has ever been tried by a jury of his peers."

Poetry and Theater

The black arts movement had its most significant impact in poetry and theater. The movement had three geographical centers: Harlem, Chicago and Detroit, and San Francisco.

The Chicago-based *Negro Digest/Black World,* edited by Hoyt Fuller and published by John Johnson, promoted the new generation of creative artists. In 1970 Fuller changed the magazine's name to *Black World* to signal the rejection of "Negro" and the adoption of "black" to designate people of African descent. The new name identified African Americans with both the African Diaspora and Africa itself.

In Detroit, Naomi Long Madgett's Lotus Press and Dudley Randall's Broadside Press republished the previous generation of black poets, notably Gwendolyn Brooks, Margaret Walker, and Sterling Brown. In Chicago, poet and literary critic Don L. Lee, who changed his name to Haki Madhubuti, launched Third World Press, which published many of the black arts poets and writers.

The Chicago–Detroit publishing nexus promoted new poets like Nikki Giovanni, Etheridge Knight, and Sonia Sanchez. These and other poets produced some of the most accomplished and experimental work of the black arts movement. It resonated with the sounds of the African-American vernacular, combining the rhythmic cadences of sermons with popular music and black "street speech" into a spirited new form of poetry that was free, conversational, and militantly cool.

Theater was another prominent genre of the black arts movement. Playwright Ed Bullins edited a special issue of the journal *Drama Review* in the summer of 1968 that featured essays and plays by most of the major activists in black arts. This volume became the textbook of black arts. In his plays, Bullins, who was greatly influenced by Baraka, portrayed ordinary black life and explored the inner forces that prevented black people from realizing their own liberation and potential. He showed how racism had deformed the black experience and consciousness. Across the country, local black communities formed their own theater groups, including Val Gray Ward's Kuumba Workshop in Chicago and Baraka's Spirit House Theater in New Jersey. These groups hosted seminars, guest appearances, fashion shows, art exhibits, dance recitals, parades, and media parties.

On the West Coast, in 1969, Robert Chrisman and Nathan Hare launched *The Black Scholar,* the first serious journal to promote black studies. Chrisman compared the black arts movement with the Harlem Renaissance of the 1920s: "More so than the Harlem Renaissance, in which Black artists were always on the leash of white patrons and publishing houses, the black arts movement did it for itself. Black people going out nationally, in mass, saying we are an independent Black people and this is what we produce."

22-1

22-2

22-3

22-4

22-5

22-6

Listen on
MyHistoryLab
Audio: "Liberation/
Poem" by Sonia Sanchez

Music

The cultural nationalists in the black arts movement championed modern jazz musicians as icons of the quest for black freedom. Baraka argued that jazz and other black music were the language that black people developed to give uncensored accounts of their experiences. He and other cultural nationalists believed music could promote black identity and encourage the pride that was vital for political struggle. Above all, jazz appeared to challenge Western conceptions of harmony, rhythm, melody, and tone. In jazz you have to improvise, to create your own form of expression by using whatever information inspires you. The emphasis is not on an original score but on individual articulation.

Cultural nationalists perceived jazz to be a self-consciously engaged, economically independent, politically useful art form.

This outlook explains why Miles Davis's legendary album *Kind of Blue* (1959), one of the most progressive jazz albums ever produced, also became one of the most popular. Davis showed that art could be accessible without sacrificing excellence and rigor. For black cultural nationalists, Davis projected an image of uncompromising and uncompromised black identity.

Jazz, however, tended to appeal to intellectuals. Most black people preferred rhythm and blues, gospel, and soul. During the height of the black consciousness movement, black popular musicians gave performances to raise funds and assert racial pride. Aretha Franklin and Ray Charles, for example, allowed SNCC workers to attend their concerts for free. Just as the freedom songs had done, the soul music of the black power era helped unify black people.

No history of the era would be complete without mentioning the performances of the "Godfather of Soul," James Brown; the "Queen of Soul," Aretha Franklin, best known for her powerful rendition of the song "Respect"; and the financial contributions of Berry Gordy of Motown. James Brown's "Say It Loud, I'm Black and I'm Proud" became an anthem for the era. Brown linked commercial marketing to social commentary, confronting American racism with racial pride and righteous indignation. Brown was "totally committed to black power, the kind that is achieved not through the muzzle of a rifle but through education and economic leverage."

Berry Gordy contributed to black freedom struggles both artistically and financially. To support King's Chicago movement, Gordy arranged for Stevie Wonder to give a benefit concert at Soldier Field in Chicago. He contributed to black candidates, the NAACP and its Legal Defense and Educational Fund, and the Urban League.

With Gordy's encouragement, his performers flirted just enough with black radicalism to gain a patina of militancy. During the late 1960s and early 1970s, the musical and lyrical innovations of the Temptations, Stevie Wonder, and Marvin Gaye reflected Motown's politicization. In an address to one of the sessions launching Jesse Jackson's People United to Save Humanity (PUSH) in 1971, Gordy declared, "I have been fortunate to be able to provide opportunities for young people. . . . Opportunities are supposed to knock once in a lifetime, but too often we have to knock for an opportunity. The first obligation we (as black businessmen) have is to ourselves and our own employees, the second is to create opportunities for others."

The Black Student Movement

The most dramatic expression of militant assertiveness after 1968 occurred among black college students. The black power generation of students was committed to transforming society and institutions of higher education by agitating for curricula reform and the

22-1

22-2

22-3

22-4

22-5

22-6

South Carolina State College Massacre, 1968, Orangeburg, South Carolina. The three young men killed in the Orangeburg Massacre were Henry Smith and Samuel Hammond, both 18, and 17-year-old high school student Delano Middleton. See *Scarred Justice* (2008), a powerful and illuminating PBS documentary film by Judy Richardson.

establishment of Black Studies programs and departments. Some observers describe the period of activism between 1968 and 1975 as the "second phase" of the black students' movement.

The Orangeburg Massacre

In this view, students at southern black colleges launched the first phase in the early 1960s. It began with the sit-ins in Greensboro, North Carolina, and the Freedom Rides and culminated in the Mississippi Freedom Summer of 1964. By 1968, however, many of the student organizations that had grown out of the civil rights movement were invested in mobilizing local communities to overthrow the remaining vestiges of overt discrimination and segregation. The massacre of black students at South Carolina State College in Orangeburg on February 8, 1968, was an appalling demonstration of state violence and a failure of the justice system. Students attending the historically black institution had protested a local bowling alley's whites-only admission policy. When the tension and protests escalated, state officials deployed the highway patrol and National Guard. On the evening of February 8, the students assembled at the front of the campus and taunted the officers. Some threw rocks, bricks, and bottles. One officer was hit by a piece of lumber. Later, without warning, nine highway patrolmen opened fire on the students with shotguns. The officers killed three young men and wounded 28. Most of them were shot in the back. All the officers involved were later acquitted, but a young black activist and SNCC leader, Cleveland Sellers, was convicted of rioting and served nearly a year in prison.

Black Studies

The movement for Black Studies and the transformation of college curriculums owed some of its inspiration to the black power and black arts movements. The Black Studies revolution on campus began with the enrollment of large numbers of black students in predominantly white institutions across the country. These students demanded courses in black history, culture, literature, and art as alternatives to the "Eurocentric" bias of the average university curriculum. Many black students also formed all-black student organizations.

The overall status of black people in education reflected the accomplishments of the classic phase of the civil rights movement, but the black power generation was determined to make its own mark on the struggle. In 1960 only 227,000 black Americans attended the nation's colleges (including those at predominantly black institutions). By 1970, enrollments had increased by 100 percent, and in 1977, 1.1 million black students attended America's universities. This was an almost 500 percent increase over 1960. This generation of students was politically diverse, but they shared the sense of being strangers in a white-controlled environment. Many found the campuses hostile, alien places and discovered little there with which they could identify. They resolved to change this.

At San Francisco State College, Nathan Hare, formerly a professor at Howard University, and black students demanded not only curriculum changes but also the structural transformation of the college. In the 1966–1967 academic year, the Black Student Union orchestrated a strike that involved thousands of students of diverse ethnic and racial backgrounds. The students chose to strike rather than take over buildings so that they could circulate on the campus, increasing their support and maintaining their momentum. Among their demands were the creation of an autonomous degree-granting black studies department and the admission of more black students. The college ultimately created the first black studies department in 1968, with Hare as its head.

Black students also took over administration buildings at other institutions such as Northwestern University, demanding not only that the schools offer more black studies courses and programs and hire more black faculty but also insisting that classrooms and facilities be made available to local black communities. The upheavals that shut down Columbia University in 1968 began when black student members of the Students Afro-American Society and Students for a Democratic Society demonstrated to block construction of a university gymnasium in nearby Morningside Park. The demonstrators argued that the gym would impinge on one of the few parks in Harlem and that the Harlem community vehemently objected to it.

In 1968 Yale University's Black Student Alliance sponsored a symposium to discuss the need, status, and function of Afro-American studies. Conference organizer Armstead Robinson saw it as an attempt to create a viable program of Afro-American studies. In December 1968 the faculty voted to make Yale one of the first major universities in the country to institute a degree-granting African-American studies program. In 1969 Harvard University created an Afro-American Studies Department, and other schools soon followed. By 1973 some 200 black studies programs existed in the United States. By the late 1980s, several of the programs, such as those at Cornell, Yale, and the University of California, Los Angeles, offered master's degrees in African-American studies. In 1988 Temple University in Philadelphia, under the leadership of Dr. Molefi Kete Asante, became the first university to offer a Ph.D. in African-American studies. By 2012 there were at least a dozen doctoral programs in African and African-American Studies.

While there is no universally accepted definition of Black Studies, the discipline has continued to evolve. James E. Turner, founder of Africana studies at Cornell, viewed Black Studies as a collective, interdisciplinary, scholarly approach to the experiences of people of African descent throughout the African Diaspora and the world. History, in black studies, constituted the foundation for analyzing common patterns of life and thought that reflected the social and material conditions of black people. Africana studies or black studies theoreticians have generally agreed on four goals for this new field: (1) it should develop solutions to the problems facing black people in the African Diaspora; (2) it should provide an analysis of black culture and life that challenges and replaces preexisting Eurocentric models; (3) it should promote social change and educational reform throughout the academy; and (4) it should institutionalize the study of black people as a field with its own theories, methods, ideologies, symbols, language, and culture. In short, the first generation of advocates envisioned black studies as a revolutionary, historically grounded, educational reform movement that sought to make the study of African descendants—their culture, problems, belief systems, internationalism, radical traditions, and spirituality—a serious scholarly endeavor with practical implications for improving black people's lives.

22-1
22-2
22-3
22-4
22-5
22-6

The Presidential Election of 1968 and Richard Nixon

22-5 | What specific policies did President Nixon initiate that affected the civil rights of African Americans?

In the presidential campaign of 1968, the Democrats provided the excitement but lost the election. In late 1967 Senator Eugene McCarthy of Minnesota entered the race as the antiwar alternative to Lyndon Johnson, Senator Robert Kennedy of New York entered the race in mid-March, after most of the convention delegates had been pledged to Johnson. When Johnson withdrew, these delegates aligned with Humphrey. Whether Kennedy could have gained the nomination will never be known. In the second traumatic assassination of 1968, Robert Kennedy was killed on June 6 in Los Angeles.

A combustible mixture of grief, anger, bitterness, and antiwar sentiment became the fuel for a Chicago explosion. It was the most tumultuous political convention in modern American history, with Chicago policemen clubbing, gassing, and arresting antiwar demonstrators. In November, Republican Richard Nixon narrowly defeated Humphrey.

Of all modern presidents, Richard Nixon is probably the hardest to pin down with neat ideological labels. By the standards of the early twenty-first century, much of his record seems progressive. He created the Environmental Protection Agency, endorsed an equal rights amendment to the Constitution that would have prohibited gender discrimination, and signed more regulatory legislation than any other president. His naming of Daniel Patrick Moynihan, one of Johnson's experts on social policy, to be his domestic policy adviser illustrates his willingness to innovate in policies affecting African Americans. But Nixon also pursued a "southern strategy" that realigned the Republican Party with the white southern backlash to civil rights and weakened the New Deal coalition.

The "Moynihan Report"

Moynihan first attracted national attention as assistant secretary of labor in the Johnson administration when a confidential memorandum he wrote was leaked to the press. It would later be published as "The Negro Family: The Case for National Action" and is popularly known as the "**Moynihan Report**." Moynihan's guiding assumption was that civil rights legislation, necessary as it was, would not address the problems of the inner city. There, he argued, the breakdown of the "lower-class" black family had led to the "pathology" of juvenile delinquency, illegitimacy, drug addiction, and poor performance in school. He attributed the vulnerability of the black family to "three centuries of almost unimaginable treatment" by white society: exploitation under slavery, the strain of urbanization, and persistent unemployment.

These forces, he argued, weakened the role of black men and resulted in a disproportionate number of dysfunctional female-headed families. In the report's most-often repeated passage, Moynihan declared that the black community had been forced into "a matriarchal structure, [which] because it is so out of line with the rest of American society, seriously retards the progress of the group as a whole, and imposes a crushing burden on the Negro male. . . ."

Although based on the work of black scholars, such as E. Franklin Frazier, Moynihan's condemnation of "matriarchy" drew fire. Black social scientists, such as Joyce Ladner, Andrew Billingsley, and Carol Stack, countered that the structure of the black family reflected a

Moynihan Report Report attributing many of the problems of poor black communities to the breakdown of the "lower-class" black family.

functional adaptation that black people had made to survive in a hostile and racist American society. Historians Herbert Gutman and John Blassingame argued that Moynihan underestimated the prevalence of two-parent black families in the past. Although many of the criticisms of the report were deserved, they diverted attention from its positive thrust. Moynihan wanted to eliminate poverty and unemployment in the black community, and he recommended vigorous enforcement of the civil rights laws to achieve equality of opportunity. Moynihan was one of the first policymakers to appreciate how white resentment of the CAPs and the expansion of the welfare rolls would make both programs politically unfeasible.

Intrigued with Moynihan's independence, Nixon told him to develop a plan to assist poor families. Under the **Family Assistance Plan (FAP)** that Nixon unveiled in the summer of 1969, each family of four with no wage earner would receive an annual payment of $1,600 plus $800 of food stamps. With its across-the-board guarantee of income, the plan eliminated an oppressive welfare bureaucracy and reduced the invidious comparison between "welfare recipients" and everyone else.

Family Assistance Plan (FAP) Plan giving financial assistance to families with no wage earner.

Had it passed, FAP would have promoted two-parent families by removing the prohibition against assistance to dependent children whose fathers were alive, well, and living at home. It would also have encouraged work by requiring able-bodied recipients to accept jobs or vocational training and by providing benefits to those accepting low-paying jobs. But although the House approved the plan, the Senate—under pressure from conservatives who objected to any government programs for the poor and from welfare-rights advocates who complained the payments were too low—killed it.

Busing

Yet, however flexible he might have been on many issues, Nixon was acutely aware that he moved in a changed political environment and particularly in a far more conservative Republican Party. In 1968 it was an influx of southern segregationists whom Barry Goldwater had attracted to the Republican Party in 1964 who Nixon had to appease. For example, South Carolina's Senator Strom Thurmond and his allies demanded that Nixon slow down court-ordered school desegregation in the South.

The Nixon administration crafted a southern strategy and embarked on a collision course with civil rights organizations such as the NAACP, which supported busing to achieve school integration. Thus, the major battle over civil rights in the early 1970s was over the federal courts' willingness to implement desegregation goals by busing students across district lines. Nixon, in 1971, advised federal officials to stop pressing to desegregate schools through "forced busing." He argued that such efforts were ultimately "counterproductive, and not in the interest of better race relations."

Educational segregation in the North reflected residential segregation. In Boston, site of some of the most acrimonious busing protests, schools in black neighborhoods received less funding than their white counterparts. Buildings were derelict, overcrowded, and deficient in supplies and equipment, even desks. In 1974 U.S. Judge W. Arthur Garrity ruled in favor of black parents who had filed a class-action suit against the Boston School Committee. To achieve racial balance in the Boston schools, the judge ordered the busing of several thousand students between mostly white South Boston, Hyde Park, and Dorchester and mostly black Roxbury.

Read on **MyHistoryLab**
Document: The Supreme Court Rules on Busing, *Swann v. Charlotte-Mecklenburg Board of Education,* 1971

White people who opposed busing organized demonstrations and boycotts to prevent their children from being bused into black communities, as well as to prevent black children from being bused into white schools. During the first week of busing, white students and their mothers clashed with police officers outside South Boston High School. Hostilities

Read on **MyHistoryLab**
Document: Ione Malloy Describes the Conflict over Busing in Boston, 1965

continued for weeks despite the arrests of dozens of people and the closing of bars and liquor stores. Sporadic violence persisted for another two years in Boston.

Nixon and the War

Meanwhile, the war in Vietnam seemed to drag on endlessly, with the peace negotiations that had begun in Paris in May 1968 making no apparent progress. Nixon realized that what most Americans disliked about the war was that it was killing their sons and husbands. So in 1969 he began to phase out direct U.S. involvement in the war. This "Vietnamization," he claimed, was made possible by the growing ability of the South Vietnamese to fight for themselves. Along with his domestic record, Nixon's promise to "wind down the war" assured his reelection. In 1972 he defeated South Dakota Senator George McGovern in a landslide.

Few in the Nixon administration, however, took South Vietnam's military capability seriously, and Nixon, just as much as Johnson, was unwilling to "lose" Vietnam. Between 1969 and 1971, Nixon stepped up the war. Even as American soldiers were being sent home, he escalated the air war.

But each time Nixon escalated the war—in 1970 with a joint American–South Vietnamese invasion of Cambodia, in 1971 with American air support for an invasion of Laos, and in 1972 with the bombing of North Vietnam and the mining of its harbors—opposition to it grew. Antiwar demonstrations kept Nixon off balance and may have deterred him from further escalation.

The most dramatic protests came after the invasion of Cambodia in April 1970, which triggered antiwar demonstrations on many campuses. In one such protest, on May 4, Ohio National Guardsmen shot and killed four white students at Kent State University. The response of students across the country was electric: the first nationwide student strike in American history. Ten days later in Mississippi, the shooting and killing of two black students at Jackson State University attracted much less attention from either white students or the media. Finally, in 1973, the United States and North Vietnam signed a peace agreement. Congress then prohibited the reintroduction of American troops or the resumption of bombing, and in 1974 it began cutting off military aid to South Vietnam. The result was predictable: in 1975 the communists launched another offensive, and South Vietnam collapsed.

Nixon became president in 1969 with popular mandates to restore law and order. The disorder that irritated the American public included many things: the inner-city riots, the antiwar demonstrations and campus protests, and the rise in crime. Responding to this mood, Nixon pushed legislation through Congress that gave local law enforcement officials expanded power to use wiretaps and enter premises without advance warning.

But Nixon's personality—a combination of paranoia and ruthlessness—pushed him beyond what the public would tolerate and even beyond the law itself. He confused criminals with principled protesters and political opponents and decided to punish them all. He created an extralegal ring of burglars, operating out of the White House, to gather incriminating information about his opponents. In June 1972 these burglars were caught breaking into Democratic National Committee headquarters in the Watergate apartment complex in Washington. Full details emerged in a Senate investigation in 1973–1974, and on August 9, 1974, threatened with impeachment, Nixon resigned. His downfall, however, left no one of his stature or with his flexible attitude toward public policy to resist the takeover of the Republican Party by more dogmatic conservatives. One early

Read on **MyHistoryLab**
Document: Mayor Maynard Jackson Talks about Race and Politics in Atlanta, 1975

intimation of this was the difficulty Nixon's successor, Gerald Ford, had in securing the 1976 Republican presidential nomination against the right's new hero, former California Governor Ronald Reagan.

The Rise of Black Elected Officials

22-6   **What were some of the political accomplishments of the black power movement in the 1970s?**

In the black power movement that followed the civil rights movement, a new generation of black leaders gained prominence. They were determined to mobilize the newly enfranchised black electorate to win political office. After the Voting Rights Act of 1965, Vernon Jordan, director of the Voter Education Project, coordinated registration drives across the South.

By 1974 there were 1,593 black elected officials outside the South and 2,455 by 1980. Although black people in northern cities had been able to vote for a century and had been slowly developing political muscle and winning representation in state legislatures and on city councils, they had not been able to command an equal voice in city governance. The rise of black power and the Voting Rights Act, however, signaled a new departure. People now eagerly engaged in the electoral process to achieve the political influence to which their numbers entitled them. In 1967 in Cleveland, where the black population had skyrocketed after World War II, Carl Stokes became the first black mayor of a major American city (see Table 22–1), winning with the support of white business leaders and the solid backing of the black community. In the same year prosecutor

TABLE 22-1 BLACK POWER POLITICS: THE ELECTION OF BLACK MAYORS, 1967–1990

Cities	Names	Years in Office
Atlanta, Georgia	Maynard H. Jackson	(1974–82) ; (1990–94)
	Andrew J. Young	(1982–90)
Chicago, Illinois	Harold L. Washington	(1983–90)
Cleveland, Ohio	Carl B. Stokes	(1967–72)
Compton, California	Doris A. Davis	(1973–77)
Detroit, Michigan	Coleman A. Young	(1973–93)
Gary, Indiana	Richard G. Hatcher	(1967–87)
Los Angeles, California	Thomas J. Bradley	(1973–93)
Memphis, Tennessee	Willie W. Herenton	(1991–2009)
Newark, New Jersey	Kenneth A. Gibson	(1970–86)
New Orleans, Louisiana	Ernest N. Morial	(1978–86)
New York, New York	David N. Dinkins	(1990–94)
Raleigh, North Carolina	Clarence E. Lightner	(1973–75)
Roanoke, Virginia	Noel C. Taylor	(1975–92)
Washington, DC	Walter E. Washington	(1974–79)
	Marion S. Barry, Jr.	(1980–90); (1994–98)

African American Mayors of Metropolitan Cities with Populations over 50,000

22-1

22-2

22-3

22-4

22-5

22-6

Richard G. Hatcher became mayor of Gary, Indiana, where the black population had also increased greatly after the war.

The Gary Convention and the Black Political Agenda

These victories made possible one of the most significant events of postwar black political history, the Gary National Black Political Convention of 1972. The co-chairs of the convention were Detroit Congressman Charles Diggs, Hatcher, and writer Amiri Baraka. Political scientist Ronald Walters, who helped plan the convention, recalled that various ideological factions had to be placated to make it work. The nationalists interpreted "black power" to mean that black people should control their own communities and create separate cultural institutions distinct from those of white society. These views clashed with those of the black elected officials represented by Stokes and Hatcher. According to Walters, "It was this body of people who really were contending for the national leadership of the black community in the early seventies. And in the seventies this new group of black elected officials joined the civil rights leaders and became a new leadership class, but there was sort of a conflict in outlook between them and the more indigenous, social, grass roots-oriented nationalist movement."

Approximately 8,000 people gathered to develop an agenda for black empowerment. The discussions about bloc voting, the efficacy of coalitions, and the feasibility of a third party inspired scores of individual African Americans to run for local office. The convention was not homogeneous, however, and no unified black consensus emerged.

Discussions over strategies to secure common interests revealed deep-seated internal divisions that allowed ancillary issues to provoke even more impassioned disagreement. Coleman Young and other Michigan delegates walked out to protest a proposal for African Americans to reject "discriminatory" unions and form their own. Others walked out over a resolution condemning Israel for its "expansionist policy" toward the Palestinians. Others argued that "forced racial integration of schools" through busing insulted black students and would cost black teachers their jobs.

Nonetheless, the Gary convention signaled a shift in the political focus of the black community toward electoral politics and away from mass demonstrations and protests. Unity continued to elude subsequent conventions, however, and delegates at the last National Black Convention at Little Rock, Arkansas, in 1974 abandoned the idea of a black political party. Deep ideological differences and institutional cleavages precluded coalitions and cooperation between black nationalists and the rising numbers of black elected officials. These same differences prevented some nationalists and elected officials from taking seriously the 1972 Democratic Party presidential bid of New York Congresswoman Shirley Chisholm.

Shirley Chisholm: "I Am the People's Politician"

Shirley Anita St. Hill was born on November 20, 1924, in Brooklyn, New York, to Charles St. Hill, a factory laborer from

Shirley Chisholm was outspoken against the Vietnam War and a fierce advocate of women's rights.

VOICES Shirley Chisholm's Speech to the U.S. House of Representatives

Excerpts from "The Business of America Is War, and It Is Time for a Change," March 16, 1969

"Secretary of Defense Melvin Laird came to Capitol Hill. . . . His mission was to sell the antiballistic-missile insanity to the Senate. . . . Mr. Laird talked of being prepared to spend at least two more years in Vietnam. Two more years, two more years of hunger for Americans, of death for our best young men, of children here at home suffering the lifelong handicap of not having a good education when they are young.

Two more years of high taxes, collected to feed the cancerous growth of a Defense Department budget that now consumes two-thirds of our federal income. Two more years of too little being done to fight our greatest enemies, poverty, prejudice and neglect, here in our own country. Two more years of fantastic waste in the Defense Department and of penny pinching on social programs. Our country cannot survive two more years, or four, of these kinds of policies. It must stop— this year—now. . . .

We Americans have come to feel that it is our mission to make the world free. We believe that we are the good guys, everywhere—in Vietnam, in Latin America, wherever we go. We believe we are the good guys at home, too. When the Kerner Commission told white America what black America had always known, that prejudice and hatred built the nation's slums, maintain them and profit by them, white America would not believe it. But it is true. Unless we start to fight and defeat the enemies of poverty and racism in our own country and make our talk of equality and opportunity ring true, we are exposed as hypocrites in the eyes of the world when we talk about making other people free.

We are now spending eighty billion dollars a year on defense—that is two-thirds of every tax dollar. At this time, gentlemen, the business of America is war, and it is time for a change."

1. **What reasons does Chisholm give for her opposition to the war in Vietnam?**
2. **What connections does she draw between support for the war and poverty and racism in the United States?**

SOURCE: Warren J. Halliburton, ed., *Historic Speeches of African Americans* (New York: Franklin Watts, 1993). 141–43.

22-1
22-2
22-3
22-4
22-5
22-6

Guyana, and Ruby Seale St. Hill, a seamstress from Barbados. She earned a B.A. from Brooklyn College in sociology in 1946 and worked as a nursery school teacher and then as director of two day care centers. In 1949 she married Conrad Q. Chisholm, a private investigator. From 1964 to 1968 she served in the New York State Assembly. In 1968 Chisholm defeated James Farmer, former leader of CORE, to become the first African-American woman to serve in Congress. Chisholm retired from politics in 1983. In the late 1960s and early 1970s, she remained an outspoken critic of the Vietnam War and a fierce proponent of the war on poverty.

Black People Gain Local Offices

Despite the demise of the National Black Convention movement, African Americans registered impressive gains in electoral politics. Statistics indicate the success of black politicians. When the leaders first convened the Gary convention, there were 13 African-American members of Congress. By 2010 there were 42. In 1972 there were 2,427 black elected officials, among them Texas state senator Barbara Jordan. By 2001 there were 9,101.

22-1

22-2

22-3

22-4

22-5

22-6

An amendment to the Voting Rights Act in 1975 enabled minorities to challenge at-large voting practices that diluted the impact of bloc voting. This helped increase the number of black elected officials. Districts were redrawn with race as the predominant factor. On November 5, 1985, state senator L. Douglas Wilder was elected lieutenant governor in Virginia, making him the first African-American lieutenant governor in a southern state since Reconstruction. In 1989 he was elected governor, making him the first black governor of any state since Reconstruction.

Between 1971 and 1975, the number of African-American mayors rose from 8 to 135, leading to the founding of the National Conference of Black Mayors in 1974. In 1973 Coleman Young in Detroit and Thomas Bradley in Los Angeles became the first African-American mayors of cities of more than a million citizens. Ten years later, in 1983, Chicago swore in its first black mayor, Harold Washington. The era of the black elected official had arrived.

Economic Downturn

The 1970s were a decade of recessions and economic instability. Many black people experienced this economic downturn as a depression. During the 1970s, as the gap between the incomes of the upper 20 percent of African Americans and their white counterparts narrowed, the gap between black men and women at the bottom of the economic ladder and their white counterparts expanded. Poor black people were losing ground. In 1969 approximately 10 percent of white men and 25 percent of black men earned less than $10,000 (in 1984 constant dollars). In 1984 about 40 percent of black men between age 25 and 55 earned less than $10,000 compared with 20 percent of comparable white men. Put a different way, between 1970 and 1986, the proportion of black families with incomes of less than $10,000 grew from 26.8 to 30.2 percent. Still, there were some improvements. The black middle class grew. In 1970, 4.7 percent of black families had incomes of more than $50,000. By 1986 the number had almost doubled to 8.8 percent. But, in general, the relative economic status of black workers did not improve.

Black Americans and the Carter Presidency

In 1976 the United States celebrated its bicentennial. For African Americans, it was an important year, but for another reason. For the first time since 1964, the man most of them voted for was elected president—Jimmy Carter, a former governor of Georgia. Ninety percent of African-American voters favored the soft-spoken, religious Democrat over President Gerald Ford. As in 1960, their votes were crucial. Without them, Carter could not have even carried his native South.

Black Appointees

Carter acknowledged his debt to the black electorate by appointing African Americans to highly visible posts. He named Patricia Harris secretary of housing and urban development, making her the first black woman to serve in the cabinet. Carter appointed Andrew Young, former congressman from Georgia and a longtime political ally, ambassador to the United Nations. Clifford Alexander, Jr., became the secretary of the army. Eleanor Holmes Norton became the first woman to chair the Equal Employment Opportunity Commission (EEOC). Ernest Green, who had been one of the nine students to desegregate Little Rock's Central High School, was appointed assistant secretary of labor. Wade McCree was appointed solicitor general in the Justice Department. Drew Days III became assistant attorney general for civil rights. Historian and former University of Colorado chancellor Mary Frances Berry was appointed assistant secretary for education. Carter also named Louis Martin his special

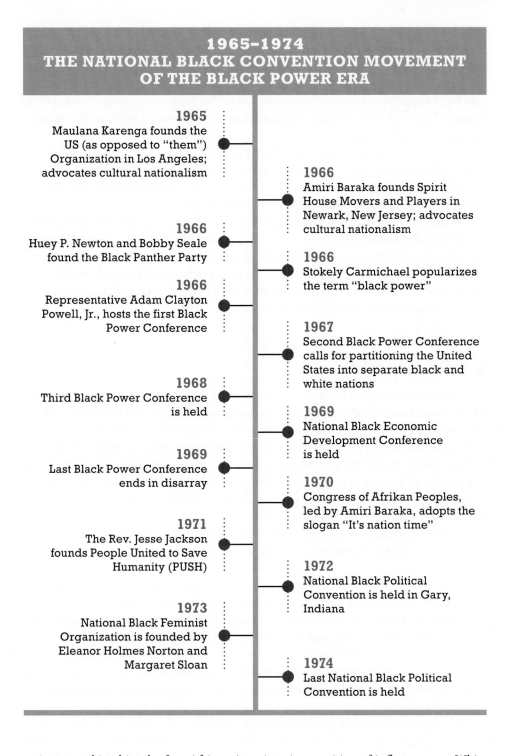

1965–1974
THE NATIONAL BLACK CONVENTION MOVEMENT OF THE BLACK POWER ERA

1965
Maulana Karenga founds the US (as opposed to "them") Organization in Los Angeles; advocates cultural nationalism

1966
Amiri Baraka founds Spirit House Movers and Players in Newark, New Jersey; advocates cultural nationalism

1966
Huey P. Newton and Bobby Seale found the Black Panther Party

1966
Stokely Carmichael popularizes the term "black power"

1966
Representative Adam Clayton Powell, Jr., hosts the first Black Power Conference

1967
Second Black Power Conference calls for partitioning the United States into separate black and white nations

1968
Third Black Power Conference is held

1969
National Black Economic Development Conference is held

1969
Last Black Power Conference ends in disarray

1970
Congress of Afrikan Peoples, led by Amiri Baraka, adopts the slogan "It's nation time"

1971
The Rev. Jesse Jackson founds People United to Save Humanity (PUSH)

1972
National Black Political Convention is held in Gary, Indiana

1973
National Black Feminist Organization is founded by Eleanor Holmes Norton and Margaret Sloan

1974
Last National Black Political Convention is held

22-1

22-2

22-3

22-4

22-5

22-6

assistant, making him the first African American in a position of influence on a White House staff.

Carter's Domestic Policies

There are many ways to judge the significance of the Carter presidency to African Americans. Carter's black appointments were practically and symbolically important. Never had so many black men and women occupied positions that had direct and immediate impact on the day-to-day operations of the federal government. Carter also helped cement gains for civil rights. When Congress passed legislation to stop busing for schoolchildren as a means of integrating the schools, Carter vetoed it. He tried to improve fair employment practices by strengthening the powers of the EEOC. His Justice Department chose cases to prosecute under the Fair Housing Act that involved widespread discrimination, to make the greatest possible impact.

Yet most African Americans found Carter's overall record unsatisfactory. He failed to help Democrats in Congress pass either full-employment or universal healthcare bills. Under his watch Congress cut social welfare programs to balance the budget, and the cuts included school lunch programs and student financial aid.

A sluggish economy diminished Carter's popularity, but it was the Iran hostage crisis in 1979 that doomed his chances for reelection. For many black people, Carter had become a disappointment, who had done little to bring about greater social justice and economic advancement. Republicans' nomination of the conservative Ronald Reagan, however, left black voters no alternative to Carter. In the election of 1980, 90 percent of black voters again supported Carter, but could not prevent his defeat.

CONCLUSION

The black power and black arts movements continued the struggle for freedom in northern and western cities and states where housing discrimination, high unemployment, and unrelenting police brutality sparked rebellions that resulted in many deaths and widespread destruction in Los Angeles, Newark, Detroit, and other cities. Although African Americans did not create a third party, they were able to elect an impressive number of black mayors and send the first two black women to the United States House of Representatives. Thus, one of the black power era's most enduring political legacies was the rise of black elected officials and the perfection of coalition building.

Clearly the most triumphant dimension of the black studies movement was the revolutionary change in academic knowledge and in the expansion of opportunities for black students and professors. Black student militancy resulted in structural changes in the academy with the establishment of black studies departments and cultural centers. The legacies of the Black Panther Party, including its social service experiments in providing free breakfasts to school children in impoverished communities and operating free healthcare clinics for residents, have yet to be fully appreciated and were often overshadowed by the relentless vilification of party leaders and members by white police authorities and media. Throughout the late 1960s and 1970s, the black arts movement opened up new venues for cultivations of black unity and an empowering positive black identity.

The legislative successes of the civil rights movement, the Civil Rights Act of 1964, the Voting Rights Act of 1965, and affirmative action were important steps in the long journey toward an egalitarian society. To varying degrees, Presidents Johnson, Nixon, and Carter attempted to address the needs of the poor. Their efforts produced mixed results, hampered by the disastrous war in Vietnam and massive white backlash against school busing and government-mandated desegregation. In the 1980s, Republicans reaped the benefits of the Democratic Party's disarray, and the plight of the black poor worsened.

22-1
22-2
22-3
22-4
22-5
22-6

CHAPTER TIMELINE

AFRICAN-AMERICAN EVENTS

NATIONAL EVENTS

1965–1966

1965

Malcolm X assassinated

Watts riot

Voting Rights Act of 1965 enacted

1966

Black Panther Party formed

Stokely Carmichael coins the slogan "black power"

Martin Luther King's Chicago campaign begins

Edward Brooke of Massachusetts elected
the first black U.S. senator since Reconstruction

Robert C. Weaver becomes first black cabinet officer

Strike at San Francisco State University results
in first black studies program

1965

President Johnson authorizes the bombing of
North Vietnam

1966

National Organization for Women (NOW) formed

1967–1968

1967

Uprisings in Newark, Detroit, and other cities

Muhammad Ali refuses to be drafted

Thurgood Marshall confirmed as first black
Supreme Court justice

Adam Clayton Powell, Jr., denied his seat in
Congress

1968

Kerner Commission Report

Poor People's Campaign in Washington, DC

Orangeburg Massacre

Martin Luther King, Jr., assassinated

Shirley Chisholm elected to the U.S. House of
Representatives

Carl Stokes elected mayor of Cleveland and Richard
Hatcher elected mayor of Gary, Indiana

1968

North Vietnam launches Tet Offensive

United States and North Vietnam begin peace talks

Johnson declines to run for another term

Robert Kennedy assassinated

Richard M. Nixon elected president

Secret bombing of Cambodia

1969–1970

1969

Harvard establishes an Afro-American studies
program

Maulana Karenga writes *Introduction to Black
Studies*

Black Panther leaders Fred Hampton and Mark
Clark killed in Chicago police raid

1970

U.S. incursion into Cambodia

Kent State killings

CHAPTER TIMELINE

AFRICAN-AMERICAN EVENTS

NATIONAL EVENTS

1970
Jackson State killings
Angela Davis placed on the FBI's Ten Most Wanted list

1971–1972

1971
Jesse Jackson founds PUSH

Busing to achieve integration begins

1972
First National Black Political Convention
held in Gary, Indiana

Shirley Chisholm makes a bid for the
Democratic presidential nomination

Angela Davis acquitted

1972
Watergate break-in

Nixon reelected president

1973–1974

1973
Thomas Bradley elected mayor of Los Angeles

Coleman Young elected mayor of Detroit

1974
National Council for Black Studies formed

1974
Watergate hearings

Nixon resigns

1975–1976

1975
Antibusing protests in Boston

1977
Andrew Young named ambassador
to the United Nations

1975
South Vietnam falls

1976
Jimmy Carter elected president

On MyHistoryLab

✓ Study and Review on MyHistoryLab

REVIEW QUESTIONS

1. Why did African Americans in Watts, Newark, and Detroit rebel in 1965–1967? What did these rebellions suggest about the value of the civil rights movement victories?

2. How did the visions and ideals, successes and failures of Martin Luther King, Jr., compare with those of Lyndon Johnson? Why were these men at odds with each other?

3. What role did African Americans play in the Vietnam War?

4. In what ways can the presidency of Richard Nixon be considered progressive? Which reforms initiated by President Johnson did Nixon advance once he took office? What was "the southern strategy"?

5. What were the major ideological concerns of the artists of the black arts movement? To what extent did James Baldwin and Amiri Baraka have similar views about art, consciousness, aesthetics, and politics?

6. Why did African Americans not form a third political party? Why was the rise of black elected officials so significant?

7. Why were African Americans disappointed with the presidency of Jimmy Carter?

23

African Americans in the Twenty-First Century 1980–2010

LEARNING OBJECTIVES

23-1 Why are so many African Americans less wealthy and healthy than white Americans?

23-2 What are some of the reasons for continued poverty among African Americans?

23-3 What achievements have African Americans made in the areas of music, literature, and film from the 1980s through the twenty-first century?

23-4 Why has rap music achieved international popularity?

23-5 What is the main philosophy of Afrocentricity?

23-6 What are the strengths and tensions operating within the black church today?

23-7 What are Louis Farrakhan's views and how has he been instrumental in helping African Americans?

23-8 Why has black identity become more complicated in the twenty-first century?

In *The Souls of Black Folk,* W. E. B. Du Bois dreamed of a nation in which black people could be both African and American, embracing their own rich cultural heritage and sharing it with America while becoming full-fledged citizens. This merging of the "two-ness" of the African and American "souls" did not happen in Du Bois's lifetime, but at his death in 1963, the civil rights movement was poised on the edge of its greatest successes. Had Du Bois lived to the dawn of the twenty-first century, he would have been both pleased by the progress made toward fulfilling his dream and saddened by the extent to which the ideals of that dream remain unfulfilled for so many African Americans.

Co-headlining the "Heart of the City" tour, "Hip-Hip Royalty" Mary J. Blige and Jay-Z brought the house down in Detroit (2008).

In the 2000s, many African Americans advanced to the top ranks of government, the military, sports, entertainment, business, the professions, and academia. The African "soul" that Du Bois urged black Americans to take pride in moved from the shadowy edges of American culture to its heart, and black Americans were honored for their contributions to the nation's music, language, and fine arts.

As a result of the legislative successes of the modern civil rights movement, laws now prohibit racial segregation, disfranchisement, and job discrimination. In their wake, millions of black men and women escaped the deep poverty to which nearly all African Americans had been confined when Du Bois wrote *Souls*. Like other Americans, many more black people now complete high school and college and live healthier and longer lives, although white Americans still, on average, earn more and live longer.

Undoubtedly, Du Bois would be appalled by the extreme poverty, poor education, substance addiction, and violent crime that still plague inner-city and rural black populations. But he might not be surprised by the deep racism and ugly stereotyping that continue to define the journey of black people in America, notwithstanding the election of Barack Obama to the presidency of the United States in 2008 and his reelection in 2012.

A "two-ness" dilemma persists a century after Du Bois wrote about "double consciousness," and contemporary scholars, authors, and public intellectuals ponder questions about "post-black" and "post-racial" identities. Such debates are complicated both by the successes African Americans have achieved in recent decades and by demographic and global political changes. Tensions have always festered between a racially defined identity and the many other ways in which African Americans define themselves. Differences of class, color, ethnicity, belief, and region have divided Americans for centuries. Today, other factors further complicate identities, including sexual preference, religious affiliation, immigration status, and political philosophy. Reconciling all these self-understandings within a larger racial identity remains one of the major challenges of the continuing African-American odyssey.

Progress and Poverty: Income, Education, and Health

23-1 | **Why are so many African Americans less wealthy and healthy than white Americans?**

After the triumphs of the civil rights era, many African Americans made great strides in overcoming the economic and educational disadvantages that had plagued their ancestors. Partly as a result of this progress, they are living longer, healthier lives. Yet, the disparities between the levels of wealth, schooling, and health status of African Americans and the white majority, although narrowed, have persisted.

23-1

23-2

23-3

23-4

23-5

23-6

23-7

23-8

23-1

23-2

23-3

23-4

23-5

23-6

23-7

23-8

The late *Ebony* and *Jet* publisher John Johnson.

High-Achieving African Americans

The decades after 1970 witnessed a consolidation of black economic, civic, and political progress and the expansion of a black middle and upper class of professionals, media celebrities, and business entrepreneurs. The success of the black upper class was exemplified by the prominence of highly visible African Americans such as media mogul Oprah Winfrey, Bill Clinton's secretary of commerce Ronald Brown, chairman of the Joint Chiefs of Staff and later secretary of state Colin Powell, and his immediate successor as secretary of state, Condoleezza Rice, and Harvard University professor Henry Louis Gates. To be sure, the ultra-rich remained rare in the black community, but their ranks grew. Winfrey, Cosby, Michael Jackson, Michael Jordan, Jay-Z, and Beyoncé acquired fortunes as entertainers or athletes.

The career of Reginald Lewis illustrates the possibilities open to black people in other industries. Armed with a degree from Harvard Law School, he purchased the McCall Pattern Company in 1984. In 1987 he bought Beatrice Foods, an international packaged goods company, for $2.5 billion. At the time it was the largest leveraged buyout in U.S. history, and Lewis became the wealthiest African American. Before his death in 1993, Lewis gave back to his community by donating millions of dollars to Howard University and the NAACP.

African Americans' Quest for Economic Security

The achievements of the most successful African Americans are impressive, but the increase in job opportunities, income, and wealth for a broad cross section of working African Americans is more significant. Before the 1960s most black men worked in the lower rungs of agriculture, construction, transportation, and manufacturing. Black women predominantly worked in domestic and food service jobs.

Antidiscrimination laws and affirmative action programs allowed millions of black people to climb up the rungs of career ladders. In 1940, for example, only 5.2 percent of black men and 6.4 percent of black women worked in white-collar occupations. Today, those figures have risen to 35.3 percent for black men and 62.3 percent for black women. Many black people have moved into jobs in government, education, and banking, and into professions including engineering, law, and medicine.

Middle-class black family income increased dramatically. In 1940 only 1 percent of black families, compared with 12 percent of white families, had incomes at least twice as high as the government's poverty line. By 1998, 50 percent of black families did, compared with 73 percent of white families. The disparity of income between similar families also decreased. In 1960 two-parent black families earned 61 percent as much as two-parent white families, but by 1998 they earned 87 percent as much. The economic boom of the Clinton presidency, from 1993 to 2001, was particularly beneficial to black people. Although the median income of black families remains well below that of white families, it has risen substantially (see Figure 23–1).

During the 1990s many African-American families narrowed the income gap, yet their average wealth remained far behind that of white families. This was due partly to the long heritage of poverty during which most black people accumulated little property or other wealth to pass on to their children. It was also closely tied to differences in the proportions of black and white people who owned their own homes because for most American families, their house is their primary asset. Because of low incomes and systematic discrimination, only 35 percent of African-American families owned their homes in 1950. By 2005, thanks to rising incomes, laws that barred discrimination in housing, and government programs,

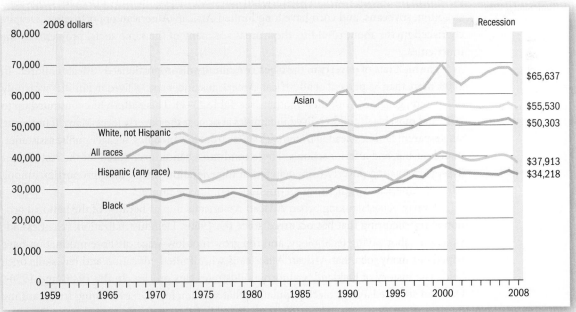

FIGURE 23–1 MEDIAN INCOME OF BLACK, ETHNIC, AND WHITE HOUSEHOLDS, 1967–2011

SOURCE: *U.S. Census Bureau,* Income, Poverty and Health Insurance Coverage in the United States: 2011 *(September 2011), 5.* http://www.census.gov/prod/2011pubs/p60-243.pdf.

46.8 percent of African Americans owned their own homes (the figure for white owner-ship was 70.7 percent). However, the economic recession that began in 2008 devastated black communities. Unethical bank lending practices along with an array of bad decisions left millions of African-American home owners vulnerable to foreclosures. The economic downturn dramatically increased the unemployment rates among African Americans to percentages unseen since the Great Depression of the 1930s. Almost 16 percent of African Americans were unemployed at the end of 2012 compared to around 7.9 percent of white Americans.

The Persistence of Black Poverty

23-2   **What are some of the reasons for continued poverty among African Americans?**

Although many African Americans enjoyed greater absolute and relative increases in in-come by the turn of the millennium, too many remained mired in poverty. The poverty rate for black people had dipped to a low of 22.7 percent during the Clinton boom but rose to 24.5 percent during George W. Bush's presidency and continues to outpace all other groups under President Obama. Equally as alarming, more poor black people remain trapped in inner-city neighborhoods plagued by gang warfare, crime, substance abuse, and HIV/AIDS.

In the urban impoverished communities where so many of the young live, they are cut off from meaningful participation in the social and economic life of the nation and ex-perience fewer educational and other opportunities that might allow them to escape from poverty. Another large concentration of black poverty is found in depressed rural areas, es-pecially in the South, where mechanization and declining commodity prices for crops such as cotton, soybeans, and corn have long limited African-American opportunities. Despite cherished myths about rural life, these areas see many of the same social problems as the inner cities.

The high rate of poverty in the black community disproportionately affects children. In 2008, more than 55 percent of all African Americans under age 18 lived in families with only one parent, generally with their mother (see Table 23–1). This pattern has continued up to 2012 and most black children lived in families at or near the poverty level. Many, if not most, single-parent families headed by females suffer from low incomes, meager public assistance, poor housing, and inferior schools. These conditions handicap children for the rest of their lives, perpetuating poverty from generation to generation. Given their proportion among African-American youth, this is an ominous sign for the future.

Poverty persists among urban African Americans in part because of the national eco-nomic restructuring that has occurred since the 1960s. Deindustrialization, relentless ad-vances in labor-saving technology, and the growth of low-wage offshore production have wiped out many jobs that African Americans with limited education and few skills once held. The history of Oakland, California, illustrates this process. In the 1940s and 1950s, Oakland attracted a large black population that was employed in everything from canning food to assembling automobiles. Thousands of black laborers unloaded ships at the ports or worked in the vast yards and repair facilities of the railroads. By the 1960s, however, manufacturing in Oakland was already in flight to lower-wage areas in the United States or overseas; in addition, the port was mechanized, which reduced both the need for longshore-men and the cost of importing foreign goods. Highways, often built through the heart of

Read on **MyHistoryLab**
Document: A Black
Sociology Professor Talks
About Teenage Pregnancy in
the Black Community, 1995

Read on
MyHistoryLab
Document:
Exploring America:
Growing Inequality

TABLE 23–1 BLACK CHILDREN UNDER AGE 18 AND THEIR LIVING ARRANGEMENTS, 1960–2012 (NUMBERS IN THOUSANDS)

Year	Children under 18 Years Old, Total	Two Parents	Living with One Parent			No Parents	
			Total	Mother Only	Father Only	Other Relatives	Nonrelatives
1960	8,649	5,795	1,896	1,723	173	826	132
1970	9,423	5,508	2,996	2,783	213	822	97
1980	9,375	3,956	4,297	4,117	180	999	123
1990	10,019	3,781	5,485	5,132	353	655	98
2000	11,412	4,286	6,080	5,596	484	879	167
2010	11,273	4,424	6,006	5,601	405	740	103
2012	11,196	4,255	6,160	5,687	473	679	102

The increase in the number of children under age 18 living with their mothers only demonstrates the change in the composition of the African-American households in the post-civil rights era. In 2012, most (over 50 percent) black children under age 18 lived with their mothers only. In 1960 only approximately 30 percent of black children lived with their mothers only, while 70 percent lived in two-parent households.

SOURCE: U.S. Census Bureau, Living Arrangements of Black Children Under 18 Years Old: 1960 to Present, Table CH-3. http://www.census.gov/hhes/families/data/children.html.

black business districts, replaced much of Oakland's rail traffic while displacing residents and weakening neighborhoods.

By 2000, Oakland had become a predominantly residential city through which goods made around the globe would flow but in which relatively little was produced or sold. This shift created wealth for some and provided jobs for many middle-class African Americans, but it left many of the once thriving black districts in the city without legitimate work. This paved the way for the rise of drug-related crime that plagued parts of the city. The economic boom of the late 1990s did improve the lot of many inner-city residents, but the staying power of this renewal was weakened in the face of the severe recession that began in 2008 and persisted through the end of President Barack Obama's first term (see Figure 23–2).

Impact of the 2008–2010 Economic Recession on Employed Black Women

In 2008, 7 out of 10 mothers with children under age 18 were in the labor force. In 2008 1 out of every 10 women maintaining a family was unemployed, a rate that exceeded the highest rate (9 percent) experienced during the 2001 recession and the "jobless recovery" that followed it. Black and Hispanic women in this group experienced unemployment at rates of 13.3 percent and 11 percent, respectively. Black female heads of household started both the 2001 and 2008 recessions with an unemployment rate just under 10 percent, well above the average for all female heads of household. In 2009 the unemployment rate for black female heads of household was 3.7 percentage points higher than it was in 2008.

Extended unemployment benefits, nutrition programs, Medicaid, and tax cuts will bring some immediate relief for these families. Jobs created in education, health care, and child care tend to disproportionately employ women. This will help ensure that as the economy slowly begins to recover, female-headed households will not be left behind.

Read on MyHistoryLab Document: The Bottom of the Economic Totem Pole: African American Women in the Workplace

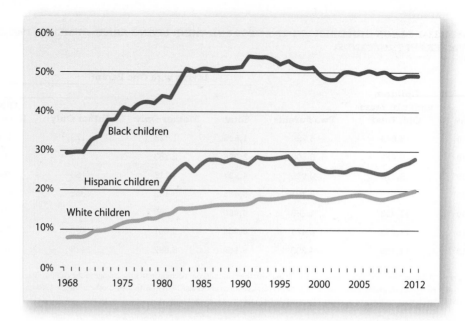

FIGURE 23–2 PERCENTAGE OF CHILDREN UNDER AGE 18 LIVING WITH THEIR MOTHERS, 1968–2012

NOTE: *Direct identification of both parents began in 2007, resulting in the ability to identify children living with two unmarried parents.*

SOURCE: *U.S. Census Bureau,* Current Population Survey, Annual Social and Economic Supplements, *1968–2012. Figure CH-2-3-4.* http://www.census.gov/hhes/families/files/graphics/CH-2-3-4.pdf

Racial Incarceration

The growth in crime in inner-city communities throughout the 1980s and 1990s combined with a national shift toward aggressive policing and harsher sentencing to vastly increase the imprisonment rates of African-American boys and men. From 1954 to 2005, the black prison population increased by almost 900 percent, from 98,000 to 910,000. As Table 23–2 shows, while the absolute numbers of both black and white prisoners have begun to fall, African Americans still, in 2011, make up almost half of the nation's prisoners even though only about 12 percent of Americans are black.

Education One-Half Century after *Brown*

Education is the key factor that distinguishes the African Americans who achieve economic success from those who do not. Black rates of school completion have advanced tremendously in the past half century. Many more black youths graduate from high school than ever before. In 1960 only 37.7 percent of African Americans between ages 25 and 29 had completed high school, but by 2007 the U.S. Department of Education estimated that 88.8 percent had completed high school, compared to 93.6 percent for white Americans. Black enrollment in college also rose from a mere 136,000 in 1960 to almost 2 million in 2009. These rates of achievement placed African Americans among the most educated groups of people in the world. African Americans between the ages of 25 and 34 are now more likely than young adults in Canada, France, Italy, and Britain to have completed high school, and they are more likely than those in Italy, Britain, Germany, and France to have completed college.

Yet, despite these encouraging figures, black people who want an education, particularly those in poor inner-city and rural areas, still face severe problems. Schools starved of funds

TABLE 23-2 RATES OF BLACK INCARCERATION

Estimated number of prisoners held in state or federal prison, by gender and race per 100,000 (December 2010).

	Males				Females		
Total	White	Black	Hispanic	Total	White	Black	Hispanic
4,791	459	3,074	1,258	257	47	133	77

Estimated number of prisoners held in state or federal prison, by age, gender, and race per 100,000 (December 2010).

	Males				Females			
Age	Total	White	Black	Hispanic	Total	White	Black	Hispanic
20–29	**17,200**	1,618	10,967	4,615	**1,002**	197	481	324
30–39	**21,249**	2,056	13,899	5,294	**1,200**	260	598	342
40–49	**16,139**	1,704	10,388	4,047	**988**	187	528	273
50–59	**9,105**	899	5,680	2,526	**436**	67	226	143
60–64	**2,174**	233	1,262	679	**74**	12	33	29

This table reflects the disproportionately larger number of young African-American males held in prisons and jails compared to white males. The largest number of black women in prison is between 30 and 39 years of age. The largest number of black men is between 30 and 39 years of age.

SOURCE: *U.S. Department of Justice, Bureau of Justice Statistics.* Prisoners in 2010, *Revised 2/9/12. Appendix Table 14-15. http://bjs.ojp.usdoj.gov/content/pub/pdf/p10.pdf.*

by regressive tax policies and the movement of wealthier people—both black and white—to the suburbs are almost predestined to fail. Affirmative action programs that made a place for African-American students have been cut in many states, resulting in declining enrollments among black students at the top schools. For impoverished black youth, the combined effect of failing schools and few opportunities results in dropout rates sharply higher than those for more affluent African Americans.

Challenging *Brown*

For over 50 years, conservative groups challenged the meaning and intent of the 1954 Supreme Court decision in *Brown v. Board of Education.* In two 2007 decisions, the justices appointed to the Court by both Presidents Bush moved to end the practice of racial classification as a means to achieve racial diversity in public schools. The two cases involved school assignment plans developed by the boards of education in Seattle, Washington, and in Jefferson County, Kentucky, which

Today African-American students pursue education in diverse fields. The Irwin S. Chanin School of Architecture at Cooper Union for the Advancement of Science and Art in New York City offers one path to a brighter future.

includes the city of Louisville. The Seattle school district classified children as white or nonwhite and used this system as the basis for allocating slots to attend the better city high schools. On the other hand, the Jeffers on County school district classified children as either black or as "other" and used that system to assign students to elementary schools and to inform decisions about transfer requests.

The Court ruled that both plans violated the Fourteenth Amendment, which guarantees equal protection of the laws. Chief Justice John Roberts, writing the majority opinion, declared, "The way to stop discrimination on the basis of race is to stop discriminating on the basis of race." In a separate opinion, Justice Clarence Thomas insisted, "Racial imbalance is not segregation," adding, "there is no danger of re-segregation."

In a spirited dissent, Justice Stephen Breyer called the majority decision a reversal of precedent and a fundamental weakening of *Brown.* Breyer argued that the majority opinion amounted to a retreat from the principle that allowed local school districts to exercise discretion about the best means to end racial segregation, curb resegregation due to segregated housing patterns, and overcome class division and racial exclusion.

The Court's decisions had affected hundreds of school districts across the country. School systems will now have to struggle to devise their own strategies to avoid or reduce racial concentration, to reverse the wide gaps between white and black students on state tests in reading and math, and to resist the resegregation of schools that has arisen from the growing patterns of housing segregation.

The Health Gap

Read on MyHistoryLab Document: Health Issues in the Black Community, 2005

As in income and education, African Americans have made significant progress toward living longer, healthier lives, but they still suffer greater incidence of disease and mortality for most major illnesses. In 1970, the first year for which we have statistics, life expectancy was 60 years for black men and 68.3 years for black women. By 2009 it had risen to 69.5 and 76.5 years, respectively. Improvements in the quality of care accessible to black people are partly responsible for these increases, but higher infant mortality rates and greater numbers of deaths from diseases kept them well below the 75.7-year life span for white men and 80.8 years for white women.

Cancer and HIV/AIDS infections remain among the greatest threats to black health. African-American men are more likely than white men to develop cancer and die from the disease within five years of diagnosis. Black women have a lower incidence of cancer than do white women, but those black women who do get cancer die at a higher rate from it than white women. Cancer is a complicated disease caused by a variety of factors. Some of the higher rate of its incidence among African Americans is related to risky behaviors common to all impoverished people: smoking, heavy drinking, obesity, and ignorance of health care. A lack of access to insurance or quality health care compounds the impact of these behaviors. Many African Americans also mistrust the healthcare system, while medical workers tend to treat black cancer patients less aggressively than white patients.

African Americans are more likely to have HIV/AIDS than any other group in the United States, as Table 23–3 shows. Although HIV/AIDS first spread in the United States primarily among gay men, and unprotected sex between men is still the primary form of transmission, only about one-third of African Americans contract the disease in this manner. Most acquire HIV/AIDS through intravenous drug use and unprotected heterosexual sex.

Although African Americans have had high rates of HIV infection from the beginning of the epidemic in the early 1980s, consciousness of this health crisis for black people only

TABLE 23-3 **ESTIMATED NUMBER OF DIAGNOSED CASES OF HUMAN IMMUNODEFICIENCY VIRUS (HIV) / ACQUIRED IMMUNODEFICIENCY SYNDROME (AIDS), PER 100,000 IN THE UNITED STATES, 2010**

Gender	Black	White
Male	15,444	12,111
Female	6,268	1,733
Total	21,712	13,844

SOURCE: *CDC 2012. HIV Surveillance Report: Diagnoses of HIV Infection and AIDS in the United States and Dependent Areas, 2010, v. 22. Table 3a. http://www.cdc.gov/hiv/surveillance/resources/reports/2010report/pdf/2010_HIV_Surveillance_Report_vol_22.pdf*

U.S. Department of Health & Human Services—The Office of Minority Health—"HIV/AIDS and African Americans." http://minorityhealth.hhs.gov/templates/content.aspx?ID=3019.

began to rise in the 1990s. At first many black leaders declared that the disease affected only gay white men and thus was not a crisis for black communities. This began to change when Los Angeles Lakers' star Earvin "Magic" Johnson told the world he had HIV in 1991. The deaths from AIDS of tennis star Arthur Ashe in 1993 and rapper Eric "Eazy-E" Wright in 1995 also shocked the black community into action.

Identity issues that concerned sexual orientation, feminine and masculine sexual roles, and male/female relationships acquired a new urgency when reports in 2003 and 2012 indicated that African-American women registered more new cases of HIV/AIDS than any other sector of the population. Clearly, heterosexual African-American women sought testing to a greater extent than black men. While women received treatment and understanding, their male partners remained in denial and avoided programs that could prolong their lives. While denying they were gay or bisexual, self-described straight men were having sex with both men and women and were spreading the virus that causes HIV/AIDS to their unsuspecting female partners.

The future health of the black community demands open conversation and creative measures to address the HIV/AIDS crisis. That such conversations are now occurring is due in no small measure to the work of gay rights activists and to the support provided to the gay community by President Barack Obama and Vice President Joe Biden, who in spring 2012 announced their support for marriage equality, that is, the right of members of the LBGT communities to marry.

African Americans at the Center of Art and Culture

23-3 What achievements have African Americans made in the areas of music, literature, and film from the 1980s through the twenty-first century?

Cultural triumphs are consistently among the most positive developments for black Americans. Beginning in the 1980s, cultural renaissances emerged in virtually every American community that had a substantial African-American presence. Black consciousness institutions proliferated and flourished. They included black history and culture museums, festivals, expositions, publishing houses, bookstores and boutiques, freedom schools, concerts, theaters, and dance troupes. By 1994 there were dozens of African-American publishing companies. In 1998 the National Literary Hall of Fame for Writers of African Descent opened at Chicago State University.

During the last days of the civil rights movement, attention shifted to another group of culture workers. Black playwrights were in the vanguard of a cultural explosion that helped revitalize American theater. August Wilson had begun writing overtly political plays in the 1960s and 1970s but focused on broader themes of race and personality as his work matured. His first great success came in 1984 with the Broadway production of *Ma Rainey's Black Bottom,* which explored racism in the music industry. He had four other plays on Broadway, two of which won Pulitzer Prizes—*Fences* in 1987 and *The Piano Lesson* in 1990. Charles Fuller also made race the center of his plays, attacking stereotypes and exploring the complexity of racial identity in modern America. His best-known play is the 1982 *A Soldier's Tale,* which also won a Pulitzer Prize. It was made into a motion picture titled *A Soldier's Story,* which was nominated for two Academy Awards. George C. Wolfe is a playwright, director, and producer whose achievements helped demolish racial barriers in the theater. His plays, such as *The Colored Museum* and *Jelly's Last Jam,* won critical acclaim, and he received a Tony Award in 1994 as best director for *Angels in America.* Anna Deavere Smith pioneered new forms of theater with her powerful one-woman plays. Her first major success was *Fires in the Mirror,* about tensions between blacks and Jews in Brooklyn's Crown Heights neighborhood. This was followed by *Twilight: Los Angeles, 1992,* a portrayal of the Rodney King riots (see Chapter 24). Smith's achievements in drama and teaching were rewarded with a MacArthur genius grant in 1996.

The new cultural renaissance differed from the black arts movement of the 1960s and 1970s. The contemporary flowering was more inclusive and more appreciative of women artists. It also included the work of openly gay and lesbian artists, such as documentary filmmaker Marion Riggs, choreographer Bill T. Jones, and novelist E. Lynn Harris. Whereas poets and dramatists dominated earlier movements, novelists took center stage in the 1980s. Much of the new work in all fields appealed as much to white audiences as to black, providing insights into the lives of people of African heritage in a predominantly Eurocentric society.

A new wave of African-American women novelists emerged as early as 1977 when Toni Morrison's *Song of Solomon* became a Book-of-the-Month-Club selection, the first by a black author since Richard Wright's *Native Son* in 1940. Then Barbara Chase-Riboud made waves with *Sally Hemings* (1979), a fictional account of a real-life woman who was both slave to and mistress of President Thomas Jefferson. In 1980 Toni Cade Bambara won the American Book Award for *The Salt Eaters.* At least as significant as these individual books was the founding in 1981 of a new publishing house, Kitchen Table: Women of Color Press. Then, in 1982, Alice Walker won the Pulitzer Prize and the American Book Award for *The Color Purple.* In 1993 she became America's poet laureate, and in the same year Toni Morrison became the first African American to win the Nobel Prize for Literature. President Bill Clinton invited Maya Angelou to read one of her poems at his first inauguration. In 2009 President Obama invited Elizabeth Alexander to read a poem at his inauguration.

Critics were not the only ones interested in these works. In 1992 three African-American women novelists—Morrison, Walker, and Terry McMillan—made the *New York Times* best-seller list simultaneously. In 2001 the works of four African Americans made the *Times* best-seller list and revealed the growing appreciation of black literature, biography, and history across the racial spectrum. In the 2000s, African-American performers earned recognition for their work on stage and in film that previous generations would have deemed unthinkable. In 2005, Oprah Winfrey spearheaded a new Broadway production of *The Color Purple,* and more than one million people saw the play in New York before it reopened in Chicago in 2007. Also in 2007, Forest Whitaker won the Academy Award for best actor for his depiction of Uganda's dictator Idi Amin in *The Last King of Scotland,* and Jennifer Hudson won the academy award for best supporting actress in *Dreamgirls.* Two years earlier Jamie Foxx had won an Oscar for best actor for his role in *Ray,* a film about the singer Ray Charles, and Morgan Freeman won best supporting actor for his role in *Million Dollar Baby.* Playwright Tyler Perry turned his popular plays about the pistol-packing but wise female-in-drag character Madea into box office gold. Tyler Perry's *Madea Goes to Jail* earned $41,030,947 in its opening week in 2009.

The Hip-Hop Nation

23-4 Why has rap music achieved international popularity?

Rap was the most commercially successful genre of black music to emerge in the late twentieth century. It became emblematic of the post–civil rights and black power movement generations of African Americans, known collectively as the hip-hop nation. There are many varieties of rap music. At its least complex, rap is a form of rhythmic speaking in rhyme. Hip-hop refers to the backup music for rap that is often composed of excerpts or "samples" from other songs.

Origins of a New Music: A Generation Defines Itself

The rap musical style arose in 1973 in New York City's South Bronx. Its original purpose was to promote musical and dance competitions among the area's inner-city youths, who had few outlets for their creative energies. Rap pioneer Kool Herc (aka Clive Campbell) began using simple raps to cover a mix of beats played from two turntables. At the same time, Afrika Bambaataa developed a political version of rap by merging the ideology of the Nation of Islam with the Black Panthers' cultural nationalism.

The first commercial rap hit, "Rapper's Delight" by the Sugar Hill Gang, came out in 1979 and popularized the term **hip-hop**. This was followed by the rise to stardom of Grandmaster Flash and the Furious Five, which grew out of 1970s funk but added rap vocals and the technique of "scratching"—moving a record back and forth under a needle to produce a rhythmic, jarring sound and manipulating turntable speeds. Much of this music was made primarily for entertainment in the clubs, but some rappers offered a political critique of American society wrapped in taunting humor.

For African-American youths, whom the world had seemingly left behind and ignored, hip-hop became the most important cultural happening of their lives. It was a creative force in which a dispossessed generation discussed the things that mattered most to them, their lives in cities burdened by racial poverty, heightened violence, and failed schools. In the Reagan years (1981–1989), few middle-class Americans acknowledged the millions left behind in urban decay. Conditions in inner cities worsened during this period, as crack cocaine flooded neighborhoods and gang warfare erupted over drug turfs. The "keeping it real" lyrics of hip-hop artists helped forge a sense of community and common destiny among a trapped generation.

Listen on MyHistoryLab Audio: Zum Zum (Street and Gangland Rhythms) from Beats and Improvisations by Six Boys in Trouble

hip-hop The backup music for rap. It is also the term for the youth culture that developed with the rise of rap music.

Rap Music Goes Mainstream

Ironically, white indifference allowed the first hip-hop entrepreneurs to take control of the production, dissemination, and profits connected with this new music. Russell Simmons saw the potential of rap street music in the mid-1970s and recognized that the mainstream entertainment industry was not aware of it. He became a concert promoter, encouraging early rap groups to stay close to the dress styles and language of the inner-city African-American community. In 1984 he and a partner formed Def Jam Records. Simmons expanded his business to include marketing hip-hop clothing under the label "Phat Farm" and promoting poetry and comedy acts. In 2000 he sold his share of Def Jam for over $100 million. Like Simmons, P. Diddy (aka Sean "Puff Daddy" Combs) found success by working within the mainstream recording industry.

Commercial success brought new groups to the fore, and the genre expanded. Rap bands such as Run-DMC, which dominated the charts in the mid-1980s, brought the sound to MTV and to a larger public, which soon included white suburban teens. Hip-hop culture quickly spread beyond New York to other African-American urban centers, and each developed a distinctive and often more graphic variant of the original. With the music came changes in clothing style, such as baggy, loose-fitting jeans, that trend-hungry fashion designers quickly adopted.

By 2000, hip-hop had become a global cultural force and the source of astonishing profits for men such as Simmons and Combs—and for white-owned business and music companies. The recurrence of the tension between black creativity and white profits fueled new debate.

Gangsta Rap

gangsta rap A genre of rap music characterized by violent and sexist lyrics.

The southern California group N.W.A. (Niggaz wit Attitudes) was one of the most successful new rap bands in the late 1980s. Their 1988 album *Straight Outta Compton* heralded the rise of **gangsta rap**. Its song "Gangsta Gangsta" shocked many with its sexist and violent lyrics. Particularly troubling, however, was the persistent objectification of women in hardcore rap music and films. The widespread use of "bitch" and "ho" by rappers to describe black women reflected broader gender divisions within the black community. Still, many rap bands explicitly rejected hard-core obscenity and violence. Artists like Queen Latifah, for example, avoid denigrating other African Americans even as they promote a message of empowerment for black women and men.

Even more noteworthy was the extent to which hip-hop migrated beyond the United States and became a global cultural force—"hip-hop planet." It influenced music worldwide, particularly across the African Diaspora. The ability of rap to combine with other musical forms to create compelling hybrids, together with the global penetration of American popular culture, ensure that hip-hop will continue to thrive and evolve.

African-American Intellectuals

23-5 **What is the main philosophy of Afrocentricity?**

The civil rights and black power movements forced predominantly white academic and cultural institutions to open their doors to African Americans. With a beachhead established, black scholars gained a prominence as public intellectuals unknown in earlier eras.

These individuals go beyond their roles as academics to participate in public debate on major issues. In the past, most public intellectuals were white males. In the past five decades, however, many of the most prominent public intellectuals to emerge have been African American. Among them are Cornel West, Henry Louis Gates, Jr., Melissa Harris-Perry, Johnnetta Cole, Beverly Guy-Sheftall, William Julius Wilson, Robin D. G. Kelley, Michael Eric Dyson, and Mary Frances Berry. Their views range across the ideological gamut but they all strive to define black identity in the United States and explore the role of race in its social, economic, and political life. Their emergence and the acclaim accorded to them mark the end of America's long refusal to acknowledge the intellectual accomplishments of African Americans.

Many African-American scholars were connected to the Black Studies programs founded in the late 1960s and early 1970s. Initially marginalized and few in number, these programs now exist in nearly every major university and college. They have become institutionalized—even prized—by institutions that once resisted them.

Afrocentricity
A philosophy of culture that celebrates Africa's role in history and stresses the enduring African roots and identity of black America.

As befits a vibrant intellectual movement, there are several main approaches to understanding the path of African Americans through U.S. history and in contemporary society. Three broad approaches predominate: Afrocentrist; what might be loosely termed an "intersectional" or "inclusionist" approach that has gained prominence more recently as an approach that emphasizes class, sexuality, and gender; and comparative race and diaspora studies.

Afrocentricity

In the 1980s and 1990s, a philosophy of culture referred to as **Afrocentricity** captured wide attention. Afrocentricity had been prominent in the political movement that created black studies, but Temple University professor Molefi Kete Asante gave it a presence and a personality. Asante argued that an African-centered perspective was needed to reorient African Americans from the Eurocentric periphery to the center of their own history. In its most extreme form, Afrocentrists argue that much of European civilization originated in Africa, particularly from the culture of ancient Egypt. They also point to evidence of advanced cultures in other parts of Africa to refute assertions of African cultural inferiority.

Many black educators embraced Afrocentricity as a way to celebrate and reclaim a positive African identity and to unite the peoples of the African Diaspora. Afrocentrists rejected the idea of America as a melting pot. Assimilation, they argued, meant rejecting their African cultural heritage. At the heart of this position is an indictment of American ideas and institutions for their complicity in the long oppression of black people.

Many black scholars, however, insist that Afrocentricity is regressive and fosters self-segregation. Earl Ofari Hutchinson, for example, concedes that Asante's ideas merit attention, but he is skeptical about the claims of some Afrocentrist academics: "In their zeal to counter

Molefi Kete Asante changed his name from Arthur Lee Smith in 1973 to better reflect his African heritage. He served as professor and chair of the Department of African American Studies at Temple University from 1984 to 1996. About Afrocentricism, Asante elaborated, "It's a very simple idea. African people for 500 years have lived on the intellectual terms of Europeans. The African perspective has finally come to dinner."

23-1

23-2

23-3

23-4

23-5

23-6

23-7

23-8

the heavy handed 'Eurocentric imbalance of history,' some have crossed the line between historic fact and fantasy." White and black critics alike caution that the Afrocentrist desire to fabricate "a glorious past" for black people obscured the truth and fostered a narrow notion of race ill-suited for studying Africans in America.

African-American Studies Come of Age

While the African-American studies department at Temple was the center of the Afrocentric approach and remained one of the largest black studies programs in the nation, many other programs adopted a more ideologically flexible approach. Under the leadership of Henry Louis Gates, Jr., Harvard University followed the integrationist tradition. Gates took charge of the department and the W. E. B. Du Bois Institute in 1991. His goals for the department focused on recovering and making accessible a usable black African and diasporic past. He supports and advocates for a rigorous multidisciplinary study of the black experience. Apart from intellectual rigor, what held the department together was a belief that race is a malleable category of identity to be analyzed critically and that effective scholarship in the field does not depend on the scholar's racial profile.

As with American intellectual life as a whole, the emergence of scholarship that questioned prevailing gender assumptions also influenced African-American studies. Just as the black studies movement challenged racial ideology, women's studies forced a reconsideration of deeply held gender beliefs while raising historical and social science questions that went unasked in an earlier era. African-American scholars in "womanism" studies, a term Alice Walker popularized to describe the intellectual projects of women of color, pay particular attention to how gender interacted with racial and class hierarchies to shape the historical experiences and contemporary lives of black women. Early journals such as *SAGE* and organizations such as the Association of Black Women Historians advanced scholarship in black women's studies. Gradually, their scholarly, literary, historical, and polemical works attracted general readers and secured a place in women's studies curricula. The field of black women's history has grown rapidly: scholarly monographs, reference works, anthologies, conferences, and exhibitions have all been devoted to the contribution black women have made to the political struggles and artistic accomplishments of African Americans. In 2007, the journal *Black Women, Gender & Families*, edited by Jennifer Hamer, began as an official organ of the National Council of Black Studies. In 2008 the Organization of American Historians announced the establishment of the Darlene Clark Hine Award for the best book published annually in African American Women's and Gender History. Black woman historian Wanda Hendricks spearheaded the fund-raising effort to make concrete the legitimization of black women's history.

Black Religion at the Dawn of the Millennium

23-6   **What are the strengths and tensions operating within the black church today?**

Read on
MyHistoryLab
Document: Building
a Black Christian
Community from
Scratch, 1999

Religion remains at the heart of the African-American experience. Black churches remain by far the largest black-controlled institutions in the nation. Houses of worship ranging from storefront operations with a few dozen congregants to "megachurches" with thousands of members are the sinew that binds together nearly every African-American community. The major denominations remain those with roots in the nineteenth century. Among the largest are the African American National Baptist Convention of America, Inc.; the Progressive National Baptist Convention, Inc.; the African Methodist Episcopal (AME) Church; the National Missionary Baptist Convention of America; the Churches of Christ; and the AME Zion Church. Immigration from the Caribbean and Africa has increased African-American membership in some predominantly white denominations. For example, black worshipers make up more than 9 percent of the Catholic Church and over 10 percent of the Episcopal Church.

African-American men and women have become leaders within predominantly white denominations since the 1960s. Harold R. Perry was consecrated a bishop in the Roman Catholic Church in 1966, and Wilton Gregory became the first African American to head the United States Conference of Catholic Bishops in 2002. Recognizing the importance of Africans and African Americans to the future of the church, in 1993 Pope John Paul II apologized for the Catholic Church's support of slavery. In 1970 African-American John M. Burgess became the first black bishop to head an Episcopal diocese in America. His leadership in Massachusetts was followed by John T. Walker in Washington, DC, in 1977. African Americans made similar gains in other denominations as churches worked to rid themselves of racist practices.

Despite this continuity with the past and the successes of black religious leaders, African-American religious life has changed in the past several decades. Most African Americans remain Protestants, but demographic and social changes have challenged the mainline denominations. One difficulty is the movement of middle-class parishioners from the close-knit urban communities that once supported churches with people from many different walks of life. Greater levels of education and different life experiences combine with geographical distance to create large suburban megachurches with a distinct character and worship practice. Often Pentecostal, these churches' theology emphasizes the individual's relationship to God. Their ministers speak to the tensions and anxiety of people with stressful lives and careers or with problems such as substance abuse or difficult relationships. They also provide community services for their parishioners.

Black Christians on the Front Line

Faced with the problems of the black community and with a changing population, African-American Christians in both traditional and nontraditional religious institutions have developed outreach programs to create supportive communities for the embattled and the vulnerable. Some of the new megachurches are in or near black inner-city communities and remain committed to local action. For example, the Salem Baptist Church in Chicago has over 17,000 members, many of whom patrol neighborhoods to discourage prostitutes and drug dealers.

Rev. Eugene Rivers has developed a different approach from that of the megachurches. Along with former students at Harvard University, he founded the small Azusa Christian Community in a crime-plagued neighborhood in Boston. An evangelical Christian, Rivers believes "the church is the last best hope that black people have." He turned a former crack house into a Christian settlement named the Ella J. Baker House. Its primary goal is to keep children from killing one another. He and fellow black clergy entered into a partnership with the police. The collaboration helped eliminate juvenile murders for two and a half years. Rivers advocates a pragmatic black nationalism aimed at developing a rich, viable black civil society centered on the church.

Tensions in the Black Church

Tensions have arisen within many black churches over their socially conservative message, patriarchal structure, staid ritual, and lack of social engagement. Gender and sexuality are two key sources of this tension. Along with other conservative Christians, the black church has long advocated the subordination of women to men. Although most black churchgoers are women, men overwhelmingly dominate church leadership. Although a few men and women have always challenged patriarchal assumptions in the churches, only in recent decades has the chorus grown too loud to ignore.

The AME Church has been at the forefront of this reform. Although the AME has ordained women since 1898, the number of women ministers has only recently become significant. Now 3,000 of the AME's 8,000 ministers are female; in 2000 the church elected Vashti M. McKenzie bishop of its Southern African district. Women's achievements in the churches have not come without conflict, and this promises to be at the center of black religious life in the twenty-first century.

Black churches also face conflicts over sexuality. Their theology has traditionally limited legitimate sexual activity to monogamous, heterosexual marriages. Baptist minister and Georgetown University professor Michael Eric Dyson lists the challenges for black Christians over sexuality: "The guilt and shame that result from unresolved conflicts about the virtues of black sexuality. . . . The role of eroticism in a healthy black Christian sexuality. The revulsion to and exploitation of homosexuals. The rise of AIDS in black communities. The sexual and physical abuse of black women and children by black male church

With the support of the Delta Sigma Theta sorority, family, and the Baltimore, Maryland, church community, Vashti Murphy McKenzie broke through "the stained-glass ceiling" (her words) to become the first woman in the history of the AME Church to be appointed a bishop. She is a graduate of the University of Maryland, earned a master of divinity from Harvard University's Divinity School, and earned a doctorate in ministry at the United Theological Seminary in Dayton, Ohio.

members. The resistance to myths of super black sexuality." Of all of these challenges, those surrounding the HIV/AIDS crisis are most pressing but also the most difficult to address, given the church's traditional refusal to do more than denounce, or remain silent about, nontraditional sexualities.

Black Muslims

Although still a relatively small phenomenon among African Americans, Islam has been gaining converts. The Nation of Islam is the best known of the many African-American Muslim groups, but its 20,000 to 40,000 members make up only a small percentage of the estimated 1.5 million black American Muslims. The clarity and discipline of the Muslim faith and the solidarity African-American Muslims feel with Muslims around the world have attracted an estimated 18,000 converts per year in the United States.

With growing immigration from Islamic countries, African-American Muslims have become more closely connected to the larger trends in Islam. This is evident in the rise of more orthodox Islamic beliefs among American blacks. The attacks on the World Trade Center and the Pentagon on September 11, 2001, and the wars in Iraq and Afghanistan, two Muslim countries, have left many African-American Muslims conflicted. On the one hand, most denounce the attacks and the ideology that led to them. On the other hand, many African Americans are troubled by what they perceive to be an indiscriminate anti-Muslim feeling in the United States and are concerned the nation's war on terror might become a holy war against Islam at home and abroad.

Louis Farrakhan and the Nation of Islam

23-7 **What are Louis Farrakhan's views and how has he been instrumental in helping African Americans?**

Beginning in the 1980s, the Nation of Islam's minister Louis Farrakhan became a potent source of racial division in the United States. After Malcolm X's rupture with Elijah Muhammad and his murder in February 1965, Farrakhan became minister of Harlem Mosque No. 7 and Muhammad's national representative. In 1978 he became leader of the Nation. Under Farrakhan's direction, the Nation developed media ventures, restaurants, clothing stores, and companies to provide security for apartment buildings, distribute soap and cosmetics, and manufacture pharmaceuticals. Farrakhan recruited among poor and marginalized urban African Americans and black prisoners. The national move to the right during the Reagan era complemented the reconstituted Nation's conservative social ideas, which harked back to those that Booker T. Washington advanced in the late nineteenth century. Like Elijah Muhammad, Farrakhan downplayed the struggle for political rights.

Until 1984 most white Americans were barely aware of Farrakhan's existence. In that year, however, he broke the Nation of Islam's long-standing abstention from politics to support Jesse Jackson's bid for the Democratic presidential nomination and ignited a firestorm of controversy. When Jews took offense at Jackson's off-the-record reference to New York as "Hymietown" during a conversation with African-American reporters, Farrakhan, whose Fruit of Islam organization provided security for Jackson's campaign, defended him and made matters worse by claiming that criticism of Jackson was an attack on all black people.

Farrakhan's verbal assaults against Jews, whom he called a principal enemy of African Americans, attracted support from ultra-right-wing anti-Semitic forces and condemnation from Jewish Americans and the Anti-Defamation League. Dredging up anti-Semitic

23-1
23-2
23-3
23-4
23-5
23-6
23-7
23-8

23-1

23-2

23-3

23-4

23-5

23-6

23-7

23-8

📖 **Read** on **MyHistoryLab Document**: Louis Farrakhan on Education, 2007

Louis Farrakhan and the Nation of Islam. Always controversial, Farrakhan achieved the greatest feat in the history of black mass mobilization, the Million Man March. The actual numbers of black men who heeded his call on October 16, 1995, to attend the Million Man March may forever be in dispute. The figures range from 400,000 to 1.2 million.

shibboleths reminiscent of Hitler's Germany, Farrakhan blamed Jews for many of the ills plaguing African Americans. Jewish Americans, many of whom had been among the principal allies of African Americans during the civil rights movement, called on African-American organizations and leaders to repudiate Farrakhan.

Millennium Marches

In the 1990s Farrakhan reached out to a broader group of African Americans. He called a Million Man March in Washington, DC. Farrakhan framed this march as a "Holy Day of Atonement and Reconciliation . . . to reconcile our spiritual inner beings and to redirect our focus to developing our communities, strengthening our families, working to uphold and protect our civil and human rights, and empowering ourselves through the Spirit of God, more effective use of our dollars, and through the power of the vote."

The estimated 400,000-strong crowd at the October 16, 1995, march made it a symbolic success and generated positive coverage even in the mainstream media. It inspired many black men to become more engaged with their communities and to speak out against oppression. On this occasion, the Nation's conservative philosophy of religion, self-respect, family values, community responsibility, and bootstrap capitalism found a responsive audience. Even though many marchers did not support the Nation's program, the peaceful solidarity of the gathering gave them hope.

Some of the goodwill dissipated, however, when, three months after the march, Farrakhan embarked on a "World Friendship Tour" to Africa and the Middle East. To the consternation of many, he met with the leader of the brutal military regime in Nigeria, General Sani Abacha. At home, Farrakhan's intemperate rhetoric made news, but he failed to forge a coherent strategy to resolve African America's continuing social problems.

The Million Man March inspired women to organize their own march. Initiated by two Philadelphia women—Phile Chionesu, a small-business owner, and Asia Coney, a public housing activist—an estimated 300,000 black women gathered in Philadelphia on October 25, 1997, to listen to speeches by California congresswoman and president of the Congressional Black Caucus Maxine Waters, rapper Sister Souljah, and South African activist Winnie Mandela. The march was a celebration, a call to unity, and a forum for black women to denounce domestic violence and inadequate access to quality health care and educational opportunities. The march got less media attention than the Million Man March, perhaps because the organizers were relatively unknown. The march nonetheless symbolized the struggle of black women to be seen and heard in American society and to counter negative stereotypes and derogatory images of black womanhood. Like the Million Man March, there was little in the way of specific policy demands, but the women marchers did gain a feeling of solidarity.

Complicating Black Identity in the Twenty-First Century

23-8 Why has black identity become more complicated in the twenty-first century?

The 2000 census counted 281,421,906 Americans, a 13.2 percent increase from 1990. African Americans numbered 34.7 million, or about 12 percent of the total. For the first time in U.S. history, they were no longer the largest minority group: the 35.3 million Americans who identified themselves as Hispanic slightly outnumbered them.

As in the past, most black Americans (54 percent) live in the South; about 19 percent live in the Midwest, 18 percent in the Northeast, and 10 percent in the West. A look beyond these raw numbers, however, reveals important information about the evolving nature of African-American identity in an increasingly multiethnic nation.

For the first time, the 2000 census allowed respondents to choose more than one racial designation for themselves. Since the first census in 1790, the politics of race have shaped such classifications. Before the Civil War, an accurate count of slaves was important because they counted for three-fifths of a person in determining the representation of states in the House of Representatives. Throughout the nineteenth century, fears about miscegenation led census takers to identify individuals as black, white, or mixed race. With the rise of segregation in the late nineteenth and early twentieth centuries, the "one-drop" rule—the belief that any black ancestry, no matter how slight, made a person black—hardened, and the census takers' list of questions dropped the classification of "mulatto." During the early civil rights movement, the American Civil Liberties Union and other groups attempted to remove racial classifications altogether from the census data, reasoning that the only purpose of such distinctions was to disadvantage black people.

The civil rights laws of the 1960s changed the purpose of gathering data by racial classification. Reliable statistics on racial characteristics of people were now necessary to combat discrimination. With the rise of affirmative action programs, identifying oneself as an

African American could be beneficial. The black power movement led many to embrace their identity as African Americans and reject the assimilation implied by abandoning racial categories.

In 1977 the Office of Management and Budget addressed the government's need for standard racial categories with its Statistical Policy Directive 15. This set up the familiar racial classifications: white, black, Asian and Pacific Islander, and Native American. "Hispanic" was chosen to denote an ethnicity and could be selected in addition to one of the four racial categories. Because there is no scientific backing for any biological racial distinctions, these categories are bureaucratic approximations of socially relevant distinctions designed to serve administrative needs. They were not necessarily meant to reflect the complex identities of many individuals included in them. Over the quarter century after their adoption, these categories became incorporated into identities and social understandings and influenced business and government programs.

Two groups sought to change the categories. The first group saw an end to racial categories as the true legacy of the civil rights movement. These advocates point to the rhetoric of Martin Luther King, Jr., and the language of the Civil Rights Act of 1964, which forbade any discrimination on the basis of race, as evidence of the need to eliminate racial classifications by the government. Some adherents of this view want to abolish the notion of race altogether. They want a color-blind society that they believe will not arrive until a person's race ceases to affect access to education, government programs, or employment. Others who advocate this position, however, are ideological conservatives who want to limit the power of the federal government to redress inequality. They have bankrolled state referendums and court cases to end racial classifications and see this as a way to roll back the gains of the civil rights era.

Those who are biracial also oppose the old classification scheme. Racial mixing is nothing new in America. Many black women slaves were compelled to bear children to their white masters. There have also been consensual sexual relationships and marriages between African Americans and other ethnic and racial groups. The number of such unions and their social acceptance have grown precipitously since the civil rights movement destroyed many of the old racial barriers and the Supreme Court struck down the last **antimiscegenation** laws in *Loving v. Virginia* in 1967. There are now more than 1.5 million mixed-race marriages in the United States and many children growing up in these households. Mixed-race marriages are much more common among younger generations and seem likely to increase rapidly.

There is a sharp debate over biracial and multiracial identities in the African-American community. One of the most significant concerns is that fundamental changes in the classification system will undermine the projects they were designed to advance. As poverty researcher John A. Powell put it, "Without racial statistics, we will not know how distributions of resources affect racial and ethnic groups. Without them, racism, which is still very much a part of our society, will be that much more difficult to eradicate, and that much more likely to remain a societal norm." The programs that use these statistics include the Equal Employment Opportunity Act, the Civil Rights Act of 1964, the Voting Rights Act of 1965, the Public Health Act, the Job Partnership Training Act, the Equal Credit Opportunity Act, the Fair Housing Act, and many others. Some argue that offering mixed-race people the option of not being black might undermine the racial solidarity that has been the basis for black advances.

Although only 1.8 million Americans opted for the biracial designation in the 2000 census, the existence of the designation raises questions about the nature of racial

antimiscegenation
Laws that denied men and women of different racial identities to marry and to risk imprisonment for having sex across the color line during the era of legal segregation.

identity. Clearly racism exists, and black Americans experienced centuries of discrimination that distinguishes them from other groups. But many who would have been considered black under the traditional American system of racial classification no longer think of themselves in the same way and may be increasingly able to assert a multiple identity. Immigration to the United States from Latin America, Asia, and Africa is also undermining what had once been a largely biracial dynamic.

Immigration and African Americans

Because of immigration restrictions and the general oppression of people of African descent in America, few blacks, either from the Western Hemisphere or from Africa, immigrated to the United States before the past few decades. Changes in immigration laws, particularly the landmark 1965 Hart-Cellar Act, which abandoned the racially exclusive restrictions of the past, helped open the door. Military, economic, health, and environmental crises that have roiled Africa and the Caribbean since the 1960s have pushed substantial numbers from these regions through the door. These new black Americans often do not fit their identity neatly into the traditional African-American category.

The number of black immigrants from the West Indies increased dramatically after the 1960s. In the 1950s, only 123,000 Caribbean people immigrated, but during the 1990s nearly one million did so. The Caribbean islands were one of the main areas of importation of African slaves. The islands' sugar production was the economic engine of the Spanish, French, Dutch, and British New World empires into the nineteenth century. These empires all abandoned slavery by the late 1800s, and the retreat of British colonialism from the Caribbean in the twentieth century left many micro-nations largely populated by people of African descent whose cultures have remained more influenced by Africa than was true of black people in the United States. Although a racial hierarchy is not unknown in these societies, racial identity is less important than class and merit-based achievement. Upon immigration, mostly to New York, Florida, and other parts of the East Coast, Caribbean immigrants soon learn the importance of race in the United States, but they have also carved out a separate identity from other African Americans. First-generation West Indians tend to have more economic success than native African Americans, in part because employers often favor them. The second generation has often had a more difficult time as discrimination and poor schools take their toll.

Voluntary immigrants from Africa once were few, and before 1980 they were mainly European colonials or North Africans from nations such as Egypt. In the 1950s only 14,000 Africans came to the United States, but during the 1990s over 350,000 arrived.

In 2003 the New York Haitian American community celebrated the two-hundredth anniversary of the Haitian Revolution. This Haitian flag-waving group of celebrants congregate on the Eastern Parkway in Brooklyn.

23-1
23-2
23-3
23-4
23-5
23-6
23-7
23-8

Most of these new immigrants were men and tended to be well educated. Part of their reason for coming to the United States was the destabilization of many African nations and oppression by autocratic regimes.

Black Feminism

The feminist and gay rights movements have challenged traditional ideas of racial identity in recent decades. Both arose as part of the broader "rights revolution" that began with the civil rights movement, but each highlights different aspects of a person's identity—gender or sexuality—in addition to race.

A new wave of feminism in the 1960s and 1970s transformed gender relations. This movement arose, in part, out of the successes of the African-American civil rights struggle. The 1964 Civil Rights Act outlawed sexual as well as racial discrimination in employment. Although this had not been a goal of the civil rights movement at that time and its inclusion was meant, in part, to lessen the prospect that Congress would enact the law, it helped open discussions of gender oppression that had lain dormant for decades. Many white women activists in the Student Nonviolent Coordinating Committee and other civil rights groups became leaders in the emerging feminist movement, often using the same strategies and tactics that had worked to fight racism.

Second-wave feminism achieved many changes. The National Organization for Women, founded in 1966, fought to end job discrimination against women, expand access to safe and effective birth control, legalize abortion, and secure government support for child care. One of the movement's most important early successes was Title IX of the Educational Amendments Act of 1972, which required colleges and universities to ensure equal access for women. Another was the Supreme Court's decision legalizing abortion in 1973 in *Roe v. Wade*. Beyond these victories, the feminist movement opened up choices for women in nearly every aspect of their lives that traditional gender roles had precluded. It also engendered a backlash as conservative men and women fought passage of the Equal Rights Amendment to the Constitution, access to abortion and legalized abortion itself, and sex education in schools.

Black women shaped modern feminism from the start. The core of black feminist thinking is a dual critique of the women's and black liberation ideology. Black women scholars argued that a critique of patriarchy had to include race and class. Whereas white leaders of the women's movement were silent on race, many male leaders in the African-American freedom movement were all too forthright about gender. As Black Panther leader Elaine Brown put it, "A woman in the Black Power movement was considered at best irrelevant. A woman asserting herself was a pariah."

Responding to sexism in the black power movement, many black women writers and activists sought to make the struggle against sexism as important as that against racism. Between 1973 and 1975, the National Black Feminist Organization (NBFO) articulated many of the concerns specific to black women, from anger with black men for dating and marrying white women; to internal conflict over skin color, hair texture, and facial features; to sexual violence and harassment against black women; to differences in the economic mobility of white and black women. Black feminists also attacked the myth of black matriarchy and stereotypical portrayals of black women in popular culture. Although the NBFO was short lived, it broke the silence black liberation movements had imposed on black women. Black feminists also helped other women talk openly about domestic violence, rape, and sexual harassment in employment.

23-1

23-2

23-3

23-4

23-5

23-6

23-7

23-8

Gay and Lesbian African Americans

The success of the civil rights movement encouraged gays, lesbians, bisexual, and transgender (LGBT) black Americans to fight openly against the discrimination they had faced for centuries. Their movement was small and quiet until 1969, when gay men at the Stonewall Inn, a bar in New York's Greenwich Village, resisted a police raid. The multiracial crowd's refusal to continue submitting to the kind of police harassment that gays had long been subjected to in the United States sparked an explosion of activism. By the 1980s, many states and cities had decriminalized homosexual behavior and forbade discrimination in employment on the basis of sexuality. Although tensions arose between lesbians and gay men, they worked together to pursue the full range of civil rights heterosexuals enjoy despite persistent opposition from conservative groups.

LGBT African Americans have struggled against their marginality within the larger gay rights movement and homophobia in their own communities. Like the women's movement, the early gay and lesbian rights movement tended to be predominantly white and middle class. Although not explicitly racist, it tended to see racial issues as secondary to or separate from the goal of ending discrimination based on sexual preference.

Despite hostility toward the LGBT rights movement by some African Americans, many black leaders, such as Jesse Jackson, Eleanor Holmes Norton, and John Lewis, and civil rights organizations, such as the NAACP, have embraced its agenda. They do so in part because they accept the analogy between the struggle against repression based on sexual preference and that based on race. The debate between black feminists and gay rights activists, who argue that gender and class identities must be taken into account in political and scholarly analysis, and nationalists, who focus on black identity as primary, continues to rage and will influence our understanding of African-American life in the twenty-first century. As Coretta Scott King put it in a 2002 speech to the National Gay and Lesbian Task Force, "I believe very strongly that all forms of bigotry and discrimination are equally wrong and should be opposed by right-thinking Americans everywhere. Freedom from discrimination based on sexual orientation is surely a fundamental human right in any great democracy, as much as freedom from racial, religious, gender, or ethnic discrimination." In 2008 California voters approved a referendum overturning a decision of the California Supreme Court that had legalized same-sex marriage in the state. To the dismay of the gay community, African Americans were instrumental in passing this referendum, which restricted marriage to unions between a man and a woman. In 2011 President Barack Obama announced his support of same-sex marriage. Over a dozen states have adopted supportive legislation guaranteeing the rights of members of the LGBT community.

CONCLUSION

The closing of the twentieth century saw remarkable progress for African Americans even as part of the community remained mired in poverty. African Americans still experienced the burden of racism that was so familiar to W. E. B. Du Bois at the nadir of the nineteenth century. Black people confronted those challenges by engaging in collective political action and maintaining predominantly black churches, colleges, and social action groups. The black soul that Du Bois thought had so much to give America now flows freely through its art, language, scholarship, and popular culture, and especially in the Hip-Hop National

23-1

23-2

23-3

23-4

23-5

23-6

23-7

23-8

VOICES E. Lynn Harris

E. Lynn Harris (1955–2009) was born in Flint, Michigan, and grew up in Little Rock, Arkansas. He was a best-selling writer whose novels explore what it is like to be gay and black in America. His first novel, Invisible Life, *was published in 1991. In this account about his own childhood, Harris is eight years old when he learns a painful lesson about perceptions of sexual difference.*

Easter Sunday, 1964, finally arrived. After my bath, I raced into the tiny room I shared with my two younger sisters and saw the coat laid out on my twin bed. It was red, black, and green plaid with gold buttons. Daddy and I had picked the coat out together at Dundee's Men's Store. I quickly put on my new clothes, and I could see my sisters, Anita and Zettoria, who were five and three, slip on new dresses over their freshly pressed hair. Anita had on a blue taffeta dress, and Shane (our nickname for Zettoria, since her name was so hard to pronounce) had on an identical one in pink. Their dresses were pretty but didn't compare to my coat. After Anita and Shane had accepted their compliments from Daddy, he called me in for inspection. "Where is my little man? Come out here and let Daddy see that new coat," he said. I quickly buttoned up each of the three gold buttons and dashed to the living room for Daddy's endorsement of my outfit. "Look, Daddy. Look at me," I said with excitement as I twirled around like my sisters had a moment before. Suddenly Daddy's bright smile turned into a disgusted frown. What was wrong? Didn't he like my new coat? Had Easter been canceled? "Come here. Stop that damn twirling around," Daddy yelled. I stopped and moved toward Daddy. He was seated on the armless aqua vinyl sofa. Before I reached him, he grabbed me and shouted. "Look at you. You. . . . little sissy with this coat all buttoned up like a little girl. Don't you know better? Men don't button up their coats all the way." Before I could respond or clearly realize what I had done wrong, I saw Daddy's powerful hands moving toward me. His grip was so quick and powerful that I felt the back of my prized coat come apart. A panic filled my tiny body when I saw his hand clutching the fabric. I began to cry as my sisters looked on in horror. I could hear Mama's high heels clicking swiftly as she raced to the living room from the kitchen. "If you don't stop that damn crying, I'm going to make you wear one of your sister's dresses to church." I caught myself and stopped crying. Daddy meant what he said. I would be the laughing stock of the entire neighborhood. . . . I could see all my friends pointing and laughing at me. I don't remember what I wore that Easter Sunday or many Easters that followed. All I recall is that I wasn't wearing a dress, and I remember what my daddy had said to me. I didn't know what a sissy was and why Daddy despised them so. All I knew was that I was determined never to be one.

1. **How does Harris's father conceive of masculinity and manhood?**
2. **Why is this Easter Sunday so important to Harris's self-development and sexual identity?**
3. **How are Harris's sisters treated differently from him?**

SOURCE: From *What Becomes of the Brokenhearted: A Memoir* by E. Lynn Harris. Used by permission of Doubleday, a division of Random House, Inc.

and International Culture Movement. At the same time, increasing diversity in the ways that African Americans live their lives has led to differences in how individuals understand their identities. Some long for the possibility of asserting those identities in ways not limited by race, sexuality, gender, and class. The tension between racial, class, gender, sexual, and racial-ethnic identities, however, is likely to persist and will profoundly shape the course of the African-American odyssey in the twenty-first century.

23-1
23-2
23-3
23-4
23-5
23-6
23-7
23-8

CHAPTER TIMELINE

AFRICAN-AMERICAN EVENTS

NATIONAL EVENTS

1960–1969

1964
Civil Rights Act outlaws sexual discrimination in employment

1966
National Organization for Women founded

1969
Stonewall riot in New York

1970–1979

1973
National Black Feminist Organization founded

1978
Louis Farrakhan becomes head of Nation of Islam

1980–1989

1982
Alice Walker and Charles Fuller win Pulitzer Prizes in fiction and drama

1984
Russell Simmons forms Def Jam Records

1987
August Wilson wins Pulitzer Prize for drama

1988
N.W.A.'s *Straight Outta Compton* marks the rise of gangsta rap

1980
Ronald Reagan elected president

1981
Recession settles in; Economic Recovery Tax Act passed

1984
President Reagan reelected

1988
George H. W. Bush elected president

1990–1999

1990
Anna Deavere Smith and August Wilson win Pulitzer Prizes for poetry and drama

1993
Toni Morrison becomes the first black woman to win the Nobel Prize for literature

1995
Million Man March

1997
Million Woman March

1990–1999
1.4 million Caribbean and African immigrants move to the United States

1991
Operation Desert Storm against Iraq

1992
Bill Clinton elected president

1994
Republicans gain control of Congress

1996
Clinton reelected; Clinton signs welfare reform legislation

1998
Clinton impeached by the House of Representatives

1999
Senate acquits Clinton

CHAPTER TIMELINE

AFRICAN-AMERICAN EVENTS

NATIONAL EVENTS

2000–2009

2000
Vashti M. McKenzie elected first woman AME bishop

African-American college enrollment tops 1.5 million

2001
AIDS becomes a leading cause of death among young African-American men

2002
Wilton Gregory heads U.S. Catholic bishops

2004
Carol Moseley Braun and Al Sharpton run for president

Barack Obama elected to U.S. Senate

Condoleezza Rice appointed secretary of state

2009
Barack Obama inaugurated as the forty-fourth president of the United States

President Obama receives the Nobel Peace Prize

Annette Gordon-Reed wins Pulitzer Prize in history

2000
Hispanics become the largest minority group in the United States

George W. Bush elected president

Bush names Condoleezza Rice national security adviser and Colin Powell secretary of state

September 11, 2001
Terrorists demolish the World Trade Center and attack the Pentagon

2004
George W. Bush reelected president

2005
Hurricane Katrina devastates New Orleans

On MyHistoryLab

 Study and Review on MyHistoryLab

REVIEW QUESTIONS

1. What social, economic, and material gains did African Americans make after the civil rights era? Why did some black Americans do better than others during this period? How are tensions surrounding class stratification manifested within the black community?

2. Why do white Americans tend to live longer than black Americans? How has the black community dealt with the problems of HIV/AIDS?

3. Who were some of the most important African-American writers, performers, and social critics in the late twentieth century? What is hip-hop, and what is meant by the term the "hip-hop planet"?

What is the relationship between rap music and hip-hop?

4. What are the goals of the Afrocentricity movement? Why is it controversial?

5. Why has the church remained so important to African Americans? How are women's roles changing in the black church?

6. Were the Millenium Marches a success? Why has Louis Farrakhan been so controversial?

7. How has immigration from the Caribbean and Africa affected black America? What factors gave rise to black feminism? What problems do black gays and lesbians face in the black community?

Black Politics from 1980 to the Present: The President Obama Era 1980–2012

The evolution of black politics from the passage of the Voting Rights Act of 1965 to the election (2008) and reelection (2012) of the first black president of the United States, Barack Obama, is best understood in four phases. The first phase was marked by the rise of black elected officials on local and state levels. In this first post-civil rights movement phase, the black voting bloc solidified in support of the Democratic Party and pushed for policies that would strengthen their communities and secure their recently won citizenship rights. The second phase was highlighted by Jesse Jackson's two unsuccessful bids for the Democratic Party's nomination for president in 1984 and 1988 and the efforts of mobilized black communities and their leaders to make the black presence felt on the national level. The third phase witnessed both the rise of black conservatives and the election in 2008 of the first African-American president. The emergence of a fourth phase since 2008 has been characterized by contradictory impulses. While more than 90 percent of black voters supported President Obama's reelection in 2012, black progressives debate whether he has significantly improved the lives of black people. They question Obama's seeming lack of sustained attention to issues that affect African Americans,

LEARNING OBJECTIVES

How did Jesse Jackson rise within the Democratic Party?	24-1
How did Reagan and Bush attempt to dismantle the "Great Society" and undermine social welfare programs?	24-2
What role did black conservatives play in the Republican Party in the 1980s and 1990s?	24-3
What are the "old" and "new" civil rights?	24-4
What were the focal points of black activism during the Reagan and Bush years?	24-5
How did general white perceptions of young black men shape trends in criminal justice in the 1990s?	24-6
Why did African Americans remain supportive of Bill Clinton's presidency and remain loyal Democrats?	24-7
How did the events of 9/11, the wars in Iraq and Afghanistan, Hurricane Katrina, and the election of Barack Obama affect black political consciousness?	24-8
In what ways does the election and reelection of Barack Obama represent a triumph of black politics?	24-9

President Barack Obama enjoys a respite from battles with Republican Congressmen over universal health care to play football with the family dog, Bo. (May 12, 2009).

563

including chronic economic distress; relentless political assaults; the deterioration of black communities; the social, health, and workplace concerns of black women; and shrinking educational opportunities for black children.

Jesse Jackson and the Rainbow Coalition

24-1 How did Jesse Jackson rise within the Democratic Party?

24-1
24-2
24-3
24-4
24-5
24-6
24-7
24-8
24-9

Rainbow Coalition
Political coalition of African Americans, workers, liberals, feminists, gay people, environmentalists, and others formed by Jesse Jackson in the 1980s.

In 1983, Jesse Jackson announced his campaign for the presidency of the United States. Jackson's preparation for battle was not the traditional climb from one elective office to another. Rather, he rose through the ranks of the civil rights movement, working alongside Martin Luther King, Jr., in the Southern Christian Leadership Conference and heading Operation Breadbasket, an organization that attempted to mobilize Chicago's black poor. After King's death, Jackson founded People United to Save (later Serve) Humanity (PUSH).

In 1983, angered by Ronald Reagan's social welfare and civil rights rollbacks, Jackson and PUSH began a drive to register black voters. Jackson's charismatic style engendered enthusiasm, especially as the Democrats searched for a presidential candidate who could challenge Reagan in 1984.

Read on **MyHistoryLab Document**: Jesse Jackson Urges Americans to Seek Common Ground, 1988

In 1988 Rev. Jesse Jackson addressed the Democratic National Convention. He made two unsuccessful bids for the White House (1984, 1988) but remained a powerful force in the Democratic Party because of his success in registering and mobilizing voters and building coalitions.

On November 4, 1983, Jackson declared his candidacy for the Democratic nomination and honed an effective style of grassroots mobilization. He began by appealing to what he would call a "rainbow coalition" of people who felt politically marginalized and underrepresented. The **Rainbow Coalition** was composed of diverse groups, including black people, white workers, liberals, Latinos, feminists, students, and environmentalists. Jackson developed a comprehensive economic policy focusing on tax reform, deficit reduction, and employment. The Jackson platform was well within the tradition of American liberal reform but far more progressive than anything his competitors proposed. In January 1984, Jackson gained credentials in international affairs when he traveled to Syria to plead for the release of U.S. Air Force pilot Robert Goodman, who had been held captive there for a year after being shot down in Syrian-controlled airspace. Jackson returned to America in triumph with the freed pilot.

Jackson eventually garnered almost one-fourth of the votes in the Democratic primaries and caucuses and one-eighth of the delegates to the convention. His speech to the convention cemented his position as a voice for progressive change. Walter Mondale, Jimmy Carter's vice president, who won the nomination, broke new ground when he made Congresswoman Geraldine Ferraro his running mate and the first woman on a major party's presidential ticket. But many Jackson supporters had hoped Mondale would pick Jackson.

In November 1984, black voters overwhelmingly favored the Democratic ticket, but Reagan nonetheless won by a landslide. Clearly, most white Americans backed Reagan's conservative policies. Undeterred by defeat, Jackson worked to build his Rainbow Coalition, reaching out to a variety of constituencies, including the unemployed, militant trade unionists, small farmers, and gay, lesbian, bisexual, and transgender communities. Perhaps most important, Jackson's campaign registered enough new voters to help Democrats retain control of the House of Representatives in 1984 and regain a majority in the Senate in the 1986 midterm elections.

By the time Jackson announced he would again run for president in October 1987, he had become a serious contender. He won 15 presidential primaries and caucuses and garnered seven million votes, one-third of all those cast. His Rainbow Coalition, however, never materialized. His victories in the primaries were based on mobilizing his black supporters. Almost all of his white support tended to come from college towns. Jackson's campaign strategies, nevertheless, were a precursor to those devised by the strategists for Barack Obama in 2008.

Despite Jackson's voter registration drive and the hopes of the black community, Reagan's vice president, George H. W. Bush, triumphed in the 1988 election. The most memorable feature of Bush's campaign, was a polarizing television ad that featured Willie Horton, a black convict who had raped a white woman while on furlough from a Massachusetts prison as part of a program approved both by Bush's opponent Governor Michael Dukakis and his Republican predecessor as governor. Jackson and other black leaders attacked the ad as a blatant appeal to white racism, but it helped elect Bush.

The second phase in the evolution of black politics witnessed both the solidification of black support for the Democrats and the resurgence of a more conservative, increasingly southern-dominated Republican Party that was determined to roll back the progress that civil rights leaders and activists had so painfully won in the 1950s and 1960s. Republican domination was also marked by the emergence of a small but prominent cadre of black neoconservatives. The overwhelming mass of black voters, however, remained bound to the Democratic Party and helped elect William Jefferson Clinton president in 1992 and 1996. Although Republican George W. Bush appointed several African-American conservatives to his cabinets between 2001 and 2008, most black people remained solidly committed to the Democratic Party.

Second Phase of Black Politics
African Americans anticipated that the Clinton victory in 1992 represented the solidification of the Rainbow Coalition of progressive forces that Jesse Jackson had championed. Clinton was undoubtedly a friend to African Americans, but many of their hopes were only partly fulfilled. Yet as political strategist Donna Brazile asserted, the Clinton 1990s appeared to be a new era of black power. In retrospect, given what occurred under President George W. Bush, this may have been true. The conservative triumph in the 2000 and 2004 elections caused many African-American leaders to reassess black political strategies. The NAACP and other social justice and civil rights organizations crafted a broad national and international political agenda during the 2004 presidential race. A new generation of black politicians, such as Barack Obama of Illinois and Governor Deval Patrick of Massachusetts, addressed the economic, healthcare, education, and security concerns of black and white America in a healing new centrist voice. The 2008 victory that catapulted

Barack Obama into the White House represented the triumph of "Rainbow Coalition" building. The radical right Tea Party faction of the Republican Party won enough local elections to regain control of the House of Representatives and pursued a strategy of obstruction that derailed many of the initiatives that the Obama administration advocated to address the country's fiscal crisis.

The third phase of black politics helped to elect Barack Obama to the presidency and preserved a Democratic Party majority in the U.S. Senate. In both his 2008 and 2012 election campaigns, Obama won in no small part because he successfully mobilized black and Latino voters. Obama represented a new type of black leader, one who, as some argued, was "post-black" or "post-race," who represented a shift from "color-blind politics" or "pluralism" to a politics of "hybridity." Both of his presidential campaigns were supported by a majority of racial minority, women, and gay voters.

The Present Status of Black Politics

In 2007 Senator Barack Obama of Illinois launched his campaign to become the Democratic presidential candidate. The closing decades of the twentieth century were characterized by sharp divisions between white and black Americans and between the Democratic and Republican parties, and by growing economic disparities between working-class and middle-class Americans and the rich. The conservative right used these years to create political organizations that supported school prayers, attacked women's reproductive rights and their right to choose, and denied the civil rights claims of gays, lesbians, and bisexual and transgendered Americans.

Throughout the 1980s white conservatives nurtured and mobilized their base of disillusioned southerners, alienated northerners, and wealthy elites to reverse liberal-progressive policies. African Americans, throughout the presidencies of Ronald Reagan and George H. W. Bush (1981–1993), witnessed a consolidation of Republican Party power. Black American leaders and community activists developed and adhered to a liberal-progressive agenda that emphasized jobs, universal health care, access to better education, environmental justice, and freedom of opportunity. African Americans did not develop a race-conscious third party movement. Instead, black voters overwhelmingly put their hopes in the Democratic Party.

To be sure, the access to greater opportunities in education and employment helped to fuel growing divisions within black America. Not all black Americans benefited equally from the gains of the civil rights movement. Fractures along class lines within the black community became more visible. While the ranks of the urban black poor swelled, the growing black middle and upper class embraced electoral politics to win a greater share in America's educational, social, and political institutions.

By 2000, a white conservative backlash, combined with inadequate housing, lack of health insurance, resource-starved schools, and reduced funding for welfare and job training programs, dampened the expectations and damaged the health and dignity of many poorer black people. In sum, as scholar Nikhil Pal Singh noted, "Despite the growth of a black middle class [during the prosperous 1990s], three decades after the passage of the Civil Rights Act the median net worth of whites—which includes inherited assets as well as income—is a staggering twelve times that of blacks." To be sure, the 2008–2010 recession delivered a major blow to black people in every income bracket, although those in service professions and holding low-skilled jobs fared far worse. The high unemployment of black women-headed households, and the so-called welfare-reform policies pursued during the Clinton presidency, especially devastated families and communities.

Ronald Reagan and the Conservative Reaction

24-2 How did Reagan and Bush attempt to dismantle the "Great Society" and undermine social welfare programs?

Just as African Americans began mobilizing their communities for full participation in the country's political life in the late 1970s, American politics took a hard turn to the right. This shift had a devastating impact on African Americans, particularly the poor. With the 1980 election of Ronald Reagan (1911–2004) to the presidency, the executive branch sought to curtail civil rights. It reduced welfare programs and staffed key agencies and the federal judiciary with opponents of affirmative action. An overwhelmingly white Republican Party became increasingly entrenched in the South and ended the Democratic Party's' long dominance. The political landscape of the 1980s and 1990s was thus marked by a hardening of ideological conflict between liberal and progressive Democrats on one side and conservative, indeed radical, Republicans on the other.

Ronald Reagan's defeat of Jimmy Carter paved the way for the dominance of the New Right. In the 1980s, powerful conservative political organizations found a home in the Republican Party. These groups were opposed to equal rights for women, especially their reproduction rights. They sought to overturn Supreme Court decisions protecting the rights of the accused and prohibiting compulsory prayer from the public schools. Many white southerners opposed labor unions, and they joined forces with white northerners who objected to school busing, affirmative action programs, and the tax burden they associated with welfare and entitlement policies.

The King Holiday

Many African Americans invested symbolic importance in making Martin Luther King, Jr.'s birthday a national holiday, elevating him to the stature of George Washington and Abraham Lincoln, both of whom are honored with a holiday. At first Reagan resisted the idea, but he eventually gave in to pressure from African Americans and their white allies. On January 20, 1985, the United States officially observed Martin Luther King, Jr., Day for the first time. In 2011 President Barack Obama unveiled the Martin Luther King, Jr., statue, the first African-American monument on the Washington National Mall.

Dismantling the Great Society

One of the New Right's chief goals was to dismantle the social welfare programs created during and after the New Deal and Johnson's Great Society. From 1981 to 1992, Reagan and George H. W. Bush halved federal grants to cities. As a result, inner-city neighborhoods where 56 percent of poor residents were African Americans became more unstable. Reagan advanced a trickle-down theory of economics. He believed that if the wealthiest Americans got richer, their increased prosperity and the spending associated with it would percolate through the middle and working classes to benefit the poor. Unemployment statistics soon challenged this theory. By December 1982, the unemployment rate had risen to 10.8 percent, and the rate for African Americans was twice that of white Americans. The annual income of the highest-paid 1 percent of the nation, meanwhile, increased from $312,206 to $548,970 by 1988.

Reagan and Bush often cloaked their intent to undermine rights-oriented policies by appointing black conservatives to key positions. Reagan chose William Bell, for example, to replace Eleanor Holmes Norton as chair of the Equal Employment Opportunity Commission (EEOC). Bell had few qualifications for the post, and civil rights organizations protested his appointment. Reagan simply replaced Bell the following year with yet another black conservative, Clarence Thomas, who opposed affirmative action. Thomas reduced the commission's staff and allowed the backlog of affirmative action cases to grow to 46,000 and the processing time for a case to increase to 10 months.

Black Conservatives

24-3 **What role did black conservatives play in the Republican Party in the 1980s and 1990s?**

Read on MyHistoryLab Document: Richard Viguerie, Why the New Right Is Winning, (1981)

William Bell and Clarence Thomas were members of a vocal cadre of black, middle-class, conservative intellectuals, professionals, and politicians who came to prominence during the Reagan years. There was a critical difference, however, between elite black Republican and black Democratic politicians: black Republicans rarely exercised meaningful power within their party. They were expected to embrace the values and support the goals of the white party leaders. In contrast, black Democratic politicians could and often did make their influence felt. Moreover, black Democrats represented a large and essential constituency within the party. Following Obama's victory in 2008, the Republican Party elected black conservative Michael Steele as chair of the Republican National Committee to create an illusion of racial inclusion within the party. Steele was replaced in 2011 by an even more conservative white chairman who was more closely aligned with the Tea Party insurgents.

The Thomas–Hill Controversy

The role of black conservatives was highlighted when, in 1991, President George H. W. Bush nominated Clarence Thomas to the Supreme Court. The symbolism of Thomas, who opposed the expansion of civil rights, replacing Thurgood Marshall, the greatest civil rights lawyer of the twentieth century, could not have been more dramatic.

Thomas's nomination precipitated a public display of gender conflict within the black community. While Marshall had been one of the Court's great liberals and a staunch defender of civil rights, Thomas was a black conservative whose record on civil rights did not endear him either to white liberals or many within the black community. His credentials for the Court were questioned. He had served only 15 months as an appellate court judge. Nevertheless, the black community was loath to openly contest his nomination or to challenge the cynical tokenism of the Bush administration. Some civil rights organizations expressed reservations about the Thomas nomination.

The anticipated easy confirmation process derailed when black law professor Anita Hill appeared before the Senate

Anita Hill, a law professor at the University of Oklahoma, testified before the U.S. Senate Judiciary Committee confirmation hearings that Supreme Court nominee Clarence Thomas had sexually harassed her. Thomas was confirmed in spite of these sexual harassment charges.

Judiciary Committee, which heard testimony on Thomas's confirmation. Hill accused Thomas of sexually harassing her when she worked for him at the EEOC.

Both Anita Hill and Clarence Thomas were conservative Republicans, and both had earned law degrees at Yale. Hill did not volunteer to testify about Thomas's sexual harassment. She had answered questions put to her in a confidential investigation. When her answers were leaked to the press, she agreed to appear before the committee. Some senators questioned her character and integrity. Thomas charged that he was a victim of a "high-tech lynching" in the media and that Hill's accusations were false. Although many in the black community supported Thomas, progressive feminists, white liberals, and some black people supported Hill. Activist black women were incensed by the treatment that Hill received from the Senate and were determined to voice their opposition to Thomas's political views. Despite the opposition, Thomas won confirmation to the Court by a narrow 52 to 48 majority. On the Court, Justice Thomas remains an archconservative who unwaveringly votes with the conservative majority. He adamantly opposes affirmative action.

Debating the "Old" and the "New" Civil Rights

24-4 What are the "old" and "new" civil rights?

The Reagan and Bush administrations distinguished between what might be called the "old civil rights law," which they claimed to support, and the "new civil rights law," which they opposed. Developed between the *Brown* decision in 1954 and the Voting Rights Act of 1965, the old civil rights law prohibited intentional discrimination, be it legal segregation in the schools, informal discrimination in the workplace, or racial restrictions on voting. The new civil rights law was concerned with discriminatory outcomes, as measured by statistical disparities, rather than with discriminatory intent.

The remedies for such historic discrimination, collectively labeled **affirmative action**, tend to be statistical in nature. They include increasing the number of minority pupils, minority employees, or minority elected officials (by redrawing the districts from which they were elected) to correspond to the percentage of the relevant minority population. In employment (and in admissions to colleges and universities), the methods used in reaching these goals became known as affirmative action "guidelines." Sometimes guidelines were imposed by court order. More often, they were the result of voluntary efforts by legislatures, government agencies, businesses, and colleges and universities to comply with civil rights laws and court rulings.

affirmative action Civil rights policy or program that seeks to redress the effects of past discrimination due to race or gender by giving preference to women and minorities in education and employment.

Affirmative Action

Few civil rights policies in the twentieth century proved more controversial than affirmative action. Many white Americans argue that it runs contrary to the concept of achievement founded on merit and amounts to reverse racial or sexual discrimination. Affirmative action's chief advocates have been African Americans who view it as a remedy for centuries of discrimination. The debate over affirmative action not only led to racial polarization, it divided the black community.

President Lyndon Johnson had first used the term "affirmative action" in a 1965 executive order that required federal contractors to "take affirmative action" to guarantee that

Days after Anita Hill appeared before the Senate Judiciary Committee, a group of black women led by Elsa Barkley Brown, Barbara Ransby, and Deborah King raised more than $50,000 to print this statement in the New York Times, *"In Defense of Ourselves." Appearing on November 17, 1991, it was signed by 1,603 black women. Five black newspapers—the* San Francisco Sun Reporter, *the* Los Angeles Sentinel, *the* New York City Sun, *the* Atlanta Inquirer, *and the* Chicago Defender—*also published the declaration.*

As women of African descent, we are deeply troubled by the recent nomination, confirmation and seating of Clarence Thomas as an Associate Justice of the U.S. Supreme Court. We know that the presence of Clarence Thomas on the Court will be continually used to divert attention away from the historic struggles for social justice through suggestions that the presence of a Black man on the Supreme Court constitutes an assurance that the rights of African Americans will be protected. Clarence Thomas's public record is ample evidence that this will not be true. Further, the consolidation of a conservative majority on the Supreme Court endangers the working class people and the elderly. The seating of Clarence Thomas is an affront not only to African American women and men, but to all people concerned with social justice.

We are particularly outraged by the racist and sexist treatment of Professor Anita Hill, an African American woman who was maligned and castigated for daring to speak publicly of her own experience of sexual abuse. The malicious defamation of Professor Hill insulted all women of African descent and sent a dangerous message to all women who might contemplate a sexual harassment complaint.

We speak here because we recognize that the media are now portraying the Black community as prepared to tolerate the dismantling of affirmative action and the evil of sexual harassment in order to have any Black man on the Supreme Court. We want to make clear that the media have ignored and distorted many African American voices. We will not be silenced.

Many have erroneously portrayed the allegations against Clarence Thomas as an issue of either gender or race. As women of African descent, we understand sexual harassment as both. We further understand that Clarence Thomas outrageously manipulated the legacy of lynching in order to shelter himself from Anita Hill's allegations. To deflect attention away from the reality of sexual abuse in African American women's lives, he trivialized and misrepresented this painful part of African American people's history. This country, which has a long legacy of racism and sexism, has never taken the sexual abuse of Black women seriously. Throughout U.S. history Black women have been sexually stereotyped as immoral, insatiable, perverse, the initiators in all sexual contacts—abusive or otherwise. The common assumption in legal proceedings as well as in the larger society has been that Black women cannot be raped or otherwise sexually abused. As Anita Hill's experience demonstrates, Black women who speak of these matters are not likely to be believed. In 1991, we cannot tolerate this type of dismissal of any one Black woman's experience or this attack upon our collective character without protest, outrage, and resistance.

As women of African descent, we express our vehement opposition to the policies represented by the placement of Clarence Thomas on the Supreme Court. The Bush administration, having obstructed the passage of civil rights legislation, impeded the extension of unemployment compensation, cut student aid and dismantled social welfare programs, has continually demonstrated that it is not operating in our best interests. Nor is this appointee. We pledge ourselves to continue to speak out in defense of one another, in defense of the African American community and against those who are hostile to social justice no matter what color they are. No one will speak for us but ourselves.

1. Why did the African-American women who signed this letter feel they needed to defend themselves?
2. Why did they oppose the confirmation of Clarence Thomas to the Supreme Court?
3. Why were they unsympathetic to Thomas's claim that he had been a victim of a "high-tech" lynching?

SOURCE: *New York Times,* November 17, 1991, 53.

job seekers and employees "are treated without regard to their race, color, religion, sex, or national origin." In 1969 Arthur A. Fletcher, a black assistant secretary of labor in the Nixon administration, developed the "Philadelphia Plan," in which firms with federal construction contracts were obligated to set and meet hiring goals for African Americans or be penalized. The plan became a model for subsequent "set-aside" programs that reserved some contracts for minority-owned businesses or that favored hiring women and minorities. Setting goals and timetables to achieve full compliance with federal civil rights requirements appealed to large corporations and accounted for the early success of affirmative action initiatives.

The Backlash

Although it produced more litigation, affirmative action in employment proved less contro-versial than affirmative action in college and university admissions. State higher-education institutions occupied the center of the controversy both because they were narrowly bound by the Fourteenth Amendment's prohibitions against racial discrimination and because they, far more than elite private institutions, were the gateways to upward mobility for many Americans, white and black, Asians, and Latino/as. Nevertheless, both to aid disadvantaged minorities and increase racial and cultural diversity on campus, admissions offices were forced to employ different admission criteria. Conservatives called these criteria "racial pref-erences" that promoted unfairness and white resentment.

The case of *Regents of the University of California v. Bakke* reflected the white back-lash to affirmative action. The medical school at the University of California set aside 16 of its 100 places in each entering class for disadvantaged and minority students. They were considered for admission in a separate system. A white student named Alan Bakke sued the University for discrimination after it rejected his application. In 1978 the U.S. Supreme Court ruled in Bakke's favor. Of the nine justices, five agreed that the university violated Bakke's rights. However, only one justice declared that affirmative action cases should be judged on the same strict level of scrutiny applied to "invidious" (intentionally harmful) discrimination. All the other justices stated that race-conscious remedies could be used in some circumstances to correct discrimination.

California was at the center of the affirmative action storm because of its multiracial popula-tion. In 1995 Republican Governor Pete Wilson ended affirmative action in state employment. In 1996 California voters approved Proposition 209, the so-called California Civil Rights Initiative, which banned all state agencies from implementing affirmative action programs.

Its effect and that of similar laws or court rulings around the nation is now known. The number of African Americans and other protected minorities admitted to the University of California system dropped, and the numbers at Berkeley, the University of California's most prestigious campus, fell precipitously. In both California and Texas, which abandoned affir-mative action in its university system after a court challenge, administrators have attempted to assure a diverse student body by offering admission to their top schools to all students in the top ranks of their high school class.

On June 23, 2003, the Supreme Court, in two separate decisions, handed the University of Michigan both a victory, when it upheld the law school's practice of using race as a crite-rion in admissions procedures to create a diverse student body, and a defeat, when it banned the university from awarding points based on race as a criterion for admitting undergradu-ates. In the first case, *Grutter v. Bollinger,* a five-to-four decision declared that the law school could use race to achieve diversity. However, writing for the majority in the second case, *Gratz v. Bollinger,* Chief Justice Rehnquist maintained that in admitting undergraduates the university crossed the line of what was permissible by giving points to black applicants.

24-1
24-2
24-3
24-4
24-5
24-6
24-7
24-8
24-9

1979–2009
SUPREME COURT CASES ON AFFIRMATIVE ACTION IN EMPLOYMENT

1979
United Steelworkers v. Weber upheld preferential treatment in hiring and training by private firms

1980
Fullilove v. Klutznick upheld government programs that reserved places for minorities

1982
American Tobacco Co. v. Patterson upheld seniority plans in place before 1964 unless discriminatory intent could be shown

1986
Wygant v. Jackson Board of Education rejected a school board's plan for laying off white teachers while retaining less senior black teachers, but it also rejected the Reagan administration position that affirmative action be limited to actual victims of discrimination, thus broadly upholding affirmative action

1986
Local 93 of International Association of Firefighters v. City of Cleveland upheld the promotion of minorities ahead of white applicants with higher test scores and greater seniority

1986
Local 28 of Sheet Metal Workers v. EEOC upheld the order that unions meet minority quotas for membership

1987
U.S. v. Paradise upheld a judicial order imposing racial quotas in hiring and promotions of Alabama state troopers

1987
Johnson v. Transportation Agency of Santa Clara County upheld a plan that promoted women over men

1989
Martin v. Wilks ruled that employees may challenge an affirmative action plan after it has gone into effect. Congress overruled this decision in the Civil Rights Act of 1991

1989
Richmond v. J. A. Croson Co. ruled that the Fourteenth Amendment prohibited set-asides for minority contractors, thus going against the spirit of *Weber* and the letter of *Fullilove v. Klutznick* and implying that all such plans face "strict scrutiny (intense examination)"

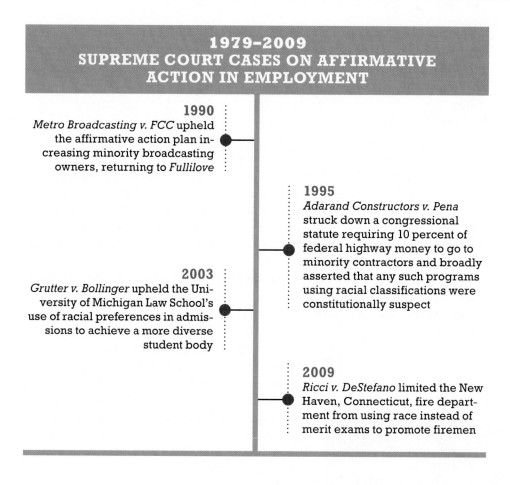

1979–2009
SUPREME COURT CASES ON AFFIRMATIVE ACTION IN EMPLOYMENT

1990
Metro Broadcasting v. FCC upheld the affirmative action plan increasing minority broadcasting owners, returning to *Fullilove*

1995
Adarand Constructors v. Pena struck down a congressional statute requiring 10 percent of federal highway money to go to minority contractors and broadly asserted that any such programs using racial classifications were constitutionally suspect

2003
Grutter v. Bollinger upheld the University of Michigan Law School's use of racial preferences in admissions to achieve a more diverse student body

2009
Ricci v. DeStefano limited the New Haven, Connecticut, fire department from using race instead of merit exams to promote firemen

24-1
24-2
24-3
24-4
24-5
24-6
24-7
24-8
24-9

Black Political Activism at the End of the Twentieth Century

24-5   **What were the focal points of black activism during the Reagan and Bush years?**

The increased participation of black men and women in the upper echelons of the Democratic Party reflected the success of black electoral politics and the internal mobilization of black communities. While in 1964 the nation had only 103 black elected officials, by 1994 there were nearly 8,500. By 2010, 43 African Americans were serving in Congress. By the mid-1990s, black men and women held the mayor's office in 400 towns and cities. Clearly, the days of black political powerlessness had ended—or had they?

By the 1990s African Americans had become an indispensable base of the Democratic Party. Reflecting the importance of African-American voters to the party, congressional Democrats passed equal rights legislation to solidify gains that blacks had won. The Civil Rights Restoration Act of 1988 authorized withholding federal funds from an entire institution if any program within it discriminated against women, racial minorities, the aged, or the disabled. The Fair Housing Act of 1988 stipulated that either an individual or the Department of Housing and Urban Development could bring a complaint of housing discrimination and authorize administrative judges to investigate housing complaints, issue injunctions and fines, and award punitive damages. These laws and the Civil Rights Act of 1991 were a response to Supreme Court decisions that narrowed the scope of earlier civil rights legislation.

Reparations

While party politics attracted attention, many African Americans focused on specific issues, including reparations for slavery, and the spread of HIV/AIDS in the United States and Africa. In 1969 James Foreman, in his "Black Manifesto," called on America's churches and synagogues to collect $500 million as "a beginning of the reparations due us as a people who have been exploited and degraded, brutalized, killed, and persecuted." Four years later, Boris Bittker, a Yale Law School professor, argued in *The Case for Black Reparations* that slavery and the persistence of government-sanctioned racial discrimination justified a program to compensate black Americans. Since 1993 black Democratic Congressman John Conyers from Detroit has introduced a bill in every session of Congress—not to pay reparations but to establish a federal commission to investigate slavery and the legacy of racial discrimination.

In 2000 the issue of reparations for slavery received widespread attention when Randall Robinson, founder and president of TransAfrica, published *The Debt: What America Owes to Blacks*. Robinson reasoned that because Jews and Japanese Americans have been compensated for the indignities and horrors they experienced in World War II, African Americans were also due financial indemnification for slavery. Robinson maintained that many African Americans still bear the scars of slavery in terms of poor housing, inadequate health care, and insufficient educational opportunities. He insists that reparations would remedy the effect of such inequalities.

Some black writers and journalists reject arguments that reparations are a realistic resolution of the nation's slave and racist legacy. Two black journalists, William Raspberry and Juan Williams, objected to the very idea of reparations. Williams declared, "The suffering of long-dead ancestors is not a claim check for a bag full of cash. I don't want any money that belongs to any slave. That is obscene. The struggle of African-Americans for civil rights is not about selling out for a check."

TransAfrica and Black Internationalism

Black activism persisted on the international as well as the national front. Much of this effort focused on ending the oppressive conditions of apartheid—the complete social, political, and economic isolation and subjection of black people—in South Africa and its glorification of white racial supremacy.

Randall Robinson sought to link African-American liberation struggles with those that Africans in South

(•)) 📖 Read on **MyHistoryLab** Document: Nelson Mandela Speaks after Being Released from Prison, 1990

Nelson Mandela's release from prison was celebrated around the globe as the event that signaled the final days of South Africa's system of racial apartheid.

Africa and elsewhere waged. In 1977 he founded TransAfrica to lobby for black political prisoners in South Africa, chief among them Nelson Mandela. In 1984 Mary Francis Berry, Eleanor Holmes Norton, and others joined Robinson for a series of sit-ins at the South African embassy in Washington, DC, during which hundreds were arrested.

The anti-apartheid movement became a major priority for African-American activists. They enlisted the sympathy and help of white Americans on college campuses and pressured universities into divesting their investments in South Africa. Similar pressures were put on corporations, especially those vulnerable to consumer boycotts. In 1986 the Black Congressional Caucus persuaded its colleagues to enact a trade embargo against South Africa and to sustain it over President Reagan's veto.

In 1990, bowing to international pressure, black activism, and a souring domestic economy, South African President F. W. de Klerk removed the ban on the African National Congress, the key opposition party, and ended the 28-year incarceration of Nelson Mandela. Soon thereafter, South Africa became a multiracial democracy, and Mandela was elected its president.

The Rise in Black Incarceration

24-6   **How did general white perceptions of young black men shape trends in criminal justice in the 1990s?**

The general white perception of black men as criminals increased following Bush's election. Even during the Democratic Party's resurgence in the 1990s, the perceptions of black youths as criminals acquired potent political currency, resulting in the mass incarceration of young black men and an increase in police brutality and racial profiling. After the disputed 2000 presidential election, the black community became even more aware of the adverse consequences of mass incarceration because many states deny the right to vote to convicted and incarcerated felons, and 1.8 million of the 5.9 million felons and former felons in the United States are black. (For the statistics on black incarceration, see Table 23–2 in Chapter 23.)

Reformers have sought to draw attention to the brutal conditions within U.S. prisons, especially the violence and high incidence of inmate rape. Yet they have achieved little. In 1994 Supreme Court Justice Clarence Thomas argued, in voting to dismiss claims that prisons failed to protect inmates, that "prisons are necessarily dangerous places, they house society's most antisocial and violent people in close proximity with one another. Regrettably, some level of brutality and sexual aggression among [prisoners] is inevitable no matter what the guards do . . . unless all prisoners are locked in their cells twenty-four hours a day and sedated."

Policing the Black Community

In March 1991 Los Angeles police pulled Rodney Glen King from his car after a high-speed chase and beat him with nightsticks. A bystander captured the incident on videotape, which television newscasts broadcast repeatedly, fueling long-simmering anger over police brutality among African Americans in Los Angeles. When a jury of 11 white Americans and one Hispanic American acquitted the four police officers involved in the incident of all but one of the charges brought against them, south-central Los Angeles erupted in protest. The verdict highlighted the gulf between the perceptions of white and black Americans about the police and the criminal justice system. Where the mostly white jury had seen the police maintaining law and order, black Americans saw police repression and racism. Altogether,

24-1
24-2
24-3
24-4
24-5
24-6
24-7
24-8
24-9

24-1

24-2

24-3

24-4

24-5

24-6

24-7

24-8

24-9

The videotaped beating of Rodney King by Los Angeles police—shown repeatedly on national television—bolstered charges by African Americans in Los Angeles that they were frequent victims of police brutality. Despite the graphic evidence, the officers were acquitted of using excessive force.

52 people were killed in the outbreak that followed the verdict. Thousands of people were injured, 4,000 were arrested, and an estimated half-billion-dollar's worth of property was damaged or destroyed. The four officers were later retried in federal court on charges of violating King's civil rights. This time juries found two of them guilty and acquitted the other two. Meanwhile, a jury in King's civil suit ordered Los Angeles to pay him $3.8 million in damages.

Black Men and White Injustice

Several such high-profile cases focused public attention on the relation of black communities to white police authorities from the 1980s into the 2000s. Police repression was a long-festering cause of tension and hostility that had been behind many of the riots of the 1960s. On November 16, 1992, two Detroit police officers were charged with the murder of Malice Green, a 35-year-old black resident of the city. In 1997 a Haitian immigrant, Abner Louima, was beaten and sodomized while in custody at a Brooklyn police station. In 1999 New York police shot Amadou Diallo, a West African immigrant, 41 times when they mistook his reaching for a wallet for going for a gun. A jury in Albany, New York, acquitted the four police officials charged in the Diallo killing. Also in 2000, Patrick Dorismond (another Haitian immigrant) was shot and killed in New York after he got into an argument with undercover police officers after he refused to buy drugs from them. In 2006 New York police officers killed unarmed 23-year-old Sean Bell, who was on his way to marry the mother of his two children. Apparently Bell was caught in the middle of an undercover sting operation. Police fired at least 50 bullets into his car. In each instance, an enraged black community protested the police profiling as another instance of bias toward black men and one that targeted all minorities for illegal detention. At a protest rally over Bell's shooting, Rev. Al Sharpton declared, "We cannot allow this to continue to happen. We've got to understand that all of us were in that car."

Human Rights in America

In October 1998 the human rights group Amnesty International, known for condemning human rights abuses in countries with repressive governments, reported on police brutality in the United States. The report covered local and state police, the FBI, the Immigration and Naturalization Service, and the prison system. Its contents came as no surprise to most black Americans or, indeed, to any resident of America's poor urban neighborhoods. The report detailed violations of the UN Code of Conduct for Law Enforcement Officials and the UN Basic Principles on the Use of Force and Firearms. Among the violations cited were the following:

- The shooting of unarmed suspects fleeing a minor crime scene
- Excessive force used on mentally ill or disturbed people
- Multiple shootings of a suspect, sometimes after the suspect was apprehended or disabled
- The beating of unresisting suspects
- The misuse of batons, chemical sprays, and electroshock weapons

These violations all involved the misuse of force during arrests, traffic stops, searches, and so forth. The report also cited sexual abuse of prisoners and the denial of food and water to them. The report noted that while most victims of American law enforcement abuse were members of racial and ethnic minorities, most police officers were white.

It is too easy to interpret these findings as showing that American police officers, as a group, are racists who oppress people they do not like. In fact, the issue of police brutality is not nearly so simple. Police officers are under tremendous pressure and live dangerous lives, in part because guns are so widely available in America. No one can be expected to have perfect judgment about using force, and the cumulative effect of years of dealing with violence can destroy a person's sense of perspective and moral equilibrium.

Neither is the problem of crime by black Americans a simple one. The level of crime in black communities is high. The murder rate, for example, for African Americans in 2009 is seven times that of whites, and black victims accounted for 46.9 percent of all those murdered, even though African Americans make up only 12 percent of the population. Over 90 percent of those who murder, rape, and assault black people are black themselves.

Crime devastates black neighborhoods. High crime rates raise the costs of business, driving jobs and investment dollars out of the areas that most need them. Fear of violence leads many in the inner cities to barricade themselves inside their homes. Crime has transformed once vibrant neighborhoods into virtual ghost towns where only the sound of gunfire disturbs the silence of the streets. Filmmaker Spike Lee was shocked in 1994 when he returned to the Brooklyn neighborhood in which he had grown up to shoot his film *Crooklyn*. He found the streets had become so unsafe that the local children he used as extras had to be taught how to play the games he had played growing up in the 1970s because they had never been allowed to play outside. Even Rosa Parks, heroine of the civil rights movement, was not immune to the urban crime wave. In 1994 she was beaten and robbed in her Detroit home by a 28-year-old unemployed black man. Her assailant recognized Parks but assaulted her anyway.

Being disproportionately the victims of crime, most African Americans have looked to the nation's police departments for aid. Because of their growing political power, they have sought, not always successfully, to make the police both responsive to crime and fair in enforcing the laws. One key for changing the behavior of law enforcement officials has been the appointment of black police chiefs.

24-1

24-2

24-3

24-4

24-5

24-6

24-7

24-8

24-9

Black Politics, 1992–2001:
The Clinton Presidency

24-7 **Why did African Americans remain supportive of Bill Clinton's presidency and remain loyal Democrats?**

Watch on
MyHistoryLab
Video:
The Clinton Years

During his first campaign for the presidency in 1992, black Americans welcomed Arkansas Governor Bill Clinton into their churches, schools, and homes. Black citizens and the civil rights leadership embraced Clinton's candidacy against incumbent Republican George H. W. Bush, who had done little to win their loyalty. White Americans, too, were dissatisfied with the Bush presidency. Although he enjoyed high approval ratings in early 1991 following American military success in evicting Iraq from Kuwait in the first Gulf War, by early 1992 his popularity had slumped in the face of an economic downturn. Still, at first, few operatives believed Clinton would unseat Bush.

Shrewdly, however, Clinton positioned himself as a centrist within the mainstream of American politics. This required him to at least appear to place some distance between himself and the liberal-progressive arm of the Democratic Party represented by Jesse Jackson and the Rainbow Coalition. Clinton attacked Bush's record and promised to make government more responsive to the needs of Americans. The strategy worked. Clinton won in November 1992 with just 43 percent of the popular vote to Bush's 38 percent and third-party candidate H. Ross Perot's 19 percent. The election was not a clear mandate. Although Democrats maintained control of Congress, they gained no seats in the Senate and lost seats in the House. Republicans used the ambiguous outcome to launch a relentless campaign to undermine Clinton's presidency.

Most black people, however, considered Clinton the best president on race issues since Lyndon Johnson. Writer Toni Morrison called Clinton the first black president, and in some

President William Jefferson Clinton is seen here with members of the Little Rock Nine, who, as teenagers, defied hostile mobs to desegregate Central High School in Little Rock, Arkansas, in 1957. African Americans claimed Clinton as the first black president, given his comfort around black people and the number of African Americans he considered friends.

circles he was called the first woman president because of his support for equal rights for women, both black annd white. Clinton appointed women, including many black women, to 37 percent of the 500 upper-level positions in the White House and federal bureaucracy. During the campaign, he had visited the riot-torn ruins of south-central Los Angeles, played the saxophone on *The Arsenio Hall Show*, and worshiped in black churches, where he was warmly received. In Clinton, black Americans had a friend. Clinton created a cabinet that mirrored the diversity of the American population, in some cases—such as Hazel O'Leary as secretary of the Department of Energy, Alexis Herman as secretary of labor, and Ron Brown as secretary of commerce—appointing black people to posts that had nothing to do with race. Clinton also gave to Washington, DC, delegate to Congress Eleanor Holmes Norton the prerogative, normally reserved to U.S. senators, of selecting U.S. district court judges, U.S. marshals, and the U.S. attorney for the District of Columbia. Moreover, not only did Clinton appoint many African-American officials and judges, he was the first American president to visit sub-Saharan Africa.

"It's the Economy, Stupid!"
In 1996 Clinton became the first Democratic president to win a second term since Franklin Roosevelt. Throughout his two terms in office, Clinton focused attention on the economy, a strategy that won grudging support from moderate Republicans. His objective was to strengthen the economy, since a stronger economy would improve economic opportunities for black Americans. In a significant departure from the policies of his predecessors, Clinton increased the taxes of higher-income Americans and pushed for an expansion of the earned income tax credit. His college student-aid program increased federal loan benefits. When Clinton left office in 2001, the country had the lowest poverty rate in 20 years.

Clinton's economic programs were supported by the Congressional Black Caucus (CBC). In 1993 CBC chairman Representative Kweisi Mfume of Maryland and the highest-ranking black congressman, Representative John Lewis of Georgia, delivered the caucus vote that saved Clinton's $500 billion economic budget in both the House and the Senate. In return, black congressmen gained financial support for inner cities, poor families, children, and the elderly.

Unemployment plummeted from 7.2 percent when Clinton took office to 4.0 percent when he left it. American businesses created 10 million new jobs, and many black people who feared they would never gain a foothold in the economy found work, some for the first time. Reduced federal spending and the 1993 tax increase helped cut the annual federal deficit in half.

The Welfare Reform Act and "Three Strikes"
Prior to his reelection in August 1996, and to the chagrin of his African-American political base, Clinton opportunistically signed the Personal Responsibility and Work Opportunity Reconciliation Act, a welfare reform bill. African Americans and many white political progressives were disappointed. The legislation combined Clinton's own ideas with those espoused by conservative Republicans. The main target of the Personal Responsibility Act was Aid to Families of Dependent Children (AFDC), a program created in 1935 as part of the Social Security Act to prevent children from suffering due to the poverty of their parents. Critics claimed AFDC stipends discouraged poor mothers from finding work, that it was responsible for the breakdown of the family among the nation's poor, and that it did little to reduce poverty. They insisted the states did not have enough flexibility in administering welfare. The conservative welfare "reform" measure ended guarantees of federal aid to poor

24-1

24-2

24-3

24-4

24-5

24-6

24-7

24-8

24-9

children, turning control of such programs over to the states along with allocations of block grants. The Welfare Reform Act denied benefits to legal immigrants, mandated drastic reductions in food stamp appropriations, and limited families to five years of benefits. It also required most adult welfare recipients to find employment within two years.

There were no good reasons to believe the welfare reform bill would accomplish its sponsors' objectives. Most of the people who would be "encouraged to find work" by having their benefits reduced or cut entirely were among the least employable people in the labor force. As for the bill's effect on families, it is true that most women on welfare had their first children when they were unmarried teenagers, but little evidence indicated that cutting welfare prevented teenage pregnancies. There was, however, evidence that the reforms which targeted improving the collection of child support payments for divorced mothers did reduce welfare costs far more effectively and humanely.

Clinton's support of the welfare act was consistent with his centrist ideology. Furthermore, it immunized him from Republican attacks while leaving black support intact. Clinton endorsed other policies that had a negative impact on African Americans and seemed, at least symbolically, to reassure white moderates. He signed a crime bill that allowed local communities to hire more police officers and build more prisons. He supported the implementation of a "three-strikes" policy of stiffer penalties for those who had at least two prior criminal convictions. Meanwhile, Clinton failed, in the teeth of intense Republican opposition, to enact comprehensive healthcare legislation.

The preliminary results of the new welfare reform strictures indicated that, within a couple of years, half of those who had taken jobs had returned to lives of unemployment, poverty, and quiet desperation. As the economy took a downturn at the end of Clinton's second term, conditions for poor mothers and children deteriorated steadily. The debate over welfare policy receded to the back burner during the 2000 election campaign and disappeared completely after George W. Bush entered the White House.

Black Politics in the Clinton Era

Congressional Republicans and radical conservatives hated Clinton's presidency, and many of them hated Clinton himself. They vowed to take back the White House. Republicans raised huge sums of money and organized local constituencies, especially in the South. The Democrats seemed demoralized and did little to mobilize their base, especially in the black community. Their passivity had predictable results. Many African Americans did not vote in the congressional elections in 1994, and the Democrats lost control of Congress. For the first time in 40 years, the Republicans could implement their conservative agenda, which included rolling back environmental protection policies, reducing taxes for the rich, cutting benefits for the elderly, increasing military spending, establishing the primacy of Christianity over other religions, and advancing white supremacy.

Belatedly awake to the peril of black political alienation, younger Democratic leaders began to fight back. In 1994 Jesse Jackson, Jr., won a seat in Congress from Chicago, held until his resignation in 2012. Jackson outlined a comprehensive social democratic agenda for black America. Progressive Democrats understood that race was no longer a matter of just black and white people. Many other groups and movements were emerging, including Asian/Pacific Island-Americans, Arab-Americans, and Native Americans. Immigrants, especially migrant workers from Mexico, were forming labor organizations to fight for immigrant rights and social justice. But Democrats were now in the congressional minority, and party leaders seemed loath to knit together these diverse constituencies into viable grassroots organizations and to foster solidarity projects and efforts crucial to social change.

While Democrats unraveled, Republicans drew strength from the appointment of Kenneth Starr as an independent counsel to investigate allegations surrounding Bill and Hillary Clinton's investment in an Arkansas land development deal known as Whitewater. As the investigations escalated, Clinton became caught up in a sex scandal. He denied sexual involvement with a White House intern, Monica Lewinsky. On December 19, 1998, the Republican majority in the House narrowly voted to impeach Clinton for perjury and obstruction of justice for tampering with witnesses to conceal his relationship with Lewinsky. The Senate, however, refused to convict him.

Black Politics and the Contested 2000 Election

The election of 2000 revealed fault lines of culture and geography, and the changing demographics of race, class, and gender. A gender gap of about 11 percent reflected the fact that men strongly supported Republican candidates and women favored Democratic candidates. The middle of the country and the South voted for Republican Texas Governor George W. Bush. Democratic candidate Vice President Albert Gore, Jr., carried the states of the upper Midwest, the Northeast, and the Pacific coast. Gays and lesbians voted 70 percent for Gore, whereas those who identified themselves as conservative Christians voted 80 percent for Bush. The campaign focused largely on economic issues—social security, taxes, health care, and education.

Black community leaders and organizations worked hard to register voters and increase turnout for the 2000 election. The NAACP, for example, spent $9 million on Operation Big Vote. Organizers even registered more than 11,000 inmates in county jails in the South.

Gore v. Bush

In a hotly contested election, the outcome hung on one state: Florida. In the end, the Supreme Court, in a five-to-four ruling (*Bush v. Gore*), decided the issue by halting the recount of ballots in Florida. The Court's majority based its ruling on the Fourteenth Amendment's prohibition of states denying citizens equal protection of the law. The Court insisted the recount had to be stopped because the Florida Supreme Court, which had authorized it, had failed to provide uniform standards for determining the intent of the voters. Bush was declared the winner in Florida by fewer than 600 votes, which gave him a four-vote majority in the Electoral College.

Bill Clinton called *Gore v. Bush* "an appalling decision" and compared its impact on African Americans to the infamous *Dred Scott* and *Plessy v. Ferguson* decisions of the nineteenth century. Indeed, African Americans reported serious discrimination and interference with their voting in Florida. A lawsuit in Jacksonville, Florida, claimed that many votes were thrown out as "undervotes" or "overvotes," especially in the four districts with the highest concentration of African Americans in the state. According to the lawsuit, 26,000 ballots were not counted in Duval County, and more than 9,000 of those were cast in largely African-American precincts where Gore had captured more than 90 percent of the vote. Indeed, the U.S. Civil Rights Commission found that tens of thousands of African Americans were disfranchised in Florida.

Republican Triumph

24-8 How did the events of 9/11, the wars in Iraq and Afghanistan, Hurricane Katrina, and the election of Barack Obama affect black political consciousness?

In the 2000 elections, Republicans also retained narrow majorities in Congress. *Gore v. Bush* thus not only put George W. Bush in the White House but also meant that for the first

Watch on
MyHistoryLab
Video: The Election
of 2000

Explore on
MyHistoryLab
Activity: The
Election of 2000

Watch on
MyHistoryLab
Video: Politics in the
New Millennium

24-1

24-2

24-3

24-4

24-5

24-6

24-7

24-8

24-9

time since 1954, the Republican Party was in control of the presidency and both houses of Congress.

George W. Bush's Black Cabinet

President Bush was aware that few African Americans had voted for him. But this did not prevent him from appointing well-educated, articulate, and accomplished black men and women to key posts. Such appointments tended to mute black criticism and placate white swing voters who disdained racial exclusion. Bush named General Colin L. Powell to be secretary of state. Powell, the son of Jamaican immigrants, had served as chairman of the Joint Chiefs of Staff (1989–1993), the highest military position in the Department of Defense. During his tenure he oversaw Operation Desert Storm, the victorious 1991 Persian Gulf War.

Bush also appointed Condoleezza Rice to be his national security adviser. Rice was the first African American and the first woman to hold this post. During the 2000 election, Rice had formed a strong personal bond with Bush, and this relationship became the foundation of her power in his administration.

In the 2000 campaign, Bush had vowed to reform public education. This was an issue of vital importance to both black and white families. Black parents were especially alarmed over the de facto resegregation of black children in urban schools. Thus, many were heartened when Bush selected black Texan Rod Paige as the secretary of education.

Paige introduced the No Child Left Behind Act, an education reform that Bush ardently embraced. This legislation, signed into law in 2002, required all schools to test students at regular intervals in reading, math, and science. States also had to publish the test results and sanction schools whose students failed to do well on the tests. Implicitly, the measure rejected integration as a primary social policy objective and retreated from mandatory busing while promoting parents' freedom to enroll their children in the schools of their choice through voucher programs.

No Child Left Behind was soon mired in controversy. Critics, including many conservatives, blasted it for setting unrealistic goals and for not including sufficient federal funding to help schools meet the higher standards. In 2007 Congress increased funding under the act, but No Child Left Behind remains controversial, and many critics would still like to see it repealed or substantially modified.

September 11, 2001

Americans were stunned on September 11, 2001, when terrorists seized four commercial airliners and crashed them into New York's World Trade Center, the Pentagon in Washington, and rural Pennsylvania. Hundreds of African Americans were among the more than 3,000 people who died that day. If the debate over reparations dramatized the separate pasts that black and white Americans have experienced, then September 11, 2001, reminded them of their common future. But the sense of national unity did not last.

War

Americans expected President Bush to devise an effective strategy against the Taliban regime in Afghanistan and to destroy Osama bin Laden and the al-Qaeda network, which was responsible for 9/11. The president pledged retribution, and the war in Afghanistan began on October 7, 2001. The Taliban were easily overthrown, but bin Laden and the Taliban leader, Mullah Omar, escaped.

Still, the Bush administration called its Afghan foray a success even though the Taliban launched a new guerrilla war and much of Afghanistan remained in the control of warlords and insurgents. Critics, such as Richard A. Clarke, the former chief counterter-rorism adviser to Presidents Clinton and George W. Bush, argued that the Bush admin-istration's real target after 9/11 was not Afghanistan and al-Qaeda but Saddam Hussein's Iraq. Clarke charged that Bush and National Security Adviser Condoleezza Rice had failed to heed the reports of a planned terrorist attack before September 11, 2001. Rice denied these charges, but early in 2002 the administration began to shift the nation's attention from Afghanistan to Iraq.

The prospect of war in Iraq aroused mass protests at home and vociferous opposition abroad and at the United Nations, which refused to back the United States despite strenuous lobbying led by Secretary of State Colin Powell. In a speech before the UN Security Council in February 2003, Powell argued, based on what turned out to be misleading and possibly distorted intelligence reports, that Saddam not only had weapons of mass destruction but also had ties to international terrorist networks, including al-Qaeda. The Security Council was not convinced and voted against the invasion, but the United States invaded Iraq any-way on March 19, 2003. Only Britain gave it significant support.

As in Afghanistan, victory in Iraq appeared to come quickly, and Bush declared the mission there accomplished when Baghdad was occupied after a few weeks of fighting. However, it proved much easier to overthrow Saddam than to pacify Iraq. The country quickly descended into chaos. Insurgents attacked American occupation forces and those Iraqis who cooperated with them. Critics blasted the administration for failing to develop a coherent peace plan. The war, they charged, had actually strengthened terrorism, while the failure to secure UN support or to find weapons of mass destruction or establish ties between Saddam and al-Qaeda had damaged America's credibility and weakened the fabric of international cooperation.

Black Politics in the Bush Era

Massachusetts Senator John F. Kerry won the Democratic Party's nomination for presi-dent in 2004. The war in Iraq dominated other issues, including gay marriage and abor-tion rights. Kerry selected Senator John Edwards from North Carolina to be his running mate against incumbents George W. Bush and Dick Cheney. While these men cam-paigned, African Americans registered an important but subtle shift in their status within the Democratic Party as it became clear that they would play a key role in determining the outcome of the election.

The process of political transformation begun in the 1960s peaked in the 2004 presiden-tial primaries. In these contests, African Americans emerged as the most reliable Democratic base and made their views heard and their power acknowledged. They wanted Americans to understand that little divided blacks and whites when it came to regaining the White House from the Republicans. In 2004 they demanded acknowledgment of their central role as Democratic standard-bearers. Two of the nine contenders for the Democratic nomination were African Americans: Carol Moseley Braun, former U.S. senator from Illinois, and Rev. Al Sharpton of New York. Braun and Sharpton participated in all of the primary debates before throwing their support to Kerry.

In the spirit of presenting a united front, Braun, Sharpton, and Jesse Jackson addressed the delegates at the Democratic National Convention in Boston. The black star of the convention, however, was the little-known 42-year-old state senator from Illinois, Barack Obama, who was running for the U.S. Senate. Obama's keynote speech, claiming that good and efficient government would improve the life chances of all Americans, catapulted him into the limelight.

24-1
24-2
24-3
24-4
24-5
24-6
24-7
24-8
24-9

Bush's Second Term

On November 4, 2004, Americans reelected George W. Bush by a three-million-vote margin. After the election Colin Powell resigned. In repayment for her loyalty and experience in international affairs, President Bush appointed Condoleezza Rice to replace Powell as secretary of state. However, Bush's popularity soon began to plummet. Scandals rocked the administration. But it was Bush's mishandling of the Iraq War and the fumbling and inadequate federal response in 2005 to the devastation wrought by Hurricane Katrina to parts of the Gulf Coast and the city of New Orleans that defined his second term. In the 2006 midterm elections, the Democrats regained control of Congress. Nancy Pelosi became the first woman Speaker of the House, and several African Americans became chairs of House committees. Democrats also captured most of the state governorships. Deval Patrick of Massachusetts became the second African American to be elected a governor in history.

The Iraq War

At the outset of his second term, Bush insisted again that America was on the right course in Iraq and that victory would soon be achieved there. Events soon proved him wrong. As the death toll in Iraq mounted, most Americans lost faith in the administration's handling of the conflict, which had become a bloody civil war among Iraq's sectarian and ethnic groups. Civic life in Iraq all but collapsed amid daily suicide bombings, attacks on U.S. troops, kidnappings, murders, and other acts of terrorism. Corruption was rampant. Millions of Iraqis had become refugees. International opinion turned solidly against America.

By 2007, in response to Bush's low poll numbers and the unpopularity of the war, eight Democrats had launched campaigns for their party's presidential nomination. The prospective candidates included a woman, Senator Hillary Rodham Clinton of New York; an African American, Senator Barack Obama of Illinois; and a Hispanic-American, Governor Bill Richardson of New Mexico. This was the most diverse roster of presidential candidates of any party in American history.

Hurricane Katrina and the Destruction of Black New Orleans

View on
MyHistoryLab
Closer Look:
Hurricane Katrina

Political decisions have consequences. The decision to invade Iraq and the years of combat there, together with questionable appointments to head the agencies charged with providing federal disaster relief, left the government unprepared in August 2005 to deal with the catastrophic devastation Hurricane Katrina caused. Although Katrina also hit the Mississippi and Alabama coasts hard, New Orleans suffered the worst effects. Federal funding for flood control in New Orleans had been reduced by 44 percent since 2001 when Bush took office. State and federal emergency services were so reduced and disorganized that they offered almost no protection from natural disasters. The plan to evacuate New Orleans if a major hurricane threatened the city ignored the fact that most of its poor residents, who were overwhelmingly black, lacked the means to flee. Moreover, one-third (35 percent) of the Louisiana National Guard, who would be needed to furnish aid and keep order in a disaster, was in Iraq.

What suddenly became apparent to the nation and the world after Katrina struck was that most of the people trapped in New Orleans were poor and black. Although most black residents of New Orleans had always been poor, the city also had a thriving black

Many African-American residents in New Orleans found themselves stranded literally and figuratively when the levees broke in the wake of Hurricane Katrina and the federal and state governments failed to provide prompt and sufficient relief and rescue efforts.

professional middle class, private black colleges and universities and black businesses. Over three centuries, the city's black community had produced a rich culture, famous for its food, music, literature, and artistic heritage. In addition to taking more than 1,500 lives in the city, Katrina damaged or destroyed much of that legacy.

Katrina moved ashore on Monday, August 29, 2005, and caused the highest storm surge in U.S. history. It punctured the levees that protected New Orleans in 53 places and inundated 80 percent of the city under 20 feet of water. Most of New Orleans's more affluent residents had escaped before the hurricane hit, leaving behind an estimated 100,000 people to weather the storm. With nowhere else to go and no means with which to get there, thousands of black people made their way to the Louisiana Superdome and the Convention Center, where they found wretched conditions—inadequate food, water, electricity, and poor sanitation. Violence erupted, and chaos loomed. As bad as the hurricane proved to be, the aftermath was worse. President Bush cut short his vacation and flew over the wrecked city, but he did not visit New Orleans until September 2, when he praised Michael Brown, the director of the Federal Emergency Management Agency (FEMA), for doing "a heck of a job." Since it was already apparent that FEMA's response and Brown's performance were ineffectual, the president's words outraged the nation—and black people in particular. Hip-hop rapper Kanye West departed from the script of a nationally televised program to raise funds for the displaced victims to charge that "George Bush does not care about black people." His comments made Katrina an "Emmett Till" moment for the hip-hop generation.

In the face of government ineptitude, individuals and groups used their own resources to bring relief to those trapped in New Orleans. Local community organizations mobilized to promote recovery, rebuilding, and renewal. Media stars such as Oprah

Winfrey pledged funds to rebuild homes; Jesse Jackson led a caravan to transport hundreds to safety in Chicago. Eleven thousand homeless residents of New Orleans were bused 350 miles away to shelter at the Houston Astrodome. Churches and international relief organizations such as the Red Cross sent supplies, money, and clothes to those who had lost jobs, homes, and loved ones. Universities across the country welcomed students and faculty from historically black institutions, and professional organizations launched book drives to reconstruct libraries.

Yet this aid could not make up for the failure of the government's response. Today, much of residential New Orleans has still not recovered. Whole neighborhoods have disappeared. The city has lost almost a third of its pre-Katrina population. Most of the former residents who have not returned are black people. For the first time in centuries, New Orleans may no longer have a black majority, and in 2010 the city elected its first white mayor since 1978.

Black Politics in the Present Era: Barack Obama, President of the United States

24-9   **In what ways does the election and reelection of Barack Obama represent a triumph of black politics?**

Barack Obama accepted the nomination of the Democratic Party as its presidential candidate on August 28, 2008, in Denver, Colorado. In his acceptance speech, he promised if elected to usher in a new era: "We meet at one of those defining moments—a moment when our nation is at war, our economy is in turmoil, and the American promise has been threatened once more."

Obama versus McCain

The 2008 presidential election campaign was unlike any other in recent American history. The differences between the one-term Illinois Senator Barack Obama and the multi-termed Arizona Senator John McCain quickly became apparent. Obama used his matchless oratorical skills to call for change and inspire hope for a better future. He attacked George W. Bush's failed economic, educational, and social policies relentlessly. He also attacked the administration's rush to war in Iraq, its support for tax cuts for the wealthy, and a series of questionable cabinet appointments and scandals. He shrewdly selected Delaware Senator Joseph Biden as his vice-presidential running mate. Biden's 36 years in the Senate and foreign policy expertise made him a formidable candidate in his own right.

McCain touted his experience and military background, especially his five years as a prisoner of war in North Vietnam. McCain insisted that he was ready to be commander-in-chief on day one if elected president. In contrast, the Republicans cited Obama's lack of experience and emphasized his "celebrity" to suggest that he was all fluff and little substance. Moreover, McCain predicted that Obama would raise the taxes of middle-class workers and indulge in wasteful spending.

McCain stunned the nation and delighted his supporters by selecting Sarah Palin, the first-term governor of Alaska, as his running mate. McCain believed she would attract white women who were disillusioned by Obama's victory over Hillary Clinton in the Democratic primaries. Palin was the first woman to share a Republican Party presidential ticket. Her opposition to abortion rights, conservative rhetoric, and anti-Washington

Read on
MyHistoryLab
Document: Barack Obama, A More Perfect Union, 2008

Read on
MyHistoryLab
Document: Dirty Politics in the 2008 Election, 2007

stand on government spending enthralled the Republicans' Evangelical Protestant base and energized McCain's campaign. However, Palin failed to win broad support from women, and interviews with journalists quickly revealed her ignorance of political, economic, and foreign affairs and raised doubts about her ability to be president should McCain die in office.

The turning point in the campaign occurred when the nation suffered the worst financial crisis since the Great Depression. McCain suspended his campaign to rush to Washington to help pass a huge federal government rescue plan for Wall Street banks. He tried to assure Americans that the "fundamentals of the economy are strong," though every indicator suggested the opposite. McCain appeared erratic, impulsive, and out of touch. By contrast, Obama seemed calm, steady, reasonable, reliable, and capable. Obama won the three televised debates between the candidates.

More than 120 million Americans voted on November 4, 2008. Approximately 67 million voted for Barack Obama, giving him one of the largest winning percentages in American history. The electoral college registered the extent of the Obama victory. He won 367 electoral votes to McCain's 173. Obama redrew the old electoral blue states/red states map by carrying states in every region of the country, including Virginia and Indiana (which no Democratic presidential candidate had won since 1964) and North Carolina, which the Democrats had not carried since Jimmy Carter won it in 1976 (see Map 24–1). He received an unprecedented 95 percent of the African-American vote.

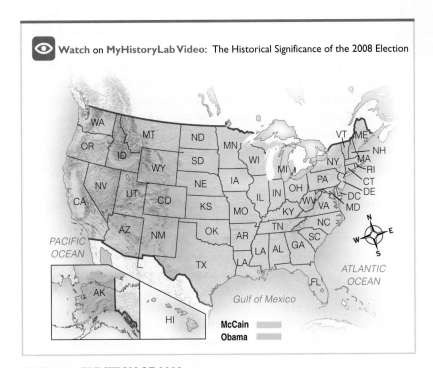

MAP 24–1 ELECTION OF 2008
This map captures the magnitude of Obama's presidential election triumph. It redraws the decades-long alignment of Republican red states and Democratic blue states. In the 2008 election, Americans moved closer to realizing the dream of one nation.

Which southern states most notably voted for Obama?

PROFILE Barack Obama

BARACK OBAMA was born in Honolulu on August 4, 1961. His father was an immigrant from Kenya who married a white American from Kansas. When his father abandoned the family to complete his studies at Harvard, two-year-old Barack and his mother moved in with her family. In 1967, Obama and his mother relocated with her second husband to Indonesia, where Obama attended both a Roman Catholic and a Muslim school. Obama and his mother later returned to Hawaii, where he lived with his maternal grandparents and completed high school in 1979.

Twice elected (2008, 2012) President Barack Obama secured enactment of the Patient Protection and Affordable Care Act and ended the War in Iraq.

After high school, Obama entered Occidental College in Los Angeles before graduating from New York's Columbia University in 1983. His father, whom he had seen only once in the interim, died in an automobile accident in Kenya before his graduation. Obama became a community organizer in Chicago, working to start a job placement and training center. His experiences as a community organizer taught him "that meaningful change always begins at the grassroots, and that engaged citizens working together can accomplish extraordinary things." He decided to pursue a law degree "to learn power's currency in all its intricacy and detail."

In 1991 Obama graduated from Harvard Law School, where he was the first African-American editor of the *Law Review.* He returned to Chicago and married Michelle Robinson, a native of Chicago's South Side who had also graduated from Harvard Law School. They have two daughters, Malia and Sasha.

In 1996, Obama was elected to the Illinois State Senate, where he voted to ban racial profiling and supported increased funding for child health care. In 2004, as a candidate for the U.S. Senate, Obama electrified the Democratic National Convention with an impassioned keynote speech. He declared, to thunderous applause, "The pundits like to slice-and-dice our country into Red States and Blue States. . . . But I've got news for them . . . We worship an awesome God in the Blue States, and we don't like federal agents poking around our libraries in Red States. We coach Little League in the Blue States and have gay friends in the Red States. . . . We are one people." A national political star was born.

In February 2007 Obama announced his candidacy to become the presidential nominee of the Democratic Party. He was a formidable campaigner, raising enormous amounts of money and attracting enthusiastic support from a wide spectrum of Americans. He addressed many of the key issues—the war in Iraq, health care, and public education—that were equally as important to African Americans as they were to others. Yet some African Americans were ambivalent about his candidacy. When asked to explain this, Obama said, "It's interesting that the people who are most hesitant about this oftentimes are African Americans because they feel protective of me. They're either concerned about the attacks I'd be subjected to or they are skeptical oftentimes that America is prepared to elect a black president."

Listen on MyHistoryLab Audio: *The Audacity of Hope* by Barack Obama, excerpt

2009 TO 2012
SELECT FIRST TERM ACCOMPLISHMENTS OF PRESIDENT OBAMA

January 2009
Lily Ledbetter Fair Pay Act: This act made it illegal for employers to pay unequal wages to men and women who perform the same work

2009
The Resurgence of the American Automotive Industry: This government financial intervention prevented the death of the automobile industry and saved tens of thousands of American jobs. Thanks to this legislation, Chrysler and GM rebounded from near bankruptcy

May 2009–2010
President Obama appointed Sonia Sotomayor and Elena Kagan to the U.S. Supreme Court: These appointments brought the number of female justices on the U.S. Supreme Court to three, an historic high

March 2010
Patient Protection and Affordable Care Act: This act established universal health care

December 2010
The Don't Ask, Don't Tell Repeal Act of 2010: This legislation allowed LBGT military personnel to serve openly in the United States Armed Services

May 2011
"Osama bin Laden is Dead!": The president made this announcement after he had ordered Navy Seals to kill a secluded bin Laden, who was the architect of the September 11, 2001, terrorist attack on America

July 2011
President Obama supported the Respect for Marriage Act, which was introduced by Senator Dianne Feinstein and Congressman Jerrold Nadler. This legislation upheld the principle that the federal government should not deny gay and lesbian couples the same rights and legal protections as straight couples

December 2011
The president withdrew troops from Iraq and ended America's long-standing war in Iraq

May 2012
President Obama announced plans for complete withdrawal from the Afghanistan War in 2014 through a systematic reduction of U.S. Armed Forces

June 2012
The president supported the DREAM Act (Development, Relief, and Education for Alien Minors), explaining, "It makes no sense to be using our enforcement resources against young people who have known no other country but this one, and who have shown their desire to study and serve"

President Obama, against opposition of Republican Party Leaders who were determined to make him a one-term President, accomplished an impressive array of transformational policies

24-1
24-2
24-3
24-4
24-5
24-6
24-7
24-8
24-9

SOURCE: The White House.

PROFILE   Michelle LaVaughn Robinson Obama

First Lady Michelle Obama made health, education, safety of children, and military families a top priority on her "Mom-in-Chief" agenda.

THE FIRST LADY OF THE UNITED STATES, MICHELLE LAVAUGHN ROBINSON, was born in Chicago in 1964 to working-class parents. She graduated from Princeton University with a major in sociology and a minor in African-American studies in 1985. In 1988 Michelle earned her law degree at Harvard. In June 1989, she began dating Barack Obama. They married in 1992 and have two daughters, Malia Ann and Natasha (Sasha).

After three years working in corporate law, in 1991 Michelle became an assistant commissioner of planning and development and a member of Chicago Mayor Richard M. Daley's staff. In early 1993, she became the founding executive director of the Chicago Office of Public Allies, a nonprofit organization that trained young adults for public service. In 2002, she became executive director of community affairs for the University of Chicago Hospitals. In 2007 she took a leave of absence to work on her husband's campaign for the presidency.

For 21 months, she played an invaluable role in humanizing, normalizing, and explaining her husband to a sometimes skeptical public that often questioned his ethnicity, citizenship, religion, experience, and vision and challenged her pride in her country.

In her official capacity, Mrs. Obama has focused on the needs of military families, women's efforts to balance work and family, improving public education and nutrition, fighting against childhood obesity, and serving as a role model for young, marginalized, and disadvantaged Americans.

The youngest first lady since Jacqueline Kennedy in 1961, Mrs. Obama is an important agent of change in American society's perception of black women and a strong role model for girls and women across the globe.

Read on MyHistoryLab Document: Darlene Clark Hine, Mystic Chords of Memory

For many Americans, Obama's victory signaled that "race" or "blackness" was no longer an insuperable barrier to the highest political office. His election heralded the dawn of a new day, the beginning of a new chapter in the United States and in the African-American odyssey. On election night, Obama stood in Grant Park in Chicago and told the world, "If there is anyone out there who still doubts that America is a place where all things are possible, who still wonders if the dream of our founders is alive in our time, who still questions the power of our democracy, tonight is your answer."

On January 20, 2009, before a global televised audience of billions and before the two million who gathered on the National Mall in Washington, Barack Obama placed his hand on the bible that Abraham Lincoln had used and took the oath of office to become the first black president of the United States of America.

Obama versus Romney

In the 2008 campaign, Obama was helped by the support of his wife Michelle, who became an exceptionally popular and revered first lady. She was an even stronger and more powerful asset in his reelection bid. Again, black social and political icons from Oprah

Winfrey and Tyler Perry to Colin Powell ardently supported both of Obama's election bids. Political supporters touted the fact that he had saved the American automobile industry. Others emphasized the national Affordable Health Care Act, the support for rebuilding America's infrastructure, the granting of citizenship to children of illegal immigrants, and his repudiation of the military's anti-gay policy, referred to as "Don't Ask, Don't Tell." Obama raised hundreds of millions of dollars in his second campaign. He used a considerable amount of this money early in the campaign to define the Republican Party candidate Mitt Romney as being hopelessly out of touch with the everyday realities of the lives of most Americans. Romney cemented this depiction in remarks (caught on tape) in which he dismissed 47 percent of Americans as being hopelessly dependent on government handouts and people who refused to take responsibility for their own lives.

In both the 2008 and 2012 bids, Obama's calm and steadfast demeanor, his eloquent and passionate oratory (at times resonant of the best of black preaching), and his manifest intelligence enabled him to capture the imagination, spirit, and yearning for change in an America weary of war and government incompetence, indifference, and economic insecurity. Prior to the November 2012 election, the fury of Hurricane Sandy wreaked havoc on the lives and property of millions of citizens in New York, New Jersey, Connecticut, and Maryland. Through it all, President Obama remained vigilant, supportive, and on the ground with residents and political leaders including New Jersey Governor Chris Christie, a Republican. The images of Obama being an active and caring president determined to alleviate suffering and to restore lives were powerful reminders of how much capable and compassionate leadership matters.

On November 6, 2012, the American public voted to retain Barack Obama as president of the United States. One of the most important occurrences during 2012 was the great lengths Republican politicians on both the state and national level went to in order to enact voter identification laws to suppress the black vote and reduce black electoral clout. The voter suppression movement had the opposite effect, however; through unrelenting mobilization, black voters turned out in a higher percentage than any other demographic group to return Obama and his family to the White House. This resilience and determination to keep their hands on the freedom plow bodes well for the future of black politics in America, and by extension across the diaspora. At the dawn of "the Obama Era," African, African-American Studies, and History Professor Paul Tiyambe Zeleza anticipated the emergence of "a more global and nationalistic world," a world that is "impatient with the old injustices and hungry for development, democracy, and self-determination."

Factors Affecting the Elections of 2008 and 2012

Many factors contributed to Obama's improbable presidential victories both in 2008 and in 2012. The most important were his skilled, dedicated, and cohesive staff and a mastery of computer technology. His use of the Internet gave him a decisive advantage over McCain in 2008, and again in 2012 over former Massachusetts Governor Mitt Romney. In both the 2008 and 2012 elections, Obama's campaign staff executed a masterful ground game strategy that increased minority voter turnout. It was the higher black voting rate that, when combined with Hispanic votes and those of Asian Americans, proved decisive in 2012. Obama appealed to millions of new voters in both elections while the white vote continued to decline (see Map 24–2). In 2012, Obama won 80 percent of the non-white vote.

Read on
MyHistoryLab
Document: Barack
Obama, Inaugural
Address, 2009

24-1

24-2

24-3

24-4

24-5

24-6

24-7

24-8

24-9

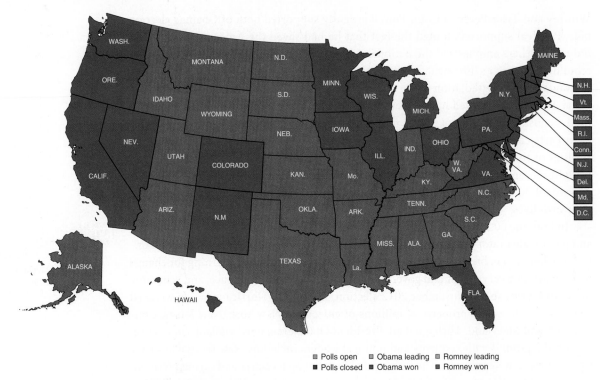

Polls open   Obama leading   Romney leading
Polls closed   Obama won   Romney won

MAP 24–2   ELECTION OF 2012
This map captures the extent of Obama's presidential election triumph. It underscores the realignments of Republican red states and Democratic blue states.

Which states returned to the Republican fold according to the election map?

Obama's presidential campaigns were the most technologically and computer-savvy in history. His background as a community organizer, his support of new immigration policies (especially the DREAM Act), and his embrace of the rights of same-sex couples to marry expanded his support in key demographic groups. His grassroots movement of volunteers on local and national levels and the use of celebrity supporters including hip-hop mogul Jay-Z appealed to younger voters while performer Bruce Springsteen attracted white working-class support. The Republican Party's cavalier attitude toward women's concerns, especially the negative remarks by Tea Party candidates challenging women's rights to make their own reproductive decisions, alienated white women voters who turned out in record numbers to support Democratic candidates. In the presidential reelection campaign, white women also voted overwhelmingly for Barack Obama (see Table 24–1).

CONCLUSION

Jesse Jackson, whose Rainbow Coalition reflected a quest for unity amid diversity, asked at the 1988 Democratic convention, "Shall we expand, be inclusive, find unity and power; or suffer division and impotence?" The Hurricane Katrina disaster in 2005 reminded the black community of how precarious life remained for those trapped in poverty and perched at the intersection of race, class, and gender in America. The 2007 Democratic primary campaign illustrated the political importance of black Americans and the extent

TABLE 24-1 2012 ELECTION RESULTS: VOTING DEMOGRAPHICS

Total Popular Vote—Obama		65,455,010	**51.0% Wins**
Total Popular Vote—Romney		60,771,703	**47.0%**

Ethnicity	Percentage	Ethnicity	Percentage
Black—Democratic	93%	Black—Republican	6%
Asian—Democratic	73%	Asian—Republican	26%
Hispanic—Democratic	71%	Hispanic—Republican	27%
Other—Democratic	58%	Other—Republican	38%
White—Democratic	39%	White—Republican	59%

Age	Percentage	Age	Percentage
18–29—Democratic	60%	18–29—Republican	37%
30–44—Democratic	52%	30–44—Republican	45%
45–64—Democratic	47%	45–64—Republican	51%
65–100—Democratic	44%	65–100—Republican	56%

Gender	Percentage	Gender	Percentage
Men—Democratic	45%	Men—Republican	52%
Women—Democratic	55%	Women—Republican	44%

Location	Percentage	Location	Percentage
Urban—Democratic	62%	Urban—Republican	36%
Suburban—Democratic	48%	Suburban—Republican	50%
Rural—Democratic	39%	Rural—Republican	59%

SOURCE: CNN, Huffington Post, *and* Mail Online.

to which the Democratic Party had embraced its diverse constituency. African Americans remained committed to a progressive political agenda that emphasized universal health care, quality education, urban economic development, job training, safe environments, an end to racial profiling and police brutality, and reform of the prison-industrial complex that had disfranchised and oppressed so many black Americans and members of other minority groups. It marked another stage in the black odyssey toward freedom and the transformation of American society. In 2008, with the election of Barack Obama and his inauguration on January 20, 2009, to become the forty-fourth president of the United States, black politics came of age.

Few black Americans anticipated the depth of animosity that circulated within the Republican Party and among those whites who supported the rise of the Tea Party. Many Republican politicians vowed to make Barack Obama a "one-term president." They vigorously pursued an obstructionist stand and tried to block every progressive measure that Obama supported or advocated.

The election campaign of 2012 became a referendum on the policies Obama pursued in his first term. The success of the 2012 campaign, and Obama's 51 to 47 percent victory over his opponent Romney, underscored the triumph of coalition politics and the importance of grassroots community organizing and mobilization strategies in the twenty-first century.

CHAPTER TIMELINE

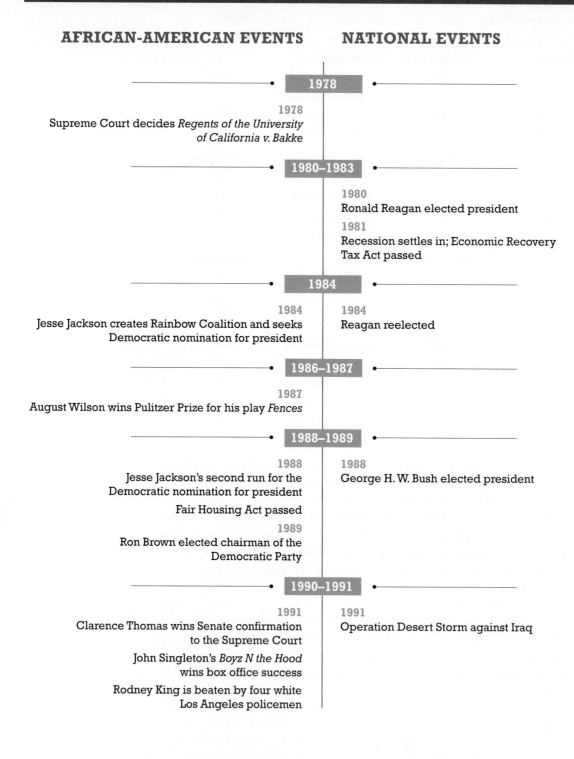

AFRICAN-AMERICAN EVENTS   **NATIONAL EVENTS**

1978

1978
Supreme Court decides *Regents of the University of California v. Bakke*

1980–1983

1980
Ronald Reagan elected president

1981
Recession settles in; Economic Recovery Tax Act passed

1984

1984
Jesse Jackson creates Rainbow Coalition and seeks Democratic nomination for president

1984
Reagan reelected

1986–1987

1987
August Wilson wins Pulitzer Prize for his play *Fences*

1988–1989

1988
Jesse Jackson's second run for the Democratic nomination for president

Fair Housing Act passed

1989
Ron Brown elected chairman of the Democratic Party

1988
George H. W. Bush elected president

1990–1991

1991
Clarence Thomas wins Senate confirmation to the Supreme Court

John Singleton's *Boyz N the Hood* wins box office success

Rodney King is beaten by four white Los Angeles policemen

1991
Operation Desert Storm against Iraq

CHAPTER TIMELINE

AFRICAN-AMERICAN EVENTS

NATIONAL EVENTS

1992–1993

1992

Los Angeles riots after King's police assailants are acquitted

Carol Moseley Braun of Illinois is the first black woman elected to the Senate

1993

Clinton names Ron Brown and Hazel O'Leary to cabinet

1992

William Jefferson Clinton elected president

1994–1995

1994

Jesse Jackson, Jr., elected to Congress

1994

Midterm elections give Republicans control of Congress

1996

1996

Clinton reelected, signs welfare reform legislation

1998–1999

1998

Clinton impeached

1999

Senate acquits Clinton

2000–2001

2000

Donna Brazile manages the presidential campaign of Al Gore

2000

George W. Bush becomes president

2001

Bush names Condoleezza Rice national security adviser and Colin Powell secretary of state

September 11, 2001

Terrorists demolish the World Trade Center in New York City and attack the Pentagon

October, 2001

United States invades Afghanistan

CHAPTER TIMELINE

AFRICAN-AMERICAN EVENTS

NATIONAL EVENTS

2002–2003

2003
Supreme Court upholds use of racial preferences in admission to University of Michigan Law School

2002
No Child Left Behind Act

2003
United States invades Iraq

2004–2005

2004
Carol Moseley Braun and Al Sharpton run for president

Barack Obama elected to Senate

Condoleezza Rice appointed secretary of state

2004
George W. Bush reelected president

2005
Hurricane Katrina devastates New Orleans

2006–2013

2006
James Brown dies; Deval Patrick elected governor of Massachusetts

2009
Barack Obama inaugurated as forty-fourth president of the United States

Obama receives the Nobel Peace Prize

Michael Jackson dies

2008
New York Governor Eliot Spitzer resigns and is replaced by David Paterson

Michael Steele elected chairman of Republican Party National Committee

Roland W. Burris replaces Barack Obama as senator

2009
Edward M. Kennedy dies

Barack Obama secures passage of an Affordable Healthcare Act

Sonia Sotomayor becomes first Latina to be appointed to the United States Supreme Court

On MyHistoryLab

 Study and Review on MyHistoryLab

REVIEW QUESTIONS

1. To what extent and in what key areas did the Reagan and Bush presidencies nullify or dismantle Great Society legislation? How did African Americans respond to the Republican conservative reaction?

2. What was the significance of Jesse Jackson's campaigns for the Democratic presidential nomination? Why did African Americans become so important for the Democratic Party?

3. How did the welfare reform legislation passed under Clinton and George W. Bush's No Child Left Behind Act affect African Americans?

4. Why did affirmative action become so controversial in the 1990s? How did affirmative action in the workplace differ from affirmative action in education?

5. How did the Rodney King case illuminate the differences between how black and white Americans saw the police and the justice system?

6. How did the Hurricane Katrina disaster expose the fault lines of race, class, and gender in American society?

7. Why did Barack Obama defeat John McCain in 2008? Why was Obama's election so significant for African Americans?

CONNECTING THE PAST

The Significance of Black Culture

John Coltrane (1926–1967) was one of the most profound and remarkable jazz musicians in the twentieth century. A master of the tenor and soprano saxophone to be revered for his instrumental improvisation. His most celebrated album, *A Love Supreme* was released in 1965.

IN AN ADDRESS CELEBRATING BLACK HISTORY WEEK in 1935, Kirkland W. Green, Dean of Arts and Sciences at South Carolina State College, declared, "The Negro has traveled through four hundred years of American history amidst thorns of torture, ridicule, scorn, degradation, and shame. These thorns have torn his flesh and wounded his soul. Bathed in blood and tears, he prayed and sang for the coming of a new day when he would come into his own, in possession of his birthright, freedom, recognition of a man's chance—the right to live his best self to fulfill his God given mission. Millions waited for this day and died."

Across the centuries, African Americans created and forged significant black culture movements at pivotal turning points in their long odyssey from slavery to full citizenship. In the twentieth century there were black renaissances in 1920s Harlem and in Chicago from the 1930s through the 1950s against the backdrop of the Great Depression and World War II. Across the United States in the first half of the twentieth century, the cultural achievements of talented black writers and performers made black people feel at home and proud in their new urban environments created by the Great Migration from the rural South to northern and western cities. The southern rural, agricultural-based Negro evolved into first, "The New Negro," then into the "black metropolitan," and finally into empowered members of an "industrial working class" who became activists for social change through their membership in labor unions. At each stage in this evolution or transformation, black cultural workers, artists, writers, and performers forged new weapons that enabled black people to achieve a sense of belonging both to their own community and to the nation as a whole. It also enabled them to shake off the demeaning and dehumanizing stereotype of blackness that centuries of oppression had forced on them.

Indeed, the U.S. government, especially the State Department in the early years of the Cold War against Soviet Communism, recognized this and tried to harness the power and appeal of black culture to win allies in Third World countries. The State Department sponsored international tours and cultural programs by representative black entertainers and spokespersons, including musicians such as Louis Armstrong, Count Basie, and Ella Fitzgerald; painters and writers; actors and dancers like Katherine Dunham; and sportsmen, from Joe Louis to Jackie Robinson, to testify that America was not the most racist country on Earth as depicted in communist propaganda.

In the 1960s and 1970s, the Black Arts Movement flourished in New York, Chicago, Detroit, Los Angeles, and Washington, DC. It was the creative and artistic counterpart to the Civil Rights and Black Power movements. Black musicians produced two strands of art during these decades when the rhythm and blues and soul music of artists like James Brown, Stevie Wonder, and Aretha Franklin flourished alongside the innovative jazz of giants like Miles Davis and John Coltrane.

More recently, the hip-hop cultural movement expressed the hopes and needs of a generation that felt it had received little benefits from the Civil Rights and Black Power movements. Globalization and deindustrialization, which destroyed the jobs that previous generations of black people had depended on, meant that too many black boys and girls of the millennial generation lived in communities with rising rates of poverty and heightened measures of social distress. Because their songs, poetry, body piercings, clothes, body language, movies, paintings, and even humor depicted an alternate reality that few adults could fathom or appreciate, they were repudiated for their use of profanity, sexist language, and seeming glorification of violence.

In each cultural movement of the twentieth and early twenty-first centuries, African-American artists and cultural workers rescued black consciousness from despair and oppression and gave birth to new identities and political awareness. Black cultural innovations reflected resilience and rebirth even when the future seemed most bleak, and the institutional, racist, and ethnic barriers seemed too high to be overcome. Thus, the poems, novels, essays, paintings, and sculpture, and the new styles of music and dance, the changing religious practices and theology, the oratory, and the employment of old and new technology and media emerged just in time to nurture the seeds of progressive black political activism and generate community mobilization, coalition politics, and the creation of empowering communal and individual identities.

Spike Lee, director, and activist, directing one of his ground-breaking films.

At each stage, black culture movements not only helped destroy demeaning racial stereotypes. They also transformed the black community. In the 1990s, the hip-hop movement showcased fundamental human and citizenship rights whose appeal went far beyond the borders of the United States. Hip-hop was enthusiastically adopted by a youth generation across the globe that was battling post-colonial domination, oppressive governments, and economic exploitation, and in the United States had to endure mass incarceration, educational failure, substance addiction, deportation, bullying, and sexual abuse. In other words, hip-hop gave a voice to the disinherited and dispossessed youth not only in the African diaspora, but in Asia, Latin America, the Caribbean, and Europe. But hip-hop was also, at its birth, just plain fun.

Culture is intimately connected with political awareness. The black cultural movements of the twentieth and early twenty-first centuries merged the "double consciousness" that W. E. B. Du Bois talked about in *The Souls of Black Folk* into "better and truer" black selves. Black cultural productions have continually provided new "intellectual equipment" that black people have used to examine, showcase, and discuss the realities and experiences of their lives and dreams. In this way, the lives and art of African-American culture workers have inspired oppressed people around the world.

Black culture has sometimes been dismissed as superficial and inconsequential. Yet the innovative, dynamic, and resonant productions of black artists, musicians, and performers have been in the vanguard of those movements whose appeal cuts across borders and smashes the negative social and political barriers that divide Americans along the fault lines of race, class, gender, and sexuality. The writers, musicians, and artists of the Harlem and Chicago Renaissances humanized black people, raised individual and group pride, and helped expand and preserve democracy for all Americans. They built bridges that connected the resolve of black people in disparate communities, nationally and internationally, to resist and reject dehumanization. Black culture workers from those Renaissances to the creators of the hip-hop movement were not only entertainers and artists. They also strengthened opposition to racial oppression, economic exploitation, political powerlessness, and social injustice. The complex, compelling, and inclusive nature of black culture is one of the great African-American achievements. It deserves to be studied with the same seriousness that we bring to the study of black migration, the struggles for political, social, and economic rights, and the history of sports.

Epilogue

Since the first Africans were brought to America's shores in the seventeenth century, black people have been a constant and distinct presence in America. During the prolonged course of the Atlantic slave trade, approximately 600,000 Africans were sold into servitude in what became the United States. By the outbreak of the Civil War in 1861 there were nearly four million African Americans in the United States. Today black people number over 30 million and make up slightly over 10 percent of the nation's population. Initially regarded merely as an enslaved labor force to produce cash crops, and not as a people who would or could enjoy an equal role in the political and social affairs of American society, African Americans constituted a separate ethnic, racial, and cultural group. For more than two centuries they remained outcasts.

People of African descent developed decidedly ambivalent relationships with the white majority in America. Never fully accepted and never fully rejected, black people relied on their own resources as they created their own institutions and communities. In 1852 Martin Delany declared, "We are a nation within a nation." A half century later, W. E. B. Du Bois observed that the black man wanted to retain his African identity and to be an American as well. "He would not Africanize America, for America has too much to teach the world and Africa. He would not bleach his Negro soul in a flood of white Americanism, for he knows that Negro blood has a message for the world. He simply wishes to make it possible for a man to be both a Negro and an American, without being cursed and spit upon by his fellows, without having the doors of Opportunity closed roughly in his face."

Sometimes in desperation or disgust, some black people have been willing to abandon America or reject assimilation. The slaves who engaged in South Carolina's 1739 Stono rebellion attempted to reach Spanish Florida. From the 1790s to the start of the Civil War, visions of nationhood in Africa attracted a minority of African Americans. During the 1920s, Marcus Garvey and the Universal Negro Improvement Association glorified Africa while seeking black autonomy in the United States. By the 1950s, Elijah Muhammad, Malcolm X, and the Nation of Islam emphasized a separate black destiny.

Yet in spite of the horrors of slavery, the indignity of Jim Crow, and the violence and discrimination inflicted, most African Americans have not rejected America. African slaves accepted elements of Christianity, and their descendants found solace in their spiritual beliefs. Black Americans have embraced American principles of brotherhood, justice, fairness, and equality before the law. The nation within a nation has never been homogeneous. There have been persistent class, gender, and color divisions. There have been tensions and ideological conflicts among black leaders and organizations. Some leaders, such as Booker T. Washington, have emphasized self-reliance and economic advancement, while others, including W. E. B. Du Bois and leaders of the NAACP, have advocated full inclusion in American society.

Furthermore, African Americans have been far more than victims, than an exploited labor force, than the subjects of segregation and stereotypes. They have contributed enormously to the development and character of American society and culture. As slaves, they provided billions of hours of unrequited labor to the American economy. Black people established churches, schools, and colleges that continue to thrive as they demonstrate a willingness to fight and die for their country. African Americans continue to make innovative contributions to art, music, literature, science and technology, athletics, and politics.

Although we are now in the twenty-first century, the long odyssey of people of African descent continues. While African Americans have been and remain "a nation within a nation," the election of Barack Obama in 2008, and his reelection in 2012, represent a remarkable milestone. Michelle Obama gives her husband's presidency an even deeper meaning, as America's first black first lady. Now, with an African-American family occupying the White House, black people will continue to help mold and shape our American civilization.

The Declaration of Independence

When in the course of human events it becomes necessary for one people to dissolve the political bands which have connected them with another and to assume, among the powers of the earth, the separate and equal station to which the laws of nature and of nature's God entitle them, a decent respect to the opinions of mankind requires that they should declare the causes which impel them to the separation.

We hold these truths to be self-evident, that all men are created equal; that they are endowed by their Creator with certain unalienable rights; that among these are life, liberty, and the pursuit of happiness. That, to secure these rights, governments are instituted among men, deriving their just powers from the consent of the governed; that, whenever any form of government becomes destructive of these ends, it is the right of the people to alter or to abolish it, and to institute a new government, laying its foundation on such principles, and organizing its powers in such form, as to them shall seem most likely to effect their safety and happiness. Prudence, indeed, will dictate that governments long established should not be changed for light and transient causes; and, accordingly, all experience hath shown that mankind are more disposed to suffer, while evils are sufferable, than to right themselves by abolishing the forms to which they are accustomed. But when a long train of abuses and usurpations, pursuing invariably the same object, evinces a design to reduce them under absolute despotism, it is their right, it is their duty, to throw off such government and to provide new guards for their future security. Such has been the patient sufferance of these colonies, and such is now the necessity which constrains them to alter their former systems of government. The history of the present King of Great Britain is a history of repeated injuries and usurpations, all having, in direct object, the establishment of an absolute tyranny over these States. To prove this, let facts be submitted to a candid world:

He has refused his assent to laws the most wholesome and necessary for the public good.

He has forbidden his governors to pass laws of immediate and pressing importance, unless suspended in their operation till his assent should be obtained; and, when so suspended, he has utterly neglected to attend to them.

He has refused to pass other laws for the accommodation of large districts of people, unless those people would relinquish the right of representation in the legislature, a right inestimable to them and formidable to tyrants only.

He has called together legislative bodies at places unusual, uncomfortable, and distant from the depository of their public records, for the sole purpose of fatiguing them into compliance with his measures.

He has dissolved representative houses, repeatedly for opposing, with manly firmness, his invasions on the rights of the people.

He has refused, for a long time after such dissolutions, to cause others to be elected; whereby the legislative powers, incapable of annihilation, have returned to the people at large for their exercise; the state remaining, in the meantime, exposed to all the danger of invasion from without and convulsions within.

He has endeavored to prevent the population of these States; for that purpose, obstructing the laws for naturalization of foreigners, refusing to pass others to encourage their migration hither, and raising the conditions of new appropriations of lands.

He has obstructed the administration of justice by refusing his assent to laws for establishing judiciary powers.

He has made judges dependent on his will alone for the tenure of their offices and the amount and payment of their salaries.

He has erected a multitude of new offices and sent hither swarms of officers to harass our people and eat out their substance.

He has kept among us, in time of peace, standing armies, without the consent of our legislatures.

He has affected to render the military independent of, and superior to, the civil power.

He has combined with others to subject us to a jurisdiction foreign to our Constitution and unacknowledged by our laws, giving his assent to their acts of pretended legislation—

For quartering large bodies of armed troops among us;

For protecting them, by mock trial, from punishment for any murders which they should commit on the inhabitants of these States;

For cutting off our trade with all parts of the world;

For imposing taxes on us without our consent;

For depriving us, in many cases, of the benefits of trial by jury;

For transporting us beyond seas to be tried for pretended offences;

For abolishing the free system of English laws in a neighboring province, establishing therein an arbitrary government, and enlarging its boundaries, so as to render it at once an example and fit instrument for introducing the same absolute rule into these colonies;

For taking away our charters, abolishing our most valuable laws, and altering, fundamentally, the powers of our governments.

For suspending our own legislatures and declaring themselves invested with power to legislate for us in all cases whatsoever.

He has abdicated government here by declaring us out of his protection and waging war against us.

He has plundered our seas, ravaged our coasts, burnt our towns, and destroyed the lives of our people.

He is, at this time, transporting large armies of foreign mercenaries to complete the works of death, desolation, and tyranny already begun with circumstances of cruelty and perfidy scarcely paralleled in the most barbarous ages, and totally unworthy the head of a civilized nation.

He has constrained our fellow citizens, taken captive on the high seas, to bear arms against their country, to become the executioners of their friends and brethren, or to fall themselves by their hands.

He has excited domestic insurrections amongst us and has endeavored to bring on the inhabitants of our frontiers, the merciless Indian savages, whose known rule of warfare is an undistinguished destruction of all ages, sexes, and conditions.

In every stage of these oppressions, we have petitioned for redress in the most humble terms; our repeated petitions have been answered only by repeated injury. A prince whose character is thus marked by every act which may define a tyrant is unfit to be the ruler of a free people.

Nor have we been wanting in attention to our British brethren. We have warned them, from time to time, of attempts made by their legislature to extend an unwarrantable jurisdiction over us. We have reminded them of the circumstances of our emigration and settlement here. We have appealed to their native justice and magnanimity, and we have conjured them, by the ties of our common kindred, to disavow these usurpations, which would inevitably interrupt our connections and correspondence. They, too, have been deaf to the voice of justice and consanguinity. We must, therefore, acquiesce in the necessity which denounces our separation, and hold them, as we hold the rest of mankind, enemies in war, in peace, friends.

We, therefore, the representatives of the United States of America, in general Congress assembled, appealing to the Supreme Judge of the world for the rectitude of our intentions, do, in the name and by the authority of the good people of these colonies, solemnly publish and declare, that these united colonies are, and of right ought to be, free and independent states: that they are absolved from all allegiance to the British Crown, and that all political connection between them and the state of Great Britain is, and ought to be, totally dissolved; and that, as free and independent states, they have full power to levy war, conclude peace, contract alliances, establish commerce, and to do all other acts and things which independent states may of right do. And, for the support of this declaration, with a firm reliance on the protection of Divine Providence, we mutually pledge to each other our lives, our fortunes, and our sacred honor.

Proposed Clause on the Slave Trade Omitted from the Final Draft of the Declaration

He has waged cruel war against human nature itself, violating its most sacred rights of life and liberty in the person of a distant people who never offended him; captivating and carrying them into slavery in another hemisphere, or to incur miserable death in their transportation thither. This piratical warfare, the opprobrium of infidel powers, is the warfare of the Christian king of Great Britain. Determined to keep open a market where men should be bought and sold, he has prostituted his negative for suppressing every legislative attempt to prohibit or restrain this execrable commerce.

The Constitution of the United States of America

(with clauses pertaining to the status of African Americans highlighted)

We the people of the United States, in order to form a more perfect union, establish justice, insure domestic tranquility, provide for the common defense, promote the general welfare, and secure the blessings of liberty to ourselves and our posterity, do ordain and establish this Constitution for the United States of America.

Article I

SECTION 1. All legislative powers herein granted shall be vested in a Congress of the United States, which shall consist of a Senate and House of Representatives.

SECTION 2. 1. The House of Representatives shall be composed of members chosen every second year by the people of the several States, and the electors in each State shall have the qualifications requisite for electors of the most numerous branch of the State legislature.

2. No person shall be a representative who shall not have attained to the age of twenty-five years, and been seven years a citizen of the United States, and who shall not, when elected, be an inhabitant of that State in which he shall be chosen.

3. Representatives and direct taxes[1] shall be apportioned among the several States which may be included within this Union, according to their respective numbers, which shall be determined by adding to the whole number of free persons, including those bound to service for a term of years, and excluding Indians not taxed, three fifths of all other persons.[2]

The actual enumeration shall be made within three years after the first meeting of the Congress of the United States, and within every subsequent term of ten years, in such manner as they shall by law direct. The number of representatives shall not exceed one for every thirty thousand, but each State shall have at least one representative; and until such enumeration shall be made, the State of New Hampshire shall be entitled to choose three, Massachusetts eight, Rhode Island and Providence Plantations one, Connecticut five, New York six, New Jersey four, Pennsylvania eight, Delaware one, Maryland six, Virginia ten, North Carolina five, South Carolina five, and Georgia three.

4. When vacancies happen in the representation from any State, the executive authority thereof shall issue writs of election to fill such vacancies.

5. The House of Representatives shall choose their speaker and other officers; and shall have the sole power of impeachment.

SECTION 3. 1. The Senate of the United States shall be composed of two senators from each State, chosen by the legislature thereof,[3] for six years; and each senator shall have one vote.

2. Immediately after they shall be assembled in consequence of the first election, they shall be divided as equally as may be into three classes. The seats of the senators of the first class shall be vacated at the expiration of the second year, of the second class at the expiration of the fourth year, and of the third class at the expiration of the sixth year, so that one third may be chosen every second year; and if vacancies happen by resignation, or otherwise, during the recess of the legislature of any State, the executive thereof may make temporary appointments until the next meeting of the legislature, which shall then fill such vacancies.[4]

3. No person shall be a senator who shall not have attained to the age of thirty years, and been nine years a citizen of the United States, and who shall not, when elected, be an inhabitant of that State for which he shall be chosen.

4. The Vice President of the United States shall be President of the Senate, but shall have no vote, unless they be equally divided.

5. The Senate shall choose their other officers, and also a president pro tempore, in the absence of the Vice

---

[1]See the Sixteenth Amendment.
[2]See the Fourteenth Amendment.

[3]See the Seventeenth Amendment.
[4]See the Seventeenth Amendment.

President, or when he shall exercise the office of the President of the United States.

6. The Senate shall have the sole power to try all impeachments. When sitting for that purpose, they shall be on oath or affirmation. When the president of the United States is tried, the chief justice shall preside: and no person shall be convicted without the concurrence of two thirds of the members present.

7. Judgment in cases of impeachment shall not extend further than to removal from office, and disqualification to hold and enjoy any office of honor, trust or profit under the United States: but the party convicted shall nevertheless be liable and subject to indictment, trial, judgment and punishment, according to law.

SECTION 4. 1. The times, places, and manner of holding elections for senators and representatives, shall be prescribed in each State by the legislature thereof; but the Congress may at any time by law make or alter such regulations, except as to the places of choosing senators.

2. The Congress shall assemble at least once in every year, and such meeting shall be on the first Monday in December, unless they shall by law appoint a different day.

SECTION 5. 1. Each House shall be the judge of the elections, returns and qualifications of its own members, and a majority of each shall constitute a quorum to do business; but a smaller number may adjourn from day to day, and may be authorized to compel the attendance of absent members, in such manner, and under such penalties as each House may provide.

2. Each House may determine the rules of its proceedings, punish its members for disorderly behavior, and, with the concurrence of two thirds, expel a member.

3. Each House shall keep a journal of its proceedings, and from time to time publish the same, excepting such parts as may in their judgment require secrecy; and the yeas and nays of the members of either house on any question shall, at the desire of one fifth of those present, be entered on the journal.

4. Neither House, during the session of Congress, shall, without the consent of the other, adjourn for more than three days, nor to any other place than that in which the two Houses shall be sitting.

SECTION 6. 1. The senators and representatives shall receive a compensation for their services, to be ascertained by law, and paid out of the Treasury of the United States. They shall in all cases, except treason, felony, and breach of the peace, be privileged from arrest during their attendance at the session of their respective Houses, and in going to and returning from the same; and for any speech or debate in either House, they shall not be questioned in any other place.

2. No senator or representative shall, during the time for which he was elected, be appointed to any civil office under the authority of the United States, which shall have been created, or the emoluments whereof shall have been increased, during such time; and no person holding any office under the United States shall be a member of either House during his continuance in office.

SECTION 7. 1. All bills for raising revenue shall originate in the House of Representatives; but the Senate may purpose or concur with amendments as on other bills.

2. Every bill which shall have passed the House of Representatives and the Senate, shall, before it become a law, be presented to the President of the United States; if he approves he shall sign it, but if not he shall return it, with his objections, to that House in which it shall have originated, who shall enter the objections at large on their journal, and proceed to reconsider it. If after such reconsideration two thirds of that House shall agree to pass the bill, it shall be sent, together with the objections, to the other House, by which it shall likewise be reconsidered, and if approved by two thirds of that House, it shall become a law. But in all such cases the votes of both Houses shall be determined by yeas and nays, and the names of the persons voting for and against the bill shall be entered on the journal of each House respectively. If any bill shall not be returned by the President within ten days (Sundays excepted) after it shall have been presented to him, the same shall be a law, in like manner as if he had signed it, unless the Congress by their adjournment prevent its return, in which case it shall not be a law.

3. Every order, resolution, or vote to which the concurrence of the Senate and the House of Representatives may be necessary (except on a question of adjournment) shall be presented to the President of the United States; and before the same shall take effect, shall be approved by him, or being disapproved by him, shall be repassed by two thirds of the Senate and House of Representatives, according to the rules and limitations prescribed in the case of a bill.

SECTION 8. The Congress shall have the power

1. To lay and collect taxes, duties, imports, and excises, to pay the debts and provide for the common

defense and general welfare of the United States; but all duties, imports, and excises shall be uniform throughout the United States.

2. To borrow money on the credit of the United States;

3. To regulate commerce with foreign nations, and among the several States, and with the Indian tribes;

4. To establish a uniform rule of naturalization, and uniform laws on the subject of bankruptcies throughout the United States;

5. To coin money, regulate the value thereof, and of foreign coin, and fix the standard of weights and measures;

6. To provide for the punishment of counterfeiting the securities and current coin of the United States;

7. To establish post offices and post roads;

8. To promote the progress of science and useful arts, by securing for limited times to authors and inventors the exclusive right to their respective writings and discoveries;

9. To constitute tribunals inferior to the Supreme Court;

10. To define and punish piracies and felonies committed on the high seas, and offenses against the law of nations;

11. To declare war, grant letters of marque and reprisal, and make rules concerning captures on land and water;

12. To raise and support armies, but no appropriation of money to that use shall be for a longer term than two years;

13. To provide and maintain a navy;

14. To make rules for the government and regulation of the land and naval forces;

15. To provide for calling forth the militia to execute the laws of the Union, suppress insurrections and repel invasions;

16. To provide for organizing, arming, and disciplining the militia, and for governing such part of them as may be employed in the service of the United States, reserving to the States respectively, the appointment of the officers, and the authority of training the militia according to the discipline prescribed by Congress;

17. To exercise exclusive legislation in all cases whatsoever, over such district (not exceeding ten miles square) as may, by cession of particular States, and the acceptance of Congress, become the seat of the government of the United States, and to exercise like authority over all places purchased by the consent of the legislature of the State in which the same shall be, for the erection of forts, magazines, arsenals, dockyards, and other needful buildings; and

18. To make all laws which shall be necessary and proper for carrying into execution the foregoing powers, and all other powers vested by this Constitution in the government of the United States, or any department or officer thereof.

SECTION 9. 1.The migration or importation of such persons as any of the States now existing shall think proper to admit, shall not be prohibited by the Congress prior to the year one thousand eight hundred and eight, but a tax or duty may be imposed on such importation, not exceeding ten dollars for each person.

2. The privilege of the writ of habeas corpus shall not be suspended, unless when in cases of rebellion or invasion the public safety may require it.

3. No bill of attainder or ex post facto law shall be passed.

4. No capitation, or other direct, tax shall be laid, unless in proportion to the census or enumeration herein-before directed to be taken.[5]

5. No tax or duty shall be laid on articles exported from any State.

6. No preference shall be given by any regulation of commerce or revenue to the ports of one State over those of another: nor shall vessels bound to, or from, one State be obliged to enter, clear, or pay duties in another.

7. No money shall be drawn from the treasury, but in consequence of appropriations made by law; and a regular statement and account of the receipts and expenditures of all public money shall be published from time to time.

8. No title of nobility shall be granted by the United States: and no person holding any office of profit or trust under them, shall, without the consent of the Congress, accept of any present, emolument, office, or title, of any kind whatever, from any king, prince, or foreign State.

SECTION 10. 1. No State shall enter into any treaty, alliance, or confederation; grant letters of marque and reprisal; coin money; emit bills of credit; make any thing but gold and silver coin a tender in payment of debts; pass any bill of attainder, ex post facto law, or law impairing the obligation of contracts, or grant any title of nobility.

---

[5]See the Sixteenth Amendment.

2. No State shall, without the consent of the Congress, lay any imposts or duties on imports or exports, except what may be absolutely necessary for executing its inspection laws: and the net produce of all duties and imposts laid by any State on imports or exports, shall be for the use of the treasury of the United States; and all such laws shall be subject to the revision and control of the Congress.

3. No State shall, without the consent of the Congress, lay any duty of tonnage, keep troops, or ships of war in time of peace, enter into any agreement or compact with another State, or with a foreign power, or engage in war, unless actually invaded, or in such imminent danger as will not admit of delay.

Article II

SECTION 1. 1. The executive power shall be vested in a President of the United States of America. He shall hold his office during the term of four years, and, together with the Vice President, chosen for the same term, be elected, as follows:

2. Each State shall appoint, in such manner as the legislature thereof may direct, a number of electors, equal to the whole number of senators and representatives to which the State may be entitled in the Congress: but no senator or representative, or person holding any office of trust or profit under the United States, shall be appointed an elector.

The electors shall meet in their respective States, and vote by ballot for two persons, of whom one at least shall not be an inhabitant of the same State with themselves. And they shall make a list of all the persons voted for, and of the number of votes for each; which list they shall sign and certify, and transmit sealed to the seat of the government of the United States, directed to the president of the Senate. The president of the Senate shall, in the presence of the Senate and House of Representatives, open all the certificates, and the votes shall then be counted. The person having the greatest number of votes shall be the President, if such number be a majority of the whole number of electors appointed; and if there be more than one who have such majority, and have an equal number of votes, then the House of Representatives shall immediately choose by ballot one of them for President; and if no person have a majority, then from the five highest on the list the said House shall in like manner choose the President. But in choosing the President, the votes shall be taken by States, the representation from each State having one vote; a quorum for this purpose shall consist of a member or members from two thirds of the States, and a majority of all the States shall be necessary to a choice. In every case after the choice of the President, the person having the greatest number of votes of the electors shall be the Vice President. But if there should remain two or more who have equal votes, the Senate shall choose from them by ballot the Vice President.[6]

3. The Congress may determine the time of choosing the electors, and the day on which they shall give their votes; which day shall be the same throughout the United States.

4. No person except a natural born citizen, or a citizen of the United States, at the time of the adoption of this Constitution, shall be eligible to the office of President; neither shall any person be eligible to the office who shall not have attained to the age of thirty-five years, and been fourteen years a resident within the United States.

5. In case of the removal of the President from office, or of his death, resignation, or inability to discharge the powers and duties of the said office, the same shall devolve on the Vice President, and the Congress may by law provide for the case of removal, death, resignation or inability, both of the President and Vice President, declaring what officer shall then act as President, and such officer shall act accordingly until the disability be removed, or a President shall be elected.

6. The President shall, at stated times, receive for his services a compensation which shall neither be increased nor diminished during the period for which he shall have been elected, and he shall not receive within that period any other emolument from the United States, or any of them.

7. Before he enter on the execution of his office, he shall take the following oath or affirmation:—"I do solemnly swear (or affirm) that I will faithfully execute the office of president of the United States, and will to the best of my ability, preserve, protect and defend the Constitution of the United States."

SECTION 2. 1. The President shall be commander in chief of the army and navy of the United States, and of the militia of the several States, when called into the actual service of the United States; he may require the opinion in writing, of the principal officer in each of the executive departments, upon any subject relating to the duties of their respective offices, and he shall have power

---

[6]See the Twelfth Amendment.

to grant reprieves and pardons for offenses against the United States, except in cases of impeachment.

2. He shall have power, by and with the advice and consent of the Senate, to make treaties, provided two thirds of the senators present concur; and he shall nominate, and by and with the advice and consent of the Senate, shall appoint ambassadors, other public ministers and consuls, judges of the Supreme Court, and all other officers of the United States, whose appointments are not herein otherwise provided for, and which shall be established by law; but the Congress may by law vest the appointment of such inferior officers, as they think proper, in the President alone, in the courts of laws, or in the heads of departments.

3. The President shall have power to fill up all vacancies that may happen during the recess of the Senate, by granting commissions which shall expire at the end of their next session.

SECTION 3. He shall from time to time give to the Congress information of the state of the Union, and recommend to their consideration such measures as he shall judge necessary and expedient; he may, on extraordinary occasions, convene both houses, or either of them, and in case of disagreement between them with respect to the time of adjournment, he may adjourn them to such time as he shall think proper; he shall receive ambassadors and other public ministers; he shall take care that the laws be faithfully executed, and shall commission all the officers of the United States.

SECTION 4. The President, Vice President, and all civil officers of the United States, shall be removed from office on impeachment for, and conviction of, treason, bribery, or other high crimes and misdemeanors.

Article III

SECTION 1. The judicial power of the United States shall be vested in one Supreme Court, and in such inferior courts as the Congress may from time to time ordain and establish. The judges, both of the Supreme and inferior courts, shall hold their offices during good behavior, and shall, at stated times, receive for their services, a compensation, which shall not be diminished during their continuance in office.

SECTION 2. 1. The judicial power shall extend to all cases, in law and equity, arising under this Constitution, the laws of the United States, and treaties made, or which shall be made, under their authority;—to all cases of admiralty and maritime jurisdiction;—to controversies

to which the United States shall be a party;[7]—to controversies between two or more States;—between a State and citizens of another State;—between citizens of different States;—between citizens of the same State claiming lands under grants of different States, and between a State, or the citizens thereof, and foreign States, citizens or subjects.

2. In all cases affecting ambassadors, other public ministers and consuls, and those in which a State shall be party, the Supreme Court shall have original jurisdiction. In all the other cases before mentioned, the Supreme Court shall have appellate jurisdiction, both as to law and fact, with such exceptions, and under such regulations as the Congress shall make.

3. The trial of all crimes, except in cases of impeachment, shall be by jury; and such trial shall be held in the State where the said crimes shall have been committed; but when not committed within any State, the trial shall be such place or places as the Congress may by law have directed.

SECTION 3. 1. Treason against the United States shall consist only in levying war against them, or in adhering to their enemies, giving them aid and comfort. No person shall be convicted of treason unless on the testimony of two witnesses to the same overt act, or on confession in open court.

2. The Congress shall have power to declare the punishment of treason, but no attainder of treason shall work corruption of blood, or forfeiture except during the life of the person attained.

Article IV

SECTION 1. Full faith and credit shall be given in each State to the public acts, records, and judicial proceedings of every other State. And the Congress may by general laws prescribe the manner in which such acts, records and proceedings shall be proved, and the effect thereof.

SECTION 2. 1. The citizens of each State shall be entitled to all privileges and immunities of citizens in the several States.[8]

2. A person charged in any State with treason, felony, or other crime, who shall flee from justice, and be found in another State, shall on demand of the executive authority of the State from which he fled, be delivered up to be removed to the State having jurisdiction of the crime.

---

[7]See the Eleventh Amendment.

[8]See the Fourteenth Amendment, Sec. 1.

3. No person held to service or labor in one State under the laws thereof, escaping into another, shall, in consequence of any law or regulation therein, be discharged from such service or labor, but shall be delivered up on claim of the party to whom such service or labor may be due.[9]

SECTION 3. 1. New States may be admitted by the Congress into this Union; but no new State shall be formed or erected within the jurisdiction of any other State, nor any State be formed by the junction of two or more States, or parts of States, without the consent of the legislatures of the States concerned as well as of the Congress.

2. The Congress shall have power to dispose of and make all needful rules and regulations respecting the territory or other property belonging to the United States; and nothing in this Constitution shall be so construed as to prejudice any claims of the United States, or of any particular State.

SECTION 4. The United States shall guarantee to every State in this Union a republican form of government, and shall protect each of them against invasion; and on application of the legislature, or of the executive (when the legislature cannot be convened) against domestic violence.

Article V

The Congress, whenever two thirds of both Houses shall deem it necessary, shall propose amendments to this Constitution, or, on the application of the legislatures of two thirds of the several States, shall call a convention for proposing amendments, which in either case shall be valid to all intents and purposes, as part of this Constitution, when ratified by the legislatures of three fourths of the several States, or by conventions in three fourths thereof, as the one or the other mode of ratification may be proposed by the Congress; Provided that no amendment which may be made prior to the year one thousand eight hundred and eight shall in any manner affect the first and fourth clauses in the ninth section of the first article; and that no State, without its consent, shall be deprived of its equal suffrage in the Senate.

Article VI

1. All debts contracted and engagements entered into, before the adoption of this Constitution, shall be as valid against the United States under this Constitution, as under the Confederation.[10]

2. This Constitution, and the laws of the United States which shall be made in pursuance thereof; and all treaties made, or which shall be made, under the authority of the United States, shall be the supreme law of the land; and the judges in every State shall be bound thereby, any thing in the Constitution or laws of any State to the contrary notwithstanding.

3. The senators and representatives before mentioned, and the members of the several State legislatures, and all executive and judicial officers, both of the United States and of the several States, shall be bound by oath or affirmation to support this Constitution; but no religious test shall ever be required as a qualification to any office or public trust under the United States.

Article VII

The ratification of the conventions of nine States shall be sufficient for the establishment of this Constitution between the States so ratifying the same.

Done in Convention by the unanimous consent of the States present the seventeenth day of September in the year of our Lord one thousand seven hundred and eighty-seven, and of the independence of the United States of America the twelfth. In witness whereof we have hereunto subscribed our names.

Articles in addition to, and amendment of, the Constitution of the United States of America, proposed by Congress, and ratified by the legislatures of the several States, pursuant to the fifth article of the original Constitution.

Amendment I [First Ten Amendments Ratified December 15, 1791]

Congress shall make no law respecting an establishment of religion, or prohibiting the free exercise thereof; or abridging the freedom of speech, or of the press; or the right of the people peaceably to assemble, and to petition the government for a redress of grievances.

Amendment II

A well regulated militia, being necessary to the security of a free State, the right of the people to keep and bear arms, shall not be infringed.

Amendment III

No soldier shall, in time of peace be quartered in any house, without the consent of the owner, nor in time of war, but in a manner to be prescribed by law.

---

[9]See the Thirteenth Amendment.

[10]See the Fourteenth Amendment, Sec. 4.

Amendment IV

The right of the people to be secure in their persons, houses, papers, and effects, against unreasonable searches and seizures, shall not be violated, and no warrants shall issue, but upon probable cause, supported by oath or affirmation, and particularly describing the place to be searched, and the persons or things to be seized.

Amendment V

No person shall be held to answer for a capital or otherwise infamous crime, unless on a presentment or indictment of a grand jury, except in cases arising in the land or naval forces, or in the militia, when in actual service in time of war or public danger; nor shall any person be subject for the same offense to be twice put in jeopardy of life or limb; nor shall be compelled in any criminal case to be a witness against himself, nor be deprived of life, liberty, or property, without due process of law; nor shall private property be taken for public use, without just compensation.

Amendment VI

In all criminal prosecutions, the accused shall enjoy the right to a speedy and public trial, by an impartial jury of the State and district wherein the crime shall have been committed, which district shall have been previously ascertained by law, and to be informed of the nature and cause of the accusation; to be confronted with the witnesses against him; to have compulsory process for obtaining witnesses in his favor, and to have the assistance of counsel for his defense.

Amendment VII

In suits at common law, where the value in controversy shall exceed twenty dollars, the right of trial by jury shall be preserved, and no fact tried by a jury shall be otherwise reexamined in any court of the United States, than according to the rules of the common law.

Amendment VIII

Excessive bail shall not be required, nor excessive fines imposed, nor cruel and unusual punishments inflicted.

Amendment IX

The enumeration in the Constitution of certain rights shall not be construed to deny or disparage others retained by the people.

Amendment X

The powers not delegated to the United States by the Constitution, nor prohibited by it to the States, are reserved to the States respectively, or to the people.

Amendment XI [January 8, 1798]

The judicial power of the United States shall not be construed to extend to any suit in law or equity, commended or prosecuted against one of the United States by citizens of another State, or by citizens or subjects of any foreign State.

Amendment XII [September 25, 1804]

The electors shall meet in their respective States, and vote by ballot for President and Vice President, one of whom, at least, shall not be an inhabitant of the same State with themselves; they shall name in their ballots the person voted for as President, and in distinct ballots, the person voted for as Vice President, and they shall make distinct lists of all persons voted for as President and of all persons voted for as Vice President, and of the number of votes for each, which lists they shall sign and certify, and transmit sealed to the seat of the government of the United States, directed to the President of the Senate;—The President of the Senate shall, in the presence of the Senate and House of Representatives, open all the certificates and the votes shall then be counted;—The person having the greatest number of votes for President, shall be the President, if such number be a majority of the whole number of electors appointed; and if no person have such majority, then from the persons having the highest numbers not exceeding three on the list of those voted for as President, the House of Representatives shall choose immediately, by ballot, the President. But in choosing the President, the votes shall be taken by States, the representation from each State having one vote; a quorum for this purpose shall consist of a member or members from two thirds of the States, and a majority of all the States shall be necessary to a choice. And if the House of Representatives shall not choose a President whenever the right of choice shall devolve upon them, before the fourth day of March next following, then the Vice President shall act as President, as in the case of the death or other constitutional disability of the President. The person having the greatest number of votes as Vice President shall be the Vice President, if such number be a majority of the whole number of electors appointed, and if no person have a majority, then from the two highest numbers on the list, the Senate shall choose the Vice President; a quorum for the purpose shall consist of two thirds of the whole number of Senators, and a majority of the whole number shall be necessary to a choice. But no person constitutionally ineligible to the office of President shall be eligible to that of Vice President of the United States.

Amendment XIII [December 18, 1865]
SECTION 1. Neither slavery nor involuntary servitude, except as punishment for crime whereof the party shall have been duly convicted, shall exist within the United States, or any place subject to their jurisdiction.

SECTION 2. Congress shall have power to enforce this article by appropriate legislation.

Amendment XIV [July 28, 1868]
SECTION 1. All persons born or naturalized in the United States, and subject to the jurisdiction thereof, are citizens of the United States and of the State wherein they reside. No State shall make or enforce any law which shall abridge the privileges or immunities of citizens of the United States; nor shall any State deprive any person of life, liberty, or property, without due process of law; nor deny to any person within its jurisdiction the equal protection of the laws.

SECTION 2. Representatives shall be apportioned among the several States according to their respective numbers, counting the whole number of persons in each State, excluding Indians not taxed. But when the right to vote at any election for the choice of electors for President and Vice President of the United States, representatives in Congress, the executive and judicial officers of a State, or the members of the legislature thereof, is denied to any of the male inhabitants of such State, being twenty-one years of age, and citizens of the United States, or in any way abridged, except for participating in rebellion, or other crime, the basis of representation there shall be reduced in the proportion which the number of such male citizens shall bear to the whole number of male citizens twenty-one years of age in such State.

SECTION 3. No person shall be a senator or representative in Congress, or elector of President and Vice President, or hold any office, civil or military, under the United States, or under any State, who having previously taken an oath, as a member of Congress, or as an officer of the United States, or as a member of any State legislature, or as an executive or judicial officer of any State, to support the Constitution of the United States, shall have engaged in insurrection or rebellion against the same, or given aid or comfort to the enemies thereof. But Congress may by a vote of two thirds of each House, remove such disability.

SECTION 4. The validity of the public debt of the United States, authorized by law, including debts incurred for payment of pensions and bounties for services in suppressing insurrection or rebellion; shall not be questioned. But neither the United States nor any State shall assume or pay any debt or obligation incurred in aid of insurrection or rebellion against the United States, or any claim for the loss or emancipation of any slave; but all such debts, obligations, and claims shall be held illegal and void.

SECTION 5. The Congress shall have the power to enforce, by appropriate legislation, the provisions of this article.

Amendment XV [March 30, 1870]
SECTION 1. The right of citizens of the United States to vote shall not be denied or abridged by the United States or by any State on account of race, color, or previous condition of servitude.

SECTION 2. The Congress shall have power to enforce this article by appropriate legislation.

Amendment XVI [February 25, 1913]
The Congress shall have power to lay and collect taxes on incomes, from whatever source derived, without apportionment among the several States, and without regard to any census or enumeration.

Amendment XVII [May 31, 1913]
The Senate of the United States shall be composed of two senators from each State, elected by the people thereof, for six years; and each senator shall have one vote. The electors in each State shall have the qualifications requisite for electors of the most numerous branch of the State legislature.

When vacancies happen in the representation of any State in the Senate, the executive authority of such State shall issue writs of election to fill such vacancies: Provided, That the legislature of any State may empower the executive thereof to make temporary appointments until the people fill the vacancies by election as the legislature may direct.

This amendment shall not be so construed as to affect the election or term of any senator chosen before it becomes valid as part of the Constitution.

Amendment XVIII[11] [January 29, 1919]

After one year from the ratification of this article, the manufacture, sale, or transportation of intoxicating liquors within, the importation thereof into, or the exportation thereof from the United States and all territory subject to the jurisdiction thereof for beverage purposes is thereby prohibited.

The Congress and the several States shall have concurrent power to enforce this article by appropriate legislation.

This article shall be inoperative unless it shall have been ratified as an amendment to the Constitution by the legislatures of the several States, as provided in the Constitution, within seven years from the date of the submission hereof to the States by Congress.

Amendment XIX [August 26, 1920]

The right of citizens of the United States to vote shall not be denied or abridged by the United States or by any State on account of sex.

Congress shall have the power to enforce this article by appropriate legislation.

Amendment XX [January 23, 1933]

SECTION 1. The terms of the President and Vice President shall end at noon on the 20th day of January and the terms of Senators and Representatives at noon on the 3d day of January, of the years in which such terms would have ended if this article had not been ratified; and the terms of their successors shall then begin.

SECTION 2. The Congress shall assemble at least once in every year, and such meeting shall begin at noon on the 3d day of January, unless they shall by law appoint a different day.

SECTION 3. If, at the time fixed for the beginning of the term of president, the President-elect shall have died, the Vice President-elect shall become President. If a President shall not have been chosen before the time fixed for the beginning of his term, or if the President-elect shall have failed to qualify, then the Vice President-elect shall act as president until a President shall have qualified; and the Congress may by law provide for the case wherein neither a President-elect nor a Vice President-elect shall have qualified, declaring who shall then act as President, or the manner in which one who is to act shall be selected, and such person shall act accordingly until a President or Vice President shall have qualified.

---

[11]Repealed by the Twenty-first Amendment.

SECTION 4. The Congress may by law provide for the case of the death of any of the persons from whom, the House of Representatives may choose a President whenever the right of choice shall have devolved upon them, and for the case of the death of any of the persons from whom the Senate may choose a Vice President whenever the right of choice shall have devolved upon them.

SECTION 5. Sections 1 and 2 shall take effect on the 15th day of October following the ratification of this article.

SECTION 6. This article shall be inoperative unless it shall have been ratified as an amendment to the Constitution by the legislatures of three-fourths of the several States within seven years from the date of its submission.

Amendment XXI [December 5, 1933]

SECTION 1. The Eighteenth Article of amendment to the Constitution of the United States is hereby repealed.

SECTION 2. The transportation or importation into any State, Territory, or possession of the United States for delivery or use therein of intoxicating liquors in violation of the laws thereof, is hereby prohibited.

SECTION 3. This article shall be inoperative unless it shall have been ratified as an amendment to the Constitution by conventions in the several States, as provided in the Constitution within seven years from the date of the submission thereof to the States by the Congress.

Amendment XXII [March 1, 1951]

No person shall be elected to the office of the President more than twice, and no person who has held the office of President, or acted as President, for more than two years of a term to which some other person was elected President shall be elected to the office of the President more than once.

But this article shall not apply to any person holding the office of President when this article was proposed by the Congress, and shall not prevent any person who may be holding the office of President, or acting as President, during the term within which this article becomes operative from holding the office of President or acting as President during the remainder of such term.

This article shall be inoperative unless it shall have been ratified as an amendment to the Constitution by the legislatures of three-fourths of the several States within seven years from the date of its submission to the States by the Congress.

Amendment XXIII [March 29, 1961]

SECTION 1. The District constituting the seat of Government of the United States shall appoint in such manner as the Congress may direct:

A number of electors of President and Vice President equal to the whole number of Senators and Representatives in Congress to which the District would be entitled if it were a State, but in no event more than the least populous State; they shall be in addition to those appointed by the States, but they shall be considered, for the purposes of the election of President and Vice President, to be electors appointed by a State; and they shall meet in the District and perform such duties as provided by the twelfth article of amendment.

SECTION 2. The Congress shall have power to enforce this article by appropriate legislation.

Amendment XXIV [January 23, 1964]

SECTION 1. The right of citizens of the United States to vote in any primary or other election for President or Vice President, for electors for President or Vice President, or for Senator or Representative in Congress, shall not be denied or abridged by the United States or any State by reason of failure to pay any poll tax or other tax.

SECTION 2. The Congress shall have power to enforce this article by appropriate legislation.

Amendment XXV [February 10, 1967]

SECTION 1. In case of the removal of the President from office or of his death or resignation, the Vice President shall become President.

SECTION 2. Whenever there is a vacancy in the office of the Vice President, the President shall nominate a Vice President who shall take office upon confirmation by a majority of both Houses of Congress.

SECTION 3. Whenever the President transmits to the President pro tempore of the Senate and the Speaker of the House of Representatives his written declaration that he is unable to discharge the powers and duties of his office, and until he transmits to them a written declaration to the contrary, such powers and duties shall be discharged by the Vice President as Acting President.

SECTION 4. Whenever the Vice President and a majority of either the principal officers of the executive departments or of such other body as Congress may by law provide, transmit to the President pro tempore of

the Senate and the Speaker of the House of Representatives their written declaration that the President is unable to discharge the powers and duties of his office, the Vice President shall immediately assume the powers and duties of the office as Acting President.

Thereafter, when the President transmits to the President pro tempore of the Senate and the Speaker of the House of Representatives his written declaration that no inability exists, he shall resume the powers and duties of his office unless the Vice President and a majority of either the principal officers of the executive departments or of such other body as Congress may by law provide, transmit within four days to the President pro tempore of the Senate and the Speaker of the House of Representatives their written declaration that the President is unable to discharge the powers and duties of his office. Thereupon Congress shall decide the issue, assembling within forty-eight hours for that purpose if not in session. If the Congress, within twenty-one days after receipt of the latter written declaration, or, if Congress is not in session, within twenty-one days after Congress is required to assemble, determines by two-thirds vote of both houses that the President is unable to discharge the powers and duties of his office, the Vice President shall continue to discharge the same as Acting President; otherwise, the President shall resume the powers and duties of his office.

Amendment XXVI [June 30, 1971]

SECTION 1. The right of citizens of the United States who are eighteen years of age or older to vote shall not be denied or abridged by the United States or by any State on account of age.

SECTION 2. The Congress shall have power to enforce this article by appropriate legislation.

Amendment XXVII[12] [May 7, 1992]

No law, varying the compensation for services of the Senators and Representatives, shall take effect until an election of Representatives shall have intervened.

---

[12]James Madison proposed this amendment in 1789 together with the ten amendments that were adopted as the Bill of Rights, but it failed to win ratification at the time. Congress, however, had set no deadline for its ratification, and over the years—particularly in the 1980s and 1990s—many states voted to add it to the Constitution. With the ratification of Michigan in 1992 it passed the threshold of the states required for adoption, but because the process took more than 200 years, its validity remains in doubt.

The Emancipation Proclamation

By the President of the United States of America:

Whereas, on the twenty-second day of September, in the year of our Lord one thousand eight hundred and sixty-two, a proclamation was issued by the President of the United States, containing, among other things, the following, to wit:

> That on the first day of January, in the year of our Lord one thousand eight hundred and sixty-three, all persons held as slaves within any State or designated part of a State, the people whereof shall then be in rebellion against the United States, shall be then, thenceforward, and forever free; and the Executive Government of the United States, including the military and naval authority thereof, will recognize and maintain the freedom of such persons, and will do no act or acts to repress such persons, or any of them, in any efforts they may make for their actual freedom.

> That the Executive will, on the first day of January aforesaid, by proclamation, designate the States and parts of States, if any, in which the people thereof, respectively, shall then be in rebellion against the United States; and the fact that any State, or the people thereof, shall on that day be, in good faith, represented in the Congress of the United States by members chosen thereto at elections wherein a majority of the qualified voters of such State shall have participated, shall, in the absence of strong countervailing testimony, be deemed conclusive evidence that such State, and the people thereof, are not then in rebellion against the United States.

Now, therefore I, Abraham Lincoln, President of the United States, by virtue of the power in me vested as Commander-in-Chief, of the Army and Navy of the United States in time of actual armed rebellion against the authority and government of the United States, and as a fit and necessary war measure for suppressing said rebellion, do, on this first day of January, in the year of our Lord one thousand eight hundred and sixty-three, and in accordance with my purpose so to do publicly proclaimed for the full period of one hundred days, from the day first above mentioned, order and designate as the States and parts of States wherein the people thereof respectively, are this day in rebellion against the United States, the following, to wit:

Arkansas, Texas, Louisiana, (except the Parishes of St. Bernard, Plaquemines, Jefferson, St. John, St. Charles, St. James Ascension, Assumption, Terrebonne, Lafourche, St. Mary, St. Martin, and Orleans, including the City of New Orleans), Mississippi, Alabama, Florida, Georgia, South Carolina, North Carolina, and Virginia, (except the forty-eight counties designated as West Virginia, and also the counties of Berkley, Accomac, Northampton, Elizabeth City, York, Princess Ann, and Norfolk, including the cities of Norfolk and Portsmouth), and which excepted parts, are for the present, left precisely as if this proclamation were not issued.

And by virtue of the power, and for the purpose aforesaid, I do order and declare that all persons held as slaves within said designated States, and parts of States, are, and henceforward shall be free; and that the Executive government of the United States, including the military and naval authorities thereof, will recognize and maintain the freedom of said persons.

And I hereby enjoin upon the people so declared to be free to abstain from all violence, unless in necessary self-defense; and I recommend to them that, in all cases when allowed, they labor faithfully for reasonable wages.

And I further declare and make known, that such persons of suitable condition, will be received into the armed service of the United States to garrison forts, positions, stations, and other places, and to man vessels of all sorts in said service.

And upon this act, sincerely believed to be an act of justice, warranted by the Constitution, upon military necessity, I invoke the considerate judgment of mankind, and the gracious favor of Almighty God.

In witness whereof, I have hereunto set my hand and caused the seal of the United States to be affixed. Done at the City of Washington, this first day of January, in the year of our Lord one thousand eight hundred and sixty-three, and of the Independence of the United States of America the eighty-seventh.

By the President: Abraham Lincoln
William H. Seward, Secretary of State

Key Provisions of the Civil Rights Act of 1964

An Act

To enforce the constitutional right to vote, to confer jurisdiction upon the district courts of the United States to provide injunctive relief against discrimination in public accommodations, to authorize the Attorney General to institute suits to protect constitutional rights in public facilities and public education, to extend the Commission on Civil Rights, to prevent discrimination in federally assisted programs, to establish a Commission on Equal Employment Opportunity, and for other purposes.

Be it enacted by the Senate and House of Representatives of the United States of America in Congress assembled, that this Act may be cited as the "Civil Rights Act of 1964."

Title I—Voting Rights

SECTION 101 . . . (2) No person acting under color of law shall—

(A) In determining whether any individual is qualified under State law or laws to vote in any Federal election, apply any standard, practice, or procedure different from the standards, practices, or procedures applied under such law or laws to other individuals within the same county, parish, or similar political subdivision who have been found by State officials to be qualified to vote;

(B) deny the right of any individual to vote in any Federal election because of an error or omission on any record or paper relating to any application, registration, or other act requisite to voting, if such error or omission is not material in determining whether such individual is qualified under State law to vote in such election;

(C) employ any literacy test as a qualification for voting in any Federal election unless (i) such test is administered to each individual and is conducted wholly in writing, and (ii) a certified copy of the test and of the answers given by the individual is furnished to him within twenty-five days of the submission of his request made within the period of time during which records and papers are required to be retained and preserved pursuant to title III of the Civil Rights Act of 1960 (42 U.S.C. 1974–74e; 74 Stat. 88): Provided, however, That the Attorney General may enter into agreements with appropriate State or local authorities that preparation, conduct, and maintenance of such tests in accordance with the provisions of applicable State or local law, including such special provisions as are necessary in the preparation, conduct, and maintenance of such tests for persons who are blind or otherwise physically handicapped, meet the purposes of this subparagraph and constitute compliance therewith.

Title II—Injunctive Relief Against Discrimination in Places of Public Accommodation

SECTION 201. (a) All persons shall be entitled to the full and equal enjoyment of the goods, services, facilities, and privileges, advantages and accommodations of any place of public accommodation, as defined in this section, without discrimination or segregation on the ground of race, color, religion, or national origin.

(b) Each of the following establishments which serves the public is a place of public accommodation within the meaning of this title if its operations affect commerce, or if discrimination or segregation by it is supported by State action:

(1) any inn, hotel, motel, or other establishment which provides lodging to transient guests, other than an establishment located within a building which contains not more than five rooms for rent or hire and which is actually occupied by the proprietor of such establishment as his residence;

(2) any restaurant, cafeteria, lunchroom, lunch counter, soda fountain, or other facility principally engaged in selling food for consumption on the premises, including, but not limited to, any such facility located on the premises of any retail establishment; or any gasoline station;

(3) any motion picture house, theater, concert hall, sports arena, stadium or other place of exhibition or entertainment;

(4) any establishment (A)(i) which is physically located within the premises of any establishment otherwise covered by this subsection, or (ii) within the premises of which is physically located any such covered establishment, and (B) which holds itself out as serving patrons of such covered establishment. . . .

(d) Discrimination or segregation by an establishment is supported by State action within the meaning of this title if such discrimination or segregation

(1) is carried on under color of any law, statute, ordinance, or regulation; or

(2) is carried on under color of any custom or usage required or enforced by officials of the State or political subdivision thereof; or

(3) is required by action of the State or political subdivision thereof. . . .

SECTION 202. All persons shall be entitled to be free, at any establishment or place, from discrimination or segregation of any kind on the ground of race, color, religion, or national origin, if such discrimination or segregation is or purports to be required by any law, statute, ordinance, regulation, rule, or order of a State or any agency or political subdivision thereof.

SECTION 203. No person shall (a) withhold, deny, or attempt to withhold or deny, or deprive or attempt to deprive, any person of any right or privilege secured by section 201 or 202, or (b) intimidate, threaten, or coerce, or attempt to intimidate, threaten, or coerce any person with the purpose of interfering with any right or privilege secured by section 201 or 202, or (c) punish or attempt to punish any person for exercising or attempting to exercise any right or privilege secured by section 201 or 202.

Section 204. (a) Whenever any person has engaged or there are reasonable grounds to believe that any person is about to engage in any act or practice prohibited by section 203, a civil action for preventive relief, including an application for a permanent or temporary injunction, restraining order, or other order, may be instituted by the person aggrieved and, upon timely application, the court may, in its discretion, permit the Attorney General to intervene in such civil action if he certifies that the case is of general public importance. Upon application by the complainant and in such circumstances as the court may deem just, the court may appoint an attorney for such complainant and may authorize the commencement of the civil action without the payment of fees, costs, or security. . . .

SECTION 206. (a) Whenever the Attorney General has reasonable cause to believe that any person or group of persons is engaged in a pattern or practice of resistance to the full enjoyment of any of the rights secured by this title, and that the pattern or practice is of such a nature and is intended to deny the full exercise of the rights herein described, the Attorney General may bring a civil action in the appropriate district court of the United States by filing with it a complaint

(1) signed by him (or in his absence the Acting Attorney General),

(2) setting forth facts pertaining to such pattern or practice, and

(3) requesting such preventive relief, including an application for a permanent or temporary injunction, restraining order or other order against the person or persons responsible for such pattern or practice, as he deems necessary to insure the full enjoyment of the rights herein described. . . .

Title III—Desegregation of Public Facilities

SECTION 301. (a) Whenever the Attorney General receives a complaint in writing signed by an individual to the effect that he is being deprived of or threatened with the loss of his right to the equal protection of the laws, on account of his race, color, religion, or national origin, by being denied equal utilization of any public facility which is owned, operated, or managed by or on behalf of any State or subdivision thereof, other than a public school or public college as defined in section 401 of title IV hereof, and the Attorney General believes the complaint is meritorious and certifies that the signer or signers of such complaint are unable, in his judgment, to initiate and maintain appropriate legal proceedings for relief and that the institution of an action will materially further the orderly progress of desegregation in public facilities, the Attorney General is authorized to institute for or in the name of the United States a civil action in any appropriate district court of the United States against such parties and for such relief as may be appropriate.

And such court shall have and shall exercise jurisdiction of proceedings instituted pursuant to this section. The Attorney General may implead as defendants such additional parties as are or become necessary to the grant of effective relief hereunder. . . .

Title IV—Desegregation of Public Education

SECTION 401. As used in this title—. . . .

"Desegregation" means the assignment of students to public schools and within such schools without regard to their race, color, religion, or national origin, but "desegregation" shall not mean the assignment of students to public schools in order to overcome racial imbalance. . . .

Survey and Report of Educational Opportunities

SECTION 402. The Commissioner shall conduct a survey and make a report to the President and the Congress, within two years of the enactment of this title, concerning the lack of availability of equal educational opportunities for individuals by reason of race, color, religion, or national origin in public educational institutions at all levels in the United States, its territories and possessions, and the District of Columbia. . . .

Title V—Commission on Civil Rights. . . .
Duties of the Commission

SECTION 104. a. The Commission shall—

(1) investigate allegations in writing under oath or affirmation that certain citizens of the United States are being deprived of their right to vote and have that vote counted by reason of their color, race, religion, or national origin; which writing, under oath or affirmation, shall set forth the facts upon which such belief or beliefs are based;

(2) study and collect information concerning legal developments constituting a denial of equal protection of the laws under the Constitution because of race, color, religion or national origin or in the administration of justice;

(3) appraise the laws and policies of the Federal Government with respect to denials of equal protection of the laws under the Constitution because of race, color, religion or national origin or in the administration of justice;

(4) serve as a national clearinghouse for information in respect to denials of equal protection of the laws because of race, color, religion or national origin, including but not limited to the fields of voting, education, housing, employment, the use of public facilities, and transportation, or in the administration of justice;

(5) investigate allegations, made in writing and under oath or affirmation, that citizens of the United States are unlawfully being accorded or denied the right to vote, or to have their votes properly counted, in any election of presidential electors, Members of the United States Senate, or of the House of Representatives, as a result of any patterns or practice of fraud or discrimination in the conduct of such election;. . . .

Title VI—Nondiscrimination in Federally Assisted Programs

SECTION 601. No person in the United States shall, on the ground of race, color, or national origin, be excluded from participation in, be denied the benefits of, or be subjected to discrimination under any program or activity receiving Federal financial assistance.

SECTION 602. Each Federal department and agency which is empowered to extend Federal financial assistance to any program or activity, by way of grant, loan, or contract other than a contract of insurance or guaranty, is authorized and directed to effectuate the provisions of section 601 with respect to such program or activity by issuing rules, regulations, or orders of general applicability which shall be consistent with achievement of the objectives of the statute authorizing the financial assistance in connection with which the action is taken. No such rule, regulation, or order shall become effective unless and until approved by the President. Compliance with any requirement adopted pursuant to this section may be effected

(1) by the termination of or refusal to grant or to continue assistance under such program or activity to any recipient as to whom there has been an express finding on the record, after opportunity for hearing, of a failure to comply with such requirement, but such termination or refusal shall be limited to the particular political entity, or part thereof, or other recipient as to whom such a finding has been made and, shall be limited in its effect to the particular program, or part thereof, in which such non-compliance has been so found, or

(2) by any other means authorized by law:

Provided, however, that no such action shall be taken until the department or agency concerned has advised the appropriate person or persons of the failure to comply with the requirement and has determined that compliance cannot be secured by voluntary means. In the case of any action terminating, or refusing to grant or continue, assistance because of failure to comply with a requirement imposed pursuant to this section, the head of the federal department or agency shall file with the committees of the House and Senate having legislative jurisdiction over the program or activity involved a full written report of the circumstances and the grounds for such action. No such action shall become effective until thirty days have elapsed after the filing of such report. . . .

Title VII—Equal Employment Opportunity. . . .

Discrimination Because of Race, Color, Religion, Sex, or National Origin

SECTION 703. a. it shall be an unlawful employment practice for an employer—

(1) to fail or refuse to hire or to discharge any individual, or otherwise to discriminate against any individual with respect to his compensation, terms, conditions, or privileges of employment, because of such individual's race, color, religion, sex, or national origin; or

(2) to limit, segregate, or classify his employees in any way which would deprive or tend to deprive any individual of employment opportunities or otherwise adversely affect his status as an employee, because of such individual's race, color, religion, sex, or national origin.

(b) it shall be an unlawful employment practice for an employment agency to fail or refuse to refer for employment, or otherwise to discriminate against, any individual because of his race, color, religion, sex, or national origin, or to classify or refer for employment any individual on the basis of his race, color, religion, sex, or national origin.

(c) it shall be an unlawful employment practice for a labor organization—

(1) to exclude or to expel from its membership, or otherwise to discriminate against, any individual because of his race, color, religion, sex, or national origin;

(2) to limit, segregate, or classify its membership, or to classify or fail or refuse to refer for employment any individual, in any way which would deprive or tend to deprive any individual of employment opportunities, or would limit such employment opportunities or otherwise adversely affect his status as an employee or as an applicant for employment, because of such individual's race, color, religion, sex, or national origin; or

(3) to cause or attempt to cause an employer to discriminate against an individual in violation of this section.

(d) It shall be an unlawful employment practice for any employer, labor organization, or joint labor-management committee controlling apprenticeship or other training or retraining, including on-the-job training programs to discriminate against any individual because of his race, color, religion, sex, or national origin in admission to, or employment in, any program established to provide apprenticeship or other training. . . .

Other Unlawful Employment Practices

Section 704. (a) It shall be an unlawful employment practice for an employer to discriminate against any of his employees or applicants for employment, for an employment agency to discriminate against any individual, or for a labor organization to discriminate against any member thereof or applicant for membership, because he has opposed any practice made an unlawful employment practice by this title, or because he has made a charge, testified, assisted, or participated in any manner in an investigation, proceeding, or hearing under this title.

(b) It shall be an unlawful employment practice for an employer, labor organization, or employment agency to print or publish or cause to be printed or published any notice or advertisement relating to employment by such an employer or membership in or any classification or referral for employment by such a labor organization, or relating to any classification or referral for employment by such an employment agency, indicating any preference, limitation, specification, or discrimination, based on race, color, religion, sex, or national origin, except that such a notice or advertisement may indicate a preference, limitation, specification, or discrimination based on religion, sex, or national origin when religion, sex, or national origin is a bona fide occupational quali-fication for employment.

Equal Employment Opportunity Commission

SECTION 705. (a) There is hereby created a Commis-sion to be known as the Equal Employment Opportunity Commission, which shall be composed of five members, not more than three of whom shall be members of the same political party, who shall be appointed by the Pres-ident by and with the advice and consent of the Senate. One of the original members shall be appointed for a term of one year, one for a term of two years, one for a term of three years, one for a term of four years, and one for a term of five years, beginning from the date of enactment of this title, but their successors shall be ap-pointed for terms of five years each, except that any in-dividual chosen to fill a vacancy shall be appointed only for the unexpired term of the member whom he shall succeed. The President shall designate one member to serve as Chairman of the Commission, and one member to serve as Vice Chairman. The Chairman shall be re-sponsible on behalf of the Commission for the adminis-trative operations of the Commission, and shall appoint, in accordance with the civil service laws, such officers, agents, attorneys, and employees as it deems necessary to assist it in the performance of its functions and to fix their compensation in accordance with Classification Act of 1949, as amended. . . .

Title VIII—Registration and Voting Statistics

SECTION 801. The Secretary of Commerce shall promptly conduct a survey to compile registration and voting statistics in such geographic areas as may be rec-ommended by the Commission on Civil Rights. Such a survey and compilation shall, to the extent recommended by the Commission on Civil Rights, only include a count of persons of voting age by race, color, and national origin, and determination of the extent to which such persons are registered to vote, and have voted in any state-wide primary or general election in which the Members of the United States House of Representatives are nomi-nated or elected, since January 1, 1960. Such information shall also be collected and compiled in connection with the Nineteenth Decennial Census, and at such other times as the Congress may prescribe. The provisions of section 9 and chapter 7 of title 13, United States Code, shall apply to any survey, collection, or compilation of registration and voting statistics carried out under this title: Provided, however, that no person shall be com-pelled to disclose his race, color, national origin, or questioned about his political party affiliation, how he voted, or the reasons therefore, nor shall any penalty be imposed for his failure or refusal to make such disclo-sure. Every person interrogated orally, by written survey or questionnaire or by any other means with respect to such information shall be fully advised with respect to his right to fail or refuse to furnish such information.

Lyndon B. Johnson July 2, 1964

Key Provisions of the Voting Rights Act of 1965

An Act

To enforce the fifteenth amendment to the Constitution of the United States, and for other purposes.

Be it enacted by the Senate and House of Representatives of the United States of America in Congress assembled, That this Act shall be known as the "Voting Rights Act of 1965."

SECTION 2. No voting qualification or prerequisite to voting, or standard, practice, or procedure shall be imposed or applied by any State or political subdivision to deny or abridge the right of any citizen of the United States to vote on account of race or color.

SECTION 3. (a) Whenever the Attorney General institutes a proceeding under any statute to enforce the guarantees of the fifteenth amendment in any State or political subdivision the court shall authorize the appointment of Federal examiners by the United States Civil Service Commission in accordance with section 6 to serve for such period of time and for such political subdivisions as the court shall determine is appropriate to enforce the guarantees of the fifteenth amendment (1) as part of any interlocutory order if the court determines that the appointment of such examiners is necessary to enforce such guarantees or (2) as part of any final judgment if the court finds that violations of the fifteenth amendment justifying equitable relief have occurred in such State or subdivision: Provided, That the court need not authorize the appointment of examiners if any incidents of denial or abridgment of the right to vote on account of race or color (1) have been few in number and have been promptly and effectively corrected by State or local action, (2) the continuing effect of such incidents has been eliminated, and (3) there is no reasonable probability of their recurrence in the future.

(b) If in a proceeding instituted by the Attorney General under any statute to enforce the guarantees of the fifteenth amendment in any State or political subdivision the court finds that a test or device has been used for the purpose or with the effect of denying or abridging the right of any citizen of the United States to vote on account of race or color, it shall suspend the use of tests and devices in such State or political subdivisions as the court shall determine is appropriate and for such period as it deems necessary. . . .

SECTION 4. (a) To assure that the right of citizens of the United States to vote is not denied or abridged on account of race or color, no citizen shall be denied the right to vote in any Federal, State, or local election because of his failure to comply with any test or device in any State with respect to which the determinations have been made under subsection (b). . . .

(b) The provisions of subsection (a) shall apply in any State or in any political subdivision of a state which (1) the Attorney General determines maintained on November 1, 1964, any test or device, and with respect to which (2) the Director of the Census determines that less than 50 per centum of the persons of voting age residing therein were registered on November 1, 1964, or that less than 50 per centum of such persons voted in the presidential election of November 1964. . . .

(c) The phrase "test or device" shall mean any requirement that a person as a prerequisite for voting or registration of voting (1) demonstrate the ability to read, write, understand, or interpret any matter, (2) demonstrate any educational achievement or his knowledge of any particular subject, (3) possess good moral character, or (4) prove his qualifications by the voucher of registered voters or members of any other class. . . .

SECTION 6. Whenever (a) a court has authorized the appointment of examiners pursuant to the provisions of section 3 (a), or (b) unless a declaratory judgment has been rendered under section 4 (a), the Attorney General certifies with respect to any political subdivision named in, or included within the scope of, determinations made under section 4 (b) that (1) he has received complaints in writing from twenty or more residents of such political subdivision alleging that they have been denied the right to vote under color of law on account of race or color, and that he believes such complaints to be meritorious, or (2) that in his judgment (considering, among other factors, whether the ratio of nonwhite persons to white persons registered to vote within such subdivision appears to him to be reasonably attributable to violations of the fifteenth amendment or whether substantial evidence exists that bona fide efforts are being made within such subdivision to comply with the fifteenth amendment), the appointment of examiners is otherwise necessary to enforce the guarantees of the fifteenth amendment, the Civil Service Commission shall appoint as many examiners for such subdivision as it may deem appropriate to prepare and maintain lists of persons eligible to vote in Federal, State, and local elections. . . . Examiners and hearing officers shall have the power to administer oaths. . . .

Lyndon B. Johnson August 6, 1965

Executive Order 13050 President's Advisory Board on Race

By the authority vested in me as President by the Constitution and the laws of the United States of America, including the Federal Advisory Committee Act, as amended (5 U.S.C. App.), and in order to establish a President's Advisory Board on Race, it is hereby ordered as follows:

SECTION 1. Establishment. (a) There is established the President's Advisory Board on Race. The Advisory Board shall comprise 7 members from outside the Federal Government to be appointed by the President. Members shall each have substantial experience and expertise in the areas to be considered by the Advisory Board. Members shall be representative of the diverse perspectives in the areas to be considered by the Advisory Board.

(b) The President shall designate a Chairperson from among the members of the Advisory Board.

SEC. 2. Functions. a. The Advisory Board shall advise the President on matters involving race and racial reconciliation, including ways in which the President can:

(1) Promote a constructive national dialogue to confront and work through challenging issues that surround race;

(2) Increase the Nation's understanding of our recent history of race relations and the course our Nation is charting on issues of race relations and racial diversity;

(3) Bridge racial divides by encouraging leaders in communities throughout the Nation to develop and implement innovative approaches to calming racial tensions;

(4) Identify, develop, and implement solutions to problems in areas in which race has a substantial impact, such as education, economic opportunity, housing, health care, and the administration of justice.

(b) The Advisory Board also shall advise on such other matters as from time to time the President may refer to the Board.

(c) In carrying out its functions, the Advisory Board shall coordinate with the staff of the President's Initiative on Race.

SEC. 3. Administration. (a) To the extent permitted by law and subject to the availability of appropriations, the Department of Justice shall provide the financial and administrative support for the Advisory Board.

(b) The heads of executive agencies shall, to the extent permitted by law, provide to the Advisory Board such information as it may require for the purpose of carrying out its functions.

(c) The Chairperson may, from time to time, invite experts to submit information to the Advisory Board and may form subcommittees or working groups within the Advisory Board to review specific matters.

(d) Members of the Advisory Board shall serve without compensation but shall be allowed travel expenses, including per diem in lieu of subsistence, as authorized by law for persons serving intermittently in the Government service (5 U.S.C. 5701–5707).

SEC. 4. General. (a) Notwithstanding any other Executive order, the functions of the President under the Federal Advisory Committee Act, as amended, except that of reporting to the Congress, that are applicable to the Advisory Board shall be performed by the Attorney General, or his or her designee, in accordance with guidelines that have been issued by the Administrator of General Services.

(b) The Advisory Board shall terminate on September 30, 1998 unless extended by the President prior to such date.

William J. Clinton June 13, 1997

Glossary Key Terms and Concepts

54th Massachusetts Regiment   This all-black volunteer infantry regiment was recruited in the northern states for service with Union military forces in the Civil War. This regiment, made up almost entirely of black men who had been free, was commanded by white officers.

Affirmative action   Civil rights policy or program that seeks to redress the effects of past discrimination due to race or gender by giving preference to women and minorities in education and employment.

African Methodist Episcopal (AME) Church   Founded in Philadelphia in 1816, this was the first black church and eventually became the largest independent black church.

Afrocentricity   A philosophy of culture that celebrates Africa's role in history and stresses the enduring African roots and identity of black America.

Age of Revolution   A period in Atlantic history that began with the American Revolution in 1776 and ended with the defeat of Napoleonic France in 1815.

Agricultural Adjustment Act (AAA)   A federal program that provided subsidies to farmers to grow less to help stabilize prices.

American and Foreign Anti-Slavery Society (AFASS, 1840–1855)   An organization of church-oriented abolitionists.

American Anti-Slavery Society (AASS, 1833–1870)   The umbrella organization for immediate abolitionists during the 1830s and the main Garrisonian organization after 1840.

American Colonization Society (ACS, 1816–1912)   An organization founded in Washington, DC, by prominent slaveholders. It claimed to encourage the ultimate abolition of slavery by sending free African Americans to its West African colony of Liberia.

American Missionary Association   This religious organization sent teachers and clergymen throughout the South following the Civil War to tend to the spiritual and educational needs of former slaves.

Amistad   A Spanish schooner on which West African Joseph Cinque led a successful slave revolt in 1839.

Antimiscegenation   Laws that enforced racial segregation at the level of marriage and intimate relationships by criminalizing interracial marriage and sometimes also sex between members of different races.

Asiento   The monopoly over the slave trade from Africa to Spain's American colonies.

Assimilation   The process by which people of different backgrounds become similar to each other in culture and language.

Battery Wagner   This defensive fortification guarded Fort Sumter near the entrance to Charleston Harbor in South Carolina. It was the scene in July 1863 of a major Union assault by the 54th Massachusetts Regiment, a black unit. The assault failed, but the bravery and valor of the black troops earned them fame and glory.

Black arts movement   Artistic movement that seeks to promote black art by black artists for black people.

Black cabinet   Informal group of highly placed African-American advisers to President Franklin D. Roosevelt.

Black codes   Laws that were passed in each of the former Confederate states following the Civil War that applied only to black people. While conceding such rights as the right to marry, to contract a debt, or to own property, the codes severely restricted the rights and opportunities of former slaves in terms of labor and mobility.

Black Committee   An organization of prominent black men in the North who assisted in recruiting African Americans to fight for the Union in the Civil War.

Black English   A variety of American English that is influenced by West African grammar, vocabulary, and pronunciation.

Black laws   Laws passed in states of the Old Northwest during the early nineteenth century banning or restricting black settlement and limiting the rights of black residents.

Border ruffians   Pro-slavery advocates and vigilantes from Missouri who crossed the border into Kansas in 1855–1857 to support slavery in Kansas by threatening and attacking antislavery settlers.

Brotherhood of Sleeping Car Porters (BSCP)   Black men and women who worked on Pullman passenger coaches on the nation's railroads organized this labor union in 1925 with A. Philip Randolph as its leader.

Brownsville Affair   In 1906, a shooting in Brownsville, Texas, was blamed on black soldiers from the 25th Infantry Regiment. President Theodore Roosevelt summarily dismissed 167 black men from the U.S. Army. Later investigations exonerated the men.

Buffalo soldiers   Four regiments of black soldiers that served with the U.S. Army on the western frontier from the 1870s to the 1890s. The Plains Indians called them the buffalo soldiers.

Call-and-response An African-American singing style rooted in Africa. A solo call tells a story to which a group responds, often with repeated lyrics.

Carpetbagger The derogatory term used during Reconstruction to describe northerners who came South following the Civil War to take advantage of political and economic opportunities. They were labeled "carpetbaggers" because they ostensibly carried all of their possessions in a solitary carpetbag.

Cash crop A crop grown for sale rather than subsistence.

Chattel slavery A form of slavery in which the enslaved are treated legally as property.

Chicago Renaissance Flourishing of the arts that made Chicago the center of black culture in the 1940s.

Church of England A Protestant church established in the sixteenth century as the English national or Anglican church with the English monarch as its head. After the American Revolution, its American branch became the Episcopal Church.

Civil Rights Act This act nullified the black codes and made African Americans citizens with the basic rights of life, liberty, and due process.

Civil Rights Act of 1875 This federal legislation outlawed racial discrimination in public accommodations such as hotels and restaurants, and in transportation, including railroad coaches and steamboats. The Supreme Court invalidated it in 1883.

Civil Rights Act of 1964 Federal law banning discrimination in places of public accommodation.

Civil Rights Act of 1968 Federal law banning discrimination in housing.

Coffle A file of slaves chained together that was typical of the domestic slave trade.

Colored Farmers' Alliance A large organization of black southern farmers in the 1880s and 1890s that had as many as one million members who agitated for improved conditions and income for black landowners, renters, and sharecroppers.

Committee for Industrial Organization (CIO) Labor organization that was committed to interracial and multiethnic organizing.

Community Action Programs (CAPS) Anti-poverty programs involving "maximum feasible participation" by the poor themselves.

Compensated emancipation Emancipation accompanied by the monetary compensation of former slave owners.

Compromise of 1850 An attempt by the U.S. Congress to settle divisive issues between the North and South, including slavery expansion, apprehension in the North of fugitive slaves, and slavery in the District of Columbia.

Compromise of 1877 An informal arrangement between national Democrats and Republicans to settle the disputed presidential election of 1876.

Confederacy Association of slave states that left the Union in 1861.

Continental Army The army created by the Continental Congress in June 1775 to fight British troops. George Washington was its commander in chief.

Continental Congress A representative assembly that first met in October 1775 and served as the de facto central government of the United States during the Revolutionary War.

Contraband Slaves who escaped to the Union or were captured by Union troops early in the Civil War, who were considered enemy property.

Convict lease system Southern states and communities leased prisoners to privately operated mines, railroads, and timber companies. These businesses forced the prisoners, who were usually black men, to work in brutal, unhealthy, and dangerous conditions. Many convicts died of abuse and disease.

Cotton gin A simple machine invented by Eli Whitney in 1793 to separate cotton seeds from cotton fiber. It greatly speeded this task and encouraged the westward expansion of cotton-growing in the United States.

Creoles Persons of African and/or European descent born in the Americas.

Disfranchisement White southern Democrats devised a variety of techniques in the late nineteenth and early twentieth centuries to prevent black people from voting. Those techniques included literacy tests, poll taxes, and the grandfather clause as well as intimidation and violence.

Divination A form of magic aimed at telling the future by interpreting a variety of signs.

Domestic slave trade A trade dating from the first decade of the nineteenth century in American-born slaves purchased primarily in the border South and sent overland or by sea to the cotton-growing regions of the Old Southwest.

"Double V" campaign Slogan during World War II that stood for victory over fascism abroad and over racism at home for blacks.

Dred Scott v. Sandford The 1857 U.S. Supreme Court case that ruled against Missouri slave Dred Scott by declaring that black people were not citizens, that they possessed no constitutional rights, and that they were considered to be property.

Economic Opportunity Act of 1964 Federal law creating the Office of Economic Opportunity and a number of programs aimed at poor communities.

Ellenton Massacre A conflict in which between 30 and 100 African Americans were killed by marauding white men in September 1876 in Aiken County, South Carolina. The event took place after an alleged assault by a black man on an elderly white woman.

Enforcement Acts Also known as the Force Acts, these measures were passed by Congress in the early 1870s to undermine the Ku Klux Klan and other terrorist organizations by authorizing the president to use military force and to suspend the writ of *habeas corpus*.

Executive Order 8802 Order issued by President Franklin D. Roosevelt in 1941 banning discrimination in employment in defense industries and the federal government.

Executive Order 9981 Order issued by President Harry Truman in 1948 desegregating the armed forces.

Exodusters   Black migrants who left the South during and after Reconstruction and settled in Kansas, often in all black towns.

Fair Employment Practices Committee (FEPC)   A committee created by Franklin Roosevelt to investigate complaints of discrimination.

Fair Play Committee   Organization formed to promote black actors in the movie industry and improve the image of blacks in film.

Family Assistance Plan (FAP)   Plan giving financial assistance to families with no wage earner.

Federal Arts Project   New Deal agency formed to promote the creation of public art.

Federal Elections bill   A measure, also known as the Force bill, to protect the voting rights of black men in the South by providing federal supervision of elections. It passed in the House of Representatives but failed in the Senate.

Fetish   A natural object or an artifact believed to have magical power; a charm.

Fifteenth Amendment   This constitutional amendment stipulated that the right to vote could not be denied on account of race, color, or because a person had been a slave.

First Confiscation Act   This 1861 act stated that any slaves used by their masters to benefit the Confederacy would be freed.

First South Carolina Volunteers   This black military unit consisted of former slaves recruited in the South Carolina and Georgia low country in 1862 and 1863 for service with Union military forces in the Civil War.

Fort Pillow   This fort on the east bank of the Mississippi River north of Memphis, Tennessee, was the scene of a massacre of black Union troops as well as some white soldiers and officers by Confederate cavalry in April 1864.

Forty-Niners   The men and women who rushed to California in 1849 after gold had been discovered there.

Fourteenth Amendment   This amendment ratified during Reconstruction made any person born in the United States a citizen of the United States and of the state in which he or she lived.

Free labor   Mid-nineteenth-century Americans who were free and worked for income or compensation to advance themselves, as opposed to slave labor, which was work done with no financial compensation by people who were not free.

Free papers   Proof of freedom that free black people had to carry at all times in the southern states prior to emancipation. The papers, issued by state governments, identified an individual by name, age, sex, color, height, and so forth.

Freedmen's Bureau   Congress established the Bureau of Refugees, Freedmen, and Abandoned Lands in February 1865 to assist black and white southerners left destitute by the Civil War.

Freedmen's Savings Bank   A private financial institution chartered by Congress in 1865. Many black people and organizations deposited funds in the bank, which went bankrupt in 1874.

Freedom suits   Legal cases in which slaves sued their master or master's heirs for freedom.

French and Indian War   A war waged by Great Britain and its American Indian allies against France and its American Indian allies, fought between 1754 and 1763 for control of the eastern portion of North America.

Fugitive Slave Act of 1793   An act of Congress permitting masters to recapture escaped slaves who had reached the free states and, with the authorization of local courts, return with the slave or slaves to their home state.

Fugitive Slave Law, 1850   Part of the Compromise of 1850 that required law enforcement officials as well as civilians to assist in capturing runaway slaves.

Fur trade   A North American colonial industry involving American Indians trapping fur-bearing animals (chiefly beavers) and exchanging their pelts for European products.

Gang system   A mode of organizing labor that had West African antecedents. In this system, American slaves worked in groups under the direction of a slave driver.

Gangsta rap   A genre of rap music characterized by violent and sexist lyrics.

General Order 11   Order threatening retaliation for the mistreatment of black soldiers by Confederate forces.

Grandfather clause   A method southern states used to disfranchise black men. It stipulated that only men whose grandfathers were eligible to vote were themselves eligible to vote. The U.S. Supreme Court invalidated the grandfather clause in 1915.

Great Dismal Swamp   A heavily forested area on the Virginia–North Carolina border that served as a refuge for fugitive slaves during the eighteenth and nineteenth centuries.

Griot   A West African self-employed poet and oral historian.

Guinea Coast   The southward-facing coast of West Africa, from which many of the people caught up in the Atlantic slave trade departed for the Americas.

Habeas corpus   A court order indicating that a person arrested or detained by law enforcement officers must be brought to court and charged with a crime and not held indefinitely.

Hamburg Massacre   White Democrats attacked black Republicans in July 1876 in the village of Hamburg, South Carolina. Five black men were murdered as the Democrats began a violent effort to redeem the state.

Harlem Renaissance   As New York City became a destination for black migrants before, during, and after World War I, most of them settled in Harlem—a large neighborhood in the northern portion of Manhattan Island. By the 1920s it became a center of African-American cultural activities including literature, art, and music.

Hierarchical   Refers to a social system based on class rank.

Hieroglyphics   A writing system based on pictures or symbols.

Hip-hop   The backup music for rap. It is also the term for the youth culture that developed with the rise of rap music.

Hired their own time   Refers to a practice in which a master allowed slaves to work for wages paid by someone other than the master himself.

House of Burgesses   A representative body established at Jamestown, Virginia, in 1619.

House Un-American Activities Committee (HUAC)   Congressional committee formed to investigate the activities of communists and "communist sympathizers" in America.

Hunting and gathering societies   Small societies dependent on hunting animals and collecting wild plants rather than engaging in agriculture.

Import duties   Taxes on goods brought into a country or colony.

Impressment   During the Civil War, Southern states and the Confederate government required slave owners to provide slaves to work on such public projects as fortifications, roads, and wharves. The owners (not the slaves) were usually compensated for the work.

Incest taboos   Customary rules against sexual relations and marriage within family and kinship groups.

Indentured servant   An individual who sells or loses his or her freedom for a specified number of years.

Indigo   A bluish-violet dye produced from the indigo plant.

Industrial Revolution   An economic change that began in England during the early eighteenth century and spread to Continental Europe and the United States. Industry rather than agriculture became the dominant form of enterprise.

Jim Crow   Jump Jim Crow was a nineteenth-century dance ridiculing black people that was transformed by the twentieth century into a term meaning racial discrimination and segregation.

John Brown's raid   Brown's raid on Harpers Ferry, Virginia, in October 1859 failed to lead to a major slave insurrection, but it inflamed the controversy over slavery in the North and South.

Joint-stock companies   Primitive corporations that carried out British and Dutch colonization in the Americas during the seventeenth century.

Kansas-Nebraska Act, 1854   Legislation introduced by Democratic Senator Stephen Douglas to organize the Kansas and Nebraska territories. It provided for "popular sovereignty," whereby settlers would decide whether slavery would be legal or illegal.

"Know-Nothing Party"   The nickname applied to members of the American Party, which opposed immigration in the 1850s.

Ku Klux Klan   A secret society founded by former Confederates in Pulaski, Tennessee, in 1866. It transformed itself into a terrorist organization during Reconstruction to drive black and white Republicans from political power in southern states.

Liberty Party (1840–1848)   The first antislavery political party. Most of its supporters joined the Free-Soil Party in 1848, although its radical New York wing maintained a Liberty organization into the 1850s.

Lien   Black and white farmers purchased goods on credit from local merchants. The merchant demanded collateral in the form of a lien on the crop, typically cotton. If the farmer failed to repay the loan, the merchant had the legal right to seize the crop.

Lincoln-Douglas debates   Abraham Lincoln and Stephen Douglas debated seven times in the 1858 U.S. Senate race in Illinois. They spent most of their time arguing over slavery, its expansion, the *Dred Scott* decision, and the character of African Americans. Douglas won the election.

Lineage   A type of clan, typical of West Africa, in which members claim descent from a single ancestor.

Low country   The coastal regions of South Carolina and Georgia.

Lowndes County Freedom Organization (LCFO)   Political organization founded in 1965 by Stokely Carmichael.

Loyalists   Those Americans who, during the Revolutionary War, wished to remain within the British Empire.

Manumission   The act of freeing a slave by the slave's master.

March on Washington Movement (MOWM)   Movement created by A. Philip Randolph to pressure the federal government to end discrimination in the defense industry and government.

Market revolution   The process between 1800 and 1860 by which an American economy based on subsistence farming, production by skilled artisans, and local markets changed into an economy marked by commercial farming, factory production, and national markets.

Matrilineal   Descent traced through the female line.

Middle Passage   The voyage of slave ships (slavers) across the Atlantic Ocean from Africa to the Americas.

Militia Act of 1862   The 1862 Act authorizing Lincoln to enlist black soldiers for the military.

Mississippi Freedom Democratic Party   Interracial group set up to challenge Mississippi's all-white delegation to the Democratic National Convention in 1964.

Missouri Compromise, 1820   A congressional attempt to settle the issue of slavery expansion in the United States by permitting Missouri to enter the Union as a slave state, admitting Maine as a free state, and banning slavery in the rest of the Louisiana Purchase north of the 36° 30' line of latitude.

Montgomery Bus Boycott   Refusal of African Americans in Montgomery, Alabama, to ride the city's buses from 1955 to 1957 until the bus lines were desegregated.

Moral suasion   A tactic endorsed by the American Anti-Slavery Society during the 1830s. It appealed to slaveholders and others to support immediate emancipation on the basis of Christian principles.

Moynihan Report   Report attributing many of the problems of poor black communities to the breakdown of the "lower-class" black family.

Nation of Islam   Religious movement that combines Islam with black nationalism.

National Industrial Recovery Act (NIRA)   Federal law intended to promote the revival of manufacturing by allowing for cooperation among industries.

National Negro Congress (NNC)   Organization founded in 1936 to unite African-American protest groups.

Negro National League   A professional baseball league for black players and teams organized in 1912.

New York City draft riot   In early July 1863, in opposition to the forthcoming military draft, rioting erupted in New York City. Many of the victims were black men, women, and children.

North Atlantic Treaty Organization (NATO)   Military alliance formed to counter the threat posed by the Soviet Union and its allies.

North Star   A weekly newspaper published and edited by Frederick Douglass from 1847 to 1851. *Fredrick Douglass's Paper* (1851–1860) succeeded it.

Northwest Ordinance   Based on earlier legislation drafted by Thomas Jefferson, it organized the Northwest Territory, providing for orderly land sales, public education, government, the creation of five to seven states out of the territory, and the prohibition of slavery within the territory.

Nuclear family   A family unit consisting solely of one set of parents and their children.

Pan-Africanism   A movement of people of African descent from sub-Saharan Africa in the early twentieth century that emphasized their identity, shared experiences, and the need to liberate Africa from its European colonizers.

Patriarchal   A society ruled by a senior man.

Patrilineal   Descent through the male line.

Patriots   Those Americans who, during the Revolutionary War, favored independence.

Peace Mission Movement   Religious movement led by Father Major Jealous Divine.

Peonage   The system that forbade southern farmers, usually sharecroppers and renters, who accumulated debts to leave the land until the debt was repaid—often an impossible task.

Pidgin   A simplified mixture of two or more languages used to communicate between people who speak different languages.

Planter elite   Those who owned the largest tobacco plantations.

Plessy v. Ferguson   In 1896 in an eight-to-one decision, the U.S. Supreme Court ruled that segregation did not violate the equal protection clause of the Fourteenth Amendment. The "separate but equal" doctrine remained the supreme law of the land until the 1954 *Brown v. Board of Education* decision overturned *Plessy*.

Polygynous family   A family unit consisting of a man, his wives, and their children.

Poor People's Campaign   Project supported by Martin Luther King involving the march of tens of thousands of poor people on Washington.

Populist Party   Also known as the Peoples' Party, the Populists supported inflation; the free and unlimited coinage of silver and gold; government ownership of railroads, telephone, and telegraph companies; and an eight-hour workday. They won state and congressional elections but lost the presidential contests in 1892 and 1896.

Port Royal Experiment   An effort by northern white missionaries, educators, and businessmen in the Sea Islands near Beaufort, South Carolina, to transform former slaves into educated, reliable, and industrious wage earners. Most of the freedmen did not acquire the land they worked.

Preliminary Emancipation Proclamation   Proclamation issued on September 22, 1862, declaring that slaves residing in states still in rebellion on January 1, 1863, would be freed.

Prince Hall Masons   A black Masonic order formed in 1791 in Boston under the leadership of Prince Hall. He became its first grand master and promoted its expansion to other cities.

Project 100,000   Military project with the goal of reducing the number of African Americans rejected by the military.

Race films   Movies made for African-American audiences in the 1930s and 1940s.

Radical Republicans   Members of the Republican Party during Reconstruction who vigorously supported the rights of African Americans to vote, to hold political office, and to have the same legal and economic opportunities as white people.

Rain forest   A dense growth of tall trees characteristic of hot, wet regions.

Rainbow Coalition   Political coalition of African Americans, workers, liberals, feminists, gay people, environmentalists, and others formed by Jesse Jackson in the 1980s.

Reconstruction   The 12 years (1865–1877) following the Civil War during which the former Confederate states were restored to the Union and former slaves became citizens and gained the right to vote and hold political office.

Red Scare   The widespread fear among many Americans in the years immediately after World War I from about 1918 to about 1924 that Russia's 1917 Bolshevik Revolution might result in communists attempting to take over the U.S. government.

Redemption   The term used for the process, often violent, by which white conservative Democrats regained political control of a southern state from black and white Republicans during Reconstruction.

Rochester Convention, 1853   African-American leaders assembled in Rochester, New York, to discuss slavery, abolition, the recently passed Fugitive Slave Law, and their prospects for life in America.

Savanna   A flat, nearly treeless grassland typical of large portions of West Africa.

Scalawag   The derogatory term used during Reconstruction to identify a native white southerner who supported black and white Republicans. They were considered traitors to their people and the Democratic Party.

Scottsboro Boys Nine young African-American men unjustly accused of raping two white women in Alabama in 1931. The Supreme Court overturned their convictions in 1937.

Seasoning The process by which newly arrived Africans were broken in to slavery in the Americas.

Secret societies Social organizations that have secret ceremonies that only their members know about and can participate in.

Segregation The separation of people based on their race in the use of such public facilities as hotels, restaurants, restrooms, drinking fountains, parks, and auditoriums. In many instances, segregation meant the exclusion of black people.

Semitic Refers to people who speak languages, such as Arabic and Hebrew, native to southwest Asia.

Sharecropping The system following the Civil War in which former slaves worked land owned by white people and "paid" for the use of the land and for tools, seeds, fertilizer, and mules by sharing the crop—usually cotton—with the owner.

Shotgun policy In Mississippi in 1875, white men resorted to violence and intimidation against black and white Republicans to regain political control of the state for conservative Democrats.

Slaver A ship used to transport slaves from Africa to the Americas.

Social Darwinism Derived from Charles Darwin's theory of evolution, Herbert Spencer and William Graham Sumner asserted that life in modern society was competitive and only those individuals who were mentally, emotionally, and physically strong would prevail.

Sons of Liberty A secret American organization formed in the Northeast during the summer of 1765 and committed to forcible opposition to the Stamp Act.

Southern Christian Leadership Conference (SCLC) Organization spearheaded by Martin Luther King, Jr., to provide an institutional base for the civil rights movement.

Southern Regional Council (SRC) Organization that conducted research and focused attention on social, political, and educational inequality in the South.

Spanish Armada A fleet that unsuccessfully attempted to carry out an invasion of England in 1588.

Special Field Order #15 General William Tecumseh Sherman issued this military directive in January 1865. It set aside lands along the coast from Charleston, South Carolina, to Jacksonville, Florida, for former slaves. President Andrew Johnson revoked the order six months later.

Spirit possession A belief rooted in West African religions that spirits may possess human souls.

Student Nonviolent Coordinating Committee (SNCC) Civil rights organization founded by black college students in 1960 at the initiative of Ella Baker.

Syracuse Convention A meeting of black leaders in Syracuse, New York, to discuss the future of African Americans following the abolition of slavery. They insisted that black people had earned and deserved the same political and legal rights as white Americans.

Term slavery A type of slavery prevalent in the Chesapeake from the late 1700s to the Civil War in which slaves were able to purchase their freedom from their masters by earning money over a number of years.

Terrell law A Texas law banning African-American participation in the Democratic primary.

Thirteenth Amendment This amendment to the U.S. Constitution outlawed slavery and involuntary servitude.

Three-Fifths Clause A clause in the U.S. Constitution providing that a slave be counted as three-fifths of a free person in determining a state's representation in Congress and the electoral college and three-fifths of a free person in regard to per capita taxes levied by Congress on the states.

Tuskegee Airmen All-black combat air unit during World War II.

Tuskegee Machine As the president of Tuskegee Institute, Booker T. Washington developed an extensive network of contacts that gave him extraordinary influence with white political leaders and philanthropists as well as with black businesspeople, journalists, and college presidents.

Tuskegee Study A medical study by the U.S. Public Health Service of the effects of syphilis on 622 black men. The study ran from 1932 to the 1970s, and the men were given only placebos and no treatment for the disease.

Uncle Tom's Cabin This antislavery novel by Harriet Beecher Stowe was a best seller in the 1850s and it helped inflame the controversy over slavery.

Underground railroad Refers to several loosely organized, semisecret biracial networks that helped slaves escape from the border South to the North and Canada. The earliest networks appeared during the first decade of the nineteenth century; others operated into the Civil War years.

Union League A social and fraternal organization that stirred political interest and support among black and white Republicans in the South during Reconstruction.

Universal Negro Improvement Association (UNIA) Established in 1914 in Jamaica by Marcus Garvey, the UNIA fostered racial pride, African heritage, Christian faith, and economic uplift.

Voting Rights Act of 1965 Federal law banning the methods that had systematically excluded African Americans from registering or voting in southern elections.

Wilmot Proviso A measure introduced in Congress in 1845 to prohibit slavery in any lands acquired from Mexico. It did not pass.

Presidents and Vice Presidents of the United States*

PRESIDENT	VICE PRESIDENT
1. George Washington (1789)	John Adams (1789)
2. John Adams (1797)	Thomas Jefferson (1797)
3. Thomas Jefferson (1801)	Aaron Burr (1801) George Clinton (1805)
4. James Madison (1809)	George Clinton (1809) Elbridge Gerry (1813)
5. James Monroe (1817)	Daniel D. Tompkins (1817)
6. John Quincy Adams (1825)	John C. Calhoun (1825)
7. Andrew Jackson (1829)	John C. Calhoun (1829) Martin Van Buren (1833)
8. Martin Van Buren (1837)	Richard M. Johnson (1837)
9. William H. Harrison (1841)	John Tyler (1841)
10. John Tyler (1841)	
11. James K. Polk (1845)	George M. Dallas (1845)
12. Zachary Taylor (1849)	Millard Fillmore (1849)
13. Millard Fillmore (1850)	
14. Franklin Pierce (1853)	William R. King (1853)
15. James Buchanan (1857)	John C. Breckinridge (1857)
16. Abraham Lincoln (1861)	Hannibal Hamlin (1861) Andrew Johnson (1865)
17. Andrew Johnson (1865)	
18. Ulysses S. Grant (1869)	Schuyler Colfax (1869) Henry Wilson (1873)
19. Rutherford B. Hayes (1877)	William A. Wheeler (1877)
20. James A. Garfield (1881)	Chester A. Arthur (1881)
21. Chester A. Arthur (1881)	
22. Grover Cleveland (1885)	Thomas A. Hendricks (1885)
23. Benjamin Harrison (1889)	Levi P. Morton (1889)

PRESIDENT	VICE PRESIDENT
24. Grover Cleveland (1893)	Adlai E. Stevenson (1893)
25. William McKinley (1897)	Garret A. Hobart (1897) Theodore Roosevelt (1901)
26. Theodore Roosevelt (1901)	Charles Fairbanks (1905)
27. William H. Taft (1909)	James S. Sherman (1909)
28. Woodrow Wilson (1913)	Thomas R. Marshall (1913)
29. Warren G. Harding (1921)	Calvin Coolidge (1921)
30. Calvin Coolidge (1923)	Charles G. Dawes (1925)
31. Herbert C. Hoover (1929)	Charles Curtis (1929)
32. Franklin D. Roosevelt (1933)	John Nance Garner (1933) Henry A.Wallace (1941) Harry S Truman (1945)
33. Harry S Truman (1945)	Alben W. Barkley (1949)
34. Dwight D. Eisenhower (1953)	Richard M. Nixon (1953)
35. John F. Kennedy (1961)	Lyndon B. Johnson (1961)
36. Lyndon B. Johnson (1963)	Hubert H. Humphrey (1965)
37. Richard M. Nixon (1969)	Spiro T. Agnew (1969) Gerald R. Ford (1973)
38. Gerald R. Ford (1974)	Nelson A. Rockefeller (1974)
39. James E. Carter Jr. (1977)	Walter F. Mondale (1977)
40. Ronald W. Reagan (1981)	George H. Bush (1981)
41. George H. Bush (1989)	James D. Quayle III (1989)
42. William J. Clinton (1993)	Albert Gore (1993)
43. George W. Bush (2001)	Richard B. Cheney (2001)
44. Barack H. Obama (2009)	Joseph R. Biden (2009)

* Year of inauguration

Historically Black Four-Year Colleges and Universities

INSTITUTION AND LOCATION	YEAR FOUNDED	LAND-GRANT, PUBLIC, PRIVATE, OR CHURCH-AFFILIATED DENOMINATION
Alabama A&M University, Normal, Alabama	1875	Land-grant
Alabama State University, Montgomery, Alabama	1867	Public
Albany State University, Albany, Georgia	1903	Public
Alcorn State University, Lorman, Mississippi	1871	Land-grant
Allen University, Columbia, South Carolina	1870	AME
Arkansas Baptist College, Little Rock, Arkansas	1884	Baptist
Barber-Scotia College, Concord, North Carolina	1904	Presbyterian
Benedict College, Columbia, South Carolina	1870	Baptist
Bennett College, Greensboro, North Carolina	1873	United Methodist
Bethune-Cookman College, Daytona Beach, Florida	1904	United Methodist
Bluefield State College, Bluefield, West Virginia	1895	Public
Bowie State University, Bowie, Maryland	1865	Public
Central State University, Wilberforce, Ohio	1887	Public
Cheyney University, Cheyney, Pennsylvania	1837	Public
Claflin College, Orangeburg, South Carolina	1869	United Methodist
Clark Atlanta University, Atlanta, Georgia	1988	United Methodist
Concordia College, Selma, Alabama	1922	Lutheran
Coppin State University, Baltimore, Maryland	1900	Public
Delaware State University, Dover, Delaware	1891	Land-grant
Dillard University, New Orleans, Louisiana	1930	Congregational/United Methodist
Edward Waters College, Jacksonville, Florida	1866	AME
Elizabeth City State University, Elizabeth City, North Carolina	1891	Public
Fayetteville State University, Fayetteville, North Carolina	1867	Public
Fisk University, Nashville, Tennessee	1866	United Church of Christ
Florida A&M University, Tallahassee, Florida	1887	Land-grant
Florida Memorial College, Miami, Florida	1879	Baptist
Fort Valley State College, Fort Valley, Georgia	1895	Land-grant

(continued)

INSTITUTION AND LOCATION	YEAR FOUNDED	LAND-GRANT, PUBLIC, PRIVATE, OR CHURCH-AFFILIATED DENOMINATION
Grambling State University, Grambling, Louisiana	1901	Public
Hampton University, Hampton, Virginia	1868	Private
Harris-Stowe State College, St. Louis, Missouri	1857	Public
Howard University, Washington, DC	1867	Public
Huston-Tillotson University, Austin, Texas	1952	United Church of Christ/United Methodist
Jackson State University, Jackson, Mississippi	1877	Public
Jarvis Christian College, Hawkins, Texas	1913	Disciple of Christ Christian Church
Johnson C. Smith University, Charlotte, North Carolina	1867	Presbyterian
Kentucky State University, Frankfort, Kentucky	1886	Land-grant
Knoxville College, Knoxville, Tennessee	1875	Presbyterian
Lane College, Jackson, Tennessee	1882	Christian Methodist Episcopal
Langston University, Langston, Oklahoma	1897	Land-grant
LeMoyne-Owen College, Memphis, Tennessee	1870	United Church of Christ
Lincoln University, Jefferson City, Missouri	1866	Land-grant
Lincoln University, Lincoln, Pennsylvania	1854	Public
Livingstone College, Salisbury, North Carolina	1879	AME
Miles College, Birmingham, Alabama	1908	Christian Methodist Episcopal
Mississippi Valley State University, Itta Bena, Mississippi	1946	Public
Morehouse College, Atlanta, Georgia	1867	Baptist
Morgan State University, Baltimore, Maryland	1867	Public
Morris Brown College, Atlanta, Georgia	1881	AME
Morris College, Sumter, South Carolina	1908	Baptist
Norfolk State University, Norfolk, Virginia	1935	Public
North Carolina A&T State University, Greensboro, North Carolina	1892	Land-grant
North Carolina Central University, Durham, North Carolina	1909	Public
Oakwood College, Huntsville, Alabama	1896	Seventh Day Adventist
Paine College, Augusta, Georgia	1882	United Methodist
Paul Quinn College, Dallas, Texas	1872	AME
Philander Smith College, Little Rock, Arkansas	1877	United Methodist
Prairie View A&M University, Prairie View, Texas	1878	Land-grant
Rust College, Holly Springs, Mississippi	1866	United Methodist
Saint Augustine's College, Raleigh, North Carolina	1867	Episcopal
Saint Paul's College, Lawrenceville, Virginia	1888	Episcopal

(continued)

INSTITUTION AND LOCATION	YEAR FOUNDED	LAND-GRANT, PUBLIC, PRIVATE, OR CHURCH-AFFILIATED DENOMINATION
Savannah State College, Savannah, Georgia	1890	Public
Selma University, Selma, Alabama	1878	Baptist
Shaw University, Raleigh, North Carolina	1865	Baptist
Sojourner-Douglass College, Baltimore, Maryland	1980	Private
South Carolina State University, Orangeburg, South Carolina	1896	Land-grant
Southern University and A&M College, Baton Rouge, Louisiana	1880	Land-grant
Southern University at New Orleans, New Orleans, Louisiana	1956	Public
Southwestern Christian College, Terrell, Texas	1949	Church of Christ
Spelman College, Atlanta, Georgia	1876	Presbyterian
Stillman College, Tuscaloosa, Alabama	1876	Presbyterian
Talladega College, Talladega, Alabama	1867	United Church of Christ
Tennessee State University, Nashville, Tennessee	1912	Land-grant
Texas College, Tyler, Texas	1894	Christian Methodist Episcopal
Texas Southern University, Houston, Texas	1947	Public
Tougaloo College, Tougaloo, Mississippi	1869	United Church of Christ/United Missionary Society
Tuskegee University, Tuskegee, Alabama	1881	Land-grant
University of Arkansas at Pine Bluff, Pine Bluff, Arkansas	1873	Land-grant
University of the District of Columbia, Washington, DC	1977	Public
University of Maryland Eastern Shore, Princess Anne, Maryland	1886	Land-grant
University of the Virgin Islands, St. Thomas, United States Virgin Islands	1962	Public
Virginia State University, Petersburg, Virginia	1882	Land-grant
Virginia Union University, Richmond, Virginia	1865	Baptist
Voorhees College, Denmark, South Carolina	1897	Episcopal
West Virginia State College, Institute, West Virginia	1891	Public
Wilberforce University, Wilberforce, Ohio	1856	AME
Wiley College, Marshall, Texas	1873	United Methodist
Winston-Salem State University, Winston-Salem, North Carolina	1892	Public
Xavier University of New Orleans, New Orleans, Louisiana	1925	Roman Catholic

Photo and Text Credits

CHAPTER 1: Library of Congress, Rare Book and Special Collections Division, 1; HO/Reuters/Corbis, 4; Galyna Andrushko/Shutterstock, 6; Detail from the Catalan Atlas, 1375 (vellum), Cresques, Abraham (1325-87)/ Bibliotheque Nationale, Paris, France/The Bridgeman Art Library, 10; Arterra Picture Library/Alamy, 12.

CHAPTER 2: Library of Congress, Prints & Photographs Division, [LC-DIG-ppmsca-15836], 22; Werner Forman/ Art Resource, NY, 25; North Wind Picture Archives, 30; Library of Congress Rare Book and Special Collections Division, 32; Library of Congress, Prints & Photographs Division, [LC-USZ62-15392], 38; Library of Congress, Prints & Photographs Division, [LC-USZ62-19607], 29.

CHAPTER 3: MPI/Getty Images, 50; Francis G. Mayer/ Fine Art Value/Corbis, 65; Thomas Jefferson Runaway Slave advert, from 'The Virginia Gazette', 14th September 1769 (litho), American School, (18th century)/Virginia Historical Society, Richmond, Virginia, USA/The Bridgeman Art Library, 67.

CHAPTER 4: James Lafayette Armistead (engraving), Martin, John (1789-1854)/Virginia Historical Society, Richmond, Virginia, USA/The Bridgeman Art Library, 75; Library of Congress, Prints & Photographs Division, [LC-USZC4-1583], 75; Library of Congress, Prints & Photographs Division, [LC-USZ62-56850], 78; Image Asset Management Ltd./Alamy, 83.

CHAPTER 5: Library of Congress, Prints & Photographs Division, Detroit Publishing Company Collection, [LC-D4-500180], 90; Library of Congress, Prints & Photographs Division, [LC-USZ62-103801], 98; The New York Public Library/Art Resource, NY, 101; Absalom Jones, 1810 (oil on paper), Peale, Raphaelle (1774-1825)/Delaware Art Museum, Wilmington, USA/Gift of Absalom Jones School/The Bridgeman Art Library, 103; PETER TOBIA KRT/Newscom, 105; Library of Congress Prints And Photographs Divisions, [LC-USZ62-7860], 107; Library of Congress, Prints and Photographs Division, [LC-USZ62-30794], 114; Bettman/Corbis, 115.

CHAPTER 6: Library of Congress, Prints & Photographs Division, [LC-USZ62-76385], 116; Library of Congress, Prints & Photographs Division, [LC-USZ62-98515], 125; Library of Congress, Prints & Photographs Division, [LC-USZ62-2574], 127; Library of Congress, Prints & Photographs Division, [LC-USZ62-76081], 128; Library of Congress, Prints & Photographs Division, [LC-USZ62-75650], 129.

CHAPTER 7: A Barber's Shop at Richmond Virginia (coloured engraving), Crowe, Eyre (1824-1910) (after)/ Private Collection/© Look and Learn/Bernard Platman Antiquarian Collection/The Bridgeman Art Library, 137; The Granger Collection, NYC, 143; Picture History/ Newscom, 147; Library of Congress, Prints & Photographs Division, [LC-USZ62-118946], 148; Thomas Waterman Wood, American, 1823-1903. Market Woman, 1858. Oil on canvas. 23 3/8 [times] 14 1/2 in. Fine Arts Museum of San Francisco, gift of Henry K.S. Williams, 1944.8, 156.

CHAPTER 8: American School, (19th century)/Private Collection/Peter Newark American Pictures/The Bridgeman Art Library, 159; Library of Congress, Prints & Photographs Division, [LC-USZ62-63867], 165; The Bridgeman Art Library, 167; Library of Congress, Prints & Photographs Division, [LC-USZ62-10320], 170; American School, (19th century)/Private Collection/ Peter Newark American Pictures/The Bridgeman Art Library, 172.

CHAPTER 9: Anti-Slavery Society, including Lucretia Mott (b/w photo), American Photographer, (19th century)/Schlesinger Library, Radcliffe Institute, Harvard University/The Bridgeman Art Library, 179; Library of Congress, Rare Book and Special Collections Division, 180; Library and Archives Canada/C-029977, 188; Picture History/Newscom, 188.

CHAPTER 10: Library of Congress, Prints & Photographs Division, [LC-USZ62-84545], 194; Library of Congress, Prints & Photographs Division, [LC-USZ62-1286], 200; Library of Congress, Prints & Photographs Division, [LC-USZ62-90750], 201; Library of Congress,

Prints & Photographs Division, [LC-USZ62-79305], 206; North Wind Picture Archives/Alamy, 209; Border Ruffians from Missouri invading Kansas, 1856 (etching), American School, (19th century)/Private Collection/ Peter Newark American Pictures/The Bridgeman Art Library, 211; Aurora Photos/Alamy, 216; The Beinecke Rare Book & Manuscript Library, 217.

CHAPTER 11: Library of Congress, Prints & Photographs Division, [LC-DIG-cwpb-04279], 218; Library of Congress, Prints & Photographs Division, [LC-USZ62-98515], 220; Library of Congress, Prints & Photographs Division, [LC-DIG-cwpb-01930], 227; U.S. Library of Congress, Prints & Photographs Division, [LC-DIG-pga-01949], 229; Library of Congress, Prints & Photographs Division, [LC-USZ62-105560], 237.

CHAPTER 12: The Granger Collection, NYC, 241; PICA 05496, Austin History Center, Austin Public Library, 249; Library of Congress, Prints & Photographs Division, [LC-USZ62-117891], 250; Fotosearch/Getty Images, 251; Library of Congress, Prints & Photographs Division, [LC-USZ62-108067], 252; Library of Congress, Prints & Photographs Division, [LC-USZ62-117139], 258; Library of Congress, Prints & Photographs Division, [LC-USZ62-125422], 262.

CHAPTER 13: Library of Congress, Prints & Photographs Division, [LC-DIG-ppmsca-17564], 265; Library of Congress, Prints & Photographs Division, D.C, LC-USZ62-100971, 266; Library of Congress, Prints & Photographs Division, [LC-USZC4-681], 267; Library of Congress, Prints & Photographs Division, [LC-USZ62-119565], 273; Henry Clay Warmoth Papers #752, Southern Historical Collection, Wilson Library, University of North Carolina at Chapel Hill., 273; Library of Congress Prints & Photographs Division, [LC-USZC4-973], 276; Library of Congress, Prints & Photographs Division, [LC-DIG-ppmsca-31598], 287; Bruce Davidson/Magnum Photos, 288.

CHAPTER 14: Solomon D Butcher/Getty Images, 289; Stock Montage/Getty Images, 294; Bettmann/ Corbis, 297; Everett Collection Historical/Alamy, 301; Library of Congress, Prints & Photographs Division, [LC-USZC4-4647], 302; Library of Congress Prints & Photographs Division/[LC-USZ62-26365], 304; Courtesy of SC State Historical Collection & Archives, 309.

CHAPTER 15: Glasshouse Images/Alamy, 314; Library of Congress, Prints & Photographs Division, [LC-USZ62-49568], 318; National Archives, 324; Historic Florida/Alamy, 326; Everett Collection/Newscom, 331; Schomburg Center, NYPL/Art Resource, NY, 334; Bettmann/Corbis, 335; Library of Congress, Prints & Photographs Division, [LC-USZ6-1824], 336.

CHAPTER 16: Library of Congress, Prints & Photographs Division, [LC-USZ62-64712], 341; Library of Congress, Prints & Photographs Division, [LC-DIG-stereo-1s02155], 344; Library of Congress, Prints & Photographs Division, [LC-USZ62-16767], 347; Bettmann/Corbis, 349; Courtesy of the Queens Borough Public Library, Archives, Lewis H. Latimer Papers, 354; Library of Congress, Prints & Photographs Division, [LC-USZ62-47385], 355; Library of Congress, Prints & Photographs Division, [LC-USZ62-116442], 357; Everett Collection Historical/Alamy, 362.

CHAPTER 17: *Photos:* Corbis, 372; Paris Pierce/Alamy, 374; Library of Congress, Prints & Photographs Division, Carl Van Vechten Collection, [LC-USZ62-42498], 376; Bettmann/Corbis, 378; Michael Ochs Archives/ Getty Images, 391; National Baseball Hall of Fame & Museum, 392; Chicago History Museum/Getty Images, 396; Mondadori via Getty Images, 397.

Text: "If We Must Die," by Claude McKay, 1919, 385.

CHAPTER 18: Margaret Bourke-White/Masters/Time Life Pictures/Getty Images, 398; Everett Collection Inc/ Alamy, 405; Washington Bureau/Staff/Hulton Archive/ Getty Images, 412; Library of Congress, Prints & Photographs Division, Carl Van Vechten Collection, [LC-USZ62-128514], 412; Library of Congress, Prints & Photographs Division, FSA/OWI Collection, [LC-USE6-D-006321], 414; Everett Collection Historical/Alamy, 417; National Archives, 419.

CHAPTER 19: AP PhotoMatty Zimmerman, 422; Library of Congress, Prints & Photographs Division, [LC-USW33-054941-ZC], 423; STF/AFP/Getty Images, 425; Clarice Durham, 429; Library of Congress, Prints & Photographs Division, Carl Van Vechten Collection, [LC-USZ62-92598], 433; David Lees/Corbis, 435; Hulton Archive/Getty Images, 435; Library of Congress, Prints & Photographs Division, FSA/OWI Collection, [LC-USW3-030278-D], 438; Bettmann/Corbis, 439.

CHAPTER 20: Library of Congress, Prints & Photographs Division, [LC-USZC4-4344], 446; Library of Congress, Prints & Photographs Division, [LC-USZC4-2328], 451; National Archives, 453; Moorland-Spingarn Research Center, 453; Bettmann/Corbis, 458; National Archives,

Index